this book belongs to
Kathryn Ruth Self

John 8:32

A HISTORY OF CHRISTIANITY

Volume I: to A.D. 1500

A HISTORY OF CHRISTIANITY

KENNETH SCOTT LATOURETTE

STERLING PROFESSOR OF MISSIONS AND ORIENTAL HISTORY

AND FELLOW OF BERKELEY COLLEGE IN YALE UNIVERSITY

Volume I: to A.D. 1500

HarperSanFrancisco

A Division of HarperCollinsPublishers

To my colleagues past and present
of the faculty of the
Yale University Divinity School

First HarperCollins paperback edition published in 1975.

Volume I contains through page 683 of the hardcover edition of A HISTORY OF CHRISTIANITY.

ISBN: 0-06-064952-6

LIBRARY OF CONGRESS CATALOG CARD NUMBER: 74-25693

95 96   RRD H   30 29 28 27 26 25

CONTENTS
Volume I: to A.D. 1500

CONTENTS　　　　　　　　　　　　　　vii

Volume II: A.D. 1500 to A.D. 1975

VIGOUR AMIDST STORM, A.D. 1914–A.D. 1952

INCREASING DISESTABLISHMENT, INCREASING DIVERSITY, GROWTH AND VITALITY, A.D. 1950–A.D. 1975

MAPS

FOREWORD

It seems especially fitting that a 1500-page summary of that religious movement constituting the greatest influence in the history of mankind should be written by a man who knew the Chinese intimately, the people constituting the largest bloc of population in the history of mankind. As a matter of fact, for twenty years Kenneth Scott Latourette taught every course Yale University offered on the Far East. Yet, curiously, it would be the Chinese who, of all major sectors of modern mankind, have made the least overt response to the Christian Church. In any case this book, in some respects, is his response to the Chinese.

He writes as a warm, sympathetic Christian. His many other books demonstrate his ability as an objective scholar. In this book he writes as a Christian to Christians, and while he does not overemphasize China, it is clear on every page that there is a constant concern for the way in which Christianity has, is, or will affect the *remainder of all humanity*.

But Latourette is no religious imperialist: a gentle man, he is most impressed, as he tells this massive story, when he is describing the gentlest of all Christ's servants. Nor is he a religious apologist. He exhibits a rare sensitivity and faithfulness in describing those ways, those times, those places in which Christians have fallen short of their ideals. If as a committed Christian he does not hesitate to expose weaknesses and shortcomings when he finds them, then as a loyal Baptist, he does not hesitate to give credit to church movements far removed from his own tradition.

In fact there is one bias that runs throughout all his books, and helps to explain his larger perspective. Unobtrusively, but consistently, he favors the minority, the man on the bottom, the movement without pedigree or official backing. While this bias does not lead him to attack the established movements, his narrative is much more than a story about the major Christian churches, or even about churches as such. He does not hesitate to describe events both within and without the "organized" Church. It is incredible but true that no other human being in history has achieved—or perhaps even earnestly sought to produce—this kind of appreciative, comprehensive account of the whole Christian story. Christianity for him is a movement of fascinating complexity, and he sees it in "relation to the total story of mankind." In many ways he actually describes the total story of mankind, demonstrating how hopeless it would be to try to understand that story without understanding the extensive influence of Jesus in that larger picture.

He wrote with a post-Vatican II breadth of spirit *prior* to that great series of meetings! Thus surprisingly the friendly climate of the 1970's does not outmode the attitudes he expresses in this remarkable summary. One wonders how anyone today could more effectively chronicle so many delicate situations down through history—both triumphs and failures of practically every branch of Christianity—and do so with such a combination of generosity and honesty. Thus the scope, the balance, and the modernity of his perspective leaves this treatment without parallel even in 1975. In trying to stretch the canvas he painted, over an additional quarter of a century—in an additional chapter—we have become painfully aware that no one today, unfortunately, is as comprehensively informed as Latourette customarily considered it his duty to be. Fortunately he himself helped with the task. The twenty pages of his Chapter 59 became a whole book of 468 pages in 1962, *The Twentieth Century Outside Europe* (Vol. V of *Christianity in a Revolutionary Age*), and takes us at least part of the way into the 1950–1975 period. In his sprightly, brief *Christianity Through the Ages* he leads the reader as far as 1964, covering 1914 to 1964 in the last twenty-five pages.

What makes these two volumes virtually an encyclopedia is the unusually detailed index which has close to 6000 entries, vastly more than the average book and as many as any of three recent dictionaries of the Christian movement. It is a splendid idea, too, for the entire index to be placed in each of the two volumes, since many topics run through both.

A by-product of exploding world development in the 1950–1975 period is the profusion of new books on the Christian movement which have appeared since Latourette completed this work in 1952. A very modest selection of these books is to be found in the supplemental bibliographies which have been added at the end of each volume.

RALPH D. WINTER

PREFACE

Here is both an old and a new story.

It is old. Repeatedly across its nineteen and a half centuries the history of Christianity has been told and retold. In one or another of its aspects it has called forth a voluminous and massive literature.

This is as it should be. Christianity has become the most widespread of all religious faiths. It is by no means dominant. It never ceases to be challenged. There have been times when it has seemed to be waning. Some of the major attacks on it have been made in our day. Its ideals have never been fully attained. Indeed, it at least is debatable whether they ever can be fully realized within the span of history, so high are they, and so far beyond anything actual, either in man's collective life, in small groups, or even in individuals. The one life in which they were fully embodied came to a cross, so contrary were they to current practice in religion and the state. Yet, measured by its effects, Christianity has become the most potent single force in the life of mankind.

Moreover, by its very genius, Christianity is a concern of the historian. If the Christian faith is true, it should be either central or at least be consciously kept as the setting and the point of reference for all the work of the historian. It had its inception in events and in a life which are part of the historical record. From the very first generation of Christians, there have been those who have believed that the clue to the perplexing and paradoxical human drama is to be found in Christ, that the whole of the created universe groans in travail waiting for the revealing of the sons of God, the sons of whom Christ is the first-born, and that it is the purpose of God to sum up all things in Christ, both in the heavens and upon the earth, and to put "all things in subjection under his feet." If this conviction arises from fact, to be seen in its proper perspective the entire course of mankind on the planet must be surveyed with reference to Christ, from the incarnation in Jesus of Nazareth, through his teaching, deeds, life, and resurrection, and it is no accident but of the very stuff of history that chronology is measured as B.C.—before Christ—and A.D., *Anno Domini,* the year of the Lord of men and of history.

It is not surprising that, equipped with this insight, again and again through the centuries Christian scholars have addressed themselves to the history of their faith and in the light of it have endeavoured to understand the nature of man and the course of mankind's pilgrimage. Examples can be instanced from the first to the twentieth century.

The story of Christianity is not only old: it is also ever new. In each age it must be told afresh. That is not merely because in every era a chapter is added by the ongoing current of events. It is also because at every stage of mankind's march fresh perspective is gained. Each generation of historians can say of its predecessors: "Without us they cannot be made perfect." That is partly for the reason that every historian can utilize the work of those of his craft who have gone before him. It is also because from the vantage of a later day and in the fresh setting of his times the historian can interpret anew the road which the race has thus far traversed. No historian can hope to give the final or definitive account of the course of Christianity. Those who come after him will presumably have the same advantages which he possesses over those who have earlier essayed the task. In each generation there must be those who will undertake to review for their fellows the scroll as it has thus far been unrolled.

Certain outstanding features of the mid-twentieth century make necessary now an attempt to resurvey the course of Christianity. These cannot be stated in logical order, for it is not clear that they are tied together in that fashion. One of them, probably the most pronounced at first glance, is the fact that the human race is bound together physically more closely than ever before. Decade by decade, almost year by year, rapid means of transportation and communication reduce the size of the globe in time-distances and make neighbours of people who only yesterday were remote from one another. Closely allied to the shrinkage of the planet is the emergence of what in some respects is a world culture. Civilization everywhere has been coming to have common features. These include machines, the scientific theories and processes which are closely allied with machines, nationalism, the trend towards socialism and democracy in one or another of their various forms, and the demand for universal primary education. Significantly, the immediate sources of the movements which have brought all mankind into close physical juxtaposition and of the outstanding features of the nascent world culture are to be found in the Occident, and the Occident has long been the main stronghold of Christianity, the major part of what traditionally has been called Christendom.

It is not surprising, therefore, that hand in hand with the spread of other features of the culture of the Occident, Christianity should be widely disseminated. That dissemination has not come automatically. Most of it has been achieved through the minority who have been deeply committed to the Christian faith. To be sure, much of it has been by emigration from Europe of those who have been Christians by heredity, but even of these the large majority have been Christians only in name and in the new environment have tended to drift away from the religious patterns of their fatherlands. It has been earnest Christians, usually from among the emigrants and their children, but sometimes missionaries from the mother countries who have kept the faith alive in the migrants as they have moved into a new setting. The spread of Christianity among non-Occidental peoples has been very infrequently through merchants or government officials from the Occident, but has been overwhelmingly by those giving their entire time as missionaries and by the converts of these missionaries. By whatever process, Christianity is today more widely distributed geographically and more deeply rooted among more peoples than it or any other faith has ever been.

By a strange and striking contrast, Christianity has never been as extensively challenged as in the mid-twentieth century. Not only have such traditional rivals as Islam, Hinduism, and Buddhism continued to prove resistant, but also, within "Christendom" great defections have been occurring and fresh rivals, sprung from Christendom, the chief of them Communism, have been spreading throughout the globe and have been threatening all historic religions, notably Christianity itself. Sometimes it seems that from Christianity have been issuing the forces of its own destruction.

It is against this background and from the coign of vantage which the present age affords that we will attempt to look backward and retell the history of Christianity from its beginning to our day.

Any history of Christianity, if it is to be comprehensive, must endeavour to survey the course of all the many features of the human story which can be traced in whole or even in part to Christ. We must strive to understand the fashion in which the impulses which issued from Christ have shaped the current of mankind's life.

Most of this will have to do with what we usually term Christianity. Christianity is a religion and as such is one of many religions. Its distinctive feature is that, as its name implies, it has Jesus Christ at its very heart. Yet Christianity is a synthesis of what the Christian regards as the Gospel, God's gift to man in Christ, and of the human response to it. Christianity centres about Christ but it is compounded of the faith, Judaism, from which Jesus sprang and which prepared the way for him; of Jesus himself, his birth, life, teachings, deeds, death, and resurrection; of the faith of his immediate disciples in him; and of the several aspects of the many environments into which it has moved.

Obviously a well-rounded account of the history of Christianity will narrate the story of its geographic spread, taking account of the forms of the faith which spread, the reasons for the expansion, and the methods, agents, and agencies through which the spread took place. Much of the history of Chris-

tianity will concern itself with the visible Church, the institutionalized fellowship, or, rather, the congeries of institutions which arose because of Christ. It
must tell something of the character, the life, and the work of the outstanding creators and leaders of these institutions. It must narrate the story of the
divisions within the Christian community and of the efforts to heal the divisions and to realize that unity in love which is of the essence of the Christian
Gospel. It must cover the development of Christian thought, especially what
is called doctrine, the attempts of Christians to give intellectual formulation to
their faith. Such a survey must also recount the development of both corporate
and private worship. It must tell of the means which Christians have used in
their endeavour to live to the full the ideals of their faith and to encourage
others to do so. To this end it must take cognizance of the methods and forms
of instruction in the Christian faith, the course of Christian asceticism and
mysticism both within and outside monastic movements, and the standards and
processes of the discipline applied to their members by the churches. There must
be accounts of some of the outstanding Christians, especially of those who have
been regarded by their fellows as approaching the Christian ideal and of those
who have been widely influential either within the Christian fellowship or
outside it. A well-balanced narrative of the course of Christianity must also
seek to disclose what the faith has meant to the rank and file of those who
bear the Christian name and of those, unknown to wide fame, who in communities, most of them small and obscure, have been radiating centres of the
faith. An inclusive history must say something of the effect of Christianity
upon its environment, not alone individuals, although these are the goal and
the test of the Christian Gospel, but also the many social and political institutions, movements, customs, and intellectual and emotional currents which
shape individuals. Space must be assigned to the effect of the environment
upon Christianity, for the two interact: Christianity both moulds and to some
degree is moulded by the setting in which it operates.

If it is not to be distorted, the history of Christianity must include all the
varieties of the faith. It must embrace not only those forms which have had a
wide following, but also minority groups. It must mention not merely the
numerous churches and movements which are features of the current scene in
whatever part of the world they are found, but in addition those offshoots of
Christianity which have disappeared.

From its very beginning, the course of Christianity must be viewed against
the background of the entire human race. The necessity of this perspective
should be obvious, yet often it has been ignored. Since Christians have claimed
that Christ is essential to a comprehension of the meaning of history, since the
outlook of Christianity is universal in its scope, and since from the outset the

ideal has been set before the followers of Jesus of winning all men to his discipleship, the historian must ask how far that understanding and that dream have been realized. His canvass, therefore, must be all mankind from the beginning to the present. In every major stage of his narrative, he who would survey the history of Christianity must strive to view it in its global setting.

This means, for example, that in those chapters in which we are telling the story of the first five centuries of Christianity, when that faith was winning the professed allegiance of the peoples of the Roman Empire and was developing institutions, patterns of thought, and forms of worship which have been normative for the majority of Christians from that time to the present, we must make it clear that most of mankind, both civilized and uncivilized, was not as yet so much as touched by the Gospel and was not aware of even the name of Jesus Christ. In the twelfth and thirteenth centuries, a period to which many are inclined to look back as the heyday of Christianity, we must be aware of the frequently forgotten fact that Europe, where the faith had its stronghold, and especially Western Europe, where most of the vigour was displayed, was not even as prominent in the total world scene as the Roman Empire had been a thousand years earlier, and that the major centres of wealth, population, and civilization were elsewhere. In that relatively brief span from the fifteenth into the twentieth century, when so-called Christian peoples were spreading throughout the globe and were bringing most of the human race under their control, and when, in connexion with that expansion, Christianity was having the greatest geographic extension which it had thus far enjoyed, we must endeavour to take into account all the chief movements of the day, both within and without "Christendom."

This perspective does not entail a comprehensive history of mankind. A universal history might be written from the standpoint of the Christian faith. Indeed, it has repeatedly been essayed, never more notably than by Augustine in his *De Civitate Dei*. It does, however, mean that from the very outset the effort must be made to place the story of Christianity in the setting of universal history.

If the history of Christianity is surveyed with an awareness of the total human drama, much more attention must be accorded the past few centuries than has been usual in such accounts. During the past four hundred and fifty years and especially in the last century and a half, Christianity has been more influential in the life of the human race than at any previous time.

This is contrary to an impression which has wide currency. Generally it is assumed that Christianity has been waning since the Renaissance and especially since the eighteenth century. The secularism of the present age, the extensive and often spectacular defections from the faith in so-called Christendom which have occurred in the past two centuries, and the emergence of communism and other new challenges to Christianity have appeared to justify the dismissal of Christianity by many intellectuals as an interesting phenomenon which has had its day but is now dying. Even many Christians, among them some prominent in the churches, have shared in this appraisal and have occasionally spoken of the present as the "post-Christian era."

The picture is by no means so simple. It supports neither the pessimists nor the unqualified optimists. On the one hand are the adverse phases which undoubtedly exist and to which the prophets of gloom call attention. On the other hand are the wide geographic spread of Christianity, the many movements issuing from the faith, more numerous than in any other stretch of time of corresponding length and evidence of extraordinary vitality, and effects upon more branches of the human family than in any other period. If we are to seek to understand the fashion in which the Christian Gospel operates we must pay particular attention to these later centuries.

At the proper place we must take account of frankly anti-Christian interpretations of history and inquire into their significance. They have appeared within what has traditionally been known as Christendom and have entailed a repudiation of Christianity by much of the latter's hereditary constituency. The contrast between this trend and the fact that parallel with it Christianity has grown in influence in the world as a whole presents a seeming paradox in which there may be a clue to the correct understanding of history. It is partly because of the fact that in these later centuries this paradox, always present, has become especially vivid and has displayed itself on a world-wide scale that we must devote a large proportion of our space to the centuries which lie immediately back of us and particularly to the past four or five generations.

At the very outset we must notice the severe limitations under which all must labour who seek to recount the history of Christianity. We should be given pause by the warning in the Christian Scriptures that what from their viewpoint is the true perspective differs so radically from what is customary that to attain it requires a basic reorientation which is best described as a new birth. One of the ancient Hebrew prophets represents God as declaring: "My thoughts are not your thoughts, neither are my ways your ways. . . . As the heavens are higher than the earth so are my ways higher than your ways, and my thoughts than your thoughts." In the New Testament we find the forceful declaration on no less authority than that of Jesus himself that unless one receives it as a little child, learning afresh from the very beginning, he cannot enter the kingdom of God—that order in which God's will is known and done. Putting it even more bluntly, Jesus said that unless a man be born again, not only can he not enter into the kingdom of God but he cannot even see it, presumably meaning that he does not recognize it even when it is before his eyes. Similarly Jesus rejoiced that true insight had been hidden from the wise and the prudent and had been given to babes, and Paul insisted that God has made foolish the wisdom of this world and that through the wisdom of God the world through its wisdom has failed to know God. So contrary is the perspective given by the Gospel that those trained in the viewpoint of the Greeks tended scornfully to dismiss it as foolishness, and the Jews who were stoutly loyal to what they believed to be what God had given them in their national heritage were either puzzled or enraged by it.

All this would appear to mean that from the Christian standpoint those events, movements, and institutions which usually attract the attention of men and therefore find a place in the records of the past which survive are not nearly as significant as some which are scarcely noticed and of which either little or no trace remains or which, if it is there, is normally passed over by the historian. Yet it is to events and institutions which caught the eye, and to men and women who seemed important to their contemporaries that the historian is chiefly confined, even when he is aware that, judged by Christian standards, many of them are not as significant as others whose memory has so faded that when he seeks for them he cannot discover them.

Fortunately many individuals and movements have appealed to those whose insights have been born of their Christian faith. For them, accordingly, documents have been cherished. Because of their involvement in phases of the world about them which non-Christians deem important, some men and movements have been given a place in records made and preserved by those who did not sympathize with them. Then, too, many individuals and institutions which have borne the Christian name have compromised their Christian principles by mingling with the sub-Christian or anti-Christian world about them to such an extent that the latter has paid them the doubtful compliment of so noticing them that accounts of them have been kept.

Because of these factors, any history of Christianity, when viewed from the Christian perspective, while perhaps having something of true insight, cannot but be distorted and defective.

Moreover, even if his records gave all that he could desire and his own judgement were fully clarified by the Christian faith, the historian of Christianity would still be partly frustrated. Of the essence of his faith is the conviction that the Gospel was in the plan of God before He created man and thus before history began, and that the human drama, whether for individuals, for the Church, or for the race as a whole is not and cannot be complete within history, but moves on beyond this bourne of time and space. At best the historian can only record what has thus far occurred within history. If he could see in detail what is to come and what and when the culmination is to be he could venture on interpretation with greater assurance. As it is, the full pattern is not yet perceived and for much of it he can only offer conjectures. We are reminded that both knowledge and prophecy shall be done away and that now we see as in a mirror, darkly. A profound Christian conviction is that only faith, hope, and love endure. These can be a matter of history, but we cannot understand the past fully because not yet has history been completed nor the final outcome seen of that love which the Christian believes to be the dominant characteristic of God Who made all this vast universe and Who continues to work in it.

No one can hope to write history without presuppositions. The professional historian of the nineteenth and twentieth centuries has aspired to be "objective" and to tell "what actually happened." Yet every attempt to view the human story, whether in some small segment or as a whole, involves a selection of events from the stream which constitutes the crude stuff of history. Back of the selection is a conviction of what is important. Governing this "value judgement" is, consciously or unconsciously, a philosophy. Underneath and conditioning any endeavour to determine what happened also lies a theory of knowledge, epistemology, with attempts to answer such questions as: Can we know? If so how do we know? How valid and how complete is our knowledge? There have been and still are many theories of knowledge, many different answers to these questions. Many interpretations—"philosophies"—of history have been or are held. Some are basically agnostic, declaring that there may be no pattern in history, that if there is we cannot discover it, that all one can confidently affirm about the various philosophies of history is that we cannot know which if any of them is true, and that we cannot be too sure even of the validity of agnosticism. Others are cyclical, viewing history as endlessly repeating itself. Others affirm progress in one form or another. The view associated with the name of Hegel is one of thesis, antithesis, and synthesis, the synthesis becoming a new thesis, marked by a new antithesis, issuing in a fresh synthesis, and so onwards, a combination of cycles and progress. The Hegelian philosophy contributed to the emergence of the dialectical materialistic view of history. The Hindu has traditionally regarded history, like human life itself, as illusion. The nineteenth and twentieth century effort to determine what actually happened consciously or unconsciously has assumed that we can know what happened. In general, historians of the various schools of that period have believed that they could discover relationships between events—causes and effects. More and more they have assumed that history is universal, that the race has a common origin, that increasingly mankind has become one, that what affects the individual affects all, and that what the individual does concerns the whole.

Here is not the place to endeavor to determine which if any of the several philosophies is true, or even to seek for valid criteria by which they can be judged. That effort would necessitate a separate and large treatise. At the outset, however, we must say as clearly as we know how that underlying the pages which follow there is a profound conviction that the Christian Gospel is God's supreme act on man's behalf and that the history of Christianity is the history of what God has done for man through Christ and of man's response.

If it is complained that this is not an "objective" approach, it must be remembered that pure objectivity does not exist, even in the natural sciences. One is either for or against Christianity: there is no neutral or strictly "objective" ground. Reason has a legitimate place. We must employ it in testing what are presented to us as facts and in searching for other facts. But truth is not attained by reason alone. The insight that is born of faith can bring illumination. Faith is not credulity and if that which is called faith ignores reason it does so to its peril. But uncritical confidence in reason as the sole or final criterion is a blind act of credulity which may be even more dangerous than a faith which disdains reason. Throughout the chapters which follow is the conviction that the faith which is stimulated by contact with the Christian Gospel, the faith which is the commitment to God of the whole man, body, mind, and spirit, the commitment which is the response in love to God Who is love and Who in His love has revealed Himself in Jesus Christ, opens the mind towards the true understanding of history. That we fail to understand history is due to our lack of such a commitment. That we understand it partly but imperfectly arises from a commitment which is real but incomplete. No one of us has made a full commitment. If we are honest with ourselves we know how limited our commitment is. We should, therefore, never claim infallibility for our interpretation of history. Yet so far as the faith which follows commitment has been given to us, we must seek in its light to perceive the road which man has thus far traversed.

Limitations both in the records and in the historian are inescapable in narrating the history of Christianity. Yet we can attempt it, being aware in part of our handicaps. That is what is essayed in the work to which this is the preface.

In entering upon this adventure we must, as we have suggested, see the history of Christianity in its relation to the total story of mankind. We must endeavour to view it in the setting of human history as a whole. To segregate it from the rest of the course of mankind is to do it violence. Ours must be a purview as inclusive as all mankind and from the beginning to the present.

Obviously this purpose cannot be adequately fulfilled in one or two volumes: a multi-volume work would be too small for the total sweep of time and events. However, there may be some value in the effort to summarize the story within the compass of a few hundred pages and in doing so to bring into prominence the highlights in the record of Christianity. It is hoped that such a survey will prove useful to the thoughtful student, whether he be clergyman or layman, Christian or non-Christian, and that it will be helpful as a text-book in colleges, universities, and theological schools.

The main outline of the book can be quickly discerned by reference to the table of contents. It corresponds to what the author believes to be the main divisions of the Christian story.

First of all is a section made up of three chapters which attempts to place Christianity in its setting, to see it in the stream of history, to point out the particular currents in that stream from which it had its rise, and to describe the portion of the world in which it was born. Next is an account of the beginnings of Christianity. This must centre around Jesus. It may seem to be a banality to say that Christianity cannot be understood apart from him. Yet repeatedly through the centuries and in our own day there have been those who have regarded Jesus as unimportant in the origin and initial growth of Christianity. In contrast with this view, the author is convinced that without Jesus Christianity is not only unintelligible: it would never have been. The fashion in which Jesus Christ has shaped the faith which bears his name and the degree to which his professed followers have embodied him or departed from him never ceases to be both fascinating and significant.

After its origin, the course of Christianity is treated by what the author deems to have been its major epochs. These, as he conceives them, are best seen as pulsations in the life of Christianity as reflected in its vigour and its influence upon the ongoing history of the race. The criteria which he believes to be valid for discerning these pulsations are, in the main, three—the expansion or recession of the territory in which Christians are to be found, the new movements issuing from Christianity, and the effect of Christianity as judged from the perspective of mankind as a whole. Precise dates can seldom if ever be fixed for the pulsations. The lines between the eras are fuzzy. One age has a way of running over into its successor or of being foreshadowed before it is born. The eras are realities, but there are no sharp breaks between them which can be identified by particular years. Advance and retreat often begin at different times in the several areas in which Christians are found and the first indications of revival are frequently seen before decline has been halted. Terminal dates are, therefore, only approximations. Yet approximate dates can be named.

In treating each of these periods we will endeavour to sketch first of all the contemporary world setting in which Christianity was found, with special emphasis upon conditions in the areas in which Christianity was strong. We will tell of the geographic spread of the faith, inquiring into the forms of

Christianity through which the expansion was effected, the reasons for the expansion, and the processes by which the spread took place. If there were territorial losses we will seek to describe them, their causes, and their extent. We will take account of the new movements in the institutional expressions of the faith, and will give brief accounts of the individuals who were more prominent in the Christian story. We will summarize the developments in the thought of Christians about their faith, in forms of worship, and in the means employed to mould the Christian constituency. We will also attempt to say something of the effect of Christianity on its environment and note, in turn, the effect of the environment on Christianity. Not always will these aspects be treated in precisely the order in which they are arranged in this paragraph but in one way or another they will be covered.

The first period or pulsation embraces roughly the initial five centuries. Within these years Christianity won the professed allegiance of the large majority of the population of the Roman Empire. During that time the Church came into being and its visible, institutional expressions took the forms which in their main outlines still characterize the churches in which the majority of Christians have their membership. The several books which compose the New Testament were written and assembled. Other literature was produced. Christians wrestled with the intellectual problems presented by their faith and in consequence Christian theology came into being. The main formulations then hammered out, together with the creeds in which they were summarized, have continued to be standard. Monasticism arose and spread. Forms of worship developed which have had lasting effects. Christianity made a marked impression upon the civilizations of the Mediterranean Basin but this was not as deep or as striking as was that upon other cultures in later periods. In these five centuries only a small fraction of the earth's surface and a minority of mankind were touched by the faith. The large majority of civilized mankind and almost all the uncivilized portions of the human race were not even aware of it. In consequence, Christianity became so closely associated as almost to be identified with a cultural tradition which was only one among several and it was threatened by the possibility of being a regional rather than the universal faith.

Between A.D. 500 and A.D. 950 Christianity suffered the greatest losses which it has ever encountered. Its very existence was threatened. The decay of the empire and the culture with which its phenomenal successes in its first five hundred years had almost identified it seemed to presage its demise. Christianity's very victory appeared to have become its doom. The invasion of the Mediterranean world by non-Christians, notably by Islam-bearing Arabs, tore from Christianity approximately half the areas which had been gained in the preceding period. The morale of the Christian communities declined to their lowest ebb. The story was not altogether one of loss. Additional peoples were brought to accept the faith, and outposts were established from Ireland to China and from Scotland and Scandinavia to Nubia. Some important developments occurred within the churches. Yet never again since those long, agonizing centuries has the prospect for Christianity appeared to be so bleak.

There followed, from A.D. 950 to A.D. 1350, four centuries of advance. The area across which Christianity was carried expanded. More significantly, striking developments occurred within the churches, the Christian faith produced outstanding personalities and important movements in thought and organization, and it helped to bring into being new cultures, notably in Western Europe.

Between A.D. 1350 and A.D. 1500 a decline was witnessed. Much territory was lost and disorganization and corruption appeared in the churches. Yet the recession was neither as prolonged nor as severe as the one between A.D. 500 and A.D. 950. A larger proportion of the territory covered was retained, a few advances into fresh areas were achieved, and vigorous movements issued from Christianity which were indications of vitality.

The two and a half centuries between A.D. 1500 and A.D. 1750 constituted an amazing epoch. A series of awakenings revitalized and largely altered the Christianity of Western Europe. That segment of the globe was entering a new era and Christianity had an important share in modifying the culture which emerged. To a less but still important extent changes were seen in some aspects of Eastern Christianity. Explorations, conquests, and intrepid missionaries carried Christianity over a larger proportion of the earth's surface than had previously been true of it or of any other religion.

From A.D. 1750 to A.D. 1815 a series of events and movements again menaced Christianity. The decay of Spain and Portugal, strong champions of the faith in the preceding two-and-a-half centuries, fresh intellectual movements, and a succession of wars and revolutions in Europe and America appeared to many to be about to bring Christianity to an end. However, viewed in retrospect, the years were more a pause than a recession. There were few actual losses of territory, and new movements, too small at their inception to attract general attention, were appearing and were later to bring Christianity to a new high level of vigour.

The century from A.D. 1815 to A.D. 1914 presented striking contrasts. Western civilization was again moving into a new age. Many of the forces which were moulding that civilization were either openly or tacitly hostile to Christianity. The faith was threatened in its chief strongholds. But new life in Christianity swelled to a flood. This was especially marked in the form of Christianity, Protestantism, which had come into being as recently as the sixteenth

century. It was also seen in what long had been the most active segment of
Christianity, the Roman Catholic Church. Christianity continued to be potent
in Occidental culture and among Occidental peoples. To an important degree
the Occident was still Christendom. Even more than between A.D. 1500 and
A.D. 1750 Christianity spread over the surface of the globe. It was an integral
feature of the new nations which were created by European peoples in the
Americas and Australasia. Especially through its share in shaping the United
States of America Christianity gained in the total world scene. For the first
time Christianity really penetrated Africa south of the Sahara and many of the
islands of the Pacific. It had an enlarging rôle in Asia. The fresh life within
Christianity had many expressions in various lands and wrought significant
changes in that religion. The faith also continued to shape the Occident and
had effects of varying importance upon the peoples and cultures to which it
was being carried.

The period which had its inception in A.D. 1914 and is still incomplete constitutes the latest division of our story. In spite of colossal threats and striking
losses, Christianity has moved forward. Never before at any one time have all
cultures been so shaken. The revolutions have centred in what was once termed
Christendom. Indeed, there is some reason for regarding them as the fruit,
directly or indirectly, of Christianity. Yet for the first time Christianity is
becoming really world-wide. It is entering into the lives of more peoples than
it or any other religion has ever done. Into the new and often terrifying stage
into which the human race, bewildered, is being ushered, Christianity is more
potent than in any earlier era. It is by no means dominant. Never has that
adjective been an accurate description of its place in the human scene. However, when the world is surveyed as a whole, it is more to be reckoned with
than at any previous time. It is an important factor in the world culture which
appears to be emerging.

Readers of *A History of the Expansion of Christianity* will be inclined to
regard the present work as a summary of the earlier one. The chronological pattern, already familiar to them through its volumes, will seem to confirm them
in that impression. Inevitably much that the author learned in the writing of
that survey has been carried over into the present one. But the book which
follows is by no means a condensation of its larger predecessor. It has a quite
different purpose. The one, as its title indicates, is an account of the spread of
Christianity. The chapters which follow endeavour to be a well-rounded
summary of the entire history of Christianity in all its phases and in its setting
in the human scene. In them expansion must have a place and at times be
prominent. However, it is only one aspect of a larger whole. It is a fresh effort
upon which we are embarked.

A bibliography will be attached to each chapter, usually with brief appraisals of the various titles cited. These bibliographies are by no means complete or exhaustive. To make them such would extend the book beyond all reasonable dimensions. Indeed, it would mean multiplying the work into many volumes, for the published material on the history of Christianity is enormous, and that in manuscript is even more extensive. What is attempted, rather, is a selection of the works which the reader or the student who wishes to go further in some of the subjects covered in the text may employ as references and as guides. Several of the books listed are original sources, or as near to original sources as can be obtained. More are secondary accounts based upon the sources or upon other secondary works. The larger proportion are in English, for this study is designed primarily for those who read that language. However, many are in other languages, partly because of their outstanding importance and partly because this book may be translated into other tongues and those who have it in those forms will not wish their reference material confined to English. Not every study consulted by the author in the preparation of this work has been listed. The author has, however, personally examined all those whose titles have been included in the bibliographies and the appraisals given are his own.

Specialists will probably wish that a larger documentation had been given for subjects in which they are particularly interested and may differ both from the estimates of individual books and from the presentation which has been made of the topics in which they are experts. The author can lay no claim to infallibility. He has attempted to avail himself of the best of the books, monographs, and articles of the specialists, to examine a fair proportion of the original sources, and by their use to make his pages as factually accurate as possible. He is painfully conscious, however, that he has not covered more than a small fraction of the pertinent material and that errors have almost certainly crept into what he has written. In questions of judgement and interpretation, moreover, many will almost certainly challenge much that is here put down. The author can only hope that what he has written will prove of some use to both general readers and specialists. He trusts that his survey may enable some who come after him to tell the story of Christianity with more accuracy and with greater insight than he has been able to command.

The author would express his gratitude to the many to whom he and this work are deeply indebted—to the thousands of scholars who have preceded him and from whose labours he has gleaned much of whatever of value these pages may contain, to students who have patiently submitted to having the material presented to them and by their questions have added much illumination, and to colleagues in Yale University and in many another institution of higher learning who have contributed of their knowledge. To no small degree they are in reality co-authors, although few if any of their exact words have been quoted. The title page would be quite too small to include all their names.

As again and again across the years, the author owes an incalculable debt to Mrs. Charles T. Lincoln for typing the manuscript and for suggestions in matters of style.

The author craves the privilege of dedicating this book to his colleagues, past and present, of the Yale University Divinity School. It seems almost invidious to single out any from that goodly company for special mention, for each has contributed, usually quite unwittingly, to these pages. However, the author is peculiarly under obligation to the three Deans under whom he has worked—Charles R. Brown, Luther A. Weigle, and Liston Pope—to Williston Walker, who first introduced him to the history of Christianity as a subject for serious study and whose writings have been of great assistance, to Roland H. Bainton, whose friendship and high standards of scholarship have been a continued inspiration and on whose vast erudition this book has again and again drawn, to Robert L. Calhoun, from whom the author has gained not a little of such knowledge of the history of Christian doctrine as he possesses, and to Raymond P. Morris, who as Librarian of the Yale University Divinity School has not only shown extraordinary skill and judgement in assembling and making accessible the pertinent literature but has also been unfailingly generous and wise in this counsel.

The author needs scarcely add that none of these many friends is to be held accountable for any errors which the book may contain or for any omissions of which it may be guilty.

THE PRE-CHRISTIAN COURSE
OF MANKIND

Chapter 1

THE GENERAL SETTING OF CHRISTIANITY
IN HISTORY

THE YOUTH OF CHRISTIANITY

Christianity is relatively young. Compared with the course of mankind on the earth, it began only a few moments ago. No one knows how old man is. That is because we cannot tell precisely when a creature which can safely be described as human first appeared. One estimate places the earliest presence of what may be called man about 1,200,000 years in the past. A being with a brain about the size of modern man may have lived approximately 500,000 years ago. In contrast with these vast reaches of time the less than two thousand years which Christianity has thus far had are very brief. If one accepts the perspective set forth in the New Testament that in Christ is the secret of God's plan for the entire creation, and that God purposes to "gather together in one all things in Christ, both which are in heaven and which are on earth," Christianity becomes relatively even more recent, for the few centuries since the coming of Christ are only an infinitesimal fraction of the time which has elapsed since the earth, not to speak of the vast universe, came into being.

When placed in the setting of human civilization Christianity is still youthful. Civilization is now regarded as having begun from ten to twelve thousand years ago, during the last retreat of the continental ice sheets. This means that Christianity has been present during only a fifth or a sixth of the brief span of civilized mankind.

Moreover, Christianity appeared late in the religious development of mankind. It may be something of this kind which was meant by Paul when he declared that "in the fullness of time God sent forth His son." We need not here take the space to sketch the main outlines of the history of religion. We must note, however, that of those faiths which have had an extensive and enduring geographic spread, Christianity is next to the latest to come to birth. Animism in one or another of its many forms seems to have antedated civilization. Polytheisms have been numerous, and some of them, mostly now merely a memory, are very ancient. Hinduism in its earlier aspects antedates Christianity by more than a thousand years. Judaism, out of which Christianity sprang, is many hundreds of years older than the latter. Confucius, the dominant figure in the system which the Occident calls by his name, lived in the sixth and fifth centuries before Christ. The years of the founder of Buddhism, although debated, are commonly placed in the same centuries. Zarathustra, or, to give him the name by which English readers generally know him, Zoroaster, the major creator of the faith which was long official in Persia and which is still represented by the Parsees, is of much less certain date, but he seems to have been at least as old as Confucius and the Buddha and he may have been older by several centuries. Only Manichæism and Islam were of later origin than Christianity. Of these two, Manichæism has perished. Christianity is, therefore, the next to the youngest of the great religious systems extant in our day which have expanded widely among mankind.

That Christianity emerged in the midst of a period in which the major high religions of mankind were appearing gives food for thought. Most of these faiths came into being in the thirteen centuries between 650 B.C. and A.D. 650. Of those which survive only Judaism and Hinduism began before 650 B.C. Here was a religious ferment among civilized peoples which within a comparatively brief span issued in most of the main advanced religions which have since shaped the human race. This occurred with but little interaction of one upon another. Only Christianity and Islam are exceptions. Both of these were deeply indebted to Judaism, and Islam was influenced by both Judaism and Christianity.

The youth of Christianity may be highly important. It might conceivably mean that, as a relatively late phenomenon, Christianity will be transient. The other major religions have risen, flourished, reached their apex, and then have either entered upon a slow decline or have become stationary. Hinduism is not as widely extended as it was fifteen hundred years ago. Not for five centuries have important gains been registered by Buddhism and during that time serious losses have occurred. Confucianism has achieved no great geographic advance since it moved into Annam, Korea, and Japan many centuries ago, and at present it is disintegrating. Islam has suffered no significant surrender of territory since the reconversion of the Iberian Peninsula to Christianity, a process completed about four centuries ago, and in the present century has pushed its frontiers forward in some areas, notably in Africa south of the Sahara. Yet its advances have been much less marked than in the initial stages of its spread. It might be argued that Christianity is to have a similar fate and the fact of its youth may mean that for it the cycle of growth, maturity, and decay has not reached as advanced a stage as has that of other faiths. To this appraisal the fact of the emergence of the high religions, including Christianity, in the comparatively brief span of thirteen centuries may lend support. The grouping of their origins in one segment of time and the progressive weaken-ing of so many of them might be interpreted as an indication that all religions, in the traditionally accepted use of that term, and including even Christianity, are a waning force in the life of mankind. Some, indeed, so interpret history and declare that the race is outgrowing religion. The losses in Europe in the present century might well appear to foreshadow the demise of Christianity.

On the other hand, the brief course of Christianity to date may be but a precursor to an indefinitely expanding future. The faith may be not far from the beginning of its history and only in the early stages of a growing influence upon mankind. As we are to see more extensively in subsequent chapters, the record of Christianity yields evidence which can be adduced in support of this view. As we hinted in the preface and will elaborate more at length later, the faith has displayed its greatest geographic extension in the past century and a half. As the twentieth century advances, and in spite of many adversaries and severe losses, it has become more deeply rooted among more peoples than it or any other faith has ever before been. It is also more widely influential in the affairs of men than any other religious system which mankind has known. The weight of evidence appears to be on the side of those who maintain that Christianity is still only in the first flush of its history and that it is to have a growing place in the life of mankind. In this Christianity is in striking con-trast with other religions. Here are much of its uniqueness and a possible clue to its significance.

A third possible interpretation, and one to which many Christians subscribe, is that Christianity will neither disappear nor fully triumph within history, but that it will continue, sometimes waning, sometimes waxing in its influence upon individuals and mankind as a whole, until, perhaps early, perhaps mil-lenniums hence, history comes to an end. To this view also much in the record appears to lend support.

The comparative youth of Christianity means that the history which is sum-marized in the subsequent chapters, complex and rich though it is, compasses only a small fragment of the total span of the story of the human race and, if mankind goes on, is merely an introduction to what later millenniums are to witness. If Christianity is only near the beginning of its course it may be that the forms which it has developed, whether institutional, intellectual, or ritual, are by no means to be final or continuously characteristic. This, however, is prophecy, and upon that dangerous road the historian ought not to venture.

The Limited Area of Early Christianity

The cultural area in which Christianity arose, that of the Mediterranean Basin, was merely one of the centres of contemporary civilization and embraced only a minority of mankind. It is important that this fact be recognized if we are to see the history of the faith in its true perspective. Since during the past four and a half centuries the Occident and its culture have been progressively dominant throughout the globe, and since in connection with it Christianity has had its world-wide spread, we are inclined to regard that condition as normal. In view of the circumstance that during its first five centuries Christianity won the professed allegiance of the Roman Empire, which then embraced the Occident, many have thought of it as having at this early date conquered the world. This is entirely mistaken. East of the Roman Empire was the Persian Empire which for centuries fought Rome to a stalemate. Its rulers regarded Christianity with hostile eye, partly because of its association with their chronic rival, and fought its entrance into their domains. India, although not united into one political realm, was the seat of a great culture which influenced the Mediterranean area but which, in spite of extensive commercial contacts, was but little affected religiously by the Occident. China had a civilization all its own. At the time when the Roman Empire was being formed, China was being welded into a political and cultural whole under the Ch'in and the Han dynasty. In area it was about as large as the Roman Empire. In wealth and population it may not have equalled its great Western contemporary, but in cultural achievements it needed to make no apology to India, Persia, or Rome. In the Americas were small beginnings of civilized states. In its first five centuries neither China nor America was reached by Christianity. These civilizations, even when taken together, occupied only a minority of the surface of the earth. Outside them were the vast masses of "primitive" mankind, almost untouched by Christianity until after its first five centuries were passed. It is against this background that we must see the rise and early development of Christianity. In its initial centuries the geographic scope of Christianity was distinctly limited.

The Unpromising Rootage of Christianity

When we come to the area in which Christianity began, we must remind ourselves that even there, in that geographically circumscribed region, the roots from which it sprang appeared to promise no very great future for the faith. It is one of the commonplaces of our story that Christianity was an outgrowth of the religion of Israel. Israel was never important politically. Only for a brief time, under David and Solomon, between nine hundred and a thousand years before Christ, did it achieve a domain of considerable dimensions. Even then it did not rank with the major empires. That realm soon broke up into two small states, the Northern and Southern Kingdoms, insignificant pawns in the contests among the great powers in the valleys of the Nile and of the Tigris and Euphrates Rivers. Except for what came through its religion, Israel was of slight consequence culturally. When contrasted with its neighbours in Mesopotamia and Egypt it occupied a small and infertile area in the Palestinian uplands. Its cities were diminutive and its buildings unimpressive. Its art was not distinguished. Today the monumental ruins of Egypt, Nineveh, Babylon, and even Syria dwarf those of Israel's past and make clear the relative insignificance, from the political and economic standpoint, of the land in which was the stock from which Christianity sprang.

In this respect Christianity was in striking contrast with those faiths which became its chief rivals. The polytheisms which it displaced in the Mediterranean Basin had the support of old and politically powerful cultures and states. Zoroastrianism was associated with Persia, for centuries one of the mightiest empires on the globe. Hinduism was indigenous to India, one of the major cultural centres of mankind. Buddhism was also a native of India and early won wide popularity in the land of its birth. Both Hinduism and Buddhism owed much of their extension outside India to the commerce and the cultural prestige of that land. Confucianism was for two thousand years so closely integrated with China, one of earth's mightiest civilizations, that its spread on the periphery of that realm seemed assured. Islam early brought unity to the Arabs and within a century of its origin was supported by one of the three largest and strongest empires of the day. At its outset Christianity had no such potent associations to commend it. Not until, after more than three centuries, it had, through its first amazing victories, become dominant in the Roman Empire did it achieve such an influential cultural and political alliance as these other faiths early possessed.

It is sometimes said that Israel owed its unique religious development to the fact that it was of the family of Semitic peoples and was on the land bridge between the great civilizations of Egypt and of Mesopotamia and so was stimulated by contributions from each of them. But there were other Semitic peoples who were in much the same favored position, the Phoenicians among them, and it was only in Israel that the religious development occurred which issued in Judaism and Christianity.

Moreover, it was in a minority, even within the comparatively obscure people of Israel, that the stream which issued in Christianity had its rise and its early course. The prophetic monotheism which was the source of Christianity long commanded the undivided support of only a small proportion of Israel.

The loyal minority were sufficiently numerous to cherish and hand down the writings of the prophets. Through them came the main contributions of Israel to the world. Within this minority we find the direct antecedents of Christianity. Yet the majority of Israel either rejected the prophets outright or devitalized their message by compromise. Even among the relatively insignificant people within which Christianity arose, only the numerically lesser part could be counted in the spiritual ancestry of the faith. Fully as significantly, it was largely those who believed themselves to be in the succession of that minority who so opposed Jesus that they brought him to the cross.

Christians have seen in this story the fashion in which God works. They have believed that always and everywhere God has been seeking man and has been confronting man with Himself and with the standard which He has set for man. Yet man, so they have held, persistently rebels against God and becomes corrupt. God, of His mercy and love, has wrought for man's redemption. This He has not done in the way which men would have predicted. Even those whom men have accounted wise have been so blinded by sin, especially by pride and self-confidence, that they could not clearly see or hear God. For reasons known only to Himself, so Christians have maintained, God chose as His channel for man's salvation a small, insignificant minority among the people of Israel, themselves of slight consequence in physical might. As the culmination of His revelation of Himself and His redemption of man, He sent His son, who, the heir of this humble minority and building on the foundations laid by them, became the centre of the Christian faith.

The story, as seen from a Christian standpoint, might also be put in the following fashion. God has always, from the beginning of the human race, been seeking to bring men into fellowship with Himself and into His likeness. He has respected man's free will and has not forced Himself on man. Only thus could He produce beings who are not automata, but are akin to Himself. In response to God's initiative, men everywhere were stimulated to grope for God. As a result of their seeking, various religions arose. All of these, clouded by man's sin, were imperfect and could not meet man's need or fulfil God's purpose. For some inscrutable reason, God found among the people of Israel a minority who responded to Him and, therefore, was able to disclose Himself fully through one who came out of that succession and through him made possible the salvation of man.

These interpretations, arising from Christian faith, might be suspect as biased. Yet, more than any others, as we are to see in a later stage in our story, they seem to make intelligible the facts presented by the course of Christianity on the planet.

BIBLIOGRAPHY

The literature on the history of religion is enormous. As good a comprehensive survey as any is G. F. Moore, *History of Religions* (New York, Charles Scribner's Sons, 2 vols., 1913–1919).

Chapter 2

THE IMMEDIATE BACKGROUND OF
CHRISTIANITY: JUDAISM

It was from Judaism that Christianity sprang. Indeed, at the outset it appeared to be only one of several sects of Judaism.

The Rise of Judaism

Judaism arose out of the religion of Israel. It came through lawgivers, priests, and prophets and was the outgrowth of centuries of development.

For many generations, as we have suggested, the faith of which it was the fruitage obtained the undivided allegiance of only a minority of the folk who bore the name of Israel, but eventually it was held tenaciously by the majority of those who were called Jews. The disasters of the eighth and sixth centuries b.c. which erased the two small states that had been the political centres of the people led to a purification of the faith of the community which survived the debacle. The downfall of the Northern and Southern Kingdoms was the work of conquerors from the Tigris-Euphrates Valley and was accompanied and followed by the deportation of the leading elements and some of the masses. Others fled to Egypt. Only small and politically unimportant groups remained. Then, under the friendly tolerance of the Persian monarchs who brought Palestine within their boundaries, a new temple was built at Jerusalem which became the centre not only for the Jewish population of that region but also for the thousands of Jews who were scattered in other parts of Western Asia and of the Mediterranean Basin. The tie which held the Jews together was religious and the religion was Judaism.

The loyalty of the Jews to their religion was heightened by persecution. Antiochus Epiphanes, one of the Seleucids who in succession to Alexander the Great built a realm in Syria and adjacent lands, sought to force Greek culture and manners on the Jews. This was met by a revolt led by the Maccabees and was followed by the setting up of a small state in which the high priest was the central figure. It also intensified among many the zeal for their faith.

Later, in the first century before Christ, the Jewish state was brought within the growing power of Rome. Herod, of non-Jewish stock but married into the Maccabeean family, with the consent of Rome established himself over the little state and rebuilt the temple in Jerusalem. Here was a sad ending of the Maccabeean dream. That dream had envisioned a community in which God's will as expressed in the Jewish law and prophets was to be perfectly observed. The outcome was a state governed by an alien ruler whose chief ambition was his own power and the establishment of a dynasty. Yet it was during the reign of Herod that Jesus was born and under Herod's descendants that Christianity had its inception.

JEWISH BELIEFS AND LITERATURE

The Judaism of the centuries immediately before the birth of Christianity was strictly monotheistic and made much of the Law and the Prophets. Into the long story of its development we must not take the time to go, even in brief summary. For our purposes we must confine ourselves to such bare features of Judaism as are essential to an understanding of the beginnings of Christianity and the nature and characteristics of that faith.

Judaism regarded the Jews as especially favoured by God. Originally, at least for many, their god was a tribal deity, one of many gods, but choosing Israel for his own. With him Israel was believed to have entered into intimate covenant relations through which they were to be loyal to him and he, in return, was to aid them. Early, perhaps from the outset, some among Israel were monotheists. They regarded their god, Yahweh, a name mistakenly put into English as Jehovah, as the God of the universe, the maker and ruler of heaven and earth. Other peoples had their gods, but Yahweh was regarded by these monotheists as far more powerful than they. They were either false gods or were completely subordinate to him. To the Jew the core of his faith and the chief commandment were found in the declaration: "Hear, O Israel: The Lord our God is one Lord: and thou shalt love the Lord thy God with all thy heart, and with all thy soul, and with all thy might." God, so the devout Jew believed, had made man in His own image, but man had sinned against God and thereby had incurred His wrath. That sin, so the Jew held, began with the transgression of the first human couple, Adam and Eve. It was basically rebellion against God. God, however, of His great mercy chose Abraham, and of him and his descendants made a nation, His peculiar people. He also, the Jew maintained, gave him His law to control his conduct. That law had to do both with what are usually called morals and with ritual. It was briefly summarized in the Ten Commandments, but it had much more elaborate

formulations. It included the regulation of food and diet and the observance
of days, especially the Sabbath. The latter was to be kept with great strictness,
free from the usual occupations of the rest of the week. Circumcision was
universal and was regarded as a symbol of the covenant between Yahweh and
His people.

The prophets were honoured as spokesmen for Yahweh. They not only foretold the future. The greatest of them also, and more especially, rebuked wickedness, both private and public, and, on occasion, sought to direct the policy of
the community and the state and to encourage those who were obedient. They
denounced the rich for oppressing the poor. Believing as they did that Yahweh
is ruler of all the earth, they spoke out against the sins of the surrounding
nations, but they were particularly vehement in their arraignment of Israel.

The law-givers and prophets were claimed by Christians as forerunners of
Jesus. Their names and histories, as well as their teachings, became the property
of Christianity and entered into its warp and woof. Outstanding were Moses,
who led his people out of their captivity in Egypt, and through whom came
the initial formulation of the Jewish law; Elijah, an heroic figure who stood as
the champion of Yahweh and of the poor against the corruptions of the court
of the Northern Kingdom and who captured the imagination of succeeding
generations; Isaiah, who rebuked the wickedness of his people, especially those
of the Southern Kingdom, called them to repentance, and heartened its king to
withstand an Assyrian invasion; the latter part of the book which bears the
name of Isaiah, with stirring chapters in which Christians have seen a pre-
vision of Jesus and his vicarious sufferings; Amos, who sternly denounced the
evils of the peoples of his world and especially of Israel; Hosea, who in his
bitter experience with a faithless wife perceived something of the way in which
Yahweh viewed a rebellious Israel; Jeremiah, who, in the last days of the
Southern Kingdom, became an unpopular preacher of doom and in his own
sufferings foreshadowed the experience of Jesus; and Ezekiel, the prophet of
the exile, who spoke to those who had been carried to the Tigris-Euphrates
Valley.

Judaism also gave rise to great poetry. The standard collection of its hymns,
the Psalms, became the cherished possession of Christians and held and continues to hold a prominent place in their public and private worship. *The Book
of Job,* with its wrestling with the problem of evil, passed over to the Christians. So also did *The Song of Songs,* which, allegorized, became a cherished
treasure house of Christian mystics. What was known as the Wisdom literature
of the Jews was also claimed by the Christians. Its proverbs and its glorification of Wisdom became a part of the Christian heritage.

Apocalypse, Eschatology, and Messiah

Prominent in the Jewish faith were apocalypses and a belief in the Messiah. The two were often associated but were by no means inseparable. The apocalypses were a kind of literature which flourished in Jewish circles in the centuries immediately preceding and following the time of Christ. The word meant to uncover or to reveal. An apocalypse claimed to be a divine revelation of the future. It arose from the Jewish conception of history. The Jews believed God to be at work in the affairs of men. Indeed, they held that He controlled all history. They saw much in life which was contrary to what they conceived to be the will of God. The wicked often lorded it over the righteous. Indeed, the righteous were repeatedly overwhelmed by the unrightous. The disobedient appeared to prosper. Moreover, misfortunes of other kinds, such as sickness, overtook the good. The Jews were concerned to reconcile these uncomfortable facts with the sovereignty of God. They held that human history is a drama which begins with the creation of man, which early sees the rebellion of man against God, and which has its culmination in the victory of God in an era in which God's will is fully done. It was the future steps of this process which the apocalypses professed to reveal. They were based upon a profound conviction that God must ultimately triumph. They speak of "the age to come." This would be introduced by a great catastrophe with judgement beyond which would lie a new heaven and a new earth. They deal with what is technically known as eschatology, "last" or final things, at the end of history and beyond it, such as judgement and the life of the age to come.

As an agent for God's victory some of the Jews cherished the hope of a Messiah. Various views of the Messiah were held, but all agreed that he was the "anointed"—for that is what the word meant—a king who was to reign under divine commission. In the periods of subjugation to foreign rulers the Messiah was anticipated as the deliverer from the alien and as one who would set up the ideal realm in which God's will would be perfectly done. The Greek word used to translate Messiah was the one from which the English word Christ is derived.

The Synagogue

By the time of the birth of Christianity Judaism had developed an institution, the synagogue, which was to have a profound effect upon the nascent Christian Church. The synagogue had arisen between the revival of Judaism after the fall of the Northern and Southern Kingdoms and the time of Jesus. Synagogues were the chief centres of Jewish worship. Until its destruction a generation or so after the time of Jesus, the temple in Jerusalem was the main shrine of

Judaism. Yet both in Palestine and among the Jews of the "dispersion," scattered through much of the Mediterranean world and Western Asia, the synagogues were the places where most of the Jews worshipped and were taught. They had regular forms of service. In them the Law and the Prophets were read and expounded. Through them and the instruction given in them Judaism was perpetuated. Schools were associated with the synagogues and in them the Scriptures and the unwritten law were taught.

THE SCRIBE

A class which had developed by the time of Christ and which had great influence upon the Judaism of that period was the Scribes. The Scribes were professional teachers and scholars who concerned themselves with the Scriptures and particularly with the Jewish law, both in its written form and in its oral tradition. They might also be priests but most of them were laymen. They were by no means an hereditary caste, as were the priests, but any one through personal competence might enter their ranks.

VARIETIES OF JUDAISM

When Christianity came into being, Judaism was not all of one pattern. In it were to be found several trends, schools, and sects. Not all of them were important in the development of Christianity. We need notice, therefore, only those which were significant for the history of that faith.

A trend of primary importance was towards the penetration of Judaism by Hellenism. The Jews were widely scattered in the Mediterranean world. Here they fell under the influence of the Greek thought which was so potent in that region, especially after the conquests by Alexander the Great in the fourth century before Christ. Outstanding as a centre of Greek culture was Alexandria, in Egypt.

The preëminent representative of this trend was Philo, or Philo Judæus. An Alexandrian, born late in the first century before Christ and doing most of his work in the first century of the Christian Era, he was a contemporary of Jesus. He was profoundly influenced by Greek thought, especially by Platonism, but also by the Stoics and the Pythagoreans. Indeed, he knew Greek much better than he did Hebrew and could almost be counted as a Greek philosopher. He was of the Hellenistic world, that cultural atmosphere, a mixture of the Orient and Greece, which arose from the spread of Greek thought and manners into the Orient. It was Hellenism in which Philo was nurtured. Yet Philo was a loyal Jew by birth and religion and sought through his writings to commend his faith to the Hellenistic world. In interpreting the Jewish scriptures he employed the device of allegory, a method which he did not originate and which was to persist long after him, in Christian as well as in other circles. With the aid of allegory he sought to show that the profoundest speculations of Greek thought were to be found in Jewish law. He insisted that Moses was the source of much of Greek philosophy. This, too, became the attitude of some of the Christian writers of the first centuries of that faith.

The Hellenistic Judaism of which Philo was the leading representative at once found expression and was reinforced through what was known as the Septuagint. The Septuagint was made up of translations of Jewish sacred books into Greek. The name is derived from the tradition that the task of translation was accomplished in the third century B.C. in seventy-two days by seventy-two scholars sent from Jerusalem to Alexandria at the request of one of the Ptolemies. This tradition is found in a letter which is undoubtedly spurious. The translation was actually the work of many different hands. It was made piecemeal and in several centuries. It was obviously needed for the many Jews for whom Greek was the language of everyday life and to whom the Hebrew of the original was either unfamiliar or understood only with difficulty.

Hellenistic Judaism was varied. A certain amount of unity was given it by the synagogue and the use of the Septuagint in teaching and in the services of the synagogue. Yet the penetration of Judaism by Hellenism differed from community to community and even from individual to individual. Moreover, Hellenism itself was far from uniform. Hellenistic Judaism, therefore, had many aspects, most of which are now lost us through the ravages of time.

Through Hellenistic Judaism many converts were won from the surrounding non-Jewish communities. The Jews were profoundly convinced that theirs was the only true religion and that it would sometime become the faith of all mankind. They probably had few professional missionaries whose assignment it was to win the Gentiles, but in their intercourse with the non-Jews—the "Gentiles"—many Jews sought to bring the latter to their faith. Their synagogue services were open to all, whether Jew or Gentile. Many Gentiles were attracted to Judaism. Some of them partly adopted Judaism but did not become full members of the Jewish community. They abandoned idolatry and the worship of other gods, they observed the Sabbath and the Jewish regulations of clean and unclean foods, they attended the services of the synagogue, and, in general, observed Jewish ethics. Others went the whole way and became full proselytes. They not only conformed as did those who might be described as on the fringes of Judaism. In addition they were circumcised, were baptized (the baptism was by immersion), and offered a sacrifice in the temple in Jerusalem. They thus were accepted into the Jewish community as equals of those who were Jews by birth.

Many converts came from less than religious motives. Some were forced by the political authorities to accept Judaism. Numbers entered through marriage. Still others wished to share in the special privileges which were accorded the Jews in some regions and periods. However, many adopted Judaism from profound religious conviction.

Eventually, as we are to see, Christianity had much of its early spread through the circles of Hellenistic Judaism, both among those who were Jews by long heredity and those who had either become full proselytes or were on the fringes of the synagogue.

In general, the penetration of Judaism by Hellenism was less marked within Palestine than outside it. Some permeation there was, even in this traditional stronghold of the Jews. Many in its very home would have Judaism conform to Hellenism. However, as we have suggested, strong resistance was put up against the attempts at partial or complete conformity and especially against the efforts of Antiochus Epiphanes to assimilate the Jews to Hellenism.

Within Palestine the Hebrew religious heritage was shared by several groups. Some of these became significant for Christianity.

One of which we hear mention in the first century was the Samaritans. The Samaritans were not Jews. They were regarded by the latter as outsiders, partly akin and yet to be classed with the Gentiles. They were descendants of some of the Israelites who had composed the Northern Kingdom and who had not been carried away captive at the time of the downfall of that state. They accepted the Law as contained in the Pentateuch, the first five books of the Jewish scriptures, but they rejected Jerusalem as the centre of true worship and would not venerate some of the writings contained in the Jewish scriptures.

Another group of which we hear something in the New Testament was the Sadducees. They were aristocrats, a kind of hereditary caste, who entered into political life and for a time controlled the temple in Jerusalem. They tended to conform to Hellenism and to lead the Hellenistic party, so far as such a party could be said to exist. Yet in some ways they were, as are most aristocrats, conservatives. As such they held to the written and repudiated the oral Jewish Law. They also rejected personal immortality, judgement after death, angels, and devils. They displayed little deep religious conviction and did not have enduring influence.

Far more important for Christianity were the Pharisees. They wished to keep the inherited faith pure from alien contamination. They stood for the strict observance of the Law. Theirs was a personal as well as a national religion, for they showed a sense of sin, recognized the need for repentance, and made much of the grace and forgiveness of God. In contrast with the Sadducees they believed in a future life with rewards and punishments. They stressed oral tradition and by it elaborated and supplemented the written Law. The rank and file of the Palestinian populace were more influenced by them than by any other of the competing kinds of Judaism. It was with them that Jesus and the early Christians had their chief conflicts. In his teaching Jesus and the Pharisees seemed to have much in common, but in the contest with a school which it appeared so closely to resemble some of the essential characteristics of Christianity stood out. To these we are to recur later.

A form of Judaism which seems to have included only a comparatively few was the Essenes. They appear to have lived together in groups, holding all things in common. The majority were celibates. They possessed no slaves, hated war, and refused to hurt man either voluntarily or at the command of another. They were austere in both food and clothing, worked hard, and denied themselves pleasure. They prized honesty and, except for the vows which they assumed on entering the Essene fellowship, would not take oaths but simply give their unsupported word. They preferred agricultural occupations, but were also to be found in towns and villages. They gave generous assistance to the deserving poor. Much that we know of the Essenes is akin to Christian teaching. Yet there is no proof of Essene influence upon the Christian faith.

JUDAISM SUMMARIZED

This brief description of Judaism may seem to be a dry summary of bare facts. If it is no more than that it has failed to give a true picture of that religion. Perhaps no words can do Judaism justice or fully disclose the inwardness of the faith. The Jewish scriptures themselves do not attempt to compress all into a simple or brief formula. Indeed, words fail adequately to convey what a high religion, or perhaps any religion, means to those who have been really caught by it.

Yet certain passages out of the Jewish sacred writings, taken together, can serve to give at least an inkling of the genius of the faith. "In the beginning God created the heaven and the earth." "The heavens declare the glory of God and the firmament showeth His handiwork." "It is He . . . that stretcheth out the heavens as a curtain and spreadeth them out as a tent to dwell in; that bringeth the princes to nothing; he maketh the judges of the earth as vanity." "Thou shalt have no other gods before Me. Thou shalt not make unto thee any graven image . . . thou shalt not bow down thyself to them or serve them; for I the Lord thy God am a jealous God, visiting the iniquity of the fathers upon the children unto the third and the fourth generation of them that hate Me; and showing mercy unto thousands of them that love Me and keep My commandments." "Thou shalt not take the name of the Lord thy God in vain, for the Lord will not hold him guiltless that taketh His name in vain." "Remember the Sabbath day to keep it holy." "Honor thy father and thy mother."

"Thou shalt not kill." "Thou shalt not commit adultery." "Thou shalt not steal." "Thou shalt not bear false witness against thy neighbour." "Thou shalt not covet." "Thou shalt love thy neighbour as thyself." "Cease to do evil; learn to do well; seek judgement, relieve the oppressed, judge the fatherless, plead for the widow." "The feast of unleavened bread shalt thou keep." "Thou shalt not plow with an ox and an ass together." "Thou shalt not muzzle the ox when he treadeth out the corn." "Whatsoever parteth the hoof . . . and cheweth the cud . . . that shall ye eat. . . . The swine . . . is unclean to you." "You only have I known of all the families of the earth: therefore will I punish you for all your iniquities." "The Lord is merciful and gracious, slow to anger and plenteous in mercy. . . . He hath not dealt with us after our sins nor rewarded us according to our iniquities. . . . As far as the east is from the west so far hath He removed our transgressions from us." "The Lord is my shepherd; I shall not want." "They that wait upon the Lord shall renew their strength: they shall mount up on wings as eagles; they shall run, and not be weary; and they shall walk and not faint." "The fear of the Lord is the beginning of wisdom." "He hath showed thee, O man, what is good; and what doth the Lord require of thee, but to do justly, and to love mercy, and to walk humbly with thy God?" "The souls of the righteous are in the hands of God." "I know that my Redeemer liveth, and that He shall stand at the latter day upon the earth: and though after my skin, worms destroy my body, yet in my flesh shall I see God."

Here are God, the creator and governor of the universe; His choice of the Jewish people for His own, yet the responsibility which went with this favour; His requirements of the Jews, in worship, in morals, in the observance of days, and in food; His mercy and forgiveness; His protection and the strength which comes from Him; the reverence for Him which is the source of true wisdom; and the assurance of immortality, late in appearing and not universally held.

JUDAISM AND CHRISTIANITY

However, it was not Judaism which became the most widely influential of the faiths of mankind. It was Christianity. In one sense Christianity was the outgrowth of Judaism. Yet in a very real way it was not the offspring of Judaism but was new. It was the culmination of Judaism, but it was more. It regarded the lawgivers, psalmists, and prophets of Judaism as its own and as preparing the way for Christ. It was the fulfilment of Judaism, but it went beyond Judaism. At the outset it appeared to be another Jewish sect, although very small. Yet eventually it far outgrew in dimensions and influence all the Jewish sects combined. It did this because of distinctive qualities which at once related it to Judaism and distinguished it from Judaism. It was not just another

Jewish sect. It was a new and fresh faith. An understanding of Judaism is essential to a full knowledge of Christianity. But Judaism does not explain Christianity. Even a complete knowledge of Judaism would by no means ensure a knowledge of Christianity. Indeed, it might make difficult a real understanding of Christianity. Christianity was built on Jewish foundations, yet it was radically different. In this difference lies the secret of Christianity and of its phenomenal history.

SELECTED BIBLIOGRAPHY

E. R. Goodenough, *Introduction to Philo Judæus* (Yale University Press, 1940, pp. xii, 223). By an outstanding specialist on Philo and Hellenistic Judaism.

G. H. C. MacGregor and A. C. Purdy, *Jew and Greek: Tutors Unto Christ. The Jewish and Hellenistic Background of the New Testament* (New York, Charles Scribner's Sons, 1936, pp. 366). A competent survey intended for non-specialists.

G. F. Moore, *Judaism in the First Centuries of the Christian Era. The Age of the Tannaim* (Harvard University Press, 3 vols., 1927–1930). A standard work of great erudition.

T. H. Robinson and W. O. E. Oesterley, *Hebrew Religion. Its Origin and Development* (New York, The Macmillan Co., 2 vols., 2d ed., 1937). One of the better of the many standard treatises, primarily for non-Jewish readers.

Chapter 3

THE IMMEDIATE BACKGROUND OF CHRISTIANITY: THE GRÆCO-ROMAN WORLD

If Christianity was radically different from Judaism, the religion which in some degree was its parent, the gulf which separated it from the Græco-Roman world into which it was born was still wider. It was an alien environment into which Christianity came.

Yet much in that environment favoured the spread of Christianity. Moreover, the environment placed its stamp on Christianity. We must, therefore, seek to understand something of the main outline of the life and thought of the portion of the globe outside of Judaism in which Christianity had its beginning.

THE SCENE OF THE BIRTH OF CHRISTIANITY

First of all, we must remind ourselves again that the basin of the Mediterranean, the region in which Christianity came into being, in which it had its first great triumphs, and in which it long had most of its strength, embraced only a small fraction of the earth's surface. Moreover, when Christ was born it was the home of considerably less than half of civilized mankind. Culturally it presented a great variety, but in general it was dominated by two traditions, those of Greece and Rome. To the east lay Mesopotamia and Persia. Both made their contributions to the Græco-Roman world, but they were quite distinct from it. For centuries the Roman and Persian Empires were deadly rivals, with Mesopotamia, the scene of one of the oldest of the civilizations of mankind, as debated ground which was chiefly in possession of Persia. More remote was India, and still farther away was China. India exerted but little influence on Greece and Rome, and China still less.

Since it had its birth, its first triumphs, and its initial chief stronghold in the Græco-Roman world, Christianity was profoundly moulded by it. In organization and in thought it conformed in part to it. It came to be largely identified with what is called the Occident, that portion of mankind which is the heir of Greece, Roman, and itself. Only occasionally did it spread extensively among non-Occidental peoples. Not until recently has it gained substantial footing in all the other great cultural units and among the majority of the primitive groups of mankind. Only within the past few decades has it become actually world-wide. It still has its main centres in the Occident. While lately it has made tremendous strides towards becoming universal, it has not yet divested itself of the integuments which it acquired during its Occidental pilgrimage.

Conditions Favourable to the Spread of Religion

At the time when Christianity came into being, much in the basin of the Mediterranean favoured the spread of religions, either new or old. Jesus was was born in the reign of Augustus. After a long period of wars which had racked the Mediterranean and its shores, political unity had been achieved and the Roman Empire had become roughly coterminous with the Mediterranean Basin. Here and there it was soon to spread beyond it. Augustus was the first Emperor. Building on the foundations laid by his uncle, Julius Cæsar, he brought peace and under the guise of the chief citizen of a restored republic ruled the realm which for several generations Rome had been building. The internal peace and order which Augustus achieved endured, with occasional interruptions, for about two centuries. Never before had all the shores of the Mediterranean been under one rule and never had they enjoyed such prosperity. The *pax Romana* made for the spread of ideas and religions over the area where it prevailed.

With the *pax Romana* went the building of roads and the growth of commerce. Highways of solid construction traversed the Empire and made possible more extensive travel and trade than the region had ever known. The pirates had been curbed who had imperilled shipping in the Mediterranean. Roads, travel, and commerce facilitated cultural and religious as well as political unity.

Travel and trade were accompanied by the spread of two languages, Greek and Latin. Greek was spoken among one or more groups in most of the cities of the Empire where commerce was to be found. The Greek-speaking and Greek-reading groups were most numerous in the eastern part of the Mediterranean. Alexandria in Egypt was a particularly prominent focus of Greek culture. Yet those for whom Greek was a primary tongue were also present in Rome, in Sicily and the south of Italy, in some of the cities of the south of Gaul, and in several other centres in the western portions of the Mediterranean. The Greek was the *koine* in one or more of its varieties. Latin was more prevalent in the West. In the first centuries of the Christian era, while Christianity was expanding in the Empire, it was increasingly the speech of much of the population on the western borders of the Mediterranean. A religion which employed Greek and Latin, and especially Greek, had advantages over rivals which did not and might gain an Empire-wide hearing.

Important also was the religious and moral hunger which characterized much of the populace of the basin of the Mediterranean in the centuries in which Christianity was having its early development. The formation of an all-embracing empire promoted the decay of the local religious cults of the several states and cities which were brought within the inclusive political unity. To be sure, many were maintained as a matter of custom or civic pride, but the heart had largely gone out of them. Then, too, the advancing intelligence and moral sensitivity of the times cast doubt upon the stories about the gods. Many of these were both incredible to an educated mind and offensive to the morally sensitive. The gods were not as good as the best men of the period and could command respect only if the stories about them were treated as myths and allegorized. The age had in it much of moral corruption. Yet it also had consciences which revolted against the excesses of the day. A religion which offered high moral standards and the power to attain them would be welcomed by the more serious.

The times brought with them much of insecurity. In the comprehensive political unity many individuals were uprooted from their accustomed environment and either as slaves, as soldiers, or by free choice found themselves unsupported by the social group in which they had been reared. While in part outwardly preserved and even strengthened, the old city states which had characterized the Mediterranean world and which gave their free citizens a sense of community were basically weakened, absorbed in the large impersonal Empire. Millions were disinherited and deracinated, slaves on the great landed estates or in city mansions, many of them from distant parts of the Empire. They were hungry for a faith which would bring them self-respect. They sought sustaining companionship, many of them in fellowships which combined religious with social purposes. Longing for the assurance of personal immortality was widespread and reached out wistfully for satisfaction through religious faith and ceremonial. As cities multiplied and grew in size, made up as many of them were of strangers and their children, and, like the Empire, impersonal, they provided favourable environment for novel religious ideas and for religious fellowships. They were melting pots into which many religions entered.

When, towards the close of the second century, disasters began to overtake the Roman Empire and society was threatened with progressive disintegration, many turned to religion for the remedy. Augustus and his successors had not solved the basic problems of the Mediterranean world. They had obscured them. For what appeared to be a failure in government they had substituted more government, and government was not the answer. Confidence in man's ability and reason was shaken. There was a widespread "loss of nerve." Religion was looked to for the sense of safety which had been lost. Moreover, there was a groping towards some kind of theism, towards a unifying principle or deity which could bring cohesion and in the confusion yield an inkling of a universe which would correspond to the political and economic unity which the Roman Empire had brought to the Mediterranean world. Distrusting themselves and their reason, men looked for the answer in antiquity and in religions which could claim the sanctions of the ancients and of long generations of believers.

RELIGIOUS RIVALS FOR THE ALLEGIANCE OF THE GRÆCO-ROMAN WORLD

Although conditions in the Græco-Roman world favoured the spread of a faith, they did not necessarily mean that Christianity would be the religion which would triumph. The competitors were many. Several of these appeared to have a marked advantage over Christianity. Indeed, at its outset, Christianity seemed to be one of the least of many rivals and with no promise of success against the others. We cannot undertake here even to name all the contenders for the religious allegiance of the Mediterranean Basin. We must, however, say something concerning the more prominent of them.

Some cults were maintained by the state. These included the gods of Rome and those of the cities of the Empire. The Roman Empire was in part a congeries of city states. Many of these cities had existed before the formation of the Empire and had been autonomous. Each had felt itself dependent upon the favour of its gods and had seen to it that the worship of its official divinities was maintained. As we have suggested, the state religions were no longer believed in as strongly as formerly. However, the continuance of their rites was believed to be necessary for the welfare of society. They were, accordingly, kept up, often with great pomp.

Outstanding among the officially supported cults was that of the Emperor. The East had long been familiar with a ruler who was also a divinity. Alexander the Great had been accorded that rôle, as had many another potentate in the Orient. It was natural that Augustus, who had brought peace to the distraught Mediterranean world, should be hailed as an incarnation of divinity. Statues of him were erected and religious ceremonies were instituted for him.

An imperial cult followed. It might call forth little personal devotion. However, it was regarded as a safeguard of law and order and important for the preservation and prosperity of the realm. Dissent from it might well be interpreted as treasonable and anarchistic.

Prominent, too, were the mystery religions, but in a different way and with distinctive purposes. They were secret in many of their ceremonies and their members were under oath not to reveal their esoteric rites. Since after a few centuries they completely disappeared, we know them only imperfectly. They arose chiefly in the East—in Egypt, Syria, Anatolia, and Persia. Numbers of them centred about a saviour-god who had died and had risen again. The god and the story about him varied from cult to cult. As the cults spread within the Empire they copied from one another in the easy-going syncretism which characterized much of the religious life of that realm and age.

Several of the mysteries were built around Dionysus. According to the stories told about him, Zagreus, the son of Zeus by Persephone, was born in the form of a bull. He was destined to rule the world, but was torn apart and eaten by the jealous Titans. But Athena saved his heart, Zeus swallowed it, and when Semele bore Dionysus to Zeus, Dionysus was Zagreus reborn. He was also often given the name Bacchus. The reason for the association of the bull with fertility cults is obvious. In the cruder of Dionysiac mysteries, the devotees drank of the fruit of the vine, for Dionysus or Bacchus was the god of wine as well as of animal and vegetable life. They also ate of the flesh of a newly slain bull, still dripping blood, and thus partook of the life of the god. They engaged in sacred dances which induced ecstasy and in which they were supposedly possessed by the spirit of the god.

Various sects associated with the name of Orpheus, who by his playing charmed men and beasts, also had the Dionysus myth at their heart. Less orgiastic and more ethical than the crasser Dionysiac cults, they assumed as axiomatic a conviction widely held in the Hellenistic world that matter and flesh are evil and that the soul of man must be free from contamination with them. They also taught that men are born and reborn, in each reincarnation imprisoned in the flesh and subject to those ills to which flesh is heir, unless the soul can be freed from the body. That separation accomplished, the soul would live forever in bliss. The emancipation was to be achieved through initiation into the cult, with cleanliness and asceticism. After a ritualistic meal of raw meat, the votaries remained vegetarians. Thus they avoided further contamination with flesh.

Prominent among the mysteries were those associated with *Magna Mater,* the Great Mother, who loved the virgin-born shepherd Attis. Attis died, slain either by his enemies or by his own hand (if the latter, by emasculation).

Magna Mater mourned for him, effected his resurrection, and he became im-mortal. Postulants for full-fledged initiation mourned for Attis, and then, as the climax of a wild dance, emasculated themselves. This was followed by a day in which the resurrection of Attis was celebrated, and the devotees felt themselves united with Attis and so participants of his immortality. There was a lay membership of men and women which did not entail mutilation. Asso-ciated with this cult, but borrowed from elsewhere, was the *taurobolium*. In this a bull was killed and the devotees bathed in its blood as means of dying to the old life and being born again.

Somewhat similar cults had as their centre a young god whom the Greeks called Adonis and who died and rose again. In like manner another set of mysteries clustered around the myth of Osiris, a king who had been killed by his brother. His widow, Isis, mourning, sought him, until, finding his body, she revived it, and Osiris became the ruler of the dead. In the religion which developed around this myth, Serapis replaced Osiris and Isis was emphasized. The chief shrine was the Serapeum, obviously named for Serapis, in Alex-andria. From that leading mart it spread by the trade routes to much of the Empire.

The Eleusinian mysteries, developed near Athens, had as their inspiring focus rites which dramatized the death of vegetation in the autumn and winter and the resurrection of life in the spring. This they did through the nature myth of Persephone, who was carried off by Hades to the underworld, was sought by her mourning mother, Demeter, was restored to the world of light, but was compelled to return to the underworld for part of each year.

Very widespread was the mystery religion which had Mithra for its main figure. Mithra, a god of Persian origin, was usually represented as bestriding a bull and slaying it. From the dying bull issued the seed of life for the world, and hence the act became the symbol of regeneration. The cult practised bap-tism and had a sacramental meal. Its membership was restricted to men and its places of worship, crypts or underground caverns, were too small to accom-modate more than a very few at a time.

Almost all the mystery cults eventually made their way to Rome, the capital and chief city of the Empire. They also penetrated much of the Empire. Their appeal seems to have been the assurance of immortality which they gave to their members, combined with a fellowship which many craved in a world in which large numbers were uprooted individuals.

Akin to the mystery religions was Hermeticism, represented by a body of literature which claimed as its author Hermes Trismegistus. This literature presented a way of redemption of the spirit from the trammels of matter which issued in immortality. Like the mysteries and much of the thought of the day, it held as axiomatic a dualism which regarded matter as evil and spirit as good. Seeking to obtain emancipation from the flesh, it was strongly ascetic, inculcating abstinence from the pleasures of the flesh and opposing malice, envy, deceit, anger, and avarice. Like so much of the religious life of the Græco-Roman world, it was syncretistic. It mixed polytheism, pantheism, and astrology.

Hermeticism was representative of a religious strain known as Gnosticism which was greatly to influence Christianity in its earlier centuries. Although the majority of Christians ultimately rejected it, Gnosticism and the struggle with it had enduring effects upon Christianity. Pre-Christian in its origin, Gnosticism assumed, as did so much of Hellenistic thought, a sharp disjunction between matter and spirit. It offered a way of emancipation from the material world into the realm of pure spirit, and into freedom from the fatalistic control by the astral powers which underlay the current belief in astrology. It claimed possession of a secret *Gnosis,* or knowledge, through which this could be obtained, and made much af sacraments, ceremonial washings, and other rites. Like the mystery religions, it was for the privileged few who shared the knowledge through which emancipation was to be achieved. It took over from any source whatever it deemed of value.

Philosophy was popular in the Mediterranean world into which Christianity came. Very little which was fresh was being thought or said. The only major new school of philosophy which emerged after the birth of Jesus was Neoplatonism, and that, as its name indicates, was largely a development from Platonism and had in it little if anything that was basically original. Indeed, it represented a tendency which can be traced back at least as far as the first century of the Christian era. In its flowering it incorporated borrowings from more than one of the schools which had gone before it.

The philosophies which were most prominently represented in the world into which Christianity came were Stoicism, Epicureanism, the Peripatetics (carrying on the Aristotelian tradition), the Pythagoreans, the Platonists, and the Cynics.

Stoicism was very influential among many in high places. It drew much from Aristotle. It believed the universe to be a universe, an organic whole, with both body and soul, and governed by Reason which expresses itself in natural law. Stoicism was a pantheistic philosophy which regarded God as permeating all things but not being independent of them. Every man, it held, should live in accordance with the universal Reason which pervades nature. This would entail rational self-control and make one independent of outward circumstances. It meant self-discipline and, for those in public office, a high sense of responsibility. The Stoics held that a bit of the universal Reason is to be found in every man, that ideally men and gods are members of one society, the city of Zeus, and that all differences of nationality should be merged in the common brotherhood of man. They taught that all men are equal by divine right, declared that in the sight of God the slave is of as much value as the monarch, and maintained that all are entitled, as sons of God, indwelt by the universal Reason, to share in the good things of life. Stoicism was to have a marked effect upon many Christians and was to leave traces of its beliefs in some phases of Christianity.

Of the Epicureans and Pythagoreans we need say nothing except to mention them. Of the Peripatetics we may simply remark that Aristotle was later to have a striking influence on Christian thought, an influence which proved very persistent. Nor must the Cynics engage our attention. Unlike the Stoics and the Epicureans, who were largely aristocratic, they addressed themselves to the common folk. Rude of speech, living simply, often rebels against society and not above reproach morally, they harangued audiences wherever they could gather them, denouncing the objects for which men usually strive, including wealth and fame.

Platonism was of very great importance, partly because of the contributions which it made to some other schools through the borrowing which was common in the intellectual world, partly because of its contribution to Neoplatonism, and to no small degree because of the effect of its patterns of thought upon Christian theology.

Neoplatonism, while younger than Christianity, combined, as we have suggested, much from philosophies which had gone before it, including Platonism, Aristotelianism, Stoicism, and Neopythagoreanism. It had a deeply religious quality with a strong mystical trend. It sought through asceticism to curb the flesh and its desires, to purify the human soul of the taint acquired by its departure from its original estate, and by contemplation to attain union with God. Again and again through the centuries Christian mysticism was to be deeply indebted to it.

All these philosophies had a Greek rootage and were developed further in the Hellenistic world into which Christianity early moved. In one way or another they had a strain of dualism. Most of them tended to regard matter as evil, believed the soul of man to be contaminated by it, and sought the emancipation of the soul from its corrupting association.

While most of the philosophies appealed primarily to the educated, those who dabbled in the intellectual life were very numerous. Teachers of philosophy often enjoyed a large popular following and lecture halls for them and their listeners were widespread. The religious aspects of philosophy attracted many of those who suffered from the hunger for a satisfying faith which was so prominent in the Roman Empire.

Judaism must also be reckoned among the more formidable of the competitors for the religious allegiance of the peoples of the Roman Empire. In the preceding chapter we have said something about it. As a faith identified with one ethnic group and stressing its belief that Israel was a peculiar people, especially chosen by God, it could scarcely hope to win all the human race, even had it desired to do so. To be sure, some of its prophets had regarded it as having a universal mission and as destined to embrace all men in its fellowship and its blessings. Yet the majority of Jews did not follow them. However, as we have seen, Jewish communities were numerous and widely scattered, the Jewish scriptures had been translated into Greek, and thousands of non-Jews were attracted by the Jewish faith and either sought full incorporation into the Jewish people or constituted a fringe who had accepted many Jewish beliefs.

It was in this Roman Empire, newly formed, this portion of civilized mankind in which the heritages of Greece and Rome were dominant, that Christianity had its rise. It profited by the features of that world which made for the spread of religious faiths, but it faced the competition of many systems which appeared to have a much better prospect for survival and growth.

Selected Bibliography

A GENERAL PICTURE OF THE GRÆCO-ROMAN WORLD

S. Dill, *Roman Society from Nero to Marcus Aurelius* (London, Macmillan & Co., 1904, pp. xii, 639). Well-written and authoritative.

M. I. Rostovtzeff, *A History of the Ancient World,* translated from the Russian by J. D. Duff (Oxford, The Clarendon Press, 2 vols., 1930). By an eminent specialist.

M. I. Rostovtzeff, *The Social and Economic History of the Roman Empire* (Oxford, The Clarendon Press, pp. xxv, 695).

THE GENERAL RELIGIOUS PICTURE

C. N. Cochrane, *Christianity and Classical Culture. A Study in Thought and Action from Augustus to Augustine* (Oxford, The Clarendon Press, 1940, pp. vii, 523). Learned, with stimulating interpretations.

Franz Cumont, *Astrology and Religion Among the Greeks and Romans* (New York, G. P. Putnam's Sons, 1912, pp. xxvii, 208).

Franz Cumont, *The Oriental Religions in Roman Paganism,* translated from the 2d French ed. (Chicago, The Open Court Publishing Co., 1911, pp. xxiv, 298). By a distinguished specialist.

W. Warde Fowler, *The Religious Experience of the Roman People from the Earliest Times to the Age of Augustus* (London, Macmillan & Co., 1911, pp. xviii, 534). The Gifford Lectures for 1909–1910.

T. R. Glover, *The Conflict of Religions in the Early Roman Empire* (London, Methuen & Co., 1909, pp. vii, 309). Charmingly written, pro-Christian, based upon a wide knowledge of the sources.

Gilbert Murray, *Five Stages of Greek Religion* (Columbia University Press, 1925, pp. 276). By an eminent classicist.

A. D. Nock, *Conversion. The Old and the New in Religion from Alexander the Great to Augustine of Hippo* (Oxford University Press, 1933, pp. xii, 309). Competent, with some fresh points of view.

THE EMPEROR CULT

Kenneth Scott, *The Identification of Augustus with Romulus-Quirinus,* in *Transactions and Proceedings of the American Philological Association,* Vol. XLVI, pp. 82–105.

Lily Ross Taylor, *The Divinity of the Roman Emperor* (Middletown, Conn., American Philological Association, 1931, pp. xv, 296). Well done.

THE MYSTERY RELIGIONS

S. Angus, *The Religious Quests of the Græco-Roman World* (New York, Charles Scribner's Sons, 1929, pp. xx, 444). Scholarly, with a pro-Christian bias.

Franz Cumont, *The Mysteries of Mithra,* translated from the second revised French edition by T. J. McCormack (Chicago, The Open Court Publishing Co., 1903). Semi-popular lectures by an outstanding authority.

J. G. Frazer, *Adonis Attis Osiris* (Part IV of *The Golden Bough,* London, Macmillan & Co., 1907, pp. xix, 452).

W. K. C. Guthrie, *Orpheus and Greek Religion. A Study of the Orphic Movement* (London, Methuen & Co., 1935, pp. xix, 287). Excellent.

R. Reitzenstein, *Die hellenistischen Mysterienreligionen nach ihren Grundgedanken und Wirkungen* (Leipzig, B. G. Teubner, 3d ed., 1927, pp. viii, 438).

HERMETICISM

Jos. Kroll, *Die Lehren des Hermes Trismegistos,* in *Beiträge zur Geschichte der Philosophie des Mittelalters,* Vol. XII (Münster i.W., Aschendorffsche Verlagsbuchhandlung, 1914, pp. xii, 441).

Walter Scott, *Hermetica. The Greek and Latin Writings which Contain Religious or Philosophic Teachings Ascribed to Hermes Trismegistus, edited with English translations and notes* (Oxford, The Clarendon Press, 4 vols., 1924–1936). The standard work in English.

JUDAISM

G. F. Moore, *Judaism in the First Centuries of the Christian Era. The Age of the Tannaim* (Harvard University Press, 2 vols., 1927). By a distinguished specialist.

W. O. E. Oesterley and G. H. Box, *The Religion and Worship of the Synagogue* (London, Sir Isaac Pitman & Sons, 1907, pp. xv, 443). Scholarly, for non-Jewish readers.

E. Schürer, *Geschichte des judischen Volkes im Zeitalter Jesu Christi,* 4th ed. (Leipzig, Hinrichs, 3 vols., 1901–1911), translated as *History of the Jewish People in the time of Jesus Christ* (New York, Charles Scribner's Sons, 5 vols., 1891). Still a standard work.

JESUS AND THE GOSPEL

Chapter 4

JESUS AND THE GOSPEL: THE FOUNDATION OF CHRISTIANITY

Christianity had what looked like a most unpromising beginning. The contemporary observer outside the little inner group of the disciples of Jesus would have thought it impossible that within five centuries of its inception it would outstrip its competitors for the religious allegiance of the Roman Empire and become the professed faith of the rulers and of the overwhelming majority of the population of the realm. Still less would he have dreamed that within less than two thousand years it would become world-wide, with a more extensive geographic spread and a greater influence upon mankind than any other religion.

This failure of this hypothetical observer to foresee the future place of Christianity in the life of mankind can be readily understood. The faith appeared to begin as one of the many sects of Judaism. Although, as we have seen, the Jews were numerous and widely spread in the Roman Empire and here and there were found beyond its bounds, there seemed to be no possibility of their winning the realm to their faith. To be sure, Judaism was making many proselytes, but in spite of some tendencies to conform to the syncretistic trend of the times and adjust itself to the prevalent religious and intellectual patterns, basically it was exclusive and intolerant of its rivals and was too much the faith of one ethnic group ever to become universal. If that were true of Judaism as a whole, presumably it would also be true of its sects.

Even within Judaism Christianity seemed to have little future and still less did it give promise of outstripping Judaism. Jesus, the figure around whom Christianity centred, was of humble birth. At the very beginning of his public career he deliberately spurned as an unworthy temptation the suggestion that he seek to carry through his aims by political means. Although he performed many miracles, he always did so to meet an obvious human need, meticulously avoided any display of his power to call attention to himself or to prove his divine commission, and at times endeavoured to keep secret his astounding works of healing. He chose for his intimates men from the humble walks of life and had few friends among the influential. His public career was brief, at most probably no more than three years and possibly compressed within a year. He wrote no book. As far as the surviving records show, he gave little or no thought to a continuing organization to perpetuate his teaching and his influence. He gathered about him a group of intimates, known to history as the Twelve Apostles, and he is reported as having declared that they were entrusted with large powers, but our earliest documents contain no certain proof (although this has been hotly debated, and the precise opposite has been and is held by the majority of Christians) that he intended these powers to be transmitted by them in a continuing succession that would make for a permanent, visible institution. Jesus appears not to have taught systematically, but to have spoken as the occasion required—at dinner parties, to a woman of dubious reputation whom he chanced to meet at a well, to a stranger who appealed to him to intervene in a family dispute, and to those who at the height of his brief popularity sought to join themselves to him and were told so sternly of the high requirements that, dismayed, they turned back. He came to an ignominious death which seemed to be not so much tragic as futile. The authentic records of his life and teachings are so brief that they could easily be printed in a single issue of one of our larger daily papers, and in these a substantial proportion of the space is devoted to the last few days of his life. No proper biography of him exists, if by that we mean a book which conforms to what in modern times are set as standards. So brief are our accounts that there have been scholars who have declared that we cannot really know Jesus and that he is not essential to Christianity. Even a thoughtful visitor in Jerusalem in the first few years of the Christian Church would scarcely have predicted that from such a beginning this Jesus, the centre of loyalty of this Jewish 'sect, would be long remembered.

Yet that life is the most influential ever lived on this planet and its effect continues to mount. Here is the most thought-provoking fact of human history.

Our Knowledge of Jesus

Although our accounts of Jesus are brief, they enable us to know him and his teachings as well as we can know any figure of like antiquity. He made so profound an impression upon those who were his intimates that their memories of him, some of them put into written form within a very few years after the events they record, enable us to have a vivid picture of him and his characteristics. His sayings, given as they were in pithy sentences or in stories of extraordinary beauty and imagery, could not fail to fasten themselves in the memories of the more thoughtful who heard them. They lent themselves to the kind of repetition which did not blur or distort them and were early collected in written form. Even if we did not have the four brief accounts which we call the Gospels we could gain a fairly adequate impression of him and of the salient points of his life, teachings, death, and resurrection from references in letters of his followers written within a generation of his death.

It seems almost presumptuous to attempt to compress what we know of the life and teachings of Jesus into a few pages and to expect within that short compass to give anything like an accurate and well-balanced summary of them. Yet that is what we must essay, for without such an account any sketch of the history of Christianity would lack the essential foundation for the entire story.

Birth, Boyhood and Youth

Born in a manger in Bethlehem, the town associated with the name of David, the most glamorous of the Jewish kings, and reared in the village of Nazareth, Jesus grew up in a humble family. From the hills back of Nazareth a commanding view could be had of the plain of Esdraelon, crammed with history, and of snowy Hermon. From what we know of his later years, we may be fairly certain that Jesus often climbed these hills and, always sensitive and observing, fed his soul on the beauty around and below him and thought deeply on the life unrolled before him.

We catch very few glimpses of Jesus until, when about thirty years of age, he began his public career. From the names of his brothers which have come down to us, we gather that the family cherished the Maccabeean tradition and were loyal to the Jewish faith. That the household was deeply religious is borne out by many bits of evidence—the account of the conception and birth of Jesus in *The Gospel according to Luke,* much of which could only have come from his mother, Mary; the other narrative of his birth, in *The Gospel according to Matthew,* which was presumably, at least in part, from Joseph, his reputed father; the delicacy, beauty, and deep religious feeling of the nativity stories, especially those in Luke, which appear to reflect the character of Mary and Joseph, notably of the mother who, we are told, "kept all these things, pondering them in her heart"; the fact of the relationship of Mary to the mother of John the Baptist and to that earnest little household, dedicated completely to God; careful compliance with the Jewish law in circumcision and in the ceremony of consecrating Jesus to God in the temple, as Mary's first born; the welcome given the infant on that occasion by members of the circle of the devout who were looking for "the consolation of Israel" and the "redemption of Jerusalem," folk who were quietly waiting for God to bring about the consummation of history expected by faithful Jews; and the custom of Mary and Joseph to go every year, and not semi-occasionally, to Jerusalem to the feast of the Passover. We are not surprised that Jesus formed the habit of going to the synagogue, that he learned to read, that his chief reading was in the sacred books of his people, and that, even at the age of twelve, he had meditated profoundly on the issues raised by them. Since, after Jesus began his public career, we hear no mention of Joseph as living, we may assume that he had died and that Jesus had been left to earn the living for his mother and the younger brothers and sisters. It is, indeed, conceivable that the delay in entering upon his itinerant ministry was due to his feeling of responsibility for shelter and daily food for the dependent members of the family.

It was a stirring day and a stirring section of the world in which to live. The Roman Empire had only recently been established. It is part of the familiar Christmas story that Jesus was born during the rule of the first Roman Emperor, Augustus Cæsar. His own little corner of the earth was seething with unrest against Roman domination. Not far from Nazareth the city of Sepphoris was being rebuilt during his boyhood after its destruction by Roman forces to quell one of the recurrent uprisings. During the adult life of Jesus resentment against Rome was mounting and within the generation after his crucifixion it was to break out in a mad revolt which was to end in enormous slaughter and in the destruction of Jerusalem and its temple. The unrest was accentuated and in part was given direction by apocalyptic hopes with their accompanying expectation of direct intervention by God on behalf of the Jews. In these hopes the dream of a Messiah loomed prominently.

Now and again we can gain hints of what Jesus may have been thinking in those hidden years at Nazareth. The parables in which he couched so much of his teaching may have embodied some of his observations and reflections as he viewed the scene about him—farms which he knew as he watched from the hill-tops the clouds march inland from the Mediterranean and drop their rain regardless of whether the owners were good or bad, evidence to him of the impartial love of God for all men; a woman seeking for a lost coin; children playing in the market place; a king going to a far country to receive for himself a kingdom, perhaps an echo of the journey of the Herods to Rome to ask for confirmation of their claims; a pearl merchant; and the father and the two sons, the younger errant but appealing and the elder correct but forbidding. Then, too, must have been acquired the familiarity with the sacred books of his people which Jesus later displayed.

The Public Career Begins

In whatever way they were occupied, the years of obscurity ended abruptly. Jesus' kinsman, John the Baptist, had become the centre of a religious awakening which deeply moved the region. An ascetic, he denounced the sins of those about him, spoke of imminent judgment with reward for the righteous and destruction for the wicked, urged repentance, and on the confession of their sins baptized the penitents in the Jordan. He gathered disciples about him, leading them in fasting and teaching them methods of prayer.

Jesus came to John and was baptized by him. The motive for that step is not clear, but John is represented as reluctant, declaring, perhaps on the basis of knowledge acquired through earlier contact, that he should be baptized by Jesus. Whatever his reason in seeking baptism, to Jesus the experience was profound. We can only conjecture its full meaning to him, but from the accounts which have come to us it at least brought a deepened realization of the significance of his sonship to God.

So soul-shaking was that day that immediately Jesus felt impelled to seek solitude, there to wrestle with the issues which it presented to him. So absorbed was he that, whether through preoccupation or deliberate choice, he did not eat. What seems to have been the climax were three urges which as he faced them he came to recognize as temptations. His mind was one which thought in pictures, as his parables witness, and these testings, as he narrated them later to his intimates—for they could have become known in no other way—were presented to him in that characteristic form. Should he use his power as God's son to meet his own physical needs? Should he seek in some startling fashion to test God's protecting power, expecting exemption from whatever disastrous results would normally follow foolhardy action, thereby seeking to convince the gaping multitude of his unique mission? Should he compromise his principles to gain earthly dominion and thus establish his righteous rule? He faced the urges, appraised them, and rejected them.

Again and again Jesus later met situations which confronted him with one or another of these issues in various forms, but at the outset of his public career he had seen once for all what was involved and he never wavered from the decisions then made. He refused to be an agent of the multitude's wishes for easy food, he rejected the repeated demand that he demonstrate the authenticity of his mission by a "sign" wrought especially for the purpose, and he would have nothing to do with political methods.

JESUS AND THE KINGDOM OF GOD

Returning to the haunts of men, Jesus began preaching and teaching. He believed that the kingdom of God was about to be inaugurated, and it was this which constituted the recurrent theme in his message. Obviously the kingdom of God meant a society in which God's will would prevail. As Jesus conceived it, the kingdom of God was to be the gift of God and was not to be achieved by men's striving. It was being inaugurated through Jesus and was both a present reality, already here, and a future hope. Like grain, it was to grow of itself and not by men's striving. Men were to prize it as the gem merchant would eagerly exchange all that he had for the exceptional pearl. While it was a society, men were to enter it one by one, and (although on this point some Christians have held otherwise and have identified it with the organized Church) it was not a visible institution but an inward possession.

Membership in the kingdom was not hereditary, for "the sons of the kingdom," presumably those born into it but having no other claim on it than birth, were to be "cast into outer darkness," while those who had been deemed aliens to it, "from the east and west," were to "sit down" in it. The kingdom of God was so important that men were "to seek it first," before food or clothing, and were to give up all that they possessed to obtain it. To Jesus the kingdom was "gospel" and "evangel"—great "good news." The terms "gospel" and "evangel," while technically correct as designations of the kingdom, have become so stereotyped by long pedestrian usage that in them the wonder and the exuberant joy which Jesus gave to them are often missed. To Jesus, men had not really begun to live until they had entered the kingdom of God, and to be in it was to have abounding, eternal life.

Jesus devoted much attention to describing the characteristics of those who had "entered the kingdom." If men were to enter the kingdom, or even to see it, they must gain a fresh perspective and make a new start. In the vivid, forceful language which was normal to him and which was an indication of one of his outstanding qualities, Jesus declared that men must "repent" (literally, "change their minds"), be "born anew," and "become as little children." It was those who were "poor in spirit," who recognized their inadequacies and who were painfully aware that they had fallen far short of the ideal which God had set for men, of whom it could be said that "theirs is the kingdom of heaven." The kingdom meant great joy; Jesus compared himself and his companions to a wedding party. Yet the joy was not incompatible with deep pain. Indeed, the former might not be possible except for the latter. He himself knew both and recognized that his disciples, as members of the kingdom, would also have both in their experience.

What Jesus called "the world" was obviously in opposition to the kingdom. It was for that reason that entrance to the kingdom entailed so drastic a reorientation, a re-creation, of those who came into it from the world. Persecution would, therefore, be the lot of members of the kingdom. Such persecution, if it were for the sake of the righteousness which Jesus proclaimed, would be evidence of membership in the kingdom. However, Jesus is declared to have been sent by God into the world not to condemn the world, but that the world through him might be saved, and he said that those who had entered the kingdom were the light of the world.

Members of the kingdom were to strive to be examples of the life which God deemed ideal for men. They were to be single-minded—pure in heart. They were to be so eager for righteousness that their longing could be described as both hunger and thirst. They were to be clean in thought, to be so sincere that their word would require no adventitious support but would need only "yes" and "no." They were to be merciful, endeavouring to make peace, not seeking retaliation but returning good for evil, loving even their enemies. The word for "love" is not one meaning "liking" but one which involves an abandon in self-giving. They were never to seek the applause of men, but were to shun publicity in acts of mercy or in such religious exercises as praying and fasting. They were not to have anxious fear of what the morrow might bring, but were to seek first of all the kingdom and the kind of conduct approved by God, quietly confident that God would supply their physical needs.

Here was no asceticism, no condemnation of the body and of matter as evil, no attempt, as in the thought and religions so prevalent in the Hellenistic world and in much of the stricter side of current Judaism, to "free" the soul from what was deemed the contamination of the flesh and the material part of the universe. In contrast with John the Baptist who was clearly an ascetic and enjoined asceticism on his followers, Jesus and his intimate disciples both ate and drank and went freely to dinners, frankly enjoying them. While Jesus taught that men should never make their goal the accumulation of material possessions, that wealth imperilled the highest attainments of men, and that those who would follow him must be prepared to abandon all, whether property, home, or kindred, he embedded in the short model prayer which he gave his disciples, immediately after the petition for the coming of the kingdom and the accomplishment of God's will, a request for physical sustenance. Among the tests that he gave for character was the use that was made of money and the care that was either shown or denied to those in physical need.

Jesus' Concern for Individuals

Although Jesus had much to say of the kingdom of God, and in that must have meant, if not a visible social structure, at least the relations of men to one another, he was deeply and primarily interested in individuals and saw society, customs, and institutions only as they affected individuals. To him the Jewish respect for the Sabbath must not be permitted to stand in the way of helping individuals, whether that entailed healing them or relieving their hunger. He declared that he had "come to seek and to save that which was lost," and by that he meant individuals.

Some of the best remembered parables of Jesus centre about care for the individual. He compared his concern for "the lost" with the shepherd's leaving the ninety-nine in his flock who were safe in the fold and going into the wilderness to look for the one stray until he found it and with the woman sweeping her house meticulously in search of a missing coin and then, when she had discovered it, calling in her neighbours and friends to rejoice with her. He told of the father waiting for his wayward son and running to greet him when he saw him far off, returning. He commanded his disciples not to despise even one of "these little ones." He declared that God noted the fate of every sparrow, so that not one of them could fall to the ground without His will, and that since human beings are of more value than many sparrows, God must surely care for them. Again and again, although he talked collectively to multitudes and although on two memorable occasions he took care that they were fed, Jesus addressed himself to individuals and gave them of his best—the woman of the street, the short-statured tax-gatherer who had climbed a tree to see him, the Roman officer with a sick servant, the child who seemed to be lying dead and her distraught parents, many an unfortunate demoniac, the rich young ruler who came running to him and whom he loved at first glance. Almost all of his recorded healings, and there were many of them, were of individuals. Only once, in the case of a group of lepers, do we read of his healing as many as ten at a time, and what stands out in that incident was the gratitude of the one, a Samaritan, who returned to give him thanks.

JESUS AND MAN

Closely allied with his attitude towards the individual was the view which Jesus held of man. He was vividly aware of the strange mixture which is man. He fully recognized the depravity in man and declared that human fathers had to face the fact that they are evil. He saw and stated emphatically the tragic disaster that is the climax of the way of life which many, presumably most men pursue. Some of his sayings seem to disclose him as a hopeless pessimist. There would be many, he said, who would fail to respond to the invitation to enter the kingdom and when, all too tardily, they sought to retrieve their mistake would find that they were too late.

But Jesus held that men could enter into life, that men could, if they would, have a confident faith through which the seemingly impossible could become a reality. He appealed to men to think, sure that if they properly employed their reason it would lead them to correct conclusions. He believed that infinite possibilities were available to men if they would take the right way towards attaining them. His works of healing both body and spirit Jesus regarded as demonstrations of God's power, but he declared that this power was available to others if they would only reach out in faith and claim it. Life would be sheer wonder and joy if men would only enter the door which was there for them, the door into God's kingdom of light and love. Pain might also be there, but it was not incompatible with the fullness of life. Indeed, it could be made to contribute to a richer and a deeper harmony. Jesus never entered into the age-long debate of determinism as against indeterminism, of predestination and free will, but he quietly assumed that men had sufficient power of choice either to reject or to meet the conditions of entering upon the life which God had designed for them.

THE CONSUMMATION OF THE KINGDOM

Did Jesus expect the kingdom fully to come within history? Did he look for the transformation of society, either gradually or by progressive stages, until it would entirely conform to the will of God? Or did he expect history to be consummated abruptly in judgement to be followed by a display of the power of God in condemnation of the wicked and their separation from those who had conformed to God's will? The answer is not clear and appears to be a paradox.

Jesus obviously believed the kingdom to be already present. He saw his healings, especially his cure of those troubled by demon possession, as evidence that it had come. To him the forces of evil were intensely real and personal. He accepted Satan as an existent being, an enemy of God, and he addressed the demons whom he cast out, not as delusions of sick minds, but as actual. To him the fact that the demons were being deprived of their baleful power over men was clear proof that the kingdom of heaven, the rule of God, was beginning. Jesus taught his disciples to pray that God's will might be done on earth as it is in heaven and commanded them to make fellow-disciples of all nations, baptizing them, and teaching them to observe all that he had commanded the little inner group of his followers. By his comparison of the kingdom of God with "leaven which a woman took and hid in three measures of meal, till the whole was leavened" he might well be supposed to be implying that all human society would be fully transformed by a progressive process. There is, too, the confident statement by one who was very close to the mind of Jesus, that God sent his son into the world not to condemn the world but that the world might be saved through him.

On the other hand, Jesus declared that few find the way to life and that many follow the road which leads to destruction, that both good and evil grow until the harvest, apparently a sudden consummation, in which the wicked, their character fully revealed by the ripening of their course will be dealt with as harvesters deal with noxious weeds, and the good be conserved as wheat is gathered into a granary.

Perhaps the paradox is insoluble within history. Certainly thus far in history it remains a paradox. What Jesus would have said had he been questioned about it we may not know. He certainly held that God is sovereign in the universe and that His will would be done. He also taught men to pray that it be done, as though God were dependent on their prayer.

Closely allied with the problem of whether Jesus believed that God's rule is to be acknowledged and complied with by all men within history is that other one of whether Jesus expected the consummation of history at an early date.

On the one hand is the well-known apocalypticism which pervaded the Jewish thought of the time and with which Jesus was clearly familiar. Much of it looked towards an early climax of history or at least a major, revolutionary crisis. Many sayings of Jesus can be interpreted as indicating that he shared this expectation. When speaking of what he seems to have intended to be interpreted as the end of history, he declared: "This generation shall not pass until all these things be done." He undoubtedly taught that history was to come to a climax in dramatic judgement and warned his disciples to watch, for their testing by their Lord's return might be at any time and would most certainly come when it was not expected. In this he was seemingly referring to the end of history.

Yet Jesus also most emphatically declared that the disciples were not to know precise times for the fulfilment of their expectation, and that not even he knew the day or the hour when the consummation was to come, but only God. Nor can we be sure to what extent his disciples, in remembering and handing on his sayings, expecting as they naturally did the early termination of history, misread the mind of Jesus and put together words of his which he had not intended to be interpreted in this fashion. We, too, may well misunderstand sayings in which imagery has a large part. A notable instance of this is the passage in which Jesus foretold the destruction of Jerusalem and appeared to conjoin it with the end of the world. That the destruction of Jerusalem was imminent any clear-headed man of the time must have seen. Seething resentment against Roman rule was obviously soon to break out in open revolt. Fanatics believed that God would intervene on behalf of his people, but Jesus was too much aware of the power of Rome, perhaps in part because of the ruthless and overwhelming fashion in which it had been displayed at Sepphoris, had too early in his public career come to the conclusion that it was not in accord with God's methods to step in miraculously to save even His own son if he presumed on His favour by recklessly jeopardizing his life, and was too sadly cognizant of the blind folly all about him to see anything but early doom for the people and the city that he loved. Jerusalem was rejecting the one way to peace, the way which he was offering it, and the end was tragically certain. He can be interpreted as having conjoined this with the end of history, and that has been a general understanding, especially among many recent scholars. Yet the interpreters may have failed to enter fully into his mind.

Certainly there are other sayings, so counter to current expectations that their preservation is evidence of correct reporting, which apparently imply a prolonged postponement of the final climax. Thought-provoking is the familiar parable of the five wise and the five foolish virgins who, anticipating being present at a wedding, were waiting for the coming of the bridegroom. The five who were condemned as foolish were those who, in expectation of the early arrival of the bridegroom, had come with insufficient oil in their lamps, and the five who were praised were those who were prepared for a prolonged delay, and, as the event proved, were right. It may well be that Jesus anticipated many successive crises, each a judgement, before the termination of history on this planet.

God is Central and Supreme

Whatever Jesus may have believed about the future course of history, he had never a doubt of the power and the centrality of God. His belief in God underlay and shaped all his other convictions and his teachings. For him God's will was sovereign. But to Jesus God was no arbitrary despot. He was Father. Father was Jesus' characteristic name for God. God was, to Jesus, the ruler of all nature. He might be and, indeed, was often defied by hostile powers and beings, but He would prevail.

Jesus was not a philosopher dealing in abstract terms and concepts. He never talked about "the problem of evil." He frankly recognized the presence of evil; indeed, he was acutely aware of it, but he never asked why, if God were sovereign, evil was present. He faced squarely the tragedy in the world about him. He plainly stated that sparrows fall to the ground and that lilies, so beautiful and alive today, are tomorrow cast into the oven. Judgement, terrible and certain, awaits those who do not conform to God's will.

Yet as he looked out on the world of nature Jesus saw the heavenly Father so ordering it that the birds are fed and the flowers bloom in all their radiance. To those who would so acknowledge Him and conform their wills to His ways, God would show Himself as Father. Indeed, He was always seeking men, but, presumably because He respected their wills, He did not force Himself upon them. Perhaps it was for that reason that His will in a specific issue was not immediately clear. In employing his will to seek it, the child would make progress towards maturity. Like the father in Jesus' most famous parable,

God does not pursue the wayward into the far country, but waits. The prodigal is still His son, and when, disciplined by judgement, "he comes to himself," recognizes his course for what it is—sin against God's generosity—and knows his own complete unworthiness, but, instead of being overwhelmed by despair, trusts enough in the character which he has seen in the provision made for servants to turn again to his Father and ask only that he be treated as a servant, the Father, waiting and eagerly watching, not only welcomes him, but runs to him, cuts short his rehearsed speech, and insists that he is His son.

THE MAN JESUS

What manner of man was Jesus? No one can fully enter into the consciousness of another or completely understand him. No two human beings are exactly alike. The differences are often subtle and yet the very qualities which elude observation and precise description may be the most important. How impossible it must be, therefore, adequately to understand and to describe one who stood out so markedly from his contemporaries and from all men, both before and since. In the first century and through the generations that have followed opinions have sharply differed. It is evidence of his importance, of the effect that he has had upon history and, presumably, of the baffling mystery of his being that no other life ever lived on this planet has evoked so huge a volume of literature among so many peoples and languages, and that, far from ebbing, the flood continues to mount. More men notice Jesus than ever before, but appraisals have never been as varied or as numerous as in the past two centuries. This is the more extraordinary in view of the brevity of the records which have survived from the memories of his intimates. It is not his teachings which make Jesus so remarkable, although these would be enough to give him distinction. It is a combination of the teachings with the man himself. The two cannot be separated, but if they could the man would be the more important.

While all of this is true, some characteristics stand out so distinctly in the accounts which preserve the impressions of those who had an opportunity to know him best, that they are a guarantee of authenticity, so obviously are they from life and not invented or even seriously distorted. They also reveal to us much of the man himself and help to make clear something of the problems which confront those who seek a complete understanding.

Jesus was a great lover of nature. His sayings abound in references to the sun, the clouds, the rain, the birds, the flowers, seed-time and harvest, growth and decay. He was a minute observer, recognized the pain and the beauty about him, and with a few pregnant words could make vivid to others what he saw. In the technical sense of that term, he was, perhaps fortunately, not a philosopher, but he discerned the cosmic issues beneath the passing pageantry. The sharp contrast between grain and weeds posed for him the problem of good and evil, although he would never have put it in those abstract terms, and of how the sovereignty and righteousness of God in which he so profoundly believed could be compatible with the existence of what was bad. The seeming indifference of the weather to the moral qualities of men was to him evidence of the impartial love of God.

Jesus liked to be with people. He enjoyed social gatherings and good fellowship. He craved friendship. He quickly saw through the individuals whom he met. He was quick to discern and scorn insincerity, pomposity, and pride, but he was fully as prompt to penetrate beneath the surface into hidden and bewildered frustrations and timid longing for the good.

The sympathies of Jesus were as broad as the human race. To be sure, some incidents appear to belie this generalization. On one occasion Jesus seemed to put off the plea of a woman of another nation by saying that he was sent only to "the lost sheep of the house of Israel" and in dispatching his disciples on a mission of preaching and healing he instructed them not to go to non-Jews, whether Gentiles or Samaritans, but only to these same "lost sheep of the house of Israel." Yet in each instance there is another possible explanation than that of exclusiveness. In dealing with the Canaanitish woman he rejected the suggestion of the disciples that he send her away and did as she requested when she proved herself in earnest. The mission of the twelve was for a special purpose and did not imply a continuing exclusion of Gentiles from the Gospel. Again and again there are incidents and sayings which are clear evidence that Jesus went out of his way to reprove racial bigotry and believed his message to be as broad as humanity. Among these were his initial sermon at Nazareth in which he angered his fellow-townsmen by calling attention to occasions in the Scriptures in which Gentiles had been helped by the prophets when those of the house of Israel were apparently passed by, his selection of a Samaritan as the example of a good neighbour, his healing of the servant of the Roman centurion, and his commission to his apostles after his resurrection to make disciples of all nations.

Deeply religious himself, Jesus was impatient with professional or ostentatious religiosity. He challenged those about him to apply their minds to religion and morals. While honouring the past and the great prophets and lawgivers of his nation, he rejected blind and stubborn adherence to the letter of the law and of the writings which he revered, and treated the traditions of his people with a vigour and a freedom which in some aroused anger and in others were greeted with amazed admiration. While for almost all, and perhaps all of his moral and religious teachings parallels and precedents can be found in the writings of the Jewish sages, Jesus had about him a freshness and an originality which gave them such vivid expression and put them in such proportion and perspective that they were seen as both old and new.

Jesus had a keen sense of humour which again and again bubbles out irrepressibly, all the more strikingly because it is in contrast with the complete absence of humour in those writings of the Christians of the first century which have been preserved in the New Testament. He had a keen eye for the ridiculous and could make startling what he saw—the self-righteous man with the huge beam in his eye essaying to see and pluck out a mere speck in his neighbour's eye; the solemn and meticulous legalist who was so conscientious about details and yet so blind to great moral issues that he was like a man who, anxious lest he be contaminated by his food and drink, would painstakingly strain out the most minute gnat and then, without blinking, swallow an entire camel, hair, hoofs, humps, and offensive breath. He laughed at children playing in the market place, especially at those who, pouting, refused to join in the sport, even when their companions were quite willing to adjust the game to meet their wishes. His questions to the crowds about John the Baptist—"What went ye out into the wilderness to see? A reed shaken with the wind? . . . a man clothed in soft raiment?"—must have provoked laughter, so purposely contrary were they to what all of his hearers knew.

Jesus had the soul of a poet. While few of his recorded sayings are in poetic form, again and again his words breathe the spirit of poetry. His mind thought in terms of pictures and concrete scenes, not in abstract phrases. The parables and sententious sayings in which most of his teachings were couched were such that, once heard, they could not easily be forgotten. It is said that he chose that manner of speaking deliberately, but he could not have employed it so skilfully had it not reflected the quality of his mind. It is tantalizing to speculate whether he may not in part have acquired it from his mother, either by heredity or through long association, for the narratives in the first portions of *The Gospel according to Luke* which could have come only from her have much of the same quality, but with sufficient difference to make it clear that they and those sayings which are ascribed to him were not the invention of some one author.

There were about Jesus a quickness and a directness which no observing reader of the Gospel narratives can miss. Jesus could blaze forth in anger. Men remembered his glance. It is interesting to note how often, even in our brief accounts, Jesus is described as looking at a person. Here was a characteristic which stood out in the memories about him cherished by Jesus' intimates—his looking on the rich young ruler and loving him, his look at the time of Peter's denial which set that unhappy, loyal, puzzled soul to bitter, heart-broken weeping. Jesus enjoined decisive action—the cutting off of an offending hand or the plucking out of a wayward eye, striving (the Greek is the word from which our "agonizing" is derived) to enter in by the narrow door. He condemned the aimlessly drifting, un-thought-out life. He had no use for indecision—for those who said "I will follow thee, but"—and declared that he who put his hand to the plow and looked back was not fit for the kingdom of heaven. He who would become the disciple of Jesus—namely, learn of him—must renounce all that he had. He even had admiration for the vigorous action of the steward who, when his dishonesty had been disclosed, adopted a bold method of making his future secure.

Jesus could be very patient. He could see one in whom he had sensed possibilities for good and had enrolled among his intimates disintegrate morally and eventually betray him, and yet seek to hold onto him. For his other disciples, who often tried him by their slowness to understand what was obvious to him, he had a forbearance which must have been difficult for one of his quick and keen intelligence. Paul, who probably never knew Jesus personally, but who had heard much of him from those who did, was impressed by his meekness and gentleness, qualities in striking contrast with the quick anger which cruelty or callousness to human need evoked in him.

Another quality which has often been remarked was the absence of any sense of having committed sin or of a basic corruption in himself. The one possible exception is the reply to the inquirer who calls him "good master"—"Why callest thou me good? There is none good but one, that is God;" but another version of the incident gives a different phrasing which does not include a disavowal of goodness. It is highly significant that in one as sensitive morally as was Jesus and who taught his followers to ask for the forgiveness of their sins there is no hint of any need of forgiveness for himself, no asking of pardon, either from those about him or of God. Deep struggle of the spirit Jesus knew, but it seems to have been to discover what the will of God was and not from any inward division, any inability to follow what he knew to be right, such as Paul so poignantly describes in himself, or from any sense of recurring fault or of unconquered sinfulness such as the greatest of Christian saints have confessed.

Less important but still significant is the fact that we never hear of Jesus being ill. We read of his being weary, of his being grieved, of his suffering pain in spirit and in body, but the pain was inflicted by others and we have no hint that he knew what it was to be sick. He radiated confidence and health.

Fundamental in all of Jesus' life was his belief in God, his loyalty to Him, and his utter confidence in Him. Here was the fountain of his ethical convictions and teachings. He took time to be alone with God in prayer. When he instructed his followers in praying to go into a room, shut the door, and pray to their Father who is in secret, he was but telling them to do what he himself did. We read of his spending an entire night alone in prayer, and of his rising early in the morning after a crowded day to go into a desert place and there pray. Even on that night before his trial and death, when he asked the inner group of his disciples to watch with him in the agonizing hour in Gethsemane, he went a little apart from them for prayer.

THE UNIQUE RELATION TO GOD

One of the most difficult and mooted questions about Jesus is what he conceived himself to be. Did he regard himself as the Messiah? If so, what did that mean to him? Why did he so often call himself the Son of Man? Much ink has been spilled in the prolonged discussions of these issues. Across the centuries the relation of Jesus to God has engaged some of the best minds among his followers and is still a subject of debate. That is partly because of the paucity of our records, partly because of the difficulty of penetrating fully into the mind of another, but chiefly because we here have to do with a subject which stretches our minds and our comprehension to the limit and even then cannot be fully apprehended.

It must be obvious to any thoughtful reader of the Gospel records that Jesus regarded himself and his message as inseparable. He was a great teacher, but he was more. His teachings about the kingdom of God, about human conduct, and about God were important, but they could not be divorced from him without, from his standpoint, being vitiated.

It is clear that Jesus believed himself to have a relation to God such as no other human being has ever known. Even if we did not have the many statements in *The Gospel according to John,* such as those which describe him as the *Logos* (the "Word") become flesh, and in which Jesus declares that he and the Father are one, we would have the startling assertion by Jesus preserved in *The Gospel according to Matthew* that all things have been delivered to him by the Father, that no one knows the Son except the Father and that no one knows the Father except the Son and any one to whom the Son chooses to reveal him. This is corroborated by the conscious authority with which Jesus spoke. While declaring that he had not come to destroy the Law and the Prophets, he said emphatically that he came to fulfil them, thus assuming his authority to do so. By implication he also pronounced the Law to be imperfect and for the exact justice of an eye for an eye and a tooth for a tooth enjoined more than once in the inherited standards of his people he commanded his followers not to resist one who is evil. In contrast with the Jewish prophets who regarded themselves as but the mouthpieces of God and who either by implication or expressly supported their pronouncements by "thus saith the Lord," Jesus repeatedly used the words, "I say unto you," with the quiet assumption that he had the inherent right to speak in such fashion. This was among the reasons for the indignation which he aroused among the religious leaders of the Jews. They deemed him to be blaspheming, to be arrogating to himself the functions of God. With an air of authority which angered some about him, believing as they did that he was usurping the prerogatives of God, in more than one instance he declared an individual's sins forgiven.

Again and again Jesus made it clear that he regarded himself as both in the continuity of what had preceded him in the spiritual life of the Jewish people—the Law and the Prophets—and as inaugurating something which was radically new. He saw the Law and the Prophets as pointing forward to him and as culminating in him. As we have said, he insisted that he did not come to abolish the Law and the Prophets but to fulfil them. But in the fulfilling he contrasted what was said in them with what he declared to be right in such a striking manner, as in divorce, oath-taking, and retaliation, that he seems not so much to be completing as to be supplanting. In each instance a case can be made for the use of the word "fulfil" as a description of what he was doing, but the advance over the past is so great as to appear a revolutionary departure from it. Many of those who heard him exclaimed that his was a "new doctrine." He himself lent support to this reception by a saying about new wine in old wine-skins and of unshrunk cloth on an old garment with the frank statement that in each case the attempt to combine the old with the new would be disastrous to both. He believed that what he was beginning was strikingly different even from the movement of John the Baptist, for while he spoke of the latter in terms of high praise, saying that he was "more than a prophet," and that among those born of woman there was none greater than he, he was emphatic that "he that is least in the kingdom of God is greater than" John. To be sure, Jesus spoke of scribes (or scholars) who, "instructed unto the kingdom of heaven," brought out of the treasures of their learning what was both old and new: each could be better understood in light of the other. Moreover, no one of the sayings of Jesus, if taken by itself, is without precedent or parallel in the earlier or contemporary literature of his people. Yet in the forms of statement, especially in the parables, and in the synthesis and the emphasis given them there is a freshness which bears the stamp of conscious authority and of originality and genius.

So unique did Jesus believe his relationship to God to be that he seems to have found no designation in the scriptures of his people or in common usage which exactly described it. This may account for the reluctance which some of our accounts appear to reflect in him to allow himself to be called the Messiah.

That term was associated with a variety of stereotypes and to accept it would be to lay himself open to even more grave misunderstanding than he had to face. When he welcomed the burst of insight with which Peter declared that he was the Christ (Messiah), the son of the living God, and began to point out that for him, Jesus, that meant the cross and the resurrection, that disciple showed his complete lack of comprehension of what his Master believed the Messiahship to entail. He was presumably quite astonished and bewildered when Jesus turned and rebuked him. If, after months of intimacy, Peter did not understand, how much less the thousands who had not enjoyed that association. It was not until after the crucifixion and the resurrection that even his most intimate disciples began to see what was inseparable from his mission and to comprehend who and what Jesus really was.

Conflict with the Religious Leaders

This uniqueness of Jesus and the revolutionary contrast of his teaching with the traditions of his people were the source of much of the conflict which brought Jesus to his death.

The fashion in which Jesus brushed aside some of the customs and prohibitions most cherished by the Pharisees appeared to these self-constituted guardians of Judaism to threaten all for which they and their forefathers had fought against the surrounding world of paganism. What seemed to them to be his disregard of the Sabbath, his contempt for prescribed ablutions, and his willingness, even eagerness, to associate with those whom they regarded as sinners were in their eyes unforgivable breaches of religion and good morals.

In his turn Jesus believed the attitude of the Pharisees to be basically wrong, even blasphemous, and to be leading astray not only themselves but also those who looked to them for guidance. In characteristically vivid language, all the more biting because of its humour, he described them as blind leaders of the blind, with the ditch as their destination. Their error was their belief that they would earn God's favour by their deeds, or, to put it in another way, that they could accumulate merit with God by obedience to His law. This attitude, Jesus saw, bred meticulous care to conform to a set of ethical principles and of ritualistic acts, with a satisfaction in having approximated to them which nourished the deadliest of all sins, pride. Also contributing to pride was the satisfaction of recognition by other men with its associated striving for the approval of men and for place and position, a striving which might even lead one to pray, to undertake ascetic practices, and to perform deeds of mercy for the applause of men.

All this Jesus excoriated in trenchant phrase and apt illustration. He pictured the self-satisfied Pharisee praying in the temple "with himself" and, in a fashion which must have made the Pharisees writhe, placed in contrast and with approbation a member of that class which good Jews loathed as a symbol and instrument of the hated Roman rule, a tax-collector, who, conscious of his sin, pled humbly with God for mercy. To be sure, this portrait of the Pharisee was a caricature, probably deliberately so. At least some of that party were as unhappy as were the prophets whom they honoured over emphasis upon legalism to the neglect of just dealing, mercy, and humility before God. Yet there was that in Judaism which in practice so denied what Jesus was profoundly convinced to be the only correct view of man's relation to God that he believed that he must put the contrast as sharply as possible. In a parable which must have been puzzling on first hearing, Jesus told of the owner of a vineyard who in time of harvest gave exactly the same wage to those who laboured only one hour as to those who had been at it all day. The point, so disturbing to the Pharisee, was that one could not acquire merit with God by piling up good deeds, partly at least because, as Jesus said in another parable, even if we did all that is commanded by God we would only be doing our duty and would deserve no reward.

Jesus appeared to go out of his way to antagonize those in charge of the worship of God in the temple in Jerusalem. He held up for admiration as one who had fulfilled the law of love to one's neighbour a nameless representative of that group whom the Jews despised, the Samaritans, and pilloried a priest and a Levite as having been quite callous in their failure to observe it. His choice of the *dramatis personæ* must have been with an express purpose and not casual. It would bring out with crystal clearness the contrast between God's commands and the religion of the leaders of worship.

Jesus also appeared deliberately to challenge the Sadducees, the politically influential group which controlled the temple. He was scandalized by the fashion in which God's worship in this central shrine of his people's faith was being callously prostituted as a money-making device—in profit in the very courts of the temple from the exchange of money to the temple coinage and from selling pigeons and sheep and oxen for sacrifice. It may be significant that two of the accounts of this "cleansing of the temple" stress his indignation at those who dealt in pigeons. The sale of these for sacrifice by those who could not afford the more expensive sheep and oxen offered a way of making gain from the poorest of the devout and was especially abhorrent to one sensitive to injustice to those "who had no helper." It appears that for a time Jesus and his followers so took possession that "he would not suffer that any man should carry any vessel through the temple." This both angered and alarmed the Sadducean clique which controlled the shrine, for it threatened their revenues from their share in the proceeds of the money-changers and merchants and might bring down on them the Roman authorities, hyper-sensitive as the latter were in an occupied land which was seething with unrest to any move which might lead to a popular uprising.

By his teaching in Jerusalem in these parlous days Jesus did nothing to allay the enmity and fear of either Pharisees or Sadducees. In a peculiarly sobering parable he denounced them as faithless administrators of a trust. He also made it clear that he regarded them as the descendants of those who had killed the prophets.

Maddening to both Pharisees and Sadducees was Jesus' quiet attitude of authority. Jesus would not submit himself to be controlled by them, but challenged them and for a time appeared to have popular support. He was accused of making himself equal with God and of admitting that he was the Messiah. If he were permitted to continue, so these critics argued, he would jeopardize the law and order maintained by the classes which ruled in synagogue and temple. They could rationalize the offense he had given to their pride by saying that in the tense situation which existed in Palestine where they were like men sitting on top of a volcano which might explode at any moment, it would be the part of wisdom to eliminate Jesus rather than to risk his setting off an eruption.

Crucified, Dead, and Buried

Under these circumstances it is not surprising that Jesus was arrested and executed. He himself had been expecting that outcome, for he was too clear-headed not to see that if carried through the course which he was pursuing could have no other climax. Indeed, he had declared that it was of the very essence of his mission, that apart from it his unique relationship to God could not be understood.

What is difficult and perhaps impossible fully to ascertain is the course of thought by which Jesus came to the deep conviction that he must bring the issue between himself and the dominant elements in his people to so sharp a focus at this particular time and then allow himself to be seized. The reasons for his challenge are fairly clear. Being sure as he was of God's goal for men, of God's purpose in Jewish history, law, and prophecy, confronted by entrenched privilege which, while professedly standing as the guardian of the Jewish heritage, was both blind to the true content of that heritage and was utilizing its championship to obtain for itself prestige, power, and wealth, he could no other than protest.

But why did he permit himself to be killed so soon after his public career had begun? Why did he not withdraw east of the Jordan to pursue a mission among the Jews there, or, perhaps, to the other Jewish communities which were scattered so widely within and to the east of the Roman Empire? He clearly saw that his disciples would be dismayed by his arrest and trial and, unnerved and not really understanding him and his mission, were most unlikely to become the nucleus of a growing movement to perpetuate his teachings. Why did he not take a longer time to instruct them, organize them, and add to their numbers, so that when death, whether peaceful or violent, should remove him they could continue with what he had begun?

From the viewpoint of worldly prudence the course Jesus was following was sheer madness. Having antagonized the Pharisees, both in Galilee and in Judea, by his procedure in the temple he now goaded their traditional rivals, the Sadducees, to side with them and take the initiative in eliminating him. After making his vivid demonstration in the temple and arraying the chief priests and the Sadducean clique against him, he took no measures to organize his followers permanently to support his reforms. Did he expect God to intervene on his behalf and thus to force Him to inaugurate the next stage in the kingdom of heaven? That would have been akin to what had presented itself to him months before in the wilderness when the suggestion came that he cast himself from a pinnacle of the temple that God might deliver him and thus dramatically demonstrate His Son's authority. Jesus had then dismissed it as a temptation of the evil one. It seems utterly unlikely that he would now have yielded to it.

Later, in looking back over their months with him, the disciples declared that they recalled that Jesus had foretold his death and resurrection and the proclamation of the Gospel throughout the entire world, but did they read back later events into dimly comprehended words? If their memories were correct, why the agony in the Garden of Gethsemane and the repeated petition, seemingly denied, that the cup might pass from him? Obviously here was no cowardice or weakness, for Jesus made no attempt at flight and showed no fear as he faced death. The mystery lies much deeper.

However, from our records, fragmentary though they are, it seems clear that for many months and perhaps longer Jesus had known that his course must lead him to Jerusalem and to death, that he saw it as foretold in the sacred writings of his people, and that his crucifixion was in the divine plan.

Whatever the processes by which Jesus arrived at his decision, some of the main outlines of the events of the days which are so important in the story of his life and for the future of Christianity are clear. Because from the beginning they were central in the consciousness and the faith of Christians, the accounts of the last few hours before the crucifixion, of the crucifixion itself, of the burial, and of the resurrection are fairly detailed, occupy a large proportion of each of the Four Gospels, and again and again are referred to in the others of the earliest Christian documents.

The time was the high Jewish feast of the year, that of the Passover, with its memories of the deliverance of the remote ancestors of the Jews from bondage in Egypt. On his way to Jerusalem for the feast Jesus tried to make it clear to his disciples both by his words and his attitude that a crisis was at hand. Yet the disciples were so obsessed with preconceived ideas of what the course of events must be for the Messiah and the kingdom of God that they misinterpreted him and were entirely unprepared intellectually and emotionally for what transpired.

Stimulated by the miracles which they had seen at his hands or by reports of them, an enthusiastic, spontaneous popular demonstration greeted Jesus as he rode into Jerusalem. His "cleansing of the temple" followed. Then came several days of teaching in the temple and of debates with those whom he had antagonized. The evening of his arrest Jesus had the meal with his twelve disciples which was to become famous in Christian history, art, and worship as "the Last Supper." The method of arranging for it which he took may well have been devised as a precaution against interruption by his enemies. The evening was marred by contentions among the disciples as to who was to be greatest, but Jesus himself set the example as one among them who served and demonstrated his attitude by washing their feet. As the eleven who survived after the defection and death of Judas looked back on the evening, they were aware that in the mind of Jesus it had peculiar significance. It was then that he took bread, gave thanks, broke it, and gave it to his disciples, saying that it was his body, and followed it with the cup, also giving thanks, having them drink from it, declaring that it was his blood of the new covenant. Something of fundamental importance was taking place. Around this was to develop the central rite of the Christian Church.

The group went from the supper room to Gethsemane on the Mount of Olives, perhaps to a spot looking out across the city. It was a place to which Jesus had been accustomed to go. From time to time through the months of his public career he had sought solitude for meditation and prayer, a practice which may well have been established during the years of obscurity. This night there ensued a time of agony which left an indelible mark upon the memory of his intimates, even though at the moment, heavy-eyed with sleep, they were only partly aware of it.

Into all that went on in the soul of Jesus during that bitter hour we cannot presume fully to enter. We can only venture conjectures from the imperfect record. Was it the consciousness of the seeming failure of his mission, apparently so soon to be terminated in pitiful futility? Was it the burden of the world's sin, the awful weight of man's blindness and depravity? Was it the apparent hopelessness of trying to make men realize the radiant vision of the reign of God which Jesus had endeavoured to share? Was it the seeming imminent triumph of evil, the victory within man himself of all that was ruining man, and the attendant defeat of God? Was it uncertainty, in the face of what looked like tragic frustration, of what God's will was?

Whatever the inward reason for that struggle, the hour was all the more dark because of the obtuseness of Jesus' most intimate friends. Those whom he had asked to share the watch with him were not so much indifferent as uncomprehending and slept except when, seeking fellowship, he roused them. His struggle had to be without the companionship of those upon whom, if it were to go on after his death, his mission would depend. Well-meaning enough though they were, they apparently completely failed to comprehend what he had been trying to do. His seeming failure must have been rendered all the more poignant by the realization that if the inner group with whom he had elected to share his vision were so far from comprehending it and only a few moments before had been disputing over who was to have priority in the kingdom which they were expecting, the great run of mankind would be even more blind. Yet, as he struggled alone with his burden, Jesus felt himself not alone, but in the presence of God, and like a refrain came the words, "Abba, Father, all things are possible unto Thee: take away this cup from me: nevertheless not what I will but what Thou wilt."

If there remained in the mind of Jesus any uncertainty as to what the will of God was, it was resolved by the appearance of the party who were seeking him for arrest. The cup from which only a few minutes ago he had prayed to be spared was being pressed to his lips and it was made the more bitter by the fact that the betrayer was one of the twelve intimates whom he had chosen. We shall never know why it was that Jesus picked Judas or the reason for Judas' treachery. Knowing his keen insight into character we can be sure that Jesus was never deceived in Judas. Moreover, Jesus would have been acting entirely out of character had he selected him with the deliberate purpose of having him become the betrayer and thus forever damning him. Jesus was always seeking to save men's lives and not to destroy them. It must have been that in Judas Jesus saw possibilities for great good as well as for sordid evil and had hoped by his love to evoke the one and discourage the other. If so, the outcome could only have added to the burden which was already his in the obtuseness of the other eleven and their failure to rise to the emergency. The eleven, dismayed by the unexpected turn of events, deserted Jesus. Poor, loyal Peter, in trying to keep within sight of his Master, stumbled into a triple denial. There followed in quick and sickening succession the remaining scenes of the tragedy. Jesus was tried by the Jewish religious authorities and by the Roman Procurator, Pilate. To the informed and unprejudiced observer the charges were palpably false. They obviously seemed so to Pilate. Yet Pilate yielded to expediency and ordered that Jesus be crucified, with the inscription above him which showed his contempt for the accusers—"the King of the Jews." It is thought-provoking irony that, having deliberately refused to employ political methods and having rejected an interpretation of his mission which would make him a leader in the current unrest against Rome, Jesus should have been executed on the charge of planning revolt against Roman rule. It is in part a reflection of the complete failure of the leaders of his nation and of the representative of Rome to understand him. Their blindness made vivid the contrast to which Jesus had repeatedly called attention between their perspective and his, between them and the kingdom of God.

We read, almost as though we were seeing it ourselves, of scourging, of rough, derisive soldiers pressing a crown of thorns on his brow, of a purple robe, of mock homage, of blindfolding and smiting with the challenge to the erstwhile wonder-worker to indicate who struck him, of a blood-thirsty mob demanding crucifixion, of the procession to the place of crucifixion, of the nailing to the cross, and of the casting of lots by the executioners for his garments. Through all the excruciating hours Jesus bore himself with dignity and without wincing. He spoke a word of compassion for the women who bewailed him on his way to the cross. He prayed for those who crucified him, saying, what was undoubtedly true, that they did not know what they were doing. Therein was part of the tragedy. He gave a reassuring word to one of the two criminals who were crucified with him. He commended his mother to the care of one of his disciples. Once he gave evidence of the physical distress and spoke of his thirst. At what may have been an especially black moment he cried out: "My God, my God, why hast *Thou* forsaken me?" But those are the opening words of a psalm which, while recounting intense suffering at the hands of others so like that of Jesus in some of its details that by many it is regarded as prophecy and by others as a model on which the narrators of the crucifixion shaped their story, ends in a note of consolation, triumph, and praise, and Jesus may have had in mind the entire psalm and found strength in it in the long hours of pain.

When at last death brought oblivion to the sufferer it seemed that the drama had not been so much his failure as the failure of man and God.

The crucifixion was put through by the spokesman and official representatives of as high a religion as the world had thus far seen and by a magistrate of a government which was as good as any which man had produced. Yet in blindness, selfish fear, and stupid anger they had done to death the rarest spirit ever born of woman, who in his teachings and example had shown the only way by which his own nation could avoid destruction and by which mankind could attain fullness of life. The cross stood in judgement on all the men who had anything to do with it—not only upon the Jewish leaders who had engineered it, upon the mob who demanded it, upon the Roman official who ordered it, and upon the soldiers who carried it out, but also upon those Jews such as the one who gave him burial who, lamenting the execution, did nothing to prevent it, upon the disciples who had failed to understand Jesus and who, bewildered, deserted him, upon the government which had not made impossible such a miscarriage of justice, and even upon the Jewish religion which, while it had nurtured Jesus, had not prevented its own prostitution by its professed guardians. Since those immediately responsible for the crucifixion were a cross section of mankind, both good and bad, the cross was a condemnation of the entire race, vivid evidence of its stupid perversity and its impotence to save its noblest representative from rejection and humiliating death at the hands of man.

But had not God, if God exists, also failed? Is there a God at all? Or is the universe, if it be a universe, and not unintelligent and unintelligible confusion, morally indifferent and blind to what the high-minded among the race hold to be man's finest hopes and noblest aspirations? Is the universe playing sport with beings which it has produced or has it blindly given birth to men who are more intelligent than what has produced them, orphaned victims of unknowing chance? Had the Jewish prophets been correct in declaring that God is righteous and in setting forth a description of what that righteousness is? If so, is God, as the prophets and the psalmists had also declared, sovereign? In these beliefs Jesus had shared. He had even called God Father. He had declared that in him God was in some fresh fashion inaugurating His kingdom, His reign, and that he, Jesus, was in a unique sense the Son of God. Had the prophets and Jesus been tragically mistaken? Had they cherished beliefs which would not stand the test of fact? So the cross would have seemed to demonstrate.

Risen, Ascended, Expected, and Yet Still Present

The answer came on what Christians hail as the first Easter and in events which shortly followed that Easter. By it the judgement of man by the cross was not lightened or revoked, but Christians have been convinced that in it faith in God was vindicated, and God was seen not to have been defeated but to have triumphed and to have revealed the fashion in which His sovereignty is exercised.

The records which have reached us do not make clear the precise sequence of events on that first Easter. However, from them it is obvious that the disciples did not expect the resurrection and that it took them completely by surprise. The accounts also declare explicitly or by unmistakable inference that the body of Jesus which a few hours before had been reverently and sorrowfully laid in a rock-hewn tomb and carefully sealed in it by a huge stone was not to be found, but that the guardian boulder had been rolled away and that those who had come to anoint the body found the tomb empty. It is abundantly affirmed that the disciples were profoundly convinced that they had seen the risen Jesus, had talked with him, had watched him eat, and had viewed the wounds in his hands and his side, and that one of their number, incredulous, had had his doubts removed by the invitation to put his fingers on the marred hands and his hand into the wounded side. The accounts agree that the risen Jesus commissioned his disciples to go forth as his witnesses and representatives into all the earth. The biographer, almost certainly Luke and a companion of Paul, who tells us that he had taken pains to obtain all possible information from eyewitnesses and the narratives compiled from eyewitnesses and who probably wrote within less than a generation after the events he describes, declares that during forty days Jesus appeared to the apostles whom he had chosen, "speaking of . . . the kingdom of God"—the subject which had constituted the burden of his teaching before the crucifixion—giving them instructions for their mission, and promising them power to accomplish it. After forty days Jesus disappeared from their sight in such fashion that they knew that they were not to behold him again in that manner until a reappearance, his "second coming," which was to be their continuing and joyous expectation. Yet Paul believed that not many years afterwards Jesus had shown himself to him, and the disciples were convinced that Jesus had promised his continued presence with them and would make his abode in any one who loved him.

It seems significant that Paul is the only one of whom our early records tell us who had not been a disciple of Jesus before he met the risen Lord. To be sure, hundreds of these disciples saw him, but so far as our evidence permits us to know none other outside that circle of friends was won to belief by a vision of the glorified Christ. With the single exception of Paul, and the accounts of what happened to him on the Damascus road indicate that even he was not an entire exception, only those prepared by loyalty to Jesus actually saw him after the resurrection. Yet it is also significant and one of the compelling proofs of the resurrection is that the crucifixion left the disciples in despair and that, hopeless, they were transformed by their experience of the risen Jesus. The resurrection became essential in the faith of subsequent generations of Christians. It meant assurance that because Jesus lived they also would live. Even more important was the conviction nourished in Christians that by the resurrection Jesus had been vindicated and had been shown to be the Son of God with power.

The Coming of the Spirit

The disciples, not only the eleven but also the larger circle who had been won by Jesus in the days of his flesh, were further strengthened and empowered by the fulfilment of a promise which had been given them by their risen Lord. On Pentecost, the Jewish feast which came fifty days after the second day of the Passover, there came upon the group in Jerusalem—a group which may have numbered slightly above a hundred—what they called the Holy Spirit. It was that occasion to which a large proportion of later Christians looked back as the birthday of the Christian Church. The continuing presence of the Holy Spirit was regarded by Christians as an essential feature of their life and faith.

Out of their experience with Jesus and with the Holy Spirit Christians found their conception of God enlarged and incalculably enriched. They continued to believe in one God and to name Him, as many pre-Christian Jews had done, Father. But they also believed that in Jesus they had seen God, that in Jesus the eternal *Logos* (a word which they found in current Hellenistic philosophic terminology) which was God Himself had become flesh. They likewise were convinced that the power which they found at work within them and within the Christian fellowship was also God. Jews as the early Christians were, nurtured on the great central affirmation of Judaism, "Hear, Oh Israel, the Lord thy God, the Lord is one," they were constrained, possibly to their surprise, to think of God as Father, Son, and Holy Spirit, Three in One. The intellectual issues raised by that illumination were to have perennial interest and became major subjects of thought, and, sad to relate, of controversy. The experience could never be adequately expressed in words, although some of the creeds or symbols which were devised in an attempt to do so gained wide, indeed, almost universal acceptance among those who bore the Christian name. Nor could all the questions about it be answered with entire satisfaction. Always there was mystery, yet belief in the Trinity, based upon early and continuing experience, became a distinguishing characteristic of Christianity.

The effects of the resurrection and the coming of the Holy Spirit upon the disciples were and are of major importance. From discouraged, disillusioned men and women who sadly looked back upon the days when they had hoped that Jesus "was he who should redeem Israel," they were made over into a company of enthusiastic witnesses. From them, as we are to see in the next chapter, faith in Jesus as Christ spread rapidly and spontaneously to many centres of the Græco-Roman world and even beyond it. They did not lose their individual characteristics nor were they immediately emancipated from their weaknesses. Most of the eleven apostles seem to have remained obscure. At least we do not have authentic reports of most of them after Pentecost. Except as names cherished in the memory of the Church and for stories about them which cannot be verified, the majority of them disappear from history. Indeed, we are not sure of the names of all of them, for the lists given do not fully agree. Peter, of whom we hear the most, for some time failed to grasp the full import of the universality of the Gospel which Jesus proclaimed and embodied and we read that on one occasion, either through lack of clarity of thought or cowardice, he compromised a principle which he had acknowledged. The disciples, like other men and Christians through the ages, remained human. Yet in them was a power, a life, which came to them through Jesus and which worked moral and spiritual transformation. That power, that life, proved contagious. The record of their operation in subsequent centuries is the history of Christianity.

How far were that power and that life to be effective? That they were potent within individual lives and groups is incontrovertible, but could the power displayed in the resurrection and at Pentecost remake the world which had crucified Jesus? Was history to prove that early Christian to be right when he declared that God sent not His Son into the world to condemn the world but that the world through him might be saved? That by the crucifixion the world, even at its seeming best, had been judged and found wanting is clear. But was the power that raised Jesus from the dead and which worked within the followers of Jesus completely to reshape that world and make it and all mankind to conform fully to the "high calling of God in Christ Jesus"? Could it lift even those who bore the Christian name "unto a perfect man, unto the measure of the stature of the fullness of Christ?" It is questions such as these that the history of Christianity should enable us to answer.

SELECTED BIBLIOGRAPHY

The literature on the subject of this chapter is enormous. No set of topics has more engaged the attention of scholars across the centuries. The flood of books and articles gives no indication of subsiding. Any selection from the available material lays itself open to legitimate criticism both for what is omitted and what is included. As will be readily seen from even a casual reading, the preceding pages are written from a conservative viewpoint. They have endeavoured to take account of recent as well as older scholarship, but they are frankly based upon an acceptance of the Gospel records as inspired and conveying accurate information. For instance, the virgin birth of Jesus is regarded as historical and John 21:24 is understood as confirming internal testimony for the Johannine source of the Fourth Gospel. Several of the books listed below, brilliant, reverent, able, and stimulating though they are, seem to the author to contain much of conjecture which, to say the least, is open to challenge, but which, unfortunately, is sometimes put forth with a dogmatic assurance which may mislead the unwary. Moreover, some of these books, like so many others written about Jesus, are so absorbed in the minutiæ of the various texts through which our knowledge of him has reached us, in discussions of the authenticity of particular incidents and sayings, of the factors which may have altered these in their transmission, and of the meanings of individual words and phrases that they obscure or entirely miss the main points and the central significance of the whole. They are like the scholars of Jesus' day—the "scribes"—who were condemned for their blindness. There is a kind of scholarship which is often praised but whose most highly esteemed qualities are its stumbling blocks. Yet Jesus himself said that it was possible for the "scribe"—the scholar—"to be instructed unto the kingdom of heaven." The viewpoints expressed in books which are the honest work of scholars must be taken into account by any who would delve deeply and comprehensively into a study of Jesus.

The sources of our knowledge of the life and teachings of Jesus are the Four Gospels and several of the letters in the New Testament, all of them written within seventy or at most a hundred years of the event and some of them clearly incorporating information and even fragments from still earlier sources.

Nine semi-popular and fairly recent books written by competent scholars are T. R. Glover, *The Jesus of History* (New York, Association Press, 1917, pp. xiv, 225), a sympathetic, brilliantly written interpretation; J. Knox, *The Man Christ Jesus* (New York, Harper & Brothers, 1942, pp. 100), a simple and moving summary based upon profound and extensive study; F. C. Burkitt, *Christian Beginnings* (University of London Press, 1924, pp. 152), three lectures by a distinguished authority of Cambridge University; F. C. Grant, *The Gospel of the Kingdom* (New York, The Macmillan Co., 1940, pp. xvii, 240), which reacts against the extreme eschatological view of Schweitzer; three little books by E. F. Scott, *The Gospel and Its Tributaries* (New York, Charles Scribner's Sons, 1930, pp. 295), *The Kingdom of God in the New Testament* (New York, The Macmillan Co., 1931, pp. 197), and *The Purpose of the Gospels* (New York, Charles Scribner's Sons, 1949, pp. vii, 171), by a Presbyterian, of Glasgow and Oxford training, long a teacher in the United States; C. H. Dodd, *The Parables of the Kingdom* (London, Nisbet & Co., 1935, pp. 214), persuasively putting forth a view called "realized eschatology"; and A. C. Headlam, *The Life and Teachings of Jesus the Christ* (Oxford University Press, 1923, pp. xiii, 336), a moderately conservative treatment by a bishop of the Church of England.

IN THE NATURE OF INTRODUCTORY HANDBOOKS FOR STUDENTS

C. T. Craig, *The Beginning of Christianity* (New York and Nashville, Abingdon-Cokesbury Press, 1943, pp. 366), with a comprehensive familiarity with modern scholarship and expressing positive views.

M. S. Enslin, *Christian Beginnings* (New York, Harper & Brothers, 1938, pp. ix, 533), fairly radical.

Somewhat technical and detailed is T. W. Manson, *The Teachings of Jesus. Studies of Its Form and Content* (Cambridge University Press, 1945, pp. xi, 352), by a competent and mature English scholar.

A SELECTION FROM A NUMBER OF RECENT AND CONTEMPORARY SPECIALISTS, CHIEFLY CONTINENTAL, ON THE LIFE AND TEACHINGS OF JESUS

R. Bultmann, *Jesus and the Word,* translated from the German by L. P. Smith and E. Huntress (New York, Charles Scribner's Sons, 1934, pp. xii, 226). Sympathetic with the crisis theology.

M. Goguel, *The Life of Jesus,* translated by Olive Wyon (New York, The Macmillan Co., 1933, pp. 591). By a French Protestant, written from the viewpoint of a fairly radical modern school of thought.

T. S. Kepler, *Contemporary Thinking About Jesus, An Anthology* (New York and Nashville, Abingdon-Cokesbury Press, 1944, pp. 429).

J. Klausner, *Jesus of Nazareth, His Life, Times, and Teaching,* translated from the original Hebrew by H. Danby (New York, The Macmillan Co., 1925, pp. 434). Mildly friendly to Jesus, by a Jewish scholar who attempts to show how Judaism differs from Christianity with the purpose of providing a history of Jesus in Hebrew for Hebrews.

H. A. A. Major, T. W. Manson, and C. J. Wright, *The Mission and Message of Jesus. An Exposition of the Gospels in the Light of Modern Research* (New York, E. P. Dutton & Co., 1938, pp. xxxi, 965), is a voluminous and useful statement of some modern views, with suggestive criticism of them, and also with decided views of its own.

C. G. Montefiore, *Rabbinic Literature and Gospel Teachings* (London, Macmillan & Co., 1930, pp. xxii, 442). By a liberal distinguished Jewish scholar.

A. Schweitzer, *The Quest of the Historical Jesus. A Critical Study of Its Progress from Reimarus to Wrede,* translated by W. Montgomery (London, Adam & Charles Black, 1910, pp. x, 410). Expresses extreme views of the place of eschatology in the teaching of Jesus.

Johannes Weiss, *The History of Primitive Christianity,* completed after the author's death by Rudolph Knopf, translated by four friends and edited by F. C. Grant (New York, Wilson-Erickson, 2 vols., 1937). Chiefly on Paul; approximately a third of the first volume on the Gospel narratives; makes many radical suggestions, brilliantly but often dogmatically expressed, and many of them at best hypotheses.

THE FIRST FIVE HUNDRED YEARS: CHRISTIANITY WINS THE ROMAN EMPIRE AND TAKES SHAPE

Chapter 5

THE SWEEP OF CHRISTIANITY ACROSS THE GRÆCO-ROMAN WORLD

One of the most amazing and significant facts of history is that within five centuries of its birth Christianity won the professed allegiance of the overwhelming majority of the population of the Roman Empire and even the support of the Roman state. Beginning as a seemingly obscure sect of Judaism, one of scores, even hundreds of religions and religious groups which were competing within that realm, revering as its central figure one who had been put to death by the machinery of Rome, and in spite of having been long proscribed by that government and eventually having the full weight of the state thrown against it, Christianity proved so far the victor that the Empire sought alliance with it and to be a Roman citizen became almost identical with being a Christian. It is the steps by which this consummation came which are the subject of this chapter. The equally important questions of what happened to Christianity in the process, the degree to which Christianity conformed to the Græco-Roman world, and of how far it transformed it must engage us in subsequent chapters.

Our Fragmentary Knowledge

The complete story of the spread of Christianity in its first five centuries cannot be told, for we do not possess sufficient data to write it. Especially is our information for the early part of the period provokingly fragmentary. That need not surprise us. What should amaze us is that so much information has come down to us. Christianity began as one of the numerically smallest of the religions which, stemming from the Orient, were being carried across the Empire. Our knowledge of many aspects and persons of these centuries, even of those which loomed large in the eyes of their contemporaries and so would be prominently noticed, is notoriously imperfect. Most of such records as were made have long since disappeared. The circumstance that Christianity survived the Empire accounts for much of such information about its history as has remained, for some Christians treasured the memory of those of their faith who had gone before them and handed it on to posterity. Yet so small were the first Christian groups that most of them escaped the notice of those who were commenting on their times and all but a few of such documents and inscriptions as they themselves left have perished. Even he who would only sketch the main outlines of the history of the expansion of Christianity in and beyond the Roman Empire in these years again and again finds himself baffled.

The gaps in our knowledge are made the more tantalizing by hints that are given us of what a complete record would reveal. In the accounts of Jesus' life in the Gospels we are given glimpses of hundreds, perhaps thousands of followers in Galilee, yet we have only cursory mention of the early presence of Christians there which would give us ground for inferring that from the early disciples of Jesus there arose continuing Christian communities in that region. We are informed that throngs from Tyre, Sidon, and beyond the Jordan came to hear Jesus, and we hear of churches in these areas, but we do not know that they were founded by natives who had been born during the lifetime of Jesus. Through Paul's *Letters to the Romans* and what we read in *The Acts of the Apostles* we are aware of the existence of a strong Christian community in Rome within less than a generation after the resurrection. Precisely how it came to be we are not told. It was notorious that to Rome, the political centre and the largest city in the Mediterranean world in that day, came representatives of many cults and faiths, but who first brought Christianity to the Eternal City we cannot tell, and until shortly before the end of the first century we hear almost nothing about the church there. Yet Paul declared in his *Letter to the Romans,* written between twenty-five and thirty-five years after the crucifixion, that the faith of that church "is spoken of throughout the whole world," words which seem to mean that Christianity had been long enough in the capital for the fact to become very widely known. From the travel diary of a companion of Paul which has been incorporated in *The Acts of the Apostles* we learn that there were Christians at Puteoli, on the Bay of Naples, who greeted Paul on his fateful journey to Rome, between thirty and forty years after the resurrection. We may guess that they came there, as did Paul, by one of the most travelled of the trade routes, but as to who they were and when they first arrived we are not informed. There may have been Christians in Herculaneum and in Pompeii, not far from Puteoli, before the destruction of those cities in A.D. 79 by an eruption of Vesuvius, but we can only guess at the means by which, if it was present, the faith was brought to them. Although Mark is cautiously named as the Christian pioneer in Alexandria in Egypt and we know of a strong church there by the end of the second century, we cannot be sure of the date or the source of the Christian community in that great Hellenistic metropolis.

BEGINNING FROM JERUSALEM

The documents which have been preserved make much of the spread of the faith from the church in Jerusalem and especially of the missionary labours of Paul. It was natural that the initial centre of Christianity should be in Jerusalem. Here was the geographic focus of Judaism. Here Jesus had been crucified and raised from the dead, and here, at his express command, the main nucleus of his followers had waited until the Pentecost experience brought them a compelling dynamic. Peter was their acknowledged spokesman, but before many years, presumably as his missionary travels carried him ever more frequently away from Jerusalem, James the brother of Jesus became the head of the community. During at least part of Jesus' public ministry an unbeliever, James had been won somewhere along the way, possibly by the special appearance to him of the risen Christ. To their neighbours these early followers of Jesus, for they did not yet bear the distinctive designation of Christian, must have appeared another sect of Judaism, predominantly Galilean in membership, distinguished from other Jews by their belief that Jesus was the Messiah and by their expectation of the early return of their Lord. Their leader, James, appears to have been especially conservative in his loyalty to Jewish customs. They continued to use the temple as a place of worship and observed the Jewish law, including its ceremonies, circumcision, and the dietary regulations. Even some of the Pharisees joined them. So far as we know, their numbers were recruited entirely from Jews and proselytes to Judaism.

CHRISTIANITY BEGINS TO MOVE OUT INTO THE NON-JEWISH WORLD

The dream of universality in the teachings and life of Jesus would not down. Early there were those who believed that Jesus would render obsolete the temple and the distinctively Jewish customs. Of these we hear especially of Stephen. Stoned by the orthodox Jews for his views, views which outraged their complacent assumption that they were a people peculiarly chosen by God to the exclusion of others, Stephen became, significantly, the first Christian of whom we know to suffer death for the faith. His tragic end made it clear that his convictions, inherent as they were in the Gospel and soon to be shared by the majority of Christians, would render it impossible for Christianity to be confined within the boundaries of Judaism. The conflict was unavoidable, for some of the basic features of the Gospel made of Christianity, if it were to be true to its founder, a religion quite distinct from Judaism.

The persecution set off by the death of Stephen forced some Christians to realize as they had not done before the universalism which was of the essence of the Gospel and started a missionary wave which quickly carried Christianity permanently outside Judaism. Presumably this would have happened had Stephen not had his revolutionary views so tragically dramatized. Perhaps it was already occurring, but if so, our records are too fragmentary to tell us of its beginnings. Probably the experience which soon led Peter to see that non-Jews were "granted repentance unto life" without first becoming Jews would have come to him and to others had Stephen never lived. As it was, however, some of those who were forced to flee by the persecution in Jerusalem won converts in Samaria, and, what was even more important, still others preached to Greeks in Antioch, then the largest city in Syria and an important radiating centre of Hellenistic culture. Christianity was moving outside Judaism into that element of the Mediterranean world, Greek-speaking and Hellenistic, in which it was to have its greatest early growth. It was at Antioch, fittingly, that the followers of Jesus were first given the distinctive designation by which they have ever since been known, Christian. The word, itself Greek, symbolized the emergence of the new faith into the wider world.

PAUL, MISSIONARY AT LARGE

Outstanding in carrying the faith into the non-Jewish, and especially the Hellenistic world was a Jew whose conversion is closely associated with the death of Stephen. This was Saul, or, to use the name by which he is best remembered, Paul. We know more about Paul than we do of any other Christian of the first century. Not only does *The Acts of the Apostles* make him and his mission its main theme, but we also have, most fortunately, a number of his letters which give us intimate pictures of him. Yet, much as Paul tells us about himself, and much as Luke adds, there are great gaps in our information, both about what he did, and, still more tantalizingly, in our insight into his inner life.

It is clear that Paul was of pure Jewish stock, that his father had that highly prized privilege, Roman citizenship, that the son was born and reared at Tarsus, a Hellenistic city in what we now call Asia Minor, a stronghold of Greek learning. However, far from conforming to the Greek pattern, Paul had been carefully nurtured in Phariseeism. While probably not highly educated in Greek philosophy and literature, he was thoroughly at home in the Greek language, did not use it crudely, and was steeped in the Septuagint, the famous Greek translation of the Jewish scriptures. He also knew Aramaic and his training in Phariseeism made him think naturally in the methods of interpreting the sacred books which were current in that school of thought. Ardent by disposition, the young Paul may have been all the more loyal and dogmatic in the strict adherence to the Jewish law and customs entailed by his Phariseeism because of his consciousness of the paganism which was all about him in Tarsus. As a youth he went to Jerusalem, the citadel of his religion, to study at the feet of Gamaliel, one of the outstanding teachers in Pharisaic circles. Here he came in touch with the followers of Jesus and joined in persecuting them. He stood by when Stephen was stoned and was sent to Damascus with letters from the high priest to the synagogues in that city with instructions to have arrested and brought to Jerusalem for trial those who were adherents of the Nazarene heresy.

While on his way to Damascus, just as he was nearing that city, Paul was smitten by a vision which changed his life. He believed that the risen Jesus appeared to him and spoke with him, and was convinced that the experience was as authentic as those which had earlier come to Peter, James, and the others.

Into the inner history of the processes which led to this climax we can enter only through conjecture. Yet it is fascinating to make the attempt. We know from his letters that Paul was intense, sensitive, lacking in humour, given to moments of deep depression and of high, quivering exaltation, unquestioning in his belief in God and in the validity of the Jewish law. We also are aware that, by what seems to be a strange paradox, Paul regarded himself as blameless when measured by the Jewish law yet suffered from a deep sense of frustration and inner defeat. In some of the most poignant passages in literature, passages which because of their very vividness and obvious emotion seem to be autobiographical, he speaks of having been alive once "without the law," but that the commandment proved to be death to him, for sin, "taking occasion by the commandment," deceived him and by it killed him. He goes on to say, in moving words which reflect the experience of many conscientious and high-minded souls: "I am carnal, sold under sin. For that which I do I allow not, for what I would, that do I not, but what I hate, that do I. . . . O wretched man that I am, who shall deliver me from the body of this death?" By what he honestly believed to be God's will he felt driven to persecute the Christians, yet, perhaps because of the radiance which he had seen in the face of the dying Stephen, his inner turmoil was accentuated, for he here glimpsed a life which had found the inward victory and peace to which he was a stranger. He was set to wondering whether, after all, those whom he was hounding might not be right and he mistaken as to what God's will actually was.

Moreover, Paul may have been both repelled and attracted by the universality of the Gospel which he glimpsed in the burden of the message of Stephen. Reared a strict Jew in a Hellenistic, pagan city, he was all the more proud of his Hebrew heritage because he was a member of a minority. He held that his were the chosen people bound to God by a special covenant, and presumably he was contemptuous of Gentiles as being outside the pale. That the barrier between Jew and Gentile should be erased by Christ must have outraged much that he had held as axiomatic. Yet it may also have appealed to him.

The inner debate appears to have been going on during the long ride to Damascus, for in one account of the vision the risen Christ is quoted as saying to him: "It is hard for thee to kick against the pricks," implying that he had been fighting the trend in his mind which was leading him to be, as he later gladly described himself, "a slave" and a missionary ("apostle") of Christ. Certainly in that blinding instant Paul realized that it was not so much the Christians as Jesus whom he was persecuting.

It appears to be significant that the decisive moment came as Paul was nearing Damascus, where he would be compelled to act. Seeing the risen Christ and hearing his voice, he was stricken down, sightless. Restoration of sight did not come to him until he was comforted by a Christian who, in spite of his fears of the persecutor, obeying a compelling voice, came to him, declared himself a messenger of the Lord Jesus, and welcomed him into the Christian brotherhood.

By temperament a mystic, possessed of a usually quick, incisive mind, Paul was susceptible to the kind of experience which came to him on the road and in Damascus. Again and again later at crucial times he was to hear a divine command and obey it, but never again were the consequences to be so soul-shaking and revolutionary.

To suggest the background, disposition, and psychology which prepared Paul for what happened on the Damascus road is not to deny its reality or the truth of his profound conviction that through it Christ himself had spoken to him.

Here is one of the most important events in the entire course of Christianity. It gave to that faith one of its greatest instruments. As a missionary Paul was to have a leading rôle in the planting of Christian communities. As a thinker he was to place an indelible impress upon Christianity in its conceptions of God, Christ, the Holy Spirit, and the Church. His spectacular conversion after deep struggle was to be a prototype of the spiritual autobiographies of untold thousands of men and women, most of them obscure but some of them among the most prominent in the history of Christianity.

So great has been his influence that Paul is often said to have been the chief creator of what we now know as Christianity, and so to have altered what had been transmitted to him that it became quite different from the teachings of Jesus and transformed Jesus from the Galilean teacher and martyr into the cosmic Christ. That, so it seems to the present author, is a mistaken interpretation of the facts. Paul himself emphatically declared that he and those who had accepted the faith through him had "the mind of Christ." That is entirely true. While clearly not a colourless reproduction of Jesus or one who was slavishly bound to the strict letter of the sayings of his Master, and while giving evidence on almost every page of his letters of his own distinctive characteristics, Paul was so loyal to the mind of Jesus as we see it in the Four Gospels that did we not have these documents we would still be able to know what manner of person Jesus was, what were the essentials of his teachings, and his crucifixion, resurrection, and continued presence. Without the Gospels we would not have so many of the incidents or of the specific sayings of Jesus, nor would we be so much aware of his personal characteristics, such as his humour and his piercing glance, nor was the kingdom of heaven as prominent as in the sayings of Jesus as recorded in the Gospels, but if we were confined to Paul's letters we would not be led to a picture of Jesus essentially different from that which the Gospels give us.

This is all the more so because of Paul's devotion to Christ. It was of the essence of his new faith that the old Paul had been crucified with Christ, that the new Paul lived by faith in Christ, for Christ had loved him and given himself for him. Paul was profoundly convinced that Christ lived in him, and he expected after his physical death to be with Christ. Possessed by such a controlling passion, Paul would certainly seek to know all that he could of the teachings and earthly life of Jesus and to be true to what Jesus had said and been.

Moreover, although the phrase, "the kingdom of God" or "the kingdom of heaven," was not as frequently in the writings of Paul as it was on the lips of Jesus, the idea was often there. To Paul's mind, God had a purpose which includes the entire creation, God's plan for "the fullness of times" is "to gather together in one all things in Christ, both which are in heaven and which are on earth" and "the earnest expectation of the creation waiteth for the manifestation of the sons of God." Paul depicted the whole creation as groaning in travail and pain, "for the creature was made subject to vanity, not willingly, but by reason of him who hath subjected the same in hope. Because the creature itself shall be delivered from the bondage of corruption into the glorious liberty of the children of God." In this the kingdom or reign of God was interpreted, quite certainly as Jesus viewed it, as having a cosmic sweep including not only the human race and human history, but all the vast universe.

Of the precise chronology and detailed course of Paul's life after his conversion we are not fully informed. Yet we know much. For a time Paul remained in Damascus. There, to the amazement and discomfiture of the Jewish authorities, he, the recent persecutor of the new faith, boldly declared that Jesus was the Son of God and won some to his views. Not unnaturally, there were those among the Jews who sought to kill him, and he deemed it wise to leave the city, going by night and being let down in a basket from the top of the wall to escape those who were watching the gates for him. He then went to Arabia, to which part we do not know, but presumably a portion not far from Syria. Nor are we told what he did while in Arabia or how long he was there. He informs us that from Arabia he returned to Damascus.

"After three years," he goes on to say, but whether measured from his conversion or his return to Damascus seems not entirely clear, Paul went to Jerusalem and was with Peter for fifteen days and also saw James, the brother of Jesus. We may surmise, although we cannot prove, that through these contacts he learned much of the life, teachings, death, and resurrection of Jesus. To one of Paul's temperament this brief sojourn in Jerusalem must have been deeply moving. Memories of his student days and of the persecution in which he had an active part, and scenes associated with the life and death of his new Master must have stirred him to the depths. It is not surprising that in the temple he fell into a trance and seemed to see Jesus and talk with him, and that the burden of their conversation was Paul's future work. Nor is it strange that Paul wished to be a missionary to his own people. Indeed, he never outgrew his eager longing that all Jews might become as he was, a Christian. Perhaps it was in that hour of illumination that he could see that from his birth God had been preparing him to "reveal His Son" in him.

Yet the conviction came to Paul that his mission was to be to the Gentiles, the non-Jews. He was to be a pioneer. The universalism of the Gospel which may have been one of the causes of his original antagonism had gripped him. He declared that by special revelation the insight had come to him that through Christ the wall of partition between Jews and Gentiles had been broken down, that to both the way of life had been opened in Christ, and that the prerequisite of entering upon it was not heredity but faith, faith that was open to all men. He burned to preach the Gospel where no one else had taken it.

In going into a city for the first time Paul usually went to a synagogue and there declared Jesus to be the Christ. When, as generally happened, some heeded him but the majority, outraged, drove him out, he sought the Gentiles. Nor would he have his converts become Jews and conform to the ritualistic practices of the Jewish religion. To him the contrast between Judaism and the Christian message was sharp. His experience had taught him what from the teachings of Jesus should have been obvious to any one, that the radiant life which God desires for men is not to be had through the meticulous observance of the Law, for no one could ever fully keep the commands which God had given for men's instruction and guidance, or, if they attempted to win God's favour in that fashion, they would either be in despair or deceive themselves and be proud of having done so, and thus be guilty of the most deadly of all sins. That life is, rather, so Paul declared, to be received through simple faith, a full, trusting commitment of one's entire self to God in response to God's amazing love as seen in Christ.

Paul rang the changes on what was to him the astounding "Good News" of what God had done in Christ in sending the son of His love—that Christ had emptied himself, that he had submitted himself to being crucified by the very ones whom he had come to save, that in this God Himself had revealed His love for men, men who had so sinned against Him that, blinded, they had killed His Son, that in raising Jesus from the dead God had displayed His mighty power, and that through faith, faith which God Himself inspires, sinful man might be born anew and enter upon the eternal life of love which had been manifested in Christ, that kind of love which gives itself utterly to those who, far from deserving it, have no claim whatever upon it. Moved by this vision Paul preached Jesus in Jerusalem, but, as might have been expected, aroused intense opposition.

From Jerusalem, to escape from those who were seeking to compass his death, Paul went back to Tarsus. From there he was summoned to begin the missionary career of which our records give us many glimpses. First he was called upon by Barnabas, a representative of the Jerusalem church, to help with the young Christian community in Antioch which was drawing largely from non-Jews. He so won the confidence of the church in Antioch that he was sent by that body with Barnabas to carry relief to Christians in Judea who were suffering from a widespread famine. Returning from that errand, Barnabas and Paul were set apart by the Antioch church for a mission which led them to Cyprus and to parts of what we call Asia Minor.

Now ensued a number of years in which Paul, usually with one or more companions, carried the Christian message into much of Asia Minor and into Macedonia and Greece. Some of the details of these journeys have come down to us. Of others we have only hints. Paul gave his chief attention to cities. Much, perhaps most of the time he supported himself by working at his trade of tent-maker. He took satisfaction in not preaching where other men had preached and in not being dependent upon his converts for his livelihood. His was an arduous life. Celibate by conviction, Paul devoted himself entirely to his mission, untrammeled by family ties. We hear of his spending months in one or another of the larger centres. Much of the time he was travelling. He speaks of shipwreck, of perils from rivers and from robbers, of hunger and thirst, of beatings, and of being stoned. Upon him weighed the care of the many churches which he had helped to bring into being. He kept in touch with them by oral messages and by letters. A few of the latter survive and give evidence of the white heat and the pressure under which they were written. Although possessing enormous vitality and astounding powers of endurance, Paul had some persistent physical or nervous weakness which he described as a "thorn in the flesh" and which was to him a heavy burden. He met with bitter opposition, not only from Jews and other non-Christians, but also from other Christians and within some of the churches which he had nurtured. Yet after some years he could say that from Jerusalem as far as Illyricum, on the east coast of the Adriatic, he had "fully preached the Gospel of Christ."

Then came seeming disaster, and in an undertaking to which a sense of duty called him. For some time Paul had been gathering from his churches in the Gentile world a fund to give to the poor among the Christians in Jerusalem. He planned to go to Spain from Jerusalem, on the way visiting the Christians in Rome. It became clear that the mission to Jerusalem would be fraught with peril, for he was to be there at the Passover season and was regarded by many loyal Jews who would be flocking there at that high feast from many parts of the Empire as one who was threatening Judaism and the temple. Characteristically, Paul insisted on making the journey. While he was in the temple some Jews from Asia Minor who had been angered by what they had heard of his attitude towards Judaism aroused a tumult against him. A mob was seeking to kill him when the Roman guard intervened. There followed arrest, judicial hearings, detention of at least two years, an appeal by Paul to Cæsar, as was his right as a Roman citizen, the journey to Rome under guard, a shipwreck in which the prisoner took command, the survival of himself and the ship's company, the completion of the journey, and a stay of at least two years in Rome, presumably still technically as a prisoner, but with considerable freedom to receive visitors and to present to them the Christian message. Then the curtain falls and assured information fails. The fact of eventual martyrdom in Rome seems to be well established.

Further First Century Spread of the Faith

In those first early vigorous years Paul was by no means the only one who spread the faith through the Empire. We hear more about him than of any other, but in various ways we obtain glimpses of many. Peter travelled, for we hear of him in Antioch, and what seems to be reliable tradition speaks of him as being in Rome and dying there as a martyr. Not all its representatives agreed on the essence of the faith. We read of Apollos, who, as a missionary, differed in his message from that of Paul but who was willing to receive instruction from friends of Paul and, conforming, became one of Paul's valued colleagues. Others were so apart from Paul in their understanding of the Gospel that he believed that he must denounce them as bearing a false message. Some of those who spread the faith were professional missionaries, drawing their financial support from the churches, but others, like Paul and Barnabas, earned their livelihood by trade or a handicraft, and many witnessed while giving most of their attention to other occupations.

Christianity quickly moved out of the Jewish community and became prevailingly non-Jewish. As early as the time that Paul wrote his letter to it, a generation or less after the resurrection, the church in Rome was predominantly Gentile. This in itself was highly significant: Christianity had ceased to be a Jewish sect and, while having roots in Judaism, was clearly new and different from that faith.

In becoming non-Jewish in its following, Christianity was entering into the Hellenistic world. While one eminent scholar has attempted to prove that some of the books of the New Testament were first written in Aramaic and then translated into Greek, there can be no doubt that the form in which they gained their initial wide circulation was in Greek and it may well be that all of them were first written in that language. The Greek was the *koine,* the vernacular of that language which was current at the time. Even the church in Rome, at the heart of the Latin part of the Empire, employed the *koine.* This meant that Christianity, still relatively flexible in thought forms, would tend to find expression through the ideas abroad in Hellenism and perhaps would even be moulded by them. It first attracted those elements in the Hellenistic population which were influenced by Judaism and thus for at least a generation was less shaped by the Greek mind than if its initial converts had come straight from pure paganism.

Christianity did not become any more exclusively Hellenistic in constituency than it was Jewish. Early it numbered some whose speech was Syriac, and among those who are reported as hearing the Christian message at Pentecost were Parthians, dwellers in Mesopotamia, Medes, Elamites, as well as those from regions more clearly in the circle of Hellenistic culture. While they were, presumably, either Jews, Jewish proselytes, or enough interested in Judaism to have come to Jerusalem, it may well be that through some of the converts of that memorable day the faith was carried to non-Jewish, non-Hellenistic groups and individuals.

At the outset, Christianity was predominantly urban. It moved along the trade routes from city to city. By the second decade of its second century in at least some parts of Asia Minor it had spread widely into towns and even into the countryside, but its strength was in the cities which were so prominent a feature of the Roman Empire.

SECOND AND THIRD CENTURY SPREAD

We know even less of the spread of Christianity in the second century than we do of its propagation in the first century. Yet it is clear that it continued to grow in numbers of adherents and that before A.D. 200 Christians were found not only in all of the provinces of the Empire but also outside the Empire in Mesopotamia.

In the third century the expansion of Christianity was still more marked. It was gathering momentum. Moreover, in that century the illnesses of society which were later to bring about the disintegration of the Graeco-Roman world were becoming palpable. Many, conscious of their insecurity, were seeking refuge in religion. Especially were those religions growing which stemmed from the Orient. Among them was Christianity.

By the close of the third century the chief numerical strength of Christianity was in the eastern part of the Empire. For reasons which will appear later, the church in Rome early took a leading position in the Christian fellowship, but most of the other main centres of the faith were in the eastern portions of the basin of the Mediterranean. Christianity was especially prominent in what we now term Asia Minor. Here Paul had spent many of his missionary years. Here were Greek cities and from them Hellenistic culture was permeating the countryside. Christianity, with a vital foothold in that culture, was spreading with it.

Through the accounts and writings of one of the leading Christians of Asia Minor of the third century, Gregory, later known as Thaumaturgos, or Worker of Wonders, we learn something of the propagation of the faith in Pontus, one portion of Asia Minor. A native of Pontus, born and reared a pagan, Gregory was from a wealthy and prominent family. Seeking an education to fit him for the duties of his station, in Palestine he came in touch with Origen, of whom we are to hear more in the next chapter. It was as a distinguished teacher of philosophy that Origen was sought out by the young Gregory. But Origen was more than a great teacher: he was also on fire with the Christian faith. Through him Gregory became a Christian. Returning to Pontus, Gregory was made bishop of his native city, somewhat against his will. This was about the year 240. He gave himself to completing the conversion of the populace of his diocese. When he died, about thirty years later, the overwhelming majority had accepted the Christian faith. It is said, somewhat rhetorically, that when he became bishop he found only seventeen Christians in his see and that at his death only seventeen remained pagan. In achieving this mass conversion, Gregory made the transition as easy as possible, substituting festivals in honour of the Christian martyrs for the feasts of the old gods.

In the great cities of the eastern part of the Mediterranean Basin, major centres as they were of Hellenistic culture, Christians became especially numerous. Antioch and Alexandria were notable for their strong Christian communities. Such smaller and yet important cities as Ephesus were also prominent in the early annals of the faith.

Most of those portions of the populations in the East which had been less penetrated by Hellenistic life were slow in adopting Christianity. Although, because of its historic importance, the church in Jerusalem was accorded respect in the Christian fellowship, the progress of Christianity in Palestine lagged. In Egypt Christianity was late in winning many adherents among the non-Greek-speaking elements of the population, the country folk whose tongue was the native Egyptian. Yet by the beginning of the fourth century parts of the Scriptures had been translated into more than one of the non-Greek vernaculars and the foundations had been laid of a native Egyptian (Coptic) church.

Although churches were found in some of its cities, especially in cosmopolitan Corinth, Greece as a whole delayed in becoming Christian. Athens especially, as the traditional centre for the study of Greek philosophy, long held to the old cults.

The northern shores of Africa, particularly in and around Carthage in the modern Tunis and Algeria, early had vigorous Christian churches. Here was produced the earliest extensive Latin Christian literature. It may be that the reasons are to be found partly in the conditions in that region. The Italians were immigrants or descendants of immigrants. Carthage had been a Punic or Phœnician city, the great rival of Rome. In a series of wars Rome had come out victor and Carthage had been destroyed. On the heels of the Roman conquest, Italians moved into the country, Carthage was rebuilt, largely as a Latin city, and a large Latin-speaking element came into being. Uprooted from their Italian environment, traditional Italian customs and religions may have had less hold on the immigrants and their children than in Italy and there may have been greater open-mindedness to the Christian message. Whatever the reason, Christianity became firmly planted in the Latin-using portions of the population and the church in Carthage was prominent in the Christian fellowship. With it were associated the names of such early prominent Latin writers as Tertullian and Cyprian, of whom we are to hear more later. Christianity also spread among the Punic elements, but probably more slowly, and still more slowly among the pre-Italian, pre-Punic elements, the Berber stock. This fact was to have tragic significance for the subsequent course of the faith in North Africa.

We know little of the details of the spread of Christianity in Italy outside of Rome, but by the middle of the third century the peninsula seems to have had about one hundred bishoprics, and, with the rapid growth of the faith in the second half of the third century, by A.D. 300 the number of dioceses must have greatly increased. Growth was more rapid in the Centre and the South than in the North, in the valley of the Po. Sicily had Christians in the third century and possibly in the second.

Almost nothing has survived about the planting of Christianity in Spain, but as early as the beginning of the third century the faith was well established in the South. Unfortunately some of our first pictures of Spanish Christianity are distinctly unfavourable—of bishops who absented themselves from their dioceses to engage in commerce, and of a Christian community which compromised with idolatry, homicide, and adultery. Yet, imperfect though it was, Spanish Christianity displayed more vitality than did its North African counterpart in surviving the Arab Moslem conquest of the eighth century.

In Gaul Christianity probably first entered directly from the East. In the Rhone Valley there were cities which long before the time of Christ possessed commercial connexions with Syria and the Hellenistic Orient. They were Greek colonies from Ionia, on the west coast of Asia Minor. In the second half of the second century, when we first catch authentic glimpses of it in that area, Christianity was fairly strong in the Greek-speaking communities in Lyons and Vienne. Irenæus, of whom we are to say more in a later chapter, and who flourished in the second half of the second century, was the first churchman in Gaul to achieve prominence. He was from Smyrna, in Asia Minor, where as a boy he had received instruction in the oral tradition which came to him only a generation removed from the original apostles. In Lyons, where he spent most of his working life, Irenæus learned the local vernacular and may have employed it to preach to the non-Hellenistic population. Before the end of the third century there were bishoprics in the northern parts of Gaul and in cities along the Rhine. Before that time, too, Christianity had won footholds in the Roman province of Britain, and early in the fourth century three bishops from Britain attended a council in Arles, in the south of Gaul.

CHRISTIANITY BEGINS TO OVERFLOW THE BORDERS OF THE EMPIRE

Well before the end of the third century Christianity had begun to gain adherents among peoples beyond the Roman Empire. As was to be expected, this was through contacts with Christians in the Roman Empire and was largely along the trade routes which irradiated from the chief commercial cities of that realm. Close commercial and cultural relations existed between the cities of Syria, such as Antioch and Damascus, where strong churches sprang up in the first century, and the Tigris-Euphrates Valley. It is not surprising, therefore, that by the end of the first quarter of the third century more than twenty bishoprics are known to have existed in the latter region and on the borders of Persia. They were found almost as far north as the Caspian Sea and as far south as the Bahrein Islands in the Persian Gulf. At Dura-Europos, on the Euphrates, on the great road between Antioch and Ctesiphon, twentieth century excavation has revealed a building which was used as a church at least as far back as the year 232. From the inscriptions on its walls it appears that the congregation was Greek-using. Syriac, however, became the major medium for the spread of Christianity in the Tigris-Euphrates Valley.

It was probably late in the third century that the mass conversion of Armenia was accomplished. A land the details of whose boundaries have varied with the vicissitudes of the years, Armenia is on the south slopes of the Caucasus and on the mountainous table-land north of the valley of the Tigris and Euphrates Rivers. Although its independence has been partially guarded by its topography, Armenia has had the disadvantage of being on the borders of much larger realms and has had to fight for its existence. In the first centuries of the Christian era it was a buffer state between the chronic rivals, the Roman and Persian Empires.

The precise course of the conversion of Armenia has been hopelessly be-clouded by legend. The great missionary was one Gregory, to whom the designation Illuminator was added because of his successful labours. Gregory seems to have been of the Armenian aristocracy and to have become a Christian while in exile in Cæsarea in Cappadocia, a region in which Christianity early made marked progress. Returning to Armenia and seeking to propagate his new faith, Gregory encountered persecution. Then he won the king, Tradt, Tirdat, or Tiridates by name. Why the king became a Christian we can only conjecture, but with the consent of his nobles he supported Gregory. The compliant population rapidly moved over to the new faith. Many of the shrines of the pre-Christian paganism were transferred, together with their endowments, to the service of Christianity, and numbers of pagan priests or their sons passed over into the body of Christian clergy. Some were made bishops. Gregory, obtaining episcopal consecration at Cæsarea, became the head of the Armenian Church and was followed in that post by his lineal descendants. To this day the Armenian Church has been known by his name and has been a symbol and bond of Armenian nationalism. Here was an instance of what was to be seen again and again, a group adoption of the Christian faith engineered by the accepted leaders and issuing in an ecclesiastical structure which became identified with a particular people, state, or nation.

By the end of the third century Christian communities may have been found on the northern and eastern shores of the Euxine, or Black Sea. This would be expected from the long-standing commerce of Hellenistic cities with that region and from the strength of Christianity in these cities.

Long before the end of the third century Christianity had gained adherents in Arabia. Some of them were in the parts of Arabia on the eastern borders of the Roman Empire and were presumably the fruits of commercial and cultural contacts. There were probably others in the South of Arabia, a region which had commercial intercourse with the Mediterranean world, especially through Alexandria, a city where, as we have seen, Christians were numerous.

Insistent tradition ascribes the introduction of Christianity to India to the Apostle Thomas, one of the original Twelve. Thus far this has been neither satisfactorily proved or disproved. Long before the time of Christ commerce was carried on between India and the Hellenistic world. Alexander invaded India's North-west and active Greek traders were familiar with the routes to that land. It may well have been that through some of the latter Christianity was carried to India before the end of the third century. It may even have made its way to one or more of the cities in Central Asia which had arisen in the wake of the conquests of Alexander and which were centres of semi-Hellenistic culture.

THE SOCIAL ORIGINS OF THE EARLY CHRISTIANS

From what social and economic strata did the Christians of the first two or three centuries come? The only safe answer is that we do not know. As we have said, Christianity was at first primarily urban, at the outset among the Jews and the Gentiles interested in Judaism, and then among the Greek-speaking, Hellenistic sections of the cities, but also soon among the Syriac-using peoples of Syria and the Tigris-Euphrates Valley. It is often said that Christians were drawn from the dregs of the urban proletariat—the dispossessed, the slaves, and the freedmen. Christianity has even been described as an incentive and channel for the upsurge of the underprivileged, a social movement. For this appealing thesis some evidence can be adduced. Paul rejoiced that "not many wise men after the flesh, not many mighty, not many noble are called," and in the third century Celsus, the author of a trenchant attack on Christianity, declared that the faith had its chief hold among the ignorant. Yet we know that even in the first century numbers of men and women of wealth, education, and social prominence became Christians, and that in the original Christian group in Jerusalem there were not only poor but also those who had the means to aid their less fortunate fellows. It is possible that members of some of the most prominent families in Rome were among the early converts, and that a near relative of the Emperor Domitian was a Christian and, but for his death by execution, might himself have become Emperor. It may well have been that the proportion of the educated, the socially prominent, and the poor in the Christian communities was about that in the Empire as a whole. This would entail a predominance of the uneducated, but it would not necessarily mean that Christianity was associated with a movement to win more privileges for the proletarian elements in the great cities.

Persistent Opposition and Persecution

It is one of the commonplaces of history that in its first three centuries Christianity met persistent and often severe persecution, persecution which rose to a crescendo early in the fourth century, but that it spread in spite of opposition and was even strengthened by it. The tradition of martyrdom has entered deep into the Christian consciousness. The faith centres about one who was executed as an alleged threat to the established order and throughout its course it has been punctuated by forcible attempts to curb it. Indeed, with the possible exception of Judaism, Christianity has had more martyrs than has any other religion. Jesus warned those who would follow him that persecution would be their lot, that he would be a source of division and contention, and his words have been amply fulfilled. This is not strange. So radical are the claims of the Gospel, so sweeping are its demands on the faithful, so uncompromising does it render those who yield themselves fully to it, that opposition and even persecution are to be expected.

At the outset, as we have seen, the main persecutors of the Christians were those who held to Judaism and were antagonized by the fashion in which what superficially appeared to be a sect of Judaism was undermining institutions and convictions cherished by that religion. As the separation between Judaism and Christianity became more obvious and as the majority of Christian converts began to be drawn from the Gentiles, while antagonism between Jews and Christians did not decline, persecution of Christians by Jews was less frequent.

Christians had to face the dislike and active opposition of the pagan population about them. Criticisms were on several grounds but arose very largely on the one hand from the fact that they would not compromise with paganism, but held themselves apart from it and in so doing withdrew from much of current society, and on the other hand because they won converts from that society and so could not but be noticed. To avoid unnecessary publicity and to escape so far as possible the notice of government officials, Christians held their services either secretly or without public announcement. In a broader and a deeper sense the dislike and the persecution which grew out of it and accompanied it were evidence that, as Jesus had said, in the Gospel something had entered the world with which the world was at enmity.

The accusations varied. Because they refused to participate in pagan ceremonies the Christians were dubbed atheists. Through their abstention from much of the community life—the pagan festivals, the public amusements which to Christians were shot through and through with pagan beliefs, practices, and immoralities—they were derided as haters of the human race. They were popularly charged with perpetrating the grossest immoralities in their conventicles. It was said that both sexes met together at night, that a dog was used to extinguish the lights, and that promiscuous intercourse followed. Garbled reports circulated of the central Christian rite, the Eucharist. The fact that it was celebrated only in the presence of believers fed the rumours that Christians regularly sacrificed an infant and consumed its blood and flesh. The circumstance that Christians called one another brother and sister and loved one another on the scantiest acquaintance was regarded as evidence of vice.

More sensible folk probably discounted these reports but were disturbed by the continued growth of an Empire-wide fellowship which, in an age when the political and economic order was obviously shaky, threatened the existing structure of society, for it not only withdrew itself from many of the customs which tied it together, but denounced them as stupid and wicked. Many pagans held that the neglect of the old gods who had made Rome strong was responsible for the disasters which were overtaking the Mediterranean world. Christians replied that they were law-abiding and moral, that they prayed for the Emperor, and that their prayers had reduced the misfortunes which had troubled mankind from long before the time of Christ, but their protestations did not remove the distrust.

Crude and misinformed though many of the criticisms of Christianity were, here was an awareness that a force was entering the world which if given free scope would overturn the existing culture. Dimly, to be sure, and imperfectly, but with an appreciation of the actualities, non-Christians sensed that because of its revolutionary nature, its uncompromising character, and its claim on the allegiance of all mankind, Christianity was more to be feared by the established order than any of its many competitors, not even excepting Judaism.

Some of the educated were more acute in their criticisms on intellectual grounds, but whether they came as near to an appreciation of the central issues is doubtful. Celsus, whose charges written towards the latter part of the second century in his *True Discourse* we know through the lengthy reply by Origen, said that Christians defied the law by forming secret associations, that the ethical precepts which they taught were not new but were found in existing philosophies, that their attack on idolatry had in it nothing of novelty but had been long anticipated by one of the Greek philosophers, that Christians disparaged reason and taught: "Do not examine but believe," and that the supposed resurrection appearances of Jesus were in secret and only to those who were predisposed to believe in them. He ridiculed Christians for following the precedent set by Jesus and for saying: "Everyone . . . who is a sinner, who is devoid of understanding, who is a child, and . . . whoever is unfortunate, him will the kingdom of God receive." With something of an awareness of the central amazing message of the Gospel, he scoffed at Christians for asserting that God made all things for the sake of man, that men, created by Him, are like Him, as though bats or ants or worms had believed that God had become a citizen among them alone, that they were like God, and that all things existed for their sake. Porphyry, an early leader of Neoplatonism, pointed out what he held to be some of the discrepancies in the Christian Scriptures. How, he said, can the differences in the various accounts of the death and resurrection of Jesus be reconciled? Why, when Jesus foretold the martyr's fate for John and his brother, did John die a natural death? Was Paul not inconsistent when on the one hand he commanded his fellow-Christians to "bless and curse not," and on the other hand bitterly denounced his opponents? These are but typical of the embarrassing questions which the more sophisticated critics put to the Christians.

Christians replied to the attacks on their faith, but they did more. They counter-attacked, pointing out the weaknesses in the pagan religions and giving positive reasons for holding to Christianity. Numbers of the writings of these apologists have come down to us. How widely they were circulated among non-Christians and whether they won any converts we do not know, but at least they would confirm the faith of Christians. We find them in the second and third centuries and some were written as late as the fifth century. Of the most famous of the fifth century apologies, the *De Civitate Dei,* we shall have something more to say in a moment.

Few of the second and third century apologists devoted much attention to the Jews and Judaism. By the time that they wrote, the separation of the Christian community from Judaism was almost complete and Christians were being drawn primarily from paganism. Nor did the apologists pay much attention to the mystery religions. What was said about them was not complimentary, but apparently they did not loom as prominently as rivals of Christianity as has sometimes been supposed.

Negatively the apologists attacked the current paganism. They excoriated the immoralities ascribed to the gods by the current myths, pilloried the follies and inconsistencies in polytheistic worship, and poured scorn on the anthropomorphic conceptions and images of the gods. They did not hesitate to come to grips with the philosophies which were popular with the educated. Indeed, some of the apologists had once sought satisfaction in the study of philosophy and after being disillusioned had turned to Christianity. They pointed out the moral weaknesses of some of the leading philosophers, what they deemed the inconsistencies and contradictions in the writings of Plato, the lack of agreement among the philosophers, and what they believed to be errors in their teaching. Tertullian of Carthage, a lawyer who became a Christian in middle life, held reason, the reliance of the philosophers, to be a false guide to truth. Truth was to be found in the revelation of God in Christ. "It is by all means to be believed because it is absurd," he declared. To him the Gospel was, from the standpoint of philosophy, divine foolishness—as Paul had said long ago—but, as Paul had also implied, wiser than all the philosophers of Greece.

Positively the apologists made much of Jesus and of the Christian belief in God. In contrast with the syncretizing tendencies of the age, they did not attempt to gloss over the contrasts between the Gospel and the non-Christian faiths and philosophies or to suggest a working combination of Christianity with its rivals. Some declared that since Moses antedated the Greek philosophers and that since it fulfilled him and the prophets of Israel, Christianity had that sanction of antiquity for which many, despairing of reason, were asking of religion. They stressed the fashion in which the prophecies of the Jewish scriptures were confirmed by the teachings, life, death, and resurrection of Jesus. They also placed great weight on the moral transformation wrought by the Gospel and contrasted with the pagan society about them the high character of the Christian community, the fashion in which Christians helped one another, and the bringing together in one peaceable fellowship of those of different tribes and customs who had formerly hated one another. They pointed to the fact that Christians prayed for those who persecuted them and sought to share with those who hated them the Gospel and its promise to believers of a joyful reward from God.

In spite of the apologists, persecution by the Roman government was chronic and persistent. The Christian churches were associations which were not legally authorized, and the Roman authorities, always suspicious of organizations which might prove seditious, regarded them with jaundiced eye. Christians were haled before the courts as transgressors of the laws against treason, sacrilege, membership in a foreign cult, and the practice of magic. Since they would not share in the religious rites associated with the imperial cult, they were viewed as hostile to the state. The antagonism was particularly marked, since Christians, revering Christ as *Kurios,* or lord of the whole earth, often looked upon the Emperor, for whom the same claim was made, as Anti-Christ, while the imperial authorities were hostile to them as those who gave allegiance to a rival of the Emperor. Correspondence which has survived between the Emperor Trajan (reigned A.D. 98–117) and Pliny the Younger, who was serving as imperial legate in Bithynia, in the later Asia Minor, appears to indicate that Christianity was officially proscribed, that if Christians recanted they were to be spared, but that if they persisted in their faith they were to be executed.

Usually ten major persecutions are enumerated, beginning with Nero in the first century and culminating in the one which was inaugurated by Diocletian early in the fourth century. In general they fall into two main chronological groups, the first from Nero to the year 250, in which they were largely local and probably entailed no great loss of life, and the second Empire-wide, determined attempts to extirpate Christianity as a major threat to the common weal.

The most famous of the early persecutions was that in Rome in A.D. 64 associated with the name of the Emperor Nero. Our first detailed account is in the *Annals* of Tacitus, written perhaps fifty years after the event and therefore not to be accepted without question. It says that Nero, to meet the ugly rumour that a great fire in Rome had been set by his orders, sought to fasten the blame on the Christians. The latter were also accused of hatred of the human race. Some of the Christians, so Tacitus declares, were wrapped in the hides of wild beasts and were then torn to pieces by dogs. Others, fastened to crosses, were set on fire to illuminate a circus which Nero staged for the crowds in his own gardens. Indeed, the pity of the mob was said to have been aroused and turned to criticism of Nero. Tradition, probably reliable, reports that both Peter and Paul suffered death at Rome under Nero, although not necessarily at this time. Peter's remains are supposed now to lie under the high altar in the cathedral which bears his name in what were once the gardens of Nero. It may have been that the persecution of Nero spread to the provinces.

The last book of the New Testament, *The Revelation of John*, seems to have Rome in mind when it describes "Babylon the great, mother of harlots" as "drunk with the blood of the saints and the blood of the martyrs of Jesus." The date is uncertain and may well be much later than Nero. If so, it would appear to indicate that persecutions by the imperial government were sufficiently chronic to lead some Christians to regard with horror Rome and what it stood for.

It is only occasionally in the second century and the first half of the third century that we know of express instances of persecution. From early in the second century we have the letters of Ignatius of Antioch written on his way to Rome for execution as a Christian. From a little later in that century we have the famous martyrdom in Smyrna, in Asia Minor, of the aged Polycarp, who may have been the last survivor of those who had talked with the eyewitnesses of Jesus. Shortly before the middle of the second century a Bishop of Rome suffered martyrdom.

Some of the ablest and noblest of the Emperors were numbered among the persecutors. Hadrian (reigned 117–138), to be sure, insisted that those innocent of the charge of being Christians should be protected and commanded that those be punished who brought accusations which they could not prove against alleged Christians, but he did not forbid action against real Christians. Under Antoninus Pius (ruled 138–161) Christians suffered in Rome. One of the most high-minded and conscientious of all the Emperors, Marcus Aurelius (ruled 161–180), heartily disliked Christians, possibly because he thought of them as undermining the structure of civilization which he was labouring to maintain against domestic and foreign threats, and during his reign persecutions occurred, including one in Gaul. Under Commodus, the unworthy son of Marcus Aurelius, persecution, at first continued, was later relaxed because of the intervention of his favourite, Marcia. Indeed, through her intercession a number were released from hard labour in the mines to which they had been condemned for their faith. During the first part of his regime (193–211), Septimius Severus was not unfriendly towards Christians, had some of them in his household, and entrusted to a Christian nurse the rearing of his son, Caracalla. However, in 202 he issued an edict forbidding conversions to Judaism or Christianity, and a persecution followed of which we hear a good deal from North Africa and Egypt. It was then that the father of Origen perished in Alexandria, and Origen, in his adolescent ardour desiring to share his fate, was kept from it only by the resourceful action of his mother in hiding his clothes.

We are not certain that any of the persecutions of the first two centuries was Empire-wide. Presumably Christians were always in danger, for their legal status was at best precarious, a local or provincial official might at almost any time proceed against them, and some action of an Emperor might stiffen the backbone of otherwise lenient authorities. They were chronically regarded with suspicion by large elements in the populace and among the respectable citizens. Their peril was further accentuated by a procedure which gave their possessions to those who brought a successful accusation against them. Confiscation of goods, imprisonment, and torture might overtake them at any time, followed by hard labour in the mines or by execution. Some Christians courted martyrdom. This was partly because it brought honour from their fellow-Christians and was supposed to erase any sins which had been committed. It was also partly because of the devotion of those who were ambitious to share the fate of their Lord. The majority opinion of the Christians, while reverencing true martyrs, was against needlessly seeking arrest. We even read that some churches paid money to officials to insure freedom from molestation. It may well have been that, compared with the total number of Christians, the martyrs were very few.

A BREATHING SPACE AND RAPID GROWTH

In the first half of the third century after the brief outbreak under Septimius Severus the persecution of Christians almost entirely lapsed. It was sharply revived under Maximinus Thrax (reigned 235–238) but his rule was short. The time was one in which religions from the Orient were making rapid headway. Several of the Emperors were from the eastern part of the Empire and were not concerned to maintain the Roman tradition. They encouraged the existing trend towards syncretism and monotheism. One of them, Alexander Severus (ruled 222–235) is said to have had in his chapel statues of Orpheus, Abraham, Alexander the Great, several of the Roman Emperors, and Jesus. His mother asked Origen for instruction. Philip the Arabian (reigned 244–249) is sometimes named as the first Christian Emperor. He is reported to have shared in the pascal vigil and to have been assigned to the section which was prescribed for penitents for entrance to that service.

Certainly in the first half of the second century thousands were flocking into the churches. The Christian communities had long been growing, the uncertainties of the times were moving many to seek security in religion, especially in one which was giving rise to so inclusive and strong a fellowship as the Christian Church, and the weakening of existing patterns of society and the popularity of cults from the Orient which were esteemed as having the authority of hoary antiquity were easing the path to the Church.

The Sudden Storms Under Decius and Valerian

In the year 250 the triumphant course of Christianity was brought to what appeared to be an abrupt and disastrous halt. The most severe general persecution which the faith had yet met broke out and, at imperial command, swept across the Empire. This was the act of the Emperor Decius. Decius came to the purple in the year 249. He was a native of Pannonia, north-west of Thrace, and may have represented a reaction in that region against the influences which had entered the Empire from the East. It may be significant that Maximinus Thrax, who was responsible for the brief persecution in the 230's, was from Thrace, and that Galerius, a notorious persecutor of the next century, was from the same general region.

We do not have the texts of the anti-Christian edicts of Decius, and we can only guess at the reasons for his action. Decius was acclaimed by his admirers as an embodiment of the old Roman virtues, and it may well have been that in the drift towards non-Roman religions under his immediate predecessors and in the attendant neglect of the Roman gods who, from his standpoint, had made Rome great, he believed the cause to lie of the calamities and decay which were palpably overtaking society.

Whatever the motives, in 249 imperial edicts were issued which presumably commanded all citizens of the Empire to sacrifice to the gods. Those who obeyed were given certificates as evidence that they had complied. Christians were not singled out but the sacrifices were to be made by all, of whatever faith. Obviously, however, Christians were the chief sufferers. In the easy-going syncretism of the times, pagans would not find their consciences troubled by compliance. They would simply be jarred temporarily out of any careless neglect of the traditional gods into which they might have fallen. For Christians, however, the issue was far more serious. To sacrifice would be apostasy and in current Christian belief apostasy was one of the sins for which no forgiveness was possible. Many Christians preferred their physical lives to spiritual death and fully complied. Numbers avoided so bald a departure from their faith by purchasing from venal officials certificates, or *libelli,* of compliance, without actually sacrificing. Others, how many we shall never know, braved the full displeasure of the state by failing to obey. Some of them were imprisoned, among them Origen, the Bishop of Rome, and the aged Bishop of Jerusalem. The two latter perished in prison. Others were killed outright. Some retired to places of comparative safety. Among the latter was Cyprian, the famous Bishop of Carthage of whom we are to hear more later.

Fortunately for the Christians, the persecution was of brief duration. In the year 251 Decius fell in battle with the Goths, "barbarians" against whom he was fighting to protect the Empire. In the months immediately before his death he had become too engrossed in the defence of the realm against the invaders to press his religious policy. Under his successor, Gallus (reigned 251–253), the anti-Christian measures were revived in at least some parts of the Empire, probably stimulated by a pestilence which drove terrified thousands to the altars of the old gods and led to hysteria against the Christians, who by their neglect of the gods were supposed to be accountable for the disaster. However, the persecution was not so protracted but that it proved salutary for the Church. It had been sharp enough to purge the Church of many of its weaker and more luke-warm members and yet had not been prolonged enough seriously to weaken it.

Under the Emperor Valerian (ruled 253–260) the anti-Christian storm broke out afresh and with redoubled fury. During the first few years of his reign Valerian appeared to be friendly to Christians and even had some of them in his household. Then his temper suddenly changed, possibly through the influence of one of his counsellors. The realm was still afflicted by foreign foes and domestic pestilence, and it may have been that Christians were again held responsible because of their antagonism to the gods who were believed to have made Rome strong.

The new persecution, which was begun in 257, seems to have been directed more astutely than was the one under Decius. The bishops, as the heads of the Church, were singled out and were commanded to do homage to the old gods under pain of exile. Christians were threatened with the death penalty if they so much as went to any of the meetings or services of the Church or even visited a Christian cemetery. Apparently the point of the measure against Christian conventicles was that they were still illegal, and the reason for action against Christian cemeteries was that, to have organizations which were within the law, Christians had formed themselves into burial associations, bodies which could obtain legal recognition.

In the year 258 a new and more drastic edict was promulgated. While, as in the case of its predecessor, we do not have the exact wording, presumably it ordered death for bishops, priests, and deacons; first confiscation of property and then, if this were not enough to induce apostasy, death for Christians of high rank in the state, confiscation of goods and banishment for Christian matrons, and slavery for Christian members of the imperial household. By hitting at the persons of prominence in the Church the latter would be deprived of its leadership.

Under these edicts the persecution was pressed in at least a majority of the provinces. In Rome the Bishop was taken while teaching seated in his chair in one of the catacombs and, with four of his seven deacons, was slain. The other three deacons were also soon caught and killed. One, Lawrence, is said to have been roasted on a gridiron. In Africa Cyprian was beheaded. A convert in middle life, as head of the church in Carthage Cyprian was one of the most honoured of the early bishops. In Spain a bishop who was reported to have been greatly beloved by both Christians and non-Christians was burned at a stake in an amphitheatre with two of his deacons.

The persecution ended abruptly in 260 when Valerian, at war with the Persians, was captured and disappeared from history. His son and successor, Gallienus, reversed his father's policy and either issued edicts of toleration for Christianity or rescripts to bishops which had much the same purport. Again a persecution which might have been disastrous had it been pressed over many years proved so short that the effect was rather to strengthen the Church than to injure it. The Church emerged with a fresh accretion of martyrs to reinforce its faith and courage.

A GENERATION OF PEACE AND PROSPERITY

Approximately a generation of relative peace and prosperity followed. Now and again we hear of martyrdoms, some of them in Rome and Italy, several in Gaul, others in Asia Minor, and still others in the Orient. There were efforts to purge the army of Christians, although, as we shall see, many, perhaps most of the early Christians had conscientious scruples against military service and presumably not many were in the legions. In the main, however, the

Christians were less molested by the state than they had been since the first half of the century. Through the Church Christianity now presented the strongest congeries of institutions in the Mediterranean world aside from the imperial government. Many were attracted to it and Christians were prominent even in the imperial household.

How many Christians there were at this time we have no way of knowing. Estimates vary from about five in a hundred to about half the population. The gain in two and a half centuries had been astounding.

CLIMAX OF STORM

Now, in the year 303, began the most severe persecution which Christianity had yet experienced. On the imperial throne was Diocletian, one of the strongest of the Emperors. He was from the vigorous peasant stock of Illyria, east of the Adriatic, from which had sprung his three immediate predecessors. In the interests of greater effectiveness he had reorganized the administration of the Empire.

Why Diocletian became a persecutor must be a matter of conjecture. He was then in his late fifties, at a time when he might have been supposed to be past undertaking any drastic change in programme. In addition to the Christians in his household, his wife and his daughter, wife of Galerius, one of the two men who, under the title of Cæsar, he had associated with himself and his imperial colleague in the top ranks of the government, were either Christians or favourably disposed to Christianity. Galerius is generally supposed to have been the instigator. An ardent pagan, he is said to have been ambitious to succeed Diocletian and for this needed the support of the army, which was still predominantly non-Christian.

Whatever the motives, the persecution was instituted by a decree in 303 which ordered the destruction of the church buildings, the burning of the sacred books, the demoting of Christians from places of honour, and the enslavement of Christian household servants who would not abjure their faith. Other decrees followed which ordered the imprisonment of the rulers of the churches, offered release to Christians who sacrificed to the old gods, and commanded torture for those who were obdurate. In 304 a fourth edict seems to have been issued by Maximian, joint Emperor with Diocletian.

The storm was Empire-wide, from Britain to Arabia, but was particularly severe in the East, where Christianity had its chief numerical strength. It lasted more than a decade and endured longer in the East than in the West. Apparently the death penalty was inflicted only as a last resort, but torture was freely applied to induce the victims to recant and through it many perished. It was to this time that the martyrdom of Alban, not far from London, famous for the fashion in which his memory was revered, is ascribed. On occasion there was wholesale slaughter. Thus in Asia Minor a Christian town was surrounded by soldiers and burned, together with its inhabitants. An eye witness declares that he saw wild beasts leave unharmed the Christians who had been exposed to them and turn upon those who were goading them on. In Rome the property of the church was confiscated and many of the members perished. In Egypt, Palestine, and Syria, the persecution was renewed again and again in the vicissitudes of the political situation and did not die out until the defeat (about 323) of the last of the persecutors.

As was to be expected, the response of the Christians varied. Some recanted under pressure of torture and imprisonment. Some sent pagans or friends to sacrifice for them. Others wavered, but eventually gave themselves to the authorities. Still others sought martyrdom, and that in spite of the general policy of the church officials which discouraged what was regarded as fanaticism. The courage of the victims made so great an impression on pagans that we hear of at least two of the latter, educated men, becoming Christians.

CONSTANTINE ESPOUSES CHRISTIANITY

In what must have seemed an unequal contest between naked, ruthless force and unarmed, passive resistance, it was not the imperial government but Christianity which emerged victor. Presumably this would have been the eventual outcome, for Christianity was clearly proving itself the stronger. As it was, the individual who was preëminent in the surrender of the state was Constantine. Constantius Chlorus, the father of Constantine, was governing Britain, Gaul, and Spain as Cæsar when the persecution broke out. He seems never to have had any stomach for it and to have been at best half-hearted in his enforcement of the anti-Christian edicts. When, after the abdication of his two superiors, Diocletian and Maximian, he became one of their successors under the title of Augustus, he appears to have allowed the anti-Christian measures to lapse. On the death of Constantius Chlorus, in 306, Constantine, then in York in distant Britain, already his father's known choice for the succession, was proclaimed Emperor by his troops. He was confronted with rivals and a prolonged struggle followed. He did not become sole Emperor until 323, when he defeated his last competitor, Licinius.

Constantine took the decisive step in his relation with Christianity in the year 312. He had invaded Italy on his march towards Rome and was faced with the army of his first formidable opponent, Maxentius. Apparently he knew that Maxentius was relying on pagan magic and felt the need of a more powerful supernatural force to offset it. Years later he told his friend, Bishop Eusebius, the most eminent of early Church historians, that, after noon, as he was praying, he had a vision of a cross of light in the heavens bearing the inscription, "Conquer by this," and that confirmation came in a dream in which God appeared to him with the same sign and commanded him to make a likeness of it and use it as a safeguard in all encounters with his. enemies. How accurately Constantine remembered the experience we do not know, but Eusebius is usually discriminating in his evaluation of data, and he declares that he himself saw the standard which was made in response to the vision—a spear overlaid with gold, with a cross which was formed by a transverse bar and a wreath of gold and precious stones enclosing a monogram of the letters Chi and Rho for the name of Christ. The staff also had an embroidered cloth with the picture of Constantine and his children. Constantine was victor, the winning battle being at the Milvian Bridge, near Rome, and he therefore took possession of the capital. Presumably his faith in the efficacy of the Christian symbol was thus confirmed.

In the following year, 313, Constantine and Licinius, between whom the realm was temporarily divided, met at Milan and action was taken which was later looked back upon as having ensured toleration for the Christians throughout the Empire. Precisely what was done at Milan remains controversial. Some, including Eusebius, declare that an edict of toleration was issued. On the other hand it is contended that Constantine had already granted religious freedom and that whatever was done at Milan was by Licinius and was intended only for the eastern portions of the Empire where Licinius was in control. Whatever the details, it seems clear that important measures on behalf of the Christians were taken at Milan and that Constantine was consistently friendly.

The policy of Constantine was one of toleration. He did not make Christianity the sole religion of the state. That was to follow under later Emperors. He continued to support both paganism and Christianity. In 314, when the cross first appeared on his coins, it was accompanied by the figures of *Sol Invictus* and *Mars Conservator*. To the end of his days he bore the title of *pontifex maximus* as chief priest of the pagan state cult. The subservient Roman Senate followed the long-established custom and classed him among the gods. He did not persecute the old faiths.

As time passed, Constantine came out more and more pronouncedly in favour of Christianity. Whether he was a Christian from political motives only or from sincere religious conviction has been hotly debated. Perhaps he himself did not know. However, it is clear that he granted to members of the Christian clergy the freedom from all contributions to the state which had been the privilege of the priests of other religions which were accorded official recognition. However, this soon led to so great an influx into the Christian priesthood of those from the curial class who wished relief from the heavy burdens which were crushing that once privileged stratum of society that another edict followed which limited ordination to those whose exemption would mean little loss to the government. Wills in favour of the Church were permitted. The Christian Sunday was ordered placed in the same legal position as the pagan feasts, and provincial governors were instructed to respect the days in memory of the martyrs and to honour the festivals of the churches. The manumission of slaves in churches in the presence of the bishop and clergy was legalized. Litigants might bring suit in a bishop's court and the decision rendered was to be respected by the civil authorities. Constantine forbade Jews to stone such of their co-religionists as chose to become Christians. He had his children instructed in the Christian faith and kept Christian bishops and clergy in his entourage. He built and enlarged churches and encouraged bishops to do likewise and to call on the help of civil officials. When he removed his headquarters to Byzantium, on the Bosporus, and enlarged that city and renamed it Constantinople, he built in it many churches. He prohibited the repair of ruined temples and the erection of new images of the gods. He forbade any attempt to force Christians to participate in non-Christian religious ceremonies. He took an active part in the affairs of the Church, thus establishing a precedent which was to be followed by his successors. The fashion in which he sought to promote Christian unity by calling the first general council of the Church and presiding at it will be noted in the next chapter. While Constantine did not receive baptism until the latter part of his life, the deferment of that rite seems not to have been from indifference to it, but from the conviction, then general, that it washed away all previous sins and, being unrepeatable, had best be postponed until as near death as possible.

The Continued Growth of the Christian Community Under the Sons of Constantine

The three sons of Constantine who followed him successively in the imperial purple were much more positive in furthering the Christian faith than their father had been. In 341 the second of them ordered that pagan sacrifices be abolished in Italy. The third, Constantius, commanded that "superstition cease and the folly of sacrifices be abolished" and removed from the Senate the statue of Victory which had been placed there by Augustus after the battle of Actium. He ordered temples closed. Yet of the pagan rites only sacrifices were forbidden, and processions, sacred feasts, and initiation to the mysteries, still permitted, presumably continued.

Under this prolonged patronage by the Emperors the Christian communities grew rapidly. The momentum acquired before Constantine was accelerated. Many now sought admission to the Church from other motives than purely religious conviction. Official favour and even wealth could be hoped for where formerly persecution, always in the background, tended to give pause to all but those impressed by the truth of the faith. Huge church structures were erected, some of which survive.

REACTION UNDER JULIAN AND THE COMPETITION OF OLD AND NEW FAITHS

The numerical triumph of Christianity in the Roman Empire was not yet fully accomplished. First came a brief attempt to restore paganism by Julian, one of the family of Constantine. There was also the continued competition of historic paganism, reinforced by the mounting disasters to the Empire. To this were added new religious faiths and the inroads of barbarians with their cults. As, from the vantage of the accomplished fact, we may think that the victory of Christianity in the Mediterranean world had long been assured, it did not necessarily so appear to contemporaries.

Julian, because of his record branded by Christians as "the apostate," is an extraordinarily appealing figure. Sensitive, able, studious, deeply religious, Julian had a youth which determined his scorn for Christianity and his nostalgic adherence to the traditional paganism. A scion of the Constantinian house and a cousin of the Emperor Constantius, he and his brother were left the only survivors of his branch of the family by a series of political murders which were designed to remove inconvenient rivals for the imperial purple. Kept under watchful ward by Constantius, he was instructed in the Christian faith and outwardly conformed to it. Indeed, for a time he may even have been a convinced Christian. However, reared under these unhappy circumstances, it is not surprising that Julian conceived an ardent admiration for the philosophies which were critical of Christianity and for the religions which that faith was supplanting.

Made Cæsar by Constantius and placed in command of an army on the frontier, Julian was proclaimed Augustus by his troops and was marching against Constantius when the latter's convenient death (361) left him undisputed lord of the Empire. On his march against Constantius, Julian threw off any remaining pretense of being Christian and openly acknowledged his paganism. He did not undertake a violent persecution of Christianity, but he deprived the Church and its clergy of some of the privileges accorded them by his recent predecessors, restored pagan temples, and in appointments to public office gave preference to pagans. He endeavoured to purge the revived paganism of its more palpable weaknesses and attempted to incorporate in it some of the institutional features of the Christian Church, such as a hierarchy, monasteries for meditation, penance, the sermon, and almonries. He wrote against the "Galileans," as he persisted in calling the Christians, and sought to annoy them by beginning the rebuilding of the Jewish temple in Jerusalem.

Julian failed. Paganism was too moribund to be revived by artificial stimulation. When, after a reign of about two years, he perished (363) in a war against the Persians, his troops elected in his place Jovian, of German descent. It is said that when Jovian at first demurred on the ground that he was a Christian, his troops declared that they too were Christians and refused to let him decline. Certainly Julian was the last Roman Emperor who openly avowed paganism. Some of the others were far from being Christians in character, but all of them outwardly conformed to the faith.

The ancient paganism was not yet dead. It held on in many places. It was strong in some of the rural districts and in remote mountain valleys. In the Eternal City the aristocracy, conservative as an aristocracy usually is, possibly resentful of the new Constantinople, cherished the pagan traditions associated with the days of Rome's glory. Especially in Italy, Gaul, and Spain paganism persisted, even in the cities, down into the fourth and fifth centuries.

The lament of the aristocracy seemed to be confirmed by the capture and sack of Rome by Alaric and his Goths in 410. To the Mediterranean world Rome was the symbol of civilization, order, and stability. Although Rome recovered very quickly physically, the experience further shook the morale of a portion of the globe which was being dealt many blows. Here, to the mind of the adherents of the old gods, was proof conclusive that the defection of the Christians from the ancient cults was the source of the illnesses of society.

The beginnings of the barbarian invasions which were to swell to major proportions in the fifth century often brought with them cults from beyond the borders of the Empire. As we are to see, some of the barbarians adopted Christianity before entering the Roman realms and all of those from the North were eventually to do so. However, for a time their religions brought fresh if fleeting resistance to Christianity.

New faiths were entering the lists against Christianity. One of these was Neoplatonism. An outgrowth of the ancient philosophies of Greece, especially Platonism, its first major creative figures, Ammonias Saccas and Plotinus, flourished in the third century. It was both a philosophy and a religion and in the fourth and fifth centuries was widely popular among the intellectuals. Julian was enamoured of it. It left a permanent impress upon Christianity, partly through Augustine of Hippo, partly through its share in shaping Christian thought in general, and especially in its contributions to Christian mysticism.

Formidable also was Manichæism. Manichæism had as its founder Mani, of the third century. Of Persian stock, with some of the blood of the Parthian Arsacids in his veins, Mani was reared in Seleucia-Ctesiphon, the chief city of Mesopotamia, where East and West met. Deeply religious, he was impressed by the many faiths with which he came in contact—the Zoroastrianism of his Persian ancestors, the ancient Babylonian beliefs, Judaism, and Christianity. He came to the conviction that he was commissioned by divine revelation to be a prophet. Opposed by the powerful Zoroastrianism, he was driven out of the Persian Empire and for many years was a wandering preacher of the new faith and is said to have travelled and taught widely in Central Asia and India. Returning to his native land, he is reported to have been favoured by the reigning monarch, but to have been killed under a successor. His followers went both westward and eastward and Manichæism was eventually represented from the Western Mediterranean to the China Sea. In the Mediterranean world especially it took on some Christian features. Mani is said to have begun his letters with "Mani, Apostle of Jesus Christ." He declared either that he was the Paraclete promised by Jesus or that the Paraclete spoke through him.

THE CONVERSION OF AUGUSTINE

The appeal of Neoplatonism and Manichæism as rivals of Christianity is vividly demonstrated in the spiritual pilgrimage of Augustine of Hippo (354–430). Born in North Africa of Latin stock, of a devoutly Christian mother, Monica, and a pagan father who became a Christian only late in life, as a youth Augustine was given Christian instruction. His mother did not have him baptized because, accepting the belief that baptism washed away sins committed before it was administered, she wished him to defer it until after the heat of youth was passed and with it the excesses of that ardent age. Brilliant, sensitive, intense, in his teens Augustine took a concubine who, before he was eighteen, bore him a son, named, perhaps conventionally, or deliberately by a strange perverseness, or from the religious feeling which characterized him, Adeodatus, "given by God." Unsatisfied religiously and seeking, Augustine dabbled with his inherited Christianity but was repelled by the crudity of the literary style of the Latin translation which was his only way to the Scriptures. For a time he tried Manichæism, but finding that it could not answer his intellectual questions, abandoned it. A teacher, first in North Africa, then in Rome, and eventually in Milan, he continued his religious quest. For a time his hunger seemed to be met by Neoplatonism, but that did not fully satisfy him and in Milan he came under the spell of Ambrose, the bishop of that city, a man of strong character and an impressive preacher, of whom we are to hear more in a moment. Suffering from conscious moral impotence and self-disgust because of his inability to control his sexual desires, a member of a small coterie who, with him, were searching, at the climax of his struggle Augustine rushed from his friends into a quiet nook in a garden, seemed to hear the voice of a child commanding "take, read," found before him a copy of Paul's *Letter to the Romans,* and his eye fell on the passage in the thirteenth chapter which includes the words: "not in rioting and drunkenness, not in chambering and wantonness, not in strife and envying, but put ye on the Lord Jesus Christ, and make not provision for the flesh, to fulfil the lusts thereof." This crisis precipitated conversion (386). He and Adeodatus were baptized by Ambrose at the same time (April 25, 387). While victory over the flesh was quickly achieved, Augustine later said that he still found pride a problem. He returned to Africa, became a prodigious writer, was the centre of what in effect was a monastic community, and died as Bishop of Hippo.

No other Christian after Paul was to have so wide, deep, and prolonged an influence upon the Christianity of Western Europe and those forms of the faith that stemmed from it as had Augustine. We are to recur to him again and again. Here we must simply pause to note that his *Confessions* became one of the most widely read autobiographies and maintains its place among the most moving and profound of the self-recorded records of a human soul and its struggles. His *De Civitate Dei,* written as an interpretation of history, originally as an answer to those who accused Christianity of being responsible for the fall of Rome to the Goths, remains one of the landmarks in the philosophy of history.

The Geographic Extension of the Faith Continues

In spite of the old and the new resistance, the spread of Christianity continued. By the close of its first five centuries Christianity had become the professed faith of the overwhelming majority of the population of the Roman Empire. The Jewish communities held to their ancestral religion, and here and there, usually in remote rural districts or mountain valleys, the ancient pagan cults lingered. In some groups and areas Christians were a smaller element than in others. Many of the nominal Christians paid only lip service to their ostensible faith and remained pagans at heart. Yet outwardly Christianity had triumphed. Moreover, Christianity continued to spill over the boundaries of the Roman Empire and was being carried to non-Roman peoples.

The spread of the faith within the Empire was furthered by more than one factor. As for several generations past, the momentum of early successes carried it forward. The Emperors were active in curbing the old faiths and in encouraging the acceptance of Christianity. Some were more zealous than others, but after Julian none sought to roll back the tide and the majority furthered it. There was no violent persecution of pagans comparable to that with which Christianity had formerly been confronted. Yet we hear of encouragement given by Theodosius I (reigned 379–395) to the demolition of temples. Theodosius proscribed not only sacrifices but also secret visits to pagan shrines and commanded that apostates from Christianity be deprived of all honours and of the right of inheritance and of conveying property by will. In many places temples were destroyed by Christians, often led by monks. Early in the fifth century imperial edicts forbade making official holidays of the special days of the old cults, withdrew all privileges enjoyed by pagan priests, and commanded the destruction of temples still standing in rural districts. Later the incomes of temples were ordered diverted to the army, the destruction of pagan images was decreed, and surviving temples were to be given to some other public use. Pagans were commanded to go to the churches to receive Christian instruction, and exile and confiscation of property were made the penalties for refusing to be baptized.

Jews were treated with lenience. Indeed, they were dealt with more mildly than were Christian heretics. Occasional sporadic outbreaks against them are recorded, but they were permitted to rear their children in the faith of their fathers and restrictive legislation against them was chiefly designed to estop them from what they were sometimes doing, winning Christians, usually Christian slaves in their possession, to Judaism.

Encouraged by the Emperors, bishops were active in the conversion of the non-Christians in their dioceses. Some required no incentive from the state, but were zealous on their own initiative, inspiring and directing missionaries. Thus in the fourth century Martin of Tours, whom we are to meet later as the leading pioneer of monasticism in Gaul, on becoming bishop of the see by which he is known seems to have found most of the surrounding countryside pagan. He led his monks in preaching, in destroying temples, and in baptizing. Victricius, Bishop of Rouen, a friend of Martin, established Christian outposts not far from the later Flanders. About the middle of the fifth century a synod meeting at Arles in the southern part of Gaul held that a bishop was derelict to his duty if he did not stamp out the worship of idols in his diocese.

Augustine was by no means the only convert of Ambrose of Milan. Son of a Prefect of Gaul, well educated according to the standards of the time, Ambrose (c. 340-397) was a civil official, Prefect of Upper Italy, when to his intense surprise and great reluctance and while still a layman and not yet baptized, he was constrained by the insistence of the populace to become Bishop of Milan. Entering upon a course of theological reading the better to fill his unsought post, he combined a Stoic background with Christian faith and became one of the most famous of bishops, administrators, and preachers. He was also a writer of hymns. He opposed the pagan party in Rome, won many non-Christians in his diocese, and encouraged missionaries in the Tyrol.

A contemporary of Ambrose, John Chrysostom ("the golden-mouthed," so called for his eloquence), whose dates were c.345-407, was originally headed for the career of advocate and was accordingly trained in oratory. Moved to seek Christian instruction, he was baptized in his mid-twenties, became a monk, and then, being ordained, rose to be the outstanding preacher in his native Antioch. Earnest, eloquent, he won widespread acclaim and at the instance of the Emperor was elevated to the episcopal see of Constantinople. In this post he sent missionaries to pagans, including the Goths on the borders of the Empire. Banished because of his courage in rebuking vice, he gave himself to winning non-Christians in the vicinity of his exile. He urged that the Christian owners of the great *latifundia* have chapels on their estates and work for the conversion of those who tilled their fields and vineyards. He held that the most effective means of conversion was the example of Christian living. "There would be no more heathen if we would be true Christians," he said.

In Alexandria late in the fourth century the bishop led in the destruction of temples and the Serapeum, the great shrine of Serapis which dominated the city from its hill, was turned into a church.

Although by A.D. 500 the large majority of the population of the Empire were Christians, in some areas and groups, as we have hinted, the proportion was larger than in others. In Phœnicia and Palestine there were many pagans well after the close of the fifth century. Even in Antioch, one of the strongest Christian centres, at the end of the sixth century paganism still had a recognized head. Athens long remained a stubborn citadel of the pre-Christian philosophies and numbers of the Christian youths who flocked there as students had their faith weakened or destroyed. It was not until the year 529 that the Emperor, by closing the schools in Athens, formally put an end to that focus of pagan infection. Although the sack of Rome by the Goths in 410 dealt a severe blow to the pagan party in that city, it was not until the sixth and seventh centuries that some of the remaining temples were turned into churches. At the close of the sixth century paganism survived in Sardinia and Sicily and missionary effort was still in progress in Corsica. In the seventh century there were pagans in the mountains between Genoa and Milan. At the end of the fifth century idolatry remained strong in Spain and the south of Gaul. While at the close of the fifth century paganism had by no means completely disappeared in the Roman Empire, its days seemed clearly to be numbered.

The expansion of Christianity beyond the boundaries of the Roman Empire which had begun before the time of Constantine continued in the fourth and fifth centuries. Whether it was accelerated by the official espousal of the faith by the Emperors would be difficult to determine. In at least one area, the Persian Empire, support by the Roman Empire was a handicap. Rome and Persia were chronic and deadly enemies. The Persian rulers, Zoroastrian by religion, had their natural opposition to a growing, non-Zoroastrian faith heightened by the fear that Christians would be sympathetic with Rome. Their apprehension was not allayed by the fact that Constantine, posing as the protector of the Christians, protested against their persecution by the Persian state. In general, however, the continued adoption of the faith within the Roman Empire seems to have facilitated its spread outside the Empire.

This certainly was true of the barbarians who were invading the Empire from the North. They tended to conform to the culture of the Roman world, for it was the only civilization which most of them knew. Since Christianity was increasingly associated with that civilization, it was natural that they should adopt it.

The Goths were the first of the northern peoples among whom Christianity had a marked spread. That was because, being the earliest of the Teutonic peoples extensively to harass and invade the Roman provinces, they were also the first to be brought into continued intimate contact with the religion which was rapidly becoming the faith of that realm. It may have been that Christianity was first introduced among the Goths by Christians whom they had taken captive in raids in the third century. Two of the forms of Christianity with which we are to become familiar in the next chapter made headway among the Goths, the Arian and what came to be known as the Catholic. To these was added a third, that associated with Audius, a bishop of great purity of life who was banished for what were regarded as heretical doctrines and while in exile became a missionary among the Goths. However, most of the Gothic Christians were Arians.

The most famous missionary among the Goths was one of their own number, Ulfilas (c.311–c.380). When and how Ulfilas became a Christian we do not know. The usual conjecture is that it was while he was in Constantinople as a young man. It was a mild form of Arian Christianity with which he became acquainted and which he propagated. At about the age of thirty he was consecrated bishop of "the Christians in Gothia." What seem to have been his first missionary labours were north of the Danube. After a few years, seeking to protect his converts from persecution, he obtained permission to move them into Roman territory south of that river. Ulfilas translated part or all of the Scriptures into Gothic, presumably devising an alphabet for that purpose and thus for the first time giving Gothic a written form. It is an early instance of what was to be common in succeeding centuries, for more languages have been reduced to writing by Christian missionaries than by all other agencies put together.

Arian Christianity continued to spread among the Goths until most of them belonged to that branch of the faith. It was the Visigoths among whom Christianity was first strong and it was chiefly from them that it gained entrance among the Ostrogoths, the Gepidæ, and the Vandals. When these peoples settled within the Empire, as they did in the fourth century, a large proportion of them were already Christian. The fact that they were Arians while the bulk of the Roman population were Catholics reinforced a tendency to keep the two elements of the population separate. As, however, the inevitable acculturation and assimilation proceeded, Arianism gave way to the Catholic form of the faith. That process was not completed until late in the sixth century.

Others of the Teutonic peoples adopted the Catholic form of the faith from the very outset of their conversion. Thus the Burgundians, moving south of the Rhine early in the fifth century, accepted the Catholic Christianity of the provincial population among whom they settled. A little later the Burgundians who remained on the right bank of the Rhine became Catholic Christians. The Burgundians were thus the first predominantly Catholic Germanic people. Subsequently, when they established themselves in the Rhone Valley, they turned Arian, perhaps through contact with the Arian Visigoths.

More important for the future than the conversion of the Burgundians was that of the Franks. In the fifth century the Franks became dominant in the northern part of Gaul and the lower portions of the Rhine Valley. Late in that century their leader, Clovis, made himself master of much of Gaul and laid the foundations of what for the next four centuries and more was to be the most important state in Western Europe. He took to wife a Burgundian princess, a Catholic, and acceded to her request that the first of their children be baptized. He himself was eventually baptized, the traditional date being December 25, 496. He did not constrain his warriors to follow him, but eventually they did so. Clovis adopted the Catholic rather than the Arian form of Christianity, perhaps because he wished in that way to identify himself with the Roman provincials, Catholics, over whom he was ruling.

It was in the fifth century that we first hear certainly of Christianity in Ireland, that island beyond and yet near to the western bounds of the Roman Empire. The most famous of the missionaries to Ireland was Patrick. Patrick was a native of Roman Britain, but of what part we are not sure. He was at least a third generation Christian, for he speaks of his father as having been a deacon and his paternal grandfather a presbyter. We cannot be certain of the date of his birth, but the year most frequently given is 389. Presumably reared as a Christian in fairly comfortable circumstances, perhaps with a smattering of Latin, when about sixteen years old Patrick was carried away captive to Ireland by one of those raids which, breaking through the weakening defenses of the Roman borders, were harassing Britain. For at least six years he was a slave in Ireland and was set to tending flocks. There, perhaps through the solitude and hardships of his lot, his inherited faith deepened and he filled his days and nights with prayer. Dreams came which aroused in him hopes of seeing his homeland and which nerved him to seek and obtain passage on a ship. We are not certain of his life for the next few years. He may have wandered in Italy and perhaps spent some time in a monastery on an island off the southern coast of Gaul. It is clear that he eventually made his way back to Britain and was greeted with joy by his family as one risen from the dead.

Again there came dreams, now with what seemed to him a letter, "the voice of the Irish," with the appeal: "We beseech thee, holy youth, to come and walk with us once more." Heeding the call, Patrick returned to Ireland, but how soon and when we do not know. He was consecrated bishop, but again we cannot tell by whom or when. He seems to have had many years in Ireland, for he speaks of baptizing thousands and of ordaining clergy. Although he himself was not a monk, under his influence sons and daughters of chieftains adopted that way of life. His was both an arduous and a perilous missionary career, for he had to face opposition from fellow clergy and from armed foes. He seems to have reached a ripe old age. Other missionaries shared in the conversion of Ireland. That island became a centre from which, as we shall see, Christian influence was to radiate not only to Britain but also to much of Western Europe.

Christianity continued its spread among the peoples to the east of the Roman Empire, chiefly civilized folk along its eastern borders.

In Armenia the Christianity which had been adopted *en masse* by the population and its rulers became better understood and more identified with the nation's life. Before the end of the fifth century the Bible was put into Armenian and other Christian books were translated from Greek and Syriac. For many decades paganism survived in some of the mountain fastnesses, but towards the close of the fourth century a deepening and purification of the Christianity of the nation was effected under the leadership of Nerses, a descendant of Gregory the Illuminator. In the fifth century Armenia was dominated by the Persians and the overlords attempted to impose their religion, Zoroastrianism, upon the land. Numbers of the faithful suffered martyrdom, but by the end of the century the Church breathed more easily.

It was in the fourth century that Christianity seems to have been introduced among the Georgians, in the Caucasus, north of Armenia. Progress continued, apparently under the prospering encouragement of the ruling house. As in Armenia, a Persian invasion was accompanied by an attempt to force Zoroastrianism on the country, possibly to offset Christianity with its ties with the Roman Empire. In the fifth century, however, a king led a national uprising which purged the land of the fire cult and created bishoprics and erected many churches.

In Mesopotamia, on the debated border between the Roman and Persian

Empires, Christianity had its chief hold among the Syriac-using population. It made some headway among the Persians proper and a Christian literature arose in Pahlavi, or Middle Persian. But Zoroastrianism, the state cult, did not exhibit the weaknesses of the official paganism of the Roman Empire and offered more effective resistance to new religions, such as Manichæism and Christianity, than did the latter. In the first half of the third century, when Christianity was spreading fairly rapidly, a dynastic revolution which brought the Sassanids on the throne was accompanied by a revival of national feeling and of the associated Zoroastrianism. This dimmed the prospect for Christianity. From time to time, notably under Sapor II (reigned 310–379), persecution was especially severe: the number of Christian martyrs is said to have been as many as sixteen thousand. The fortunes of Christianity varied with the state of the political relations between Rome and Persia. During the recurring wars persecutions of the Christians, as suspected supporters of Rome, were intensified. The one exception was during the brief reign of Julian, when, in spite of hostilities between the two realms, Christians, out of favour with the Roman Empire, were regarded more leniently by the Persians. However, the wars with Rome brought Christian captives into the Sassanid realms and through them facilitated the spread of the faith. In the intervals of peace the restrictions on Christianity seem usually to have lightened. Some of the Persian nobility became Christians and one from that class is said to have been a zealous and successful missionary among his fellow-Persians and to have carried the faith even to the fierce Kurds in their mountain fastnesses.

Christianity was brought into Central Asia. By the end of the fifth century it counted converts among the Turks and the Hephthalite Huns and had bishoprics in the cities of Herat, Merv, and Meshed. From these centres irradiated caravan routes along which it might be conveyed to even more distant points. It may have been furthered by remnants of Hellenistic culture left in these cities in the wake of Alexander the Great.

A national organization was achieved for Christianity in the Sassanid realms. This was accomplished at a council held in 410. At the head was a Catholicos or Patriarch with his seat at Seleucia-Ctesiphon, the Sassanid capital. The state accorded him recognition and held him responsible for the conduct of his flock. Thus the Christians constituted a recognized minority enclave within the Persian domain. At times this led to state interference in the selection of bishops and there was the ever-present danger that unworthy aspirants for the office might obtain the post by bribery or political favouritism.

The distinctiveness of this Persian (or Assyrian) Church was further accentuated in the fourth century by doctrinal differences. The Persian Church was penetrated by the views of the relation of the human and the divine in

Jesus which are associated, somewhat inaccurately, with the name of Nestorius. We are to hear of this development more in detail in the next chapter. The views which were condemned by the Catholic Church in the Roman Empire are more accurately connected with the teachings of Theodore of Mopsuestia. They gained a strong foothold at Edessa. Expelled from that city, their exponents became teachers in Nisibis, the chief centre for the training of the clergy of the Persian (or Assyrian) Church. From Nisibis they spread throughout that church, but usually they were not extremely held.

In the fourth and fifth centuries the Christian communities in Arabia grew. Some of them were on the eastern borders of the Roman realms, some on the edge of Mesopotamia, some along the Arabian margin of the Persian Gulf, and others in the south of Arabia. They represented various strains of the faith, several of them far removed from orthodox or Catholic Christianity.

Christianity also obtained a foothold on the African side of the Red Sea, in Axum, from which the Christianity of the later Ethiopia or Abyssinia seems to have had its rise. The traditional account tells of a philosopher from Tyre who, taking with him two youths, one of them Frumentius, sailed for "India." On the return voyage they were seized by the inhabitants of one of the ports on the west coast of the Red Sea. All the ship's company were massacred except Frumentius and his fellow-youth. The two rose to high posts in the service of their captors and Frumentius set himself to the spiritual care of the Christian merchants from the Roman Empire whom he found there and built for them houses of worship. He went to Alexandria, asked the archbishop of that city, Athanasius, for a bishop, and Athanasius responded by consecrating him and sending him back to his flock. Whatever may be the truth of this story, it appears to be certain that Athanasius appointed one Frumentius Bishop of Axum. It seems probable that Frumentius won the king of Axum and that in consequence Christianity became the official faith of that state. This was in the first half of the fourth century. Thus was begun a connexion between the Christianity of Abyssinia and that of Egypt which was to persist into the twentieth century.

It is probable that in the fourth and fifth centuries Christians were to be found in India and Ceylon. Some doubt exists because of the uncertainty of the identification of geographic names and the confusion of the south of Arabia with India. If there were Christians in India, their associations were probably at least in part with the Tigris-Euphrates Valley.

WHY THE PHENOMENAL SPREAD OF CHRISTIANITY?

Why was it that Christianity had this amazing expansion? How shall we account for the fact that, beginning as what to the casual observer must have appeared a small and obscure sect of Judaism, before its first five centuries were out it had become the faith of the Roman state and of the vast majority of the population of that realm and had spread eastward as far as Central Asia and probably India and Ceylon and westward into far away Ireland? Why of all the many faiths which were competing for the allegiance of the Roman Empire, many of them with a much more promising outlook, did it emerge victor? Why, of all the Jewish sects, did it alone move outside the pale of Judaism and attract the millions of many races and cultures which composed the Mediterranean world?

The motives which led non-Christians to embrace the faith were many and varied. We hear of an entire family, headed by the grandfather, who became Christian because they knew of a case of demon possession which was cured by invoking the name of Christ. In the fifth century in one section of Gaul numbers of pagans were converted because, when a plague attacked the herds, the cattle of the Christians escaped or recovered and this was attributed to the use of the sign of the cross. On the other hand, we read of a son of pagan parents, also in Gaul, who later became a distinguished bishop, who was led to the Christian faith by struggling with the question: "What is the purpose of my life?" We are told of a fourth century Roman scholar and teacher of distinction who after prolonged and careful study asked for baptism. We have noted the fashion in which Augustine came through deep religious hunger and a sense of moral impotence. Augustine also said that he was impressed by the incarnation and the humility of Jesus, both of which he failed to find in the Neoplatonism in which he had sought an answer to his long yearning. Much earlier, in the second century, Justin Martyr, a native of Samaria, who wrote one of the more famous of the apologies for Christianity, and who won his sobriquet by his death for the faith, had sought wisdom through the philosophies of his day and became a convert when he found truth in Christ, Christ in whom the *Logos* had taken individual human-historical form.

One of the factors to which is attributed the triumph of Christianity is the endorsement of Constantine. But, as we have suggested, the faith was already so strong by the time when Constantine espoused it that it would probably have won without him. Indeed, one of the motives sometimes ascribed to his support is his supposed desire to enlist the coöperation of what had become the strongest element in the Empire, the Christian community.

Another cause was the disintegration of society, especially beginning with the last two decades of the second century, with the weakened opposition of old institutions to Christianity and a loss of nerve which led millions to seek security in religion. But why was it that of all the many religions which were competing and which offered to meet this need it was Christianity which was accepted?

It is clear that the institutions which Christianity possessed in the churches proved an attraction. In spite of the divisions which we are to describe in the next chapter, the Christian churches were the most inclusive and the strongest of all the various associations in the Roman world. They cared for their poor and for those of their number imprisoned for their faith. In times of distress churches would help one another by gifts of money or food. A Christian holding membership in a local unit of the Church would be among friends in whatever city or town he found others of his communion. The only fellowship approaching that of the Christians in solidarity was that of the Jews, and in contrast with the churches, which welcomed all, regardless of race, this was as much racial and cultural as religious. But what was the source of the churches and what gave them their strength?

Christianity was inclusive. More than any of its rivals it appealed to men and women from all races and classes. In contrast with the philosophies, which were primarily for the educated, Christianity had a message for the simple and the ignorant. It also won many of the keenest and most highly trained minds. Membership in the mysteries was expensive and therefore chiefly for the well to do. Christianity was for both rich and poor. Mithraism was only for men. The Gospel was proclaimed to both men and women. Why this inclusiveness? It was not in the parent Judaism.

In a combination of flexibility and uncompromising adherence to its basic convictions Christianity surpassed its rivals. Like the latter and to a much greater extent than Judaism it accommodated itself to the Græco-Roman world. It availed itself of Greek philosophy to think through its theology. It took over and adapted much from Judaism. In its organization it fitted into the patterns of the Empire. Yet, in striking contrast with the easy-going syncretism of an age in which one religion borrowed what it liked from its neighbours and all except Judaism permitted their adherents to share in the worship of the cults endorsed by the state, Christianity was adamant on what it regarded as basic principles. It held some sins to be unforgivable to Christians, among them any participation in non-Christian worship. As time passed, as we are to see, and the numbers of Christians multiplied, ways were found by the Catholic Church, the largest of the Christian communions, of declaring even the most serious of sins forgiven if there were true repentance, but severe penance was entailed. Some of the Christian groups broke from the Catholic Church in insisting on stricter procedures.

The constancy of the martyrs under torture impressed many non-Christians. As we have seen, by no means all Christians stood up under trial. Many wilted. Yet enough remained firm to give convincing evidence of a power which nerved children, old men, and weak women as well as stalwart youths to hold to their faith under gruelling and prolonged torment and to do so without bitterness towards their enemies. One of the apologists was obviously speaking truth when he declared that when reviled, the Christians blessed.

Moreover, Christianity worked the moral transformation which it demanded. Augustine was by no means the first or the only morally defeated individual who found victory in the Gospel. This was so frequent as to be almost normal. The apologists rang the changes on the welcome given by the Christian community to the tarnished, weak dregs of society and on the regenerating vigour of the faith.

It was not only to miracles of moral rebirth to which Christians could point. Pagans were also attracted by the miracles of healing wrought in the name of Christ.

Better than its rivals, Christianity gave to the Græco-Roman world what so many were craving from a religion. To those wishing immortality it pointed to the historic Jesus, risen from the dead, and to the promise that those who believed in him would share with him in glorified, eternal life. To those demanding high morality it offered standards beyond the full attainment of men and the power to grow towards them. To those craving fellowship it presented a community of worship and of mutual aid, with care for the poor, the infirm, and the aged. To those who, distrustful of reason, longed for a faith sanctioned by immemorial antiquity, it pointed to the long record preserved in what it termed the Old Testament, going back to Moses and beyond him and pointing forward to Christ. To those demanding intellectual satisfaction it could present literature prepared by some of the ablest minds of the day.

Whence came these qualities which won for Christianity its astounding victory? Careful and honest investigation can give but one answer, Jesus. It was faith in Jesus and his resurrection which gave birth to the Christian fellowship and which continued to be its inspiration and its common tie. It was the love displayed in Christ which was, ideally and to a marked extent in practice, the bond which held Christians together. The early disciples unite in declaring that it was from the command of Jesus that the Gospel was proclaimed to all, regardless of sex, race, or cultural background. The new life in Christ might express itself in many forms, but its authenticity was to be proved by high, uncompromising moral qualities as set forth by Jesus. Hence the combination of flexibility and inflexibility. As against the mystery religions, those cults which had so much superficial similarity to Christianity, it was partly belief in God, partly a theology, a metaphysic, which gave the latter its advantage, but it was chiefly that as against the mythical figures at the heart of the mysteries, Christians could point to Jesus, an historical fact. Through the Holy Spirit promised by Jesus came the moral transformations which were so marked in the Christian fellowship. The loyalty of the martyrs was to

Christ, and his example and the promise of eternal life through him were their sustaining strength. It was through the sign of his cross or by the use of his name that miracles were wrought. It was a true insight, even if exercised in derision, which named the members of the new faith Christians and in the city where non-Jews were first won in large numbers. Without Jesus Christianity would never have been and from him came the distinctive qualities which won it the victory.

We must not end this chapter without calling attention to what should be obvious, that in this victory of Christianity was also something of defeat. The victory had been accompanied by compromise, compromise with the world which had crucified Jesus, compromise often made so half-consciously or unconsciously that it was all the more serious a peril to the Gospel. In later chapters we must return to this more in detail and also to the attempts of Christians to meet the peril.

SELECTED BIBLIOGRAPHY

ON THE GENERAL SUBJECT OF THIS CHAPTER

For the pre-Constantinian period the standard work is A. Harnack, *Die Mission und Ausbreitung des Christentums in den ersten drei Jahrhunderten* (Leipzig, J. C. Hinrichs'sche Buchhandlung, 1902, pp. xii, 561), translated and edited by James Moffatt under the title, *The Mission and Expansion of Christianity in the First Three Centuries* (New York, G. P. Putnam's Sons, 2d ed., 2 vols., 1908).

For the entire period see K. S. Latourette, *A History of the Expansion of Christianity. Volume I, The First Five Centuries* (New York, Harper & Brothers, 1937, pp. xxiv, 412), with its footnote citations and its bibliographies. The present chapter is very largely a condensation and rearrangement of chapters III, IV, and V of this work.

For a Roman Catholic treatment see the pertinent sections in A. Fliche and V. Martin, *Histoire de l'Eglise depuis les Origines jusqu'a nos Jours,* Vols. I, II, III, IV (Paris, 1946–1948).

TEXTS OF THE SOURCES

J. P. Migne, *Patrologiæ . . . Latinæ* (Paris, 221 vols., 1844–1864) and J. P. Migne, *Patrologiæ . . . Græcæ* (Paris, 161 vols., 1857–1866).

ENGLISH TRANSLATIONS OF MANY OF THE EARLY CHRISTIAN DOCUMENTS

The Ante-Nicene Fathers (the American reprint and revision of the Edinburgh edition, Buffalo, The Christian Literature Publishing Co., 10 vols., 1885–1887).

The Church History of Eusebius, translated by A. C. McGiffert (New York, The Christian Literature Society, 1890, pp. x, 403). A translation of this most famous of early church histories, is especially valuable for its critical notes, although some of them are now out-dated.

See also a convenient collection, C. R. Haines, *Heathen Contact with Christianity during Its First Century and a Half, being All References to Christianity Recorded in Pagan Writings during that Period* (Cambridge, Deighton, Bell & Co., 1923, pp. 124).

Philip Schaff, editor, *A Select Library of Nicene and Post-Nicene Fathers of the Christian Church* (New York, The Christian Literature Co., first series, 14 vols., 1886–1890, second series, 14 vols., 1890–1900).

SECONDARY WORKS ON CERTAIN GENERAL ASPECTS

S. J. Case, *The Social Triumph of the Ancient Church* (New York, Harper & Brothers, 1933, pp. vii, 250). By a well-known expert, presenting stimulating, somewhat radical views.

C. N. Cochrane, *Christianity and Classical Culture. A Study in Thought and Action from Augustus to Augustine* (Oxford, The Clarendon Press, 1940, pp. vii, 523). A most stimulating discussion.

A. D. Nock, *Conversion. The Old and the New in Religion from Alexander the Great to Augustine of Hippo* (Oxford University Press, 1933, pp. xii, 309). Competent, with some fresh points of view.

G. Uhlhorn, *The Conflict of Christianity with Heathenism,* edited and translated by E. C. Smyth and C. J. H. Ropes (New York, Charles Scribner's Sons, 1879, pp. 508). Still useful although old and strongly Protestant and Christian in its bias.

PAUL

A. Deissmann, *Paul. A Study in Social and Religious History,* translated by W. E. Wilson (London, Hodder & Stoughton, 2d ed., 1926, pp. xv, 323). A standard work by an expert.

C. H. Dodd, *The Epistle of Paul to the Romans* (New York, Harper & Brothers, 1932, pp. xxxv, 246). With deep religious insight, by a thoroughly competent scholar.

T. R. Glover, *Paul of Tarsus* (New York, Harper & Brothers, 1925, pp. 256). A popular account by a competent scholar.

F. C. Porter, *The Mind of Christ in Paul* (New York, Charles Scribner's Sons, 1930, pp. xiii, 323). A work of ripe scholarship and mature religious insight, arguing the fidelity with which Paul reproduced and interpreted the mind of his Master.

FURTHER FIRST CENTURY SPREAD OF CHRISTIANITY

Hans Lietzmann, *Petrus und Paulus in Rom* (Berlin, Walter de Gruyter und Co., 2d ed., 1927, pp. viii, 315). Critical, careful, thorough.

A. C. McGiffert, *A History of Christianity in the Apostolic Age* (New York, Charles Scribner's Sons, 1897, pp. xii, 681). Standard, but partly out-dated by more recent scholarship.

SECOND, THIRD, FOURTH, AND FIFTH CENTURY SPREAD

A. Alföld, *The Conversion of Constantine and Pagan Rome,* translated by H. Mattingly (Oxford University Press, 1948, pp. vi, 140). A useful monograph.

A. Hauck, *Kirchengeschichte Deutschlands* (Leipzig, J. C. Hinrichs'sche Buchhandlung, 5 vols., 1922–1929). Standard.

T. Scott Holmes, *The Origin and Development of the Christian Church in Gaul during the First Six Centuries of the Christian Era* (London, Macmillan & Co., 1911, pp. xiv, 584). Carefully done.

H. Leclerq, *L'Afrique Chrétienne* (Paris, Librairie Victor Lecoffre, 2 vols., 1904). Competent.

H. Leclerq, *L'Espagne Chrétienne* (Paris, Librairie Victor Lecoffre, 1906, pp. xxxv, 396). Based upon careful research.

J. Mesnage, *Évangélisation de l'Afrique. Part que Certaines Familles Romano-Afriques y ont Prise* (Algiers, Adolphe Jourdan, 1914, pp. 98). Excellent, by a modern Roman Catholic missionary to Africa.

G. La Piana, *Foreign Groups in Rome during the First Centuries of the Empire* (*Harvard Theological Review,* Vol. XX, pp. 183–403).

W. M. Ramsey, *The Cities and Bishoprics of Phrygia, being an Essay on the Local History of Phrygia from the Earliest Times to the Turkish Conquest* (Oxford, The Clarendon Press, 2 vols., 1895, 1897). Based upon extensive archeological research.

AMBROSE

F. H. Dudden, *The Life and Times of St. Ambrose* (Oxford, The Clarendon Press, 2 vols., 1935).

CHRYSOSTOM

W. R. W. Stephens, *Saint Chrysostom, His Life and Times* (London, John Murray, 1872, pp. xiv, 474).

OUTSIDE THE EMPIRE

F. C. Burkitt, *Early Christianity Outside the Roman Empire* (Cambridge University Press, 1899, pp. 89).

F. C. Burkitt, *Early Eastern Christianity* (New York, E. P. Dutton & Co., 1904, pp. viii, 228). Popular lectures by an expert.

J. B. Bury, *The Life of St. Patrick and His Place in History* (London, Macmillan & Co., 1905, pp. xv, 404). The standard critical biography.

W. Germann, *Die Kirche der Thomaschristen* (Gütersloh, C. Bertelsmann, 1877, pp. x, 792). Scholarly, fairly critical.

J. Labourt, *Le Christianisme dans l'Empire Perse sous la Dynastie Perse* (Paris, Librairie Victor Lecoffre, pp. xix, 372). Standard.

Victor Langlois, *Collection des Historiens Anciens et Modernes de l'Armenie* (Paris, Librairie de Firmin Didot Frères, Fils et Cie, Vol. I, 1867, pp. xxxi, 421).

A. Mingana, *The Early Spread of Christianity in Central Asia and the Far East. A New Document* (Manchester University Press, 1925, pp. 80).

E. Sachau, *Zur Ausbreitung des Christentums in Asien (Abhandlungen der preus. Ak. der Wis. 1919 phil. hist. Klasse*, pp. 1–80). A scholarly summary.

C. A. Scott, *Ulfilas, Apostle to the Goths, together with an Account of the Gothic Churches and Their Decline* (Cambridge, Macmillan & Bowers, 1885, pp. xiv, 239). Excellent.

M. Tamarati, *L'Église Géorgienne des Origines jusqu'a nos Jours* (Rome, Imprimerie de la Société Typographico—Editrice Romaine, 1910, pp. xv, 710). Based upon extensive research.

W. A. Wigram, *An Introduction to the History of the Assyrian Church or the Church of the Sassanid Empire 100–640 A.D.* (London, Society for Promoting Christian Knowledge, 1910, pp. 318). By an English missionary to the Assyrians.

PERSECUTION

P. Allard, *Histoire des Persecutions pendant la Première Moitié du Troisième Siècle* (Paris, Librairie Victor Lecoffre, 1886, pp. xv, 524).

P. Allard, *Les Dernières Persécutions du Troisième Siècle (Gallus, Valérien, Aurélien) d'après les Documents Archéologiques* (Paris, Librairie Victor Lecoffre, 1887, pp. xvii, 411). Standard, by a Roman Catholic scholar.

L. H. Canfield, *The Early Persecutions of the Christians* (Columbia University Press, 1913, pp. 215). An excellent critical summary.

E. G. Hardy, *Christianity and the Roman Government. A Study in Imperial Administration* (London, George Allen & Unwin, 1905, reprint of 1894 ed., pp. xiii, 161). Carefully done with no extreme views.

K. J. Neumann, *Die römische Staat und die allgemeine Kirche bis auf Diocletian* (Leipzig, Veit und Co., 2 vols., 1890). Based upon the sources.

H. B. Workman, *Persecution in the Early Church* (Cincinnati, Jennings and Graham, 2d ed., preface 1906, pp. xx, 382). An excellent survey.

ATTITUDES AND ACTIONS OF THE EMPERORS

C. B. Bush, *Constantine the Great and Christianity* (Columbia University Press, 1914, pp. 258). Based upon extensive use of the sources.

The Life of Constantine by Eusebius . . . a revised translation by E. C. Richardson, in *Nicene and Post-Nicene Fathers of the Christian Church, Second Series*, Vol. I (New York, The Christian Literature Society, 1890).

E. J. Martin, *The Emperor Julian. An Essay on His Relations with the Christian Religion* (London, Society for Promoting Christian Knowledge, 1919, pp. 126). Objective, judicious.

W. C. Wright, *The Works of the Emperor Julian with an English translation* (London, William Heinemann, 3 vols., 1913–1923).

Chapter 6

CHRISTIANITY TAKES SHAPE IN ORGANIZATION AND DOCTRINE

Two of the most striking features of the history of Christianity in the first five hundred years of its existence were the development of visible organization and the intellectual formulation of belief. The two were so intimately interrelated that the course of their growth can best be treated together. By the time that the majority of the population of the Roman Empire had adopted the Christian name, the main features of the structure of the Christian community had appeared and the major verbal expressions of the Christian faith, including the Apostles' Creed and the Nicene Creed, which remained standard for the large majority of Christians from then onward, had been framed. While the faith was spreading and winning the population, the organization of the Church and the formulation of the intellectual statements of the faith were proceeding. Here were parallel, reciprocally interacting movements.

THE RETICENCE OF JESUS ON ORGANIZATION AND CREED

So far as our records enable us to determine, Jesus gave little thought to a continuing organization and did not put the heart of his teaching in any single verbal formula which was to be binding upon his followers. To be sure, the word "church" is twice in the sayings of his which were remembered. Yet this is in only one of the Gospels, that according to Matthew, and it is not so much as mentioned in the other three. The one of these two sayings on which greatest stress has since been placed is that in which after Peter's declaration that Jesus was "the Christ, the Son of the living God," Jesus is reported as saying: "Thou art Peter, and upon this rock I will build my church, and the gates of hell shall not prevail against it. And I will give unto thee the keys of the kingdom of heaven: and whatsoever thou shalt bind on earth shall be bound in heaven; and whatsoever thou shalt loose on earth shall be loosed in heaven." Whatever else this passage may mean, it does not so much as hint that there was to be a series of successors to whom Peter was to have authority to transmit the "power of the keys." In the final chapter of *The Gospel according to John* we have the command of Jesus to Peter to tend and feed his sheep, but there is no indication that he meant this exclusively for Peter or that he gave Peter the authority to transmit the responsibility to others.

In still another passage, also in *The Gospel according to John,* the risen Christ is recorded as saying to "the disciples," presumably although not explicitly the eleven who survived the betrayal and suicide of Judas: "As the Father hath sent me, even so I send you. . . . Receive ye the Holy Ghost: whosesoever sins ye remit, they are remitted unto them; and whosesoever sins ye retain, they are retained." Yet here again there is not the slightest suggestion that the disciples to whom these words were uttered were given the right to hand on that dread power to successors. Here was no clear word of an organization which was to continue across the centuries. To be sure, on the night of his betrayal Jesus prayed that his disciples might be one and that all those who were to believe in him through their word might be one, as the Father was in him and he in the Father. This certainly implied a close and continuing fellowship, but it did not specify what visible structure, if any, that fellowship was to take. In choosing precisely twelve disciples for his intimates Jesus seems to have had in mind a community not unlike that of Israel, with its twelve tribes, a divinely chosen people. For this, however, he outlined no detailed structure nor did he sketch even its general outlines.

Still less did Jesus put the gist of his teachings into a compact statement which was to be remembered and repeated as final. The one set of words which he is recorded as giving to his disciples is what has been traditionally called the Lord's Prayer. That is a prayer and not a creed, and even it was not phrased as something which was to be held to with slavish accuracy, but as a suggested outline—"after this manner . . . pray," not "using these precise words pray."

THE NEW TESTAMENT IDEAL OF THE CHURCH

After his death and resurrection a fellowship of the followers of Jesus came into being which was called the Church. Beliefs about it arose almost immediately and it took a variety of visible forms.

The ideal of the Church appears again and again in the early Christian documents which compose the New Testament and which reflect the convictions of leaders in the primitive Christian fellowship. To these leaders the Church was to be inclusive and one. They shared the purpose of Jesus which was transmitted through *The Gospel according to John* that all believers in him should be as united as were he and the Father. More than once, carrying out this same conception, Paul spoke of the Church as the body of Christ. Obviously, as he saw it, it was to be one, knit together, each member contributing to the whole. *The Epistle to the Ephesians* declares that Christ is the head of the Church and dreams of the Church as ultimately being without spot, wrinkle, or blemish. The Christian fellowship, so the New Testament held, was to be a new Israel, a chosen people, but it was to be drawn from all mankind. In Christ both Jews and Gentiles were to be members of "the household of God," growing into "an holy temple." Not only was the Church to embrace both Jews and Gentiles, but in it there was also to be no distinction on the basis of race, nation, cultural status, servitude, freedom, or sex. It was to be gathered from every nation, and from all tribes, peoples, and tongues.

THE CHURCH AS IT WAS

Actually, also as the writers of the New Testament clearly recognized, the Church was far from fully attaining this ideal. It was badly divided. On the very night of the prayer of Jesus for the unity of all Christians and only a few hours before that prayer was voiced, the disciples who were to be the nucleus of the Church were quarrelling over who of them should have precedence and one of them had gone out to complete his preparation for the betrayal of his Master. Even in the first generation of its existence the Church was torn by dissensions. In one local unit of the Church, in Corinth, there were factions between those who professed adherence respectively to Paul, Apollos, Peter, and Christ, and between rich and poor. As we are to see more particularly in a moment, the Church was deeply and bitterly divided between those who held that to become Christians Gentiles must adhere to Judaism through the symbolic act of circumcision and those who maintained, with Paul, that this was completely to misunderstand and pervert the Gospel. Before the first century of the Church was out, some were denying that Christ had come in the flesh, presumably foreshadowing movements, notably Gnosticism, which in the second century were to be major sources of division. Morally the Church was far from perfect. Some of those who wished to be regarded as Christians were adopting the attitude, technically called antinomianism, which was drawn from a misconception of man's response to God's grace and which was to recur again and again through the centuries, that the Christian need not be bound by any moral law. In at least one local congregation at the time of the common meal, some became drunk. We hear, too, of members of the Church being accused of fornication. In one congregation we have the spectacle, later to be almost chronic, of an outstanding member who was eager for power and control.

In this contrast between the ideal and the actual in the Church we have another example of the seeming paradoxes which are so familiar in the teachings of Jesus and in the New Testament in general. It is the setting up of perfection as the goal towards which Christians are to strive for themselves and for all men, paralleled by the frank recognition of the degree to which performance falls short of the goal.

THE ORGANIZATION OF THE EARLY CHURCH

The precise forms of the Christian community in the first century or so of its existence have been and remain a topic of debate. This is partly because in subsequent generations Christians sought in the organization of early Christianity the authority for the structure of their particular branch of the Church. It is also because the evidence is of such a fragmentary character that on many important issues it does not yield incontestable conclusions.

For the first two or three generations, the Christian community exhibited great variety. There was a consciousness, at least among some of the leaders, of the inclusive unity which, as we have seen, was the ideal set forth in the New Testament. Yet no central administration existed as the instrument for knitting together the many local units of the Church into a single articulated structure. The church in Jerusalem, as the initial centre of the Christian fellowship, endeavoured to exercise some measure of control, especially on the contested question of the degree to which Christians should conform to the Jewish law. To some extent it was heeded, perhaps after the pattern of the respect shown for the Jewish authorities in Jerusalem by the Jewish communities in various parts of the Gentile world, but it possessed no administrative machinery for extensive oversight. Its authority was more that of prestige than of precise canon law. Under these conditions, no comprehensive or uniform pattern of church practice and government existed.

Before the first century of its existence was out, the Church began to display certain organizational features which, developed, have persisted, with modifications, into the twentieth century. We hear of offices and officials. Prominent among them were deacons (from the Greek διάκονος meaning a servant or minister), elders (the English translation of the Greek πρεσβύτερος, from which the word presbyter is derived, and from which, in turn, comes the word priest), and bishops (from the Greek ἐπίσκοπος, with something of the meaning of overseer or superintendent).

It was early maintained that the precedent for the deacons was to be found in the seven who are described as having been appointed by the Twelve Apostles in the early days of the Jerusalem church to take charge of the daily distribution to the widows from the common store. While the historic continuity between the seven and the later diaconate has by no means been fully demonstrated, and in the New Testament we never have clear mention of deacons in the church in Jerusalem, it is indisputable that within a generation or two in some of the local units, or churches, deacons were regarded as characteristic officers, and it may have been that women as well as men served in that capacity.

The office of presbyter, or elder, may have been suggested by the organization of the synagogue, where elders were a regular part of the structure. In at least several of the local churches there was more than one bishop and the evidence seems to support the view that at the outset in some and perhaps all of the churches the designations of "elder" and "bishop" were used interchangeably for the same office.

Uniformity of structure was far from coming into being at once. In the earliest mention of what appear to be officers or leaders in the great Gentile church in Antioch, we hear of prophets and teachers, but not of deacons, elders, or bishops. In one of his letters to the church in Corinth, where he appears to be naming the offices in the church, Paul says nothing expressly of deacons, elders, or bishops, although some of his words can be so interpreted, but he speaks of apostles, prophets, and teachers. In his *Letter to the Romans* prophets, ministers, teachers, exhorters, givers (perhaps deacons), and rulers are named as what appears to be the order with which Paul is familiar. In another letter the list is apostles, prophets, evangelists, pastors, and teachers. In the first generation of the church in Jerusalem, James the brother of Jesus was regarded as its head, but not until later was the title of bishop attached to him. It is also clear that the church in Jerusalem had elders. It is likewise obvious that Paul exercised jurisdiction over the churches which he had founded. Whoever the author may be of the letters which bear the traditional designation of the first and second epistles of John, and this is much in dispute, he calls himself "the elder" and as such writes with acknowledged authority. He also speaks of a certain Diotrephes as loving preëminence in a church and refusing to recognize the power of the author.

In the fore part of the second century the picture began to change. While no single form of structure as yet prevailed, we now hear indisputably of what soon came to be the accepted pattern, a bishop governing a particular church and of at least one bishop, that of the church in Antioch, acting as though it were his acknowledged right to address himself with authority to other churches. In the first quarter of the second century Ignatius, bishop of the church in Antioch, while on a journey to Rome under guard for martyrdom, wrote letters to several churches, most of them in Asia Minor. In these is seen something of the organization of the churches and of the conception which Ignatius had of it. It is clear that in several of the churches which he addressed there was a single bishop. Presumably, although not certainly, there was only one bishop in a city. Ignatius enjoined obedience to the bishop. He spoke of presbyters and deacons as though they were the recognized officers in the church and commanded that they also be heeded. He declared that the bishop is representative of God the Father and that the presbyters are the sanhedrin of God, the assembly of the apostles. Nothing was to be done without the bishop and the Eucharist was to be administered either by the bishop or by some one to whom he had entrusted that function. Ignatius held that it was not lawful to baptize or to celebrate a love-feast without the bishop. He declared that he who honours the bishop shall be honoured by God. Ignatius writes as though the bishop, the presbyters, and the deacons had come to be essential to the existence of a church. Presumably that was true of such churches as he knew. These, naturally, were in Asia Minor and Syria. In his *Letter to the Romans* he does not mention any of these officers, but his silence does not necessarily argue that the church in Rome did not have them. The emphatic fashion in which he stressed these officers and respect for them may be evidence that the position which he advocated for them had not yet won general acceptance.

A letter from the church in Rome to the church in Corinth with which the name of Clement is associated and which may date from late in the first century and be earlier than the letters of Ignatius declares that Christ was sent forth by God, the apostles were sent by Christ, and the apostles, preaching through countries and cities, "appointed their first fruits . . . to be bishops and deacons of those who should afterwards believe." The letter also says that the apostles gave instructions that when these bishops and deacons appointed by them should "fall asleep, other approved men should succeed them in their ministry." The letter indicates that the bishops were appointed by the apostles "or afterwards by other eminent men, with the consent of the whole Church." It seems to imply that bishops were presbyters and that the church in Corinth had more than one of them. If this is true, the church in Corinth did not have the oversight of a single bishop as did the churches with which Ignatius was familiar. It may be that Clement himself, although the leader of the church in Rome, was only the chief of a group of presbyters in that city. In later lists he is given as one of the bishops of Rome in succession to Peter, but this may be reading back into the first century the institution as it existed before the close of the second century.

Another early Christian document, the *Didache ton Dodeka Apostolon,* or *Teaching of the Twelve Apostles,* describes a church organization which knew of travelling apostles and prophets and of resident prophets and teachers. It instructs the Christians to appoint for themselves bishops and deacons and to hold them in honour, along with the prophets and teachers. There were several bishops, not one, and no presbyters. It has been suggested that here was a transition from an earlier structure of the churches to the later one, either in communities apart from the main centres where old customs lingered, or perhaps mirroring the change in some of the larger urban churches.

In any event, the latter part of the first century and the fore part of the second century still saw variety in the forms of organization of the churches.

THE CHURCH OF ROME

Well before the end of the second century the Church of Rome was occupying an outstanding place in the total Christian fellowship. This was to be expected. Being in the capital and chief city of the Empire, if it were at all strong it would naturally be regarded with deference by a religious community which was found principally within that Empire. As we have seen, it appears to have been vigorous before Paul reached it. So important did Paul deem it that he felt it advisable when he had been hoping to come as a free man and not a prisoner to precede his visit by the most carefully thought out and deliberately written letter which we have from him. In addressing the Church of Rome, he declared that the news of its faith was already being "spoken of throughout the whole world." Presumably, since "all roads led to Rome," and the city was extraordinarily cosmopolitan and attracted representatives of most if not all of the many regions and races of the Empire, the Church of Rome would, through its members, have ties with many different portions of the realm. For several generations its language was Greek, the most generally used of the tongues of the Empire, and this would further its widely extended contacts. Although not founded by either, the Church of Rome enjoyed the prestige of the presence of both Peter and Paul, and what appears to be dependable information declares that Rome was the scene of the martyrdom both of the outstanding member of the original Twelve Apostles and of the chief missionary of the early Church. The epistle of Clement which we have already mentioned was written partly to ease a difficult situation in one of Paul's churches, that in the great commercial city of Corinth. It is evidence that the Church of Rome felt a responsibility for the peace of this sister church and that it believed that an expression of its concern would not be regarded at Corinth as an impertinence. It may well have been that it thought of itself as being under similar obligation to other churches. Certainly in the third quarter of the second century Irenæus, Bishop of Lyons, in Gaul, and who, coming from Asia, would not be biased by Roman origin, declared that "it is a matter of necessity that every church should agree with this church [i.e., of Rome] on account of its preëminent authority." This does not mean that the Church of Rome had the wide supervisory and directive functions which it later claimed and exercised through its bishops. However, the foundations for that eventual supremacy go back to the first century.

IDEAL UNITY AND ACTUAL DIVISION: THE CONTINUING PROBLEM

As we have suggested, Christianity early displayed one of the most striking features of its history, the contrast between the dream of complete unity, the unity of the kind of self-giving love seen in Christ, and division. No other religion has so high an ideal of an inclusive community of love. Yet, as we are to see again and again in the course of our story, no other religion has had as many divisions and as many bitter controversies between its adherents.

This contrast between dream and actuality was probably inevitable. It arose from the very essence of the Christian Gospel and was witness to the accuracy of the Christian insight into the nature of man and God's purpose. As the Christian faith sees it, man owes his nature to God's purpose and God's creative act, and God's purpose is to create man in his own image. If, as the Christian Gospel declares, God is love, the kind of love which is revealed in Jesus Christ and which is utterly self-giving, the Christian ideal must be the full realization of this love in individuals. Since to find its full expression this love must be both towards God and among individuals in their inter-relations, this love will give rise to a collective life of mankind which, if God's purpose is completely carried out, will be wholly controlled by love, love which arises from response to God's love. This is what is meant by the model prayer given by Jesus to his disciples: "Our Father which art in heaven, hallowed be Thy name. Thy kingdom come, Thy will be done on earth as it is in heaven." It is clearly implied in the commission to make disciples of all the nations, teaching them to observe all that Jesus commanded the inner group of his disciples. That love should be expressed first of all in the redeemed worshipping community of the disciples, and that community of faith and love is to seek to win the world. This is but a paraphrase of the well-known words of the Gospel that all who believe in Christ "may be one, even as thou, Father, art in me, and I in thee, that they also may be one in us: that the world may believe that thou hast sent me." This ideal has haunted the Church from the beginning.

The Gospel also frankly faces the sombre reality of man's sin, of the perversion of the free will with which God has endowed man, with its rebellion against God, its seeking to usurp the place of God, its self-centredness, and its basic corruption of man's nature. That sin, provoked by the unmerited love of God in Christ, is seen most dramatically and tragically in nailing Jesus Christ to the cross. By God's act in Christ, so the Gospel goes on to declare, his incarnation, his cross, and his resurrection, God has wrought the redemption of men and through His Holy Spirit is beginning to display its working in transformed lives gathered into a new community. But the individuals who compose that community are, as Paul so clearly saw, only in process of "being saved." They and the community which is the Church have not yet been entirely freed from sin, nor have they fully attained to the "high calling of God in Christ Jesus." The Church, as discerning Christians have long said, is still *in via* and not yet *in patria:* it is on the road, but has not yet reached its true home and goal and, presumably, will not do so within history, until that final culmination of history which is also the culmination of both God's judgement and His redeeming love.

Because of the compelling attraction of the ideal, compelling because it appeals to the nature with which man has been endowed by God, Christians are always lured by the dream of the complete unity of the Church and of its effective witness to mankind. By various roads they have endeavoured to attain it—usually by seeking to devise one organizational structure which will embrace all Christians, by verbal statements which will accurately and briefly put into words the Christian Gospel and to which all Christians will be induced to agree, by disciplinary measures to constrain all Christians to full conformity with the conduct to which the Gospel calls men, or by one form of worship. Yet so hampered have Christians been by the sin from which they have been only partially freed that each of these efforts has given rise to fresh divisions. The Lord's Supper, or Eucharist, which with its "table of the Lord" should be a symbol and bond of unity, by the very act of being made such a symbol has also become a symbol of division.

THE CONFLICT OVER THE RELATION TO JUDAISM

It was natural that the first major conflict within the Church should be over the issue of whether Christianity should remain within Judaism as one of the many sects of that faith, or whether its genius demanded that it become an independent and distinct religion. If Christianity were simply a variant of Judaism, Gentile converts to it should submit themselves to circumcision as an accepted initiatory step for admission to the Jewish community and as essential to sharing in the special covenant which Jews believed had been made between God and their progenitor. They should also observe all aspects of the Jewish law, including the Sabbath and the distinctions between clean and unclean foods. This was the conviction, held in moderation by their leaders but more extremely by others, of the majority of the Christian community which remained in Jerusalem after the persecution which began with the stoning of Stephen. On the other hand, an increasing number of Christians, of whom Paul was the outstanding spokesman, maintained that to insist that disciples of

Christ become members of the Jewish community and submit themselves to the Jewish law was utterly to fail to grasp the essence of the Gospel. They declared that in Christ and the Gospel God had done something quite new, foretold, to be sure, in the Jewish scriptures, but a fresh and unique act. They said that men were to enter into the fullness of life, not by earning it through the observance of God's commands as expressed in the Jewish law, but by faith in the love and forgiveness of God as seen in the death and the resurrection of Jesus. That faith would issue in gratitude and love towards God, and God's commands would be obeyed out of love and with no thought of winning a reward from Him. Many Christians in practice took positions between these two extremes.

Attempts were made to reach an agreement and maintain unity. Paul and his companion missionary, Barnabas, journeyed to Jerusalem to consult with the leaders of the Christians in that city, for that church, as the mother body, had, as we have seen, a degree of prestige. A compromise was reached which yielded most of what Paul had stood for. It did not demand circumcision.

The overwhelming majority of Christians took a view which claimed loyalty to Paul but which in practice had legalistic features and held to some aspects of Judaism. Indeed, for many of its adherents Christianity seemed to be primarily obedience to a moral code, a code which embraced some of the Jewish law, but which went beyond it and was, therefore, higher. Such, for instance, was the implication of *The Epistle of James* in the New Testament, of the *Didache,* and of other writings of the first generations of Christians.

Waning minorities, probably overwhelmingly Jewish in ancestry, clung to one or another variation of the conviction that disciples of Jesus should remain within the Jewish fold. The church in Jerusalem, headed by James the brother of Jesus, tended to do so. Indeed, early tradition declares him to have been highly regarded by the Jews. But he is said to have suffered martyrdom at the hands of the Jews in the year 62 and to have been succeeded in the leadership of the church at Jerusalem by another blood relation of Jesus. The church moved to Pella, a Gentile city east of the Jordan, and there survived for a time. Some of the Jewish Christians, referred to by one or more early Christian writers as Nazarenes, held that Jesus was the Messiah, the Son of God, and that his teachings are superior to those of Moses and the prophets, but that Christians of Jewish descent should observe the Jewish laws of circumcision, Sabbath observance, and foods. Others, called the Ebionites, maintained that Jesus was merely a man, a prophet, a spokesman for God, as were the great Hebrew prophets of the past. Although some of them accepted the virgin birth of Jesus, others are said to have taught that Jesus was the son of Joseph and Mary, that at his baptism Christ descended upon him in the form of a dove, that he then proclaimed the unknown Father, but that Christ, who could not suffer, departed from him before his crucifixion and resurrection. The Ebionites repudiated Paul, declaring him to be an apostate from the law. They used a Hebrew gospel of Matthew. There were several kinds of them. Some of these may have been continuations of pre-Christian varieties of Judaism. They persisted, as small minorities, until at least the latter part of the fourth century and perhaps much longer.

The waning and disappearance of the groups of Christians who sought to remain within Judaism made it clear that the radical newness of the Gospel was not to be obscured by reducing Christianity to a Jewish sect. Christianity was now unmistakably a separate religion, having rootage in Judaism and honouring the Jewish scriptures, but interpreting them as preparing for the basic and revolutionary novelty of Jesus and the Gospel.

The Greek Menace

Scarcely had the course of events made it clear that Christianity was not to lose its distinctive message by absorption into the parent Judaism when the faith was confronted with an even greater menace. As it moved out into the non-Jewish world it was in danger of so far conforming to that environment that it would sacrifice the essential features of the Gospel. The threat was especially acute from Hellenism and the atmosphere of the Hellenistic world, for, as we have seen, it was in the portions of the population of the Empire where Hellenistic influences were especially strong that Christianity had its first major spread.

The danger was not conformity to polytheism, for against that Christians were quite adamant. It was more subtle and therefore more to be feared. It was the incorporation of some of the attitudes of the Hellenistic mind. One of these was the confidence in philosophy as the way to truth, or, in a less thorough-going conformity, the attempt to think through and present the Gospel in the categories of Greek philosophy. In the process the Gospel might be distorted or obscured. Another was the sharp disjunction between spirit and matter which was a basic assumption in much of Hellenism. This seemed to have come into Greek thought through the Orphic movement centuries before Christ. It was perpetuated through Platonism and Neoplatonism. By its presence in that cultural tradition, it had so moulded the thinking and the attitude of Christian converts from a Hellenistic background that it often came over with them. Through them and the continued study of Platonism and Neoplatonism it has persisted in the thought, practice, and worship of a large proportion of Christians.

In contrast with much of the Jewish tradition and, especially of Jesus himself, this attitude regarded matter, including flesh, as evil, and pure spirit as good. It conceived of man as a compound of flesh and spirit. To it, therefore, the goal of every man's striving must be salvation by the emancipation of the spirit from the contamination of the flesh. Here was a way of accounting for the presence of evil, that perennial problem for thoughtful and sensitive souls, which made a great appeal and had sufficient resemblance to the issue presented by the incarnation and the cross to attract many Christians. Again and again we shall find it as a recurring theme in the asceticism, thought, and mysticism of those who have borne the Christian name, among them some of the most devoted Christians, men and women who have been esteemed ideal exemplars of the Christian faith.

THE GNOSTIC THREAT

A somewhat related threat, Gnosticism, had wide vogue in the first few centuries of Christianity. Foreshadowings of it are recorded in the first century and in the second century it attained major proportions. As we saw earlier, Gnosticism was not a phenomenon which was to be found only in the guise of Christianity, but was widely prevalent in the Mediterranean world into which Christianity was ushered. This pagan Gnosticism was protean, taking many forms and drawing from a wide variety of sources. Into one or another of its varieties entered contributions from Orphic and Platonic dualism, other schools of Greek thought, Syrian conceptions, Persian dualism, the mystery cults, Mesopotamian astrology, and Egyptian religion. It was highly syncretistic. When combined with certain elements from Christianity, Gnosticism proved so attractive that, while no accurate figures are obtainable, the suggestion has been made that for a time the majority of those who regarded themselves as Christians adhered to one or another of its many forms.

The Gnosticism which essayed to knit Christ into its speculations included many different systems. Indeed, it is evidence of the power inherent in the Gospel and the excitement produced by it that it stimulated the formation of these multitudinous expressions.

Among the names that have come down to us as prominent in the creation of Gnosticism is Simon Magus, of whom we hear in *The Acts of the Apostles* as a magician in Samaria who professed conversion and was denounced by Peter for his attempt to buy the power to confer the Holy Spirit. Tradition, possibly authentic, declares that he was the father of several aberrant variants of Christianity. We also hear much, among others, of Basilides of Alexandria and of Valentinus, an Alexandrian who attained fame as a teacher in Rome and who had many disciples. Some of the Gnostics seem to have been men of better than average intellect and of deep religious feeling. We read of such schools as the Naassenes, who worshipped the serpent as the principle of generation, and their sub-groups, the Sethians and the Perates, the latter esteeming the serpent as midway between the Father and unformed matter.

In general the Gnostics believed in a *Gnosis,* which was not a philosophy which issued from man's striving, but a knowledge that had been revealed and was transmitted to those who were initiated into it. It had the fascination which for so many inheres in a secret disclosed to the privileged few. It professed to be universal, incorporating whatever of truth had been disclosed in any of the faiths to which mankind gave allegiance. It regarded pure spirit as good, but thought of that spirit as having become imprisoned in corrupt matter. Salvation was the freeing of spirit from matter. This salvation was to be attained by the teaching of revealed truth which was presented in the form of mysteries and which by stages was to emancipate the possessor and bring him back to the realm of pure spirit. Justification for the Gnostic beliefs was sought in the Christian and Jewish writings, allegorically interpreted, and in supposed teachings of Jesus which had not been committed to writing, but which had been handed down secretly through oral tradition.

To the modern mind the systems of which these were general characteristics seem complicated and even bizarre. In general they held that there exists a first Principle, the all-Father, unknowable, who is love, and who alone can generate other beings. Since love abhors dwelling alone, this first Principle brought into existence other beings, æons, which together with the first Principle constitute the Pleroma, "Fullness," true Reality. From this world of the spirit the present world appeared. According to one system this was through the work of one of the æons who, moved by pride, wished to do what the all-Father had done, and create something on her own. The present world was ascribed to a subordinate being, the Demiurge, who was identified with the God of the Old Testament. This present world, the world of matter, so this view held, has in it some traces of the spirit world. Men belong to this present world, and are compounded of spirit and matter, soul and flesh. Some have more of spirit than do others. Salvation, the freeing of spirit from the contamination of matter, is through Christ the redeemer. Many different accounts, conceptions, and interpretations were given of Christ. Some held that Christ was never associated with flesh, but that he merely seemed to be man and was really pure spirit. Another system conceived Christ as an æon. This view separated Christ from Jesus, but held the latter also to have been an æon in whom something of all the other æons was included. It also taught that another Jesus, sent to be the saviour of men, was born of the Virgin Mary. Not all men are saved, so the Gnostics went on to say, for many have little or nothing of spirit in them and in due time they will be destroyed. Others, having a portion of spirit in them, will be saved by being taught the hidden knowledge, or *Gnosis,* and through faith and works. They will be freed from the contamination of the flesh and mount to the Pleroma.

The Gnostics had no well knit, inclusive organization. They were too divided and too varied to be brought together. Some remained within the existing churches, teaching their doctrines, until they were cast out as heretics. Others formed themselves into separate congregations. These had special rites, distinct from those of the churches which did not hold their views, and some resembled the mystery cults which were widespread in the contemporary Roman Empire. Several were strictly ascetic in their morals. Others, claiming that, being predominantly spiritual by nature, they could not be corrupted, felt free to go to pagan festivals and to gladiatorial contests, and even to have irregular unions with women who had accepted their doctrines. Such at least were the accusations of their critics.

Obviously Gnosticism tended to minimize the historical element in Christianity and to divorce the faith from the life, acts, teaching, death, and resurrection of Jesus of Nazareth. It was a group of attempts at a universal religion which would take advantage of contributions from many sources, but which would hold as a basic assumption a sharp distinction between spirit and matter and would give to Christ a central place in achieving man's salvation. It was an effort, perhaps not consciously recognized as such, to acclimatize Christianity in a popular religious trend of the day and to show it to be consistent with it and a fulfilment of it. In doing so, by omission and interpretation it so badly distorted Jesus as to make him quite different from the Jesus recorded in the Gospels. Had Christianity come to be identified with Gnosticism, presumably it would have disappeared as the contemporary beliefs of non-Christian origin which were the outstanding features of Gnosticism ceased to have currency.

Marcion and the Marcionites

A movement sometimes classified, probably mistakenly, with Gnosticism, and even in starker contrast than the latter with Judaism, was that begun by Marcion. Marcion is said to have been a native of Sinope, a seaport in Pontus, on the south coast of the Black Sea, the country of the famous Cynic, Diogenes. He is reported to have been the son of a bishop and thus to have been reared a Christian. He came to Rome, a man of considerable wealth, about the year 138 or 139. He joined himself to the church in that city and made it a generous gift. He began teaching the distinctive views which brought him fame and attracted a large following in the church. However, he failed to win the majority and after a few years, probably about 144, he was cut off from the church's communion. Yet he carried with him a number of members and formed them into a separate church.

Marcion is reported to have been influenced by one of the Gnostics and Gnostic conceptions can be found in him, but much in his teachings was quite distinct from Gnosticism. To be sure, with the Gnostics he was a sharp dualist, but he drew the dualistic line in somewhat different fashion from them and his explanation of dualism was quite at variance from theirs. Unlike them he did not profess to possess a secret body of knowledge. Like them, and, indeed, like the Christian churches as a whole, he was deeply concerned with the salvation of men. This, however, he conceived to be not, as did the Gnostics, through initiation into a mystery, but by simple faith in what he believed to be the Gospel. He held that the Gospel had been lamentably distorted by the Church as he knew it, and he sought to recall the latter to what he was profoundly convinced was the simplicity and truth of the Good News.

Marcion insisted that the Church had obscured the Gospel by seeking to combine it with Judaism. He maintained that the God of the Old Testament and of the Jews is an evil God. Recalling the words of Jesus that a good tree cannot bring forth evil fruit, he argued that a world which contains the suffering and cruelty which we see all about us must be the work of some evil being and not of a good God. This God, whom he called by the Platonic term *Demiurgos,* a word also employed by the Gnostics, had created the world, with its revolting evils. This Demiurge, Marcion held, also created men, both their souls and their bodies. Marcion thus differed from the Gnostics in putting man's spirit as well as his body in the realm of evil. Yet, in a self-contradiction, perhaps as a result of his contacts with the Gnostics, he saw an antithesis between spirit and flesh. He also noted that the God of the Old Testament commanded bloody sacrifices to him, and, a God of battles, rejoiced in bloodshed and was vindictive. He taught that this God had given a stern and inflexible law for the governance of men, demanded obedience to it, was rigorous in his enforcement of it, and was arbitrary in his choice of favourites. "Good men," he held, were those who yielded obedience to the law of the Demiurge, but they, too, were the creation of that evil God. Marcion refused to evade the difficulties presented in the Jewish scriptures by the easy and popular device of regarding their text as allegory: he took them at their face value.

Marcion held that in contrast with the God of the Jews there is a second God, hidden until he revealed himself in Christ. This God is a God of love. Out of the pure mercy which is an essential part of his love, seeing the sad plight of men, he undertook to rescue them, beings for whom he had no responsibility, since they were not his, but were creatures of that other God, the Demiurge. This God of love, hitherto unknown to men, and perhaps even to the Demiurge, disclosed himself in Christ. Christ, so he taught, owed nothing to the Demiurge, and therefore was not born as men, the creatures of the Demiurge, are born, and only seemed to have a body. This view, technically dubbed docetism, from a Greek word meaning "to appear," that Christ was only a phantom who seemed to be a man, was, as we have noted, also found among the Gnostics. Nor was it limited to Marcion and the Gnostics, for it was a belief which was congenial to those who regarded flesh as evil and spirit as good and believed that the Redeemer, to be effective, must have nothing of the taint of the flesh about him.

Christ, so Marcion contended, came down from heaven and began teaching, proclaiming a new kingdom and deliverance from the rule of the malevolent Demiurge. However, those who were loyal to the Demiurge crucified Christ, thus unwittingly contributing to the defeat of the former, since the death of Christ was the price by which the God of love purchased men from the Demiurge and enabled them to escape from the latter's kingdom into his own. Christ also rescued from the under-world those who had previously died and who in their life-time had not been obedient to the Demiurge and thus from the standpoint of his law were wicked. All that the good God asks of men if they are to escape from the rule of the Demiurge is faith in response to his love. Men have been emancipated from the legalistic requirements of the Demiurge and of his creature, Judaism.

Marcion believed that Paul had understood this Gospel. In Paul he saw the sharp disjunction between law and grace, the grace which is the unmerited favour of God, which Marcion was passionately convinced was of the essence of the Gospel. He declared that the church of his day had obscured the Good News and he regarded himself as commissioned to proclaim the truth in its uncontaminated purity. To this end he made a collection of the letters of Paul, expurgating from them what he held to be the corrupting additions of later hands. He added to these *The Gospel according to Luke,* editing it in such fashion as to free it from what he viewed as accretions inconsistent with the Gospel. Here was an attempt to recall the Church to the primitive Gospel by summoning it to a restudy of the original sources. Marcion seems to have been the first to bring together an authoritative collection of the earliest documents of Christianity.

Marcion was also an organizer. He gathered his followers into churches. To the members of these churches all sexual union was forbidden. Husbands and wives were required to separate and chastity and celibacy were enjoined. Martyrdom was prized. Eloquent witness is borne to the compelling appeal of

Marcion and his teachings by the fact that the latter enjoyed a wide spread and persisted for centuries. Marcionite churches were especially numerous in the eastern part of the Empire. Although, because of the requirements of celibacy, they could be continued only by fresh conversions and not by heredity, they were to be found at least as late as the fifth century. Some of the Marcionites may have been absorbed into Manichæism and have contributed to the emphasis which in the West that religion gave to Christ.

THE MONTANIST MOVEMENT

A movement quite distinct from both the Gnostics and the Marcionites, but which had wide vogue in the latter part of the second century and persisted for more than two centuries and which brought division in the Church, took its name from Montanus, of Phrygia, in Asia Minor, who flourished in the second half of the second century. Because of the region of their origin, the Montanists were often referred to as Phrygians. They represented a revival of the prophets who were prominent in the first few decades of the Church, a call to Christians to stricter living, and a vivid belief in the early end of the world, in the second coming of Christ, and in the establishment of the ideal society in the New Jerusalem.

At his baptism Montanus "spoke with tongues" and began prophesying, declaring that the Paraclete, the Holy Spirit, promised in *The Gospel according to John,* was finding utterance through him. Two women, his disciples, were also believed to be prophets, mouthpieces of the Holy Spirit. The three taught that the Spirit had revealed to them the early end of the world, and that the New Jerusalem would "come down out of heaven from God," as had been foretold in *The Revelation of John,* and that it would be fixed in Phrygia.

The belief in the early second coming of Christ was not new nor was it exclusively a tenet of the Montanists. Ground for it was found in more than one of the Gospels and New Testament epistles and in *The Revelation of John.* Many held to the view that before the final end of history and the full accomplishment of God's purpose in the perfect doing of His will, a hope which was common to all Christians, Christ would return, set up his kingdom on earth and reign for a thousand years. The centre of this kingdom was often placed at Jerusalem. The return of Christ was associated with the resurrection and the last judgement. The conception of an age or ages of a thousand years' duration was not confined to Christians, but was also to be found in Judaism. Nor did all Christians who held the view agree upon the order of the events connected with the thousand year reign of Christ. The expectations associated with the millennial reign of Christ are technically known as chiliasm.

Not far from the time of Montanus at least two bishops, one in Pontus and one in Syria, were expecting the early return of Christ. The one declared that the last judgement would come in two years and those who believed him ceased to cultivate their fields and rid themselves of houses and goods. The other led his flock into the wilderness to meet Christ. Since the return of Christ and the last judgement were regarded as being so imminent, believers were urged to be strict in their living. Celibacy was encouraged, fasting was enjoined, and martyrdom was held in high honour.

The Montanist movement spread widely. It was especially popular in Asia Minor and persisted there and in Carthage into the fifth century. It was found in other sections of the Mediterranean world, including Rome, Gaul, and North Africa. It had itinerant preachers supported by the gifts of the faithful, and in time seems to have been fairly well organized, with a head living in Phrygia. It prized the records of the teachings of Christ and his apostles, but it believed, although not contradicting what had been said there, that the Holy Spirit continued to speak through prophets, and among these it included women. It stressed a high standard of Christian living among Christian communities into which laxity was beginning to creep.

The most eminent convert to Montanism was Tertullian. Born in Carthage not far from the middle of the second century, of wealthy pagan parents, he was widely read in philosophy and history, knew Greek well, and practised law in Rome. In early middle life he was converted and became a presbyter. Much of the remainder of his life he spent in his native city. There he wrote voluminously and was the first to employ Latin extensively on Christian subjects. Possibly because of the cast which his legal training had given to his mind, Tertullian's literary style was systematic, precise, and vigorously polemical. Pronouncedly orthodox, he composed an extensive treatise against Marcion. Early in the third century, in late middle life, he became a Montanist and remained critical of the majority church until his death, towards the close of the first quarter of the century.

The Development and Clarification of Catholic Organization and Doctrine by Competition

The popularity of Gnosticism, the teaching of Marcion, and the Montanist movement forced others who regarded themselves as Christians to develop a tighter organization and to give added attention to the clarification and formulation of their beliefs. At the outset, in the middle of the first century or earlier, all that was required for admission to the Christian fellowship represented by the Church was repentance, the affirmation that Jesus is Lord, baptism, and the reception of the Holy Spirit. The wide variety which was appearing in bodies which claimed the Christian name, especially the Gnostics and the Marcionites, seemed to call for a more detailed definition of the Gospel and additional tests for admission to the Church and continued membership in it. Thus came notable steps in the development of what was early called the Catholic Church and which soon, if it did not already do so, embraced the majority of those who thought themselves to be Christians.

The word Catholic as applied to the Church only gradually came into circulation. The earliest known use of the term is in the letter of Ignatius to the church in Smyrna. In this he declared that "wherever Jesus Christ is, there is the Catholic Church." We next find the term in a letter from the church in Smyrna written about the year 155, describing the martyrdom of Polycarp. There it is employed at least three times, twice where it might be taken to mean simply "universal," but once where it clearly has the connotation of orthodox. By the end of the second century the word Catholic was increasingly applied to the Church and in a technical manner, meaning both universal and orthodox. In the latter sense it was intended to distinguish the body which was regarded by its leaders as orthodox as against bodies and individuals which were thought of as heretics, in other words, professed Christians who were deviating from true Christianity.

In the development of the Catholic Church three motives were present. One was the desire to unite all Christians in conscious fellowship. A second was to preserve, transmit, and spread the Christian Gospel in its purity, that men may enter into the fullness of the life which it reveals and makes possible. The third was to bring all Christians together into a visible "body of Christ." In practice the three proved to be reciprocally contradictory, for in the process of defining the faith and of developing an organization bitternesses arose which were a palpable contradiction of the love which is the chief evidence of Christian unity. Those who regarded themselves as Christians separated into organizations which denounced one another and as an indication of their disagreement excommunicated, that is, refused to admit to the rite instituted by their professed Lord, those from whom they differed. They endeavoured to make of the Lord's Supper, the Eucharist, the memorial of Christ's sacrificial death, a sign and bond of unity, but by that very effort they rendered it an outstanding evidence of their divisions.

The claims of the Gnostics, the Marcionites, and the Montanists compelled those Christians who did not agree with them to seek to determine and make unmistakably clear what the Gospel is. To do this they sought, naturally, to go back to Christ himself. To determine what Christ had been, taught, and did they attempted, also quite understandably, to discover what had been said by the most intimate friends of Christ, the apostles, those who were believed to have been commissioned by him to perpetuate and spread his teachings.

They endeavoured to do this in three ways: (1) by ascertaining lines of bishops who were in direct and uninterrupted succession from the apostles and could therefore be assumed to be transmitters of the apostolic teachings, (2) by determining which writings were by the apostles or clearly contained their teachings and bringing them together in a fixed and authoritative collection, and (3) by formulating as clearly and briefly as possible the teachings of the apostles so that Christians, even the ordinary unlettered ones among them, might know what the Christian faith is, especially on the points in which the Catholic Church differed from Gnostics and Marcionites. Thus an impulse was given to what from that time to the present have been distinguishing marks of the churches in which the majority of those who profess and call themselves Christians have had membership—the apostolic succession of the episcopate, the New Testament, and the Apostles' Creed. These three features of the Catholic Church were by no means entirely due to the effort to ascertain what the true faith is: they were already present in embryo. However, their development was assisted and their form in part determined by the struggle to ensure that the Gospel should be preserved and transmitted in its pristine integrity.

APOSTOLIC SUCCESSION

In the fourth quarter of the second century, we have the case for the apostolic succession stated forcefully and clearly by Irenæus. A native of either Syria or Asia Minor, Irenæus had in his youth seen Polycarp, Bishop of Smyrna. Polycarp, he informs us, had been instructed by the apostles and had talked with many who had seen Christ. Coming to Gaul, Irenæus in time became Bishop of Lyons. Distressed by what he regarded as the errors and corruptions of the Gospel which he knew in Gaul and by the headway which he found on a visit to Rome was being made by them, he wrote an extensive treatise "against heresies," describing them and refuting them by setting forth what he believed to be the true faith. He insisted that the apostles had transmitted faithfully and accurately what had been taught them by Christ and had not, as the heretics asserted, intermingled with them extraneous ideas. He was emphatic that the apostles had appointed as successors bishops to whom they had committed the churches and in doing so had undoubtedly passed on to them what had been entrusted to the apostolic company by Christ. These bishops had been followed by others in unbroken line who were also guardians and guarantors of the apostolic teaching. He hints that he could, if there were space, give the lists of the bishops of all the churches, but he singles out that of the Church of Rome, which he holds to have been founded and organized by Peter and Paul. Peter and Paul, so he says, appointed Linus. Linus in turn, so Irenæus declared, was followed by others in unbroken line to the twelfth in the succession who was bishop when the book was being composed.

Writing in the first quarter of the fourth century, Eusebius, the most famous of the early historians of the Church, gave the lists of the bishops of several of the churches. We need not stop to enquire whether these were accurate. That they existed is evidence of the conviction which lay back of their compilation and preservation, that a succession of bishops from the apostles was assurance that the Gospel had been conserved and handed down and that it was one of the marks of the Catholic Church.

Bishops began coming together for consultation and common action. The first of these gatherings, or synods, of which we have record, although we are not entirely clear that it was made up of bishops or only of bishops, was held in Asia Minor to deal with Montanism. That movement was condemned as heretical and its adherents were expelled from the Church and debarred from the communion.

In its response to all three of these movements which it deemed heretical— Gnosticism, Marcionism, and Montanism—the Catholic Church quickened a process which was already in progress, the development of an administrative system which centred about its bishops. Gone were the days when in at least some churches presbyter and bishop were interchangeable terms and when there might be several bishops in a church, or, perhaps, a church without a bishop. Now bishops were becoming a characteristic feature of the Catholic Church, with a single bishop in a given city or area. If a city had more than one bishop, others beyond the one would be assistants.

The bishop was more than administrator. He also was in charge of the worship and supervised the entire life of the church within his territorial jurisdiction. As Christians increased the number of bishops grew. In some areas, notably in North Africa and Italy, every town had its bishop, and the bishops in one of these areas might number several hundred. However, another system was emerging, with territorial subdivisions, parishes, in charge of a resident presbyter or priest supervised by the bishop in the neighbouring city.

Whatever the organization, succession in direct line from the apostles was deemed of the essence of the episcopate. Even Tertullian, who became a Montanist, stoutly maintained that only those churches were valid which agreed in their teaching with those which had been founded by the apostles and where the faith had been kept pure by a succession of bishops going back to the apostles. Cyprian, Bishop of Carthage and a martyr in the third century, held that there was only one Church, that the episcopate founded upon the rock by Christ was in the Church and the Church in the bishop, and that if any were not with the bishop he was not in the Church. Moreover, Cyprian insisted that he who was not in the Church was not a Christian and that outside the

Church, authenticated by the presence of the episcopate, there was no salvation. The bishops were more and more becoming prominent as essential features of the Catholic Church.

As the third century wore on, and after the Gnostics, the Marcionites, and the Montanists had ceased to become a major menace, the Catholic Church continued to develop its structure. As early as the beginning of the second century a distinct cleavage had begun to appear between clergy and laity, and this in spite of the fact that in the first century every Christian was held to be a priest unto God. By the end of the second century the clergy had clearly become a separate "order," that designation having probably been derived from the designation given to Roman magistrates in a tightly stratified society. The election of a bishop was usually by the presbyters and other clergy of the city, was ratified by the congregation, and was approved by other bishops of the neighbourhood. When so chosen, the bishop was consecrated by other bishops. The bishop selected and ordained the subordinate clergy. Among the latter the chief ranks were presbyters and deacons. Below them were the minor orders, such as sub-deacons, acolytes, exorcists, readers, and janitors. Deaconesses were to be found in the eastern part of the Empire, with the responsibility of caring for members of their sex. In both East and West there were "widows," who were charged with the duty of prayer and nursing the sick. Cyprian, the famous Bishop of Carthage whom we have already met, while looking up to Rome as the chief church in dignity, regarded every bishop as having all the powers of the group and at most esteemed the Bishop of Rome as only the first among equals. But the Bishop of Rome claimed greater authority, and it was natural that the bishops of the larger cities, especially Rome, should be more prominent than those of the smaller cities and towns.

The Canon of the New Testament Is Determined

From the very beginning the Christians had revered the Jewish scriptures, had seen in them the preparation for Christ, and had read them in their services. Gradually, by common usage and consent, books of Christian authorship were also brought together. From a very early date several of the letters of Paul were read in the assemblies of Christians. The Four Gospels won acceptance, so that Irenæus, writing in the second half of the second century, while recognizing that some questioned the position of *The Gospel according to John,* stoutly maintained that there must be four Gospels, no more and no less. Marcion, as we have noted, seems to have been the first to assemble some of the Christian writings into a well-defined collection. This, as we have seen, included *The Gospel according to Luke* and some of the letters of Paul, edited to make them conform to Marcion's convictions.

It is possible that Marcion's initiative accelerated the formation of an authoritative collection by the Catholic Church. The Catholic Church obviously wished to have a recognized body of documents to which it could appeal as containing the records of the life and words of Jesus and what had been taught by the original apostles. As against Gnostics and Marcionites it could point to them for dependable data to determine what the Gospel was on which the Christian faith was based. The test for inclusion in the collection was authorship by an apostle or a close friend of an apostle.

Only gradually was universal assent given to the twenty-seven books which now comprise the New Testament. Some books were later than others in winning inclusion. *The Gospel according to John,* as Irenæus is evidence, was not accepted as quickly as were the first three Gospels. *The Revelation of John,* the only prophetic book to be admitted, was long questioned. The letters called *Hebrews, James, II Peter,* and *II* and *III John* were included in some lists but one or more of them were omitted in others. Several books not now among the twenty-seven were for a time here and there used in public reading as though they belonged in the canon. Among them were the letter of Clement to the Corinthians, already noted, the *Didache, The Shepherd of Hermas* (a series of revelations originating in Rome), the *Apocalypse of Peter,* and the *Epistle of Barnabas.*

It may be that *The Revelation of John* was viewed with suspicion and that the other writings of Christian prophets did not find a permanent place in the canon because of the distrust with which those prophets claiming to be the mouthpieces of the Holy Spirit were viewed by the bishops and their clergy. The Montanists, with their assertion that Spirit-inspired prophets continued to arise in the Christian community, were a challenge to the administrative regularity represented by the bishops, and their rejection by the Catholic Church may have accentuated the distrust for the prophets and their writings. Certainly prophets, accorded a place in the early Church next to the apostles, were no longer granted recognition by the Catholic Church. Inspiration through prophets was supposed to have ceased with the apostolic age.

The first list which has come down to us of the twenty-seven books which embraces only those which appear in our New Testament is in a letter written by Athanasius, Bishop of Alexandria, in the year 367. While it was not until long after that date that uniform agreement on the list was found among all teachers in the Catholic Church, by at least the end of the second century a body of writings embracing a majority of the present twenty-seven was being regarded in the Catholic Church as the New Testament and was being placed alongside the Jewish scriptures. The latter were thought of as the Old Testament and were interpreted in the light of the former.

It was, then, by the slow consensus of the Church that the New Testament was assembled and accorded recognition as especially inspired. It was not merely supposed actual apostolic authorship which ensured for a book inclusion in the New Testament. This had an important place. It was also by the test of experience through long use that the Christian community came to recognize in the writings which were admitted to the accepted canon a quality which distinguished them from those books which were rejected, a quality which to the Christian mind was and continues to be evidence of a peculiar degree of divine inspiration, the crown of the process of revelation recorded in the Old Testament.

THE APOSTLES' CREED

The present form of what we know as the Apostles' Creed probably did not exist before the sixth century. However, the essential core has a much earlier origin. It seems to be an elaboration of a primitive baptismal formula, the one given in the last chapter of *The Gospel according to Matthew*—"baptizing them in the name of the Father, and of the Son, and of the Holy Ghost." It may go back to an Eastern development of that formula, but more probably it had its inception in Rome. Certainly a briefer form, known as the Roman Symbol, was in use in the Church of Rome at least as far back as the fourth century. With the exception of two or three phrases it was known to Irenæus and Tertullian, and so was employed in the latter part of the second century.

The term "symbol" comes from a word which in one of its usages meant a watchword, or a password in a military camp. As applied to a creed, it was a sign or test of membership in the Church. Assent to the creed or symbol was required of those who were being baptized.

The Roman Symbol may well have been an elaboration of an earlier form which went back to the primitive baptismal formula, modified in such fashion as to make it clear that the candidate for baptism did not adhere to the beliefs in which Marcion, who had a strong following in Rome, differed from the Catholic Church. The opening affirmation, "I believe in God the Father almighty" (in the original Greek the word translated "almighty" means "all governing" or "all controlling," as one who governs all the universe), quite obviously rules out Marcion's contention that the world is the creation of the Demiurge and not of the loving Father. The phrases which follow, "and in Jesus Christ his son, who was born of Mary the Virgin, was crucified under Pontius Pilate, on the third day rose from the dead, ascended into Heaven, sitteth on the right hand of the Father, from which he cometh to judge the living and the dead," clearly do not permit the Marcionite teaching that Christ was a phantom, but assert positively that he was the Son, not of the previously unknown God, but of God who is also the Creator, that he was born of woman, and so from his conception shared man's flesh, that as sharing man's flesh as an individual human being he had a specific place in history, having been crucified and buried under a Roman official whose name is known. This, of course, does not deny that he is also the Son of God and so divine, but, as against Marcion, it asserts the fact that Jesus Christ was also fully human. The symbol likewise declares that the risen Christ is seated by the right hand of the Father, the God Who is the creator and ruler of the universe, so stressing the conviction that there is only one God, not two gods. By emphasizing the belief that Christ, the Son of the Father, is to be judge, the creed is repudiating, either deliberately or without that view explicitly in mind, the Marcionite contention that it is the Demiurge, not the Father of the Son, who is the judge. Of the concluding phrases, [I believe] "in the Holy Spirit, and the resurrection of flesh," the first was not in controversy and so was not amplified, but the second, an addition to the primitive formula, seems to have been intended as a protest against the view which counted flesh as evil.

Although the development was in part due to the conflict with the Marcionites and although several generations were still to elapse before all the phrases were added which make it as it stands today, it must not be forgotten that the Apostles' Creed had as its nucleus words going back to the first century and first explicitly stated in the post-resurrection command of Jesus to the apostles. It was meant to be simply a further interpretation to meet particular challenges as they arose. Thus it clearly is an expression of what was taught by the apostles, and the designation "Apostles' Creed" is not an accident or a mistake. Moreover, in those few words, "Father, Son, and Holy Spirit," is succinctly summarized the heart of the Christian Gospel—God Who is Father, Who once in history revealed Himself in one who was at once God and man and Who because of that continues to operate in the lives of men through His Spirit. In this is the uniqueness of Christianity.

The Continuation of Conflict within the Church

The methods to which resort was had against Gnostics, Marcionites, and Montanists to preserve the integrity of the Gospel and the efforts to further the unity of Christians in one fellowship were by no means entirely successful. To be sure, as organized bodies these three dissident groups eventually died out, although not until several centuries had elapsed. However, other causes of contention arose and, indeed, have continued to arise across the centuries. Some of them were healed without a visible breach in the Church, but others were so potent that the acceptance by all parties to the dispute of the apostolic succession of the episcopate, the authority of the New Testament, and the

Apostles' Creed did not estop formal and permanent division. Still less was the rupture prevented of that unity envisaged by Christ and such of his early exponents as Paul, that based upon love.

THE EASTER CONTROVERSY

An acute early controversy, one which ran concurrently with those aroused by Gnosticism, Marcionism, and Montanism, was over the time for the celebration of Easter. Although our first certain notice of Easter is from the middle of the second century, that festival, commemorating the resurrection of Christ, was presumably observed by at least some Christians from much earlier times.

Differences arose over the determination of the date. Should it be fixed by the Jewish passover and be governed by the day of the Jewish month on which that feast was set regardless of the day of the week on which it fell? This became the custom in many of the churches, especially in Asia Minor. In contrast, many churches, including that of Rome, celebrated Easter on the first day of the week, Sunday. It was the first day of the week when Christ rose from the dead and which because of that fact was early observed as the Lord's Day. Disputes also developed over the length of the fast which was to be observed preceding Easter in commemoration of the crucifixion and as to whether Christ's death occurred on the fourteenth or on the fifteenth day of the Jewish month of Nisan.

In various parts of the Empire, probably not far from the end of the second century, synods met to decide the issue. In general the consensus was for Sunday, but in Asia Minor the bishops held to the other method of reckoning. Thereupon Victor, Bishop of Rome in the last decade of the second century, sought to enforce uniformity by breaking off communion with the dissenting bishops and churches. Irenæus expostulated with Victor on the ground that the differences in practice had long existed without causing a breach in unity. Ultimately the observance of Easter on Sunday prevailed and probably the prestige of Rome was thereby enhanced. Yet the controversy, called Quarto-decimanian from the fourteenth day of Nisan, long remained an unpleasant memory.

THE NOVATIAN AND DONATIST DIVISIONS

More serious were two schisms, one which began in the third century and which is usually given the name of Novatian, and the other which had its origin in the fourth century and is called Donatist. For both the primary source was dissatisfaction with what they regarded as the lax moral practices of the majority and both came into being as protests against the lenient treatment of those who had denied the faith in time of persecution.

In its earlier days the Church maintained rigorous standards for its membership. As we have seen, baptism was believed to wash away all sins committed before it was administered. After baptism, the Christian was supposed not to sin, and some sins, if indulged in after that rite had been administered, were regarded as unforgivable. Tertullian listed the "seven deadly sins" as "idolatry, blasphemy, murder, adultery, fornication, false-witness, and fraud." Both Hermas and Tertullian conceded that forgiveness might be had for one such sin committed after baptism, but allowed only one.

Modifications began to be made in this rigour. The guilty might obtain remission even for apostasy and sex offenses if they were truly repentant—although assurance of forgiveness and readmission into the full fellowship of the Church might be deferred until the penitent had demonstrated his sincerity by prolonged demonstration of sorrow for his sin. Pardon might be had through the officers of the Church. Those about to suffer death or who had endured imprisonment and torture for the faith were often looked upon as competent to assure forgiveness to the repentant, especially to those who had lapsed. The exercise of this function sometimes proved annoying to the bishops, among them to the Cyprian whom we have met as Bishop of Carthage. Again and again there were Christians who protested against this laxity. Part of the appeal of the Montanists was their insistence upon strict moral standards.

In the first quarter of the third century Callistus, Bishop of Rome, seems to have declared that no sin is unforgivable if the sinner is genuinely contrite. He is said to have appealed to Scripture for authority for his practice, finding as he did so ample precedent in the parables of the lost sheep and the prodigal son and in Paul's letters. He is also reported to have declared that the Church is like the field which has both wheat and tares and like Noah's ark, in which were many kinds of animals. In the next quarter of a century the principles of Callistus won wide although by no means universal acceptance in the Church.

In the middle of the third century the Decian persecution brought the issue starkly before the Church, for thousands yielded to pressure and compromised their faith. Many of them, terrified or deeply grieved by what they had done, sought readmission to the Church. In Rome the bishop, Cornelius by name, was prepared to permit the restoration of the lapsed. However, there was opposition led by Novatian, a presbyter of the Roman Church, no mean theologian, and of impeccable orthodoxy. Chosen bishop by critics of Cornelius, he gathered about him many who shared his convictions about exacting ethical requirements for church membership and rebaptized those who came to him from the Catholic Church. The movement spread and in part coalesced with the Montanists. Novatian appointed bishops for the emerging communities, and churches in sympathy with him arose in North Africa, the West, and especially the East. They persisted for several generations. In the fifth century there were three Novatian churches in Constantinople and even more in Rome. In the first half of the fifth century the Bishop of Rome took possession of their churches in that city and they could henceforth meet only secretly and in private homes. Yet their churches were still permitted in Constantinople.

The Donatist schism appeared after the persecution which began with Diocletian in the first quarter of the fourth century and had its main centre in North Africa. A Bishop of Carthage was consecrated in 311 by one whom the strict elements in the Church declared to have been a traitor during the persecution. These elements chose a counter bishop who in 316 was succeeded by Donatus, from whom the movement took its name. A number of factors combined to give the Donatists an extensive following in North Africa. It may have been that they were drawn largely from the non-Latin and the Catholics from the Latin elements in the population, and that the cleavage was in part racial and cultural. It is said that at one time they had 270 bishops. Synods called by Constantine at the request of the Donatists decided against the latter and for a time the Emperor sought to suppress them by force. Augustine endeavoured, without avail, to bring about a reconciliation. They regarded themselves as the true Catholic Church and continued at least until the Vandal invasion of the fifth century and possibly until the Moslem Arab invasion late in the seventh century.

Out of the controversy came the enunciation of the principle, formulated by one of the councils called to deal with the issues raised by the Donatists, that, contrary to the latters' contention, ordination and baptism are not dependent for their validity upon the moral character of the one through whose hands they are administered. This continued to be upheld by the Catholic Church.

A schism in Egypt about the same time as that of the Donatists and for a similar reason was that of the Meletians, named for the bishop who was their first leader. They, too, stood for a rigorous attitude towards those who had denied the faith.

As we have suggested, the majority in the Catholic Church took the attitude that no sin is beyond forgiveness if it is followed by true penitence. It may be that it was this conviction which led to the addition to the Roman Symbol of the phrase [I believe in] "the forgiveness of sins," now so familiar a part of the Apostles' Creed.

The Effort to Define the Trinity

A problem which long vexed the Church, and which even now has not been solved to the satisfaction of all who bear the Christian name, is that of the Trinity. As we hinted in an earlier chapter, through their deepest experiences the first Christians were confronted with the fact of Christ and of the Holy Spirit. How were Christ and the Holy Spirit related to God? The Christians were sure that God is one. Most of them were also convinced that in some unique way in Christ were both man and God and that the Holy Spirit was from God and is God. How could one hold to a belief in one God and make room for what had become known of Christ and of the Holy Spirit? The phases of the question which most engaged the attention of Christians were the relation of Christ to God and the work of Christ. This was as it should be, for Christianity had Christ as its central figure. Here, to the Christian, was the completely new and decisive fact in history. How could it be put adequately into the categories of existing human knowledge, thought, and speech? Inevitably Christians endeavoured to use terminology with which they were already familiar and sought analogies in existing philosophies and religious beliefs. Yet nothing which they found ready to their hands exactly met their needs. Christ was too novel to be fitted into what had been previously experienced without doing him violence. To Christians it was clear that he was fully man, an historical human individual, and that he was also God. How could these two convictions be reconciled?

As Christians wrestled with these problems differences arose which led to sharp controversies. The discussions and the controversies continued intermittently through the entire first five centuries and even beyond them. In their course the Catholic Church came officially to a common mind on most of the questions which had been raised and incorporated its conclusions in creeds and statements some of which to this day remain standard for the overwhelming majority of Christians. Yet the controversies led to fresh divisions, several of them of large proportions and some of which still survive.

Early Christian Views of Christ

The early Christians, including those who had been his most intimate companions, came to cherish very exalted views of Jesus. They named him Messiah, Christ, the anointed one. They called him *Kyrios* (Κύριος), "Lord." Indeed, the only creedal affirmation which seems to have been asked of the first converts was subscription to the declaration, "Jesus is Lord." While to those reared in a Greek or a non-Jewish Oriental background this term would bring to mind the many "lords" of the mystery religions with the assurance of immortality through being joined in union with the central figure of one or another of these cults, to those with a Jewish heritage the word *Kyrios* was the Greek term employed for the Hebrew *Adonai*, which meant God Himself, or, in one passage from the Psalms which Christians remembered, the Messiah as well as God. Sometimes Jesus was called the Wisdom of God, reminiscent of the *Sophia* ("Wisdom") in much of late Jewish thought which had been influenced by Hellenism, and in which Sophia had been almost personalized. Repeatedly he was called Son of God. In a famous passage in one of Paul's letters he is declared to have existed in the form of God but as emptying himself and being made in the likeness of man. In another well-known passage Christ is described as having been appointed by God to be "heir of all things, by whom also he made the worlds," and as "the brightness of his glory and the express image of his person." In the even more famous passage at the outset of *The Gospel according to John*, Jesus is identified with the *Logos* (Λόγος) or "Word," which "was in the beginning with God" and "was God," by whom all things were made. The *Logos* is described as having become flesh in Jesus.

Scholars are by no means agreed as to the source from which the term *Logos* came into this passage and, therefore, as to the precise meaning which it had for the author. Some maintain that it was from a strain in current Hellenistic thought to which several schools of Greek philosophy contributed, and which in Judaism had its outstanding exponent in Philo. This held that the God Who is far beyond man's knowing maintains His contact with the created world through the *Logos*, who is subordinate to God. Another view identifies the *Logos* with the Wisdom which is found in Hebrew literature. Still another conjecture sees the influence of religious conceptions in contemporary non-Christian Syria and Asia Minor and which stressed the unity of God and yet His nearness in the life forces.

What *The Gospel according to John* emphasized, and where it differs from all these other conceptions, is its declaration that the *Logos* became flesh, and became flesh in a particular man, Jesus of Nazareth. While in places it seems to view the *Logos* so incarnated as subordinate to God, it makes much of the intimacy of the incarnate Son with the Father and declares that the two are one.

The early Christians stated in various ways what they believed to be the specific work of Christ. "God was in Christ reconciling the world unto Himself"; "He hath made him to be sin for us who knew no sin that we might be made the righteousness of God in him"; "The blood of Jesus Christ his son cleanseth us from all sin"; "God commendeth his love towards us in that while we were yet sinners Christ died for us"; "Jesus Christ . . . the propitiation of our sins and not for ours only, but also for the sins of the whole world"; "God so loved the world that he gave his only begotten son, that whosoever believeth in him should not perish but have everlasting life"; "For as in Adam all die, even so in Christ shall all be made alive"; he "abolished death and brought life and immortality to light through the Gospel"—these are some of the phrases which at once come to mind. Christ was pictured as a judge. He was also named as saviour and as priest who once for all had offered up himself as a sacrifice and continues to make intercession for the faithful to God "who spared not his own son but delivered him up for us all." Jesus was also a prophet, speaking for God. He was king. He was alpha and omega, the beginning and the end. As God had created all things through him, so it was also the purpose of God to sum up all things in him, whether in heaven or on earth.

These first century Christians did not attempt to make a complete orderly statement of their beliefs about Christ. Here and there, as in *The Gospel according to John* and in Paul's *Letter to the Romans,* something of what they believed to be the place of Christ in the human drama and in the universe is set forth. Yet these early disciples were so carried away with the breath-taking vision of what they believed Christ meant and of what God had done and was doing in him that they could not put it in sober intellectual terms, nor did they attempt to answer all the questions which Christians would inevitably raise as they struggled with the problems presented by this unique and climactic person whom they had come to know. In their writings were passages to which appeal has been made to support divergent and even contradictory views. Across the centuries Christians have continued to be moved by the words in which the New Testament writers attempted to express what they believed Christ to be and what God had wrought through him. Again and again they have come back to them in the endeavour to enter fully into the reality to which they bore witness.

CHRIST AND THE LOGOS

In the second and third centuries widely divergent views of the relation of Jesus to God were put forward, even by those who regarded themselves as being within the Catholic Church.

A group of these convictions centred on the identification of Christ with the *Logos.* Not all those who made that identification agreed as to precisely what it implied. Some, including the convert, Justin Martyr, whom we have earlier mentioned, whose spiritual pilgrimage had led him through Greek philosophy to Christ, and who had become acquainted with views of the *Logos* which were akin to those taught by Philo, held the *Logos* to be "the second God." To be sure, Justin Martyr's Christian faith led him to an affirmation which was not to be found in Philo, that the *Logos* was incarnated in an historical individual, Jesus Christ, for the salvation of men. Yet the *Logos* which had become flesh in Jesus Christ, while not different in kind from God the Father, was a second God.

On the other hand, Irenæus held that the *Logos* which became incarnate in Jesus Christ was the Son of God, the Mind of God, and was the Father Himself. In contrast with those against whom he especially argued, the Gnostics with their belief that Christ was a phantom, not man, and the Marcionites, with their particular form of dualism, Irenæus stressed his conviction that Jesus Christ was both man and God, fully man and from the beginning the incarnation of the *Logos,* that in Jesus God Himself suffered for men (who deserved nothing from Him), and that at the same time Jesus as man at every stage of his life, by what is known as *recapitulation,* or "summing up," perfectly fulfilled what God had intended man and His entire creation to be, and so, as representative of man, won for man the right to be recognized by God as having met His demands.

Irenæus is representative of a trend which, in reacting against the thinly veiled polytheism of the Gnostics and the two gods of the Marcionites, emphasized the unity of God. That trend, possibly reinforced by other factors, in some of its extreme forms known as Monarchianism, formulated a conception of the Trinity which was eventually condemned by the Catholic Church as untrue. Monarchianism was, in general, an attempt to stress monotheism against those who would make Jesus Christ, as the incarnation of the *Logos,* a second God, or would solve the problem presented to Christian thought by the belief in God the Father and Creator, the deity of Jesus Christ, and the action of the Holy Spirit by what was in effect tritheism, a belief in three Gods. While emphasizing the unity of God, the Monarchians also wished to honour Jesus and to explain the uniqueness of his life.

The Monarchians did not necessarily recognize a kinship among themselves, nor did they constitute a movement with a unified organization. While differing sharply from the Gnostics, they were, somewhat like the latter, diverse in the details of their views. Several of their leaders were expelled from the fellowship of the Catholic Church for their convictions, and others, more moderate, but with Monarchian tendencies, continued to be highly esteemed in that church.

In general, Monarchianism is usually said to have been of two types, dynamic (from the Greek *dynamis*—"power") and modalistic. The Dynamistic Monarchians believed that Jesus Christ was a man born of the Virgin Mary, and that in him was an impersonal power (*dynamis*) which issued from God. God's unity was thus preserved, for the power was not in any sense personal. Some of them have been styled Adoptionists, because they held that this power came upon Christ at his baptism, or, according to others, after his resurrection from the dead. This strain of thought was represented at Rome late in the second century and in the first half of the third century. Its leaders were excommunicated by the Bishop of Rome and attempted to found a separate church with their own bishop.

The most famous advocate of Dynamistic Monarchianism was Paul of Samosata, Bishop of Antioch in the third quarter of the third century, and also a civil official. Paul was accused by his enemies in the Church of loving pomp and power, of having acquired wealth by reprehensible means, of permitting in his entourage questionable relations with women, and of craving applause for his oratory. Whether these accusations were true we cannot know, for his critics were looking at him with jaundiced eyes. Apparently he sought to stress the humanity of Jesus. He held that in God are the *Logos* and Wisdom, but the *Logos* is not a distinct being and is what reason is in a man. The Wisdom dwelt in the prophets, but was uniquely in Christ as in a temple. Jesus was a man, but was sinless from his birth. The Holy Spirit was in him, he was united in will with God, by his struggles and sufferings he overcame the sin of Adam, and he grew in his intimacy with God. Three successive synods assembled to go into Paul's life and views and the third condemned and deposed him. However, he held on to his bishopric until, about 272, the Emperor Aurelian forced him to give up the church property, perhaps because he had been of the party of Zenobia, the famous queen in Palmyra, whom the Emperor had defeated.

Modalistic Monarchianism is also called Patripassianism, because it held that the Father suffered, and Sabellianism, from Sabellius, its most famous exponent. Noetus and Praxeas, who were early advocates, held that the Father was born as Jesus Christ, thus becoming the Son, and that He died and raised Himself from the dead. Sabellius held that Father, Son, and Holy Spirit are three modes or aspects of God, much as the sun is bright, hot, and round.

This form of Monarchianism made its way to Rome at the end of the second century and in the first quarter of the third century. It gained partial support from two Bishops of Rome, Zephyrinus (198–217) and Callistus (217–222). Although he excommunicated Sabellius, Callistus gave out a statement which declared that the Father and the Son are the same, and that the Spirit which became incarnate in the Virgin Mary is not different from the Father, but one and the same. While denying that the Father suffered, it asserted that the Father suffered along with the Son. It seems to have been a modified form of Modalistic Monarchianism. Hippolytus, a contemporary of Zephyrinus and Callistus in Rome, a prolific writer and a theologian of distinction, bitterly denounced the views of Callistus and, an uncompromising rigorist in morals, also accused him of being too lenient with sinners in the Church, since, as we have seen, he permitted the restoration to the fellowship of the Church of those who had been guilty of even the most serious offenses. Hippolytus, emphasizing the role of the *Logos,* was accused by Callistus of believing in two Gods. He would not recognize Callistus as bishop and for a time was set up by his followers as a rival bishop.

Monarchianism came to Rome from the East and here and there remained in Asia Minor, Syria, Libya, and Egypt for many years. It was especially persistent in Egypt. In the fifth century Augustine leaned towards Modalistic Monarchianism.

TERTULLIAN AND THE TRINITY

One who gave much thought to the problem presented by the relationship of Father, Son, and Holy Spirit, and who contributed substantially to the conception which became dominant, was Tertullian. With his legal mind, Tertullian had the gift of precise and clear statement. He also employed terms with which he was familiar in the law courts to give expression to Christian conceptions. He was polemical and, like an advocate, not always fair to his opponents. Often emphatic and startling, he was at times betrayed into inconsistencies. While pouring scorn on philosophy, he owed a great debt to the Stoicism in which he must have been nurtured in his youth, and his ideas were sometimes moulded by Stoic thought and expressed in Stoic terms. Yet he sought to base his beliefs squarely upon the Scriptures and argued from Scriptural passages and texts.

Like the Monarchians, whom he attacked, Tertullian believed in the *monarchia,* or sole government, of God. As to the Monarchians, so to him, God is one. In connection with God Tertullian employed the Latin word *substantia,* taken from Roman legal terminology and meaning a man's status in a community. He declared that in his *substantia,* or substance, God is one. Father, Son, and Holy Spirit, so Tertullian said, are three *personæ,* or persons. In *persona* Tertullian seemed to have in mind the use of that word in Roman law, where it meant a party in a legal action. These *personæ,* or parties, have their place in the οἰκονομία (economy), or administrative activity of God. They are seen in the government through which the *monarchia,* the rule of the one God, operates. Here is unity of *substantia,* but a unity distributed in a trinity, a unity of substance, but a trinity in form and in aspect. Before the world was created, Tertullian went on to say, God was alone, but always, since God is rational, there was in Him Reason, the Greek *Logos.* This Reason was God's own thought. The Reason expressed itself in Word, Word which consists of Reason. This Reason or Word is identical with what the Scriptures call Wisdom. Wisdom and Reason became also the Son of God. Yet there was a time when the Reason had not yet expressed itself in Word, when, namely, the Son was not. Here was a point which, as we are to see, later became a centre of contention. The Son was conceived by Tertullian as being subordinate to the Father, and the Holy Spirit proceeded from the Father through the Son.

In Jesus, so Tertullian averred, quoting *The Gospel according to John,* the Word became incarnate. Yet in Jesus the divine and the human did not fuse, as do gold and silver to form a new metal, *electrum,* for in that case Jesus would be a *tertium quid,* a third something which would be neither God nor man. Instead Jesus was both God and man. In Jesus Christ there is one *persona,* but two "substances" or natures, the divine and the human, the Spirit and the flesh. In the one "person," Jesus, the Spirit and the flesh exist together, without either the Spirit becoming flesh or flesh becoming Spirit. Yet, so Tertullian insisted, Jesus Christ was only one "person." Christ was merely a designation, meaning the anointed, and did not imply a person distinct from Jesus as the adoptionists had argued. Here, as in his use of *substantia* and *persona,* Tertullian contributed to later creeds through which the Catholic Church expressed its faith.

Tertullian aided in formulating and probably also in part expressed the theological convictions which prevailed in the western part of the Empire. Certainly that part of the Church was not so torn by the theological controversies of the fourth and fifth centuries as were the Eastern portions of the Church. This may have been because the Latin mind was less speculative and more practical and ethical than was the Hellenistic mind of the East. It may be significant that the greatest schisms over questions of morals and discipline, the Novatian and Donatist, had their rise in the West, while the main divisions over speculative theology, divisions which we are soon to describe, had their birth in the East.

THE GREAT ALEXANDRIANS: CLEMENT

While Tertullian was writing in Carthage there was beginning to flower in Alexandria a school of Christian thought which was to contribute even more than did he to the intellectual formulation of the Christian faith. Alexandria was one of the chief cities of the Roman Empire. Founded by Alexander the Great in the fourth century before Christ, it had become a cosmopolitan centre of commerce and of Hellenistic culture. Here was one of the great libraries of the world. Here Greek and Oriental philosophies met and here the latest of the Græco-Roman non-Christian philosophies, Neoplatonism, was born. Here the Jewish Philo had lived and had interpreted his hereditary faith in Greek forms. In the Museum was the equivalent of a university, famous throughout the Græco-Roman world. Before the end of the second century Christianity was represented by vigorous but divided communities. Alexandria was a stronghold of the Catholic Church and Gnosticism also flourished. In contrast with Tertullian, who, although influenced by Stoicism, professed to scorn philosophy, in Alexandria Christian thinkers regarded Greek philosophy as a tool to be used and the greatest of them became experts in it.

In Alexandria the main focus and stimulus to Christian intellectual life was in a catechetical school, made famous through two of its heads, Clement and Origen. This catechetical school was already in existence late in the second century. As its name indicates, its primary purpose was the instruction of candidates for Church membership in the principles of the Christian faith. Yet it also became a centre for advanced and creative thought and extensive literary activity. The first head of the school of whom we hear was Pantænus, a Stoic philosopher who had become a Christian. His most distinguished pupil was Titus Flavius Clement, a contemporary of Tertullian.

We do not know the precise year or place of Clement's birth or death. He may have been a native of Athens. It seems certain that he was born a pagan and that he was reared in the atmosphere of Hellenistic culture and thought. Possessed of an eager, inquiring mind, Clement appears to have conformed gladly to the eclectic temper of the Græco-Roman world of his day. He dipped into the various philosophical schools with which he came into contact and read extensively in some of them, notably in Platonism. Either before or after he became a Christian, he travelled widely in the eastern part of the Empire, seeking out those who could tell him what the apostles had taught. He was especially attracted by Pantænus and succeeded the latter as head of the catechetical school. Again exact dates are uncertain, but the last decade of the second century appears to have seen the height of Clement's Alexandrian career. He left Alexandria some time before the year 203, perhaps because of a persecution instituted by the Emperor Severus. We hear of him in Jerusalem and Antioch, called "the blessed presbyter," and praised by the Bishop of Jerusalem as having "built up and strengthened the Church of the Lord." When and where he died we cannot say.

Clement's three major surviving works are the *Protreptikos,* urging pagans to become Christians, the *Paidagogos,* translated, but not with entire accuracy, as the *Instructor,* intended to teach Christians the kind of conduct to be expected of those of their faith, and the *Stromateis,* or miscellanies, an admittedly poorly organized collection of notes, giving more advanced instruction in Christianity.

In these books Clement so far conceded to those Christians who cherished an aversion to philosophy as to agree with Paul that "the wisdom of the world is foolishness with God," and to admit that Jeremiah was right in insisting that the wise man is not to glory in his wisdom. Yet he contended that the philosophy of the Greeks was a preparation for the Gospel, to those who were familiar with it paving the way for perfection in Christ. He held that God is the source of all good things, of philosophy as well as of the Old and New Testaments. Indeed, he held that the Greek philosophers had learned much from Moses. It is possible, so he said, for one who is unlearned to become a Christian believer, but it is impossible for one without learning to comprehend fully what has been made known in the Christian faith. While he repudiated those who are usually called Gnostics, he held that there is a truly Christian *Gnosis*, or knowledge, a *Gnosis* which comes by faith and not through reason. He who has this *Gnosis*, so Clement declares, imitates God so far as possible, exercises self-restraint, loves God and his neighbour, and does good, not out of fear, but out of love. The Christian, Clement says, will gladly learn all that he can from all branches of human knowledge, whether music, mathematics, astronomy, dialectics, or Greek philosophy.

God, so Clement held, is knowable only through the *Logos*, His mind. The *Logos* has always existed and is the perfect mirror of God. The *Logos* is the face of God by whom God is manifested and made known. The *Logos* inspired the philosophers. Jesus is the *Logos*, the Word, who is holy God, the guide to all humanity, the *paidagogos*, or instructor, of Christians. Clement said that the *Logos* had shed his blood to save humanity. Yet Clement seems not to have thought of Jesus as really a man, but as merely in human form because he chose to appear so. Clement spoke of the Holy Spirit, but in such fashion that it is difficult to gain a clear picture of what he conceived the Spirit to be. He declared that "the universal Father is one, and one the universal Word" (*Logos*), "and the Holy Spirit is one and the same everywhere, and one is the only virgin mother . . . the Church." He affirmed that the Lord Jesus is the Word (*Logos*) of God, the Spirit made flesh.

Like Tertullian, Clement believed that every individual is free and is able to respond to God or to refuse to do so. Man may and does miss the mark, but he is capable of repentance. Yet, like Tertullian, he taught that after the initial repentance when one becomes a Christian only a single additional repentance is possible for a grievous sin.

THE GREAT ALEXANDRIANS: ORIGEN

Clement's successor as head of the catechetical school in Alexandria, Origen, was to be much more influential than he. His was, indeed, one of the greatest of Christian minds.

Origen was born of Christian parents, probably not far from the year 185.

A precocious child and the oldest of seven sons, he was instructed by his father in the Scriptures and in Greek learning. Possessed of an eager mind, he perplexed his father by questions about the deeper meanings which he believed lay behind the words of Holy Writ. When Origen was slightly less than seventeen years of age, his father was imprisoned and killed and the family's property was confiscated in the persecution by Severus which seems to have been the occasion for the termination of Clement's residence in Alexandria. In his youthful ardour, as we have seen, Origen wished martyrdom and was prevented only by his mother's firmness in hiding all his clothing and thus compelling him to remain at home. After his father's death, Origen continued his study of Greek literature and in part earned his living by teaching it.

Since, because of the persecution, no one was left in Alexandria to give instruction in the Christian faith to those who sought it, Origen began to undertake it and in his eighteenth year was in charge of the catechetical school, a post in which he was confirmed by the bishop. During the renewed persecution he boldly visited those imprisoned for their faith and accompanied some as they went to their death. He himself escaped only by shifting his home from house to house. He lived with extreme asceticism, curtailing his hours of sleep and giving himself exclusively to the catechetical school and to the continued study of the Scriptures and of Greek philosophy, including Neoplatonism. Partly to avoid the possibility of scandal in teaching women catechumens, he made himself a eunuch.

Origen visited Rome and Arabia and, later, Greece and Palestine. While in Palestine he was ordained a presbyter by two friendly bishops. The Bishop of Alexandria regarded this act as a flagrant disregard of his jurisdiction and had synods banish Origen from his see and, so far as possible, depose him from the priesthood.

Henceforward Origen made his headquarters in Cæsarea in Palestine. There he taught and wrote and from there he made occasional journeys. During the Decian persecution he was imprisoned and tortured. He was released, but his health was broken and not long after the persecution he died, in his seventieth year, and was buried at Tyre.

A superb teacher, he had a profound influence upon his students. From them and through his writings issued currents which were to help mould Christian thought for generations.

Origen was an indefatigable worker and wrote prodigiously. The better to study the Old Testament, he learned Hebrew, and in his *Hexapla* placed in parallel columns the Hebrew text and various Greek translations of the Old Testament. He wrote many commentaries on the Scriptures. Believing the Scriptures to be the word of God, he held that nothing in them was to be believed which is unworthy of God. He saw in the Scriptures three levels of meaning: first, the common or historical sense which is on the surface for even the simple-minded; second, the soul of the Scriptures which edifies those who perceive it; and third, for the perfect, a meaning hidden under what superficially is repugnant to the conscience or the intellect but which, discerned, can be expressed by allegory. The allegorical interpretation of the Scriptures was by no means new, but Origen gave it a fresh impetus. Origen's *Against Celsus* was evoked by the most penetrating criticism of Christianity produced in the Græco-Roman world of which we know and, in turn, was the ablest defense of Christianity which had thus far appeared. In his *Peri Archon* (*On First Principles*) which we have in full only in a Latin translation under the title *De Principiis*, and which somewhat altered the original, Origen gave to the Church its first orderly comprehensive statement of the Christian faith. In his literary labours he was assisted by a substantial body of amanuenses made possible by the generous financial aid of a friend.

Inevitably, like so many of the early Christian thinkers, nurtured as they were in Greek philosophy, and, indeed, like still others in succeeding centuries who were familiar with Greek thought, in his writings and in the formulation of his religious beliefs Origen bore the unmistakable impress of the Greek heritage. Yet Origen believed that he found the truth primarily in the Scriptures and in what had been transmitted in orderly succession from the apostles. The apostolic teaching, Origen held, is (1) that there is one God, the Father, just and good, the creator of all things; (2) that Jesus Christ, the God-man, was the incarnation of the *Logos* who is wisdom, word, light, and truth, coeternal with the Father, for since the Father is always Father there must always have been a Son, but who, since he is the image of the Father, is dependent upon the Father and subordinate to Him; Jesus Christ was not, as so many of the Gnostics held, a phantom, but was truly born of a virgin and the Holy Spirit, truly suffered, truly died, truly rose from the dead, conversed with his disciples, and was taken up into heaven; (3) that the Holy Spirit is associated in honour and dignity with the Father and the Son and that he is uncreated. Origen distinguished the Father, the Son, and the Holy Spirit from one another, although they constitute a unity. He taught that men derive their existence from the Father, their rational nature from the Son, and their holiness, or sanctification, from the Holy Spirit.

Origen held that there had been an earlier stage of the creation, a spiritual world, in which there were spiritual and rational beings to whom God had given free will. Some of these did not turn away from God, but others used their free will to do so. To punish and reform the fallen, God created the present visible world. Salvation was the work of the Son, the *Logos,* who in becoming man united with a human soul which had not sinned in its previous existence. The Saviour, the God-man, was the self-revelation of God, making evident to sinful men what God really is. The Saviour also gave himself as a ransom for the lost and by doing so conquered evil in the hearts of the fallen. He is a propitiatory offering to God. The Holy Spirit brings light to those who believe.

Origen taught that ultimately all the spirits who have fallen away from God will be restored to full harmony with Him. This can come about only with their coöperation, for they have freedom to accept or to reject the redemption wrought in Christ. Before their full restoration they will suffer punishment, but the punishment is intended to be educative, to purge them from the imperfections brought by their sin. After the end of the present age and its world another age and world will come, so Origen believed, in which those who have been born again will continue to grow and the unrepentant will be given further opportunity for repentance. Eventually all, even the devils, through repentance, learning, and growth, will be fully saved. Origen's conception of the drama of creation and redemption was breath-taking in its vast sweep and in its confident hope.

Influential though he was in the stream of Christian thought, some of Origen's views proved repugnant to the Catholic Church. Among these were his beliefs that the created world had always been, that human souls had existed from eternity before they came into these present bodies, that all souls, not only men but also demons, are ultimately to be saved, and that beyond this present existence the growth of souls through discipline is to continue until all are perfect. In the later years of the fourth century and in the fifth and sixth centuries controversy raged over Origen. In it monks, among them the scholarly and emphatic Jerome, and high ecclesiastics were involved. It entailed violent words and bitternesses. It contributed to the expulsion of John Chrysostom from Constantinople. Eventually, because of some of his teachings and also for others wrongly attributed to him, the Catholic Church in regional synods in Alexandria (399), Jerusalem, and Cyprus, and perhaps in one of its general or ecumenical councils, at Constantinople in 553, although this has been hotly debated, labelled him a heretic.

Post-Origenist Developments in Christian Thought and the Rise of Arianism

Origen was so outstanding a mind, so radiant a spirit, and so stimulating a teacher and author, that for more than a century after his death he profoundly moulded the minds of Christian thinkers, especially in the eastern portions of the Roman Empire. From those who came after him and who were deeply indebted to him, two main streams of thought issued which came into conflict with each other and which late in the third and through much of the fourth and fifth centuries led to the most serious division which the Catholic Church had thus far experienced. The streams were not always clearly defined, and so abounding in energy was the rapidly expanding Church of the day that each had varied currents and branches which at times appeared to intermingle.

The two streams could both claim reinforcement from Origen. As we saw, Origen taught that Christ was the only-begotten Son of God, and that since God the Father had always existed, He could never have existed, even for a moment, without having generated the Son. The Son, therefore, is coeternal with the Father and existed before all worlds. Origen had taught that "his generation is as eternal and everlasting as the brilliancy which is produced by the sun." One of the two streams stressed the conviction that Christ is the Son of God, Wisdom and the *Logos* (Word) of God, and had always been, and that the *Logos* was, accordingly, equal with the Father. Yet, as we have said, Origen seemed also to say that Christ is a creature, and that as the image of the Father he is secondary to the latter and subordinate to Him. The other stream made much of this subordination of the Son to the Father.

The second of these streams was represented by a pupil of Origen, Dionysius, head of the catechetical school in Alexandria and bishop in that city around the middle of the third century. He seems to have been a man of scholarly competence, moderate and conciliatory. He found Sabellianism very influential in his diocese and preached against it. In making clear his dissent from that school of theology which, it will be recalled, regarded Father, Son, and Holy Spirit as aspects or modes of God, he stressed the distinctness of the Son as a person and in doing so used language which appeared to imply that the Father had created the Son, that there had been a time when the Son was not, and that the Son was subordinate to the Father. His friend, another Dionysius, Bishop of Rome, wrote him urging that he be more careful in his use of language and that he make it clear that the Son was (ὁμοούσιον) (*homoousion*), namely, of the same essential being or substance with the Father and not simply (ὁμοιούσιον) (*homoiousion*), of similar substance with Him. Dionysius of Alexandria answered that, while he did not find *homoousion* in the Scriptures, he was in agreement with the idea which it contained. The lines of controversy had not yet hardened.

The second of the streams also had an important channel through Antioch. At Antioch there was a presbyter, Lucian by name, a contemporary of Origen, who was an influential teacher and who perished in 312, a victim of the last great persecution before Constantine brought toleration. Among his students who became famous were Arius of Alexandria and Eusebius of Nicomedia (to be distinguished from Eusebius of Cæsarea, the Church historian). Lucian was an earnest student of the Bible and of theology and was one of those who saw in the *Logos* a way of expressing the relation of Christ to God. Yet he seems to have taken the position which was soon to make Arius a storm-centre.

Conflict between the two streams broke out over Arius. Arius was a presbyter in the Alexandrian Church. Tall, handsome, ascetic, earnestly religious, an eloquent preacher, he gave the impression of being arrogant. He protested against what he believed to be the Sabellianism of his bishop, Alexander. Alexander, so he said, taught that "God is always, the Son is always," and the Son "is the unbegotten begotten." In contrast, Arius maintained that "the Son has a beginning but that God is without beginning" and that the Son is not a part of God. The controversy between the two men became so sharp that Alexander called a synod in Alexandria and had Arius and his friends condemned and deposed. Arius sought and found refuge with his friend, Bishop Eusebius of Nicomedia, and carried on a correspondence maintaining his views, while Alexander wrote to numbers of his fellow bishops giving his side of the story. The conflict was chiefly in the eastern part of the Empire and seriously threatened to divide the Catholic Church in that region.

The Council of Nicæa

Then the Emperor Constantine stepped in. He had recently come over to the side of the Christians and, after a long, hard struggle had united the Empire politically under his rule. The dispute over Arius threatened the disruption of what, along with the Empire, was the strongest institution in the Mediterranean world, the Catholic Church. Constantine had already intervened in the affairs of the Church over the Donatist controversy. He now felt impelled to act in this much more serious division. To that end he first wrote to Alexander and Arius, sending the letter by his adviser in church matters, Hosius, Bishop of Cordova, calling on them to compose their differences and forgive each other. When this appeal did not succeed, Constantine had recourse to a council of the entire Catholic Church. He took the initiative, had the state pay the travel expenses of the bishops to the gathering, and, although only a catechumen, presided over its opening session, and was active in its deliberations.

Whether Constantine appreciated the niceties of the questions at issue is highly doubtful, for he was a layman, a warrior and administrator, not a philosopher or an expert theologian. In his letter to Alexander and Arius he said that having made "careful inquiry into the origin and foundation of these differences" he found "the cause to be of a truly insignificant character and quite unworthy of such fierce contention," and that the discussions should be "intended merely as an intellectual exercise . . . and not hastily produced in the popular assemblies, nor unadvisedly entrusted to the general ear." Constantine's words probably reflected the attitude of the average Christian layman. We read that one of these who had suffered for his faith in the persecutions which were of recent memory and who, hearing the pre-council disputes before the gathering at Nicæa, bluntly told the debaters that Christ did not "teach us dialectics, art, or vain subtilties, but simple-mindedness, which is preserved by faith and good works."

Constantine's action established a significant precedent for what were called ecumenical or general councils of the Catholic Church and for the frequent leadership of the civil power in them. Local and regional synods or councils were, as we have seen, not new. They may well have provided a conscious precedent for the council of the entire Catholic Church. Certainly the general or ecumenical council was to become an accepted method for seeking accord on major divisive issues and other urgent problems which concerned the whole Church.

The council met at Nicæa, in Asia Minor, in the year 325. To it came about three hundred bishops. Most of them were from the eastern part of the Empire. Because of his age the Bishop of Rome was unable to attend, but he was represented by two presbyters. While the overwhelming majority of the bishops were from within the Empire, there are said to have been one from Persia and perhaps one from among the Goths. Hundreds of lesser clergy and lay folk also came. After the formal opening of the council by an address by Constantine, and when the latter had given permission for the disputants to present their views, violent controversy broke out. The large majority had not yet taken a position, but Arius was supported by a small and vocal minority of whom the most prominent was Eusebius of Nicomedia, and another, equally determined minority upheld Alexander. With Alexander was one of his deacons, the able young Athanasius. Born not far from the year 300 of upper class parentage, from childhood Athanasius had shown a deep interest in the Church and, having come to the favourable notice of Alexander, had early been brought into the latter's official family. Athanasius was to succeed Alexander as Bishop of Alexandria and to become one of the outstanding figures in the entire history of Christianity.

The Arians presented a statement of their position, but this aroused violent opposition. Eusebius of Cæsarea, who took a middle position but was against any leaning towards Sabellianism and hence was inclined to favour the Arians, suggested as a statement to which all might agree the creed which was in use in his own see and which he said had come down from his predecessors in the Cæsarean episcopate and was taught catechumens and to which, presumably, assent was required at baptism. This seemed to win general assent, including the endorsement of the Emperor. It became, therefore, the basis of what has since been known as the Nicene Creed. The main body of the creed of Cæsarea read:

We believe in one God, the Father Almighty, maker of all things, visible and invisible, and in one Lord, Jesus Christ the word [*Logos*] of God, God from God, light from light, life from life, the only-begotten Son, first-born of all creatures, begotten of the Father before all ages, by whom also all things were made; who for our salvation was made flesh and dwelt among men; and who suffered and rose again on the third day, and ascended to the Father and shall come again in glory to judge the living and the dead. We believe also in one Holy Spirit.

To this creed was added, with the approval of the Emperor and perhaps at his suggestion, the word *homoousion,* applied to Christ. The term was adopted by the council and the creed proposed by Eusebius was altered to conform with it so that it was as follows:

We believe in one God, the Father Almighty, maker of all things visible and invisible, and in one Lord, Jesus Christ, the Son of God, the only-begotten of the Father, that is, of the substance [*ousias*] of the Father, God from God, light from light, true God from true God, begotten, not made, of one substance [*homoousion*] with the Father, through whom all things came to be, those things that are in heaven and those things that are on earth, who for us men and for our salvation came down and was made flesh, and was made man, suffered, rose the third day, ascended into the heavens, and will come to judge the living and the dead.

Even a cursory comparison of the two creeds will show the nature of the changes. For *Logos,* which the Arians could use, was substituted the word "Son," and that term was emphasized by keeping the word "only-begotten," that is, begotten in a way different from the sons of God who are adopted, and also by adding that the Son is of the substance of the Father. In place of "life from life," which might be interpreted in various ways, the phrase "true God from true God" was used to make more explicit "God from God." *Homoousion* was inserted. This was of central significance, for it stated emphatically a position which was the storm centre between the two extremes and was rapidly to become the crux of the difference between them. "Came down," another addition, implied that Christ had been with God and was not subordinate to Him, possibly the reason back of the substitution of "ascended into the heavens" for "ascended to the Father." "Was made man" was also inserted, perhaps to emphasize the belief that Jesus Christ was not only "true God" but also not merely "flesh," but true "man." This would serve to make clear that through the incarnation of the Son in Jesus Christ men could share in his sonship.

As in the Apostles' Creed, so in the Nicene Creed, painfully, slowly, and through controversies in which there was often lacking the love which is the major Christian virtue, Christians were working their way through to a clarification of what was presented to the world by the tremendous historical fact of Christ. At Nicæa it was more and more becoming apparent to them that the high God must also be the Redeemer and yet, by a seeming paradox, the Redeemer must also be man. The astounding central and distinguishing affirmation of Christianity, so they increasingly saw, and what made Christianity unique and compelling, was that Jesus Christ was "true God from true God," or, to put it in language more familiar to English readers, "very God of very God," who "was made man." Thus men could be reborn and become sons of God, but without losing their individual identity.

The words were not always wisely chosen, perhaps because words could not be found which would exactly stand for the reality. For instance, *ousia* had several different connotations in Greek philosophical usage and, although *substantia* was used in translation into Latin, and for one sense of *ousia*, accurately, the latter term had no precise Latin equivalent. Existing terminology was chosen which would come as nearly as possible to the fact and then would gradually be given the connotation which would convey what Christians meant by it.

To make the position of the council towards Arius unmistakable, it was declared that the Catholic Church anathematized, namely, cursed, those who say "there was a time when he [the Son of God] was not," or "that he did not exist before he was begotten," or "that he was made of nothing," or that "he is of other substance or essence from the Father," or that he was created, or mutable, or susceptible to change.

It will be noted that the creed which today bears the name of Nicene is a further development from the one which was adopted at Nicæa. Yet the latter's essential features were preserved.

The Council of Nicæa embraced the opportunity to settle some other issues which were troubling the Catholic Church. The time for the observance of Easter was agreed upon and made uniform, thus attempting to ensure accord on what had been a subject of controversy. Here, it may be remarked, the council was not entirely successful. Steps were also taken to end the Meletian schism which we mentioned earlier, but in vain, for the Meletians persisted for at least a century longer. Several canons, or rules, were adopted for the administration and discipline of the Church, among them one which required at least three bishops for the laying on of hands, namely, the consecration of a bishop, regulations for the treatment of those who had fallen away during the recent persecutions, for a uniform handling of the excommunicated, and for improving the morals of the clergy and the bishops by more care in admission to these orders, by prohibiting the clergy from exacting usury, and by keeping other women than near relatives from their homes. These canons shed much light on the quality of the lives of Christians in the fore part of the fourth century and on the means which were taken to maintain high moral standards and orderly procedures.

To enforce the decisions of the Council of Nicæa, Constantine commanded, with the death penalty for disobedience, the burning of all books composed by Arius, banished Arius and his closest supporters, and deposed from their sees Eusebius of Nicomedia and another bishop who had been active in the support of Arius.

THE RESURGENCE OF ARIANISM

The Council of Nicæa from which so much had been hoped did not bring enduring peace to the Catholic Church. Indeed, no council which has claimed to be inclusive or "ecumenical" has ever done so. Here and there a regional council has helped to restore unity in a particular area or in a segment of the Church, but many, perhaps most, of even these have failed. "Ecumenical" councils have either hardened old divisions or have led to new ones. They have usually been marked by bitterness and recriminations and, by bringing face to face those who have differed, have sharpened dissensions rather than healed them. However, like the Council of Nicæa, they have often contributed to a clarification of the thinking of Christians, have made more apparent what the issues were or are, and have enabled the majority to reach a common mind. In this paradox is seen something of the nature of the Church as it has actually operated in history.

While, viewed from the vantage of the centuries, it is quite clear that the Council of Nicæa was an important stage in the attainment of the Catholic Church of a consensus of conviction on the relation of Jesus Christ to God, for more than a generation it was not at all certain that the definitions arrived at by the council would prevail. Indeed, it looked as though Arius, although anathematized and exiled, would win. The debate continued, the Arians accusing those who adhered to the Nicene formula of being Sabellians, and the defenders of the Nicene Creed charging the Arians with making Christ a second and subordinate God. In a sense the Arians were seeking to fit Christ into the monotheism towards which much of pagan philosophy had been moving. In contrast the Nicene party was stressing the uniqueness of Christ and the Christian revelation with its conception of God.

The outstanding defender of the Nicene position was Athanasius. To him the real issue was the salvation of men. As he saw it, salvation is the rescue of men from the mortality which sin has brought upon them to participation in the divine nature. This, he held, can be accomplished only as "true God" is united with "true man." He declared that "He [Christ] was made man that we might be made God." A man of stalwart character and deep religious faith and insight, his intrepid and unwavering support contributed notably to the eventual triumph of the form of the faith which is associated with Nicæa.

As we have suggested, for years the tide appeared to be flowing against Athanasius and the Nicene findings. By the year 328 Eusebius of Nicomedia was back from disgrace and had become a trusted adviser of Constantine. In 330, only five years after Nicæa, Eustathius, bishop of the important see of Antioch and a leader of the anti-Arians, but one whose theological convictions were Monarchian, was haled before a synod, charged with various offenses, partly his theological teachings and partly his conduct, was deposed, and was exiled by the Emperor.

The friends of Arius urged upon the Emperor his rehabilitation. Arius presented to Constantine a confession of faith which, although it avoided the chief points at issue, appeared to the Emperor to be satisfactory. He was, accordingly, permitted to return from exile and, shortly before his death, was restored to communion. Indeed, it was the bishops, summoned again by Constantine, who, meeting in Nicæa in 327, readmitted to fellowship both Eusebius of Nicomedia and Arius.

Seeing Athanasius as their chief opponent, Eusebius of Nicomedia and his supporters sought by various means to have him put out of his office. In 335, at the summons of Constantine, who continued to be disturbed by the divisions in the Church, a council convened at Tyre. It heard charges against Athanasius, largely by the Meletians, accusing him of arbitrariness and cruelty in his treatment of them. Dominated by the Arians, it ordered him deposed. The Arians eventually succeeded in having Athanasius banished to Gaul. Just how they accomplished this is not entirely clear, but perhaps they convinced Constantine that he was a disturber of the peace of the Church. Marcellus, Bishop of Ancyra, in Asia Minor, also a staunch anti-Arian, was accused by the Arians of Sabellianism and was driven from his see.

Constantine died in 337. Shortly before, he was baptized by Eusebius of Nicomedia. He was succeeded by his three sons, Constantine II, Constans, and Constantius, and they divided the Empire among themselves. They permitted the exiled bishops to return and, in consequence, Athanasius was once more in Alexandria. The death of Constantine II, in 340, was followed by the division of the realm between the two survivors, Constans, who had the West, and Constantius, who ruled in the East. In the West the Catholic Church, supported by Constans, held to the Nicene decision, while in the East the majority of the bishops seem to have been against it. Constantius sympathized with them, and the anti-Nicene cause was strengthened when, in 339, Eusebius of Nicomedia was made Bishop of Constantinople. A synod in Antioch in which Eusebius had marked influence brought about a second expulsion of Athanasius from Alexandria and put another in his place.

Athanasius took refuge in Rome and was joined there by Marcellus. The then Bishop of Rome, the first of that line to bear the name Julius, took the side of Athanasius and Marcellus. Eusebius and his associates had written Julius, presenting their case and asking him to call a synod (or council) and be the judge. This Julius did, but the Eastern bishops did not come. The synod met in Rome in 340 or 341 and exonerated the two. Anti-Nicene bishops convening in Antioch drew up statements of the faith which they apparently hoped would bridge the widening chasm between them and the supporters of Nicæa, but these did not accomplish that result.

In a further attempt to heal the breach, the two Emperors, acting at the suggestion of Julius, called a council of the entire Church which met at Sardica, the later Sophia, near the border between East and West, probably in 343. Before the council had proceeded to business, the Eastern bishops, with Arian sympathies, protesting against the seating of Athanasius and Marcellus, withdrew, perhaps because they saw themselves outnumbered by their opponents. Bishop Hosius of Cordova presided. The council once more examined the charges against Athanasius and declared him innocent, adjudged Marcellus to be orthodox, and ordered the two, along with some others who had been ejected by the Eusebian party, reinstated in their posts. In 346 Athanasius returned in triumph to Alexandria. The Council of Sardica also issued a letter to all the bishops of the Catholic Church reporting its decisions, condemning the Arian views, and making a fresh statement of what it believed the Catholic faith to be. The council adopted a number of canons, largely disciplinary and administrative, for the regulation of the bishops. Among other acts the Council of Sardica decreed that if a bishop were deposed, he might appeal his case to the Bishop of Rome, who should take steps to see that it was heard and a decision given. Rome was forging ahead in its leadership in the Catholic Church.

Athanasius, as the outstanding champion of Nicene orthodoxy, was not allowed permanently to enjoy his victory. In 353 Constantius became the undisputed ruler of the entire Empire. His sympathies were clearly pro-Arian. He sought to achieve unity in the Church by bringing the Nicene party and the Western bishops to heel. Councils were called at Arles, in Gaul, in 353, and in Milan in 355. At the latter a tumultuous scene ensued. Yet the bishops were constrained to come into accord with their Eastern colleagues. Athanasius was again sent into exile (356), although this was spent chiefly in Egypt. For refusing to comply with the imperial wishes, Liberius, the Bishop of Rome, Hosius of Cordova, and one other were also exiled. At a council held in Sirmium, the imperial residence, in 357, the second to assemble there, the bishops, some of them clearly dominated by the Arian Emperor, put forward a creed which explicitly forbade the use of *ousia, homoousia,* or *homoiousia,* on the grounds, as was the customary reason advanced by the Arians, that these were not to be found in the Scriptures. Thus the distinctive phrase of the Nicene Creed was condemned. Apparently the extreme Arians were impatient with the long effort to dodge the basic issue between themselves and the Nicene party by the utilization of words which could be interpreted in more than one way and believed themselves to be strong enough to come out unequivocally with their own position and to force through its acceptance by the entire Catholic Church. Hosius, said now to be a centenarian, signed the creed, but, it is alleged, only after he had been brought to the council against his will and had been beaten and tortured. There is some ground for belief, although this has been warmly debated, that under the stress of exile Bishop Liberius of Rome also assented to the Arian position. Obedient councils held in several cities in the next few years concurred: outwardly the unity of the Church had been restored. The official term for the relation of the Son to the Father was *homois,* "similar," that is, "the Son is like the Father."

The issue was complicated by the relations between the Church and the state. The Arians would have the Church submit to the Emperor. The Nicene party insisted on the autonomy of the Church as against the Arian rulers.

THE DEFEAT OF THE ARIANS

The seeming victory of Arianism, due as it had been to the Emperor Constantius, was illusory. However, the reversal of the tide did not come quickly. In 361 death removed Constantius. As we have seen, his successor, Julian, sought to restore paganism and was, accordingly, not averse to the weakening discord in the Church. Athanasius was able to return to Alexandria, but within the year Julian ordered him again into exile, his fourth, for his success in winning pagans to the Christian faith. On Julian's early death (363), Jovian, a Christian, was elevated to the purple, but was little interested in ecclesiastical disputes. Athanasius once more returned to Alexandria. Jovian was followed by Valentinian I, who soon made his brother Valens his colleague and put him in charge of the East. Valens was under the influence of the Arian clergy, for they were strongly intrenched in Constantinople, and Athanasius for the fifth time was exiled. Yet Valens was not as vigorous a supporter of the Arians as Constantius had been.

The Arians were weakened by internal divisions. Some took an extreme position. They would not say that the Son is like (*homois*) the Father, but frankly declared that he was unlike (*anomoios*) the Father, that he was fallible and might sin. They were known as the *anomoians*. In the middle were those who used the term *homois* and could be called the *homoians*. On the other extreme were those who approached the Nicene views and who eventually made common cause with the Nicene party. They have been called semi-Arians, but this probably is not accurate. They were reluctant to say that the Son is *homoousion* with the Father, apparently because they felt that this term meant Sabellianism, with the loss of individuality of the Son and, therefore, the unreality of the incarnation and, accordingly, the failure to realize the wonder of the Gospel in making it possible for men to share in the nature of God without themselves being absorbed into God and losing their individual identity. They were, however, prepared to say that the Son was *homoiousion*, namely, of similar "substance" with the Father. These differences among the Arians had begun to appear before the death of Constantius. As we have seen, it was the middle of the road group, the *homoians*, who won out under him and who in synods controlled by them anathematized both the *anomoians* and the *homoiousians*. These differences continued and deepened.

In their views the adherents of the Nicene formula began to approach the "semi-Arians," or, better, *homoiousians*. At a council or synod held by Athanasius in Alexandria in 362, in an effort to win over the Meletians, who were numerous in Egypt and who were apparently *homoiousians*, a way to reciprocal understanding was sought, so we gather from a synodical letter which grew out of the gathering, by declaring that it is correct to hold that in God there is only one *ousia*, but that there the three *hypostases*. *Hypostasis* (ὑπόστασις) was a term found in both Platonic and Stoic philosophy and could be used as an alternative word for *ousia*. The Synod of Alexandria, indeed, seems to have regarded the two as interchangeable. However, in the development of the thought of the Nicene party, *ousia* came to be regarded as the equivalent of the Latin *substantia* ("substance") and *hypostasis* as translatable into Latin by *persona* ("person"). At Alexandria, it will be noted, the question of the Holy Spirit became more prominent than at Nicæa. At Alexandria it was made clear that the approved belief was that the Holy Spirit is not a creature, but is inseparable from the Father and the Son.

The formulation of the position that clearly distinguished between *ousia* and *hypostasis* and said that in God there is only one *ousia*, in which Father, Son, and Holy Spirit share, but that there are three *hypostases*, Father, Son, and Holy Spirit, was largely the work of what are often called the three great Cappadocians, Gregory of Nazianzus, Basil of Cæsarea, and Gregory of

Nyssa. It was they who led the way in so interpreting the Nicene Symbol that it won the support of the large majority of the Eastern bishops, including many of those who had been classed with the Arians. They represented what might be called right-wing Origenism, that stream of thought which had been reinforced by Origen and which held that the *Logos* has always been equal with the Father.

All three men were natives of Cappadocia, in what later was known as Asia Minor, immediately to the west of Armenia. All three have continued to be held in the highest esteem by those Eastern churches which bear the name Orthodox. Their dates of birth are somewhat uncertain, but all appear to have been born soon after the Council of Nicæa. They were younger contemporaries of Athanasius.

Gregory of Nazianzus was the son of a bishop. He studied in several centres, among them Alexandria and Athens, and so was familiar with Greek philosophy and the thought of Origen. The latter made a profound impression upon him. He was also much attracted by the monastic movement which, as we are to see in a subsequent chapter, was then in the first flush of its devotion and was making a strong appeal to the more earnest among the Christian youth. Late youth and early middle life were spent in comparative obscurity, but when he was not far from fifty he became a preacher in Constantinople and there by his conviction and eloquence did much to bring about the discomfiture of the Arians. Made Bishop of Constantinople not long thereafter, he held the post only a short time. Distressed by the criticism aroused by his promotion, he resigned and retired to the land of his birth.

Basil of Cæsarea, sometimes called the Great, and Gregory of Nyssa were brothers, the latter somewhat the younger. They were scions of a prominent family. A younger brother was also a bishop, an older brother a distinguished Christian jurist, and a sister was noted for her saintly life. Basil had an eager mind and was a fellow student in Athens with Gregory of Nazianzus. Like the latter, he was deeply influenced by Origen. The two joined in compiling a selection from Origen's writings. He was also strongly drawn to monasticism, for a time lived as a monk, and the rules for that life which are ascribed to him still constitute the basic guide for the monastic communities of the (Eastern) Orthodox Church. Not until middle life, however, was he ordained a priest. Naturally a leader and an eloquent preacher, he was made bishop of the important see of Cæsarea in Cappadocia and as such, imperious and vigorous, he did much to rout the Arians. He wrote extensively and improved the liturgy of his church.

Gregory, who was ordained by Basil as Bishop of Nyssa, a small town near Cæsarea, was not as able an administrator as his brother nor as eloquent a preacher as Gregory of Nazianzus, but he was a prolific writer and, like them stimulated by Origen, was a greater theologian than either.

Through long friendship and discussion the three Cappadocians worked out an interpretation of the Nicene formula which removed the doubts of many who had thus far questioned it. They were loyal to the wording of that formula, including *ousia* and *homoousion,* the words which were such a stumbling block to the Arians and which were regarded by the latter as smacking of Sabellianism, that is, as we may remind ourselves again, making Father, Son, and Holy Spirit modes or aspects of God. As we have suggested, they overcame this difficulty by saying that in God there is only one *ousia,* but that there are three *hypostases,* Father, Son, and Holy Spirit. They held that there are not three Gods, but only one, and that the one is to be found equally and identically in Father, Son, and Holy Spirit. For these three the Cappadocians preferred the term *hypostasis,* although they also gave as an alternative term *prosopon* (πρόσωπον).

The difficulty with the Cappadocian effort was that it tended to make God a somewhat vague, colourless abstraction. To one trained in the Platonic philosophy this might not seem alien or untenable, for Platonism held that ideas or forms are real. The generalized term "man," to use an example given by Gregory of Nyssa, has reality. Peter, James, and John seem to be three separate men, but they partake of a common humanity, a single *ousia,* "man." For one not schooled in Platonism, this conception of God might place an obstacle to that love of God which is both the primary obligation and high privilege of men. The Cappadocians did not entirely overcome the difficulty of finding words to compass the facts of Christian experience.

Although the Cappadocians did not fully succeed in making clear in language what Christians believed to be basic to their faith, they prepared the way for the final defeat of the Arians and the triumph in the Catholic Church of what was associated with the name of Nicæa. In the year 380 the Emperor Theodosius issued an edict on ecclesiastical affairs. Born in Spain and reared by parents who were attached to the orthodoxy of the West, he was anti-Arian by heredity and conviction. He ordered that all his subjects follow the faith which "Peter delivered to the Romans," "the deity of the Father and the Son and the Holy Spirit of equal majesty in a Holy Trinity." Congregations of those who varied from this faith were not to be recognized as churches and were to be prohibited. The following year, at his call, a council convened at Constantinople which confirmed the Nicene formula and anathematized those who would not accept it, naming specifically, among others, the *anomoians,* the Arians, and the semi-Arians.

The Nicene Creed

The gathering of 381 was eventually esteemed the Second Ecumenical Council, the first being that at Nicæa in 325. It is doubtful whether this rating can be fully justified. There came to be associated with it, mistakenly believed to have been adopted by it, the creed which today is given the name of Nicene and which is held as authoritative by the Roman Catholic, Orthodox, and several other communions. That creed seems to have been based, not directly upon the Nicene formula, but indirectly upon a fourth century creed which was in use in Jerusalem and which in turn was influenced by the Nicene formula. The major change from the latter were additions at the end. It read, in the form familiar in the Book of Common Prayer: "I believe in the Holy Ghost, the Lord, the Giver of Life, who proceedeth from the Father ['and the Son' was a later Western addition], who with the Father and the Son together is worshipped and glorified, who spake by the prophets. And I believe one Catholic and Apostolic Church. I acknowledge one baptism for the remission of sins. And I look for the resurrection of the dead, and the life of the world to come." The amplification of the clause about the Holy Spirit was put in to make it clear that the Spirit is not subordinate, for while the term *homoousion* was not applied to the Spirit, the intent is clear: the Father, Son, and Holy Spirit are uncreated and are to be worshipped together as one God.

This creed came into general use. The Arian cause was irretrievably lost. For several generations Arianism persisted as the faith of most of the Germanic peoples who, beginning with the latter part of the fourth century, were invading the Empire. Its adherents insisted that it was the true Catholic Church. But the overwhelming majority of Roman citizens held to the Nicene Creed, and Arianism eventually disappeared: its adherents died out or became Catholic (Nicene) Christians. By a slow and often stormy process the overwhelming majority of Christians had come to believe that the formula which bore the Nicene name contained the correct statement of the Christian faith on the questions which had been at issue. Today most of those who are called Christians continue to honour it, along with the Apostles' Creed, as the official authoritative formulation of their faith and as such employ it in public worship.

Further Christological Controversies: the Relation of the Divine and Human in Jesus: Apollinaris, Nestorius, Cyril

The general acceptance in the Catholic Church of what came to be called the Nicene Creed did not bring peace. That creed had been concerned primarily with the Trinity and with the relations within the Trinity of Father, Son, and Holy Spirit. There remained the problem of the relation of the divine and the human in Jesus Christ. Here was to be the storm centre of a controversy which was to continue into the seventh century. It was to issue in divisions some of which persist into the present. Here, as in the struggles over the inter-relations of the members of the Trinity, the majority came to the position which prevailed in the Western portion of the Church and in whose formulation the thought of Tertullian had been of marked assistance. Here, too, the dissensions were the most pronounced in the East. It was in the East that the enduring cleavages were seen.

In general, the participants in the controversy accepted the Nicene formula as authoritative. Within that pattern, however, with its declaration that "the only begotten Son of God . . . very God of very God . . . being of one substance with the Father . . . came down from heaven . . . and was made man," there was room for various interpretations of the fashion in which the Son of God and the human had been found in Jesus of Nazareth. One major trend, with its chief focus at Alexandria, stressed the divine element, at times apparently to the exclusion of the human. Another, strongly represented at Antioch, where the historical study of the Gospels had gone forward, emphasized the human element and tended to regard the divine and human as so distinct from each other that some of its representatives seemed to say that in Jesus there were two separate beings.

It was the first of these views which initially came to the fore. It was associated with Apollinaris, Bishop of Laodicea in Syria, a younger friend of Athanasius. Apollinaris felt that in one being, Christ, two complete and contrasting natures could not exist, namely, the divine, eternal, unchangeable, and perfect, and the human, temporal, corruptible, finite, and imperfect. Along with many others, he held each human being to be composed of body, soul, and mind or reason, the last being what distinguishes man from the lower animals. If the two natures were both in Jesus, the latter would really have in him two beings. Moreover, the human side of Jesus might sin, much as the extreme Arians declared to be possible. This, to Apollinaris, would make man's salvation impossible. He solved the problem of the relation of the divine and human in Jesus by saying that in him the divine *Logos* was the rational element. This, of course, would make Christ less than fully human and would leave the divine nature in him complete. Yet Apollinaris believed that he had remained true to Nicene orthodoxy, and that he had successfully solved one of the unresolved riddles.

The Cappadocians came out in opposition to Apollinaris. They saw that he had sacrificed the full humanity of Christ and said so. Gregory of Nazianzus insisted that only a Christ who had all the elements of human nature could redeem all of man, and that if every phase of man's nature were not redeemed, redemption would not be a fact. Those of the school of Antioch also vigorously disagreed. They held that the divine and human natures were both complete in Jesus and that the *Logos* dwelt in Jesus much as God dwells in a temple. God had thus been in the prophets and is in Christians, but the relation was unique in Jesus, for Jesus willed what God willed and in him the unity had become indissoluble. The school of Antioch was seemingly more affected by Aristotle than by Plato and made more of the historical facts of the life of Jesus. That of Alexandria, to which Apollinaris belonged, had been more under the influence of Plato. The Antioch school was concerned with the study of the historical accounts of the life of Christ. Diodorus of Tarsus was an outstanding teacher of these views and among his students were Theodore, Bishop of Mopsuestia from 392 to 428, John Chrysostom, and Nestorius, a presbyter and monk of Antioch who in 428 was called from his monastery to become Bishop of Constantinople.

Emphatic decisions against the views of Apollinaris were pronounced by various synods, among them ones in Rome in 374, 376, and 382, and in 381 by the Council of Constantinople which condemned the Arians.

Yet the struggle between the convictions represented by Alexandria and Antioch was not terminated by the anathemas against Apollinaris. It was kept up and out of it issued two extremes, on the one hand the several varieties of Monophysites and on the other that associated with the name of Nestorius. They failed to find favour with the Catholic Church and were ruled out and joined with geographic, political, and cultural factors in distinguishing churches which were separated from the Catholic Church and which have had a continuing existence.

The chief leader in the position associated with Alexandria was Cyril, bishop of that city from 412 to 444. He seems to have been moved not only by theological conviction but also, perhaps unconsciously or half-consciously, by ambition for leadership in the Catholic Church for himself and his see and by jealousy of the other great episcopal sees of the East, Antioch and Constantinople, both of them occupied by men who endorsed views from which he sharply dissented. Cyril shared in the refusal to accept the solution of Apollinaris, for he maintained that in Christ the divine and the human nature were both complete and that the latter included the rational element. But the unity in Christ, so Cyril held, was through the *Logos* who became incarnate in Christ, and who in becoming incarnate took on the general characteristics of man. The humanity in Christ was not so much an individual man as humanity in general. Salvation was accomplished by the personal *Logos* who assumed impersonal human nature, thus uniting it with the divine nature. It is thus, so Cyril taught, that human nature is enabled to become a partaker of God and of immortality. In this Cyril seemed to be following in the footsteps of Athanasius. He applied to the Virgin Mary a term which had long been in current use, *Theotokos* (Θεοτόκος), "God-bearing," or, as usually translated, "Mother of God," a term which, unfortunately, was to become a battle cry in as sharp and bitter a theological conflict as the Church had known.

As Bishop of Constantinople, Nestorius was zealous in attacking heresy, especially the remnants of the Arians. However, reared as he had been in the theological atmosphere of Antioch, he was reluctant to employ *Theotokos* in his sermons, but preferred instead *Christotokos* (Χριστοτόκος), "Christ-bearing," or "Mother of Christ," not "God-bearing," or "Mother of God." This aroused Cyril. Apparently he was all the more keen to scent heresy because his critics were complaining about him to the Emperor and to Nestorius. Nestorius had interested himself in the situation, and Cyril, partly moved by injured pride, welcomed an opportunity to shift attention from himself to the challengeable views of his rival. Nestorius was not always tactful, circulated his convictions widely, and dealt harshly with monks who dared to denounce him. Cyril came out in favour of *Theotokos* and a sharp exchange of letters took place between himself and Nestorius. Both men wrote to their fellow bishop, Celestine of Rome. Celestine found against Nestorius, possibly because the latter had not been as deferential to him as had Cyril and possibly also because Nestorius had displayed a certain degree of hospitality to some Pelagians, of whom we are to hear more a little later, who had fled to Constantinople. In 430 a synod at Rome ordered Nestorius either to recant or be excommunicated. Also in the year 430 Cyril convened a synod in Alexandria which condemned the positions which he maintained were those of Nestorius. Among them were the failure to use *Theotokos* and the separation of the divine and human nature in Christ in such fashion that Christ was viewed as a "God-bearing man," and that "Jesus is, as a man, energized by the *Logos* of God." Except for the reluctance to use *Theotokos,* Nestorius had not taught them.

The dispute waxed so warm that a general council was called—by imperial order—to deal with it. The bishops assembled at Ephesus in 431 (in what is usually called the Third Ecumenical Council). Cyril and his supporters reached the city first. Without waiting for the friends of Nestorius, a party of bishops from Antioch, the council convened under the presidency of Cyril and, when Nestorius declined to appear before it until the other bishops arrived, under the leadership of his chief accuser in a single long day's session it condemned and deposed him. Stirred up by their bishop, Memnon, the Ephesian populace committed acts of violence against Nestorius and his supporters. When, not long thereafter, John, the Bishop of Antioch, and the bishops with him came, they organized themselves, claiming to be the legitimate council, and condemned Cyril and Memnon as Arians and Apollinarians and deposed and excommunicated them. The bishops in Cyril's council numbered about two hundred and those in John's forty-three. A few days later, when the representatives of Bishop Celestine of Rome reached Ephesus, the majority council resumed its sessions and excommunicated Bishop John and his party.

Both sides appealed to the Emperor and the latter for the moment confirmed the deposition of Cyril, Memnon, and Nestorius and endeavoured to bring the two factions together and heal the breach. Nestorius was commanded henceforth to live in a monastery. A temporary peace was patched up when in 433 John of Antioch sent to Cyril a creed which declared Jesus Christ to be "true God and true man, consisting of a reasonable soul and a body," and the Virgin to be *Theotokos*. To this creed Cyril subscribed.

Nestorius remained in exile, most of the time, apparently, in Egypt, and often in great physical and mental distress. In his painful seclusion he wrote extensively in his own defense, setting forth his version of the unhappy controversy and elaborating a statement of his faith. From this it is not entirely clear whether he held the views which have been associated with his name—the presence of the divine and human in Jesus Christ in such fashion that there were in Him two distinct beings or persons rather than, as the majority view held, two natures concurring in one person (*prosopon*) and one substance (*hypostasis*).

One of the works written by Nestorius in exile bore the title *Tragedy*. That might be a description of the life of the author and of the group of which he was a central figure, and also be illustrative of one aspect of the course of the Gospel. In his youth giving himself completely to Christ and in pursuance of that dedication caught up in the monastic movement, in the prime of his manhood Nestorius was called to one of the most exalted positions in the Catholic Church, the leadership of the Church in the Empire's second capital, Constantinople. There in his zeal for Christ as he understood him Nestorius aroused the bitter enmity of fellow Christians who also believed themselves to be loyal to Christ and held that by his preaching Nestorius dishonoured him. The leader of the opposition, Cyril, in part confused allegiance to Christ with personal ambition. Scenes followed which were a denial of the love and therefore of the faith to which both parties were theoretically committed. Nestorius, defeated, languished long years in exile. Outraged and perhaps perplexed, he again and again went over the events and the convictions which had brought him to that pass. He believed himself to have been right, but his thinking appears either to have been too subtle or not clear cut. Dragging out his years in his banishment Nestorius perished in obscurity while his successful rival continued in office and died amidst the trappings of ecclesiastical splendour.

Neither man was perfect, either in his adherence to Christian moral standards or in his thinking. Through both the Church was further divided. Yet both had been, in their own eyes, sincere. In a sense they were typical of the entire Christian Church and epitomized the problem presented by the Gospel in the world.

"NESTORIANISM" FINDS A REFUGE IN THE PERSIAN EMPIRE

Nestorius was not entirely to fail. When once he was safely out of the way and John and Cyril were reconciled, the latter sought to bring about the condemnation of Diodorus of Tarsus and Theodore of Mopsuestia (now dead) whom he charged as authors of the Nestorian heresy. In this he was aided by the Bishop of Edessa. Moreover, Armenian monks with Monophysite tendencies came out vigorously against Theodore. John of Antioch, as might have been expected, rose to the defense of Theodore, and the Emperor, presumably at his instance, ordered that no one should be calumniated who had died in the communion of the Catholic Church—thus supporting John.

There were some, including bishops, who held views akin to those of Theodore and Nestorius who refused to subscribe to the creed through which Cyril and John had composed their differences. Because they were regarded by the imperial authorities as disturbers of the peace of the Church and thus of the realm, they were exiled. A number of them sought refuge in the Persian Empire. Among them were several who found a home at Nisibis, the chief training school for the clergy in the Persian domains. Eventually many of the leading ecclesiastical posts in that realm were filled by their students and, after something of a struggle, their doctrines became the accepted teaching of the Mesopotamian-Persian Church. That church now tended to regard the Catholic Church as heretical. This was of advantage to it, for ever since Constantine had espoused Christianity it had been looked at askance by the Persian monarchs as a possible supporter of their chronic enemies, the Roman Emperors. The Mesopotamian-Persian Church could now affirm that, since its ties with the church of the Roman Empire had been dissolved, that fear was baseless. It is said that on this ground one of the Sassanian monarchs of Persia decreed that Nestorian Christianity should be the only form of the faith granted official recognition in his possessions.

How far the teachers at Nisibis dissented from what was endorsed by the Catholic Church is debatable. The variation may not have been as great as has sometimes been said. Whatever the degree of the difference, the Mesopotamian-Persian Church came to be known as the Nestorian Church. As we have seen and are to see in later chapters, it was the means of an extensive eastward spread of the Christianity which in subsequent centuries carried the faith to the shores of the China Sea. The influence of Nestorius, therefore, did not disappear with his pitiful death, but was felt across the vast reaches of Asia.

The Continuation of the Christological Controversy: "The Robber Synod" of Ephesus and the Council and Creed of Chalcedon

So long as Cyril of Alexandria and John of Antioch lived, the peace which had been effected between the theologies which they represented was fairly well preserved. However, that peace proved to be only a truce. After death had removed them from the scene the struggle broke out with renewed fury. Here were two tendencies which could scarcely be reconciled. The one, represented by the scholarship which had been strong at Antioch, stressed the historical study of the Gospel records of the life of Jesus and hence made much of his humanity. The other, with its traditional centre at Alexandria, interpreted the Scriptures allegorically, minimized the historical and therefore the human side of Christ, and gave great weight to the divine in him. It was in part an outgrowth of the position of Athanasius and had been carried further by Cyril, even though the latter had anathematized its extension in the form represented by Apollinaris. As we have suggested, the tension was heightened by rivalries between the great sees of the Orient, especially between Alexandria and the New Rome at Constantinople, for from the standpoint of the former the latter was an upstart. Moreover, Constantinople made itself conveniently obnoxious by drawing a large proportion of its bishops from men trained in the Antiochene tradition.

In 444 Cyril was succeeded at Alexandria by Dioscurus, a man fully as zealous as himself for the prestige and theology of his see and who went beyond Cyril in emphasizing the divine nature in Christ. In 446 Flavian, whose sympathies seem to have been with Antioch, was placed in the bishop's chair in Constantinople. Conflict soon arose over a monk of Constantinople, Eutyches. Eutyches denounced as Nestorian the creed of 433 in which John of Antioch and Cyril had reached agreement and declared that before the union (the incarnation) there were the two natures, divine and human, but that after the union (the incarnation) the two so blended that there was only one nature, and that was fully divine. In other words, Jesus Christ was *homoousion* with the Father but not with man. Eutyches was denounced at a synod in Constantinople in 448 over which Flavian presided, was excommunicated as a reviler of Christ, and was deposed from every priestly office. Eutyches presented his case to the Emperor and to a number of bishops, including the Bishop of Rome. Flavian also wrote to fellow bishops, as was the custom in the Catholic Church, among others to the Bishop of Rome.

The Bishop of Rome was one of the ablest men who have ever sat on the throne of Peter, Leo I, "the Great." Leo supported Flavian and sent him a long letter, known as the *Tome,* in which he set forth the view which had been generally held in the West and which had been clearly stated by Tertullian years before, that in Christ Jesus there was neither manhood without true Godhead nor the Godhead without true manhood, that in Christ two full and complete natures came together in one person, "without detracting from the properties of either nature and substance."

Dioscurus sided with Eutyches. The Emperor called a council of the whole Church to deal with the issue. The council convened at Ephesus in 449. Dioscurus presided and was dominant. Leo was not present but was represented by two legates. His *Tome* was denied a reading. The gathering professed allegiance to the creed of Nicæa, by a large majority declared Eutyches exonerated, and deposed Flavian and some of his supporters. Dioscurus excommunicated Leo and appointed an Alexandrian priest in his stead. It is not strange that in circles loyal to Rome the council was dubbed "the robber synod."

Leo was not to be so easily thwarted. He sought to have another council called, and in Italy. In 451 a council was indeed summoned by the Emperor, but it met, not in Italy, but at Chalcedon, immediately across the Bosporus from Constantinople, and was later known as the Fourth Ecumenical Council. About six hundred bishops were present, more than had previously come together at any one gathering, almost all of them from the East. Leo did not come, but was represented by legates. The latter were given the first place in the roll-calls. The imperial commissioners presided. Dioscurus was present, but was clearly out of favour. The *Tome* of Leo was approved and a creed was adopted which incorporated its views. The heart of it read:

Following the holy fathers we all, with one voice, define that there is to be confessed one and the same Son, our Lord Jesus Christ, perfect in Godhead and perfect in manhood, truly God and truly man, of rational soul and body, of the same substance [*homoousion*] with the Father according to the Godhead, and of the same substance [*homoousion*] with us according to the manhood, like to us in all respects, without sin, begotten of the Father before all time according to the Godhead, in these latter days, for us and for our salvation, born of the Virgin Mary, the Mother of God [*Theotokos*] according to the manhood, one and the same Christ, Son, Lord, Only-begotten, in two natures, inconfusedly, immutably, indivisibly, inseparately, the distinction of natures being by no means taken away by the union, but rather the peculiarity of each nature being preserved and concurring in one person [*prosopon*] and one substance [*hypostasis*], not parted or separated into two persons, but one and the same Son and Only-begotten, divine word [*Theon Logon*], the Lord Jesus Christ; as from the beginning the prophets declared concerning him, and the

Lord Jesus Christ has taught us, and the creed of the holy fathers has transmitted to us.

It will be seen that in this the distinctive views of Apollinaris, Eutyches, and those ascribed to Nestorius are condemned.

Flavian, now dead, was exonerated, Eutyches was denounced as a heretic, and Dioscurus was deposed and excommunicated.

In other legislation of the council, various regulations or canons were enacted for the administration of the Church. Moreover, the Bishop of Constantinople was placed second in precedence to the Bishop of Rome, thus promoting his see above the more ancient ones of Antioch, Alexandria, and Jerusalem.

The Further Progress of Monophysitism

In spite of Chalcedon, the view represented by Alexandria continued to spread. To be sure, the West, led by Rome, and such of the East as acknowledged Constantinople held by the decision of that council. But large elements in the East dissented. They were called Monophysites, for they stressed the divine nature in Christ, holding that it transformed the human nature in such fashion that the whole became divine, although with some human characteristics. The Monophysites varied in the degree to which they emphasized the divine in Christ, but they could not accept Chalcedon.

The division was largely regional. Most of Egypt, Ethiopia, and much of Syria became Monophysite, thus further breaking the unity of the Catholic Church and threatening that of the Empire. Armenia also tended in that direction. The Roman Empire, within which whatever unity the Catholic Church possessed had been achieved and to which it was deeply indebted, was already suffering from the disintegration which was to become permanent in the centuries after A.D. 500. In later chapters we shall see how the divisions in the Church and in the political structure interacted to reinforce one another. The efforts to achieve Christian unity through doctrinal statements, ecclesiastical organization, and the aid of the state were proving illusory.

Yet the state did not give up the struggle. In 476 the Emperor Basilicus in his *Encyclion* condemned the *Tome* of Leo and Chalcedon. In 482 the Emperor Zeno, in an attempt to heal the breach between Monophysites and the Chalcedonians, took a partly opposite tack and issued what was known as the *Henoticon,* a document which was purposely capable of various interpretations and which satisfied some of the moderate Monophysites. However, the more extreme of the Monophysites would not accept it, and the Bishop of Rome, believing it to be a rejection of Chalcedon, broke off communion with the Bishop of Constantinople, who supported it. To carry the story to its end would take us far into the period which followed the year 500. We must, accordingly, defer its completion to a later chapter.

AUGUSTINE AND PELAGIANISM

While the conflict over Nestorius and between the Alexandrian and Antiochene schools was raging in the eastern part of the Catholic Church, another struggle was being waged mainly in the Western portions of the Church. It seems to have been characteristic of the Latin West that this was primarily over the nature of man rather than, as in the Hellenistic East, over the relation of the human and the divine in Christ.

One of the striking facts of the history of Christianity is that after the fifth century creative, original thought became less and less frequent in the Eastern sections of the Church, but that it continued in the West and, with occasional sterile periods, has persisted into the present. This does not mean that thought and discussion on the great issues presented to the human mind ceased in the East. It was still to be found there, but except for some minority groups it took as final the conclusions reached in the "ecumenical" councils of the first eight and especially the first five centuries and it operated within the framework arrived at through those councils and raised few if any basically new questions.

Some reasons for this partial sterility are fairly obvious and will be pointed out in a subsequent chapter. Others must be largely conjectural and, therefore, debatable. It may be that they are to be found to some degree in the circumstance that the East addressed itself primarily to the relation of the divine and the human in Christ and was more concerned with the divine element in Christ and in the end, even beyond circles which were known as Monophysite, tended to stress the divine in him and to give less attention to his humanity. In contrast, the West, while agreeing in principle on the relation of the divine and the human in Christ as formulated in the findings of the councils in which it had joined with the Eastern portion of the Catholic Church, concerned itself also with problems of human nature and of the fashion in which the "grace"—the unmerited love of God in Christ—operated in relation to human nature.

This concern of the Western, or Latin, part of the Catholic Church with the nature of man and the manner in which God through Christ redeems and transforms it was vividly seen in the fifth century in Augustine.

In the preceding chapter we saw something of the early life and the conversion of Augustine. Here was a sensitive spirit and a first-class mind which, after a prolonged quest for moral victory, an answer to the riddle of life, and inner peace, first through Manichæism (which he hoped would satisfy him intellectually and give him moral power but which failed to do either) and then through Neoplatonism (which gave him a convincing intellectual framework from which he never long departed but could not meet his moral needs), at last found what he craved, in dramatic fashion, in the Gospel. In later years, through a long life, Augustine gave himself to a study of various aspects of the Christian faith.

No other single Christian thinker after Paul was to influence so profoundly the Christianity of Western European peoples. Individuals such as Thomas Aquinas, Luther, and Calvin were to have as great or greater effect on particular branches of the Christianity of the West, but no other after the apostolic age was so deeply to mould all the major forms of the Western wing of the faith. He combined deep personal Christian experience with an acute and disciplined intellect which had been quickened to profound activity by the Gospel and which was equipped with a knowledge of Neoplatonism, familiarity with the best Roman thought, and the Roman tradition of emphasis upon morals and action. Significantly, Augustine was to have little influence in Eastern Christianity. By helping to shape and by epitomizing much of Western Christianity, he contributed to the incipient divergence between the Christianity of the western and eastern portions of the Mediterranean world. His thought was dominant in Latin Christianity for at least eight centuries, has since remained prominent in the Roman Catholic Church, and was to make major contributions to Protestantism.

We have noted the conversion of Augustine at Milan in 385 and his baptism by Ambrose, the great Bishop of Milan, together with that of his son, Adeodatus, and a friend, at Easter, 387. Soon thereafter, Augustine, with his mother, Monica, Adeodatus, and some of his friends set out for his native place in Africa. On the way, while waiting at Ostia for their ship, Monica died. Adeodatus followed her a few months later, after the party's arrival in Africa. In Africa, at his family estate in Tagaste, the group lived in community in study and prayer. Within a little less than three years (in 391), while Augustine was visiting Hippo Regius, a port about two hundred miles west of Carthage, popular demand led to his ordination as presbyter. Four years later, after much hesitation on his part, at the insistence of the Bishop of Hippo he was consecrated bishop with the right of succession to that see. The following year, 396, on the demise of his predecessor, he became Bishop of Hippo and remained in that post until his death, August 28, 430.

At Hippo Augustine faithfully performed his episcopal duties—preaching, administering discipline, caring for the poor, and adjudicating disputes among his flock. He gathered clergy about him who lived together under a common rule. He also carried on an enormous correspondence and through this and his other writing made of the otherwise obscure port of Hippo one of the chief centres of Christian thought of his day. He was a prolific author. Although troubled with insomnia and often ill, he accomplished a prodigious amount of work.

In all his writing, although it bore the mark of his genius and contributed fresh insights, Augustine held to views which were already widely accepted in the Catholic Church. He had a high conception of the Catholic Church. He held that God's attitude towards man can be known only through faith, that faith is a guide to truth, and that faith is belief in what is taught by the Scriptures and the Church. He said that he would not have believed the Scriptures had the Church not declared them to be true. His youthful repugnance to them disappeared, partly because he had learned from Ambrose the method, so widespread in the Church, of interpreting allegorically passages, especially in the Old Testament, which had repelled him.

Although there were other important ones, including a treatise on the Trinity, Augustine's most distinctive works were on the interrelated subjects of human nature, the character of sin, the redemption of man, the attitude of the Church towards the sinner and the penitent, the Church within history, and history. His autobiography, the *Confessions,* is not so much narrative, although it contains it, as meditations on human nature as seen in himself and on the fashion in which God had dealt with him. His extensive polemics against the Donatists were on the burning issues on which the latter separated from the Catholic Church. These were not what are usually called doctrinal questions, for on such points as those on which Gnostics, Marcionites, Arians, and Monophysites differed from the Catholic Church Donatists were in accord with the latter. The contention, rather, as we have seen, was over the moral character of the priesthood and the treatment which the Church should accord to those Christians who, having been guilty of serious lapses, repented.

Augustine believed profoundly in the Catholic Church as a visible institution distributed throughout the world, continuous from the church of the apostles through its bishops, whom he esteemed the successors of the apostles. To be sure, Augustine held that bishops, including the Bishop of Rome, might err, but the Catholic Church, he maintained, was the Body of Christ, tangible, and outside it there was no salvation.

One of Augustine's most widely read works was the *City of God (De Civitate Dei)*. Provoked by the sack of Rome by Alaric and his Goths in 410, and the insistence by the pagans that the fall of the Eternal City had been due to the abandonment by the growing body of Christians of the gods who had made Rome great, the *City of God* was not only an attempted refutation of that charge. It was also a positive and comprehensive philosophy of history, an interpretation of the entire human drama. In contrast with the Greek view which regarded history as a series of cycles, endlessly repeating itself, Augustine, in accordance with the Biblical view, maintained that it had a beginning and a culmination. Contradicting his non-Christian contemporaries who prized the Roman Empire as the citadel and guarantor of order in the midst of a chaotic world, a society held together by a divine ruler, and who viewed its decline with deep dismay, Augustine regarded the passing of the Empire with confident hope, believing that the Roman realm was to be replaced by an infinitely better order, that to be established by God. Augustine held that from the time of man's first rebellion against God two cities, the earthly and the heavenly, had existed, the first typified by Cain and the other by Abel. The earthly was formed by love of self and pride. It was not entirely bad, for Babylon and Rome, its highest representatives, and other governments had, out of regard for self-interest, brought peace and order. The heavenly city, on the other hand, is dominated "by the love of God even to the contempt of self." Men enter it here and now and it is represented by the Church, although not all in the Church are its citizens. The earthly city must fade as the heavenly city grows. As Augustine saw it, from its very inception all history has been directed and governed by God and moves to a climax in a society in which God's will is perfectly to be accomplished. Although his general conception of meaning in history was derived from the Scriptures, the boldness of his pattern, with its contrast between the city of the world and the city of God, and the fashion in which he fitted history into that framework was a striking contribution to the thought of mankind.

It is significant that the *City of God* concerned itself with man. To be sure, its subject was the dealings of God with man, but its emphasis was upon what happens to man. In this interest in man, visible institutions, and history Augustine differed from the thinkers of the Eastern sections of the Catholic Church. They focussed their attention upon God and tended to minimize man.

In his emphasis Augustine was more than an individual. He was typical of a major trend in the Western portions of the Catholic Church, of what might be called Latin Christianity. While this Latin Christianity fully assented to the creeds of Nicæa and Chalcedon and, indeed, as we have seen, contributed decisively to the latter, it was more concerned with historical man and human society than were the Greek and other branches of the Eastern sections of the Catholic Church. It was more activistic, more intent upon moulding society here and now than were these others. To be sure, Eastern Christianity had pronounced social effects and now and again had movements, such as that associated with the name of Joseph Volotsky in Russia in the sixteenth century, which sought to shape the entire life of a country, but in general, perhaps in part because of the practical Roman tradition, Western Christianity gave more thought and effort to man within history than did its Eastern counterpart. This may have been because of the Roman tradition, with its concern for empire and for the practical administration of human affairs.

The controversy of Augustine with Pelagius and the discussions over what was termed Pelagianism, were, characteristically, most marked in the Western or Latin portion of the Catholic Church. They were known in the East and Eastern synods dealt with them, but they were most pronounced and continued longest in the West.

The issue was the freedom of man's will and the manner in which the grace of God operates. In general the East, while by no means denying the grace of God, believed in the freedom of man's will and in the ability of the individual man to do what God commands. The great preacher of the Eastern Church, John Chrysostom, for example, insisted that men can choose the good and that when they do so grace comes to their aid to reinforce them in their effort to do what God commands. In the West, however, even before the time of Augustine, Tertullian, Cyprian, and Ambrose had declared for what is usually known as original sin. Ambrose, for instance, taught that through the sin of the first man, Adam, all Adam's descendants come into the world tainted with sin. "Adam perished and in him we all perished," he said. He held that no one is conceived without sin and that, therefore, the new-born infant has it. In contrast with Chrysostom, who maintained that man by his free will turns to God and that then God supports man's will, Ambrose believed that God's grace begins the work of salvation and that, when grace has initiated it, a man through his will coöperates.

Augustine went much further than Ambrose. That was probably in part because of his personal history of prolonged moral impotence against the sin which he believed had been with him from his conception and his infancy and because of his experience of having been sought by God's grace until he could not but yield to it. Augustine held that at the outset angels and men were created rational and free, the only created beings of which that could be said. In the beginning, moreover, so Augustine, true to his Neoplatonic background, taught, there was no evil anywhere. What we call evil, he said, is but the absence of good. In this he revolted from his Manichæan stage with its belief in a primal dualism, with an evil as well as a good principle in nature. Evil, as he saw it, is degradation, a decline from one's proper rank. His capacity for rational free choice, so Augustine went on to hold, is at once man's highest quality, a gift from God intended for his own good, and his chief peril. Only men and angels have rational free choice. They can exist without being wicked, but because they alone possess rational free will, only they can be wicked.

Employing his divinely given capacity for rational free choice, so Augustine further taught, the first man, Adam, fell into sin. This was not primarily a yielding to sub-rational instincts and emotional drives, as the Greeks would have held, but a choice made deliberately through the use of reason. Basically man's sin is pride, the desire of the creature to put himself in the centre rather than God, to do his will rather than God's will. Through his own bitter experience Augustine saw this degradation especially in sexual lust.

This falling away from man's God-given status into a lower level of being, so Augustine believed, is not one from which man can recover by his own effort. Every endeavour of man to restore himself to his primal rank is marred and made impotent by the degradation worked by that original sin. Man cannot raise himself by his own boot-straps. Having once put himself in the centre, his every effort to extricate himself is nullified by the fact that it arises from continuing concern for himself, and thus he is mired ever more deeply in the morass into which he has fallen. Man is still free, but only free to sin, to sink ever lower. He is not free to turn wholly to God. The sin of Adam and its resulting degradation are, so Augustine believed, passed on to all Adam's descendants, namely, all the human race. All of us have not only a tendency to sin, but through Adam's sin we share his loss of status, his self-centredness, his inability to choose God, and, therefore, his guilt in the sight of God. We can be rescued only through a second birth. This cannot be except by a fresh act of God.

Since by Adam's fall the wills of all Adam's descendants have been in bondage to sin and death, so Augustine said, freedom can come only by the grace of God. This grace of God was in Christ, Christ who was in God incarnate, fully God and yet fully man. The man Christ Jesus is the only mediator between God and man. Born of the Virgin Mary, he was not stained by the sin which accompanies ordinary human generation, and lived and died without sin. Christ is the second Adam, for in him God made a new start. Through the sin of the first Adam, Augustine declared, "the entire mass of our nature was ruined and fell into the possession of its destroyer. And from him no one—no, not one—has been delivered, or ever will be delivered, except by the grace of the Redeemer." Quoting Paul, to the effect that "the gift of God is eternal life through Jesus Christ our Lord," Augustine insisted that "a gift, unless it is wholly unearned, is not a gift at all," and that, therefore, even "man's good deserts are themselves the gift of God, so that when these obtain the recompense of eternal life, it is simply grace."

Augustine was profoundly convinced that all men share the sin of Adam and therefore deserve judgement. Of His great mercy, however, God has predestined some to salvation. The others He has predestined to the punishment which their sin deserves. All men, being stained by sin, deserve damnation, but God, of His grace, has by His free choice selected some to be saved and also has chosen those whom He will not save. Augustine, therefore, seemed to teach "double predestination," namely, the determination by God of those on whom He will have mercy and those on whom He will not have mercy. Augustine held that God has predetermined the exact number of those who are to receive His grace, and that that "number is so certain that one can neither be added to them nor taken from them . . . that the number of the elect is certain and neither to be increased nor diminished." Those who are of the elect will, accordingly, be saved. Of His grace God will accord them the gift of perseverance, so that even though they commit sins they will repent. Eventually those to whom perseverance has been assigned will not be able to sin. Before his fall Adam had been able not to sin, was able not to die, and might have persevered if he would. This was a blessing which was from God. The culminating blessing given to the elect will be that they will not be able to forsake good and not be able to die. This is the highest freedom of all. Here are convictions which we are to meet again and again in the course of Christianity in the West—"predestination," "irresistible grace," and "the perseverance of the saints."

No one can here certainly know, so Augustine taught, whether he is among the elect. He may be among the believers, for, quoting from one of the parables in the Gospels, "many are called." "But," to quote again from that parable, "few are chosen." Not all those who are "called" and "believe" will persevere. By baptism original sin and the sins committed before baptism are washed away. Augustine, indeed, advocated the baptism of infants on the ground that baptism is the prescribed way of washing away original sin—the sin inherited from Adam. Augustine taught that both baptism and the Lord's Supper are necessary to salvation. By God's grace men are enabled to do good works which God rewards as though they were theirs. A gradual transformation is wrought by His grace. Yet one may be baptized and partake of the communion, good works and spiritual growth may be seen, and still one may not be among those elected to receive the gift of perseverance and ultimate salvation. If one were to be confident of being among the elect, this might well lead to pride, a renewal of the basic sin. Therefore it is necessary that so long as a man is in this mortal flesh he shall be uncertain where he is "in the number of the predestined."

Some of these views of Augustine were elaborated and sharpened by his controversy with those known as the Pelagians, especially Pelagius and his associate, Cœlestius, and the Bishop of Eclanum, Julian. Pelagius was a British monk who came to Rome not far from the end of the fourth century and was there for several years. He was a layman, a man of some learning, and of austere and ascetic life. He was apparently scandalized by the loose living of many of the Roman populace and sought to persuade them to reform. He insisted that if they really desired to do so, they could keep the commandments of God. Among those whom he won was a younger man, Cœlestius, a lawyer and, like Pelagius, a layman. Cœlestius was more forthright and less tactful in expressing his views than was his teacher.

Shortly after 410 Augustine's *Confessions* was having a wide reading in Rome. In it Augustine had prayed: "Give what you command: command what you will." This seemed to Pelagius to lead to moral listlessness and he protested that man had sufficient free will to perform his duty to God and should exert himself to do so.

Not far from 411 Pelagius and Cœlestius came to North Africa, perhaps because of the sack of Rome by Alaric and his Goths. There Cœlestius applied for ordination as presbyter but was accused of heretical teachings and was excommunicated by a local synod (412). Among the teachings ascribed to him and which he did not deny holding were that Adam's sin injured himself only and not the human race, that every child is born as free as Adam was before his fall and can, if he chooses, do the right, that a man can fully keep God's commandments if he will, and that some before the time of Christ had been sinless.

Both Pelagius and Cœlestius went to the East, and the latter was ordained presbyter at Ephesus. In Palestine Pelagius attracted the attention of Jerome, who was living there, and aroused his ire. A synod at Jerusalem, to which the issue was referred, took no action except to refer the matter to Rome, and in 415 a synod at Diospolis (Lydda) in Palestine acquitted Pelagius. However, in 416 synods at Carthage, Mileve (in Numidia), and Rome took adverse action and the Bishop of Rome supported them. The next Bishop of Rome, Zosimus, first sided with Pelagius and Cœlestius, but, after the Emperor Honorius had exiled them (418), he also condemned them. In 418 a synod in Carthage came out against Pelagianism. In spite of these actions, Julian continued to argue the case and so brought against him the powerful pen of Augustine. Cœlestius, again going East, won the support of Nestorius, then Bishop of Constantinople. In 431 the Council of Ephesus which condemned Nestorius also acted against Pelagius, Cœlestius, and their associates, including Julian.

Those grouped under the category of Pelagians did not completely agree among themselves and held a variety of views. Julian, for example, seems to have been as much a Stoic as a Christian and was interested in the philosophical aspects of the issue, while Pelagius and Cœlestius appear to have been more concerned for religious and moral results.

In general Pelagians differed from Augustine in denying that the taint of Adam's sin and the impairment of the will brought by it have been transmitted to all Adam's descendants, but, in contrast, declared that each man at birth has the ability to choose the good. In other words, they denounced "original sin." Some seem to have held that Adam was created mortal and that his death was not due to his sin, that new-born children need not be baptized, for they have no original sin inherited from Adam which needs to be washed away, and that some men before and after Christ have so used their free will that they have been sinless. God's grace, so at least some Pelagians held, is seen in giving man free will at his creation, in giving man the law as a guide to his choice, and in sending Jesus Christ who by his teaching and good example assists men to do good. From Augustine's standpoint, this view made grace unnecessary and differed little from Stoic morality.

The struggle between Augustine and Pelagianism is a phase, within a Christian context, of the agelong controversy between determinism and indeterminism in which in many different cultures thoughtful men have engaged. To Christians with the experience of Paul and Augustine only one answer is possible, for in their own lives they have known the impotence of their wills and the power of victory which has come from outside themselves as the free gift of God through Jesus Christ. To them it is easy to regard the action of God as initiated solely by God and at His unfathomable discretion. Others, who have not known that deep inner conflict with its bitter frustration and the amazing joy of triumph through God's grace, have been inclined to hold to man's ability to attain, through his own effort, although perhaps aided by God, to the ideal life. In one form or another the issue has again and again been raised, especially in the Christianity of Western Europe.

SEMI-PELAGIANISM

Although Pelagianism had been officially condemned by the authorities of the Catholic Church, not all Catholics fully agreed with Augustine. Some thought that his doctrine of predestination, irresistible grace, and perseverance due entirely to God would undercut all moral effort, for if God chooses those who are to be saved and no sinner can take even the first step towards repentance and God without the impulse of God's grace, and if God will find a way of making His grace effective for the elect, why should any one trouble himself to attempt to do what is right?

This stage of the controversy over election as against free will was begun by John Cassian, a monk from the East who about 415 founded monasteries in the vicinity of Marseilles, in Gaul. He declared that God wishes all men, not merely some, to be saved, that He has not so made man that the latter neither wills nor is able to do good, and that when He sees in us even the smallest spark of a will towards goodness He strengthens it. Cassian was followed by his pupil, Vincent, a monk of Lerins, who declared that Augustine's teachings were novelties and that in the Catholic Church "all possible care should be taken" to "hold that faith which has been believed everywhere, always, and by all." (*Quod ubique, quod semper, quod ab omnibus.*)

Some in Gaul came to the support of the views of Augustine and in 529 the Bishop of Arles held a synod or council at Orange whose findings were approved by Bishop Boniface II, of Rome, and thus were accorded the support of that powerful see. The Synod of Orange affirmed original sin and declared that man has lost all power to turn to God and that turning to God is wholly through God's grace. It condemned those who affirmed that our will can anticipate God's action, that the beginning of faith and the desire to believe can come apart from the free gift of grace, and that apart from God's grace we can choose the good. Yet the findings of the synod said nothing of irresistible grace and condemned the teaching that some are predestined to evil. Moreover, the Synod of Orange did not speak of man as being totally depraved by Adam's sin. It said, rather, that by that sin free will is so inclined and weakened that "no one is able to love God as he ought, or believe in God, or do anything for God which is good, except the grace of divine mercy comes first to him." Moreover, the Synod of Orange ascribed more to baptism than did Augustine. To be sure, Augustine held that baptism is essential to the remission of sins, but the Synod of Orange declared that through the grace received at baptism "all who have been baptized can and ought, by the aid and support of Christ, to perform those things which belong to the salvation of the soul if they labour faithfully." The implication is that all, and not merely, as Augustine held, those of the limited number of the elect, can, if they are baptized, through the grace which comes through baptism, if they work at it faithfully, by the aid and support of Christ, be assured of salvation. They need not be distressed by the fear that they are not of those to whom, through grace, perseverance has not been given. Man's will has not been so impaired by Adam's fall but that, healed by grace and aided by Christ, it can achieve salvation. Here were semi-Augustinianism, a weakening of pure Augustinianism, and a view of baptism which were to characterize Latin or Roman Christianity in succeeding centuries.

THE CONTINUED DEVELOPMENT OF THE STRUCTURE OF THE CATHOLIC CHURCH

While these developments were taking place in the thought of Christians about their faith, and, as we have suggested, in part through the struggle to arrive at a common mind on the issues which were raised, the structure of the Catholic Church was continuing to grow. While this growth was in part from the effort to reach unanimity on central features of the Christian faith, it was profoundly affected by the patterns of the state and the society in which the Church found itself and by the relations of the Church to the state.

The Catholic Church was the majority Church of the Roman Empire. While it reached beyond that Empire and while there were minority Christian groups which excluded themselves from the Catholic Church or were excluded by it, in the main the Catholic Church was the Church of the Roman Empire. By the close of the fifth century the Catholic Church and the Roman state had become so intimately associated that the latter had placed an impress upon the former which was to prove indelible. The Catholic Church owed what might be called its structural unity as much to the fact that it had the support of the political unity which the Roman Empire had given to the Mediterranean Basin as to the love which theoretically should bind all Christians together. Indeed, when in the centuries which immediately followed the first five hundred years of the faith the Roman Empire fell apart, the unity which ideally should have existed in the Christian Church not only was too feeble to preserve the unity of the Mediterranean world: it also was not strong enough to hold the Catholic Church together. Yet so deeply had the Roman Empire placed its stamp on the Catholic Church that to this day the various fragments into which the latter broke have preserved many of the features, especially those of outward organization, which were acquired in the days of the Empire, and the largest fragment, the Roman Catholic Church, in many ways perpetuates the genius of pre-Christian Rome.

As we have suggested, increasingly the Church centred about the clergy led by the bishops and especially around the bishops. As early as the beginning of the second century a differentiation between clergy and laity began to be seen, and as time passed a priesthood developed which was regarded as the Christian counterpart of that of the ancient Jews. Leading the clergy and, therefore, the Church, were the bishops. As we have seen, the bishops were regarded as successors of the apostles. The development of the clergy and of ranks in the clergy may in part have been influenced by the example of the kind of officialdom which characterized the Roman Empire, especially during the later years of the period which we have been describing. We have also noted something of the theory of the episcopate held by the great Bishop of Carthage, Cyprian, who expounded it in letter after letter. He insisted that the bishops were necessary to the very existence (*esse*) of the Church and were not merely a form of administration found useful for the well-being (*bene esse*) of the Church. "The Church is in the bishop and the bishop in the Church," he said. He held that each bishop was the equal of every other bishop and that while a bishop might admonish one of his brothers no one had rightful administrative authority over any other. He declared that no bishop should "set himself up as a bishop of bishops," and that a bishop "can no more be judged by another than he himself can judge another." In this he was in conflict with the claims of the Bishops of Rome, claims to which we have already referred and to which we are to recur. The bishops tended to group themselves by the administrative divisions of the Empire, and for the election and consecration of a bishop the bishops of a particular province assembled. From very early days, bishops wrote letters to one another on matters which concerned the Church. Through them, Christians in one part of the Empire helped those in other sections who suffered from persecution or famine. Bishops prayed for one another, especially at the time of the Eucharistic services. Lists of bishops, emperors, and benefactors of the Church, both living and dead, were placed on tablets, called diptychs, for commemoration at the Eucharist. Removal of a bishop's name from the diptychs of another bishop was symbolic of excommunication.

After the time when, through Constantine, the government of the Roman Empire made its peace with the Church, the Church became increasingly associated with the state. Long before it had accepted the Church, the Roman state had insisted upon controlling the religion of its citizens. Its Emperor was *pontifex maximus,* the chief priest of the cults officially acknowledged by the state. It was, therefore, natural that when the Emperors were Christians they should insist upon having similar power in the Church. To be sure, they were not members of the hierarchy and did not perform the functions which by now had become exclusively assigned to the latter. The Church was never as fully subservient to the Emperor as the former pagan state cults had been, but to a degree maintained the autonomy which it had developed in the centuries when it had not been accorded legal recognition. In theory a Christian Emperor might be cut off from communion for his misdeeds like the humblest member of the Church. This was seldom done, but on a notable occasion in 390 Ambrose, as Bishop of Milan, remonstrated with the Emperor Theodosius for a massacre which the latter had ordered in Thessalonica and excluded him from the Church until he had proved his repentance by the acts prescribed for penitents. Yet the Emperors exercised great power in the Church. We have noted how Constantine and some of his successors sought to bring internal peace in the Church by calling councils of the Church. We have pointed out that some of the Emperors hastened the formal acceptance of Christianity by encouraging bishops in their missionary activities and by proscribing paganism and its ceremonies. Eventually, the Emperor himself, as we have reported, and as we are to see especially in the case of Justinian, declared what was sound doctrine. The Emperors enforced the decrees of councils against those condemned as heretics. They had a voice in appointments to high ecclesiastical office, especially in the East, near the main seat of their authority. As time passed, the assent of the Emperor was required even for the assumption of his powers by each successive Bishop of Rome. It was under the Emperors that what came to be called "ecumenical councils" became the voice of the entire Catholic Church.

In the course of the years the bishops in the larger cities began to exercise authority over the bishops in their vicinity. In 341 the Council of Antioch ordered that in each province the bishop in the chief city, or metropolis, should have precedence over the other bishops in the province, and that the other bishops should "do nothing extraordinary without him." In this the council believed that it was not making an innovation but was simply following a time-honoured custom. The metropolitan or archbishop was to take no common action without the concurrence of the other bishops in his province. Each bishop had authority in his own diocese, namely, "the whole district which is dependent upon his city; to ordain presbyters and deacons; and to settle everything with judgement." But he was "not to undertake anything further without the bishop of the metropolis," nor was the latter "to undertake anything further" without the consent of the other bishops of the province. Any bishop might have under him what were called chorepiscopoi, appointed by himself, to supervise the churches in villages and rural districts. The chorepiscopus had been ordained to the episcopate and could ordain those in the subordinate ranks of the clergy—readers, sub-deacons, and exorcists—but not presbyters or deacons.

The bishops in the chief cities of the Empire had positions of outstanding prestige, a prestige which, with modifications, has persisted into our own day. Especially prominent were those of Jerusalem, because of its historic associations with the beginning of Christianity, Antioch, the chief city of Syria and where the disciples were first called Christians, Alexandria, Constantinople, and, particularly, Rome. The bishops of these sees were eventually known as Patriarchs.

The Increasing Importance of the Church of Rome and Its Bishop, the Pope

As the centuries passed, the Church of Rome and its bishop, or the Pope as we must now begin to call him, became increasingly prominent in the Catholic Church. We have already noted the importance of the Church of Rome and the reasons why its bishops occupied a leading place. As time went on that position was accentuated. The removal of the main centre of the administration of the Empire to Constantinople, begun by Constantine, gave added importance to the Church of Rome and its head in the ancient capital and in the West, for they were no longer overshadowed by the Emperor and his court. As we have seen, the Popes usually took an active part in the controversies of the fourth and fifth centuries over the relation of the divine and human in Jesus Christ and between Augustinianism and Pelagianism and, with two possible and brief exceptions, were on the side which the majority eventually regarded as orthodox. Rome was more and more esteemed in the Catholic Church as the representative and champion of true Christianity. When, in the fifth century, the imperial power began to decline in the West, the Popes, by contrast, loomed larger in that region, especially in Rome and Italy. This was particularly the case when, after 404, the imperial residence in the West was taken from Rome to Ravenna.

To this prestige of their office some of the Popes made outstanding contributions. Fairly typical of the pontiffs of the fifth century was Innocent I, who held the post from 402 to 417. In spite of the fact that his tenure of the office saw the sack of Rome by Alaric (although Innocent was in Ravenna at the time on business of state), he was active in the affairs of the Catholic Church in Italy, Spain, Gaul, Illyricum, North Africa, Thessalonica, and the East. He championed, although unsuccessfully, the cause of his contemporary, John Chrysostom, when the latter was deprived of the see of Constantinople.

Far more important was Leo I, who held the office of Pope from 440 to 461, and who with Gregory I, whom we are to meet in a later chapter, is known by common consent as "the Great." None of his predecessors had been as forceful or had exercised so great an influence. He insisted that by Christ's decree Peter was the rock, the foundation, the doorkeeper of the kingdom of heaven, set to bind and loose, whose judgements retained their validity in heaven, and that through the Pope, as his successor, Peter continued to perform the assignment which had been entrusted to him. We have noted how Leo's *Tome* set forth the doctrinal position which was approved by the Council of Chalcedon. Leo declined to recognize as valid the canon enacted by that body which elevated the see of Constantinople to a position substantially equal with that of Rome, thus seeming to assert the right of his office to dissent from the decrees of a general or ecumenical council, but basing his opposition in part on the finality of what had been done earlier at Nicæa. Leo was a contemporary of the invasion of Italy by Attila and his Huns and was a bulwark of order in those troubled times. He interested himself in ecclesiastical questions throughout Italy, such as the qualifications of candidates for the episcopacy. In Gaul he successfully asserted the claims of the Church of Rome even as against metropolitans. He concerned himself with affairs in Spain and North

Africa. He obtained from the Emperor Valentinian III an edict which commanded all to obey the Bishop of Rome on the ground that the latter held the "primacy of St. Peter."

In 494 a successor of Leo, Gelasius, declared that the world is ruled by the Emperor and the priests, but that the latter are more important since they will have to give an account even for kings in the day of judgement, and that the Emperor must submit to prelates in divine matters. He also insisted that the Pope was of right preëminent over all priests. He declared that in view of the founding of the Church of Christ upon Peter and of the joint consecration by Peter and Paul of the Church of Rome, the latter "has been placed before the other churches" and hence depended for that position not on any decrees of synods, but upon Christ Himself. Moreover, by their presence and martyrdom Peter and Paul, so Gelasius said, had elevated the Roman Church "over all the others in the whole world."

Probably important for the contribution which the outstanding Popes made to the leading position of Rome was the fact that they embodied the skill in administration and the sense for law and order which were the characteristics of the great Romans.

SUMMARY

We do well to remember that the developments which we have described in the chapter of which the following lines are a brief summary were taking place concurrently with the amazing spread of the faith which we attempted to cover in the chapter that immediately preceded it. While Christianity was winning the professed allegiance of the overwhelming majority of the population of the Roman Empire and was being carried beyond the Roman borders, it was developing a visible, organized fellowship, the Church, and was seeking to define what Christians deemed the essential convictions of their faith. This was accomplished within the context of the Roman Empire and of Greek and Roman patterns of thought. Always there was the dream, going back to Christ himself, of a unity of love embracing all those who bore his name.

Never was that unity fully realized. Indeed, the history of the Church was—and has been throughout—chronically punctuated by dissension, often bitter and between outstanding leaders in the Church. Bishops, synods, and councils employed emphatic language in condemning individuals and views from which they differed. Never was there a single organization which was comprehensive of all who professed themselves Christians. The efforts to define the distinctive doctrines of the Christian faith invariably sharpened divisions among Christians. By the close of the fifth century several rival bodies were in existence, each regarding itself as representative of true Christianity and most of them calling themselves Catholic and denying that designation to the others. Such unity as existed had been furthered by the development of the Church within a single cohesive political structure, the Roman Empire. Moreover, again and again Roman Emperors had intervened in the affairs of the Church in an effort, usually futile or at best ephemeral, to achieve unity. In the process it often seemed as though Christ had died in vain, that his teachings were being hopelessly compromised and, while honoured in word, were denied in practice.

Yet, by a seeming paradox which we are to witness again and again in the history of Christianity, the failure to live up to the ideals set forth by Christ and his apostles was paralleled by prodigious vitality. From being one of the smallest of scores of rival religious groups, Christians had become numerically dominant, and that within less than five centuries. In a civilization which was dying and which was ceasing to say or to do anything new, Christianity had stimulated the emergence of the Church. This Church, to be sure, was really several churches rather than one, but the very divisions were evidence of vigour and of the power which had been released in the Gospel, and almost all branches, with the possible exception of the Gnostics, had common features of organization and belief.

The organization of the Church bore the indelible impress of the political framework within which it had arisen. However, it was not a pale reflection of that framework, but a fresh creation. The creeds and the discussions out of which they were formulated were influenced by Greek and Roman thought, but they were essentially new. Forced by the fact of living in a particular intellectual climate to use terms and employ ideas which were features of that climate, Christians were saying something quite novel and even revolutionary. They were handicapped by the only terminologies which lay to their hands and by the grandeur and originality of the Gospel. None of the words which they employed quite expressed what they were struggling to understand and to express, but what they said was, like the Gospel itself, fresh and striking. Christians had not yet rethought the whole range of human knowledge in terms of Christ, but some, notably Origen and Augustine, had attempted to see Christ in the setting of Greek philosophy, and in his *City of God* Augustine had endeavoured to discern the meaning of the entire human drama as disclosed in the Scriptures and Christ.

The Church and its faith were clearly a new creation. Their appearance and their spread were only the beginning of the story, for, as we are to see later, they were to continue to expand from the narrow confines of the Mediterranean world until by the middle of the twentieth century they had won footholds in almost every corner and among almost all the peoples of the globe.

SELECTED BIBLIOGRAPHY

GENERAL WORKS

J. C. Ayer, *A Source Book for Ancient Church History from the Apostolic Age to the Close of the Conciliar Period* (New York, Charles Scribner's Sons, 1913, pp. xxi, 707). A useful selection of translations with brief introductory comments, some of which are misleading.

L. Duchesne, *Early History of the Christian Church from Its Foundation to the End of the Fifth Century* (translated from the French. New York, Longmans, Green & Co., 3 vols., 1908–1924). By a liberal French Roman Catholic scholar.

The Church History of Eusebius, Translated with Prolegomena and Notes, by A. C. McGiffert, in *Nicene and Post-Nicene Fathers,* Second Series, Vol. I (New York, Charles Scribner's Sons, 1890). The standard translation into English of this most important of the early church histories, with extremely valuable notes.

Augustin Fliche and Victor Martin, editors, *Histoire de L'Église depuis les Origines jusqu'a Nos Jours* (Paris, Bloud & Gay, Vols. 1–4, 1947, 1948, cover the period to the election of Gregory the Great). By several Roman Catholic scholars.

H. M. Gwatkin, *Early Church History to A.D. 313* (London, Macmillan & Co., 2 vols., 1909). Readable, with references to the sources.

B. J. Kidd, *A History of the Christian Church to A.D. 461* (Oxford, The Clarendon Press, 3 vols., 1922). By a high Anglican. Valuable in part for its very extensive footnote references to the sources.

H. Lietzmann, *A History of the Early Church.* This comprehensive work, planned in German in five volumes, but left incomplete by the author's death in 1943, was brought down to the close of the fourth volume by a later hand. The first three volumes have been translated by B. L. Woolf as follows: *The Beginnings of the Christian Church* (New York, Charles Scribner's Sons, 1949, pp. 303), *The Founding of the Church Universal* (New York: Charles Scribner's Sons, 1938, pp. 432), and *From Constantine to Julian* (London, Lutterworth Press, 1950, pp. 340).

THE ORGANIZATION OF THE EARLY CHURCH

A. Harnack, *The Constitution and Law of the Church in the First Two Centuries,* translated by F. L. Pogson, edited by H. D. A. Major (New York, G. P. Putnam's Sons, 1910, pp. xiv, 349). A standard work.

J. B. Lightfoot, *Saint Paul's Epistle to the Philippians. A Revised Text with Introduction, Notes, and Dissertations* (London, Macmillan & Co., 1890, pp. xii, 350). Contains an important dissertation on the Christian ministry, by an Anglican bishop.

B. H. Streeter, *The Primitive Church, Studied with Special Reference to the Origins of the Christian Ministry* (New York, The Macmillan Co., 1929, pp. xii, 323). A thoroughly competent work by an Anglican.

Teaching of the Twelve Apostles, Edited with a Translation, Introduction and Notes by R. D. Hitchcock and F. Brown. New edition (New York, Charles Scribner's Sons, 1885, pp. cxv, 85).

THE RISE OF THE CHURCH OF ROME

J. T. Shotwell and L. R. Loomis, *The See of Peter* (Columbia University Press, 1927, pp. xxvi, 737). Translations of pertinent sources for the first four centuries.

GNOSTICISM

The major contemporary description of the various Gnostic teachers and groups which, while an anti-Gnostic polemic, contains much information nowhere else obtainable, is by Irenæus, translated under the title *Against Heresies* in *The Ante-Nicene Fathers,* Vol. I, pp. 309 ff. (Buffalo, The Christian Literature Publishing Co., 1885).

A semi-popular summary treatment of Gnosticism by an expert is F. C. Burkitt, *Church and Gnosis. A Study of Christian Thought and Speculation in the Second Century* (Cambridge University Press, 1932, pp. ix, 153).

More technical and detailed is E. de Faye, *Gnostiques et Gnosticisme* (Paris, Paul Geuthner, 1925, pp. 547).

THE MARCIONITES

The standard treatment is Adolf von Harnack, *Marcion: Das Evangelium von fremden Gott. Ein Monographie zur Geschichte der Grundlegung der katholischen Kirche* (Leipzig, J. C. Hinrichs'sche Buchhandlung, 1921, pp. xv, 357).

E. C. Blackman, *Marcion and His Influence* (London, Society for Promoting Christian Knowledge, 1948, pp. x, 181), appreciates Harnack but holds that he has overestimated Marcion's influence on the formation of the New Testament canon and the Apostles' Creed.

MONTANISM

Bonwetsch, *Die Geschichte des Montanismus* (Erlangen, Andreas Deichert, 1881, pp. viii, 210).

J. de Soyres, *Montanism and the Primitive Church* (Cambridge, Deighton, Bell & Co., 1878, pp. viii, 167).

THE FORMATION OF THE NEW TESTAMENT

Two popular accounts, both by specialists, are B. W. Bacon, *The Making of the New Testament* (*The Home University Library of Modern Knowledge,* New York, Henry Holt and Co., 1912, pp. 256), and E. J. Goodspeed, *The Story of the New Testament* (The University of Chicago Press, 1916, pp. xiii, 150).

THE DONATISTS

W. H. C. Frend, *The Donatist Church. A Movement of Protest in Roman North Africa* (Oxford, The Clarendon Press, 1952, pp. xvi, 360). A very important study, carefully done.

GENERAL WORKS ON THE HISTORY OF CHRISTIAN DOCTRINE

A. von Harnack, *History of Dogma,* translated from the third German edition by E. B. Speirs, J. Millar, *et alii* (London, Williams & Norgate, 7 vols., 1894–1899). Marked by the well-known conviction of the author that the historical Jesus, the Jesus disclosed in the first three Gospels, and the conceptions of him held by Christians, were profoundly altered by Greek thought and especially by Neoplatonic philosophy and the identification of Christ with the *Logos.* Brilliant and erudite, Harnack has proved provocative, convincing to some, controverted by others, and always stimulating.

A. C. McGiffert, *A History of Christian Thought. Volume I, Early and Eastern from Jesus to John of Damascus* (New York, Charles Scribner's Sons, 1932, pp. x, 352). Written in late life by a distinguished scholar, embodying a course which he had taught for many years, much briefer than Harnack's work, somewhat less technical, but still with extensive references to the sources. The viewpoint is that of the liberalism of the latter part of the nineteenth and the fore part of the twentieth century.

R. Seeberg, *Text-Book of the History of Doctrines.* Revised, 1904, by the author, translated by C. E. Hay (Philadelphia, The United Lutheran Publishing House, 2 vols., 1905). *Volume I. History of Doctrines in the Ancient Church,* pp. xviii, 413. Not as brilliant as Harnack, and more detailed and technical than McGiffert, but probably the best comprehensive summary.

THE APOSTLES' CREED

A. C. McGiffert, *The Apostles' Creed* (New York, Charles Scribner's Sons, 1902, pp. vi, 206).

TERTULLIAN

Translations of the works of Tertullian are to be found in *The Ante-Nicene Fathers,* Vols. III and IV (New York, Charles Scribner's Sons, 1899).

CLEMENT OF ALEXANDRIA

A translation of the works of Clement of Alexandria is in *The Ante-Nicene Fathers,* Vol. II, pp. 163–605 (New York, Charles Scribner's Sons, 1899).

ORIGEN

Translations of Origen's chief surviving works are in *The Ante-Nicene Fathers,* Vol. IV, pp. 221–669 (New York, Charles Scribner's Sons, 1899).

On Clement and Origen see C. Bigg, *The Christian Platonists of Alexandria* (New York, The Macmillan Co., 1886, pp. xxvii, 304).

THE COUNCILS

C. J. Hefele, *A History of the Christian Councils,* translated from the German by W. R. Clark. The first four volumes (Edinburgh, T. & T. Clark, 1872–1895) carry the story down to A.D. 680. By a Roman Catholic scholar, more extensive than any other treatment available in English.

E. H. Landon, *A Manual of Councils of the Holy Catholic Church* (Edinburgh, rev. ed., John Grant, 2 vols., 1909). A much briefer compendium than Hefele, arranged alphabetically by councils rather than chronologically.

ATHANASIUS

Select Writings and Letters of Athanasius, Bishop of Alexandria, edited, with prolegomena, by A. Robertson in *A Select Library of Nicene and Post-Nicene Fathers of the Christian Church.* Second Series, edited by P. Schaff and H. Wace, Vol. IV (New York, Charles Scribner's Sons, 1903, pp. xci, 605).

NESTORIANISM

J. F. Bethune-Baker, *Nestorius and His Teaching. A Fresh Examination of the Evidence* (Cambridge University Press, 1908, pp. xviii, 232). Carefully done.

F. Loofs, *Nestorius and His Place in the History of Christian Doctrine* (Cambridge University Press, 1914, pp. vii, 132). A careful study by an expert, differing from Bethune-Baker in some of its conclusions.

F. Loofs, *Nestoriana. Die Fragmente des Nestorius gesammelt, untersucht und herausgeben* (Halle, Max Niemeyer, 1905, pp. x, 407). Competent.

Nestorius. The Bazaar of Heraclides. Newly translated from the Syriac and edited with an Introduction, Notes & Appendices by G. R. Driver and Leonard Hodgson (Oxford, The Clarendon Press, 1925, pp. xxxv, 425). The joint editorship of a specialist in the language and a theologian.

AUGUSTINE

Saint Augustin's The City of God, translated by Marcus Dods, and *On Christian Doctrine in Four Books,* translated by J. F. Shaw, in *A Select Library of the Nicene and Post-Nicene Fathers of the Christian Church,* edited by P. Schaff, Vol. II, pp. vi, 621 (New York, Charles Scribner's Sons, 1887).

St. Augustin: On the Holy Trinity. Doctrinal Treatises. Moral Treatises, translated by various authors, in *A Select Library of the Nicene and Post-Nicene Fathers of the Christian Church,* edited by P. Schaff, Vol. III, pp. iv, 578 (New York, Charles Scribner's Sons, 1900). This also includes the *Enchiridion.*

Saint Augustin's Anti-Pelagian Works, translated by P. Holmes and R. E. Wallis, revised by B. B. Warfield, in *A Select Library of the Nicene and Post-Nicene Fathers of the Christian Church,* edited by P. Schaff, Vol. V, pp. lxxii, 567 (New York, Charles Scribner's Sons, 1902).

L. Bertrand, *Saint Augustin,* translated by V. O'Sullivan (New York, Appleton-Century-Crofts, 1914, pp. viii, 396). A popularly, well-written biography.

C. N. Cochrane, *Christianity and Classical Culture: a Study of Thought and Action from Augustus to Augustine* (Oxford, The Clarendon Press, 1940, pp. vii, 523). A competent survey with stimulating conclusions.

Chapter 7

ADMISSION, WORSHIP, AND DISCIPLINE IN THE CHRISTIAN COMMUNITY

While Christianity was spreading and while the Christian Church was coming into being, developing its organizations, thinking through its faith, and experiencing divisions, other aspects of the Christian community were taking shape. Processes and standards were being worked out for admission to the Church, forms of worship were developing, and methods were being devised for achieving and maintaining Christian ideals of life. They are of importance not only in themselves but also because they shed light on the effect of the Christian Gospel and because many of the customs and forms which then emerged have either persisted through the centuries and characterize the churches to which the majority of Christians now belong or form the foundation for current practices. To them we now turn.

Admission to the Church

As we have seen, admission to the Church was through baptism. In the first few decades of the Church, baptism might be administered on a simple profession of faith in Christ. Thus on the famous day of Pentecost, often regarded as the birthday of the Church, when about three thousand are reported to have been added to the fellowship of the disciples, the injunction was to repent and be baptized in the name of Jesus Christ. Whether all were baptized on that day is not explicitly stated, but we hear of the Ethiopian Eunuch being baptized after only brief instruction and of a jailer at Philippi receiving the rite, with all that were in his house, on the very night in which he seems first to have heard of Christ, with the simple requirement of belief "in the Lord Jesus Christ." An early baptismal formula, in accordance with the command in the closing words of *The Gospel according to Matthew,* was "in the name of the Father and of the Son and of the Holy Ghost." Baptism seems to have been by immersion, at least normally. Whether it was by immersion only has been a matter of debate and on it no unanimity has been realized. Immersion appears to have been implied in the symbolism of death and burial to the old life and the resurrection to the new life of which Paul spoke so graphically. Baptism seems to have been regarded as requisite for the "remission of sins" and for the new birth through which alone one could enter the Kingdom of God. It was often, perhaps regularly, followed by the laying on of hands by one of the apostles, although not necessarily by one of the Twelve, and through this the Holy Spirit was held to be imparted.

By the time that the *Didache* was written, baptism, at least as that document knew it, was still comparatively simple. It was preceded by instruction. Both he who administered baptism and such other Christians as could do so were to fast before the rite was given to a neophyte. Baptism was to be "in the name of the Father, and of the Son, and of the Holy Ghost." It was normally to be in "living," that is, running cold water, but if that were not available it might be in other and even in warm water. If immersion were impossible, water was to be poured upon the head three times "into the name of the Father and Son and Holy Ghost." Another early custom was to have the candidate anointed with oil both before and after baptism.

Tertullian, writing not far from the end of the second or the beginning of the third century, describes baptism. Evidently it had been further elaborated. The rite was to be administered by a bishop or a presbyter or deacon designated by him, or, in the absence of these, by a layman. It was generally given at Easter or during the fifty days after Easter. Candidates were to prepare for it by prayer, fasting, vigils through entire nights, and the confession of all past sins. Immediately before baptism, which was in water that had previously been blessed, the convert formally renounced the devil, his pomps, and his angels. He was also anointed with oil to drive out evil spirits. After the rite the newly baptized candidate was given a mixture of milk and honey to taste and was again anointed with oil. Then a hand, preferably that of the bishop, was laid on him, invoking the Holy Spirit, and he was signed on his forehead with oil. He refrained from the daily bath for a week after having received the rite.

Baptism was by a thrice-repeated immersion, preferably in water running through the baptistry. The first immersion was preceded by a confession of faith in God the Father, the second by a confession of faith in Christ Jesus, the Son of God, and the third by a confession of faith in the Holy Spirit. In at least some churches, so we must note in passing, the candidate was baptized naked, the children first, then the men, and finally the women. No one was to take into the water anything except his body.

The post-baptismal laying on of hands for the reception of the Holy Spirit was the rudimentary form of what later came to be esteemed one of the sacraments, confirmation. In Rome by the end of the fifth century this was regularly done by the Pope, as Bishop of Rome, in a special chapel behind the baptistry. There the newly baptized were brought. Then the Pope prayed to God to send His Holy Spirit on them, and, dipping his thumb in the consecrated oil, made the sign of the cross on the forehead of each saying "In the name of the Father, and the Son, and the Holy Spirit, Peace to you."

Tertullian appears to have believed that he was describing baptism as it was generally practised in his day, but it may well have been that no such uniformity existed as he supposed. For instance, according to another early account, the bishop anointed the candidate before rather than after immersion. Tertullian vigorously opposed teaching and the administration of baptism by women, because there were Christians who advocated both.

By Tertullian's day the baptism of infants seems to have been common, so much so that he spoke of it as though all Christians were familiar with it. At baptism the children had sponsors who took vows, apparently on behalf of the children. Tertullian favoured the deferring of baptism for infants until they themselves knew Christ and asked for baptism. He also advocated that for the unmarried baptism be delayed either until they married or until the habit of continence had been established.

Some baptized infants eight days after birth, but Cyprian objected even to this postponement. In this he was supported by Augustine, who held that baptism removed the taint of original sin derived through Adam.

As we have seen in the case of Augustine, baptism was regarded as washing away previous sins and, since it could not be repeated (although martyrdom, being interpreted as a baptism by blood, might count instead of baptism by water or be a second baptism), it was by many deemed the part of wisdom to postpone it until the first heat of youth was passed or until one's final illness. Some authorities in the Church might discourage such delay, but numbers, even of eminent laymen, including more than one of the Emperors, judged it safe and adopted it.

In the years when Christianity was spreading rapidly and thousands of converts were coming from paganism, baptism was preceded by a period of instruction and probation as a catechumen. Admission to the catechumenate was eventually by a ceremony in which the priest blew on the face of the aspirant, signed his forehead with the cross, and put a grain of salt in his mouth. Catechumens were counted as Christians and were admitted to the services of the Church, but were required to leave when a certain stage in the ritual was reached, before the celebration of the Eucharist. In some places the catechumenate was for three years.

The question began to be raised in the Catholic Church of the efficacy of baptism if it were administered by one who was regarded as a heretic. Tertullian and Cyprian of Carthage stoutly maintained that such baptism was not valid. This view was held in some other sections of the Church, especially in Syria and Asia Minor. On the other hand, Rome and Alexandria regarded baptism as authentic no matter by whom it had been given, provided only that it had been with water and with the essential forms.

EARLY CHRISTIAN WORSHIP

What was done in the assemblies of the early Christians? In what did their meetings consist? In what manner did they worship? So far as we know, no single pattern was followed. There was much spontaneity, and the Holy Spirit was believed to be impelling and guiding. Here and there we have hints of what took place, but nowhere do we have a complete picture. We are told that in the first days of the Church in Jerusalem the initial large influx of converts, those who came out of the stirring events of Pentecost, "continued steadfastly in the apostles' doctrine and fellowship, in the breaking of bread and in prayers." Here were instruction, presumably a rehearsal of the sayings, deeds, death, and resurrection of Christ; fellowship or community, the "breaking of bread," which may mean the supper which had been instituted by Christ; and "prayers," as though these were already customary. We hear, too, of meetings of the Jerusalem Christians on special occasions for thanksgiving or petition. In the church in Antioch in its earliest days there were prophets and teachers, and this may have implied gatherings at which they spoke.

From Paul's first letter to the church in Corinth we have as nearly a detailed picture of the assemblies of a church of the first generation of Christians as has come down to us. Apparently there were meetings in which both men and women spoke, although Paul declared that in all the churches it was the rule that women should keep silent. Paul implies that the assemblies were open to non-Christians as well as Christians, and that they were often noisy and confusing. Several might simultaneously "speak with tongues." At the same time two or more might be "prophesying," that is, voicing a message which they believed had been given them by the Spirit, perhaps in the form of a "revelation." There were some who were gifted with the ability to "interpret tongues," or to put into the common speech the meaning of what had been spoken in an unknown tongue. There were those who broke out in spontaneous prayer in a "tongue" or in the vernacular. Apparently it was the custom for the hearers to say "Amen"—"so be it"—a sign of emphatic agreement, at the end of a prayer, especially if that were one of thanksgiving. There was singing, perhaps at times in a "tongue," at other times with a psalm. Paul strove to bring some kind of order into these gatherings. Although he himself had the gift of "tongues," he held it to be far inferior to speaking in a fashion which others could understand, so that all might profit. He would limit these speeches in a "tongue" to two or three, and one at a time, with some one on hand to interpret. If there was no one to interpret he who felt impelled to use an unknown tongue was to keep silence. He commanded the "prophets" to speak one at a time, and only two or three at one meeting.

At Corinth the Supper of the Lord was prominent in the common life of the church. It seems to have been associated with a meal, the *agape,* or "love feast." To Paul's distress, to this meal each brought his own food and drink and the better supplied did not share their provisions with those who had little or nothing, with the result that some became drunk and others went away hungry. Paul recounted the original institution of the Lord's Supper as he declared that he had "received" it "of the Lord," presumably by direct revelation, and insisted that he who partook of the Lord's Supper in an unworthy manner was guilty of the body and blood of the Lord, as though he were among those who had crucified Christ. Paul believed that in some real sense, while the bread was eaten and the wine was drunk in memory of Christ, the wine and the bread were also the blood and body of Christ. Said he: "The cup of blessing which we bless, is it not a communion in [or participation in] the blood of Christ? The bread which we break, is it not a communion in [or participation in] the body of Christ." The meaning of the Lord's Supper and the character of the presence in it of Christ were eventually to become two of the most controversial questions among Christians.

From the beginning the example and forms of worship of the Jewish synagogue had a marked influence upon Christian worship. The Christians were familiar with the Jewish scriptures, presumably in part because they were read in their services. The *Trisagion,* "Holy, Holy, Holy, Lord God of Sabaoth, heaven and earth are full of His glory. Blessed be He for ever," was used in Christian worship, probably from a very early date, and was a direct contribution from the synagogue. So, too, was the congregational response, "Amen."

LATER DEVELOPMENTS IN WORSHIP

As from the second century we gain further glimpses of the worship of the churches, we find that it was built about the Lord's Supper. This was coming to be called the Eucharist, from a Greek word meaning the giving of thanks. The Eucharist was being clearly separated from the *agape.* The emphasis upon the Lord's Supper was to be expected, for it perpetually focussed attention upon the source of the Church's origin and vigour—Christ, his death, his resurrection, his continuing life, and the new and eternal life given to the Christian through him. It was with the narrative of the death and resurrection of Christ, if we may judge from the proportion of space given it in all

Four Gospels and from the emphasis upon it in the other writings in the New Testament, that the instruction of catechumens was largely concerned and on it the thought and faith of Christians were centred.

One of the earliest descriptions of the Eucharist, that by Justin Martyr, not far from the middle of the second century, recognizes the similarity to what was seen in one of the mystery cults, Mithraism, but holds that this was because the latter had imitated the Christians. Latterly it has been repeatedly asserted that in baptism and the Eucharist Christians borrowed from the mysteries and that Christianity was simply another one of these cults, with Christ as its hero-god, slain by his enemies and raised from the dead, and, like them, drawing its appeal and power from the assurance to the initiates that through its rites the believers would share in the death and in the resurrection and immortality of its god. The similarity is striking.

Yet fully as striking are the differences. None of the others could point· to a clearly historical figure, nor could the other figures begin to match Christ in teachings and character. It was in retaining their belief in Jesus Christ as fully man as well as fully God that the majority of Christians rightly discerned that the uniqueness of their faith consisted, against the Gnostics who would minimize or reject Jesus as a particular man who lived at a particular date in history, or the Marcionites who held that he was not truly flesh, but only seemed to be man, or those who maintained that he was merely an ordinary man who somewhere in the course of his life had been adopted by the Divine Spirit.

There is no proof of either conscious or unconscious copying from the mystery religions by Christians. Indeed, the voluminous writings of Christian apologists of the early centuries which have survived make very little mention of the mystery religions. Their attacks are directed, rather, against the Greek and Roman polytheism with its pantheon and its stories of the gods, or against the Greek philosophies, as though the mystery cults did not count. Presumably many Christians were aware of the latter and might even once have been adherents of them. They may have carried over into Christianity some of the conceptions of religion derived from them. This, however, has yet to be demonstrated. Certainly Christianity was essentially different from what we know of these cults, and the similarities are only superficial.

Already in the second century the chief day of worship and of the celebration of the Eucharist was Sunday, and the reason given was that it was on this first day of the week, "the Lord's Day," that Christ had been raised from the dead. In choosing that day instead of the Jewish Sabbath (although for centuries even many Gentile Christians also observed the seventh day, or Sabbath) or of Friday, the day of their Lord's crucifixion, Christians were giving further evidence that their faith was primarily in the risen Christ.

Two somewhat detailed descriptions of the fashion in which the Lord's Supper was celebrated in the second century have come down to us. The one, in the *Didache,* was intended primarily for Christians. The other, in one of the apologies of Justin Martyr, was designed to be read by non-Christians. The two show variations from each other, an indication that uniformity had by no means been attained, but they also display striking similarities. Both, for example, speak of the rite as the Eucharist, evidence that this designation had become very widespread.

In the *Didache* the direction is given that only the baptized shall share in the Eucharist. First the cup was given, with the prayer of thanksgiving, apparently already fixed and ritualistic:

We thank Thee, our Father, for the holy vine of David Thy servant, which Thou hast made known to us through Jesus Thy servant; to Thee be the glory forever.

Then came the broken bread with the prayer:

We thank Thee, our Father, for the life and knowledge which Thou hast made known to us through Jesus Thy servant; to Thee be the glory forever. Just as this broken bread was scattered over the hills and having been gathered together became one, so let Thy church be gathered together from the ends of the earth into Thy kingdom; for Thine is the glory and the power through Jesus Christ forever.

After the communicants had been "filled" there was another prayer of thanksgiving:

We thank Thee, holy Father, for Thy holy name, which Thou hast caused to dwell in our hearts, and for the knowledge and faith and immortality which Thou hast made known to us through Jesus Thy servant; to Thee be the glory forever. Thou, Master Almighty, didst create all things for Thy name's sake; both food and drink Thou didst give to men for enjoyment, in order that they might give thanks to Thee; but to us Thou hast graciously given spiritual food and drink and eternal life through Thy servant. Before all things, we thank Thee that Thou art mighty; to Thee be the glory forever. Remember, Lord, Thy church, to deliver it from every evil and to make it perfect in Thy love, and gather it from the four winds, it, the sanctified, into Thy kingdom, which Thou hast prepared for it; for Thine is the power and the glory forever. Let grace come and let this world pass away. Hosanna to the son of David. Whoever is holy, let him come; whoever is not, let him repent. Maranatha. Amen.

Maranatha, it will be noted, appears to have been one of the earliest expressions of Christians, for we find it in Paul's first letter to the Corinthians. It seems to have been an Aramaic word meaning either the affirmation "our

Lord has come" or, as a prayer for Christ's second coming, "Our Lord, come."

There was also the instruction to "permit the prophets to give thanks as much as they will," presumably making a place for spontaneous prayers by the "prophets," either itinerant or resident, who were a feature of the Christian communities which the *Didache* depicts.

Justin Martyr, describing the Eucharist as he knew it not far from the middle of the second century and presumably in the cities of Asia Minor, among them Ephesus, says that immediately after he had been baptized, which Justin calls "illumination," the new Christian was brought to the assembly of the "brethren," for prayers in behalf of themselves, the freshly baptized, and "for all others in every place," that they might be counted worthy, by their works, and that they might "be saved with an everlasting salvation." After the prayers, the Christians saluted one another with a kiss, a custom enjoined by Paul and perhaps of even earlier origin. There was then brought to the one of the brethren who was presiding bread and a cup of wine mixed with water. He took them and gave thanks to "the Father of the universe, through the name of the Son and of the Holy Spirit," usually at considerable length, and presumably "free prayer," without prescribed form, that the communicants were counted worthy to receive these things at his hands. When he had finished, the congregation said "Amen," and the deacons gave to those present the bread and the water mixed with wine and carried portions to those who were absent.

Justin Martyr goes on to say that the bread and the wine so blessed were not received as common bread and drink, but "as the flesh and blood of that Jesus who was made flesh." He also reports that the Eucharist was observed regularly on Sunday, presumably in addition to these special celebrations for the newly baptized. On Sundays it was preceded by readings from "the memoirs of the apostles or the writings of the prophets" "as long as time permits." After the reader had ceased, he who was presiding "instructs and exhorts to the imitation of these good things." Then all rose together and prayed and there followed the service of the Eucharist in the manner described above. Justin also said that contributions made by the well to do, apparently in connexion with the Eucharist, were deposited with the presiding officer, and the latter used the fund to succour widows, orphans, the sick, prisoners, strangers visiting the Christians, and others who were in need.

The Eucharist as described by both the *Didache* and Justin was open only to the baptized, in it thanksgiving was made, and the bread and the wine were consumed. Yet there are differences, although some of these may be due to failure of one or the other account to give all the details. In the *Didache* the wine came first, the bread second, and in Justin the reverse was the case.

In the *Didache* there was place for a fixed form of prayer as well as free prayer; in the service as known to Justin only free prayer. Justin regards the bread and the wine as the body and blood of Christ, while the *Didache* does not so describe them. The former speaks of the wine as mixed with water, the latter knows nothing of water with the wine. The former tells of portions of the consecrated bread and wine being taken to the absent, of a presiding officer, and of deacons who do the distributing; the latter makes no mention of any of these. Justin describes a Sunday observance of the Eucharist as preceded by reading from what we would now call the Old Testament and the New Testament and a discourse by the one who was presiding, but the *Didache* speaks of neither. In contrast with Justin, the *Didache* tells of a prayer of thanksgiving after the bread and the wine. It also knows prayers for the unity of all Christians, while Justin mentions prayers for all Christians only in connexion with the Eucharist as it was celebrated for the newly baptized.

Hippolytus, of Rome, writing in the first half of the third century, says that immediately after baptism the neophytes were given the Eucharist. The bread came first, and then, in order, they tasted of three cups—of water, of milk mixed with honey, and of wine. Here were variations, but still a simplicity which in succeeding centuries was superseded by more elaborate forms.

Developing Liturgies for the Eucharist

Well before the end of the fifth century, the Eucharistic rite and the liturgy connected with it had been greatly enlarged. The clergy had become quite distinct from the laity and the presbyters and bishops had become priests patterned consciously after the Jewish priesthood of pre-Christian times and offering a bloodless sacrifice at an altar. The stately, huge church buildings which were erected, especially after Constantine espoused the faith, probably made for an elaboration of a ritual which would be in keeping with them. In at least some sections of the Empire, the sanctuary, which contained the altar, the bishop's throne, and the seats of the clergy, was separated from the laity by a screen and the laity were not supposed to enter it. The altar might be of wood or be a stone slab supported on pillars. The fore part of the liturgy seems to have been an adaptation of the worship in the Jewish synagogue. Variations there still were, but in the chief churches, such as Rome and Alexandria, forms had been developed which had spread widely from these centres and had become associated with particular regions, notably Syria, Egypt, and Gaul.

In general, the following appears to have been approximately the procedure common to all the varieties of the liturgy. When the congregation gathered, the men were on one side of the church and the women on the other. The clergy were in the apse, where was the altar. The youths were by themselves, sitting or standing. The older people were to sit and the mothers with children had a special place. The deacons were to see that all took their proper places and that no one whispered, laughed, nodded, or slept.

The service began with several selections from the Scriptures, by "readers" who took their stand in the ambo, a kind of pulpit or desk raised above the congregation about the middle of the church where they could be heard by all. The readings were interspersed with Psalms chanted by another of the clergy and taken up at the end by the congregation. The last of the readings was from one of the Gospels and all the congregation rose for it. Then one or more of the priests spoke, the custom apparently being that such of the priests present as desired to do so might address a homily to the assembly.

After the homilies those who were not entitled to be present at the Eucharist were dismissed. First the catechumens left, having first offered up a silent prayer at the invitation of the deacon, while the congregation joined in a prayer offered on their behalf by the deacon by answering with *"Kyrie Eleison"*—"Lord have mercy"—followed by a prayer which the catechumens offered in a form suggested by the deacon and by a blessing from the bishop. Next, after the same form, those catechumens were dismissed who were preparing for baptism. Then the penitents who had not yet been received back into communion were sent away, with similar prayers and an episcopal blessing.

The communicants alone being left, they responded to a litany led by the deacon with the words *"Kyrie Eleison."* Then came the Eucharist proper, with the bishop officiating, clad in a festal garment, with the priests around him. There were prayers by the bishop, with responses from the congregation. Among the latter was the *Trisagion, Tersanctus* or *Sanctus*—"Holy, holy, holy . . . "—in which the choir of angels was believed to join. Early in the service, at the outset of the liturgy proper, the bishop gave the kiss of peace to the clergy, and the faithful interchanged it with one another, the men to the men and the women to the women.

There was then the consecration of the bread and the wine, modelled on the account in the Gospel of the institution of the Lord's Supper. This was followed by a prayer for the Church throughout the world, the Lord's Prayer, a litany led by the deacon, and the blessing by the bishop. Somewhere in the course of the centuries there was added to the liturgy the invocation of the Holy Spirit to descend upon the bread and the wine to make of them the body of Christ.

Then came the communion, the clergy first partaking of the elements in the order of their rank, followed by the members of the congregation. The bread and the wine were given to all. During the partaking of the communion, singers chanted some of the Psalms.

After the communion the bishop again offered prayer and gave his blessing and the deacon dismissed the congregation with the words "depart in peace."

This was the Eucharist substantially as it was celebrated in the fourth century. Changes continued to be made in it. For instance, as the conversion of the Empire was completed, the catechumens diminished in numbers and their dismissal either disappeared or became, in at least one of the liturgies, purely vestigial and formal.

OTHER TIMES AND FORMS OF WORSHIP

The Eucharist was the central and chief form of Christian worship developed in these early centuries of the faith. However, it was by no means the only occasion for worship. Some practices were private, by individuals, and others were by groups or congregations. Several of the customs and forms were taken over from Judaism, often with modifications: others were of purely Christian origin.

The most frequently repeated prayer was that given by Christ himself, the Lord's Prayer. This was used both by congregations and by individuals. The *Didache* held that it should be said three times a day. In his treatise on prayer Tertullian gave first importance to it.

The times of prayer were frequent. In the second century it was the custom, presumably held up as the ideal to all the faithful, to pray at daybreak and nightfall when normally Christians came together for prayers and the singing of psalms, and at three other hours of the day—at mid-forenoon, at noon, and at mid-afternoon. We also hear of prayers being enjoined at midnight. Bible reading was commended for the individual Christian if there were no communal services on that day.

Sunday was the chief day of worship. Then the first service, at least at some places and in the second century, was before the dawn, with readings from the Scriptures, chants, homilies, and prayers. After it came the Eucharist in the early hours of the morning. As we have seen, the common meal, the *Agape* or love feast, which in Paul's day seems to have been held in connexion with the Eucharist, was eventually separated from it and held later in the day. It was soon dropped completely, but for what reason is not entirely clear.

The Eucharist was observed on other days than Sunday. Partly after the Jewish custom, two days in the week were marked by fasting and prayer, but they were not those set apart by the Jews, namely, Mondays and Thursdays, but Wednesdays and Fridays. In Latin the word "station" was applied either to these days or to the fasts connected with them. In many places these two days were occasions for the Eucharist, but some Christians felt that they would be breaking their fast if they took communion on them. The Wednesday and Friday fasts were usually concluded by mid-afternoon, and some had the bread and the wine of the Eucharist reserved for them until that hour. In numbers of churches Saturday also became a fast day, or the Friday fast was prolonged into Saturday, and in some churches the Eucharist was not celebrated on that day.

We must note that prayer was commanded before dinner in the form of a brief thanksgiving, with a petition and a dedication to "every good work." The blessing on the meal could not be given by a layman, but only by the bishop or, in his absence, by a presbyter or deacon.

First-fruits were offered to the bishop, who gave thanks for them and presented them to God.

In addition to these regular times of worship, there were special occasions which entailed Christian ceremonies. Among them were ordination, the consecration of virgins, the dedication of churches, and the blessing of marriages. Ordination to the lower ranks of the clergy was by very simple ceremonies. Even that for priests and deacons was not elaborate, but usually consisted of prayers by the congregation and the bishop, the laying of the bishop's hands on the heads of those ordained, and the kiss of peace from the bishop. The consecration of bishops was more extended. The bishop was supposed to be the choice of his flock, including his clergy, and in his consecration all were recognized. The Eucharist was part of the ceremony. The consecration was normally by at least three bishops, but in times of persecution one bishop was held to be sufficient if the act was with the permission of other bishops, and by the sixth century the Pope might officiate alone. As we are to see later, the setting apart of women to virginity and to the service of the Church went back to the first century, and long before the close of the fifth century this was by formal ceremony, often celebrated with great pomp, and always presided over by a bishop, in which the virgin was given the veil as the bride of Christ.

In the fourth century we begin to hear of the dedication of edifices for Christian worship. Buildings erected especially for that purpose multiplied after the cessation of the persecutions in the fore part of the fourth century. Many of these were constructed near or over the tomb of a martyr. Martyrs were held in veneration and either the tomb or some relic of a martyr was so highly prized that eventually, although not until after the fifth century, the presence of a relic in the altar was held to be essential to a church. Until about the close of the fifth century all that usually seems to have been considered necessary for the consecration of a church building was the celebration in it of the Eucharist. Not far from that time special services of dedication increased.

Christians were not required to seek the blessing of the Church to give validity to their marriage. However, by the time of Tertullian it seems to have become customary to have a Christian ceremony in which the Church cemented the marriage, confirmed it with an oblation, and sealed it with a benediction.

CHRISTIAN FESTIVALS AND THE BEGINNING OF "THE CHRISTIAN YEAR"

Either from the beginning or from near the beginning Christians held some days and seasons as sacred. A few of these were taken over from the Jews, such as the observance of one day in seven for special worship and Pentecost. Several other Jewish feasts were completely disregarded, such as the Day of Atonement and the Feast of Tabernacles. Because of its association with the crucifixion and the resurrection of Christ, connected as they were with it, the Passover became central in the Christian calendar, although with a quite altered connotation.

Easter, the day of rejoicing, was preceded by a fast. The pre-Easter fast varied in duration. In some sections, in the second century it was for only one or two days, although in others it was prolonged to several days. In the third century the church in Alexandria fasted for the week preceding Easter. Montanists had a pre-Easter fast of two weeks. In the fourth century the forty days before Easter, *Quadragesima* (although it might be six weeks), became common as a period of special observance, but for many the fast was only for Holy Week, and for others possibly three weeks. We also read of *Quadragesima* being kept distinct from Holy Week, separating its fast from the fast of the latter. In Antioch and much of the East the addition of Holy Week to *Quadragesima* made a fast of seven weeks. In some places Sunday and in others Saturdays and Sundays were exempted from the Lenten fasting. The observance of the Sunday before Easter, commemorating the triumphal entry of Jesus to Jerusalem, seems to have begun at Jerusalem at least as early as the fourth century and to have spread gradually from there. Maundy Thursday, the Thursday before Easter, was observed as the anniversary of the institution of the Lord's Supper and in North Africa late in the fourth century the Eucharist was celebrated on the evening of that day, rather than in the morning, which, as we have seen, had become customary. Good Friday, quite naturally, was carefully observed, although in varying manner. The lighting of the Paschal or Easter candle became common in some sections before the end of the fifth century, and the formal blessing of the candle was fairly general as a pre-Easter custom.

By the end of the fourth century two other festivals had become widespread, the Epiphany, originating in the East, and the twenty-fifth of December, radiating from the West. The Epiphany, at first celebrated on the sixth and tenth of January, but eventually only on the former date, commemorated the birth of

Jesus, the adoration of Jesus by the Wise Men, and the baptism of Jesus. Christmas, the observance of the twenty-fifth of December as the birthday of Christ, appears to have begun at Rome. The New Testament, it is scarcely necessary to say, gives no clue to the precise days of any of these events, but they were obviously of importance to Christians, and Epiphany and Christmas, although fixed conventionally, became outstanding.

The festival of the Presentation of Christ in the Temple, or the Purification of the Virgin, was observed in Jerusalem as early as the fourth century. That of the Holy Cross, commemorating the alleged discovery of the cross on which Jesus was suspended and the dedication of churches in Jerusalem erected by Constantine, began at Jerusalem and gradually spread. There were also feasts in honour of the apostles and others who were revered as saints, one for the Maccabees, and, at least as early as the sixth century, one for the Angel Michael. In different places various days were observed in memory of local martyrs. Some of the great episcopal sees had special periods of fasting which did not gain universal acceptance.

CUSTOMS OF PRAYER

The manner of public prayer developed or took over certain forms. The custom early arose of facing the East in prayer. In public prayer one attitude was that of standing with arms outstretched or upraised. Another was lying prone, face downwards. To Tertullian's disgust, some sat down after a prayer had been completed. Tertullian declared that fasting or kneeling in worship on the Lord's Day and between Easter and Whitsunday (Pentecost) was improper.

PSALMS, HYMNS, MUSIC

The Epistle to the Ephesians enjoins the use of "psalms, and hymns, and spiritual songs." Some of these hymns are to be found in the New Testament itself, imbedded in its text. From a very early date, perhaps from the beginning, Christians employed in their services the psalms found in the Jewish Scriptures, the Christian Old Testament. Since the first Christians were predominantly Greek-speaking, these psalms were in a Greek translation. We hear of at least one form of service in which, after the reading from the Old Testament, the "hymns of David" were sung. This was done as a solo, presumably as a chant. At the end of each verse the congregation would join, taking up the final words in a short refrain. Later the responses might be by a choir. In Rome the custom arose of singing a psalm from the ambo, or *gradus*, and hence this psalm was called the *gradualis*, or the gradual. Another psalm was called the *tractus*, or tract. Some distinctly Christian hymns were early written in Greek, but in prose form, conforming to the pattern of the psalms as put into Greek. At least as early as the fourth century it became customary to follow the psalm with the *Gloria*—in one of its forms translated into the familiar "Glory be to the Father and to the Son and to the Holy Ghost, as it was in the beginning is now and ever shall be, world without end. Amen."

In Gnostic circles religious poetry arose to compete with the Old Testament Psalms. Some Catholics therefore distrusted the composition of hymns after this pattern, on the ground that they might smack of heresy. Yet from at least the second century hymns were written by the orthodox which, like their Gnostic counterparts, employed the forms of Greek poetry. Clement of Alexandria concluded one of his works with a hymn to Christ in Greek classical metre. Until near the end of the fourth century, in the services of the Catholic Church only the Old Testament Psalms and the hymns or canticles from the New Testament were sung: the other hymns were for personal, family, or private use. Gradually there were prepared versical paraphrases of the Psalms, hymns with lines of equal length, and hymns which were acrostics.

In Constantinople in the days when John Chrysostom was its bishop, the Arians are said to have congregated in the city squares and around the gates, or to have paraded through the streets at night, going to their meetings outside the walls, chanting antiphonally songs which denounced the Catholic views. To counter their efforts, John encouraged some of the Catholics to chant their own hymns in nocturnal processions. As a result violent conflicts between the two factions arose, and several on both sides were killed.

Just when the custom of antiphonal singing arose is not clear. One church historian of the fifth century ascribes it to Antioch not far from the beginning of the second century. Another church historian, also of the fifth century, declares that it began in Antioch in the fourth century, when two of the laity divided the choirs into two parts to sing the psalms of David antiphonally, and that from Antioch the custom spread in all directions. It is from the antiphon that the word "anthem" is derived.

Great writers of hymns began to emerge as early as the second century. Thus Bardaisan (Bardesanes), suspected of heresy late in that century, had a collection of one hundred and fifty hymns in Syriac. In the fourth century, Ephraim, clearly orthodox, a powerful preacher, wrote many hymns in Syriac for liturgical purposes, some of which are said still to be in use. Also in the fourth century, Hilary of Poitiers, in Gaul, during a sojourn in Asia Minor was so inspired by the Greek hymns which he heard there in the churches that on his return to Gaul he began writing hymns in Latin, some of them acrostics, and others in the rhythm of the marching songs of the Roman legionaries. It was in this century that one of the most widely used hymns of the Church, the *Te Deum,* seems to have been composed. The authorship and date have been disputed, but the majority opinion appears to credit Niceta, a bishop in Dacia (north of the Danube), with the authorship. Niceta is said to have employed hymns in the winning of the pagan barbarians in his diocese. Quite undisputed is the fact that Ambrose, the great Bishop of Milan, composed hymns which he taught his flock to sing. His most famous convert, Augustine, has recorded how deeply moved he was by them. They proved extremely popular and for many centuries were the inspiration of other Latin hymns, written, as were they, in eight stanzas. A Spanish contemporary of Ambrose, Prudentius, developed what seems to have been a new type of hymn, having more warmth and glow than those of Ambrose, but for personal and domestic use and not for liturgical purposes. The so-called Athanasian Creed, beginning with the words *quicumque vult,* has by some been classified with hymns. Its precise date, author, and place of origin have not been indisputably determined, but it appears to have originated in the West, perhaps in Gaul, and possibly as early as the fifth or the beginning of the sixth century. Like the *Te Deum* it put into verbal form what were held as central convictions and was widely employed in public worship. Late in the fifth century the Nestorian Narsai (Narses) wrote many hymns, some of them for use in church services. Roughly contemporary with him was Romanus, a pioneer in Byzantine hymnody, whose compositions were to come into extensive use in Constantinople in the sixth century.

Numbers of these Christian hymns, like the *Te Deum,* were what might be termed with accuracy but still in misleading fashion, theological. They put into verbal expression either for congregational worship or for the individual, the central and distinctive convictions of the Christian faith. They were, accordingly, a witness to the effect of Christ on the human spirit. As the worship of the Christian communities centred around the Eucharist, with its commemoration of the sacrificial death of Christ, so the hymns of the Christians of the first five centuries concerned themselves chiefly with Christ and with what God was believed to have done through him.

The Emergence of Popular Cults and Forms of Worship within the Church

Before the end of the fifth century subsidiary cults and forms of worship began to appear within the Catholic Church. We have noted that Christian worship stressed the Eucharist and that the Eucharist had to do primarily with the central distinctive features of Christianity—Christ himself, his incarnation, death, and redemption and eternal life through him. We have seen that the great creeds of the Church focussed on them their attention, and that the hymns made much of them. Yet side by side with this emphasis upon Christ, although subordinate to it and in theory associated with it, there were emerging special reverence for other beings and practices of worship which were reminiscent of the non-Christian religions of the Mediterranean world.

Martyrs were held in high honour. This had been true as far back as the first and second centuries, as is vividly attested by the last book in the New Testament. Their cults grew rapidly in the fourth and fifth centuries. The last great wave of persecutions which began with Diocletian added many to their ranks. The events of those tragic days were read back into the earlier centuries when those who had suffered death for the faith were actually relatively few. Their numbers were exaggerated and their sufferings were magnified, until the Church of the first three centuries was viewed in retrospect, mistakenly, as a church of martyrs. When, in the fourth and fifth centuries, after the last persecutions, converts flooded into the Church, they tended to transfer to the martyrs some of the reverence they had given and the attributes and powers which they had ascribed to the gods of paganism. The relics of martyrs were cherished, their tombs became the goals of pious pilgrimages, and they were appealed to in prayer to intercede with God on behalf of their votaries. They were believed to work miracles and were esteemed as healers of disease, guardians of cities, and patrons of trades.

Angels, especially Michael, were also revered, and to the martyrs were added Christians of exemplary lives, especially ascetics, as among those through whom prayer could be made. The process of canonization was to wait for regularization until later centuries, but it was already in being through the consensus of the faithful in particular localities or in the Church at large.

The Virgin Mary was early viewed with great respect, but in the fourth and fifth centuries the importance accorded her rapidly mounted and her cult increased. As we have seen, she was acclaimed as the "Mother of God." In Ephesus something of the worship paid to Diana may have been transferred to the Virgin Mary and she is said to have taken possession of the Sicilian sanctuaries of Ceres and Venus.

Here and there sites sacred to pagan divinities were appropriated by Christians and were still regarded as hallowed, but by Christian saints rather than by the gods. In at least one place the temple of a non-Christian god was transformed into a Christian church and the latter was devoted to that god thinly disguised by prefixing the title "Saint" before his name.

Beliefs and practices which were either magic or closely akin to magic had wide vogue among Christians. Even the highly intellectual Origen held that the repetition of the name of Jesus, if made in faith, would expel demons. In pagan days the ill had been taken to the temples to sleep in them in the hope that in their dreams directions would be given them by the god for treatment which would heal their disease. The practice was transferred to Christian churches and became so common that the ecclesiastical authorities felt constrained to take action against it. Spells and charms, blessed in the name of Christ or one of the saints, were much used. In one recorded instance the sign of the cross was employed in Gaul to protect cattle against an epidemic and was believed to have proved efficacious.

Dionysius the Areopagite

By the end of the fifth century Christian mysticism was beginning to be profoundly moulded by Neoplatonism, an influence which has persisted into our own day. Very potent were the writings ascribed to Dionysius the Areopagite, mentioned in *The Acts of the Apostles* as a convert of Paul at Athens. Dionysius was not their author, for they seem to have been composed either in the last quarter of the fifth century or the first half of the sixth century, perhaps by a monk or a bishop. Some of the terminology is Christian, but the basic conceptions are primarily Neoplatonic. God, Who is supra-personal, supraessential Essence, above either time or eternity, Who is the source of the universe and Who pervades it, from Whom constantly issue emanations, exercises His power through nine orders of celestial beings and does so on earth through the hierarchy of the Church, which corresponds to the celestial hierarchy and which begins with bishops as the highest rank, has priests in the second rank, and deacons in the third and lowest rank. Every hierarchy culminates in Jesus Christ. The sacraments, administered by the ecclesiastical hierarchy, are the channel of the divine operation of grace. Perhaps in an effort to escape the extreme dualism in the widely prevalent Manichæism, the Pseudo-Dionysius, stressing what had come down from Platonism and Neoplatonism, held that sin is largely negative, that there is nothing that is inherently evil, and that in all evil is some good. Salvation is regarded as the deification of the saved, and deification is the highest possible resemblance to God and union with Him. It is to be sought in moral and intellectual discipline, with the sacraments as an aid and a means, and through contemplation which carries one outside of oneself, above reason, to the vision which realizes that the individual is never really separated from God. Yet the self continues to exist, even when merged with God.

Here were views which either did not emphasize or were contrary to such basic Christian convictions as the creation of the world by the will of God, the corruption of man through man's voluntary rebellion against God, the redemption of man through the self-giving of God in the incarnation, the costly sacrifice on the cross, and the new birth through the Holy Spirit.

Yet the writings of the Pseudo-Dionysius carried great weight, partly because they were believed to be by a close intimate of Paul, and were to be a handbook of Christian mysticism in both the East and the West, a major channel of a strong Platonic and Neoplatonic strain in Christian piety.

It was not only in Christian mysticism that the writings of Dionysius the Areopagite were influential. They also made an impression on Christian thought. For instance, the outstanding Western theologian of the Middle Ages, Thomas Aquinas, quoted from them extensively.

OTHER FORMS OF PRIVATE WORSHIP AND DEVOTION

It was not only or even chiefly through the Pseudo-Dionysius that the spirit of contemplation and prayer was nourished among Christians. There was much family and private reading of religious books. This was true of the writings included in the Scriptures. Books were expensive, for printing was still centuries in the future, and literacy was by no means universal, but many individuals and families had copies of the Scriptures and the temper of the Church encouraged Bible reading by individuals and groups. Translations of all or parts of the Bible were made into several of the vernaculars. Many Christian books not included in the Canon were also widely circulated. Works of a devotional nature continued to be written. Famous among these was Augustine's *Confessions*. Late in the fifth or early in the sixth century there appeared in Gaul *De Vita Contemplativa* ("The Contemplative Life") by Julianus Pomerius, who had Augustine as his model. These were only two among many from both the Western and the Eastern sections of the Church on which contemporaries and later generations nourished their faith.

THE DRESS OF THE CLERGY

How early the members of the clergy were distinguished from the laity by special garb is not clear. At the outset there seems to have been no difference in dress. Indeed, so long as persecutions lasted, such a distinction would have made the clergy conspicuous and would have singled them out for arrest. Even after persecutions ceased, in the fifth century one of the Popes expressly forbade any special ecclesiastical dress, but the fact that he found it necessary to issue this prohibition may be evidence that such costumes were beginning to be worn elsewhere and that Rome was holding to an earlier custom. At that time the outdoor dress of Roman civil officials was an undergarment, a tunic, with or without sleeves, and an immense sleeveless cloak which was without an opening in the front and was passed over the head. The undergarment might be bound around the waist by a girdle. Presumably this was the fourth and fifth century dress of the Roman clergy. In later centuries these garments, perpetuated and conventionalized, became part of the specialized clerical dress. By the end of the fifth century a second tunic, with large sleeves, called the dalmatic, worn over the undergarment and under the cloak, became a distinguishing mark of the Pope and his clergy and might have been in use elsewhere.

From at least the first half of the fifth century, and perhaps earlier, what was known as the *pallium* was regarded as a badge of the bishop's office. The *pallium* was of white wool and was a kind of scarf worn over the shoulders. It seems also to have been a mark of civil service in the Roman Empire of the time, perhaps derived from a short mantle introduced by the Greeks. The privilege of wearing the *pallium* may have been granted the bishops by the Emperors in connexion with the special recognition accorded the clergy after the Emperors had become Christians. Certainly the Emperors are known specifically to have granted to individual bishops the privilege of wearing the *pallium*. Some time after the fifth century, in the West the *pallium* came to be regarded as part of the garb of the Popes and the Pope granted it to bishops as a symbol of his approval of their election and therefore of his authority over them. It was esteemed as a kind of duplicate of the mantle of Peter and so as a token of the power of his successors, the Bishops of Rome. In the East, as early as the fourth century, bishops, priests, and deacons had the *orarium*, a conventionalized form of a handkerchief or neckcloth. It was of linen and was worn as a stole, draped over the shoulder. In the fourth century a council in Phrygia deemed it necessary to forbid its use by sub-deacons and other minor clergy, presumably because they were adopting it.

FINANCING THE CHURCH

How were the churches maintained financially? From the very outset the churches cared for the poor and the widows. This was true not only in the immediate circle of each congregation, but churches also came to the rescue of other churches which were suffering from special or chronic stress. Moreover, some of the apostles drew their support from their fellow-Christians. For a brief time in the first church in Jerusalem all the Christians shared in a community of goods. In that church the widows were given especial help. The Jerusalem church charged the Gentile churches to remember the poor, and in this the great missionary to the Gentiles, Paul, heartily concurred. Paul took pride in labouring with his own hands for his support, but seems to say that other apostles, including Peter, and the brothers of Jesus were maintained by the churches. Paul raised a substantial sum from the Gentile churches to aid the Christians in Judea, and directed that this was to be done by Christians setting aside something on the first day of the week, obviously, a form of systematic giving.

In the fourth century, following the precedent of the Old Testament and harking back in part to earlier Christian practice, we find the command to bring the first-fruits of the winepress, the threshing-floor, the oxen, the sheep, and other things to the priests, and to devote a tenth of one's increase to the widows, the poor, and strangers. We also read that every true prophet or teacher who came to a Christian community was to be maintained. These instructions were at least current in the East.

When, beginning with Constantine, the Church began to be shown special favour by the state, clergy were exempted from the public obligations which had become a burden on many, and donations to the Catholic Church through legacies were permitted. Constantine erected numerous church buildings in various parts of the Empire and endowed them. Later Emperors also erected churches. Before long, some of the clergy were being accused of using unworthy means to obtain legacies from the well-to-do. Before the close of the fifth century, whether through legacies or other channels, some of the churches, notably that of Rome, became the owners of large possessions, the management of which became a major problem of administration, and the income from which went in large part to the support of widows, orphans, and the poor.

ETHICAL IDEALS AND MORAL DISCIPLINE IN THE CHURCH

Throughout the first five centuries, as through their successors, the records disclose a marked gulf in Christians and the Christian communities between professed ethical ideals and motivation for moral action on the one hand, and performance on the other, together with continuing efforts to close the gulf either by bringing the ideals down to a level attainable in performance or by inducing performance to conform to the ideals.

In the New Testament, the motive and basic principle of action is *agape*, love, love of God and love of man, inspired by the love of God, especially as seen in His self-giving in Christ and in the death of Christ for rebellious, sinful men on the cross. The Gospel is not a new law, a fresh and higher set of moral standards through obedience to which men are to find salvation and enter into life.

To be sure, in penetrating fashion Jesus laid bare the springs of action and placed the emphasis upon the governing, inward thought and motive rather than on the outward deed. He declared that the ideal was to act like God, to be "perfect, as your heavenly Father is perfect." Here was a standard so high that it seemed impossible of attainment, and yet in it discerning souls recognized what men must be if they are to realize to the full the purpose for which

God had created them. Jesus seemed to believe that it was theoretically possible for all to reach the goal, yet he also perceived clearly and frankly the evil in men, held that men must strive (the Greek word is that from which the English word "agonize" is derived) to enter the gate to true life, and declared that only a very few find the gate and pursue the path into which it opens.

Paul recognized the impossibility of obeying entirely the moral law, the law of God, and saw in that law and the sense of moral impotence and frustration bred by its acceptance "our schoolmaster to bring us unto Christ that we might be justified by faith." When confronted by the law, especially as interpreted by Jesus, sensitive spirits were brought to see how far short of it they fell. Across the centuries one of the fruits of Christianity has been the quickening and deepening of the consciences of men. Indeed, the more discerning have recognized the basic sin to be self-sufficiency, pride, and rebellion against God, have appreciated something of the depth of man's depravity as they have seen representatives of the highest religion and the noblest of man's governments nail the Son of God to the cross, and have stood in amazed awe at the wonder of God's love and forgiveness in giving His Son thus to die for man's redemption. It is men's response in humble faith and love to God's love in Christ, so the New Testament says, which should be the well-spring of Christian living. No man can perfectly attain to God's ideal for him in this life, but accepting this as a fact, Paul declared that he pressed on to lay hold on that for which he had been laid hold on by Christ Jesus, striving "toward the mark for the prize of the high calling of God in Christ Jesus." In his *Confessions,* as he looked back over his spiritual pilgrimage, Augustine clearly recognized that, while he had been freed by the Gospel from slavery to the grosser sins of the flesh, he had not yet completely overcome man's fundamental sin, pride.

Here is not a set of commands through obedience to which men can earn anything from God. Men, so the New Testament sees, can never fully comply with God's commands, and even if they could and did they would deserve nothing from Him, but would only, like good servants, have done what it is their duty to do. The Christian Gospel is, rather, the good news of God's love and of that kingdom of God which is God's free gift to men and into which men can enter here and now by accepting that gift. Christians are to determine their actions, not by legalistic rules, but by the love of God which itself is the gift of God through His Holy Spirit and by its inevitable corollary, love for their neighbours. As the *Epistle of James* says, "Thou shalt love thy neighbour as thyself" is the "royal law." As Paul emphatically states: "Love worketh no ill to his neighbour, therefore love is the fulfilling of the law."

Yet from the outset this conviction about conduct has been confronted by two perils. On the one hand, there has been what is technically known as antinomianism, the assumption that the Christian, by being emancipated from legalism, the meticulous observance of rules, is free from all moral law and can with impunity disregard it. The other, often more subtle and in one form or another much more widely held, is the conviction that the Gospel is a new and higher law, that being a Christian primarily entails obedience to moral maxims, some of them ancient and to be found in the Old Testament and some of them new and seen in the New Testament, and that one's salvation is to be earned by that obedience. This tendency, even though only a tendency and not carried to its logical conclusion, is found in some books which were greatly prized by Christians of the first five centuries, among them the *Didache, The Shepherd of Hermas,* and extensive portions of the *Paidagogos* of Clement of Alexandria. Indeed, *The Shepherd of Hermas* declares that it is possible to do more than God commands and by so doing to gain more abundant glory.

Fully as serious as these two perils has been the failure of Christians even to approximate in practice to the high standards set forth in the New Testament. This is seen again and again in the pages of the New Testament, where the sins of professing Christians are frankly described and condemned. It is also apparent in such records as we have of succeeding generations of Christians. Sometimes these sins were excoriated and at other times, as in the language of the participants in the controversies which distressed the Church and which we described in the preceding chapter, were unrecognized or unacknowledged by those who were guilty of them, sad evidence of self-righteousness and lack of love even in some of those who were later revered as saints. Lapses multiplied as multitudes poured into the Church, especially after persecutions ceased and the Emperors espoused the faith.

The Church had early to face the problem of what should be done with those of its members who sinned. Baptism, we have noted, was regarded as washing away all offenses committed before it. But what of those sins committed after baptism? Some of these were held to be especially serious, or "deadly." Tertullian, as we have hinted, said that they were seven in number—idolatry, blasphemy, murder, adultery, fornication, false-witness, and fraud. To the early Christians the most heinous of sins were the denial of the faith, murder, and gross sexual offenses. *The Shepherd of Hermas* allowed the possibility of one repentance after baptism, a possibility in which, as we have seen, Clement of Alexandria concurred, but Hermas held that beyond that one post-baptismal repentance no other was possible. This appears to have been the view of Clement. Clement said that if allowed continual and successive repentings for sins, Christians would differ nothing from those who never have been Christians, except only in the consciousness of having sinned. Yet he repeated approvingly a story about the Apostle John who in his old age sought and won to penitence a man who as a youth had been baptized and then, falling away, had committed many sins and had become the leader of a band of robbers. Thus he at least recognized as possible repentance for a multitude of sins committed after baptism.

In the preceding chapter we have seen that some groups broke from the Catholic Church in part or entirely in protest against what they held to be too great leniency of the latter towards moral lapses, especially apostasy. Among these were the Montanists, the Novatians, and the Donatists.

In this rigour, whether in the Catholic or in other Christian bodies, there was grave danger of legalism, of equating Christianity with morality, all the more so since outward acts were more readily detected than inner motives, pride, and the failure to respond with love to God's love. Moreover, while the New Testament has severe words for those who sin against the Holy Spirit or who lapse from the faith, and while, as some early Christian writers soberly recognized, even those who have long been seemingly exemplary Christians may come to moral shipwreck in their later years, it is perfectly clear that Jesus taught that no matter how often a man sins, if in genuine repentance he turns to God, God will forgive him. The issue is not God's readiness, even eagerness to forgive, but man's ability and willingness to repent. That should be obvious from the most frequently repeated of Christian prayers, the Lord's Prayer, and from assurances given again and again in the New Testament.

The Catholic Church increasingly made provision for the restoration of the genuinely penitent. Not far from the end of the second century, Tertullian described the practice of the single repentance which was permitted after baptism. The penitents were required to fast, living on plain food, to dress in mourning garb, to lie in sackcloth and ashes, to pray, to weep, to bow before the presbyters, and to kneel before the faithful and ask their prayers. How far Tertullian was describing the customary procedure and how far he was holding up an ideal which was seldom attained is not clear.

Those who had suffered for the faith as martyrs and had survived were believed to have the power to declare sins forgiven. They were besieged by penitents and, as we have noted, their leniency was a source of embarrassment to the stricter souls and to the bishops and other clergy. We have seen that early in the third century a Bishop of Rome, Callistus (Calixtus I), permitted the restoration of those guilty of fornication and adultery if they fulfilled the conditions for pentitents. After the Decian persecution, a synod in Carthage under Cyprian ruled that to those who had denied the faith hope of restoration must be held out to keep them from reverting to paganism, but that a long penance must be imposed on them. This stand was confirmed by a synod in Rome in 251 and by another in Carthage in 252. The severe persecutions which began with that of Diocletian early in the fourth century led to many apostasies. The Council of Nicæa found it necessary to define the conditions of the read-mission of those who had thus lapsed. None who was penitent was to be for-bidden the communion on his death bed, but the others might be kept waiting for from two to ten years. For them, as for other penitents for grave offenses, there were grades through which they passed before readmission to full com-munion. Some were dismissed at particular points in the service—some after the sermon and the reading from the Scriptures, some after the prayers—while others might remain through the Eucharist.

Penance and penitents were under the direction of the bishop, and restoration was usually not easy and was only with the consent of the bishop. If the sin had been publicly known, restoration must also be public. In the churches in the West, especially in Rome, a place was appointed in which penitents stood and mourned until the completion of the service. They then cast themselves prostrate on the ground with groans and lamentations. The bishop, weeping, also cast himself on the ground, and the congregation wept and groaned. The bishop then arose, offered a prayer for the penitents, and dismissed them. The penitents were also required to fast, or to abstain from bathing, or to suffer some other deprivation for a period fixed by the bishop.

In the East, after the persecution by Decius in the middle of the third century, it became customary for the bishop to designate a special priest to hear the confessions of those who had sinned, to fix the penance, and to grant absolution. Late in the fourth century, because of a scandalous incident, this office was abolished in Constantinople and the decision of whether he should partake of the communion was left to the conscience of each Christian. From Constantinople the cessation of the appointment of a priest to hear confessions spread widely, and the result was increasing laxity in maintaining moral standards among the members of the Church. Against this laxity monasticism, of which we are to read in the next chapter, was a reaction and a protest.

The growing laxity which contributed to the monastic reaction was also seen in the clergy, both high and low. Especially beginning with Constantine and the friendship of the state, self-seeking, pomp, and luxury began to appear among them. Some of the bishops, particularly in the larger sees, lived like magnates, and the priests and deacons sought wealth. Thus in the latter part of the fourth century the Bishops of Rome kept a large establishment and set a princely table, and some of the clergy fawned on wealthy women, hoping for gifts or legacies. At least one contest for the Papal throne was accompanied by brawling and bloodshed.

Easy-going though much of the Catholic Church had become in its enforce-ment of moral standards, in its recognition of the inexhaustible mercy and love of God to the truly penitent it was holding to a central affirmation of the primitive Christian faith. It was also doing this in preserving baptism, with its witness to the new birth, the complete transformation which is of the essence of Christian faith and experience as taught at the outset of Christianity, and in putting at the heart of Christian worship the Eucharist, with its thanksgiving for the incarnation, the sacrificial death of Christ, and the power of the new life which has issued from them. In baptism, worship, and discipline the Church was seeking to preserve and to stress what was strikingly distinctive of Jesus Christ and the teaching of the apostles. Nor did all the bishops and clergy succumb to the pomp and circumstance which accompanied their posts.

SELECTED BIBLIOGRAPHY

BAPTISM, WORSHIP, AND THE EUCHARIST

A competent survey, from the Roman Catholic viewpoint and stressing the practices in the Church of Rome, is by the distinguished Roman Catholic scholar, L. Duchesne, translated by M. L. McClure, *Christian Worship, Its Origin and Evolution. A Study of the Latin Liturgy up to the Time of Charlemagne* (London, Society for Promoting Christian Knowledge, 1931, pp. xx, 593).

G. Dix, *The Shape of the Liturgy* (Westminster, Dacre Press, 1945, pp. xix, 764). Another excellent survey, of a somewhat different kind, by a staunch Anglo-Catholic.

For the *Didache* see *Teaching of the Twelve Apostles . . . edited with a translation, introduction and notes* by R. D. Hitchcock and F. Brown (New York, Charles Scribner's Sons, 1885, pp. cxv, 85).

For Tertullian, *On Baptism,* see a translation by S. Thelwall in *The Ante-Nicene Fathers,* Vol. III, pp. 669–679 (New York, Charles Scribner's Sons, 1899).

Justin Martyr's description of the Eucharist is in his *First Apology,* translated in *The Ante-Nicene Fathers,* Vol. I, pp. 185, 186 (Buffalo, The Christian Literature Co., 1885).

See also an early document on the catechumenate, baptism, the Eucharist, and other forms of worship, in *Constitutions of the Holy Apostles,* Book II, Section VII, in *The Ante-Nicene Fathers,* Vol. VII, pp. 421, 422, 465–478, 483–491 (New York, The Christian Literature Co., 1896).

Still another early document, of the third century, with a description of the Eucharist, ordinations, the catechumenate, baptism, widows, prayers, and other church customs is *The Apostolic Tradition of Hippolytus,* of which a useful translation, under that title, accompanied by an extensive introduction and notes, is by B. S. Easton (New York, The Macmillan Co., 1934, pp. 112).

On the Jewish influence on the forms of Christian worship, see W. O. E. Oesterley, *The Jewish Background of the Christian Liturgy* (Oxford, The Clarendon Press, 1925, pp. 243). Carefully done, well documented.

Also very carefully done, broader in its geographic scope than Duchesne, is J. H.

Srawley, *The Early History of the Liturgy* (Cambridge University Press, 2d ed., 1947, pp. xviii, 240), semi-technical, with an excellent bibliography and footnotes.

Translations of some of the early liturgies are in *The Liturgies of SS. Mark, James, Clement, Chrysostom, and Basil, and the Church of Malabar,* by J. M. Neale and R. F. Littledale (London, Griffith Farran & Co., 7th ed., no date, pp. xl, 256), with an introduction and notes.

Excellent, and on a limited phase of the liturgy is W. H. Frere, *The Anaphora or Great Eucharistic Prayer, An Eirenical Study in Liturgical History* (London, Society for Promoting Christian Knowledge, 1938, pp. vi, 212).

EARLY CHRISTIAN POETRY AND HYMNS

Excellent, compact articles by A. Baumstark, A. J. Maclean, and G. M. Dreves are in J. Hastings, editor, *Encyclopædia of Religion and Ethics,* Vol. VII, pp. 5–24 (New York, Charles Scribner's Sons, 1915).

A survey more limited geographically, based upon careful research and sound judgment, is F. J. E. Raby, *A History of Christian-Latin Poetry from the Beginnings to the Close of the Middle Ages* (Oxford, The Clarendon Press, 1927, pp. viii, 491). The section covering the first five centuries is pp. 1–120.

CLERICAL DRESS

In addition to a section in Duchesne, *Christian Worship,* see G. S. Tyack, *Historic Dress of the Clergy* (London, William Andrews & Co., 1897, pp. 134).

DIONYSIUS THE AREOPAGITE

C. E. Rolt, *Dionysius the Areopagite on the Divine Names and the Mystical Theology* (London, Society for Promoting Christian Knowledge, 1920, pp. viii, 223). Contains a valuable introduction and translations.

OTHER DEVOTIONAL READING

A. Harnack, *Bible Reading in the Early Church* (London, Williams & Norgate, 1912, pp. x, 159).

Julianus Pomerius, *The Contemplative Life,* translated and annotated by Mary Josephine Suelser (Westminster, Md., The Newman Bookshop, 1947, pp. 220).

P. Pourrat, *Christian Spirituality from the Time of Our Lord till the Dawn of the Middle Ages,* translated by W. H. Mitchell and S. P. Jacques (London, Burns, Oates & Washbourne, 1922, pp. x, 312). The first volume of a comprehensive survey by a Roman Catholic. An excellent introduction.

SIN, PENANCE, FORGIVENESS

Clement of Alexandria, *The Stromata,* Book II, Chap. XIII, in *The Ante-Nicene Fathers,* Vol. II, pp. 360, 361 (New York, Charles Scribner's Sons, 1899); *Who Is the Rich Man that Shall be Saved,* XLII, in *The Ante-Nicene Fathers,* Vol. II, pp. 603, 604.

C. J. Hefele, translated by W. R. Clark, *A History of the Christian Councils* (Edinburgh, T. & T. Clark, 2d ed., 1872), Vol. I, pp. 415–423. Valuable for its citations from the original documents.

The Pastor of Hermas, Book II, Commandment 4, Chap. 3, in *The Ante-Nicene Fathers,* Vol. II, p. 22 (New York, Charles Scribner's Sons, 1899).

Sozomen, *Ecclesiastical History,* Book VII, Chap. 16, in *A Select Library of Nicene and Post-Nicene Fathers of the Christian Church, Second Series,* Vol. II, pp. 386, 387 (New York, The Christian Literature Society, 1890).

Tertullian, *Against Marcion,* Book IV, Chap. X, in *The Ante-Nicene Fathers,* Vol. III, p. 356 (New York, Charles Scribner's Sons, 1899); *On Repentance,* IX–XII, in *The Ante-Nicene Fathers,* Vol. III, pp. 664, 665; *On Modesty,* in *The Ante-Nicene Fathers,* Vol. IV, pp. 74–101 (New York, Charles Scribner's Sons, 1899).

O. D. Watkins, *A History of Penance* (London, Longmans Green and Co., 2 vols., 1920). Volume I is to A.D. 450.

Chapter 8

THE RISE OF MONASTICISM

What is the perfect Christian life? Can it be lived? If so, how? Does it entail the transformation of all human society? Can individuals be immersed in a prevailingly or partially un-Christian society without compromising their principles and be fully Christian? To be fully Christian, is it necessary to withdraw from society? If so, must one live alone, or must those intent on the complete Christian life seek it in community with others? If life in community is necessary, can there be a community, a human society, which will fully embody the Christian ideal? In one form or another these questions have been raised by Christians from the outset and have been recurrent across the centuries. Beginning in the third century they became insistent and in the following two centuries were increasingly clamant.

As we have seen, the early Christians were a small minority of the population of the Roman Empire and to a large degree held aloof from the society about them, seeking to realize the ideal in the small communities which then made up the Church. By the middle of the third century thousands were pouring into the Church. The great persecutions of the second half of the third century and the first quarter of the fourth century only temporarily checked the flood and by their failure eventually accelerated it. Before the close of the fifth century the overwhelming majority of the citizens of the Roman Empire were professing themselves to be Christians, had been baptized, and were members of one or another of the bodies which bore the Christian name. As we saw at the end of the last chapter, with the progress of the mass conversion the discipline of the Church was being relaxed and the gap between the ideal and the performance of the average Christian widened.

It was partially as a reaction against this laxity and partly because of the dissatisfaction which the teachings of Jesus and the apostles aroused with anything short of perfection that monasticism arose. At first it was primarily a lay movement, not within the hierarchical structure of the clergy. To some degree it was a rebellion of the individual against the organization of the Catholic

Church, regimented as that was under the bishops and clergy. Indeed, at times its members were quite unsubmissive to the bishops and were insubordinate, even tumultuously so, against a particular bishop. Many bishops looked with unfriendly eyes on the monks. In the initial decades of monasticism numbers of monks, laymen living alone, seldom partook of the Eucharist. Yet by the end of the fifth century monasticism had spread so widely that it had become characteristic of the Catholic Church. It was being regarded as the preferred way towards the perfect Christian life and as such it was attracting many of the most ardent Christian youth. Henceforward it was to be an accepted feature of the Catholic Church and of most of the churches into which that church divided. At present, while rejected by most of Protestantism, it is found in the churches which embrace a majority of those who regard themselves as Christians. It so captured the churches that in the East eventually the bishops were normally, indeed almost if not quite universally, drawn from the monasteries. In the West many of the bishops were monks. Before the end of the sixth century Pope Gregory I, one of the strongest men to sit on the throne of Peter, was drawn, reluctant, from his monastery—although it is not certain that he ever took monastic vows—and since then many monks have been numbered among his successors.

Monasticism has displayed many variations and has been one of the chief ways in which the vitality of the Christian faith has found expression. We are, accordingly, not only to trace its beginnings, but in later chapters we are again and again to recur to it to sketch its successive stages.

To a certain degree monasticism represented the triumph of ideas which the Catholic Church had denounced as heretical. Into it crept something of the legalism, the belief that salvation can be earned and deserved, which is opposed to grace and which had been theoretically rejected when the Ebionites were appraised as untrue to the Gospel. In it was still more of the conviction that flesh and matter are evil which had been so prominent in Gnosticism, the Marcionites, and Manichæism. In the triumph of monasticism, therefore, basic attitudes and beliefs won acceptance which in other forms the Catholic Church had branded as contrary to the genius of the Christian faith.

Moreover, at its inception, and to some degree in its later history, monasticism had much in it which was in contrast with the Gospel. At the outset, for the most part it was not missionary, in the sense that it did not endeavour to win non-Christians. It did not seek to save the world but to flee from it. The primary objective of the monk was his own salvation, not that of others.

We must also note that, again in opposition to what is found in the New Testament, where all Christians are called upon to be saints and a holy priesthood, monasticism tended to divide Christians into two groups—those aspiring to perfection and those content to compromise with sub-Christian or non-Christian practices.

Yet distinctively Christian elements were in the monastic movement. On renouncing their possessions the aspirants to the monastic life distributed them among the poor. Hundreds of monks, including the most famous of the pioneers, gave spiritual counsel to those who came to them. In later centuries, especially in the West, many monastic organizations became missionary or devoted themselves to the service of others. Indeed, from the sixth century onward most of the missionaries of the Roman Catholic and Eastern Churches were men or women who had taken monastic vows.

PRE-MONASTIC CHRISTIAN ASCETICISM

Although it has been prominent in the churches in which the majority of Christians have been enrolled, monasticism was unknown in the first two centuries of Christianity. Later generations believed that they found commands and precedent for the ascetic life in the teachings and example of Jesus and in other writings in the New Testament, but the accuracy of their interpretation is at least open to question. To be sure, Jesus declared that he who would become his disciple must surrender all that he had, in one notable instance commanded a wealthy young man to sell all that he possessed and give to the poor, and by saying that there were some who had made themselves eunuchs for the kingdom of heaven's sake appeared to commend celibacy. Yet, in marked contrast with John the Baptist, who was clearly an ascetic, Jesus, as he himself remarked, came both "eating and drinking" and neither he nor his disciples fasted during his lifetime. His leading disciple, Peter, and some others of the apostles, even after the resurrection continued to live with their wives. Paul, who favoured celibacy, knew of no express command from Jesus to support him in it and said in effect that matrimony might be as much a gift of God as the unmarried state. While community of goods was practised for a time in the early days of the original Christian church in Jerusalem, the giving of one's possessions to the common store was voluntary and not compulsory, and from the very beginning private ownership of property seems to have been normal among Christians. In at least one place in the New Testament those who forbade Christians to marry and commanded them to abstain from some kinds of food were deemed untrue to the faith. While widows were accorded special recognition, no one was enrolled as such before sixty years of age and the younger widows were commanded to marry and rear children.

However, long before monasticism, and, indeed, from the first days of the Church, fasting was an accepted discipline. Widows who did not remarry and who devoted themselves to prayer and the service of the Church became customary. Moreover, celibacy was early prized by the Church. *The Shepherd of Hermas* held that while it was not wrong for Christian widows or widowers to remarry, they would "gain greater honour and glory of the Lord" if they refrained from doing so. As we have seen, the Marcionites forbade marriage. While the Catholic Church did not have that requirement for membership, in 305 a synod in Elvira, in Spain, demanded celibacy of the bishops and other clergy. Even earlier the custom had been established that a bishop, a priest, or a deacon should not marry if he had been unmarried before his ordination, and that if his wife died there was to be no remarriage. The official decrees of synods, councils, and Popes enjoining celibacy on the clergy seem to have arisen out of a growing custom and to have reinforced it rather than to have initiated it.

Gradually the tradition was developing which was later to become fixed, in the West for the celibacy of deacons, priests, and bishops, and in the East celibacy for the bishops, but marriage before ordination for deacons and priests. In 385 Pope Siricius enjoined chastity upon all priests, saying that their daily offering of the sacrifice of the Eucharist made this necessary. In 390 a council at Carthage commanded chastity for bishops, priests, and deacons. Not far from the middle of the fifth century Pope Leo the Great extended to subdeacons the rule of clerical celibacy. In the second half of the fourth century a council in the East condemned those who regarded as unlawful receiving the Eucharist from the hands of a married priest. Late in the seventh century, in 692, a council which was esteemed ecumenical by the Eastern but not by the Western section of the Catholic Church declared that any who wished might be married before ordination as subdeacon, deacon, or priest, but no one should do so after ordination, and a married man who was raised to the episcopate must separate from his wife and provide for her in a monastery.

The Beginning of Monasticism

These trends in Christianity prepared a fertile seed bed for monasticism. On the one hand, the level of the morality of the average Christian appeared to be sinking and the ardent, their consciences quickened by the high standards of the New Testament, were not content. On the other hand, Christians had long honoured and many of them had practised voluntary poverty, fasting, and celibacy. But why should it have been monasticism rather than other forms of asceticism which arose and flourished on this soil?

It was in the third century and in Egypt that monasticism sprang up on the ground so prepared. Attempts have been made to find its source in Indian, Greek, pagan Egyptian, or Jewish roots, but none of these has been supported by conclusive proof. Indeed, from the outset Christian monasticism has differed markedly from any previous asceticism or religious community. It seems probable that the impulse which led to its emergence was predominantly and perhaps entirely from the Gospel. Origen, a native of Alexandria, gave an example of extreme asceticism in self-mutilation and in austerity in food, drink, sleep, and bodily comforts, and he had a profound influence upon many of his pupils who became prominent in the Church in Egypt. Ascetic Gnostics, Marcionites, and Montanists were found in Egypt and may have contributed to the later developments.

Yet factors other than those of Christian provenance may have been responsible for the birth of monasticism in Egypt rather than in some other land. Mysticism and the contemplative life were in non-Christian circles in Egypt, including the Neoplatonism which had its origin there, and they may have stimulated that phase of the monastic life. It is possible that influences may have entered from India. Manichæism may have contributed, although probably, if at all, later. Political and economic disorders in Egypt in the third and fourth centuries may have bred a sense of insecurity which impelled many to seek escape from the world. It is conceivable that a desire to be rid of the growing burden of civic obligations contributed to the flight of some from ordinary society. Probably, too, monasteries arose in part from disgust with city life, with its dust, crowds, noise, and moral corruption. That motive certainly made a strong appeal to some in other lands when the monastic movement had spread to them. The geography and climate of Egypt favoured the life of the monk, whether solitary or in community. The fertile valley of the Nile was a ribbon flanked on either side by the desert, rain was infrequent, and the ascetic could live alone and with little shelter, with such slight food as he needed from villages near at hand or raised on his own little plot of ground. Before the third century was out, Christian hermits were beginning to be seen in Egypt. Some of these had fled to the desert to escape the Decian persecution and remained there after it was over. Others, probably more numerous, began living in solitude as ascetics near villages in huts built by themselves and there gave themselves to prayer and contemplation.

The most famous of the early monks was Anthony. We know of him chiefly from a biography which is attributed to Athanasius, the great Bishop of Alexandria, noted for his part in the Arian controversy, and which by its early and wide circulation did much to stimulate the spread of the monastic life. The account which this biography gives of Anthony can be briefly summarized. Anthony was born, of Egyptian ancestry, probably not far from the year 250, of well-to-do Christian parents, and was reared in their faith. When he was about eighteen or twenty years of age his parents died, leaving him with the care of a younger sister. One day, while in church, he heard, in the reading of the

Gospel, the command of Jesus to the rich young ruler: "If thou wilt be perfect, go and sell what thou hast and give to the poor, and thou shalt have treasure in heaven, and come, follow me." Going out from the church, he immediately gave his inherited acres to the villagers, sold his movable possessions, and distributed the proceeds among the poor, reserving only enough for the care of his sister. Later hearing in church the injunction of Jesus, "be not anxious for tomorrow," he turned over even this remaining fund to the poor and placed his sister in the care of a community of virgins. He took up his abode outside the village, working with his hands, spending part of the return for food and giving the rest to the poor, visiting the hermits of whom he had heard, and learning from one or another of them graciousness, love, kindness, endurance, meekness, freedom from anger, and the art of prayer. He fought temptation in many forms, ate and drank sparingly and only of bread, salt, and water once a day after sunset, often went without food for from two to four days, slept but little and then usually on the bare ground, and to harden his body would not anoint it with oil. Later he withdrew to a ruined fort on a mountain and there dwelt alone for nearly twenty years, seldom seen by any. His fame eventually attracted disciples who built themselves cells in the mountains and emulated him in the solitary life. With him they formed a kind of community. Demons and the Devil were very real to him and he had many a bout with them. During one of the persecutions early in the fourth century he went to Alexandria, ministering to those condemned for the faith to the mines and the prisons, and hoping for martyrdom for himself. After the persecution ceased, he increased his austerities—fasting, giving up bathing, and wearing a skin garment with the hair next to his flesh. He withdrew again to solitude. There many sought him out, some for spiritual counsel and others for the miraculous healing of their diseases. He was strongly opposed to the Arians, and, going to Alexandria, denounced their views. As his fame spread, the Emperor Constantine and two of the latter's sons wrote to him, asking and receiving his counsel. He is said to have died in 356 at the age of 105 years. Although without formal education, he possessed a vigorous mind and a retentive memory. He was humble, cheerful, with a radiant love for God and with sympathy and well-mannered courtesy for the individuals who came to him.

Anthony represented two types of monasticism. One of these was that of hermit, the eremitical life, where each monk lived in solitude. The other was a modification of the way of the hermit, in which the monks had individual dwellings—a cell, a cave, a hut, or some other shelter—yet sufficiently near one another to make fellowship possible. They might even have over them a fellow-monk as a kind of director. Such a collection of monks was known as a *laura*.

A third type of monasticism was the cenobitic, in which the monks lived in a community, or monastery, governed by a head monk and by rules. He who was looked back to as the great pioneer of that kind of life was Pachomius, a younger contemporary of Anthony, who was born c.285 or c.292 and who died in 346. The son of pagan parents in Egypt, at the age of twenty Pachomius was for a short time in the imperial army. There he was impressed with the thoughtful kindness of Christians in bringing food and drink to the soldiers. Leaving the army, he was given instruction in the faith, was baptized, and joined himself to an ascetic. Some time afterwards he began a monastery, and it became so popular that several others arose. Pachomius ruled over them from a central monastery. As he was dying he appointed a successor and the latter eventually chose a coadjutor who succeeded him in his office.

Rules were gradually developed for the operation of the community. By the end of the fourth century the Pachomian system was fairly mature and stabilized. Each monastery was surrounded by a wall. Within this wall there were the houses in which the monks dwelt, twenty-two to forty to a house, and each with his own private cell. Every house had a common room for meetings. Within each enclosure there were also a church, a refectory, a library, a kitchen, a bakery, a store house for food, various workshops, and an infirmary. All the monasteries were under a superior-general or archimandrite who appointed his own successor. He visited them, made rules for them, and to each named one of the monks as resident head. In each house were placed, so far as possible, those with the same type of work. In every house the monks were ranked by order of seniority. Dress was prescribed and was very simple. All who applied were admitted if they were willing to keep the rules, but full membership was given only after a probation of three years. Each day had its regular times for group prayers by houses. The Eucharist was celebrated twice a week. Twice a year there were assemblies of all the monks, and at one of these the custom was for each to forgive any of the others who had done him an injury. Monks slept three in a cell and in a sitting, not a recumbent position. Study and memorization of passages from the Bible were required of all and the illiterate were taught to read. Manual labour was also compulsory, partly in the weaving of rushes into mats and baskets for sale and partly for the supply of the physical needs of the community. Extreme asceticism was discouraged, although some of the monks followed a very austere diet or might greatly curtail their hours of sleep. There were two meals a day, and flesh and wine were forbidden. Twice a week there were community fasts. Strict obedience to their superiors was required of all, and there were punishments for the disorderly. Chastity and poverty were compulsory. Gossip was forbidden and conversation was supposed to be limited to spiritual subjects. Each monastery had between two and three hundred monks and the total by the time of the death of Pachomius is said to have been three thousand.

Mary, the sister of Pachomius, gathered a nunnery about her which was put under the control of the Pachomian superior-general. Soon after the death of Pachomius, two other nunneries were formed. Although they were also in the comprehensive organization, precautions were taken to keep the men and women from meeting.

The Further Development of Monasticism

In the fourth and fifth centuries monasticism spread widely and monks multiplied. Monks and monasteries were especially numerous in the East, notably in Egypt, Mesopotamia, Palestine, and Syria, partly because in the latter two countries pre-monastic asceticism had been strong in Christian circles. In Mesopotamia they seem to have had beginnings which were quite independent of influences from Egypt. They may have been indebted to Manichæan monasticism and through that to Buddhist and Hindu asceticism. Monks and monasteries were also present in the West. All three kinds of monks were found—the solitaries (who were especially numerous in Palestine), those whose cells were grouped into a loose community, a *laura,* and those dwelling in the highly organized groups of which Pachomius had been a pioneer.

Some of the monks practised extreme austerities. There were the "pillar saints," those who lived on the top of pillars. One of the earliest and quite the most famous of them was Simeon Stylites, who died in 459. He dwelt on his pillar east of Antioch for thirty-six years, is said to have touched his feet with his forehead more than 1244 times in succession, and to have dripped with vermin. His fame spread, and multitudes, including some high state officials, came to see him. Other monks were immured in cells, some of them so small that they could neither lie at full length nor stand at full height. In one group the monks are reported to have subsisted on grass which they cut with sickles. Some monks passed many nights without sleep. Others went for days without food. The extreme ascetics were popularly esteemed "athletes of God." Many were said to work miracles of healing.

More numerous than these individualistic ascetics were the monks who lived in communities according to rule. After Pachomius, the most famous pioneer in the East of this form of monasticism was Basil of Cæsarea, whom we have already met as a scion of a wealthy, earnestly Christian family and as one of the three great Cappadocian champions and interpreters of Nicene orthodoxy. In 358, then in his late twenties, Basil visited Egypt and was profoundly impressed by what he saw there of the Pachomian monasteries. During their student days at Athens he and Gregory of Nazianzus agreed to join in living the ascetic life.

The ascetic life had appeared among the Christians in his native country some time before Basil's return home, and Eustathius, Bishop of Sebaste, north-east of Cæsarea, had already founded monasteries. Although later separated on questions of doctrine, Basil and Eustathius were for a time close friends. Moreover, Basil's mother, one of his sisters, Macrina, and a younger brother began in Pontus the nucleus of a community for simple Christian living which later was to develop into a nunnery. Indeed, Macrina was looked back to as the founder of women's conventual life in the Greek portion of the Catholic Church. Basil distributed part of his property among the poor and embarked on the monastic life in a secluded spot across the river from this establishment. Others joined him. He did not condemn Christians who married, but he believed celibacy and asceticism to be the higher way.

Basil was not long permitted to give himself exclusively to the monastic discipline, for he was drawn into the general life of the Church—into its theological controversies and eventually into its administration as a bishop. In this he was a prototype of many outstanding monks, both in the East and the West. They found that they could not withdraw completely from the world or from the Church as a whole, but must participate in them. Yet in the intervals which he devoted to the monastic life Basil worked out a set of rules which helped to shape monasticism in the Catholic Church, both in the East and the West. These were not in one formal piece of legislation, but were directions for the ascetic life contained in several writings, especially what are known as *The Longer Rules* and *The Shorter Rules*.

Here is not the place for a full description or even an adequate summary of these directions. In them Basil was deeply indebted to what he had seen in the Pachomian monasteries in Egypt. Yet he was no slavish imitator but was, rather, a creator. He knit the monastery into more of a community than had Pachomius. In general Basil advocated that the ascetics dwell together in communities rather than in solitude, declaring that association with others was necessary to the full Christian life, such as the practice of the law of love to one's neighbour. In the community room was to be found for both work and prayer. Extreme austerity was to be avoided, for after testing it in his first years of the ascetic life Basil had found it unfruitful. Food was to be simple and inexpensive and during the common meal a book was to be read. Work was for the supplying of the needs of the monastery and was varied, with preference given to agriculture and chief honour paid to intellectual labour, especially the study of the Scriptures. The monastery had its officers, with a superior over them all, chosen by the heads of neighbouring monasteries and after a period of probation accepted by his brethren. The superior was to seek the counsel of senior brethren. The obedience of the monk was to be absolute and the commitment was for life. Entrance to a monastery did not necessarily entail the renunciation of all the postulant's property, but he was to distribute at least part of it to the poor, taking care to do so with wisdom, remembering that he held it in trust from God. The monks were to make frequent confession of their sins, probably to one or another of the more mature of their brethren and not necessarily to a priest. After entering the monastery, the monks were to have as little contact as possible with their families, for this would embroil them with the world and its affairs. The monastery as a whole, through its official almoner, gave aid to the poor outside its walls, more especially to those who were dedicated to God. Boys were received to be educated in a religious manner, but were largely kept separate from the monks. The monasteries did not form a closely knit order, but constituted a kind of loose federation, and in time of need the richer were supposed to come to the assistance of the poorer. The monks were mostly laymen and the bishops seem to have had no control over them or the monasteries except that the formal admission to the monastic life was in the presence of a bishop. Yet Basil himself, as we have seen, became a bishop, and he made important contributions towards bringing the monastic life into the life of the Catholic Church as a whole. He and his monks became champions of orthodoxy and he set the example of a man of learning and outstanding gifts of organization giving himself both to the ascetic life and to the Church.

As we have suggested, Basil had a profound influence upon later monasticism, in both the East and the West. The great leader and organizer in the revival of Byzantine monasticism, Theodore the Studite, whom we are to meet in the eighth century, and whose reformed monastery, an outgrowth of a church and centre of monasticism founded in Constantinople in the late fifth century by Studius, became a model throughout the Eastern or Greek wing of the Catholic Church, drew his inspiration largely from the writings of Basil. In the West, Cassian, a fifth century pioneer in developing monasticism in Gaul, was aware of the work of Basil. Basil's precedent was formative in the rules devised by Benedict of Nursia, whom we are to meet in the sixth century. Benedict took over the Basilian pattern, although not slavishly or to the neglect of other earlier forms of the monastic life, and modified it to suit the needs of himself and of the community which he founded. For centuries his rule was dominant in the monasticism of the West.

An older contemporary of Basil and apparently quite unaffected by him, but a pioneer of the monastic movement in the West, and especially in Gaul, was Martin of Tours. We have already met him as a bishop who was active in spreading the faith in his diocese. Martin was born in the first half of the fourth century, the son of pagan parents. Since his father had been a military officer, Martin, complying with the requirement which made that occupation hereditary, entered the army in his teens. He was then already a catechumen. It was while serving in northern Gaul that the most famous incident of his life is said to have occurred. He is reported to have divided his coat with a beggar on a cold winter day and that night, in a dream, to have seen Christ clothed with the half which he had given away and saying that it was he with whom the young soldier had shared his garment. Baptized and resigning from the army two years later, Martin joined himself to Hilary of Poitiers, a famous champion of Nicene orthodoxy, journeyed to his parents to try to win them to the Christian faith and, returning to Gaul, established himself as a hermit. Others were attracted to him and a community arose which became the beginning of a monastery. The Christians of Tours wished him for their bishop and, luring him into the city, constrained him to accept the post. While performing with distinction the duties of his office, he remained humble, refusing to sit on the bishop's throne but using instead a rude stool, and continued to live as a hermit in a cell outside the city and there was joined by admirers who became the nucleus of another monastery. Many miracles were attributed to him. He was active in winning non-Christians and travelled extensively outside his diocese on various errands in the interests of the faith. He believed that no one was so depraved that he was beyond the scope of God's pardon. Himself impeccably orthodox, he protested against the persecution of heretics. He died in 397 or 400, probably in his seventies or eighties, exhausted by a journey which he had undertaken to restore harmony among the clergy in a town in his diocese. A younger contemporary admirer who wrote his biography declared that "he judged none and condemned none and never returned evil for evil. No one ever saw him angry, or annoyed, or mournful, or laughing. He was always the same and presented to everyone a joy of countenance and manner which seemed to those who saw it beyond the nature of man. Nothing was in his mouth except Christ, nothing in his heart but piety, peace, and pity." This biography early had a wide circulation and helped to shape the general religious life as well as monasticism in the West. The large number of churches in Western Europe which were dedicated to Martin were evidence of the impress which he made upon the Christianity of that region.

Another, but very different Western pioneer of monasticism was Eusebius Hieronimus Sophronius, better known as Jerome. A gifted and diligent scholar, enormously erudite, a master of languages, a lover of books, wielding a facile, vigorous, and often vitriolic pen, Jerome was an eloquent advocate of the monastic life. A contemporary of Martin of Tours, Ambrose of Milan, Augustine of Hippo, John Chrysostom, and the great Cappadocians, Jerome was born about the year 342 of devout Christian parents, near Aquileia, not far from the head of the Adriatic. As a youth he studied in Rome and there his ardent na-

ture caused him on the one hand to be moved by the churches and the catacombs and on the other to succumb to some of the vices which abounded in
that capital. Baptized in Rome in his mid-twenties, he was attracted to the
ascetic life. This had already entered Rome, perhaps stimulated by the descriptions given of the monks of Egypt by Athanasius when, exiled from his see, he
took refuge with his fellow bishop, the Pope. It had won women from some of
the wealthiest circles of Roman society. Returning to Aquileia, Jerome became
one of a group of young men who gave themselves to the ascetic life. From
Aquileia Jerome journeyed east and for three years lived as a solitary ascetic
on the borders of Chalcis, southeast of Antioch, devoting himself to austerities,
correspondence with his friends, and study in the library which he had brought
with him. Restless by disposition, he lived for a time in Antioch, was there, reluctant, ordained priest, travelled to Palestine to visit the holy places of his
faith, and then made his residence in Constantinople, where he formed a friendship with Gregory of Nazianzus. Journeying again to Rome, he was secretary
of a council which aspired to be ecumenical, from 382 was secretary to Pope
Damasus until the latter's death in December, 384, and, with the encouragement of the latter, began the work on a Latin translation of the Scriptures
which was to be one of his chief claims to fame. While in Rome he continued
to wear the dress and follow the abstemious discipline of the hermit and became
spiritual director and teacher to the circle of wealthy women who were interested in the ascetic life. With one of these, Paula, he formed an especially close
friendship. Against bitter opposition, Jerome eloquently advocated the ascetic
life, praised virginity, and excoriated the luxurious and wealth-seeking among
the clergy of the city.

After the death of Damasus Jerome left Rome, perhaps because of disappointment at not being elected Pope or because of the opposition and criticism
which he had aroused. A few months later he was followed by Paula. Together
they visited the places associated with the life of Jesus, among them Jerusalem,
Bethlehem, and Egypt. Returning to Bethlehem, Jerome built a monastery and
established himself in a cave close to the reputed site of the nativity, while
Paula erected convents and a hospice for pilgrims. There Jerome gave himself
to the routine of the monk, with its prayers, austere meals, and work. His chief
labours were literary, and in them he had the encouragement of Paula and the
assistance of scribes who wrote at his dictation. He composed commentaries on
the Bible, engaged in theological polemics, and carried on a voluminous correspondence. His chief accomplishment was a fresh translation of the Bible
into Latin from the original tongues. Because of its merit, both in its scholarship
and its felicitous Latin style, this translation won its way among Latin-using
peoples and eventually became standard for the Roman Catholic Church. How-

ever, the text which circulated under the name of the Vulgate, namely, the Latin vernacular version of the Bible, did not preserve the work of Jerome in its purity. It incorporated an older version of the Psalms, in part revised by Jerome, and some of its other sections were from older translations, partly unrevised or partially revised. It was a late sixteenth century revision of the Vulgate which was eventually made standard by Papal decree. Jerome lived on until 420, surviving the death of Paula and several of his closest friends, and dying where he had spent the last thirty-four years, in Bethlehem. His was a tempestuous career, but by his ardent advocacy of monasticism he had given a great impetus to that movement, especially in the West.

Martin of Tours and Jerome were by no means the only ones responsible for the growth of the monastic movement in the West. Ambrose of Milan furthered it. In the fourth century Bishop Eusebius of Vercellæ in Italy had the clergy of his cathedral live together according to a rule. Augustine of Hippo gathered his clerical household into a community. At least two Popes of the fifth century founded monasteries in Rome. Early in the fifth century John Cassian began monasteries in Marseilles and Lérins in the south of Gaul which soon enrolled thousands.

By the end of the fifth century monasticism had become firmly established in the Catholic Church in both East and West and had begun to take on the forms which were to characterize it through the centuries. It was to undergo many modifications, but in its numerous ramifications it was to be the main channel through which bursts of new life were to find expression in the various churches which conserved the traditions of the Catholic Church of the Roman Empire. One of the best gauges of the vitality of these churches, and especially of the Roman Catholic Church, is to be found in the numbers and strength of the reforms of existing monastic houses and of the new monastic or near-monastic movements which emerge in any one era. When vigour has been at a low ebb, the monastic life has languished and become sluggish or corrupt. In times of revival, the monastic life has attracted ardent souls who wish to give themselves unreservedly to the faith and has taken on fresh variety and new forms.

Here was effort after effort to create communities which would completely realize the Christian ideal and also, in the case of increasing numbers of variations of the monastic patterns, dream after dream of making these communities centres from which the Christian faith would irradiate and transform the non-Christian world about them. Never did the effort fully reach its goal nor was the dream ever entirely fulfilled. Most monastic institutions, if they survived, fell away from the purposes of their founders and became lethargic or worse.

Yet the vision would not die. Its constraining appeal persisted and was never more compelling than in the nineteenth and twentieth centuries.

Selected Bibliography

GENERAL WORKS

A. Harnack, *Monasticism: Its Ideals and History and the Confessions of St. Augustine. Two Lectures.* Translated into English by E. E. Kellett and F. H. Marseille (London, Williams & Norgate, 1901, pp. 171). The lecture on monasticism is a general, interpretative essay.

W. H. Mackean, *Christian Monasticism in Egypt to the Close of the Fourth Century* (London, Society for Promoting Christian Knowledge, 1920, pp. 120). Soundly based upon the sources.

I. G. Smith, *Christian Monasticism from the Fourth to the Ninth Centuries of the Christian Era* (London, A. D. Innes & Co., 1892, pp. viii, 351). A competent, well-documented survey.

H. B. Workman, *The Evolution of the Monastic Ideal from the Earliest Times to the Coming of the Friars* (London, The Epworth Press, 1913, pp. xxi, 368). A well-written, scholarly survey, of which a little more than a third is devoted to the period covered by this chapter.

ANTHONY

Athanasius, *Life of Antony* (*vita Antoni*), translated by H. Ellershaw, with notes by A. Robertson, in *A Select Library of Nicene and Post-Nicene Fathers of the Christian Church,* Second Series, Vol. IV (New York, Charles Scribner's Sons, 1903), pp. 188–221.

BASIL

Saint Basil. The Letters, with an English Translation, by R. J. Deferrari (London, William Heinemann, 4 vols., 1926–1934). Greek text, English translation, and notes.

W. K. L. Clarke, *St. Basil the Great, A Study in Monasticism* (Cambridge University Press, 1913, pp. lx, 176). Carefully done, by a specialist.

W. K. L. Clarke, *The Ascetic Works of Saint Basil, Translated into English with Introduction and Notes* (London, Society for Promoting Christian Knowledge, 1925, pp. 362).

E. F. Morison, *St. Basil and His Rule. A Study in Early Monasticism* (Oxford University Press, 1912, pp. xii, 150). Carefully done, based upon the sources.

M. G. Murphy, *St. Basil and Monasticism* (Washington, The Catholic University of America, 1930, pp. xix, 112). A doctoral dissertation.

MARTIN OF TOURS

E.-Ch. Babut, *Saint Martin de Tours* (Paris, Librairie Ancienne H. Champion, no date, pp. viii, 320). Objective, carefully done.

L. Foley, *The Greatest Saint of France* (Milwaukee, Morehouse-Gorham Co., 1931, pp. xi, 321). Popularly written, based upon careful research, with critical notes.

Sulpicii Severi Vita Sancti Martini, in *Corpus Scriptorum Ecclesiasticorum,* Vol. I, pp. 109–141.

JEROME

E. L. Cutts, *Saint Jerome* (London, Society for Promoting Christian Knowledge, 1897, pp. ix, 230). Popularly written, based upon careful scholarship.

Largent, *Saint Jerome,* translated by H. Davenport (New York, Benziger Brothers, 1913, pp. x, 196).

Select Letters of St. Jerome, with an English translation by F. A. Wright (London, William Heinemann, 1933, pp. xvi, 510). Parallel Latin text and English translation.

Chapter 9

EARTHEN VESSELS . . . THE EXCEEDING GREATNESS OF THE POWER

In one of his most famous passages, Paul declares that "we have this treasure in earthen vessels, that the excellency [or exceeding greatness] of the power may be of God, and not of us." In another letter he speaks of "the exceeding greatness of His power to us-ward who believe, according to the working of his mighty power which he wrought in Christ, when he raised him from the dead and set him at his own right hand . . . far above all principality and power, and might, and dominion, and every name that is named, not only in this world, but also in that which is to come; and hath put all things under his feet."

As we come to the end in the initial period in the history of Christianity we would do well to ask just what effect the Christian Gospel was having. By the year 500, as we have seen, the overwhelming majority of the population of the Roman Empire were calling themselves Christians and the faith had begun to be carried beyond the borders of that realm. It was but a small proportion of the earth's surface which had been touched by Christianity. Only here and there had the peoples of primitive cultures who thinly occupied most of the world been reached, and of civilized mankind less than half had even so much as heard the name of Christ. Most of the Persians and the Indians and all the Chinese were as yet ignorant of it. Long before the end of the fifth century the Roman Empire had been showing signs of internal weakness and the invasions had begun which were to hasten its disintegration and, as they became more pronounced, were to usher in for Christianity an agonizing period of decline.

What was Christianity doing to the peoples who had accepted it and to their culture? Was the "exceeding greatness of His power" to be seen, and if so how? Had it been true of Christ that God had "put all things under his feet"? Had "the earthen vessels" to which "the treasure," "the light of the glorious Gospel of Christ," been entrusted so hampered it that it had been nullified or at least weakened, or had the fact that "the treasure" was in "earthen vessels" made more vivid, as Paul had declared, that there was in the Gospel a unique power, something so in contrast with human nature that it was obviously not man's creation, but from outside man, so demonstrably from Christ that it was clear that the Catholic Church was right in affirming that Jesus Christ, while fully man, was also God incarnate, the Word become flesh? Would the power prove so potent that it would survive the centuries of adversity and break out with renewed vigour, or would it be dissipated through the corruption of the earthen vessels?

It was not merely a question of striking changes, but of what kind of changes. Sweeping changes there had been before in the Mediterranean world and in other cultures, as in the wake of Alexander the Great and of Gautama Buddha, and changes there were to be again. Fully as important was the quality of the changes. How far were these to reflect the kind of life which was disclosed in Christ? Were men being transformed into likeness to Christ?

An even deeper question, one at which we cannot more than hint in this place, was that raised by Paul's confident affirmation that God had "foreordained" "them that love God . . . to be conformed to the image of His Son." Was this true? Was Christ, as the author of *The Epistle to the Hebrews* declared, "the brightness of His [God's] glory, and the express image of His [God's] person"? In the changes which were taking place was the Creator of the universe at work, fulfilling His purpose for man, and could this purpose be seen in the kind of individuals and the characteristics of the communities which were emerging?

These questions are not of antiquarian interest. It was in these five centuries that Christianity first moved out into the world. It was then that it created a literature and developed organizational features, intellectual statements of belief, and forms of worship which for the majority of those bearing the Christian name have remained standard to this day. The experience of these initial centuries should shed important, perhaps decisive light upon the questions which we raised at the close of our fourth chapter, just before we embarked upon this period, about the place of the Gospel in human history, the query as to whether in it is to be found the clue to the enigma which the universe presents to man and which man presents to himself. They should be of assistance in determining whether, to use another affirmation of Paul, "God was in Christ, reconciling the world unto himself," and, if so, just how that reconciliation has operated.

The Power Creates the Church, Christian Literature, and Christian Theology

From what has been said in the preceding chapters it must be apparent that power of extraordinary magnitude was at work. Into a civilization which had ceased to say or to do much that was new a dynamic force had entered which had brought into being a vast new literature, of which the New Testament was only a small portion, inspired by a compelling creative message, centred about Christ. This force was also responsible for the emergence of the Christian Church, a structure without parallel in history, which, while arising within the Roman Empire and in part owing its unity to that Empire, was spreading beyond the borders of that realm and with an inner vitality which enabled it to survive the breakup of that state. In connexion with the Church a new profession had arisen, the clergy. The clergyman was in part priest, modeled consciously on the pattern of the Jewish priesthood and perhaps unconsciously showing the influence of the pagan priesthood. Yet the clergyman was far more than a priest, officiating at the public services of the Church. He was also a pastor, a shepherd and guide of souls. That function was to grow as the centuries passed and was to make the profession of the Christian clergyman quite unique.

This power had stimulated the conventionalized mind of the Græco-Roman world to wrestle with the baffling new intellectual problems presented by the birth, life, death, and resurrection of Christ and to reach answers which were novel in the history of human thought. It had created new forms of worship and in monasticism had brought into being a movement which, like the Church, was to outlast the society within which it arose and against which it was a protest. Moreover, the Christian Gospel had worked moral and spiritual transformations in the lives of individuals. In some, as in Paul and Augustine, these were spectacular. In others, such as Ambrose and Tertullian, they were not as cataclysmic but were no less real. In still others, such as Origen, Anthony, and Basil of Cæsarea, reared as Christians from infancy, the product was also distinctive and contagious.

Yet No Attempt Was Made to Reshape Civilization

In addition to the effects which we have already noted, there were others which must be taken into account if anything like satisfactory answers are to be given to the questions which we have propounded.

It is significant that no thoroughgoing remaking of Græco-Roman society was achieved. Indeed, none was attempted. For the first two centuries Christians constituted a small minority. At the outset many of them expected the early visible return of their Lord, bringing with him the abrupt end of history. For several generations, as we have seen, substantial numbers of Christians continued to reassert that hope. For the most part the Church was concerned for the salvation of the individual. It sought to gather these individuals into its fellowship and it constituted a community, divided to be sure, but fairly distinct from the world about it. Their critics charged Christians with being enemies of society, but Christian apologists protested the loyalty of their co-believers to the Empire. Tertullian, for instance, declared that Christians regarded the existence of the Roman Empire as a bulwark against chaos, held that God had appointed the Emperors, and that, as commanded by the New Testament, Christians prayed for their temporal rulers, the Emperors and their ministers, and even for those who persecuted them. Against those who charged Christians and their neglect of the gods with the responsibility for the ills which were overtaking society, Tertullian boldly insisted that because of its sins the human race had always deserved ill at God's hands, that God's judgements had brought misfortunes upon mankind in pre-Christian days, and that calamities had actually declined since the advent of Christianity, for, so he said, from that time onward virtue had placed some restraint upon the wickedness of the world and men had begun to pray for the averting of God's wrath. Christians were far from attempting the overthrow and reconstruction of Græco-Roman society. To be sure, they were attacking certain features of that society—its polytheism, its immoralities, its gladiatorial contests, the indecencies of its theatre, its infanticide, and its sexual irregularities—but in doing so they believed that they were conserving and not destroying the Empire and its civilization.

When, beginning with Constantine, the Empire made its peace with the Church, it sought to control the latter and to use it as a bulwark against the mounting threats to the stability of the realm. In this the leaders of the Church acquiesced. Indeed, when the sack of Rome by Alaric and his Goths in 410 made apparent the mortal weakness of the Empire, Augustine stoutly declared that the presence of churches as sanctuaries and the Christian profession of some of the Goths had mitigated the disaster.

With the numerical triumph of Christianity through the winning of the overwhelming majority of the population of the Roman Empire to the Christian faith, it might have seemed that the Church would at last undertake the reshaping of civilization. However, the emergence of monasticism served further to preclude even the formulation of such a programme. The monks sought to withdraw from the world and either to live completely apart from society or to set up communities of their own which would perfectly embody the Christian ideal.

Although Christians did not attempt the complete remaking of Græco-Roman civilization, they attacked some of the constituent elements of the life about them and in other ways their attitudes were in stark contrast with the culture in which they were immersed and wrought not only negative but also positive changes in the Mediterranean world. Moreover, there was a striking difference between Græco-Roman civilization and the Roman state on the one hand and on the other the faith set forth in Christ and by his apostles. There were basic differences in values—what was deemed most worth while—and in conceptions of the nature and destiny of man, of the universe, of the course of history, and of power—between the kind of power seen in the cross and the resurrection and that which formed and sustained the Roman Empire. These could scarcely be reconciled. Here, as in Judaism, the parable of Jesus of the new wine in old wineskins was pertinent, perhaps tragically so. In trying to put the one into the other both might be lost.

The Profound Effect on the Religious Life

As was to be expected, Christianity had a profound effect upon the religious life of the Roman Empire and its people. Christian apologists devoted much of their energy to denouncing the pagan cults in which the Empire abounded and would have no compromise with them. As we have suggested, there was some carry over from paganism in the attitudes and practices of many Christians, but there was not the deliberate and easygoing syncretism which was so marked a feature of the contemporary religious life outside of Christianity and Judaism. The Church was officially intransigent. It held that through itself alone was salvation, the true goal of human life, to be attained. By the year 500 the pagan cults had all but disappeared. They survived chiefly in backward rural districts and remote mountain valleys, or among the barbarian invaders.

So sweeping a religious revolution had never before been seen in the Mediterranean world. It was not unique. It was later to be paralleled by the supplanting of religions, some of them "higher" than the paganism of the Roman Empire, by Islam, and by the elimination and absorption in most of India of Buddhism, also a "high" religion, by Hinduism. Yet in some ways the victory of Christianity was a more notable achievement than either of these. In contrast with Islam, the triumph of Christianity, which had really been won before Constantine espoused the faith, had been accomplished without the use of arms or the support of the state, and, unlike the success of Hinduism in India as against Buddhism, it was not the resurgence of the hereditary religion against what the latter regarded as an heretical variant from itself.

The religious effects of Christianity were not alone negative, the destruction of rival cults. Christianity contributed to new religious movements. It was a potent element in Manichæism, and in the various forms of Gnosticism. It may have had some influence on the rise and growth of Neoplatonism. Even more significant were the positive results in the conceptions of God and of human nature, in the kind of worship, and in the quality of living which the victor produced. On the conceptions of God and of human nature and on the kind of worship associated with Christianity, we have already said as much as the limitations of our space will wisely permit. However, we must add something about the basic convictions concerning the relation of the Christian community to the society in which it was immersed, convictions concerning the goal of history, and the sort of behaviour and character which issued from the religious beliefs of Christians. Here were tensions and reciprocal contradictions. While they were partially resolved as Christian thinkers achieved an uneasy reconciliation and as membership in the Church came to be almost identical with citizenship in the Empire, they never fully disappeared, but persisted, a source both of weakness and strength in the society with which Christianity had become associated.

The Tension between the Early Christians and "the World"

From the beginning, Christians felt themselves in opposition to what they called "the world." They recognized the antagonism between Jesus on the one hand and, on the other hand, the state in which they were set and which had brought about the crucifixion of Jesus and the chronic persecution of his followers. This contrast found dramatic expression in Augustine's *City of God* with its sharply drawn distinction between the city of the world and the city of God, but that famous book was the more important because it was an amplification by a first-class mind of views already cherished by Christians.

Many tended to identify the Church with the city of God. Even Augustine seemed at times to do so. Certainly as it grew the Catholic Church became a distinct society, within the Empire but not fully of it, a kind of *imperium in imperio*. It had its rules and laws, the beginnings of its canon law, administered by its own officers, the clergy, alongside the state. This contributed to the contrast between Christians and the society in which they were immersed.

Moreover, as we pointed out in a previous chapter, the Christian view of human history differed radically from that of the Græco-Roman world. It was the contrast between fate and destiny. The Greeks, and in this Roman thinkers followed them, regarded history as endlessly repeating itself in a series of cycles, so that what is now had been in some earlier stage of man's career and would be again in later eras. Blind fate determined it. Here was a weary, pessimistic appraisal of man's course. To the Christian, in striking contrast, human history has God as its sovereign, begins with God's creation of man, and will go on to a climax in which God will still be master. Christians saw in history a cosmic drama, centring about man's creation with freedom of will, man's sin, and the redemption of man through the incarnation, the cross, the resurrection, and the coming of the Holy Spirit. Through Christ, so Christians believed, fallen, sinful man could be transformed and grow into fellowship with God and in likeness to Him. This gave to man a dignity and a worth and to history a meaning which Græco-Roman thought had not known.

Christians differed as to when the climax to history would arrive and as to its precise nature. Yet the early Christians held that God was even now master, that, while the climax had not yet come, it was near. Paul said that "the day is at hand" and that Christians should even now "walk honestly as in the day" where God's will is perfectly done. Jesus seemed to say that here and now men could enter that kingdom where God's will is the rule, in a "realized eschatology," the end of history, which for them had already dawned. Many believed that the climax would be in a second coming of Christ. Some sought to discover the precise date of that coming, while others, while convinced that it would be, held that no man could know the day or the hour. Origen was convinced that the Word, the *Logos,* would "prevail over the entire rational creation, and change every soul into His own perfection" and that "the consummation of all things is the destruction of evil, although as to the question whether it shall be so destroyed that it can never anywhere arise again, it is beyond our present purpose to say." Many, among whom was Augustine, taught that perfection could never be realized within history, but only beyond it, in heaven.

The opposition between Christians and "the world" was partially allayed, as we have suggested, as the centuries wore on. Leaders of the Church held the latter to be like Noah's ark, in which were all, both good and bad. Christianity tended to fuse with Platonism and Stoicism. Stoicism was utilized by Christian thinkers to afford a theoretical foundation to ethics. To the Stoic there was in the universe a dominant Divine Reason from which came a moral natural law. Some of the Christian intellectuals held that this natural law of the Stoics was identical with Christian moral law. Yet this convenient accommodation did not entirely erase the contrast between Christianity and "the world" in which it had to operate.

CHRISTIANS AND WAR

One of the issues on which the early Christians were at variance with the Græco-Roman world was participation in war. For the first three centuries no Christian writing which has survived to our time condoned Christian participation in war. Some Christians held that for them all bloodshed, whether as soldiers or as executioners, was unlawful. At one stage in its history the influential Church of Alexandria seems to have looked askance upon receiving soldiers into its membership and to have permitted enlistment in the legions only in exceptional circumstances. Hippolytus, prominent in Rome, in putting down in writing what he believed to be the apostolic tradition and so the authentic Christian teaching, maintained that when he applied for admission to the Christian fellowship a soldier must refuse to kill men even if he were commanded by his superiors to do so and must also not take an oath, and that military commanders must resign if they were to continue as catechumens. A catechumen or baptized person, so Hippolytus said, who sought to enlist as a soldier must be cut off from the Church. Tertullian argued against Christians being members of the Roman armies on the ground that this brought one under a master other than Christ, that it entailed taking the sword, and that, even when the army was used for police purposes in peace time, it made necessary the infliction of punishment, when all revenge was forbidden to the Christian. He said that in disarming Peter Christ ungirded every soldier. Another consideration which weighed against service in the armies was the strong possibility that as a soldier the Christian would be required to take part in idolatrous rites. Some Christians would permit service in the legions in times or areas of peace when the function of the army was that of the police, but frowned upon it in war.

So clear was the opposition of the early Christians to bearing arms that Celsus, in his famous attack on them, declared that if all were to do as did the Christians the Empire would fall victim to the wildest and most lawless barbarians. In replying, Origen did not deny that Christians were pacifists. Indeed, he said that Christians do not fight under the Emperor "although he require it." Instead he argued that if all were to become Christians, the barbarians would also be Christian, and that even now, when Christians were in the minority, their love, labour, and prayers were doing more than Roman arms to preserve the realm.

For the early Christians, pacifism was largely theoretical, for they were chiefly from groups other than those from which the legions were recruited and they did not have the responsibility for formulating state policy.

In spite of the general trend among Christians towards pacifism, in the third century the numbers of Christians serving in the legions seem to have increased. This was especially the case on the frontiers, menaced as they were by invasion, and in the West.

Moreover, after the Emperors had espoused Christianity and they and Christian officials were charged with the responsibility for the body politic and for making decisions for the government, the attitude of the majority of Christians towards war changed. Christians now began to believe that some wars are just. That was the position taken by Ambrose. Augustine elaborated the theoretical basis for a just war. He held that wickedness must be restrained, by force if necessary, and that the sword of the magistrate is divinely commissioned. Not all wars are just. To be just, so Augustine said, a war must be waged under the authority of the prince, it must have as its object the punishment of injustice and the restoration of peace, and it must be fought without vindictiveness and without unnecessary violence. It must also be carried on with inward love. Yet without the authority of the prince, Augustine taught, the civilian must not use force to defend even his own life. The clergy and the monks were to be entirely exempt from military service. It was this principle of a righteous or just war which was held by a large proportion of Christians in subsequent centuries.

CHRISTIANS AND PUBLIC AMUSEMENTS

On amusements Christians also set themselves against the prevailing mores of Græco-Roman life. The theatre, gladiatorial combats, and contests between men and beasts were almost universal. Every city of consequence had prominent structures for them. The pagan Emperors, even such noble spirits among them as Marcus Aurelius, considered it part of their public duty to give gladiatorial shows and to attend them, and the crowd demanded them. Yet leading Christians unhesitatingly condemned the theatre and the sports of the amphitheatre. The theatre was opposed because of the lewdness of its plays and its hypocrisy—its simulation of love, wrath, fear, and sorrow. Tertullian gave as reasons for the prohibition to Christians of attendance at the public spectacles the fact that the games and the gladiatorial contests were in honour of the pagan gods, that they stirred up rage, bitterness, and grief, that the accompanying betting was too agitating to be wholesome, and that through them crime was not only committed but also taught. Another of the early Christian writers denounced the gladiatorial shows as "a cannibal banquet for the soul," and still another as inculcating murder. Some, including Clement of Alexandria, forbade Christians to frequent the race course. Hippolytus declared that early Christian tradition did not countenance attending or taking part in chariot races. Augustine described and condemned the blood lust aroused by witnessing the gladiatorial combats. For a time the Church refused baptism to a professional gladiator unless he would renounce that occupation and excluded from the communion those who frequented the games. Under the influence of his new faith, the Emperor Constantine forbade gladiatorial shows and abolished the legal penalties which required criminals to become gladiators. John Chrysostom, like many a lesser bishop and preacher, took up the verbal cudgels against horse-racing, popular farces, and pantomimes.

Yet these amusements were continued even after the majority of the population of the Empire had become professed Christians and when many, perhaps most of their patrons bore the Christian name. We are told that the gladiatorial combats persisted in Rome until, in the fifth century, a monk, Telemachus, leaped into the arena to stop the combatants and the mob, presumably nominally Christian, stoned him to death for interfering with their pleasure. Thereupon the Emperor ordered that the spectacles be stopped and Telemachus enrolled among the martyrs. Probably, however, the end of the gladiatorial combats and of contests in the arena between men and beasts was due as much to the growing poverty of the declining Empire and the dearth of recruits for the ranks of the gladiators as to the Christian conscience.

CHRISTIANS AND SLAVERY

Christians carried on no organized campaign against slavery. That was to wait until the nineteenth and twentieth centuries. Yet here, also, although by no means so markedly as in the case of amusements, the trend of the Christian conscience and of Christian practice was against a basic, generally accepted institution of the Græco-Roman world and mitigated its harshness.

Even the casual student of Græco-Roman culture cannot but be aware of the prominence in it of slavery. The Greek democracies had slavery, and the leisure of their free citizens for the affairs of the state was made possible by the labour of slaves. In the Roman Empire the great landed estates were worked by slaves, and slaves also did much of the urban labour and performed most of the domestic service in households which could afford them. The lot of the slaves was often unhappy and public opinion condoned the use of the lash on them, the killing of them when their usefulness was past, and the selling of them at a low price when they became old.

Few Christians condemned slavery outright, many Christians owned slaves, and some Christian masters treated their slaves harshly. Yet Christian teaching ameliorated the lot of slaves. While Paul commanded slaves to obey their masters as slaves of Christ, doing their work as unto him and not unto men, he also exhorted masters to forbear "threatening" their slaves, remembering that there is no "respect of persons" with Him who is in heaven, the Master of both earthly masters and slaves. In a very touching letter Paul returned a fugitive slave to his master, pleading with the latter to receive the runaway as a brother in the Lord. Paul also declared that in the Christian fellowship there is neither bond nor free, but that "all are one in Christ Jesus." More than once in later centuries Christian writers reminded those of their faith that in

God's sight the master has no higher status than the slave, but that both are to be judged. Ambrose said that the slave might be superior in character to his master and be really more free than he. Augustine declared that God did not create rational man to lord it over his rational fellows. In this attitude both Ambrose and Augustine may have been influenced by Stoicism, but they believed it to be in accord with Christian principles. In many places slaves might hold office in the Church. It was not unusual for pagans to free their slaves, but many Christians did likewise. That they believed that a connexion existed between their faith and this act is seen from the fact that manumission was often solemnized in a church and on one of the great festival days, especially Easter. Near the end of the first century we hear of Christians who voluntarily became slaves to ransom others from bondage.

Christianity undercut slavery by giving dignity to work, no matter how seemingly menial that might be. Traditionally, labour which might be performed by slaves was despised as degrading to the freeman. Christian teachers said that all should work and that labour should be done as to Christ as master and as to God and in the sight of God. Work became a Christian duty.

Before the end of the fifth century slavery was declining. This was not due entirely and perhaps not even chiefly to the influence of Christianity, but the latter contributed to it.

THE CHRISTIAN ATTITUDE TOWARDS PROPERTY

Could a man of wealth become and remain a Christian? Did the Christian ethic make for a revolution in the attitude towards property and the industrial and commercial structure of life? Some passages in the New Testament brought disquiet to tender consciences. Notable was the statement of Jesus to the rich young ruler that if he would be perfect he must sell all that he had and give to the poor, and his further comment that it was extremely difficult for a rich man to enter the kingdom of heaven. As we have seen, the early church in Jerusalem for a time practised community of goods. With some partial exceptions poverty was one of the rules for those who sought to be fully Christian by following the way of the monk. Christian teachers tended to regard agriculture and manual labour as preferable to trade and frowned upon the latter for those of their faith. Clement of Alexandria did not proscribe trade, but said that the Christian merchant should seek to determine what would be a just price to ask for his wares and to demand no more and accept no less.

Yet Christian teachers did not forbid private property. They held that luxury was contrary to Christian principles and commended simplicity in clothing and in eating and drinking, but they also enjoined labour and did not require the full surrender of the fruits of labour. The Church became the owner of large estates and even monasteries possessed property collectively and sold on the market the products of the work of the monks.

CHRISTIAN PHILANTHROPY

Gifts of individuals to the public weal were not a Christian innovation. Many non-Christians had been very generous. Indeed, in the Roman Empire benefactions by private individuals and public officials were a commonplace. Through them baths, temples, theatres, roads, bridges, aqueducts, markets, schools, and libraries were constructed and games and other public amusements were provided.

However, in the use of money for the general welfare, Christianity brought five significant innovations. It made giving the obligation of its adherents, poor as well as rich, for it was held that all should contribute, each according to his ability, and this was symbolized by the collection which was early part of the Eucharistic ritual. The motive that was stressed was also new: it was love in grateful response to the love of Christ, who, though he was rich, yet for the sake of those who were to follow him became poor, that they through his poverty might become rich. The objects of beneficence were also changed, at least in part. The Christian community stressed the support of its widows, orphans, sick, and disabled, and of those who because of their faith were thrown out of employment or were imprisoned. It ransomed many who were put to servile labour for their faith. It entertained travellers. One church would send aid to another church whose members were suffering from famine or persecution. In theory and to no small degree in practice, the Christian community was a brotherhood, bound together in love, in which reciprocal material help was the rule. This was more easily carried out in the years when Christians were a minority, but something of the same spirit, even though attenuated and institutionalized, carried over into the days when Christians became a majority.

Christian love and service were not restricted to members of the Church. They were also extended to non-Christians. The command to love one's neighbour was not forgotten, nor the parable by which Jesus had illustrated that command, of care for a nameless stranger upon whom misfortune had fallen. In one of the New Testament writings Christians were enjoined, as they had opportunity, to do good unto all men. We read that later, when pestilence swept great cities such as Carthage and Alexandria, and when the pagans had fled to escape it, Christians remained and cared for the sick and dying. After persecutions ceased, wealthy Christians founded hospitals.

We must note that, as a fifth innovation, Christian giving was personalized.

Springing as it did from love, it was not impersonal service to masses of men, although often, as in times of famine, it dealt with large numbers, but it poured itself out to individuals, valuing each as having distinct worth in the sight of God, one "for whom Christ died."

SEX, WOMEN, CHILDREN, MARRIAGE, AND THE FAMILY

In that important realm of human life which embraces the relations between the sexes, the status of women and children, marriage, and the family, Christianity wrought significant modifications.

Women were prominently and favourably mentioned in the cherished records of the life of Christ. While Paul would not allow them to speak in the meetings of the churches, he declared that in Christ Jesus there could be neither male nor female, and in the churches of the first generation women were honoured as prophetesses. Women seem also to have served as deaconesses, although this is not certain. As we have seen, from the very early days of the Church widows and virgins were held in high respect.

We have noted that at least from the time of Paul virginity was esteemed above the married state. Yet, except in some of the minority groups, such as the Marcionites, marriage was not proscribed. In the case of the death of one partner, a second marriage was forbidden by the stricter elements in the Church, but was eventually permitted by the more lenient. A third marriage was regarded as evil. Sexual intercourse outside of marriage was sternly interdicted and within marriage was permitted only for the procreation of children. Divorce was not allowed, except after the violation of the marriage bond by one of its partners. Sexual offenses were by no means unknown among Christians, but they were long held to exclude the offender from the Church. Later, as we have noted, restoration was permitted after due repentance and discipline. Civil law forbade a woman of high degree to marry a man of lower social rank, a freedman, or a slave, and decreed that if she disobeyed she would sink to the status of her spouse. Yet society in general winked at such unions. Early in the third century, although he was sharply criticized for it, Pope Callistus (Calixtus I), who relaxed the rule for sexual offenses, also pronounced such marriages legal from the standpoint of the Church.

Children were to be held in tender regard. Jesus himself had set the example and Paul, while enjoining them to obey their parents, commanded that the fathers should not provoke them to wrath but rear them in the "nurture and admonition of the Lord." The destruction of young life, either by abortion or infanticide, was forbidden.

In its first few centuries, within the Church which it had called into being Christianity had not only largely drawn the sting of slavery, given dignity to labour, and abolished beggary. It had also elevated the status of women and given new worth to childhood.

Should Christians study and teach the non-Christian literature—the Greek and Roman philosophers, poets, and dramatists—held in such high regard by the pagans about them, or were these writings so in contrast with the Gospel that to read them would contaminate the faith of Christians?

Here Christians did not fully agree. We have noted that such outstanding moulders of Christian thought as Clement of Alexandria and Origen were students of the Greek philosophers and, while not uncritical of them, levied tribute on them in forming their own conceptions of the Christian faith. They were by no means alone in this. We have remarked the fashion in which Ambrose was indebted to Stoicism and Augustine to Neoplatonism. The list could be lengthened. Moreover, it was through Christians that such of Greek and Roman literature as has survived to our day was preserved and transmitted. Yet Jerome came to believe that he must give up his passion for the Greek and Roman classics as a kind of idolatry. Many Christian writers poured scorn on the philosophers and denounced the accounts of the gods in the literature of the day for their immoralities and puerilities. Numbers of Christians, moreover, feared to have any contact with Greek and Roman literature, holding that the Scriptures were sufficient.

We must remind ourselves that between the Christian and the Greek approach to the intellectual life a great gulf existed, a gulf which helps to explain the distrust of many Christians for pagan philosophy. The Greeks relied on reason as the primary way to truth, but underneath that reason they had, consciously or unconsciously, certain presuppositions to which they applied reason. Among many Christians the non-Christian use of reason and its presuppositions were rejected. Jesus had thanked God that He had hid the Gospel from the wise and prudent and had revealed it unto babes, and Paul had declared that in the wisdom of God the world through wisdom had not known God. The road to the truth most important for man was held to be the acceptance by faith of what God had done in the incarnation, the cross, and the resurrection. Augustine declared: "Believe in order that you may understand." By the fifth century a loss of confidence in the Greek use of reason was fairly widespread in the Roman Empire, outside as well as within Christian circles.

Yet reason in itself was not universally disavowed either among non-Christians or Christians. In succeeding centuries the effort to determine the relation of reason to faith was to constitute a continuing problem in Christian circles. Jesus himself appealed to men to use their minds. Leading Christians, including Paul and Augustine, applied reason to the data derived through faith. In rejecting the Greek use of reason they did not reject reason itself. They maintained that through reason men could attain to an understanding of some aspects of truth. But they held that in the Gospel fresh and essential data had been given by God, of which reason must take account, that in Christ God had assumed the initiative, that it was through faith, the faith which is a full commitment of themselves to God in Christ, that men gain the central insights into the meaning of life, lay hold on true life, and enable God to lay hold of them, and that, having made this commitment and having gained these insights, they can apply reason to what has thus come to them.

CHRISTIANITY AND LANGUAGE

A phase of the influence of Christianity, although only in part in contrast with the culture in which the faith was set, was its effects on language. This was seen in a variety of ways.

One which was little short of revolutionary was the new meaning which Christianity gave to certain words, some of them in familiar use. In attempts to express their deepest convictions and central beliefs, Christians sometimes coined new terms. Often, however, they took over existing words, such as *deus* in Latin and *theos* ($\theta\epsilon\grave{o}s$) in Greek, and endeavoured to fill them with distinctively Christian content. They were not entirely successful, for many of the terms carried over with them to those who employed them something of their pre-Christian and even anti-Christian connotations. Yet in varying degrees Christians gave peculiarly Christian meanings to the words which they adopted.

In some regions Christianity assisted in the spread of a language or creating for it literary form. In Asia Minor Christianity was probably responsible for the supplanting of the numerous local tongues by Greek, and in Gaul the disappearance of the Celtic vernaculars and the triumph of Latin seem to have been closely associated with the spread of Christianity. Yet in Armenia the golden age of native literature came through the translation and composition of Christian books through an alphabet formed for that purpose. In Egypt it was the successful effort to provide the masses of the population with a literature in the speech of everyday life which halted the exclusive use of the alien Greek for the written page and which stimulated the development of an alphabet which could be quickly and easily learned by the multitude in place of the ancient hieroglyphics which could be the property only of the few. Through this medium Coptic Christian literature came into being, largely the work of monks. Its major creative period was in the latter part of the fourth and in the fifth century. Similarly, the use of Syriac in literature which had been cramped by the spread of Greek through the Hellenizing of Syria after the conquests of Alexander the Great was stimulated by the conversion of Syriac-speaking peoples to the Christian faith. The flowering of Syriac literature went hand in hand with the spread of Christianity among those for whom Syriac was the vernacular and was a concomitant to the effort to make Christian literature accessible to the rank and file. Gothic was first given a written form, so far as we know, by the Christian missionary, Ulfilas, and the Georgians owed at least two alphabets to Christians.

CHRISTIANITY AND ART

The effect of Christianity upon art was not immediately revolutionary or startling, either negatively or positively. To be sure, under the influence of the faith the construction of pagan temples and the making of images of the gods ceased, and some temples were destroyed. However, it was not until after the first five centuries that distinctively Christian forms of art and architecture began to be prominent.

Long before the year 500 paintings inspired by the Christian faith had begun to appear, and a few surviving specimens can still be seen, notably in the catacombs. The catacombs themselves represented a modification in funeral customs. Christians disapproved of cremation, the form of disposing of the dead normally followed by pagans, and held that the body should be buried intact. In Rome until the fifth century Christian burial was prevailingly in niches in the subterranean passages in the volcanic material which underlay the city, passages whose prototypes were the galleries left by excavators of building materials. In these catacombs and upon some of the Christian sarcophagi Christian scenes were often depicted, among them the nativity, and Jesus as the Good Shepherd.

However, the catacomb as a burial place was not a Christian invention, for the Jews also employed it. Moreover, the Christian scenes normally used non-Christian art forms. Thus at least some of the portrayals of the Good Shepherd are clearly modelled after pagan pictures in which Orpheus was the central figure: with some modifications a representation of Jesus was substituted for that of Orpheus. Beginning with the age of Constantine and the full toleration of Christianity, large church edifices were erected, but these generally adopted existing architectural traditions, modifying them to meet the purposes of Christian worship. It was not until the sixth century that revolutionary forms of church architecture began to appear.

CHRISTIANS AND THE STATE

What attitude did Christians take towards the state, especially towards the Roman Empire in which their faith arose and in which the large majority of them had their home? We have seen that they did not set out deliberately to supplant the Roman state or to remake the structure of society of which it was an essential part. However, did they weaken or strengthen it?

The attitude of Jesus towards the state was not one either of unqualified disapproval or approval. He certainly did not head a movement of his people to throw off the Roman yoke, although there were some who wished him to do so and he was crucified on the charge of setting himself up as a king in opposition to the Emperor. He commanded obedience to the men in authority in the Jewish community and to the law of Moses which presumably governed that community, paid his taxes, in a somewhat cryptic saying enjoined rendering unto Cæsar the things that were Cæsar's, and as a part of what has been called his teaching of non-violence directed that no resistance was to be offered if by due process of law one's cloak were taken away, even unjustly. He refused for himself or his cause to employ political methods and never advocated rebellion. Indeed, although he declared that his followers would be haled before representatives of the state, he did not advocate denial of the jurisdiction or disobedience to the findings of the courts, but, rather, commanded those so arrested to state their case and trust God to suggest to them what to say. Yet Jesus had scorn for Herod as a person, and stood in no awe of rulers, not even of Solomon, so revered in Jewish history. Moreover, his teaching and example of refusing to rely upon the power represented by the state and his dependence upon a radically different kind of power, that seen in the apparent weakness of the cross and vindicated by the resurrection, if fully carried out would make unnecessary the sort of state represented by the Roman Empire.

The attitude of the Christians of the first three centuries towards the state seems contradictory. Paul declared that government derived its authority from God and instructed Christians to be obedient to its officers and to pay their taxes. *The First Epistle of Peter* commanded Christians to honour the Emperor. Yet *The Revelation of John* regarded the Roman Empire as evil and diametrically opposed to the Christian faith. Paul forbade Christians to take disputes among themselves to the Roman courts and characterized the Roman magistrates as "those least esteemed in the Church." While Christians bore the persecutions by the state passively and, so far as we know, without opposing them with violence, and although they offered prayers for the Emperor, they regarded as apostasy participation in the cult which gave divine honours to the Emperor, and at least some of them refused to take oaths and looked upon government officials in general as evil and the state as hostile to God. Christians held that for them loyalty to God must be given priority over loyalty to the state and that on occasion the one might require disobedience to the other. Striking wholesale examples of this were seen in the thousands of Christians who refused, even at the cost of their lives, to comply with the imperial decrees to sacrifice to the gods. Although there were some Christians in public posts, there was a conviction widely held among Christians that none of their number should hold office under the state, for to do so might entail participation in pagan ceremonies or the taking of life through the infliction of the death sentence. As late as the beginning of the third century Hippolytus said that historic Christian custom required a civic magistrate to resign his office as a condition of joining the Church. As we have seen, usually Christians regarded service in the army as wrong for them. Yet where compliance with the laws of the state did not mean disloyalty to what they believed to be their allegiance to God, Christians endeavoured to be model citizens. They paid their taxes and in other ways complied with the demands of the government. Moreover, as Christians multiplied, as they did in the third century, increasing numbers of them were in public posts.

When, beginning with Constantine, the Emperors became professing Christians, and when, in the course of the next two centuries, the overwhelming majority of the population of the Empire were brought into the Church, the latter, as we have seen, entered into a kind of alliance with the state. Except for the brief interlude of Julian, the magistrates were predominantly Christians and even under Julian the majority in the legions regarded themselves as of that faith. It is probable that the state gained by that alliance, for, in spite of its internal divisions, the Catholic Church was, next to the government, the most comprehensive and well articulated body in the Roman Empire and served to reinforce a political regime which was already displaying symptoms of disintegration. Moreover, leading Christians hailed Constantine as appointed by God and by Christians the Emperor now was accorded peculiar honour and added authority as a bulwark against anarchy. Some generations later, the Emperors were crowned by representatives of the Church in a religious ceremony.

Yet the alliance of Church and state was by no means an unqualified advantage to the Roman imperial government. The internal dissensions of the Church threatened, as we have seen, to rend not only the Church but also the Empire. Indeed, in the next period they were to contribute to the break-up of the Empire. The rapid growth of monasticism in the fourth and fifth centuries withdrew thousands from ordinary society either to the solitary life of the anchorite or to communities which were virtually autonomous. Here may have been a source of weakness for the state.

Beginning with Constantine, Christianity seems to have had some influence upon the laws of the realm. Constantine appears to have endeavoured to rule as a Christian, to make the Empire safe for Christianity, and to create a world fit for Christians to live in. This is reflected in some of his modifications of the laws and additions to them. Constantine's legislation against gladiatorial combats seems to have been inspired by the Christian faith. So do his edicts in behalf of widows, orphans, and the poor, and against immorality, the separation by sale of a slave and his wife, infanticide, the selling of children into slavery, prostitution, immoral religious rites, and the ancient right of a father to kill his child. The profession of an actress normally entailed prostitution, and in the third century, by imperial decree, apparently at the instance of the Church, it was commanded that if an actress at the point of death asked for and was given the last sacraments, and then recovered, she was not to be forced to resume her former way of life.

New Wine in Old Wineskins: the Power of Christ and the Power of Cæsar

The relation of Christianity to the Roman state poses even deeper questions than those raised in the preceding paragraphs. As we have hinted, we see here two powers, the power of Christ and the power of Cæsar. In one of his parables Jesus declared that new wine could not safely be put into old wineskins, for if it were, the skins would break and the wine would be lost. Did that prove to be true in the case of the Roman Empire and the Christian Gospel? Would "the exceeding greatness of the power" destroy the "earthen vessels" and in the process itself be dissipated or be gravely and perhaps irreparably weakened?

To what extent, if at all, were the "decline and fall of the Roman Empire" due to Christianity? Again and again, as we have seen, while Christianity was spreading, the accusation was made that it was bringing mortal illness to the Empire and to the structure of Græco-Roman society. Repeatedly the Christian apologists addressed themselves to answering that charge. Outstanding was the *City of God* of Augustine, but this was not by any means the only work evoked by the complaint, nor the last. The accusation has more than once been renewed in modern times.

The Christian apologists, far from admitting the truth of the indictment, insisted that, instead of weakening the Empire, Christians were actually strengthening it. Thus in the first half of the second century *The Epistle to Diognetus* declared: "What the soul is to the body, that are Christians to the world. . . . The Soul is imprisoned in the body, yet preserves that very body;

and Christians are confined in the world as in a prison, yet they hold the world together." As we have seen, Tertullian insisted that Christians did more than pagans for the Emperor, that they regarded him as appointed by God, and held that chaos was prevented only by the continued existence of the Roman Empire. Origen said that by their prayers Christians were of more service to the realm than if they had fought for it in the legions, for by their petitions they "vanquish all demons who stir up war . . . and [who] disturb the peace." Which were right, the critics or the apologists?

In attempting to find the answer to this question, we must bear in mind several facts. First we must recall that the symptoms of mortal illness were present in the Græco-Roman world before Christ was born. Precisely what were all of the causes scholars have never agreed, but as to the sickness of that region in the first century before Christ there can be no debate. To be sure, in every culture, even at the height of its prosperity, evidences of serious weakness can be found and are by no means conclusive proof of impending collapse.

However, in the second place, in the century before Christ was born the evidences of disintegration were so palpable in wars, in the passing of the old order, and in moral corruption, that the thoughtful feared early collapse. From this disaster the Mediterranean Basin was saved by Julius Cæsar and Augustus Cæsar, especially the latter. Through the structure devised by Augustus with the Emperor as its head, peace, the *pax Romana,* was established almost coincidently with the coming of Christ. Then followed a period of material prosperity hitherto unequalled in the Mediterranean world—although paralleled by a somewhat similar era in the contemporary China under the Han dynasty. No wonder that Rome and the Empire were regarded as the bulwarks of civilization against anarchy.

Yet, in the third place, we must note that the principate devised by Augustus did not cure but only temporarily halted the course of the disease from which Græco-Roman culture was suffering. Except for the political structure given it by Augustus, that culture was ceasing to say or to do anything substantially new. In philosophy the only fresh system of consequence which emerged in the first two centuries of the Empire, so prosperous materially, was Neoplatonism, and that was chiefly a development from the earlier Platonism and may possibly have in part owed to Christianity the stimulus which brought it into being. After the first century with its Augustan Age and the generation which followed it, no contributions of first class importance were made in literature or art. It was only through Christianity that a major impulse was at work to stir spirits in a jaded world to fresh creation. By the end of the second century the remedies applied by Augustus had begun to fail. Indeed, they may have aggravated the malady. Certainly the disease was breaking out afresh.

As a fourth fact we must note that the disease could not accurately be traced to Christianity. It had appeared before that faith had been born. Its fresh outbreak in the closing decades of the second century was before Christians were sufficiently numerous to have become its inciting cause.

A fifth consideration is the fact that Christianity did not prevent the disease from running its course and bringing the demise of the Roman Empire. Christianity did not save the Græco-Roman stage of civilization. If it was not the source of the disease from which Græco-Roman culture suffered, neither did it heal that culture of its illness.

As a closely related fact we do well also to recall that at its very outset Christianity had not saved the Jewish community from which it sprang nor had it brought even a temporary pause in the mad, headlong course which led that community to futile rebellion against Roman rule and to the destruction of Jerusalem and of the temple which had been the centre of Jewish worship. Jesus had clearly foreseen the tragic climax towards which events were heading, had offered an alternative course through which the catastrophe could have been avoided, but had the heart-breaking experience of meeting blind rejection.

A seventh observation is not so much a fact as a comment. It may be that Christianity could not save either Græco-Roman civilization or the Jewish society which centred in and found its symbol in Jerusalem and the temple. Both may have been founded on presuppositions so contrary to the Christian Gospel that they had to pass before the Gospel could begin to find free expression. We do well to remind ourselves again and again that it was official representatives of Judaism and the Roman Empire who brought Jesus to his death, because they sensed more or less clearly that if he were loyally and consistently followed the religious structure and the political system of which they were the respective custodians and to which they were bound by self-interest would disappear. Certainly Jesus, as Stephen and others of the early Christians clearly discerned, rendered the temple and its elaborate sacrifices unnecessary, and, as Paul declared, had made it obvious that the legal road of earning the favour of God was worse than a blind alley and led away from the path to true life. As Augustine saw, what he called the earthly city, based upon force, pride, the love of human praise, the desire for domination, and the self-interest represented by the Roman Empire, had value in the restraint of wickedness and the preservation of order, but was basically different from the city of God, for the latter was built upon quite other foundations. The kind of power which had brought the Roman Empire into being was diametrically opposite to the power of God dramatically and decisively displayed in the cross. When Paul said that Christ crucified was a stumbling-block to the Jews and sheer folly to the Gentiles, namely, the Greeks and the Romans, and that the ways through which the Greeks were seeking wisdom did not bring them to the wisdom of God as revealed in the cross, he was stating unvarnished fact. If the Gospel was not to be obscured, Christianity had to break free from Judaism and the Roman Empire would have to pass.

An eighth set of facts is one which we are to see somewhat elaborated in our account of the next major period in the history of Christianity, but which we must briefly summarize here to enable us to give a tentative answer to the question posed to us by the coincidence of the progressive decline of Rome with the seeming triumph of Christianity. It was in the western portions of Europe, where the collapse of the Roman Empire was most marked, that Christianity was to display its greatest vigour in succeeding centuries. Indeed, the near disappearance of Græco-Roman culture in that region gave to Christianity one of its greatest opportunities. By being largely freed from the incubus of the Roman state and of the closely associated cultural heritage of Greece and Rome, the kind of power which was of the essence of the Gospel was given freer course than it had been accorded under the professedly Christian Emperors. This was akin to the fashion in which that power displayed itself in great might in that wing of Christianity which broke through its Jewish integuments and ceased to be a Jewish sect in contrast with the nervelessness of the strain of Christianity represented by the Ebionites and which attempted to remain within Judaism.

In this connexion we must also anticipate the next chronological sections of our story by noting that Christianity was the means by which the remnants of Græco-Roman civilization were transmitted to Western Europe and that in the East, where the dwindling Roman Empire continued and passed over into the Greek Byzantine Empire, it was Christianity which reinforced the state, helped to give it cohesion, and put spirit in its defense against the onslaughts of its enemies.

We shall also be recording, when that stage of our narrative is reached, that on the southern and eastern shores of the Mediterranean the conquering force, Arabic Islam, which overthrew Roman rule in those areas, proved too strong for the kind of power represented in Christianity, and the churches slowly faded out.

May we now attempt to summarize in a few words what the evidence seems to show of the relation of Christianity to the decline of the Roman Empire and of the civilization associated with it? Christianity was not the basic cause of the "fall of Rome." Yet it did not prevent that "fall." Whether it retarded or hastened it we cannot certainly know. In the segment of the Empire which continued with Constantinople as its nucleus Christianity undoubtedly prolonged the life of the Empire and later it was to aid in what purported to be a revival of that Empire in the West. In the West it became the vehicle by which much of Græco-Roman culture was transmitted to a subsequent age. Christians also were a major instrument in passing on much of that culture to the Arabs who overwhelmed the eastern and southern portions of the Empire. While Christianity helped to perpetuate more or less extensive elements of Græco-Roman civilization, it placed those elements in a new context. Where, in the West, the disintegration of the old came in such fashion that Christianity was partially emancipated, that faith had a much larger share in moulding life than the Roman Empire had permitted it.

What Happened to the New Wine?

If the old wineskins were broken by agents other than the new wine of Christianity and that wine actually preserved something of the wineskins, what happened to the wine? Was it lost or fatally denatured? Or, to change the metaphor, was the "exceeding greatness of the power" weakened by the "earthen vessels" in which it was at work? To put the question less figuratively, how far, if at all, was the Gospel compromised by elements in the culture, in many ways so in contradiction with it, into which it moved and in which it appeared to be victorious?

That the Gospel was in grave danger of being lost among those who professed to adhere to it must be obvious. It was launched into a hostile world with none of the safeguards which human prudence would have counselled. As we have more than once reminded ourselves, Jesus wrote no book, but trusted his teachings and the record of his deeds to the memories of men and women who, though loyal, while he was with them in the flesh failed really to understand him. He did not utter his words in systematic form, but spoke as the occasion seemed to demand. So far as our evidence goes, he gave almost no thought to an organization to perpetuate his mission. Certainly he did not create an elaborate organization. Under these circumstances it would have been natural to expect that, coming into a world which was either misunderstanding or hostile, or both, the Gospel, as it spread, would be hopelessly distorted and lost. That this happened, indeed, has repeatedly been said. There have been many, some of them of great erudition, who have declared that Jesus is at best a shadowy figure, early obscured by his reporters and interpreters, and that we can be certain of almost none of his deeds and sayings. They see him hidden by layers of tradition and believe the Christianity of the fifth century to have been compounded of Judaism, Græco-Roman polytheism, appropriations from the mystery cults, and Greek thought.

That Christianity was influenced by all these phases of its environment is indubitable. We have had occasion to note some of the contributions from these several sources. But that it remained distinct and owed its outstanding qualities to Jesus is both certain and important.

From Judaism issued the larger part of the Scriptures which Christians revered as the inspired word of God. From Judaism came also the belief in one God, much of the ethical standards, the seven day week with its day of rest and worship, portions of the early forms of worship, the conviction of being a chosen community distinct from the world about it, something of the dream of becoming the universal religion of mankind, baptism, much of the conception of history, and the precedents for a priesthood and of regarding Christ's death as a sacrifice which became outstanding characteristics of Christianity.

Yet it is one of the striking features of these Jewish legacies that they were thought through in the light of the life, death, and resurrection of Jesus and were interpreted in terms of these and of the teachings of Jesus. The temptation to become simply a variant of Judaism was successfully resisted and those groups which most nearly conformed to Judaism dwindled and perished. Moreover, the figure of Jesus, his teachings, and the main events of his life, death, and resurrection stand out so clearly in the records contained in the New Testament as to preclude any possibility of their invention or serious distortion.

Although some striking similarities to the mystery religions are seen in the story of a divine being slain and risen again, of immortality acquired by sharing symbolically in his death and resurrection, of initiatory rites, and of a sacred meal, there is, as we have suggested, no proof of conscious or even unconscious copying and the differences between Christianity and the mystery cults are greater than the similarities. We have also seen that Catholic Christianity fought free of absorption into the current non-Christian Gnosticism. While here and there some transfer from Greek and Roman polytheism may have occurred, as in the cults of some of the saints and in a few of the festivals, all of these contributions were profoundly altered to conform with Christian convictions. A major peril was one of attitude, for converts were inclined to expect Christianity to do for them what they had demanded of their pre-Christian gods but to do it better. Yet the trend of the teaching of the Church was towards the progressive weakening of these attitudes and the inculcation of conceptions more nearly in accord with the Gospel.

In some ways, more serious than any of these threats to Christianity from its environment was the belief in the sharp disjunction between the material and the spiritual world, or, in human terms, between flesh and spirit, which was prevalent and which appeared axiomatic to many, perhaps the majority, in those elements of the population in which Christianity first made its chief gains. In some of its most extreme forms, notably those represented by the Marcionites, the Gnostics, and the Manichæans, it was rejected by the Catholic Church. Yet it made itself felt in theology and in the attitude of the rank and file of Christians, notably in the East, and was particularly potent in monasticism and in clerical celibacy. Through these channels, especially through the last two, it has remained a permanent feature of the churches in which the majority of Christians have been members. As we have noted, it distorted the teachings of Jesus. Yet, as we have seen and are to see repeatedly in later chapters, among many of those who espoused it, Christian monasticism was not merely the negative denial of the flesh but also carried with it the propulsion to go out into the world in an effort to serve and transform individuals and society.

Probably an even greater peril came from Greek philosophy. This was the temptation to regard Christianity as a philosophy, better than that of the Greeks, but not essentially different, truth to be arrived at by the application of the human mind and of man's rational processes. Fully to yield would be to ignore the fundamental contrast which we have noted and to denature the Christian faith. Fortunately for Christianity its intellectuals who most profoundly influenced the future course of the faith never entirely succumbed to this tendency. For example, Augustine, while retaining much of the Neoplatonism which had once captivated him, held it to be basically defective in not taking cognizance of the incarnation. Moreover, as we have said, Augustine, in his famous "believe in order that you may understand," while by no means repudiating reason, was giving to it a different place than that accorded it in Greek philosophy, and, along with other Christian thinkers, was taking account of data which were unknown to the pre-Christian Greeks and which were rejected as "foolishness" by those who continued to adhere to Greek philosophy.

Yet Christians made substantial appropriations from Greek philosophy. Clement of Alexandria and Ambrose of Milan based much of their ethics on what they had learned from Stoicism. The writings of the Stoic Epictetus, somewhat modified to make them more palatable, had a wide circulation in Christian circles. To be sure, Christians took over from Stoicism only what they believed to be consistent with their faith and would have nothing to do with the basic pantheism of that philosophy which would deny the opposition of God to sin, and looked forward to the consummation of the kingdom of God, rather than backward to a Golden Age, as did the Stoics. But Christian ethics were long to give evidence of Stoic contributions. Platonism had a marked influence on Christianity. It entered from many channels, among them the Hellenistic Jew Philo, who was utilized by some early Christian writers, and through Justin Martyr, Clement of Alexandria, Origen, Augustine, and the writings which bore the name of Dionysius the Areopagite. The term *Logos,* which was extensively employed by Christians as they thought about the relation of Christ to God, came from Greek philosophy, perhaps by way of both Stoicism and Platonism. We have seen how the Christian creeds employed technical terms from Greek and Latin. With these, as with the word *Logos,* pre-Christian connotations would inevitably enter.

However, as we earlier suggested, the creeds never became really Greek. They sought to express convictions which were central in the Gospel and peculiar to it. They were distinctively Christian and not Hellenistic. Moreover, it has been suggested that Christian thinkers solved the problems of order and change, reason and emotion, the physical and the intellectual with which classical philosophy had wrestled, and did so without denying the validity of the changing, the emotional, or the physical. They thereby provided a basis for individual salvation in a world of dislocated individuals and a principle on which a stable but not a rigid society might be based.

What in many ways proved the menace which was most nearly disastrous was that presented by the kind of power on which the Roman Empire was founded, a kind of power, as we have seen, which was in complete contradiction to that seen in the cross. From the very beginning, pride of place and the desire for control in the Christian community were chronic temptations. On the very eve of the crucifixion, first on the way to Jerusalem and then at the final supper, in the inner circle, among those who were to be the apostles of the Good News, there were some who sought superior rank and recognition as "the greatest," incidents which led to characteristically vivid sayings from Jesus and which may have been the reason for the assumption by him of the menial role of washing the disciples' feet. By word and by deed Jesus put in stark contrast the two kinds of greatness, that esteemed by the "kings of the Gentiles," namely, the one in vogue in the Roman Empire, and that which should characterize his disciples. It was the contrast between those who from the vantage of visible power established and maintained by crude force professed to seek to do good and were called benefactors and those who humbly served in tasks which were despised in the other kind of society.

In one of the letters preserved in the New Testament there is evidence, as we have said, of sharp conflict between the author, who believed himself vested with authority in one of the churches, and another "who loveth . . . preëminence." Again and again, even in the brief summary of the preceding pages, we have caught glimpses of similar incidents. The various churches, including the Catholic Church, creations of Christianity and the visible vehicles by which it was transmitted, were clearly institutions. Even before Christianity was accorded toleration by the state and while it was still subject to chronic or intermittent persecutions, not a few of its bishops were accused of striving for prestige and were entering into intrigues and exerting the kind of power which was akin to that of the dignitaries of the state. Some of the bishops were surrounded by pomp and maintained households and a manner of life which rivalled those of civil officials. Indeed, it is a question whether any visible institution, especially if it becomes large, can avoid falling victim in part to trends in the direction of the power which crucified Jesus.

The danger to Christianity was augmented when the state made its peace with the Church. Until then, as we have seen, Christians tended to keep aloof from government and many, perhaps the majority of the Christians believed that loyalty to Christ was inconsistent with holding civil or military office or serving in the army. Beginning with Constantine, that attitude was weakened. The Emperors and an increasing proportion of the officials and of the troops assumed the Christian name. In these positions they, perforce, exercised the sort of power on which the state rested. Christian officials had to make choices for the state among courses none of which was in full conformity with Christian principles and to take action which entailed the use of the kind of force on which the state was built. Emperors exercised their power to interfere in the affairs of the Church. To be sure, they did this primarily in an effort to bring unity to the Church and through the prestige of their position more than through naked force, and in this may be seen something of the ameliorative influence of Christianity. Yet here was still power which was in contrast with that vividly displayed in the cross.

This peril, as we are to see, became more marked in the succeeding centuries. In the West as the Roman Empire declined, the Catholic Church took over many of the functions previously performed by the state. In the East in the area where the Empire continued, the tie between Church and state was very close and the Church was in large degree controlled by the state and was used to serve the latter's purposes.

It is clear that the Church was the product of the Gospel. It is also clear that the visible, institutionalized church, whether Catholic or one of the bodies which dissented, was shot through and through with contradictions to the Gospel. As Augustine frankly recognized, the two cities, the earthly and the heavenly, are intermingled. He held that they are to continue to be entangled until the last judgement effects their separation.

In view of these facts, necessarily succinctly stated, was the new wine being dissipated? Where was the exceeding greatness of the power? It will be remembered that the power was characterized as that which, having faced seeming defeat in the cross, was displayed in the resurrection of Christ from the dead. It is a power which is associated with seeming weakness. It is a power which does not at once destroy the religion or the state which nailed Christ to the cross, but which, by a kind of paradox, achieves a victory which would have been impossible without defeat. It is a basic Christian conviction that Christ was glorified through his death and resurrection and became far more potent than he had been in the days of his flesh.

The exceeding greatness of the power was displayed primarily in the transformation of those men and women who became followers of Christ, who put their trust in him. Even now, so Jesus had said, men might enter the kingdom of God, and, indeed, were entering it. To use other figures employed in the New Testament, men could be born again, they could die to sin and, by the same power which raised Jesus from the dead, they could be raised to walk in newness of life. The proof that they had experienced this new birth, this resurrection to a new life, was to be seen in their "fruits," in the "fruits of the Spirit." These fruits were described in one place as "love" (the Greek word is *agape,* namely, the kind of love displayed by God in Christ and by Christ in his self-giving), "joy, peace, longsuffering, gentleness, goodness, faith, meekness, temperance." Paul, who coined this list, was quite aware that these qualities would not at once be realized in any one life in their perfection and said of himself that he had not fully attained. Years after his conversion, as we have more than once said, Augustine made a similar confession. They are qualities which are not susceptible to precise measurement, at least not by men. They do not achieve complete expression in any visible institution or organization. Perhaps it was something like this which Jesus had in mind when he declared that the kingdom of God was not to come in such fashion that it can be seen or in such a manner that men could point to it and say, "Lo here or lo there" and yet that "the kingdom of God is among you" (or, in an alternative translation, "within you"). As Jesus saw it, the kingdom of God is both present now and is also a future hope. Part of the Good News is, so the New Testament documents disclose, that the exceeding greatness of the power is in the fresh creation of sinful men and the dying to sin, the sin which through man's perverse misuse of the free will with which he is endowed has brought on him, individually and collectively, the tragic aspects of human history. This fresh creation issues in the beginning of a new life.

Although that new life cannot be measured, its presence can be observed. Even in the fragmentary documents which have reached us from the first five centuries of Christianity, it is clear that the fruits of the Spirit were to be seen in many individual lives. We have pointed to a few outstanding examples, such as Paul and Augustine. Were there space, we could name many more. From the few the records of whose lives have been preserved across the wreckage of the centuries we are on safe ground in assuming that for every one of whom we know there were hundreds, perhaps thousands, of whom we do not know, for most of them were very humble folk who left no written documents behind them. The testimony of the apologists, although given with a pro-Christian bias, bears this out. They appeal to what is to them obvious fact, the moral and spiritual changes wrought through conversion. Even though in the majority of those bearing the Christian name the alteration was either slight or had not occurred, the honour accorded by the Church to the minority in whom the fruits of the Spirit were seen was indicative of a persistently held ideal and of the reality of the new life in those who had experienced it.

It was chiefly through such lives that the creative impulse was released which produced the Church and Christian literature, theology, and worship, which swept away the pagan cults of the Roman Empire, which wrestled with the problems of war and with the relation to the state, property, marriage, and the popular amusements. It was through these lives that within the Church the position of women and children was lifted, dignity was given to labour, and much of the sting was taken from slavery. No individual attained fully to the "high calling of God in Christ." The churches were by no means identical with the city of God: there was in them much of the earthly city. Yet here, in earthen vessels, was a power at work which, in spite of what looked like chronic frustration, out of human material apparently hopelessly and basically marred and twisted, was achieving the seemingly impossible, the re-creation of thousands of men and women until they displayed something of the quality of life which was seen in Jesus Christ.

It was these men and women who were, to use the language of Jesus, "the salt of the earth" and "the light of the world." In the succeeding sections of this work we will see that, as Christians have multiplied and converts have been won from more and more peoples, these characterizations have been increasingly demonstrated to be true. They do not hold for all who have borne the Christian name, but they are valid for a minority in whom "the exceeding greatness of the power" has been palpably at work.

SELECTED BIBLIOGRAPHY

WORKS WHICH COVER MOST OF THE TOPICS DEALT WITH IN THIS CHAPTER

C. J. Cadoux, *The Early Church and the World. A History of the Christian Attitude to Pagan Society and the State down to the Time of Constantius* (Edinburgh, T. & T. Clark, 1925, pp. li, 675). A comprehensive, careful work based on the sources.

C. N. Cochrane, *Christianity and Classical Culture. A Study of Thought and Action from Augustus to Augustine* (Oxford, The Clarendon Press, 1940, pp. vii, 523). A thought-provoking analysis based upon extensive reading in the sources.

I. Giordani, *The Social Message of the Early Church Fathers,* translated from the Italian by A. I. Zizzamia (Paterson, N. J., St. Anthony Guild Press, 1944, pp. x, 356). Based upon an extensive use of the sources, by a Roman Catholic, and decidedly pro-Christian.

Hippolytus, *The Apostolic Tradition of Hippolytus,* translated into English with introduction and notes by B. S. Easton (Cambridge University Press, 1934, pp. 112).

K. S. Latourette, *A History of the Expansion of Christianity. Volume I, The First Five Centuries* (New York, Harper & Brothers, 1937, pp. xxiv, 412). Chapters VI and VII deal with the subjects covered in this chapter.

E. H. Oliver, *The Social Achievements of the Christian Church* (Toronto, Board of Evangelism and Social Service of the United Church of Canada, 1930, pp. 192). Meant for class use, decidedly pro-Christian, containing excellent bibliographies.

E. Troeltsch, *The Social Teachings of the Christian Churches,* translated by Olive Wyon (New York, The Macmillan Co., 2 vols., 1931). Approximately the first half of this well known work is given to the period covered in this chapter.

CHRISTIANS AND WAR

R. H. Bainton, *The Early Church and War,* in R. M. Jones, editor, *The Church, The Gospel, and War,* pp. 75–92 (New York, Harper & Brothers, 1948, pp. xii, 169). A competent summary.

C. J. Cadoux, *The Early Christian Attitude to War. A Contribution to the History of Christian Ethics* (London, Headley Bros., Publishers, 1919, pp. xxxii, 272). A careful, well-documented study which stresses the refusal of the early Christians to sanction war or to serve in the armed forces.

A. Harnack, *Militia Christi. Die christliche Religion und der Soldatenstand in den ersten drei Jahrhunderten* (Tübingen, J. C. B. Mohr, 1905, pp. vii, 129). Marked by the scholarship for which the author is famous.

U. Lee, *The Historic Church and Modern Pacifism* (New York and Nashville, Abingdon-Cokesbury Press, 1943, pp. 249). Argues against the pacifist position.

G. H. C. Macgregor, *The New Testament Basis of Pacifism* (London, J. Clarke & Co., 1936, pp. 159). Supports the pacifist's position.

J. Moffatt, *War,* in J. Hastings, editor, *Dictionary of the Apostolic Church,* Vol. II, pp. 646–673 (New York, Charles Scribner's Sons, 1918).

CHRISTIANS AND SLAVERY

R. H. Barrow, *Slavery in the Roman Empire* (London, Methuen & Co., 1928, pp. xvi, 259). Carefully done; well documented.

SEX, CHILDREN, MARRIAGE, AND THE FAMILY

R. H. Bainton, *Marriage and Love in Christian History,* in *Religion in Life,* Vol. XVII, pp. 391–403). Has an excellent bibliography.

R. S. T. Haslehurst, *Some Account of the Penitential Discipline of the Early Church* (London, Society for Promoting Christian Knowledge, 1921, pp. vii, 162). Quotes extensively from the sources.

CHRISTIANS AND THE STATE

The Epistle to Diognetus is translated in *The Ante-Nicene Fathers,* Vol. I, pp. 25–30 (Buffalo, The Christian Publishing Co., 1885).

C. H. McIlwain, *The Growth of Political Thought in the West from the Greeks to the End of the Middle Ages* (New York, The Macmillan Co., 1933, pp. vii, 244). Excellent.

WHAT HAPPENED TO THE NEW WINE? THE INFLUENCE OF THE
ENVIRONMENT ON CHRISTIANITY

S. Angus, *The Religious Quests of the Græco-Roman World* (New York, Charles Scribner's Sons, 1929, pp. xx, 444). Carefully done, with a pro-Christian bias.

C. Clemen, *Primitive Christianity and Its Non-Jewish Sources,* translated by R. G. Nisbet (Edinburgh, T. & T. Clark, 1912, pp. xiii, 403). Careful, conservative in its judgements, employing the sources.

S. Dill, *Roman Society in the Last Century of the Western Empire* (London, Macmillan & Co., 2d ed., 1906, pp. xxviii, 459). Readable, scholarly.

F. Gavin, *The Jewish Antecedents of the Christian Sacraments* (London, Society for Promoting Christian Knowledge, 1928, pp. viii, 120).

E. Hatch, *The Influence of Greek Ideas and Usages upon the Christian Church,* edited by A. M. Fairbairn (London, Williams & Norgate, 1890, pp. xxiii, 359). The Hibbert Lectures for 1888.

C. N. Moody, *The Mind of the Early Converts* (London, Hodder & Stoughton, 1920, pp. xii, 310). A stimulating comparison between the Early Church and what the author has known about converts in Formosa.

E. F. Scott, *The Gospel and Its Tributaries* (New York, Charles Scribner's Sons, 1930, pp. 295). By a competent New Testament scholar.

THE DARKEST HOURS:
THE GREAT RECESSION,
A.D. 500 — A.D. 950

MAP TO ILLUSTRATE THE
HISTORY OF CHRISTIANITY
IN
WESTERN AND CENTRAL EUROPE
A.D. 500-1500

Scale of Miles
0   100   200   300   400

Chapter 10

THE SETTING OF THE GREAT RECESSION

The seeming triumph of Christianity in winning the professed allegiance of the Roman Empire carried with it a major threat. In the preceding chapters we noted the fashion in which Christianity was imperilled by the extent to which a large proportion of those who bore the Christian name were compromising with the non-Christian environment in which they were immersed. We also saw the manner in which the Church was being interpenetrated by ideals which were quite contrary to the Gospel, especially the conception and use of power which were in stark contrast to the kind of power exhibited in the life and teachings of Jesus and in the cross and the resurrection. A nearly related but somewhat different danger was the close association with the Roman Empire and Græco-Roman culture which that victory brought. Although before it had completed the first five centuries of its course Christianity had begun to spill over the boundaries of the Roman Empire, by the end of that period it had become almost identified with that realm and its civilization. The overwhelming majority of Roman citizens thought of themselves as Christians and the large majority of those who bore the Christian name were Roman citizens. The Catholic Church, which embraced most of those who counted themselves as Christians, had grown up within the area which had been given political unity by the Roman Empire and in its structure reflected the pattern of that Empire. While strikingly original in its essence, Christian theology had perforce employed Greek and Roman terms and had utilized concepts drawn from Greek philosophy. By the year 500 the Roman Empire and Græco-Roman culture were in decline. Christianity had both weakened them and prolonged their life. In succeeding centuries their disintegration was accelerated. Could Christianity survive their demise or would it share their growing debility and ultimate death?

That Christianity was seriously affected by the fatal sickness of the Roman Empire is one of the most palpable facts of history. For more than four centuries the outcome was by no means clear. In the numbers of those who called themselves Christian, in apparent inner vitality as expressed in fresh movements inspired by the faith, in the moral and spiritual quality of the churches which were the official vehicles of the Gospel, and in its prominence in the total human scene, Christianity lost ground.

The Roman Empire suffered from both internal weaknesses and external pressures. We have already noted that the weaknesses in part ante-dated the coming of Christianity, that they were for a time allayed by the imperial system inaugurated by Augustus Cæsar, but that from the end of the second century they began again to be apparent, were aggravated, and multiplied. The external pressures were by invaders who took advantage of the internal decay to overrun most of the Empire. Their inroads accelerated Rome's decline. The main incursions were from two directions, from the north and north-east on the one hand and from the south-east on the other. Those from the north and north-east were by peoples who were thought of as barbarians and whose cultures were of a "lower" and more nearly "primitive" stage than that of the Romans. Their cultures, including their religions, disintegrated under contacts with what was left of Græco-Roman civilization and by the year 1000 most of the northern invaders who had settled in what had once been the Roman Empire had taken on the Christian name and were in part conforming to the remnants of Græco-Roman culture which had survived their conquests. Those from the south-west, the Arabs, were the bearers of a new and vigorous religion, Islam. While in some ways they, too, were "barbarians" and took over much of the cultures of the peoples of "high" civilizations whom they subdued, their religion almost entirely supplanted the faiths of the conquered populations. From the seventh into the tenth century the Moslem Arabs mastered about half of the lands which had been ruled by Rome. This segment also embraced about half of what might be denominated Christendom. In it the Christian churches dwindled more or less rapidly. With the possible exception of Judaism, Christianity proved more resistant to Islam than the faith of any other people whom the Arabs overran, and in two regions, the Iberian Peninsula and Sicily, it did what no other religion accomplished: it eventually won back extensive areas and populations from the Prophet. However, this did not come at once. For several centuries the record was one of progressive losses of the Cross to the Crescent.

Christianity not only survived these disasters. Eventually it forged ahead to fresh advances which carried it farther geographically than it had gone in the first days of its might. Some of the gains were made while major losses were being suffered on other fronts, but most of them were not to be achieved until much later centuries. Christianity even proved to have profited by the break-up of the Roman Empire, for, in the West, largely freed from the latter, it eventually displayed renewed vigour and a long series of fresh, creative movements.

In this recovery from the disintegration of the closely allied Roman Empire and in this subsequent spread Christianity surpassed the record of any other religion. A religion is often an integral part of a particular culture. When a culture disappears the religion associated with it also tends to die out. Some religions prove to have more vitality than the cultures with which their early development had been connected and outlast them. In its ability to survive the passing of cultures with which it has been intimately related, to win back territories in which it has experienced grave losses, and to gain peoples of other cultures, Christianity has been unequalled. Buddhism, absorbed by Hinduism in its native land, India, lived on outside of India and was reintroduced into India by immigrants. Yet most of its geographic spread was prior to the assimilation of its Indian constituency by Hinduism and since then it has thrown out few new movements. Islam survived the decay of the Arab Empire through which it had its initial spread and, capturing other peoples, notably the Turks, enjoyed fresh geographic expansion through them. In Persia, partly divorced from Arab culture, it gave rise to fresh developments. Yet in general Islam has been closely tied to the Arabic language and to Arab culture and apart from that connexion it has not displayed much vitality. Judaism did not perish with the disappearance of the little Jewish state which centred in Jerusalem, but compared with Buddhism, Islam, and Christianity it has won relatively few converts outside of its own community, a community which has never been able to break away from its narrowly ethnic traditions and become universal. Hinduism and Indian culture have been inseparable and Confucianism has been identified with the particular form of Chinese civilization of which it has been the core. Christianity continues to bear the imprint of its Jewish heritage and of the Græco-Roman world into which it first moved, but more than any other of the faiths of mankind it has proved its capacity to outlast cultures with which it has seemed to be identified and some of which it has helped to create. Freed in part from the crippling compromises of the Gospel which that association entailed, it has inspired fresh movements within itself and in its milieu, it has resumed its expansion, and more and more it has approached the universality which has been of its essence.

The dates of the beginning and the end of the great recession cannot be precisely determined. We have named the end of the fifth century as the climax of the first great period of advance and as ushering in the decline, but by selecting a round number, A.D. 500, we are wishing to convey the suggestion that no single year can be pointed to as a sharply marked divide between the one era and the other. The conquest of the Roman Empire by the northern invaders is sometimes said to have begun in 378, for in that year the Goths defeated the legions and slew the Emperor Valens in the battle of Adrianople, not far from Constantinople, the capital which Constantine had created only a few decades earlier. The capture and sack of Rome in 410 was even more spectacular. However, Rome as a city was not seriously damaged and soon recovered, and while in the fifth century various Germanic peoples established kingdoms in the West—the Visigoths in Spain, the Ostrogoths in Italy, the Burgundians in the south of Gaul, the Vandals in North Africa, the Angles and Saxons in Britain, and the Franks in the north of Gaul—most of them still thought of themselves as within the Roman Empire and several of their rulers accepted titles from the Roman government.

Not far from the year 500 came various events which may be regarded as marking both the peak of the triumphal course of Christianity in the Roman Empire and the beginning of the decline and of a new age. In the year 476 Romulus Augustulus, commonly viewed as the last of the Emperors in the West, was deposed by the Herulian Odovacar (Odoacer), and while the event was not regarded as of outstanding importance by contemporaries and the Empire continued, the centre was now indisputably in Constantinople and the date has been traditionally given as marking the end of the Western Empire. In 496 Clovis, King of the Franks, was baptized, both a landmark in the conversion of the Germanic invaders and an indication that a new era had begun in which not the Roman Empire, but Germanic rulers were to become champions of the faith in the West. One era was passing and another was beginning. In the year 529 the Emperor Justinian I closed the ancient schools at Athens in which philosophy had been taught, an act symbolic of the triumph of Christianity in the very citadel of the non-Christian philosophies which had once been dominant in the Roman Empire. Not far from that same year Benedict of Nursia and a small band of his followers established themselves on Monte Cassino, the centre from which was to spread the rule which for centuries was to shape the monastic life of the West.

The decline of Christianity was not rapid nor without spurts of revival. In the second and third quarters of the sixth century, as we are to see, the generals of Justinian I renewed Roman administration in much of the West and in North Africa and Justinian himself, as an earnest Christian, added to the prestige of the Church in the East. In that century Christianity spread up the Nile into what is now called the Sudan. It also was carried eastward and early in the seventh century was planted in China. In the West in the latter part of the sixth century Pope Gregory the Great greatly added to the power of the Church of Rome, and through missionaries, some of them from Rome and some from Ireland, a beginning was made towards the conversion of the Germanic peoples who had settled in Britain and of other pagans on that island. In the seventh century the reconversion of Britain was practically completed.

Yet the seventh century also saw the spectacular and rapid Arab conquests. It is from A.D. 622 that the Moslems date the beginning of their era. Mohammed died in 632. Before A.D. 651 the Arabs had conquered Palestine, Syria, Mesopotamia, Persia, and most of Egypt. In 697 they took Carthage, the capital of North Africa, and by 715 they had overrun most of Spain. The political victories of the Arabs were accompanied by the spread of Islam and the beginning of the slow decline of the Christian communities in the Arab domains. In the meantime, in the sixth and seventh centuries, the Slavs, pagans, were moving into the regions north of Greece, filling most of the Balkan Peninsula and even much of Greece itself, and the pagan Avars effected settlements in the Balkans and raided Greece. In consequence, substantial portions of these areas were being de-Christianized. In 680 the Bulgars, an Asiatic folk, moved south across the Danube and established a non-Christian state at the expense of the eastern remnants of the Christian Roman Empire. Never again was Christianity to lose so large a proportion of the territory in which it was the dominant religion.

The eighth century witnessed a marked revival of the faith and an improvement in the morale of the Church in the West under the Carolingians, rulers of the Franks, and the conversion of much of Germany. Yet the ninth and tenth centuries saw new waves of invasions of the West by pagans. The Carolingian Empire broke up and could offer them but feeble resistance. The Scandinavians ravaged the shores of most of Europe, and established themselves in much of Britain, in the part of France, Normandy, to which they gave their name, and in the western portion of the later Russia. Wherever they went they plundered churches and monasteries. They dealt mortal blows to the flourishing monasteries of Ireland in which had been centred the Christianity of that island. Late in the ninth century the pagan Magyars made themselves masters of Hungary, to the detriment of whatever churches were found in that region.

The decline of the Carolingians and the renewed invasions were followed by decay in the quality of the life of the Church in the West. Monasteries became lax in the observance of their rules, bishops tended to be secular magnates, and the morals of the clergy deteriorated. In the middle of the tenth century, the Papacy, deprived of the support of the Carolingians, became the victim of local factions in Rome and reached an all time nadir.

In the eighth and ninth centuries the section of the Church which had its centre in Constantinople was torn by a prolonged controversy over the use of images. In the ninth century, moreover, the Moslem Arabs conquered Sicily, established strongholds in the southern parts of Italy, and took Crete. The Arab successes made for fresh advances of Islam in territories which were traditionally Christian. In China a severe outburst of persecution in 845 seriously weakened the small Christian communities in that Empire.

In spite of the disasters the ninth century was also a time when in Central Europe, the Balkans, and Constantinople the tide seemed to have turned. Notable advances of the faith were being achieved among the Slavs and Bulgars and the patriarchal throne in Constantinople was held by Photius, outstanding as scholar and churchman. From our tantalizingly imperfect knowledge of early Christianity in India comes evidence which may indicate a growth in the eighth and ninth centuries. In the West the upswing was beginning to be seen even in some of the darkest hours. The monastery of Cluny, both a centre and a symbol of renewed life, was founded in 910. In the East the Byzantine Empire, the leading champion of Christianity in that region, was enjoying a revival in the latter part of the ninth and in the fore part of the tenth century. The end of the recession might, therefore, be placed as early as 850 or 900.

On the other hand, because of events which we are to see later, such as the spread of the Cluny reforms and the revival of the Roman Empire in the West under Otto I (he was crowned Roman Emperor in 962), and the beginning of the conversion of Russia (which may be dated from the baptism of Olga c.954, or, better, from the baptism of her grandson, Vladimir, c.987), A.D. 950 seems preferable. The upswing was not sharp or sudden. By that year it was distinctly noticeable in some quarters, but in others the decline appeared to be continuing and not yet quite to have reached its lowest point. For instance, in spite of the persecution which followed an imperial edict of 845, Christians were still reported in some of the ports of China in 877–878, while not far from 987 Nestorian monks sent to China to assist the Church there declared that they could find no Christians in that land.

In A.D. 950 Christianity was far less prominent in the total human scene than it had been in A.D. 500. In A.D. 500 the Roman Empire, while tottering, was still outwardly the mightiest realm on the planet and Christianity was its professed faith. In extent and culture the Roman Empire was then rivalled only by its chronic enemy, the Persian Empire, and by the Gupta Empire in India. Neither of these controlled as much territory as was still nominally in the Roman domains, and the Gupta Dynasty was showing signs of disintegration. China was in a long period of division, civil strife, and foreign invasion.

During the first five centuries of the Christian era the expansion of Christianity was paralleled by that of Buddhism. Approximately five centuries older than Christianity, by the time of the birth of Christ Buddhism had already spread through much of India and Ceylon and had penetrated into Central Asia and China. In A.D. 500 its geographic extent was probably wider than that of Christianity. Like Christianity, but for other causes, by A.D. 950 it had fallen on evil days. In India, the land of its birth, it was decadent and was in process of the absorption and elimination by Hinduism which were to bring about the severe decline of which we have already spoken. Before A.D. 950 it had entered upon the slow decay in China which is still in progress. It was never as widely spread as was Christianity in the seventh century or as Christianity ultimately became. In the seventh century Christianity was represented by communities from Ireland in the west to China in the east, and from Scotland and Germany in the north to the Sudan and possibly South India in the south. Yet between A.D. 500 and A.D. 950 Buddhism was also spreading —in South-east Asia, the East Indies, Korea, and Japan—and in A.D. 950 it was probably more prominent in the total world scene than it had been in A.D. 500.

The four and a half centuries between A.D. 500 and A.D. 950 also witnessed the emergence of Islam, vigorous and younger than Christianity, and by the latter of those years Islam, after only three centuries, was almost as widely spread geographically as Christianity and was the official faith of states which were more powerful, in the sense in which that term is applied to states, than were any of those which were professedly Christian. During most of the period, moreover, China was ruled by the T'ang Dynasty which, during its heyday, was, along with the Arab Empire, the mightiest realm on the planet, and Confucianism, which provided the ideological foundation of Chinese culture, was on the eve of a great revival.

In A.D. 950 a religiously neutral world traveller or the hypothetical visitor from Mars might have given it as his opinion that Christianity was to share the fate of Manichæism, which, also after an extensive geographic spread, was waning. Manichæism, it will be recalled, was younger than Christianity but older than Islam. Like the latter, it was indebted to Christianity but it never had as powerful political support as that accorded Christianity through the Roman Empire or Islam through the Arabs. After a rapid expansion which carried it as far west as Carthage and as far east as the China Sea it slowly died out, although its last remnants lingered on in China at least to the beginning of the seventeenth century.

In these centuries of its great decline Christianity was espoused by a few kingdoms in Western and Southern Europe which, compared with the major empires of the day, seemed insignificant, by the Byzantine remnant of the Roman Empire, and by such minor states as Armenia and Ethiopia. Culturally Christianity seemed to be of dwindling significance. Italy had not recovered from the "barbarian" invasions and the "Christian" peoples of Western Europe, while vigorous, were crude. Constantinople was wealthy and its upper classes were polished, luxurious, and sophisticated, but were ceasing to do or say much that was new. The Nestorians in Mesopotamia had tutored their Arab conquerors in Hellenistic culture, and in the process had put some of the Greek philosophers into Arabic, but the Arabs had proved apt pupils of the Nestorians and other subject peoples and were producing a culture which appeared to be fully as "high" as that of Constantinople and "higher" than that of the Franks or others of the Germanic peoples who had been converted to Christianity. To the thoughtful non-Christian tourist Hindu and Buddhist India, although politically divided, would have seemed to be on a more advanced cultural level than any "Christian" land except the Byzantine Empire, and under the glorious T'ang Dynasty the great cities of China would have been far ahead even of Constantinople. From the standpoint of Augustine's earthly city, by A.D. 950 the political and cultural associates of Christianity had decidedly declined since the days of Constantine and his immediate successors and even since Justinian I. If its future depended upon the kind of power embodied in the earthly city and its affiliated cultures, the outlook for Christianity was grim.

The break-up of the Roman Empire was accompanied and followed by divisions in the Catholic Church. As we have seen, the Catholic Church arose within the framework of unity provided by the Roman state. When that framework fell apart, the bond of love which ideally characterizes Christians did not have sufficient strength to hold the Church together. The ostensible grounds for the divisions which emerged were doctrinal and administrative, and these intensified the divisions. However, the cleavages were largely along the cultural, racial, and national seams in the fabric which Rome had once held together. Arian Christianity became identified with some of the Germanic conquerors; the descendants of the ancient Egyptians, the Copts, found in Monophysitism reinforcement of their antipathy to the Byzantine tie. Somewhat similarly Monophysitism was the bond of a Syrian Christianity and, in another form, of the national church of Armenia as against the orthodox Greeks. Nestorianism continued to be the faith of the majority of the Christians in Mesopotamia and the regions to the east, although both Monophysites and Orthodox also had communities in Mesopotamia and the lands which lay eastward of that fertile valley.

In point of numbers the major cleavage was between the portions of the Catholic Church which centred respectively at Rome and Constantinople, the one predominantly Latin and Roman by tradition and temper, and the other Greek and Byzantine. The separation cannot be given a precise date. The two main wings of the Catholic Church drifted away from each other partly because of cultural traditions, partly because of rivalry between the two great sees, and partly because of the obstacle presented to communications by the widening of time-distances and the difficulty brought by the disruption of political unity to preserving intimate physical contact. Now and again the breach seemed to be healed, but across the centuries it deepened and widened. While various dates have been given for the final break, the ones usually offered come after this period and none of them has won universal acceptance by historians.

As we endeavour to cover the years of what we have called the great recession, it seems best to do so by summarizing the course of Christianity in each of the main divisions of the Church. First we will survey the history during these centuries of that branch which had its main centre in Constantinople, for it was here that the tradition of the relation of the Catholic Church and the Roman Empire which had been inaugurated by Constantine went on without interruption and was strengthened. Constantinople was the capital from which the Roman Empire was carried on without a lapse and by almost insensible stages became what is commonly called the Byzantine or Greek Empire. The branch of the Catholic Church officially espoused by the continuing Empire regarded itself as the Orthodox Church. Eventually, by processes which are to be discerned in this period but which matured centuries later, the Orthodox Church became a family whose main members were national churches. We will then move on to the several smaller churches in the East, especially to those of Monophysite complexion, including the Coptic, Ethiopian, Jacobite, and Armenian bodies, and to the Nestorians. Finally we will survey the course of that branch of the Catholic Church which found its cohesion in Rome and the Roman Pontiff, the Pope, for it was from this section of the Church that Christianity was to have its chief developments in the next three major periods of its history.

Here again we shall wish to ask how far the kind of power seen in the cross and the resurrection was compromised by the sort of power that expressed itself in the earthly city and where and to what degree it made the Gospel effective in particular individuals, in institutions, in regions, in cultures, and in the entire human scene. Viewed against the background of all mankind, was it really waning? The Christian faith holds that God was in Christ reconciling the world to Himself. In what fashion and to what degree, so far as the surviving records enable us to discern it, was that reconciliation working during these four and a half centuries? Was the decline as great as it might have appeared to the Martian observer who employed the criteria suggested by citizens of the earthly city and who, supposedly, would have been his chief channels of information? Or was there evidence which, assessed by the criteria set up in the New Testament, would give other results?

Chapter 11

THE BYZANTINE CONTINUATION

As we have suggested, it seems fitting that in carrying our story into the period which follows the first five hundred years we should begin with that portion of the narrative which centres about Constantinople and which leads into an account of what may be designated as the Greek or Byzantine segment of Christianity. It was through the administrative structure which had its headquarters at Constantinople that the Roman Empire persisted without a break. Through it, accordingly, the relationship between Church and state which had its inception under Constantine continued its most characteristic development. We have seen that Christianity had its first extensive spread in the Hellenistic, Greek-using elements in the Mediterranean world. It was through Greek that all of the early Christian writings incorporated in the New Testament were given their permanent and authoritative form. Greek was the language of most of the oldest leaders in Christian thought. In the course of the centuries with which this chapter is to deal Greek became the prevailing language of that continuation of the Roman Empire which, dominated by Constantinople, is usually called Byzantine, from Byzantium, the pre-Constantinian designation of that city. Through extensive geographic expansion in subsequent centuries this Greek or Byzantine Christianity was to become the faith of the majority in Eastern Europe and the Balkan Peninsula and as such was to remain one of the numerically major forms of Christianity.

THE JUSTINIAN ERA

The decline of the Roman Empire which had been so marked in the fifth century seemed to be halted in the sixth century and for a brief time that realm flowered again. The central figure in the revival was the Emperor Justinian I, who reigned from 527 to 565, dying in his eighties. A nephew of his predecessor, Justin I, an Illyrian peasant who had come to Constantinople in his youth to seek his fortune and had risen to the throne in 518 at the age of sixty-six, Justinian had been the real power during much of his uncle's tenure of the high office. Justinian was highly intelligent, enormously hard-working, paying great attention to details, friendly, usually in control of his temper, vain, autocratic, ambitious, sometimes vacillating, temperate in his private life almost to asceticism, and deeply religious. He cherished the dream of restoring the Roman domains to their former extent and of bringing unity to the Church. This last he sought to achieve by obtaining the triumph of the orthodox faith of Chalcedon over its rivals, especially the Arian Christianity held by many of the Germanic invaders and the varied kinds of Monophysitism.

Thanks very largely to able generals, during the reign of Justinian Italy, North Africa, and part of Spain were brought back under Roman, or perhaps we should now say, Byzantine rule. Wars were waged against the chronic enemy, Persia. Under Justinian this revived Roman Empire was probably the mightiest realm on the planet, for the period was one of decline for the major contemporary kingdom in India, that of the Gupta, and China had not yet emerged from the political division which had come upon that land in the third century and which had been aggravated by invasions from the north and west.

Justinian's Empress was Theodora. Theodora, like Justinian's family, was of humble origin. A contemporary, Procopius, who wrote a *Secret History* defaming both Emperor and Empress, tells scandalous stories of her youth. These may have been exaggerated, but it is regarded as certain that before her union with Justinian she had had an illegitimate child. She was indisputably a woman of great resolution, charm, beauty, ability, and force. After she was raised to the throne she seems to have remained true to Justinian, who, in turn, was devoted to her. The two differed religiously, for while Justinian was staunch in his Chalcedonian orthodoxy, Theodora was a warm supporter of the Monophysites. She was energetic in redressing wrongs, and she is given the credit for stringent legislation suppressing the sale of girls into prostitution and for founding a convent in which the unfortunates were given an opportunity to begin a better life.

Under Justinian and Theodora, perhaps because of the latter's love of luxury and display, the imperial court took on additional pomp and those coming into the imperial presence were required to prostrate themselves. This was in accord with the lavish ornateness which was to characterize Byzantine life, both secular and religious.

It was partly in this spirit that Justinian became a great builder. At his command towns came into being, extensive fortifications, roads, bridges, baths, and palaces were constructed, and many churches and monasteries were erected. His most famous architectural achievement was Saint Sophia, the cathedral church of Constantinople. Saint Sophia was the climax of a new style of architecture which made outstanding use of the dome and which was inspired by the Christian faith and had as its purpose a worthy setting for Christian worship.

Justinian was deeply interested in theology. Almost inevitably, therefore, he took a leading part in the controversies which were still raging over the relation of the divine and human in Christ. We have seen how in 482 the Emperor Zeno had attempted to compose the differences between the Chalcedonians and the Monophysites by his *Henoticon*. This had not brought peace, for while some Monophysites accepted it, others of them rejected it, and, on the other extreme, the Pope would have none of it and excommunicated the Patriarch of Constantinople for being associated with it.

Into all the complicated details of the disputes and the attempted settlements during the reign of Justinian we must not take the time to go. In general, Justinian, who was no mean theologian in his own right, endeavoured to bring about agreement on the basis of ostensibly holding to the decrees of Chalcedon but slanting the latter in the direction of the views of Cyril of Alexandria. These, it will be recalled, while conceding the human element in Christ, subordinated it to the divine. Justinian seems to have hoped that by this policy he would draw together the adherents of Chalcedon and the more moderate among the Monophysites. The latter, it will be remembered, represented varying shades of theological conviction, some leaving less room for the human in Christ than others. In this effort Justinian found support in the writings of a contemporary monk, Leo of Byzantium, who, employing Aristotelian categories, held that one could affirm two natures in Christ without going to the extreme associated with what was regarded as Nestorianism, and that, while the two natures, the human and the divine, might remain, they could be regarded as so commingled and united that in Christ there would be but one *hypostasis,* that of the *Logos.*

In 544 Justinian issued an edict in which by his own fiat he condemned three writings or groups of writings (sometimes known, not with entire accuracy, as "the three chapters"), including those of Theodore of Mopsuestia, who had had much to do with shaping the views of the two natures in Christ which had been associated with the name of Nestorius and had been rejected by the Catholic Church, and of a Theodoret who had come out against Cyril and in behalf of Nestorius. However, this edict, far from making for harmony, stirred up fresh dissension. In the West some of the bishops regarded it as an iniquitous action against men who, being dead, could not defend themselves, as a repudiation of Chalcedon, and as an endorsement of the Monophysites. The resulting controversy is known as that of "the three chapters."

In the ensuing struggle the Pope, Vigilius, came through with a record of vacillation and self-contradiction. At first he opposed the imperial edict and broke off communion with the Patriarch of Constantinople, who supported it. Then, arriving in Constantinople, he executed an about face and issued a

Iudicatum in which, while careful to support Chalcedon and not to concede to the Emperor the right to determine matters of doctrine, he independently condemned the writings which had been anathematized in the imperial edict. The *Iudicatum* met with sharp criticism from many bishops in Gaul, North Africa, Scythia, Dalmatia, and Illyria, as compromising Chalcedon, and in 550 Vigilius withdrew it. Vigilius also reversed himself in other decisions. Yet on occasion he showed courage, refused to yield to the Emperor, and stood up for the authority of the Papal see.

Eventually, after many discussions among the bishops and with Justinian, the latter called a synod of the entire Catholic Church, usually known as the Fifth Ecumenical Council. This met in Constantinople in 553. Vigilius refused to attend and insisted on giving an independent judgement on the points at issue. The gathering confirmed the condemnations of the imperial decree of 544, and, at the command of the Emperor, probably had the name of Vigilius as an individual struck from the diptychs, but without breaking off communion with Rome. The Emperor banished Vigilius, but the latter was freed when he had conceded the legitimacy of the council. This Vigilius did, condemning "the three chapters" and their defenders. Thus the Cyrillic interpretation of Chalcedon, with its leaning towards Monophysitism, was made official for the Catholic Church.

Yet the Fifth Ecumenical Council did not, as Justinian had hoped, restore unity in the Church. In spite of its endorsement by Vigilius and his successor, numbers of the bishops in Italy and Gaul refused to recognize it as authoritative and for more than a century part of the West was divided from the main body of the Catholic Church. Moreover, Justinian's dream of providing a *via media* which would win back the Monophysites was by no means entirely fulfilled. The more extreme among the latter believed that assent would mean compromise of jealously held convictions. In some areas, notably Egypt, Ethiopia, Syria, and Armenia, Monophysite views were becoming identified with a regionalism which, to use a nineteenth and twentieth century term, was a kind of nationalism. It resented control by the Greeks and from Constantinople.

What Justinian was unable to accomplish by negotiation, persuasion, and a council of all the Church he endeavoured to bring about by force. He wished an empire which would be solidly Christian and orthodox. He sought to extirpate what survived of paganism. In its formal cults, paganism was clearly dying. Yet many continued to be pagans at heart and held to the pre-Christian Greek philosophies. To rid the realm of these remnants Justinian enacted fresh legislation. He commanded both civil officials and bishops to seek out pagan superstitions and forbade any persons "infected with the madness of the unholy Hellenes" to teach any subject. There were prosecutions and confiscations of property and, as we have seen, Justinian closed the schools of philosophy in Athens. Yet many, among them some in high office, remained pagans and usually were not molested if they were not ostentatious in their faith. Justinian also placed the Samaritans under heavy disabilities and ruthlessly suppressed the revolts which his measures provoked. He was somewhat more lenient towards the Jews, but essayed to regulate their worship. He decreed the death penalty for Manichæans and for heretics who, after recanting, fell back into their former beliefs. He tried to argue with Manichæans, and, when he failed to convert them, had numbers of them killed, among them nobles and senators. He took vigorous measures against heretics, and was especially zealous against the Montanists, who after nearly four centuries still persisted in Phrygia, the region of their origin. He took action against some who, professing to follow Origen, used the name of that famous teacher to justify a pantheistic mysticism which was enjoying something of a vogue, especially in Palestinian monasteries. He labelled Origen as a heretic and either the Fifth Ecumenical Council or an earlier synod in Constantinople in 543 condemned some of the teachings ascribed to that great Alexandrian.

Justinian did not act as emphatically and consistently against the Monophysites as against other heretics. As we have seen, he sought to woo the more moderate of them and Theodora's known advocacy of their views may have softened his rigour towards them. In his last years he attempted to force on the Church a form of Monophysitism known as Aphthartodocetism. This held that Christ's body, being divine, had undergone no change from the time of its conception in the womb of Mary, and was incorruptible, incapable of suffering or of the natural and blameless passions. It thus distinctly limited Christ's humanity. Justinian tried to impose this view on the bishops of the Catholic Church, and, since the orthodox among them resisted, he was preparing to apply physical violence when death removed him.

Not only did Monophysitism continue. It also spread. Its most active missionary was a younger contemporary of Justinian, Jacob Baradæus. Born about 490, of well-to-do parents, Jacob was given a good education and had fluent use of Greek, Arabic, and Syriac. From his early youth he was committed to the ascetic life. During an episcopate of nearly a generation, from 542 to 578, he roved from Nisibis in Mesopotamia to Alexandria in Egypt, usually on foot and garbed only in a ragged horse cloth, and is said to have consecrated two patriarchs, eighty-nine bishops, and a hundred thousand priests. He extended Monophysitism, strengthened it, and did something towards giving it a sense of unity. The term Jacobite applied to a large wing of the Monophysites either perpetuates his memory or was intended to indicate the claim of the group to be the true Church, the custodians of the faith of James, or Jacob, the brother of Jesus.

In spite of the labours of Jacob Baradæus, the Monophysites were badly divided. They differed from one another in doctrine and had no comprehensive organization. Towards the end of the sixth century there were said to be twenty Monophysite sects in Egypt alone. One form was tritheism, which held that in the Trinity there are really three Gods, each with a substance and a nature different from the others.

After the death of Justinian there were attempts to unite the Monophysites. In 575 the Monophysites of Egypt chose a Patriarch of Syrian origin, but he was not generally accepted. Not far from 580, about two years after the death of Jacob Baradæus, partly through the efforts of an Arab Christian prince, a council was held which seemed for a brief time to have brought a semblance of accord. Yet that also failed. The two leading Monophysite sees were the Patriarchates of Antioch and Alexandria.

In Alexandria there was also an orthodox Patriarch, but loyalty to him was confined chiefly to Greek residents and imperial functionaries. In spite of the use of force to obtain conformity with the Catholic faith, most of the Egyptians adhered to Monophysitism in one or another of its expressions.

Justinian was not content with seeking the doctrinal unity of his realm. He also enacted a large number of laws which dealt with various aspects of the life of the Church—the election of bishops, the appointment of the heads of monasteries, the ordination of clergy, public worship, the management of church property, and the morals of the clergy (legislation which, by forbidding simony—the sale and purchase of ecclesiastical office—and the attendance of the clergy at the theatre and horse-races, is an indication that some of the clergy were given to these practices). Justinian increased the functions of bishops in the administration of civic and social matters, such as the overseeing of public works, the enforcement of legislation against gambling, and the rearing of exposed infants. In some matters they acted in place of the governors.

It will be seen that Justinian greatly accelerated a movement which had begun with Constantine for the domination of the Church by the Emperor and which made the Church an instrument of the state. This control of the Church by the Emperor, known as cæsaropapism, was so characteristic of the eastern continuation of the Roman Empire that it was also called Byzantinism. As we have suggested earlier, it was the continuation of the tradition of the pre-Constantinian Roman Empire by which the Emperor, among other titles, bore that of *pontifex maximus,* or chief priest.

It is not surprising that under Justinian, with the renewed vigour displayed by the Roman Empire, Christianity continued to spread in the outlying sections and on the borders of the realm. The re-conquest of North Africa was followed not only by the strengthening of the Catholic Church against the Arians and Donatists who flourished in that region under the Vandals. It also led to the conversion of some of the pagan Berbers, a process which continued after the death of Justinian. During the reign of Justinian Christianity was carried further up the valley of the Nile, into Nubia, in both its Catholic and Monophysite forms. Through the encouragement and initiative of Justinian at least one people in the Caucasus and a barbarian folk who crossed the Danube into Roman territory adopted the Christian faith.

THE FINAL STAGES OF THE CHRISTOLOGICAL CONTROVERSY: MONOTHELETISM

The lack of unity among Christians, and especially between Monophysites and the majority, which Justinian had failed to eliminate, continued to pose a major problem to both Church and state, and Emperor after Emperor wrestled with it. The issue became urgent when, in the seventh century, Arab invaders bearing a new religion, Islam, began their conquests. The Emperors believed it imperative to have Christians and the Empire present a common front against the invader. A fresh approach was made towards bringing Orthodox and Monophysites together, but, far from attaining its goal, it brought another wave of controversy.

The new approach was suggested by the Patriarch Sergius of Constantinople to the Emperor Heraclius and found support in the writings, then relatively new, which were attributed to Dionysius the Areopagite. These had said that the selfsame Christ and Son works divine and human deeds by one divine-human operation (*energeia*). For a time the statement that Christ acted through one *energeia* brought about union in Egypt of Orthodox and Monophysites, but it drew attack. Sergius, in an attempt to by-pass a divisive debate, suggested that the discussion of whether Christ acted through one or more than one *energeia* be dropped, but that surely all would agree that in Christ there was only one will (*thelema*). To this Pope Honorius, to whom Sergius had written, assented. Seemingly backed by the bishops of the two most eminent sees in the Church, in 638 the Emperor Heraclius issued an edict containing the views of Sergius, forbidding the discussion of one or two energies, and declaring that Christ had one will. This seemed to win the assent of the legates of the successor of Pope Honorius, but in 641 a later Pope came out against Monotheletism, the statement that there was only one will in Christ, and declared that his had really been the view of Honorius. Subsequent Popes also affirmed that there were two wills, divine and human, in Christ, and this in general was the conviction in the West. It was argued that if Christ is truly man as well as truly God, he must have a human as well as a divine will. To deny him a human will is to deprive him of his full humanity. It was, of course, held that the divine and the human will were always in accord and never in disagreement.

Since the discussion was a menace to the unity of the Church and was producing fresh division and weakness, in 648 the Emperor Constans II forbade further debate of the questions of one or two energies and of one or two wills. In defiance of this order, in 649 Pope Martin I held a synod at Rome which declared for two wills in Christ, condemned the Patriarch of Constantinople for taking the opposite view, and also came out against the imperial edicts of 638 and 648. For what he deemed the Pope's contumacy the Emperor had Martin brought to Constantinople as a prisoner, treated him cruelly, and exiled him to the Crimea. There Martin died. The Greek monk Maximus, known to later generations as the Confessor, who had been an able and outspoken opponent of Monotheletism, was imprisoned, tortured, mutilated, and exiled.

By this time most of the provinces where the Monophysites were strongest had been lost to the Arabs, and, apparently from a desire to bring peace in such of the Church as remained within the Roman Empire, the successor of Constans II called what is usually known as the Sixth Ecumenical Council. This met in Constantinople in 680 and 681. It pilloried the advocates of the Monothelete position, naming among them several Patriarchs of Constantinople and Pope Honorius as instruments of the Devil, and came out flatly for two wills and two energies in Christ, as "concurring most fitly in him for the salvation of the human race." In its distinctive findings the council declared that it was following the suggestions of the reigning Pope, Agatho, and of the synod of a hundred and twenty-five bishops which had been held under him in Rome the preceding year.

The Sixth Ecumenical Council is generally said to mark the end of the centuries-long debate over the relation of Jesus Christ to God and over the fashion in which the divine and human were to be found in him. To be sure, the issue was revived by a Byzantine Emperor early in the eighth century and a large group in the Lebanon, the Maronites, held to Monotheletism until the twelfth century, when they made their peace with Rome. Moreover, the Nestorians and various branches of the Monophysites continued their independent existence. Yet by the eighth century Arianism, the first major dissent on the issue, had largely disappeared, and for the main bodies of Christians in the West and for those in the East who had their chief centre in Constantinople the discussion had ceased and a common mind had been reached.

The positions defined in the course of the debate have since been deemed final by the churches which together embrace the large majority of Christians. Roman Catholics, Orthodox, and most Protestants hold to them. The various branches of the Monophysites cling to the findings of their spiritual ancestors of the fifth and sixth centuries. It has been mainly among some Protestants, and they small minorities of that wing of the faith, that the ancient questions have been raised afresh and answers given which differ from those of the first six ecumenical councils.

The Western and Eastern Sections of the Catholic Church Continue to Drift Apart

Although for them agreement had been reached over the nature of Christ and the relation of the divine and human in him, the Western and Eastern sections of the Catholic Church were drifting apart, the one looking to Rome and the other to Constantinople.

A stage in the separation was a council held in Constantinople in 692. It was summoned by the Emperor, but, while the East regarded it as supplementary to the Sixth Ecumenical Council and really a continuation of that body, its membership was purely from that section of the Empire. It dealt with matters of organization and discipline rather than doctrine. Its enactments have been regarded as binding by the portion of the Church led by the See of Constantinople but have never been fully accepted by Rome or by the section of the Church which has looked to Rome for guidance. The council reaffirmed the position of Chalcedon that "the See of Constantinople shall enjoy equal privilege with the see of Old Rome . . . and second after it." In open opposition to Rome it permitted the marriage of deacons and presbyters, forbade the Roman custom of fasting on Saturdays during Lent, prohibited the representation of Christ as a lamb, as was customary in the West, and ordered that Christ be depicted in human form. The final division had not yet come and East and West were usually in communion with each other. Indeed, while the then Pope refused to assent to the decisions of the council of 692, a few years later another Pope signed them with some qualifications. Yet a gulf was appearing and was widening.

The Coming of the Arabs and Islam

The disintegration of the Roman Empire which had been seemingly halted by Justinian was hastened, as we have more than once suggested, by the spectacular irruption of peoples from the south-east, the Arabs, the bearers of a new religion, Islam. Moslems reckon their era as beginning with the Hegira, A.D. 622, the traditional (but erroneous) date of Mohammed's flight from Mecca to Medina. Within a century of that year the Arabs had overrun about half of what had once been the Roman Empire and were the political masters of approximately half of what might be called Christendom, or the Christian world. The story is a familiar one, but to put it in its proper perspective in the history of Christianity we must summarize it afresh.

Islam owes its birth to Mohammed, whose years were 570–632. Deeply and sincerely religious, Mohammed believed himself to be the mouth-piece of God. By his followers, the Moslems (properly Muslims), he is revered as the Prophet, and the revelations which they believe to have been given to him by God, whom he called Allah, have been assembled preëminently in the Koran, a book which Moslems hold in fully as high esteem as Christians do the Bible. Mohammed knew much of Judaism and something of Christianity and was influenced by them both. He honoured Jesus as a prophet but emphatically denied that God could have a son, for this seemed to him to be derogatory to the greatness and uniqueness of God. Here Islam differed and still differs basically from Christianity. It declares that the gulf between God and man is too great to be bridged, while the fundamental conviction of Christianity is that the gulf, although undoubtedly great, has been bridged by God's initiative in Christ, Christ who is both God and man. Some, including especially many Christians in the early Moslem centuries, regarded Islam as a Christian heresy, but Islam is held by its adherents to be a fresh revelation from God, the final religion, and not a reinterpretation of Christianity.

The sweep of Islam across much of Western Asia and North Africa and into Europe was facilitated by the power vacuum which had been created by the chronic wars between the Roman and the Persian Empire. On the eve of the Arab invasion these two realms had recently come through a stage of their hereditary struggle which had exhausted them both. In the second decade of the seventh century, beginning in 611, when they took Antioch, the Persians had torn Syria and Palestine from the Roman Empire and had pillaged Jerusalem, looting and burning churches, killing thousands of Christians, and carrying off what the latter revered as the Holy Cross on which Christ was believed to have suffered. They also captured Alexandria, probably in 618 or 619, and thus put themselves in control of Egypt. They marched through Asia Minor, seized Chalcedon on the Sea of Marmora near the Bosporus, and encamped just opposite Constantinople. In the meantime, Avars and Slavs came in from the north and one of their raids even broke through the walls of Constantinople. The Persian successes were probably facilitated by the apathy or even hostility of the Mesopotamian Nestorians and the Monophysite Syrians and Egyptians towards the Byzantine rule, identified as that was with the Greeks and Catholic orthodoxy. Then, in the 620's, by one of the striking reverses of history, the Byzantine Empire, led by the Emperor Heraclius, reasserted its power, bought off the Avars, and, in what it deemed a holy war, retook Syria, Palestine (including Jerusalem and its sacred sites), and Egypt, invaded Persia, and extracted a peace, including the Holy Cross, from the demoralized Persians. But the struggle had impoverished and weakened both realms and had rendered them vulnerable to the new invaders.

The Arab advance was spectacular. Mohammed died in 632. He was followed in the leadership of the Moslems by a succession of men who bore the title Caliph, meaning "successor," "viceregent," or "vicar" (of Mohammed). Under the Caliphs the Arabs, although by no means all of these at first accepted Islam, moved into Byzantine and then into Persian territory. In 635 they took Damascus, in 636 all of Syria fell to them, and in 638, after a siege of two years, they captured Jerusalem, although the Holy Cross escaped them and was carried to Constantinople. In 641 or 642 Alexandria capitulated and the Arabs were thus assured of the possession of all Egypt. Their rapid conquests were facilitated not only by the near-exhaustion of the Byzantine realm through the recent Persian wars, but also, as had been the Persian advance, by resentment against the imperial efforts to establish Catholic orthodoxy against the prevailing Monophysitism. In Egypt, moreover, the Byzantine forces were poorly organized and ineptly led. By 650 Mesopotamia had been conquered and the heart of Persia had been overrun. Thus the traditional eastern rival of Roman and Byzantine power was eliminated, only to be replaced by a more dangerous foe. By 650, too, parts of Asia Minor and North Africa were under Arab sway.

The Arabs became a naval as well as a land power, occupied part of Cyprus, captured the island of Rhodes, and raided Sicily and Southern Italy. In the 670's they repeatedly attacked Constantinople itself from a nearby base and were beaten off partly through the use of "Greek fire," a new invention the formula of which was a carefully guarded Byzantine secret.

In 697 Carthage, the centre of Byzantine power in North Africa, fell to the Arabs. For a time the Berbers in that area proved a knotty problem, but by 715, with the assistance of Berber forces, the Straits of Gibraltar had been passed (indeed, they have that name from Tarik, the general who commanded the crossing) and the Visigothic rule in Spain had been overthrown. Arab arms were carried across the Pyrenees and the Moslem call to prayer was heard in southern Gaul. There the Arab Moslem tide was not halted until 732 when, in the battle of Tours (or Poitiers) the Franks, in a decisive victory, stemmed it and began the slow process of rolling it back. Early in the eighth century the Arabs penetrated the Punjab in India and far into Central Asia.

In 717–718, taking advantage of a rapid change of rulers, mutinies, and a near approach to anarchy in the Byzantine Empire, the Arabs again attacked Constantinople, but were repulsed by the able Leo III, the first Emperor of the Isaurian line. Near the middle of the eighth century the Byzantine Empire recovered Cyprus and pushed the Arabs out of Asia Minor. Not for many centuries was the Moslem threat to Constantinople renewed. Yet in the ninth century Crete was taken, Sicily fell to the Moslems, Moslems established posts on the Italian coast, and Rome was attacked more than once and on at least one occasion saved itself only by paying a ransom.

The Arabs did not remain united politically and bitter wars among them were frequent. The strongest and most brilliant of the states established by them was that of the Abbasid Caliphs, descended from Abbas, uncle of Mohammed, with its capital at Baghdad.

The conquests of the Arabs by no means meant the early extinction of the Christian communities in the realms of the Caliphs. Arab Christians, of whom there were many, were in theory required to become Moslems, for Mohammed is said to have declared that there could not be any other religion in Arabia than Islam. Yet many Arab Christians were allowed to retain their faith, and in return were heavily taxed. In principle, the Moslems regarded Christians, like the Jews, as "people of the book" and tolerated them. Indeed, for a time the Arabs looked askance at the adoption by them of Islam, for conversion would give the privileges of Moslems and deprive the Arab rulers of the proceeds of the discriminatory taxes levied against Christians. At the outset in Egypt and Syria non-Catholic Christians were better off than they had been under Byzantine rulers, for the latter had attempted to force their faith upon them. So, too, in the former Persian realms Christians, notably those who were most numerous there, the Nestorians, were freer than they had been under the Zoroastrian princes. Encouraged by their new masters, they taught the latter, as we have suggested, much of Greek civilization, translating in Arabic some of the writings of the Greek philosophers.

However, in Moslem realms Christianity was under handicaps which made for a decline of the numbers of its adherents, sometimes rapid. At the time of the Arab conquest many, particularly in North Africa where the prevailing faith of Christians was not Monophysite or Nestorian, but Catholic, took refuge with their fellow Catholics in Sicily and the south of Italy. They thereby reinforced the Greek element, already strong in those traditionally Greek regions, in the churches in these areas. Others went to Spain, Greece, Gaul, and even Germany. This exodus dealt what proved to be a fatal blow to the Christianity of North Africa. As was to be expected, nearly everywhere the Arab conquests were followed by extensive defections to Islam. Occasionally, but infrequently, these were accomplished by force. Some were from the conviction that the Moslems were right in proclaiming Mohammed to be the true prophet of God and to have a later and higher revelation than Christianity. The conviction was reinforced by the military victories, for they appeared to prove that Islam was under the peculiar favour of God. Many moved over to Islam from quite mundane reasons: from the worldly standpoint it was better to be identified with the ruling class.

Then, too, Christians were under legal disabilities which made accessions to the churches, except by birth, all but impossible, placed their worship under restrictions, and laid other galling disabilities upon them. In lands where Moslem law prevailed, unrepentant apostasy from Islam was punishable by death. Conversions to Christianity, therefore, were very rare and converts usually disappeared. Christians might retain their churches, although some of these were turned into mosques, but in theory they could not build new ones. They were prohibited from displaying their faith through public religious processions or by loud church bells. Possibly following the precedent of the Zoroastrian Persians with religious minorities, the Moslem Arabs required Christians to wear a distinctive badge or garb. Christians were not allowed to serve in the armies, but instead a special head tax was levied on men who normally would have been able to bear arms.

For purposes of administration, another device was taken over from the Zoroastrian Persians. Each of the Christian communions was treated as a distinct community and was placed under its ecclesiastical head. The latter was given authority over the members of his flock and was held responsible for them. In later centuries these communities were called *melets* or *millets*. Catholic Christians in communion with Constantinople were, quite understandably, regarded by the Arabs with especial suspicion and for many years were not allowed to have a community organization under their own head. They were known generally as Melchites or Malkites, from a Syriac word meaning "king," for they were the ones who were obedient to the imperial commands and therefore belonged to the "king's" church.

The effect of these regulations and of this administrative system was to place the churches on the defensive and to render them static, encysted minorities. They resisted change and held to the patterns which had come down to them from their fathers. They feared that any departure from the traditions of the past would be followed by the disintegration of their entire life and their faith. This meant that churches in the Arab realms were extremely conservative.

Under these circumstances, the churches in the Moslem domains, those of the Arabs and their Moslem successors of later centuries, many of them Turks, were tenaciously persistent, but slowly lost ground. The rate of decline varied from country to country. In Arabia most of the Christian communities seem to have died out before the tenth century. In North Africa the decay was marked but somewhat less rapid. In the eleventh century there were still five bishops, but late in that century the three bishops necessary for the consecration of an archbishop were not to be found and the man elected to the post by the Christians in 1074 was sent by the Moslem ruler to Rome for that rite. In Nubia, south of Egypt, Christianity persisted well beyond the thirteenth century, but eventually disappeared, not to be renewed until in the nineteenth century and then by missionaries from Western Europe. Elsewhere the churches continued but, even in the twentieth century, were still dwindling.

THE SLOWING DOWN OF THEOLOGICAL CREATIVITY IN THE CHURCH OF THE BYZANTINE EMPIRE

It is understandable that in those churches which were encircled by Moslems, embedded in Moslem states, and perpetually on the defensive, fresh thinking on theological issues would cease or, if it appeared, would be quashed by the ecclesiastical authorities. Any innovation would seem perilous. It is possible that this necessity of passive defense contributed to a somewhat similar absence of creative thought in that portion of the Catholic Church which centred about Constantinople. Theological activity did not disappear in this Byzantine, or, as we must also now call it, Greek Church. Theology remained a major concern in the intellectual circles, especially in the wealthy and highly cultured capital. Yet vigorous, fresh thinking such as was to revive and continue in the Christianity of Western Europe was not found. Certainly the successive blows dealt by the Arabs and then, centuries later, as we are to see in later chapters, the even more disastrous experiences with Christian Crusaders from the West and, after them, with the Moslem Turks, must be part of the explanation.

Whatever the cause, the Byzantine Church displayed no such theological ferment as did Western Europe. It held to what had been done in the Catholic Church in the first seven and especially the first five centuries. It regarded itself as the guardian of the true Christian faith taught by Christ and his apostles. Indeed, that to this day is the attitude of the family of Orthodox Churches in which the Patriarch of Constantinople, his effective authority and the flock over which he immediately presides sadly dwindled, is still theoretically the ranking bishop.

THE LAST GREAT FIGURE IN GREEK THEOLOGY, JOHN OF DAMASCUS

He who is usually regarded as the last great figure in the theology of the Greek wing of the Catholic Church was John of Damascus. It is significant that he is important, not for original thought, but for his systematization of that which had gone before him. John belongs to the first half of the eighth century. He was born in Damascus, the son of a high official in the court of the Caliph, then located in that city. He succeeded to his father's position, but resigned it and entered the monastery of St. Sabas, near Jerusalem. He was deeply religious, as can be seen from the important share that he had in the hymn-writing which helped to shape that part of Byzantine worship.

John's main theological work was *The Fountain of Knowledge*. In this there were three parts, first an exposition and application to theology of Aristotle's Dialectic, second a description of heresies, reproducing and bringing down to date an earlier work by Epiphanius, and, third and most important, "An Accurate Exposition of the Orthodox Faith." Here was a complete theological system based on the teachings of the fathers and the findings of the councils of the Catholic Church.

John thought of the Christian faith in its orthodox or Catholic form as having already been defined. What he attempted to do was to make a comprehensive synthesis of what had been established. In this he did not differ substantially from the great Cappadocians, Basil of Cæsarea and Gregory of Nyssa. To be sure, they had Platonic assumptions and arrived at the idea of the unity in the Trinity after stressing first the fact of Three, Father, Son, and Holy Spirit, and then coming to the insight of unity, while John, inclined to Aristotelianism, started off with the unity of the Godhead and then discerned in it the Trinity. John began with the nature of God, went on to the creation, the nature of man, providence, foreknowledge, predestination, and the salvation of man, and concluded with the resurrection and speculations as to what would develop as the entire purpose of God in the universe is disclosed.

The work was so comprehensive, so clearly written, and stated so well what was believed in the Greek wing of the Catholic Church, that it became standard in its field for that branch of the Church and through a twelfth century Latin translation also influenced the Western section of the Church, including notably Peter Lombard and Thomas Aquinas.

THE ICONOCLASTIC CONTROVERSY

The major dispute in the Greek or Byzantine wing of the Catholic Church after the seventh century was not over the nature of Christ, but over the use of images in Christian worship. In this the West also became involved, although it was not as badly divided as were the Greeks. The controversy broke out in 726 and raged, with intervals of comparative quiet, for over a century, until 843. It was concomitant with the recovery of the Byzantine Empire from the internal disorder from which the realm suffered near the beginning of the eighth century and was the result of the religious policy of the Emperor Leo III, who brought a fresh access of strength to the waning Byzantine power.

Objections by Christians to the use of images and pictures—icons as they are technically known—were by no means new. We have seen that pictures of Christian subjects, even of Christ himself, had been made long before the sixth century. Yet there had also been opposition to them on the ground that they smacked of paganism. In the sixth century, before his consecration a Syrian bishop denounced the veneration of the representations of Christ, the Virgin

Mary, the apostles, and other saints. In that same century, moreover, a bishop of Massilia (Marseilles) was reprimanded by the Pope for ordering the destruction of the images in the churches in his diocese, for that pontiff, while agreeing that they should not be adored, held that they were a valuable means of instructing illiterate Christians in the faith.

Yet icons became increasingly numerous. Christ, his mother, the apostles, saints, and scenes from the Old and New Testaments were pictured in mosaics, frescoes, bronze, and carvings in ivory. They were characteristic of churches and chapels and were in private homes.

Why the Emperor Leo decided to open a campaign against them is not entirely clear and has been much debated. It is noted that he was not a Greek but was from the East and it has been suggested that, having been faced with the taunts of Moslems and Jews that Christians were idolaters, he wished to remove the ground for that charge and thus to facilitate winning the support of Moslems and Jews for the Empire. It is also said that he hoped to reconcile the Montanists and other Christians who dissented from the Catholic Church. Leo is reported to have been moved as well by the desire to make the throne master of the Church, to reduce the power of the monks, and to eliminate the control of education by the Church. His is likewise conjectured to have been a revolt of the non-Greek elements in the Empire against the Greek dominance, for, in general, the Greeks were for the icons and Leo and the other Emperors who led in the attacks against them were of non-Greek stocks and cultures. Some have seen in the iconoclastic movement primarily an effort at religious reform.

Whatever the motives which originally actuated Leo, the struggle became complicated by many factors. In it were on the one hand abhorrence of the use of icons as idolatry and on the other popular emotional devotion to them, including veneration of some of the particular images which were singled out for destruction. The contest was in part from the conviction of many churchmen and especially of monks that the Church should be independent of the state, at least in matters of faith and religious practice, and the equally determined purpose of Emperors to assert their authority over the Church. Monks, who had separated themselves from the world, were particularly active in their opposition to the icon-forbidding Emperors. The Emperors may have wished to curb the monasteries because the latter drew so many men from the service of the state and, tax-exempt, reduced the imperial revenues. The army often sided with the iconoclasts, apparently because it wished its head, the Emperor, to be supreme and to be reverenced without the rivalry of veneration for the icons. Women were prominent in the defense of icons, perhaps because of emotionally religious temperaments. In general, as we have suggested, the Greek constituency in the Church was committed to the icons, and much of the attack on the icons came from non-Greek elements. Yet the iconoclasts tended to favour the revived study of the pre-Christian Greek literature while the monks opposed it as tending towards paganism. Personal ambitions and rivalries were always present and at times were very strong. Partisan strife in Constantinople had long been rife. Until the reforms of the Emperor Heraclius in the first half of the seventh century it had centred about the two major parties in the circus, the Blues and the Greens. It had entered into theological disputes. While the Blues and the Greens were now in the past the party spirit was still strong. At one point the putting away by an iconoclastic Emperor of his wife and the marrying of another woman gave occasion for the charge of adultery by those who favoured the icons and also was used by them to insist that an Emperor must be as obedient to the laws of the Church as the lowliest commoner. Theological issues were raised. It is said that the controversy was a split with Hellenism, that those who favoured the icons stood for the historical element in Christianity and that those who opposed them were of the Origenist, Platonic strain who were critical of efforts to confine Christianity to history.

The iconoclasts pled the prohibition of the second commandment to make "the likeness of anything" and held that to do so "draws down the spirit of man from the lofty worship of God to the low and material worship of the creature." They declared that "the only admissible figure of the humanity of Christ . . . is the bread and wine in the Holy Supper." They took a variety of attitudes towards the icons. Some were completely intolerant. The more extreme among them condemned the popular veneration of the saints and of the Virgin. Others would compromise.

To be sure, the iconoclasts did not forbid art. They encouraged pictures of birds, musical instruments, clusters of fruit and flowers, hunting scenes, chariot races, and donors to the Church, and substituted the Emperor's head on the coins for Christ or the Virgin. Some of these motifs resembled and may have been consciously drawn from early Christian art, such as is still to be seen in the catacombs in Rome. The opponents of the iconoclasts held this art to be of the Devil. They argued, too, that the iconoclasts were really Monophysites, denying the reality of the incarnation and of the humanity of Christ, for by refusing to depict the human form of Christ they laid themselves open to the charge that they were affirming that he was God but were denying that he had ever really become man.

Two important figures, both against the iconoclasts, claim special notice. One was John of Damascus. In the early days of the controversy, before he entered a monastery and while he was still a civil servant in the Caliph's government, he came forward against the iconoclast position. In the ninth century, in the later stages of the dispute, an outstanding defender of the use of icons was Theodore of Studius. Born in Constantinople of a well-to-do family, when he was twenty-two Theodore entered a monastery on Mt. Olympus, in Bithynia in Asia Minor, under the tutelage of his uncle. Eventually he succeeded the latter as abbot. Later he and some of his monks moved to Constantinople and entered a large monastery which had been founded in 463 by Studius. Under his leadership that house soon attained prominence and the Studite monks became famous.

There Theodore further developed a rule which he had received from his uncle and made it into a meticulous organization of the monastic life with a rigorous discipline. Among the features which he took over from his uncle was the prohibition of receiving not only women but also female animals into the monastery, probably to discourage the breeding of animals for sale and the accompanying employment of non-monks as servants to assist in this profit-producing activity. Theodore's changes had a wide influence in Byzantine monasticism and in the lands to which Byzantine Christianity spread.

Theodore took an uncompromising attitude in favour of the icons and he and his monks were prominent in the opposition to the imperial policy. Probably this was both out of conviction that the imperial position was wrong on that particular issue and partly from opposition to the domination of the Church by the state. Theodore was persecuted, banished, and imprisoned, but the rigours to which he was subjected did not break his spirit. A scholar, a gentleman, a leader, he attracted both men and women. Uncompromising, at times gloating over the disasters to the enemies of the causes which he espoused, he was also a writer of hymns and a spiritual counsellor to members of both sexes.

The details of the long attempt to be rid of the icons need not long detain us. The issue was raised, as we have seen, by Leo III not many years after he came to the throne. He is said to have been urged to this course by some of the bishops. An edict against the use of icons was issued in 725 or 726 and was followed by the destruction by imperial order of an image of Christ which had enjoyed great popular veneration. That act provoked a riot. In 730 a council convoked by the Emperor took further measures against the icons. The Patriarch of Constantinople was deposed for refusing to concur and one who was opposed to the icons was elevated to the see. The Popes set themselves against the imperial policy and Gregory III, the last Bishop of Rome to have his election confirmed by a Byzantine Emperor, called a council which excommunicated the iconoclasts. In retaliation for the hostility of Rome and to the great annoyance of the Popes, the Emperor transferred Greek bishoprics in Italy and Sicily from the supervision of the latter to that of the Patriarch of

Constantinople. The son and successor of Leo, Constantine V, was even more adamant against the icons than his father had been. In 753 or 754 he called a council of more than three hundred bishops which obediently condemned the icons but in which, significantly, neither the Pope nor the patriarchs of Antioch, Jerusalem, and Alexandria were represented. Severe persecutions of those who held to the icons followed, but under Constantine's son, Leo IV, icons were tolerated outside Constantinople.

On the death of Leo IV, in 780, his widow, Irene, became regent for his infant son. She favoured icons and promoted to the patriarchate Tarasius, a sympathetic civil official who, in conformity with ecclesiastical tradition, took monastic vows and so became eligible for the office. A council of the entire church was called which met in 787, for the most part at Nicæa. Tarasius presided rather than the Emperor or a civil official delegated by the Emperor. He was eager to solve the relations between Church and state by having the Church recognized as supreme in matters of dogma and by according to the Emperor authority in ecclesiastical law and administration. The Pope was represented and the gathering is generally regarded as the Seventh Ecumenical Council. The council approved the use of icons, but regulated the manner in which they should be honoured. The council also forbade the appointment of bishops by the lay power and ordered that in each ecclesiastical province an annual synod be held.

The decisions of the council did not immediately win universal acceptance. Many in the East held to their iconoclastic convictions. On the other hand, some who favoured the icons, notably Theodore of Studius and his monks, were unhappy because those bishops who renounced iconoclastic views were treated leniently and were permitted to retain their posts. Even in the West, where the Popes had consistently stood for the icons, in the Frankish domains a council at Frankfort (794), while allowing images to be set up in the churches, forbade their veneration and denounced the findings of the Council of Nicæa. In 825 a synod in Paris condemned the Pope for assenting to the findings at Nicæa. Not until the eleventh century did Northern Europe accept the Nicæan gathering as the Seventh Ecumenical Council.

Early in the ninth century, in 813, Leo V, the Armenian, came to the imperial throne and revived iconoclasm. However, he was much milder in his enforcement of the ban than had been some of his predecessors and the attack was not so much on icons in general as upon some of the uses of them, especially in worship in private houses. The veneration of icons seems to have continued outside the capital, especially in Greece, the islands, and much of Asia Minor.

In 842 another woman, Theodora, came to power as regent for an infant son, this time Michael III. Like Irene, she favoured the icons and in 843 she restored them. That act really terminated the struggle, although echoes of it were still heard and there were some who held to iconoclastic views. The day in which the icons were formally reinstated, the first Sunday in Lent, is still celebrated in the Greek Church as the Feast of Orthodoxy.

While icons were finally legitimatized, the long protest was not without lasting effect. By tacit consent, in practice after 843 in the Greek portion of the Catholic Church sculptured figures were no longer employed, and icons were confined to pictures. Yet, for good or for ill, they were permanently established in the life and worship of the Catholic Church in both East and West.

In the important and intimately related problem of relations between the Church and the state, the controversy ended in a compromise. The Emperor and the army, who wished the Emperor supreme, did not have their full way. The icons were retained, and this was a victory for the monks and those who wished to have the Church less subservient to the state. Yet in the final settlement it was the crown and not the Church which took the initiative.

THE CONTINUED MONASTICISM OF THE BYZANTINE CHURCH

We have had occasion more than once to note the prominence and something of the place which monasticism held in the Byzantine branch of the Catholic Church. That monasticism had been partly shaped by Basil. Theodore the Studite had added to it. Monks were prominent in the life of the Church and the community and were much less susceptible to control by the cæsaropapist state than was the ecclesiastical hierarchy, even though technically the bishops were drawn from the monasteries. The contrast may have been accentuated by the practice begun in the eighth century of appointing to the Patriarchate of Constantinople men who had risen through the civil bureaucracy and were thus seasoned in practical, secular administration and who in their mature years had gone through the form of assuming monastic vows. To this the more radical monks, among them the Studites, were vigorously opposed. They wished strict compliance with the canons of the Church. The monks were quite the most independent section in the official church of the Byzantine Empire.

More and more the course and the characteristics of this Eastern monasticism and those of the West diverged. Eastern monasticism tended towards contemplation and away from activism. Western monasticism displayed much greater variety. Some groups emphasized worship and contemplation, others activism, and still others combined the two. In the East, rather more than in the West, monasteries tended to be grouped together on holy mountains. They were also in the cities, but the mountain monastic communities were either without exact parallel or were more prominent than in the West. Several of the holy mountains were in Asia Minor. What came to be the most famous of all was in Europe, Athos, a rugged promontory jutting southward from the mainland into the Ægean. Mount Athos first attained prominence in years immediately preceding 950 through the exodus to it of monks from Constantinople in protest against the election to the Patriarchate of one whom they had opposed.

Hermits were revered in both East and West and were sought out by both the lowly and the eminent, and on mundane as well as spiritual questions. In the East, although they seem not to have persisted but to have been a fad that passed before many generations, "pillar saints" were prominent, those who had Simeon Stylites as their most famous prototype and inspiration. One of them was Daniel (409–493), whose years of fame were on the eve of the period with which we are now concerned. He entered a monastery at the age of twelve and spent the next twenty-five years there. For five years he visited some of the most famous of the ascetic "athletes of God" of his day, at forty-two he came to Constantinople and, after living for nine years in what had been a pagan temple, he mounted a pillar and passed his last thirty-three years on it. He was visited by multitudes, including officials, Emperors, and Patriarchs, at imperial command was ordained priest by one of the latter, and is said to have prophesied the fate of Emperors and to have been consulted not only on personal problems, but also on weighty matters of state. Many miracles were attributed to him.

A hermit, but not one of the pillar saints, was Theodore of Sykeon, of the latter part of the sixth and the first part of the seventh century. Born in Galatia in Asia Minor, the son of a prostitute, from early childhood he was very devout and began following the ascetic road. So early did he commend himself by his singleness of purpose that he was ordained priest at the age of eighteen. He journeyed to the holy places in and near Jerusalem and at his request was given the monk's habit near the Jordan. Returning to his home country, he led a life of extreme asceticism, much of the time in a narrow cage suspended from a rock, where he was exposed to the storms of winter, had himself loaded with irons, undertook prolonged fasts, and followed a severe regimen of psalm-singing. Others were attracted to him and he became the centre and the head of a monastery. He was famed for his miracles of healing, of expelling demons, and of ending a curse of locusts by killing the locusts, and for inducing repentance of sin. At the insistence of the populace of a neighbouring city he was made their bishop. After eleven years, troubled by the burdens of administration which interrupted his prayers and contemplation and prevented him from giving due attention to his monasteries, he resigned his episcopate. He was sought by many, some for physical healing and others for spiritual and moral advice. Even high officials and Emperors honoured him and asked his counsel.

We must note another trend which in subsequent centuries was to give rise to a memorable controversy. That was towards contemplation and the way of the mystic. Known technically as Hesychasm, it went back to the beginning of monasticism. It was to have many aspects, some of them bizarre, as we are to see in a later period, was to persist into modern times, and was to be very important in that child of Byzantine Christianity, the Russian Orthodox Church.

MINORITY MOVEMENTS BRANDED AS HERETICAL BY THE ORTHODOX

Not all the religious life of the Byzantine Empire inspired by the Christian faith was contained within the official church. Before the decline in vigour which marked these centuries had reached a nadir, there emerged awakenings which from the beginning were quite outside the Catholic Church. At least one of them flourished for centuries. Since they were often persecuted and eventually died out, only fragmentary information about them has survived and about some we know very little.

The most prominent and persistent of these separate groups was the Paulicians. Possibly a primitive form of Christianity cut off from later developments by geographic isolation, they are first heard of early in the second half of the seventh century on the eastern borders of the Empire, south of Armenia. They called themselves simply Christians and the designation Paulician was given them by their enemies. The first leader of whom we know was Constantine-Silvanus who, set on fire by reading the Gospels and the letters of Paul, became an itinerant preacher and eventually was stoned to death.

The Paulicians developed many leaders and divisions. Like the Marcionites, they were dualists, holding that matter, including this world and the flesh, is the creation of an evil power, the imperfect God of the Old Testament, while spirit and souls are the work of the good God. The "perfect" among them abstained from sexual intercourse and from some kinds of meats. They rejected infant baptism and, taking Jesus as their model, were baptized at the age of thirty, in a river. The "hearers," or adherents, were not required to follow this hard road, but hoped to be baptized and undertake it sometime before their death. The Paulicians rejected the honours paid by the Catholics to the Virgin Mary, the invocation of the saints, icons, incense, candles, and all material symbols. Maintaining the Eucharist and the Agape, they observed the former at night and used in it water, not wine. They would have none of the Catholic hierarchy and had only one grade of ministry. They accepted most of the New Testament. Christ was regarded as born of the good God, but as passing through his mother's body like water through a pipe and deriving nothing from her flesh. To them both his birth and his death were unreal, and his work was that of a teacher.

The Paulicians were severely persecuted, but, in resisting, they became excellent soldiers and won respect for their fighting abilities. The iconoclastic Emperors were generally tolerant of them and one of them moved Paulician colonies to the Balkan peninsula to fend off the Bulgars. They experienced a revival at the beginning of the ninth century through Sergius who, like Constantine-Silvanus, had been won by reading the Gospels and Paul's epistles. Sergius became a travelling preacher, supporting himself by working at his trade as a carpenter. In the ninth century, persecuted, some of the Paulicians took refuge in Moslem territory and from there harassed the borders of the Empire.

Still more of the Paulicians moved into the Balkans in the tenth century, especially into Bulgaria. Here they seem to have contributed to a dissident movement, Bogomilism, which continued for many centuries.

Early in the ninth century we hear of another heresy, that of the Athingani. The Athingani were in Phrygia, in Asia Minor, and may have been a branch of the Paulicians. They, too, were persecuted by the state at the instance of the official church.

The Revival of the Byzantine Church and Renewed Strains in Relations with Rome

As we have suggested, recovery to Christianity from the disasters which accompanied the disintegration of the Roman Empire began in the Eastern branch of the Catholic Church in the ninth century. It was well under way by 950, when the decisive upswing in the Western branch of the Catholic Church was about to become noticeable. The revival in the Byzantine Church was associated with the period which was spanned by the Macedonian dynasty, 867 to 1056, a period of about two centuries. The iconoclastic controversy which had so long wrought internal turmoil in the Church was ended, and external foes were less of a menace than they had been or were to be later. The capital of the Caliphate had been moved from Damascus to Baghdad, so that the threat from the Arabs to Asia Minor was not as acute as formerly. On the eastern border, Armenia, a professedly Christian state, was under strong rulers and was having its golden age. To be sure, external dangers had not passed, for in 904 the second city in the Empire, Salonika, was sacked by Moslem corsairs from Crete, in 910 a Byzantine expedition against Crete was defeated, and in the fore part of the tenth century Bulgaria, a near rival, had its great day. But, as we are to see, the height of Bulgarian power was under a Christian ruler and was evidence of the triumph of Christianity in that realm. In the second half of the tenth and the first half of the eleventh century Byzantine power attained its highest point since the beginning of the Arab conquests. The Church shared in the prosperity.

In the first half of the tenth century, that is, the last fifty years of the period with which we are here dealing, before the rise of the Holy Roman Empire of the German nation, the Byzantine Empire was the strongest state in Europe. However, neither it nor that German state which bore the Roman name was nearly as wealthy or as extensive as the Roman Empire had been in its prime, and in territory and population both were very minor powers as compared with China, united as that great land was by the Sung dynasty which came into being in 960.

The resurgence of the Byzantine realm and church was accompanied by renewed strains between the Eastern and Western wings of the Catholic Church.

An outstanding figure in the vigorous life of the Byzantine Church in the second half of the ninth century and one who became a storm centre in the relations between the Eastern and Western wings of the Catholic Church was Photius. Photius came from an eminent Byzantine family of ancient Greek stock and was related to Emperors. During the iconoclastic controversy his father had suffered persecution because of his loyalty to the icons. His uncle, Tarasius, had been the Patriarch who presided at the Council of Nicæa in 787. Photius was a distinguished scholar, the centre of the intellectual renaissance which was one of the features of the revival in Byzantine life. In his house the intelligentsia gathered for the reading and discussion of ancient and recent Greek literature, pagan and Christian. He was a favourite at court and, a civil official, was president of the imperial chancellery when, in 858, he was made Patriarch of Constantinople in succession to Ignatius, who had resigned. Like Tarasius, therefore, he came to the post from civil office.

Ignatius, the son of an Emperor and made a eunuch in his youth by political enemies, had been brought to power in the midst of bitter division in the Church by Theodora, whose part in the restoration of the icons we have already noted. Ignatius was almost immediately a centre of controversy. Honest and zealous, revered by later generations as a saint, he seems to have proved tactless and not to have been worldly-wise. Certainly he alienated many and was regarded by the intellectuals as both ignorant and contemptuous of Greek philosophy. Soon after being made Patriarch he committed, perhaps out of ignorance, the serious *faux pas* of sending a pallium to the Pope, implying that he had the right to invest the latter with that symbol of his office. The Pope, quite understandably, replied that he gave the pallium to bishops but did not receive it from others.

In the controversies between Ignatius and his opponents appeal was made to Rome by both parties, for in theory the Latin and the Greek Church were both in the Catholic Church and the Pope was recognized as having great even if not supreme authority. Among others, Ignatius had as antagonists the young

Emperor, Michael III, and the latter's uncle and most influential minister, Bardas, the successful rival of Theodora for the control of that pleasure-loving monarch. Ignatius publicly refused the communion to Bardas, alleging, perhaps on insufficient grounds, that the latter was guilty of incest. Bardas had Ignatius deported to a convenient island and the latter abdicated and urged his friends to join in electing a new Patriarch.

Photius seems to have been chosen because he was acceptable both to the opponents and to the friends of Ignatius. He was regularly elected by a synod of bishops called for that purpose. A layman, he was hurried through all the degrees of the priesthood in one week. This was contrary to canon law, but for it there was much precedent. Bishops from both the friends and opponents of Ignatius joined in consecrating the new Patriarch. His elevation seemed to have brought peace to the Church.

The concord had lasted only a few weeks when the conflict between the parties in the Church broke out more furiously than ever. Some of the prelates revolted against Photius, Bardas, and Michael III and insisted on the restoration of Ignatius. They were replaced by men who were friendly to Photius, but the vast majority of the monks would not recognize the latter's authority. The monastery of Studius, so active in advocacy of the icons, led in the opposition. In 861 a synod was held in Constantinople at which Papal legates were present, instructed by their master to investigate. Here Ignatius appeared, denied that he had appealed to Rome, and challenged the competence of the Roman representatives. The latter ratified the deposition of Ignatius. The action of Rome was based on the claim that, as recognized by a much earlier council at Sardica, the Pope had the right to re-try a case against any bishop. The synod also passed acts designed to control some of the abuses in the monasteries, and thus confirmed the enmity of many monks against Photius and his supporters.

The Pope, who was the vigorous Nicholas I, while not at first repudiating his legates in joining in the confirmation of the deposition of Ignatius, did not yet recognize Photius or enter into communion with him. He was eager to extend the control of Rome over the Bulgarians who, as we are to see, were about to be converted, and also to restore to his direct jurisdiction Illyricum, which had been transferred to the Patriarch of Constantinople by Byzantine monarchs who, as Roman Emperors, claimed that right. The Pope, presumably, would have recognized Photius had the latter acceded to his territorial desires, but this Photius would not do. In 863 the Pope held a synod in Rome which, acting on the conviction that the Papal legates had exceeded their authority in 861, stripped Photius of all ecclesiastical dignity and restored Ignatius to the

Patriarchate. The Emperor, Michael III, refused to admit the competence of Rome in such matters and said so frankly to the Pope.

In replying, Nicholas I asserted in no uncertain terms what he held to be the prerogatives of the Papal see and declared that through the clear words of Christ himself the Popes had power "over all the earth, that is, over the entire Church" and insisted that no council of the Church could be called without the Pope's consent—conveniently disregarding the fact that earlier ecumenical councils had been called by the Emperor and had been presided over either by him or his representative. Here was an assertion by the Pope of the Church's independence of the power of the state and of his authority in the Church. The latter was not new and practice, even in Constantinople, had been tending in the direction of the former.

The situation was still further complicated by developments in Bulgaria. There the king, Boris, under pressure from Constantinople, had accepted baptism from the hands of Greek clergy sent by Photius. Greeks, Armenians, and Paulicians poured into the country instructing the populace in the new faith. Boris wished to have his church free from both Rome and Constantinople, and in an effort to gain as favourable terms as possible played off each against the other. He wished a patriarch of his own but might compromise on an archbishop. Rome sent two bishops who engaged in instruction and baptism. Missionaries also came from the Franks, who adhered to the Latin form of Christianity.

The close juxtaposition of missionaries from the two wings of the Church brought into sharp relief the differences which had developed across the years. The Latins had a celibate clergy and confirmation was only by a bishop. The Greek priests were married (to them, as we have noted, the Roman insistence on a celibate clergy smacked of Manichæism) and confirmation was by the priest. Moreover, the Latins were putting *filioque* into the creed which is usually called Nicene, saying that the Holy Spirit proceeds from the Father and the Son, whereas the original of the formula spoke of the Holy Spirit only as proceeding from the Father. The insertion had developed in the West in conflict with Arian Christianity, the faith of the Goths who ruled in Spain and part of Italy. To state their position as against the Arians the Catholic Latin clergy had framed a creed (possibly, as we have seen, originally a hymn) which was commonly given the name of Athanasius, because the Arians called the Catholics Athanasians. That creed had *filioque*. The Latins added the phrase to the Nicene Symbol, presumably to bring that and the Athanasian Symbol into accord. This seems to have been done first at Toledo in Spain in 589 or 653 to signalize the conversion of the Visigoths from Arianism to Catholicism. While in St. Peter's in Rome the Popes did not use *filioque* until early in the eleventh century, the custom had gradually spread through the West and in 809 under Charlemagne a synod at Aachen had given its approval. The Greeks were not averse to saying that the Holy Spirit proceeds from the Father through the Son, but objected to saying "and the Son." Then, too, in contrast with Greek custom, the Latins fasted on Saturdays and used milk, butter, and cheese in Lent.

The struggle for Bulgaria continued. At first Boris seemed to have been won by the Pope's envoys. Partly to offset this success, in 867 Photius called a synod in Constantinople which condemned Pope Nicholas and tried to wean the Franks from him by acclaiming, with the consent of Michael and Bardas, the Carolingian Louis II of that people as joint Emperor.

Then came a sudden reversal. Basil "the Macedonian," of humble Armenian origin, murdered Bardas (866), was made joint Emperor with Michael, and in 867 had the latter assassinated while drunk. These deaths deprived Photius of his two most powerful backers and freed Ignatius, who was still living, from his most influential enemies. Basil had the support of the party of Ignatius. Under the circumstances, Photius resigned and Ignatius was reinstated as Patriarch.

Hoping to bring unity in the Byzantine Church, Basil now referred to the Pope the whole tangled issue of Ignatius and Photius. A new pontiff, Hadrian II, was now on the chair of Peter. At a synod in Rome in 869 Hadrian decided against Photius and for Ignatius. In 869–870 a poorly attended synod was held in Constantinople, some members of which assented to the Papal condemnation of Photius. However, there was no enthusiasm for conforming with Rome and in spite of the protest of the Pope's representatives, by action of Basil, to whom the synod referred the question, Bulgaria was placed under the Patriarch of Constantinople. Ignatius then consecrated an archbishop and several bishops for Bulgaria. This angered the Pope, who held that his recognition of Ignatius had been conditional upon the latter's assent to the Roman claims in Bulgaria.

A reconciliation was effected between Basil and Photius and the latter returned to court as a tutor to the Emperor's sons. Ignatius and Photius also seem to have made peace with each other. When the former died, in 877, the latter quietly succeeded him as Patriarch. From then until 886 his influence in Church and state was at its height.

In 879–880 a largely attended council met in Constantinople. Photius presided. The Papal legates, in the name of the Pope, John VIII, joined with the council and the representatives of the three other Patriarchs—Jerusalem, Antioch, and Alexandria—in recognizing Photius as the legitimate and canonically elected Patriarch. The action taken against Photius by Pope Hadrian II was repudiated by Pope John's representative. Nothing was said about *filioque*, for in Rome that had not yet been added to the creed. Pope John VIII, although admonishing Photius for his lack of humility, confirmed his reinstatement. The breach between the Western and Eastern wings of the Catholic Church was technically healed. Yet differences remained and were to come again to the fore.

As to Photius, some of the partisans of Ignatius remained recalcitrant. On the death of the Emperor Basil, in 886, the latter's son, Leo, who came to the throne, was hostile and Photius resigned. He lived on, but how long we do not know. Within a few decades after his death he was canonized by the Byzantine Church.

We have devoted to Photius and the events associated with him a much larger amount of space than may at first sight seem warranted. We have done so for several reasons. Photius himself is important, for he was one of the ablest ecclesiastics produced by the Byzantine Church. His career provides a window by which we may gain insight into that church, its politics, the fashion in which it was related to the state, and a little of its life. From it we can also glean some understanding of the state of the Catholic Church in the ninth century. We see it as continuing to think of itself as one and as intimately related to the Roman Empire. That Empire, although sadly diminished in area since the days of Constantine or even Justinian, was still regarded as inseparable from the Catholic Church. In theory there was a Christian society of which the Roman Empire was the civil phase and the Catholic Church, which included all true Christians, cared for what might be called the religious side. The Emperor had power in the Church, although that was being challenged in the West and now and then was being questioned in the East. In the Catholic Church the Pope asserted his primacy and to some degree was so acknowledged in both East and West. Yet East and West were continuing to drift apart. Even before Photius, in 781, the Popes had ceased to date their documents by the regnal years of the Emperors in Constantinople and in 800 a Pope had crowned Charlemagne as Roman Emperor. This was followed in the ninth century by the coronation by the Popes of some of the successors of Charlemagne. Carolingian Emperors regarded themselves as the Western colleagues of the Eastern monarchs and held the Empire to be still one. Towards the end of the reign of Charlemagne the Emperors in Constantinople assented to that claim. In actuality division was in progress. Not only were strains chronic, but from time to time they became so acute that actual schisms appeared. Thus far these schisms were temporary, but from the vantage of the perspective of a later age we can now see that they would eventually become permanent.

In spite of protestations to the contrary, the only true Christian unity, that of love, was largely lacking and from time to time the administrative structure which presented to the world an impressive façade and provided an opportunity for unity broke down and at best only partially hid the basic conflicts. These were primarily in sectional loyalties, in ecclesiastical customs, and in the rivalry between the sees of Rome and Constantinople. Popes and Patriarchs stood up for the authority of their respective offices and, perhaps unconsciously, under the guise of adherence to principle were jealous for their personal prestige and power. As we have seen, the Catholic Church had grown up within the inclusive political framework provided by the Roman Empire. It survived that realm, but after the scaffolding of the Empire fell away its inherent cohesion was not strong enough to hold it permanently together.

THE NORTHWARD EXPANSION OF BYZANTINE CHRISTIANITY

The expansion of the Byzantine wing of the Catholic Church to the east was long estopped by the chronic warfare between the Roman Empire and the Zoroastrian Sassanian dynasty which ruled in Mesopotamia and Persia. Beginning with the seventh century expansion to both east and south was effectively blocked by Islam.

However, to the north the situation was not so forbidding. To be sure, pagans, largely Slavs, Avars, and Bulgars, had broken through the imperial defenses and had settled in what had once been imperial and Christian territory. Slavs had infiltrated into Macedonia, Epirus, Greece, and Asia Minor. Scandinavians, the Northmen, moving southward, had taken possession of part of what was later to be Russia and were raiding the Byzantine coasts. In 860, for example, they attacked Constantinople itself. In the 890's the pagan Magyars established themselves in the modern Hungary. Yet these invaders were of a "lower" stage of "civilization" than were the Christian Greeks and tended to adopt the latter's culture and religion. Before the middle of the tenth century the conversion of all of these except the Northmen—the Varangians—north of the Black Sea was well under way. Moreover, through contacts made possible by commerce, Byzantine Christianity was spreading among the peoples of the Caucasus.

Beginning with the reconquest of North Africa, under Justinian, as we have seen, Catholic Christianity resumed the expansion in that region which had been interrupted by the Vandal occupation in the preceding century. Numbers of the Berbers were converted. However, the Arab conquest brought that to an end and, as we have noted, Christianity rapidly lost ground.

In lands which remained under the administration of the Byzantine continuation of the Roman Empire the conversion of the invaders was part of the assimilation to "Christian" Greek culture. Following Roman practice, the imperial armies were in part recruited from "barbarian" peoples. Since the state was officially Christian, festivals were regularly observed among the troops in honour of the Virgin Mary and the saints, and the armies were deemed to be fighting in behalf of the Catholic faith. Those who came into the ranks as pagans would, therefore, speedily conform. In Asia Minor, Greece, Macedonia, and Epirus, conversions seem to have come about unspectacularly and through the ordinary machinery of the diocesan organization. We hear of the monks of Mt. Athos baptizing a large body of Slavs. The Patriarch of Constantinople appointed inspectors to oversee the work of conversion in the European provinces. We read of men of Slavic blood high in the Church, among them at least one Patriarch of Constantinople.

The conversion of the Slavs outside the areas which were continuously under the political control of Constantinople proceeded more slowly, but made rapid progress in the second half of the ninth century. Some of it, as we are to see, was through German missionaries and to the Latin wing of the Catholic Church. Some, however, usually that in the regions nearest Constantinople, was by missionaries from the Greek Church.

The most famous of the early missionaries to the Slavs from the Eastern wing of the Catholic Church were the two brothers, Constantine (also known as Cyril from the name which he assumed late in life) and Methodius. Shortly before the year 852 the Moravians were won to a nominal profession of the Christian faith. Precisely how that was accomplished we do not know, but within a few years Italian, German, and Greek missionaries were said to be labouring among them. Sometime in the years 861, 862, or 863 the prince of the Moravians, Rastislav, himself a Christian, asked the Byzantine Emperor for missionaries to instruct his people. That Emperor was Michael III whom we have already met in connexion with the end of the iconoclastic controversy and with Photius. Michael, often contemptuously known as "the drunkard," was more noted for his dissipations than his piety. However, in his name and perhaps at the instance of his minister, Bardas, and on the recommendation of Photius, then in the first period of his patriarchate, the brothers were appointed.

Methodius and Constantine are said to have been sons of a prominent citizen of Salonika, an officer in the army. Methodius was the older and may have been a civil official before entering the monastic life. Constantine, the younger, is reported to have gained distinction as a teacher and philosopher and to have been a missionary to the Khazars in what is now Russia. Tradition has it that before the brothers left Constantinople Constantine had devised a script for the writing of Slavonic and had begun the translation of the Gospels into that tongue. Whether this was the first reduction of Slavonic to writing we do not know, nor are we sure which of the ancient Slavonic alphabets, the Cyrillic or the Glagolithic, was his work.

Rastislav received the brothers with honour and they began the instruction for which they had come. Constantine continued his translation and put the liturgy and some other religious literature into Slavonic. In doing this he was following the custom of the East, where the Bible and the services of the Church were customarily in the vernacular. However, in Moravia he met opposition. This was probably from German clergy who were penetrating that region. Jealous of Byzantine influence, they maintained that the only languages permissible in the Eucharist were the three which were alleged to have been in Pilate's placard on the cross of Christ—Hebrew, Greek, and Latin. This became a cause of controversy with the Germans which was to plague the lives of both brothers.

Methodius and Cyril went to Rome (868), thus acknowledging the authority of the see of Peter. This must have been balm to the soul of the Pope, then Hadrian II, as recognition of his authority by Greek priests in his dispute for jurisdiction with the Patriarch of Constantinople. Yet the Pope wished to avoid giving unnecessary offense to the powerful Germans. He is said to have received the brothers cordially, to have given approval to the Slavonic service books, to have permitted the use of Slavonic in the Eucharist in some of the churches in Rome, and to have made arrangements for the ordination of several of the candidates for the priesthood who had come to Rome with the missionaries. Constantine died in Rome (February 14, 869).

Heeding a last wish of his brother, Methodius continued the mission to the Slavs. Possibly at the request of one of the Slavic princes, the Pope revived an ancient bishopric in Illyricum and appointed Methodius to it, presumably welcoming this opportunity to strengthen, through a Greek, the jurisdiction which he claimed in that area. The Germans were offended. Methodius was tried and condemned by a synod of Germans and for two years and a half was confined in a German monastery. The Pope eventually obtained his release, rebuked two German bishops who were involved, and ordered his restoration to his see. Yet Rome compromised with the Germans and Pope John VIII, he who confirmed the reinstatement of Photius, ordered Methodius not to use Slavonic. Perhaps, in view of the needs of the mission in Bulgaria, John later relented and permitted Slavonic in the services of the Church. John (c.879) made Methodius archbishop and head of the hierarchy for the Moravians. Methodius is said to have visited Constantinople in 882 and to have been received cordially by Photius. Photius established in Constantinople a school for Slavonic studies. This became a refuge for Slavonic priests who had been sold into slavery by a hostile prince and had then been freed by Venetians and sent to Constantinople. Methodius died in 884 or 885.

The course of the pupils of Methodius continued to be troubled. Probably at the instance of German clergy, Rome again withdrew its permission for the use of Slavonic. In the year 900 the pagan Magyars crossed the Danube, soon made themselves the masters of much of the area in which Constantine and Methodius had laboured, and Christianity suffered. Yet the work of translating Christian literature into Slavonic went on and contributed greatly to the spread and nourishment of the Christian faith in Bulgaria and, after 950, in Russia.

It was through the Byzantine wing of the Catholic Church that Christianity made its chief gains among the Serbs. The Emperor Heraclius (reigned 610–641), whom we have already met in connexion with the Monothelete controversy and the Persian and Arab invasions, sent missionaries who baptized some of the Serbs. In the second half of the ninth century Basil I attacked the Serbian pirates who were preying on commerce, swept them off the seas, laid waste their strongholds, and, sending them priests, compelled them to accept baptism.

We have already had occasion to say something of the conversion of Bulgaria. That, however, is so important that it demands a more comprehensive statement. The Bulgars were a people of Asiatic origin and of Turkish or Hunnish stock. In the second half of the seventh century they had made themselves masters of extensive territories north of Constantinople. They were so near that capital that they repeatedly threatened it, especially in those perilous decades when the Arabs were making great gains. They were a minority who ruled over a population which was predominantly Slav.

As we have seen, the Khagan or King of the Bulgars, Boris, was baptized in 864 or 865. Boris seems to have been considering that step for some time. One of the Carolingians, Louis the German, whom Boris had defeated, believed that he had persuaded him to receive the rite. While the Bulgarian army was out of the country assisting Louis, the Byzantine forces invaded the country and Boris purchased peace by ceding some territory, promising to withdraw from his alliance with Louis, acknowledging the suzerainty of Michael III, and accepting baptism. Envoys of his were baptized in Constantinople and a mission of Greek clergy sent by Photius went to Bulgaria and baptized the prince himself.

This act of Boris precipitated a rebellion of the Bulgar aristocracy. It may be that Boris wished to use his new faith as a means towards introducing European civilization and of strengthening his own power as against that of the nobles. We shall see that happening in more than one kingdom in succeeding centuries. To this the nobles would quite understandably object. Boris put down the rebellion and furthered the instruction and baptism of his subjects. As we have noted, missionaries came from the Byzantine Empire—Greeks,

Armenians, and Paulicians—and a mass conversion was soon in progress. Missionaries also entered from the West.

We have remarked that Boris wished to have a patriarch of his own for Bulgaria. It may be that his motive was in part to make certain that the Bulgarian church would not be used to further the political designs of either the Byzantines or the Germans. It is probable that he at least wished to have his realm and his church on a full equality with Constantinople. We have reported how he bargained with both the Pope and the Patriarch of Constantinople to attain this ambition and took advantage of the rivalry between the two sees to gain his end. Boris did not at once obtain a patriarch, but in 870 Ignatius consecrated a Bulgar as archbishop and sent him with ten bishops and many priests to his new see. In spite of the surrender by Photius in 879–880, as part of his peace-making with Rome, of his patriarchal powers in Bulgaria, Boris continued relations with Constantinople. This was natural, for that city was much nearer than Rome. He sent a younger son, Simeon, to Constantinople to be educated as a monk, presumably with the hope that he would return to head the church in Bulgaria, thus keeping both state and church in the hands of one family.

Some of the Slavonic clergy who had been trained by Constantine and Methodius and who had found their old homes impossible were welcomed by Boris. The latter was trying to bring about an amalgamation of the Bulgars with the subject Slav majority and to that end was encouraging Slavonic literature. One of the exiles, Clement of Ochrid, probably a Byzantine Slav, was sent by Boris to Macedonia and there established a school for training clergy and translating sacred books. Later he became a bishop.

In 889 Boris resigned his throne and retired to a monastery which he had founded near his capital as a centre of Slavic Christian culture and was succeeded by his eldest son, Vladimir. However, Vladimir led a pagan reaction. Around him gathered the nobles who were opposed to the innovations of Boris—Christianity, the new customs associated with that faith, and the centralizing of authority in the monarch. After a few years Boris, thoroughly aroused, emerged from his retirement, deposed Vladimir, had him blinded and placed in confinement, called a national council, and had Simeon chosen for the vacancy. He also induced the assembly to substitute Slavonic for Greek as the language of the Bulgarian church. Feeling his life work now to be secure, Boris once more retired to his monastery.

Under Simeon Bulgaria enjoyed its golden age. Simeon renounced the monastic life for which he had been trained, but he furthered the growth of Bulgarian literature. This was in Slavonic and was made up mostly of translations from Greek. It was from Bulgaria that Slavonic literature spread to other

Slavic peoples. Under Simeon the formal conversion of the land to Christianity was completed. He also fulfilled his father's vision of a realm legally on an equality with the Byzantine Empire. He surrounded himself with the splendour and ceremonial which he had seen in Constantinople, assumed the title of "the Tsar and Autocrat of all Bulgarians," thus giving his crown a title on a par with that of the Macedonian dynasty in Constantinople, and had the Bulgarian bishops declare (918) the Bulgarian Church fully independent (autocephalous) and place a patriarch at its head. The patriarch crowned Simeon, hailing him with the imperial title. At first the Patriarch of Constantinople was unreconciled to these changes, but Rome seems to have accepted them, and in 927, the year of Simeon's death, Constantinople also assented. The Bulgarian Church was orthodox in doctrine, but independent in administration. By Simeon's initiative it was the first to establish the tradition, later characteristic of the family of Orthodox Churches, of being reciprocally independent of one another administratively, but of agreeing in doctrine and regarding the Patriarch of Constantinople as a kind of *primus inter pares* among their heads. In the first half of the eleventh century, less than a century after Simeon's death, the Byzantine Emperor Basil II conquered the country, made it a Byzantine province, and cancelled the Bulgarian patriarchate. But Bulgaria continued to be professedly Christian.

Just when and how the peoples of the Caucasus became Christians we do not know. Conversion began well before the sixth century, but it continued after that time and seems largely to have been through Byzantine influence. Some of it was in the reign of Justinian. The conversion of the Alans is said to have been in the eighth century. Contacts with Byzantine commerce and culture by way of the Black Sea, long a Greek lake, furthered the process. The birth of the largest offshoot of the Byzantine Church, that of Russia, was not to come until shortly after 950.

THE EFFECT OF THE BYZANTINE ENVIRONMENT ON CHRISTIANITY

What effects did the Byzantine environment have upon the Christianity which was so closely associated with it? We have seen that the Eastern and Western wings of the Catholic Church tended to drift apart and we have noted some of the differences which were the ostensible causes of the friction between Latin and Greek Christianity. But were there other characteristics, perhaps permeating more deeply the genius of the Eastern wing, which can be attributed to the Greek and Byzantine influence?

We must say at the outset that the Byzantine Church was Catholic. That is to say, it inherited those features of the Catholic Church which had been developed in the first five centuries. Its administrative structure, with its bishops and patriarchs, was that which had arisen in the Roman Empire and in its main outlines it remained much as we have already met it. It accepted the creeds and the doctrine which are associated with the first four ecumenical councils and assented to the findings of the three councils held in the period covered by this chapter. Its liturgy, its sacraments, and its monasticism were a continuation and outgrowth of those of the earlier centuries. Indeed, it thought of itself, as do its successors, the Orthodox Churches of today, as the guardian of true Christianity, the possessor and custodian of the Catholic faith.

Yet this Byzantine Christianity displayed features which were peculiar to it and which must be attributed in part to the milieu in which it inescapably had its existence. These were not in formal dogmas, for those remained substantially unaltered, but were, rather, in practices and in temper.

First of all we must remind ourselves of what we have again and again had occasion to notice, the effect upon the Church of the close relation with the state. Beginning with Constantine, the first formally to accept the Christian faith, the Emperors sought to control the Church and to make it serve the state and society as they had the non-Christian official cults. That tradition was strengthened in the sixth and seventh centuries by Justinian and other strong Emperors, and was what has been termed cæsaropapism. The Emperors called church councils and presided at them either in person or by deputies. They issued decrees on ecclesiastical matters. Although technically they had only the right of nomination, they often virtually appointed the Patriarch of Constantinople. No Patriarch could hold office without their consent. Until late in the eighth century elections to the Papacy were confirmed by them. The subordination of Church to state persisted and today is seen in the family of Orthodox Churches.

Yet the Church was not as fully mastered by the state as the pre-Christian official cults had been. From time to time individuals and groups within the Church protested, and by the middle of the tenth century a partial independence had been achieved. At times the Church forced the Emperor to make concessions. We have noted that the monks, who in theory had given themselves fully to the Christian faith, repeatedly refused to conform to the orders of the state. This was seen especially under the iconoclastic Emperors, when they spear-headed the opposition to the government's efforts to remove the images. The Studites, led by their most famous member, Theodore, were particularly uncompromising in the later stages of the struggle. After the controversy had been decided in their favour, they opposed the imperial policy on some other issues. The Patriarch Tarasius rather than the Emperor or one of the latter's representatives from among the civil officials presided over the Seventh Ecumenical Council, in 787. From time to time a Patriarch or some other spokesman for the Church insisted that the Emperor and other high officials must in morals be fully as subject to the discipline of the Church as the humblest Christian. The principle came to be recognized that to be valid the coronation of the Emperor must be by the Patriarch of Constantinople as the ranking bishop in the Eastern wing of the Church. A strong Patriarch might exact promises from a compliant Emperor as a condition for officiating. Thus early in the ninth century the Patriarch obtained from the incoming Emperor a written pledge to preserve the orthodox faith, not to shed the blood of Christians, and not to scourge ecclesiastics.

A second characteristic was the growing sterility in theological thought. Theology continued to be a major subject of study and writing. The Patriarch Photius, for example, was deeply learned in that field as in so many others. Yet, as we have seen, the most famous theological work of this period, *The Fountain of Knowledge* by John of Damascus, had in it little that was new, but owed its fame to its competent and comprehensive summary of views already endorsed by the Catholic Church.

Why this sterility? We do not know. As we have suggested, it may have been because of the fact that the Byzantine realm was prevailingly on the defensive, fighting to preserve its waning remnant of the Roman Empire against encroaching invaders and that this made it conservative, hostile to major change of any kind. This was especially the case after Justinian, and notably so after the beginning of the Arab invasions.

A third characteristic was the emphasis upon the public services and especially upon the liturgy through which the Eucharist was celebrated. They were marked by ornate pomp. Much of this may have been because of the prosperity of Constantinople. The Byzantine Empire centred about that city and was dominated by it. As the metropolis of Europe, living primarily by its commerce, it was wealthy and its upper classes were luxurious. The imperial court was noted for its splendour. To this Justinian had added. It was to be expected that the great church built by him, Saint Sophia, would be rich in mosaics and that ceremonies in it would match those in the imperial court. Since it was the cathedral church of the Patriarch and the leading ecclesiastical structure of the realm, in the other church edifices so far as possible efforts were made to duplicate what was done in it.

From this emphasis upon the formal public worship of the Church may have come the tendency to regard religion as primarily the correct performance of the liturgy. Religion was by no means completely divorced from ethics, nor were morals regarded as purely private. The state was supposed to follow Christian principles and ascetic anchorites gave spiritual and moral counsel, not only to private individuals on matters of faith and conduct, but also to high officials, including Emperors, on policies of state. Yet there was in this Byzantine Christianity less of activism and more of other-worldliness than in its Latin counterpart.

This other-worldliness may also have been seen in the stress on Easter and the resurrection. The Latin wing, while by no means belittling that festival, made more of the crucifixion and the atonement. This may have reflected the tendency in the Greek tradition as it developed in Hellenistic times to emphasize the distinction between matter and spirit, to regard the former as evil and the latter as good, and to think of salvation and immortality as the emancipation of spirit from flesh. Latin Christianity, on the other hand, may have reflected the Roman regard for law and administration, with the desire to realize an ideal society here and now and the conviction that conformity to good morals is one of the essential features of such a society.

A fourth characteristic of Byzantine religion, and especially of Byzantine monasticism, seemingly related to this last, was the trend towards ascetic withdrawal from the world, with mysticism and contemplation. This can easily be exaggerated. The same characteristic was to be found in the Christianity of the West. Yet as the centuries passed, the activist element in Latin monasticism became increasingly prominent and the contemplative, non-resisting, non-activist, mystical strain in Byzantine monasticism and especially in its most numerous offspring, Russian monks and monasteries, became more marked. It is significant that for centuries the most widely used writings on mysticism in Christian circles were those ascribed to Dionysius the Areopagite and that they were written in the East and were profoundly shaped by Neoplatonism.

The Effect of Christianity upon Byzantine Life and Culture

Fully as important as the question of the effect of the Byzantine environment upon Christianity is that of the influence of Christianity upon those peoples and individuals who lived under Byzantine rule.

First it must be noted that Christianity contributed markedly to the unity of the Byzantine Empire. Christianity was the official faith of that realm. Closely associated as it was from near its outset with Hellenism, it furthered the assimilation of the non-Hellenistic elements in the Empire. Especially after the Teutonic and Arab conquests lopped from the Empire most of its non-Hellenistic provinces, that realm was a Greek Christian state. The remaining non-Hellenistic constituencies were absorbed, together with those northern invaders who settled within the imperial domains. Wars against the Zoroastrian Persians and the Moslem Arabs were regarded as holy, and religious enthusiasm contributed to the resolution with which they were waged.

In the second place, Christian influence was increasingly seen in the laws of the Byzantine Empire. When the famous Institutes of Justinian are compared with those of the non-Christian Gaius of the second century, they are seen to have alterations in the laws of marriage and succession, in regard to chastity, and concerning the exposure of infants which reflect the Christian convictions of the later rulers. In the *Ecloga,* promulgated in the eighth century, after Christianity had a longer time in which to make itself felt, the marks of that faith are even more evident. References to the Scriptures for confirmation for legal principles are numerous, every concubine was made a wife, and punishment for fornication, formerly left to the Church, was included. In the *Basilics,* issued in the latter part of the ninth century, Christianity is still more prominent. The first book is devoted to the Holy Trinity and the Catholic faith, and three books are given to ecclesiastical law.

In the third place, the Christian impress on Byzantine architecture and art was profound and creative. Byzantine architecture had its most glorious expression in Saint Sophia, built, as we have seen, at the command of Justinian. It embodied a pattern which appears to have had one of its roots in the churches in Syria, Mesopotamia, and Armenia and which was developed primarily for the purposes of Christian worship. Much of pre-Christian art persisted, including pagan themes, but the mosaics and frescoes for which Byzantine churches are famous were inspired primarily by Christ, his mother, and Christian saints and stories. Manuscripts were illuminated, often with Christian scenes.

Byzantine literature was to a large degree religious and concerned itself with Christian subjects. Theology, the devotional life, hymns, lives of the saints, and sermons were obviously from Christian sources and made up a large proportion of Byzantine libraries. The hymns of Romanos of the sixth century, of Andrew of Crete of the seventh and eighth centuries, and of John of Damascus are especially memorable. Romanos developed the form of hymn which became characteristic of the Byzantine Church.

The effects of Christianity in individual lives were marked and varied. We have seen it in a few outstanding figures, some of them Patriarchs and others of them monks. Always it is difficult to measure precisely. Perhaps it is best observed in the ideals portrayed in the biographies of those who were regarded as saints. Even when men did not conform to them these standards reveal what was believed to be Christian.

We must frankly recognize, however, that Byzantine culture fell far short of the full realization of the new life stressed by Christ. There was much study of the pre-Christian Greek philosophers and many of the Byzantine scholars were basically pagan with only a superficial and quite perfunctory conformity with the official Christianity. Something of a revival of classical studies came in the ninth and tenth centuries, and this in spite of the opposition of monks who condemned it as a reversion to heathenism and associated it with the iconoclasm which was so repugnant to them. The centuries-long absorption with doctrine controversy led to an emphasis upon orthodoxy in intellectual belief and verbal profession, but tended to belittle ethical practice. Constantinople was a commercial city and its inhabitants were noted for suavity and a trickery in trade which their professed faith did little to amend. There was also much of perfidy and cruelty. Now and again an ascetic or a Patriarch would admonish an Emperor not to take life, but this seems to have had little effect upon the behaviour of the rulers or their officials.

Yet not all teaching and preaching was purely doctrinal. In the writings of the period we come across emphasis upon following the example of Christ in gentleness, humility, pardoning the sinner, not repaying evil for evil, and forgiving one's enemies. Theodore of Studius taught that the true Christian is a copy or impression of Christ. Here and there, too, comes a gleam in an individual in high ecclesiastical position. Thus, at the time of the Byzantine-Persian wars of the early years of the seventh century, the Catholic Patriarch of Alexandria was John, who was known as the Almsgiver. From an eminent family in Cyprus, a devout layman whose wife and children had died, he had been chosen for the post at the desire of the Emperor Heraclius. A prelate who refused compromising presents, he lived simply, almost austerely, and devoted the revenues of his see chiefly to the poor and to the refugees from the Persian conquest of Palestine. He humbly sought reconciliation with one of his clergy who had become alienated from him, endeavoured to enforce uniformity in weights and measures in that commercial city where variable standards had made for much dishonesty, and increased the salaries of his stewards to render it unnecessary for them to eke out their stipends by receiving bribes. The fact that his biography, recounting his deeds of virtue, could be written in popular literary style and have a wide circulation is evidence that when such a life appeared it was recognized as Christian and was held up for emulation. Presumably to every record of one such individual which has been preserved, there were hundreds, perhaps thousands of lives which bore the impress of Christ which have not left any written evidence of their existence.

Selected Bibliography

GENERAL WORKS WHICH INCLUDE IMPORTANT SECTIONS OF THE RELIGIOUS ASPECTS OF BYZANTINE HISTORY

H. H. Baynes and H. St. L. B. Moss, editors, *Byzantium. An Introduction to East Roman Civilization* (Oxford, The Clarendon Press, 1948, pp. xxxi, 436). Chapters by several experts, an extensive bibliography, and a sheaf of illustrations.

J. B. Bury, *History of the Later Roman Empire from the Death of Theodosius I to the Death of Justinian* (A.D. 395 to A.D. 565). Vol. II (London, Macmillan & Co.,

1923, pp. lx, 494). Covers the sixth century to the death of Justinian. By a master of the subject.

J. B. Bury, *A History of the Eastern Roman Empire from the Fall of Irene to the Accession of Basil I* (A.D. *802–867*) (London, Macmillan & Co., 1912, pp. xv, 530). By the same master hand as the above.

A. A. Vasiliev, *History of the Byzantine Empire. Vol. I, From Constantine the Great to the Epoch of the Crusades* (A.D. *1081*) (*University of Wisconsin Studies in the Social Sciences and History, Number 13*, Madison, 1928, pp. 457). An excellent summary, especially important for its use of Russian works.

A. A. Vasiliev, *Justin the First. An Introduction to the Epoch of Justinian the Great* (Harvard University Press, 1950, pp. viii, 439). Contains an important chapter on Justin's religious policy.

SOURCES

The writings of several of the important figures of the period are in the multivolume J. P. Migne, *Patrologiæ . . . Græca*. For instance, those of Theodore of Studius comprise Vol. 99 and those of Photius fill Vols. 101, 102, 103, and part of 104. The Greek text is given with a Latin translation.

SPECIALIZED WORKS ON VARIOUS ASPECTS OF THE STORY

E. Dawes and N. H. Baynes, *Three Byzantine Saints. Contemporary Biographies Translated from the Greek* (Oxford, Basil Blackwell, 1948, pp. xiv, 275). Not only translations illustrating Byzantine popular Christianity, but also excellent introductions.

F. Dvornik, *Les Slaves, Byzance et Rome au IXe Siècle* (Paris, Ancienne Honoré Champion, 1926, pp. v, 360). Based on a careful study of the sources.

F. Dvornik, *The Photian Schism. History and Legend* (Cambridge University Press, 1948, pp. xiv, 504). A very important detailed critical study.

G. Every, *The Byzantine Patriarchate, 451–1204* (London, Society for Promoting Christian Knowledge, 1947, pp. 212). An excellent survey, especially good on relations with Rome.

A. Gardner, *Theodore of Studium. His Life and Times* (London, Edward Arnold, 1905, pp. xiii, 284). Carefully done.

C. J. Hefele, *A History of the Councils of the Church. Volume IV* (A.D. *451 to* A.D. *680*), translated by W. R. Clark (Edinburgh, T. & T. Clark, 1895, pp. x, 498). Standard on the Fifth Ecumenical Council, Constantinople 553, and the events immediately before and after.

K. S. Latourette, *A History of the Expansion of Christianity. Volume II, The Thousand Years of Uncertainty*, pp. 158–166, 223–249, 286–307 (New York, Harper & Brothers, 1938).

M. Spinka, *A History of Christianity in the Balkans. A Study of the Spread of Byzantine Culture among the Slavs* (Chicago, The American Society of Church History, 1933, pp. 202). Thorough and competent.

Chapter 12

THE SMALLER EASTERN CHURCHES

We have repeatedly noticed the existence of churches which had broken away from the Catholic Church and had ceased to be in communion with it. Until well after the year 950, indeed until the sixteenth century, many more of these were to be found in the East than in the West. Some of these bodies completely died out and we have only fragmentary information about them. Most of that which has reached us has come down from their critics. Such were the Paulicians. Some of the movements which have disappeared differed radically from the Catholic Church not only in doctrine but also in forms of worship and in organization. However, several of the dissident bodies have survived into our own day, although with greatly diminished numbers. As we have suggested, they separated from the Catholic Church ostensibly on questions of doctrine but in reality as much from regional, national, or racial opposition to the dominance of the Byzantine Empire and the Greeks as on creedal grounds. At the outset they were larger than the more drastic dissenters. Beginning with the seventh century, all had to face Islam. Sooner or later, although for some not until after 950, almost all the territories in which they existed were subjugated by Moslems. Identified with national or racial units, they held out against the politically dominant Islam. However, eventually all dwindled in numbers and today none is as strong as it was in the era with which this chapter deals. All that have survived have preserved, with variations, the structure and forms of worship which were theirs before they separated from the Catholic Church. All have a distinct clergy with the main orders of priests and bishops. All have monks and monasteries. All have baptism and the Eucharist, and the latter is usually observed with an elaborate liturgy. Each has its creed. Each regards itself as preserving the Gospel in its purity and looks upon other churches as heretical.

In several of the lands in which these bodies enrolled the majority of those bearing the Christian name, the Catholics were to be found under their own clergy but as minorities for whom a customary designation was Melchite.

There were, as we have seen, "Melchite" or Catholic Patriarchs of Jerusalem, Antioch, and Alexandria.

It was a divided Church which faced the expanding and dominant Islam and the common danger from that rival faith did not bring its severed branches together. Indeed, by removing the common bond of political unity under a professedly Christian state, the Byzantine continuation of the Roman Empire, the Arab conquests led to an accentuation of the gulfs which kept the bodies apart. In Baghdad, for instance, the capital of the Abbasid Caliphs, there were Nestorian, Jacobite, and Melchite communities. There resided the Catholicos or Patriarch of the Nestorians. On at least one occasion when the Melchite Patriarch of Antioch appointed a metropolitan for the Melchites in Baghdad, the Nestorian Catholicos strongly objected to the action as an infringement on his see. But the Jacobites also had a bishop there.

During the earlier centuries of the period from A.D. 500 to A.D. 950, even after the Arab conquests, several of these churches displayed geographic expansion. By A.D. 950, however, and this becomes one reason for fixing that year as the terminal date of the era of the great recession, almost all and perhaps all were losing ground.

We must now take up the chief of these churches one by one and say something of their history. At best we can give them only brief mention. That is partly because the records of some of them are not available to us, but chiefly because, even as early as this period, the main stream of Christianity as measured by inner vitality and the effect upon mankind as a whole did not flow through them. We will begin in the south-west of the areas in which they were present and move northward and eastward.

MONOPHYSITES OF EGYPT, NUBIA, AND ETHIOPIA

We have already had occasion to note the winning of the peoples of Egypt to Christianity. We have seen that the faith seems first to have found rootage in Alexandria in the Greek-speaking elements of that cosmopolitan Hellenistic city and that the head of its Christian community became one of the chief patriarchs in the Catholic Church. We have noted that before the end of the fifth century the faith became rooted among the native Egyptian stock and in time was the dominant religion of the land. To facilitate the integration of the faith in the lives of the masses the Scriptures were translated and other Christian literature was prepared in the vernacular and the services of the Church were carried on in that tongue. We have remarked, too, that this Coptic population followed its leaders in refusing to accept the decisions of the Council of Chalcedon and held to Monophysite views. Monophysites by no means entirely agreed among themselves, and their dissensions, theological and personal, troubled the Coptic Church, but opposition to the Chalcedonian theology was associated with nationalistic resistance to Byzantine rule and in general only the minority, Greeks and those loyal to the Emperor, held to the Catholic faith. On the eve of the Arab conquest the imperial government, represented by the Melchite Patriarch, was taking severe measures to suppress Monophysitism.

At the outset the Arab victories brought relief to the Coptic Christians, for the latter were freed from persecution by Byzantine officials. The Arabs tolerated all the varieties of Christianity and prevented the Copts from taking vengeance on the Catholics. Under Arab rule, therefore, both Copts and Melchites continued. To be sure, Christians were placed under the disabilities which we have already noted as general under the Moslem Arabs, including a discriminatory tax. Within a generation of the conquest a large proportion of the Christian population, both Coptic and Melchite, went over to Islam. Yet Arabs employed many Christians in the government. They utilized Christian artists and architects. Indeed, what we often call Arab architecture seems to have been at least in part the creation of these Christian employees.

As the years passed, Moslem restrictions on Christians were tightened. Early in the eighth century additional financial burdens were placed on the Christians and in that same century persecutions were instituted which led to the apostasy of many, even of several of the bishops, and which were countered by futile revolts that were sternly suppressed. By at least the tenth century Christians were forbidden to attempt to convert Moslems, to marry Moslem women, to speak disparagingly of the Prophet or the Koran, to display crosses, to ring church bells or in other ways to obtrude their faith on Moslems, to erect houses higher than those of Moslems, to ride thoroughbred horses, or to drink wine in public or to allow swine to be seen, since both of these were abhorrent to good Moslems. Now and again Christians won converts from Islam, but such defections from the dominant faith were usually visited with severe penalties.

Yet Christianity persisted. Monasteries, of which Egypt had been the chief early centre, continued and were the main strongholds of the faith. From them, as was general in the Eastern Churches, the bishops were recruited. Although, in their resistance to Islam, the churches tended to hold to the Coptic language in their services, even when Arabic became the vernacular of the masses, some Christian literature was prepared in the latter tongue.

We have noted how, from Egypt, beginning chiefly in the sixth century, the Christian faith spread southward into Nubia, roughly the present Sudan, and became very strong, apparently the prevailing faith in that region. Naturally the dominant form of Nubian Christianity was that of Egypt, Monophysite.

We have also seen that Ethiopia, which we associate with the present Abyssinia, had Christian communities before the end of the fifth century. Early in the sixth century an Ethiopian prince led an expedition to South-western Arabia which had as at least one of its objects the relief of Christians who were being persecuted by rulers of Jewish faith. In the sixth and seventh centuries the Ethiopian Church continued to prosper and was in close touch with the Coptic Church and its monasteries. From the seventh to the thirteenth century we know little of the history of Ethiopian Christianity. There were attacks by pagans and Moslem Arabs and in the tenth century a princess who was zealous for Judaism instituted a severe persecution. Yet the Church lived on, obviously Monophysite.

SYRIAN MONOPHYSITES

We need add little to what has already been said about Monophysitism in Syria. Jacob Baradæus was active in spreading it, but it did not owe its strength primarily to him. Syrian Jacobites travelled eastward as merchants and perhaps to escape persecution by the Catholic Byzantine rulers. Presumably they were the chief means of the wide extension of that form of the faith as the religion of some of the Christian minorities in Mesopotamia and east of that region. They had an ecclesiastical organization in Persia, but were not as numerous there as the Nestorians.

ARMENIAN (GREGORIAN) CHRISTIANITY

Armenia, won to Christianity in the third century chiefly through the efforts of Gregory the Illuminator, owed much of its cohesion to that faith. Christianity was the national religion and had a national organization. A border state, between the two great empires of the Romans and the Zoroastrian Sassanid Persians and then between the Byzantine successor of Rome and the Arab Caliphs, Armenia was repeatedly invaded and threatened by conquest from both sides. Inhabiting a rugged country, the Armenians relied for their independence upon their armies and the fortified hilltop strongholds of their nobility. The Sassanids succeeded in extending their suzerainty over the country, and in the fifth century, perhaps to ensure complete submission, attempted to force Zoroastrianism on the land. This led to revolt and late in the fifth century the Sassanian monarch gave up the effort to de-Christianize Armenia by force and granted religious liberty.

The Armenian Church held to the faith of Nicæa as against Arianism, but it rejected Chalcedon and remained Monophysite. The definite rupture with the Catholic Church was in 491. This may have been in part from the desire to preserve the independence of the land against Byzantine rule. Chalcedon was anathematized twice in the sixth century by synods of the Armenian Church, first in 524 or 527 and then in 552. In the latter part of the sixth century an occasional Armenian prelate conformed to the Catholic faith, but brought with him no large proportion of his flock. Late in the sixth century Persia was constrained to cede part of Armenia to the Byzantine Emperor Maurice. In the portion which he controlled, Maurice had a council of Armenian bishops called which gave its adherence to Chalcedon and named an Orthodox Catholicos, or head, of the Armenian Church. Since the bishops who were in the part of the country not under Byzantine control would not assent to this action, a schism took place. In general, the Armenians held to their Monophysitism and as a symbol of their political independence of Constantinople.

The coming of the Arabs meant a new threat to Armenian political and religious freedom. After fighting which lasted from 639 to 859 the Armenians granted the Arabs the same kind of suzerainty which the Sassanids had enjoyed. This permitted the Armenians a considerable degree of autonomy. In general, the Arabs conceded to the Armenians liberty to hold to their faith. Late in the seventh and early in the eighth century there were further Byzantine efforts to bring conformity with the Catholic Church, but for the most part the Armenians remained aloof and in 719 a national council again declared itself against the Chalcedonian position. The Christianity of Armenia differed in some of its practices from that of Constantinople. Its clergy were largely hereditary, perhaps going back for precedent to the hereditary priesthood of pagan days. In the mass it used wine unmixed with water. The Armenian Church had its own literature in the language of the country and made contributions in architecture which appear to be one source of the Byzantine ecclesiastical style. It had strong monasteries, prosperous schools, and distinctive art. It spread east of the Euphrates, largely through Armenian colonies and merchants.

Nestorian Christianity and Its Eastward Extension

The form of Christianity which had the widest geographic spread in this period was the one which is usually given the name Nestorian. To be sure, it did not win the official adherence of any important state and with the possible exception of a few tribes in Central Asia and perhaps an occasional section and city of the Tigris-Euphrates Valley was never more than the faith of a minority. Yet it had some important effects and its course is of great interest.

Nestorianism owed its prominence to the fact that it constituted the major church in the realms of the Persian monarchs and then of the Abbasid Caliphs. We have seen something of the early history of Christianity in the Persian realms, of its persecution, of the introduction of doctrines associated, perhaps mistakenly, with the name of Nestorius, and of the fashion in which separation from the Catholic Church occurred and a distinct organization was set up with its Patriarch or Catholicos, at the Persian capital, Seleucia-Ctesiphon.

In their structure and customs the Nestorians were very similar to the other Eastern Churches and seem not to have stressed in their teaching the differences in their beliefs about the relation of the human and divine in Christ. They had monasteries and in the period with which we are here concerned they insisted that the bishops and Catholicos must be unmarried. They had the Eucharist. They had images of Christ and of the saints and held in reverence the relics of martyrs and other outstanding Christians.

The coming of the Arabs brought the Nestorians some relief from the chronic and occasionally severe persecutions from which they had suffered under the Zoroastrian Sassanids. To be sure, they were required to pay a special head tax, as were other Christians in Moslem realms. From time to time, especially during wars with the Byzantine Empire, church buildings of Nestorians as well as of other Christans were destroyed, particularly those which had been erected contrary to the laws which forbade fresh construction. Yet many Nestorians were employed by the Arabs and were given high places in the Arab court. Some Christians were exempted from the head tax. During the first few generations of Arab rule, before the new masters had acquired the arts of the high civilization in which they had settled, the Nestorians provided accountants for the government, and physicians, astrologers, and philosophers for the realm. Nestorians were prominent as bankers and merchants. As we have more than once noted, it was Christians who first translated into Arabic some of the works of the ancient Greek philosophers. Much that the Christians of Western Europe were later to learn from the Moslem Arabs had first been taught the latter by Nestorians.

The Nestorians engaged in extensive missionary activity. In spite of prohibitory laws they won numbers of converts from the Persian Zoroastrians, more than they were later to gain from the Moslem Arabs. South and East of the Caspian, in Central Asia, they had many communities and missionaries. There were Nestorian churches and bishops and even metropolitans in some of the caravan cities of Central Asia, among them Merv, Herat, and Samarqand. Before the Arab conquests Christianity seems to have spread widely among the non-Christian peoples of this area, notably among the Turks and the Hephthalite Huns. Until the coming of Islam its chief rival in Central Asia appears to have been Manichæism. After the military advances of the Arabs, Islam became the major competitor, but the issue of the contest between the Cross and the Crescent was not decided until well after 950, when, as we are to see, the Cross lost.

Nestorian Christianity was planted in India. Our knowledge of how and when that was done is tantalizingly fragmentary. We know that there were Christians in India before the rise of the distinctive Nestorian beliefs and that these may have come through commercial contacts with the Christians of Mesopotamia, Syria, and Egypt. As we have said, tradition even ascribes the first Christian preaching to the Apostle Thomas. In the thirteenth and fourteenth centuries travellers from Western Europe found well established Christian communities on the coasts of South India and Ceylon. The more detailed reports of Western Europeans of the sixteenth century make it clear that the ecclesiastical language of these communities was Syriac, indicating that they had been nourished and perhaps planted by Syriac-using peoples, and their church connexion was with the Nestorians of Mesopotamia. Inscriptions concerning Christians found in South India dating from the seventh into the ninth century are in Pahlavi, or Middle Persian. All of this seems to point to the growth and perhaps the introduction of Christianity in India through contacts, from the sixth century onward, with the Christians, primarily Nestorians, of Persia, Mesopotamia, and Syria. From what we know of the history of trade, it is natural to assume that the contacts were made largely through commerce, for the Christian communities were on or near the coast and in or near cities and from as far back as pre-Christian times there had been maritime trade between India and the lands to the west. The Nestorian communities in India, however, seem not to have been primarily the descendants of immigrants, but to have been of Indian stocks. This would appear to point either to extensive intermarriage of Christian immigrants with indigenous peoples or to active missions as their source, probably in association with the Christian mercantile communities.

It was through Nestorians that Christianity was introduced to China. The year of the first known coming of Christianity to that vast land was 635. At that time the T'ang dynasty had recently risen to power and T'ai Tsung, the ablest monarch of that line, was on the throne. China was entering on one of the glorious epochs of its history and for two centuries or more was the most powerful and perhaps the wealthiest realm on the planet, rivalled only by the Arab Empire, and that did not long remain as united as did China. The first missionary, A-lo-pên, came to the capital, Ch'ang-an, the present Hsianfu. Ch'ang-an, possibly the largest city in the world of that day, attracted representatives of many races and faiths. T'ai Tsung is said to have given A-lo-pên a cordial welcome and, after he had examined translations of the books which the latter brought with him, to have ordered the preaching of their contents. He may have done this because he was fairly tolerant of all religions. In succeeding years Christian monasteries were founded in several centres, Christian literature in Chinese was produced, and a metropolitanate was created for

China. Some converts were won, but the core of the Christian communities and perhaps their membership was predominantly foreign. Buddhism, then in its heyday in China, Taoism, and a reviving Confucianism were the prevailing religious systems of the Empire. Christians were a very small minority, perhaps not as numerous as Moslems, Manichæans, or Zoroastrians. Late in the ninth century there were still Christians in China, but an imperial edict of 845 which was directed primarily against the Buddhists and which also included Christians in its proscription seems to have brought a sharp reduction in the numbers of the latter. The disorders which accompanied the end of the T'ang dynasty late in the ninth and early in the tenth century may have contributed to a further decline. Monks sent in 980 to put the Church in order could find no traces of Christians in the land.

SUMMARY COMMENT

We must note that in the vast area covered by this brief chapter and especially in Mesopotamia, Syria, Palestine, and Egypt, we appear to see one of the striking failures of Christianity. Here was a major reverse, indeed, the major territorial reverse of all the history of the faith. Here Christ had lived, died, and risen again. Here the Gospel was first preached, here the original Christian churches came into being, and here the name Christian was coined. Here were three of the five great patriarchal sees of the Catholic Church—Jerusalem, Antioch, and Alexandria—and the earliest creative theological thinking. It was here that monasticism arose, with its daring and resolute dream of the complete attainment of the Christian ideal. Yet here Christians were more divided than anywhere else in the first thousand years of the faith and fell further short of the ideal of the unity of love than elsewhere. In some areas the majority adopted the Christian name but much of this was superficial and could not stand the test of adversity. When Islam came, borne by conquering Arabs, the churches shrank and slowly became fossilized and sterile. To be sure, some converts were made to the east of the Arab domains, notably by the Nestorians, but they were usually small minorities. Yet more than any other religion in Islam-dominated lands, Christianity displayed the ability to survive and to reach out into new areas and propagate itself.

SELECTED BIBLIOGRAPHY

W. F. Adeney, *The Greek and Eastern Churches* (New York, Charles Scribner's Sons, 1928 [preface 1908], pp. xiv, 634). A fairly good survey.

W. Barthold, *Zur Geschichte des Christentums in Mittel-Asien bis zur mongolischen Eroberung. Berichtige und vermerhte deutsche Bearbeitung nach dem rus-*

sischen Original herausgegeben von Dr. Rudolf Stübe (Tübingen, J. C. B. Mohr, 1901, pp. vii, 74). Excellent.

L. E. Browne, *The Eclipse of Christianity in Asia from the Time of Mohammed till the Fourteenth Century* (Cambridge University Press, 1933, pp. 198). Based upon extensive reading in the sources and secondary works.

L. Duchesne, *Les Missions Chrétiennes au Sud de l'Empire Romain* (Ecole Française de Rome, *Mélanges d'Archeologie et d'Histoire,* 1896, pp. 79–122).

J. Labourt, *Le Christianisme dans L'Empire Perse sous la Dynastie Sassanide* (Paris, Librairie Victor Lecoffre, 1904, pp. xix, 372). A standard work.

A. Mingana, *The Early Spread of Christianity in Central Asia and the Far East: A New Document* (Manchester University Press, 1925, pp. 80).

A. Mingana, *The Early Spread of Christianity in India* (Manchester University Press, 1926, pp. 82).

A. C. Moule, *Christians in China before the Year 1550* (London, Society for Promoting Christian Knowledge, 1930, pp. xvi, 293). Translations of all the known sources, with notes.

E. Sachau, *Zur Ausbreitung des Christentums in Asien* (*Abhandlungen der preuss. Ak. der Wissenschaften, phil. hist. Klasse,* 1919, pp. 1–80). A scholarly summary.

W. A. Wigram, *An Introduction to the History of the Assyrian Church or the Church of the Sassanid Persian Empire 100–640 A.D.* (London, Society for Promoting Christian Knowledge, 1910, pp. 318). By an English missionary.

Chapter 13

THE COURSE IN WESTERN EUROPE

As we move into the West we find a story which in some significant ways differs from that in the East. Here the disintegration of the Roman Empire began earlier than it did in the East and was much more marked than in the areas which remained under the Eastern continuation of that realm, the Byzantine Empire. Yet in the West Christianity eventually most strikingly proved its vitality. From the West it had its broadest geographic expansion, in the West arose the large majority of the vigorous new movements after the ninth century, and from the West came the widest and deepest influences upon mankind as a whole.

Why was this? How are we to account for the fact that in the region in which the collapse of the Empire with whose life Christianity had become so closely interrelated first became most apparent and where the earliest sweeping conquests by invaders occurred, Christianity displayed not only its most pronounced recovery but also its greatest vigour? Had an intelligent traveller from China or India journeyed through the Mediterranean world at the end of the sixth century he probably would have given a quite contrary forecast and would have looked for the revival and the renewed spread of Christianity, if they came at all, from the East. Here, with the exception of Rome, were all the most ancient and the strongest churches. Here the existing patterns of life had been far less disturbed. Here the larger part of the theological thinking and discussion had taken place and was still in progress. Here monasticism, that potent new movement in protest against the growing laxity of life in the Church, had arisen and had shown its most extensive development.

The answers to this question must be in part conjectural. Yet some factors can be pointed to as offering possible clues. One of these seems to have been that the collapse of the Empire freed Christianity from the restrictions placed on it by its close association with that regime and gave greater opportunity for its inherent genius to express itself than was true in the East, where the Roman state persisted.

Nearly allied to this factor is a second. The threat to Christianity in the West brought by the disintegration of the Empire and the inroads of invaders, while serious, was not overwhelming. Indeed, it was not as ominous as in much of the East. Situated as it was at the extreme tip of Eurasia, Western Europe was either not reached by many of the invasions which the East had to meet, arising as most of them did from the heartland of the continent, or, in the case of the Arabs, in the south-east, or it had to face them only after they had spent their main force. Thus the invasion which was most disastrous for the Christianity of the East, that of the Arabs, bringing with it a new faith, Islam, against which few counter gains have been made by Christianity or any other religion, was rolled back soon after it crossed the Pyrenees and never overwhelmed the churches of Gaul, the Iberian Peninsula, or Sicily to the extent that it did those nearer Arabia. Eventually the churches of these areas reëmerged and won or expelled all Moslems. The Bulgars, the Mongols, and the Turks penetrated effectively only to the eastern edges of Western Europe. What might have been the future of Christianity in Western Europe had invasions continued may be surmised from the fact that not until the last, that of the Scandinavians, had ended, did the recession cease which they helped bring and the resurging vitality emerge which issued in fresh advance. In contrast with the East where the major incursion, that of the Moslem Arabs, brought with it a "high" religion, Islam, all the invasions of the West were either by "barbarians" who were already in part converts to Christianity or who had more nearly "primitive" religions. It is a generalization borne out by universal human experience that a "primitive" religion yields more readily to a "high" religion than does a "high" religion to another "high" religion. Christianity won back none of the ground lost by it in the East to Islam, but, in contrast, it not only regained all of the territory in the West which it lost but pressed out beyond its former frontiers and gathered into its fold pagan peoples of "primitive" faiths and cultures.

The Main Features of the Western Europe in Which Christianity Was Set (a.d. 500–a.d. 950)

The first few generations after the fifth century witnessed a progressive disintegration of what remained of the Roman Empire and of Græco-Roman civilization in the West. The invaders established themselves in various parts of the Roman domains. At the outset their rulers usually prized Roman titles conferred on them by the Emperors and regarded themselves as still within the Empire. Actually, however, they were heads of kingdoms which for most practical purposes were independent. In Italy the Ostrogoths were masters of much of the country from the latter part of the fifth century until Justinian's generals overthrew them about the middle of the sixth century. Then came the Lombards who founded a kingdom which survived until 774. For centuries after the downfall of that kingdom Lombard nobles ruled parts of Italy. The Visigoths controlled much of the Iberian Peninsula until, in the eighth century, they gave way to the Arabs. The Burgundians were in the Rhone Valley. Germanic folk, mostly Angles and Saxons, colonized Britain and founded a number of small states.

The Franks proved to be the major power. At the outset of the sixth century they were in control of much of Gaul, especially its northern portions, and of a large part of the Rhine Valley. The ruling line, the most prominent of whom was Clovis, of whose conversion in 496 we have spoken, were known as the Merovingians. In the first half of the seventh century the authority of the Merovingians declined and that of local magnates increased. In the fore part of the eighth century the Merovingians, now become purely nominal monarchs, *rois fainéants,* were gradually replaced by a new dynasty, the Carolingians. The Carolingians had emerged in the seventh century. Near the close of that century Pepin (or Pippin) of Heristal became the virtual ruler. Charles Martel, his illegitimate son who succeeded him, exercised even more power and in 732 won lasting fame by checking the Arab advance into Gaul at the decisive battle near Tours. In 751 a son of Charles Martel, Pepin (or Pippin) the Short was crowned King of the Franks and relegated the last of the Merovingians to a monastery. Pepin the Short (died 768) was succeeded by his son, another Charles, better known as Charles the Great or Charlemagne (742–814), who brought the power of his house to its apex and was crowned Roman Emperor on Christmas Day, 800. Under the Carolingians and especially under Charlemagne the Frankish state reached its height. Compared with the Chinese Empire under the contemporary T'ang dynasty it was a small affair. Yet through it, as we are to see, Christianity displayed a new surge of life.

After Charlemagne the Frankish power declined. Although for a time it was still formidable, by the end of the ninth century the Carolingians, with whom it was closely allied, had ceased to be of major importance in the West and their disintegration left a power vacuum which was not to be filled until the second half of the tenth century. The invasions of the Scandinavians—the Northmen or Vikings—added to the confusion and brought civilization in Western Europe to a further low ebb.

Parallel with the political changes came other profound alterations in the life of Western Europe. The chronic disorder made for a decline in commerce and industry. The Roman roads fell into disrepair. Travel, whether by land or sea, was rendered perilous by robbers, either singly or in bands. Cities and towns dwindled in population and wealth. Education and the arts languished.

Crude agriculture became the main productive occupation and wealth was chiefly in land. Feudalism began to emerge, a structure by which power became fragmented into hundreds of units, large and small, and the authority of the kings suffered. Warriors were the rulers and the chief occupation of the aristocracy was fighting.

In spite of the advantages which geographic location gave it over the branches of the faith in the lands farther east, could the Christianity of the West seize the opportunity? Could it win these roistering warrior tribesmen even to a nominal allegiance? If it gained their professed adherence, could it bring them to an understanding of the Gospel and to conformity with it? Could that church which, in the course of drawing into its ample fold the majority of those bearing the Roman name, had compromised with non-Christian living, preserve enough vitality really to propagate the Gospel? Here was the challenge. It was not fully met. Perhaps, given the nature of man and of the Gospel, it could not be. Yet to an amazing degree Christianity rose to it and had a more profound effect upon the peoples of Western Europe and their culture than it had exerted upon the Roman Empire in the first five centuries.

The General Course of Christianity in Western Europe

For a time the quality of Christian living declined and the very existence of Christianity was threatened. The danger was not the immediate disappearance of a formal profession of that religion. Indeed, as we are to see, the majority of the pagan invaders were fairly quickly brought to an outward adoption of Christianity and the faith was even carried beyond what, in the year 500, had been its northern borders. The peril, rather, was the progressive denaturing of what bore the Christian name by secularization and corruption of many kinds. The decline was not sudden nor was it continuous. Numerous attempts were made to stem the trend, many individuals and groups were bright gleams in the night, and here and there partial recovery was effected. Yet by the middle of the tenth century Christianity in Western Europe was at a lower ebb than it was ever again to be.

As we attempt to picture a scene which has many details and which is very confusing, we can best do it by broad strokes, bringing out some of the main features and sketching in several of the more prominent individuals who figured in it.

The Victory of the Catholic Church over Arianism

One of the features which marked the earlier portions of these centuries was the disappearance of Arian Christianity and the bringing into the Catholic

Church of those who had professed it. Arianism had been the form of Christianity which had won a large proportion of the Germanic peoples who had settled in the Roman Empire. This was true of most of the Goths, including the Ostrogoths who ruled in much of Italy and the Visigoths who were dominant in Spain. In so far as they were Christians, the majority of the Lombards who followed the Ostrogoths as masters of much of Italy were Arians. Many of the Burgundians were of that faith. So were a large proportion of the Vandals who controlled North Africa. The Arians regarded themselves as the true Christians and their churches as the Catholic Church. However, the overwhelming majority of the Latinized Roman provincials over whom the invaders ruled were loyal to Nicæa. It was to be expected that the invaders, a minority, although the ruling minority, and of more nearly "primitive" culture, would eventually conform to the language, manners, and customs of the majority. As they did so, quite understandably they accepted Nicene Catholic Christianity.

By the end of the seventh century most of the Arian Lombards had become Catholics. In Spain the transition was earlier. Recared, the Visigothic king, near the end of the sixth century apparently decided that his realm must have one religion and that that had best be the faith of the majority. Accordingly, at a synod at Toledo he formally became a Catholic and was quickly followed by a number of Arian bishops and nobles. In Gaul the Arians among the Burgundians were beginning to turn Catholic before the end of the sixth century. The fact that Clovis, the ruler of the people who became dominant in Gaul, accepted the Nicene rather than the Arian form of the faith, was decisive in the victory of the Catholic Church in that area. The Goths who had ruled in the south of Gaul were conquered by the Franks and that meant the elimination of their Arianism. The reconquest of North Africa by the Romans under Justinian in the first half of the sixth century made for the triumph of the Catholic Church in that region.

The disappearance of Arianism facilitated the religious and cultural unity in Western Europe. Had the Arians prevailed or even persisted as a strong factor with their national churches and lack of any generally acknowledged centre of orthodoxy and administration such as the Catholics possessed in Rome, that all pervasive cohesion which the Catholic Church gave to an otherwise divided Europe might not have been achieved.

The Emergence of Western Forms of Monasticism

One of the major features of the Europe of these centuries was the extensive spread of monasticism and the development of forms of that movement peculiar to the West.

An important figure was Cassiodorus. Born late in the fifth century, his long life spanned most of the sixth century. Of noble ancestors from Antioch but a native of Italy, he served as a high official under the Ostrogoths. In his later years, when the armies of Justinian had overthrown the Ostrogothic kingdom, Cassiodorus retired to his estates in the south of Italy and there founded two monasteries. One was for those who wished to follow a solitary, ascetic life. The other he made a house of learning. He had it pleasantly equipped, collected for it a library of theology and classical literature, and encouraged the transcription of existing books and the composition of new ones. He himself wrote and compiled a number of works. In an age in which wars were bringing the neglect of learning, he strove to create a centre for the study and propagation under Christian auspices of all products of the human mind. His example may have helped to inspire scholarly pursuits in other monasteries. Certainly some of his writings were widely used in later centuries.

More influential than Cassiodorus was Ireland. Remote in its western sea, Ireland was spared most of the invasions of the sixth, seventh, and eighth centuries. Not until the Northmen came was it to suffer as severely as the rest of Western Europe. Between the time of Patrick and the sixth century we know little of the history of Christianity in the island. When our information again begins to be dependable, we see an Ireland which was the home of a vigorous monasticism. The Church did not have the kind of territorial diocesan organization under the administration of bishops which, influenced by the forms of civil government, prevailed in areas which had been in the Roman Empire. In creed, the Irish Church was in accord with the Catholic faith. In some particulars, especially the date for celebrating Easter and the form of the tonsure, it differed from the customs sponsored by Rome, but in theology it was orthodox. In contrast with that of the continent, the Christianity of Ireland was organized around the monastery. This may have been because of the prominence of the tribe in Ireland and a partial reproduction of it in the Church, where the monasteries may have been a Christian substitute for it. Whatever the reason, in Ireland monasticism was dominant. The important administrative officers were the abbots. Unless, as was sometimes the case, the abbot was also a bishop, the bishop's only distinctive function was that of ordination.

Irish monasteries were centres of learning. The chief subject of study was the Scriptures. Latin was the main language through which this was carried on, and some of the works of Latin Christian scholars were also cherished. Much attention was paid to the copying of manuscripts and their illumination.

An outstanding feature of Irish monasticism, one which we shall have occasion to note more at length later, was the migration of Irish monks to other countries. What moved them we cannot certainly know. Ostensibly they went for the "love of God," "in order to win the heavenly fatherland," "for the love of the name of Christ," and after the example of Abraham who, at the divine call, left his country and his kindred for a strange land. Compounded with this religious urge may also have been a desire to see other peoples, a kind of *wanderlust*.

The Irish *peregrini* went far. They voyaged to the Orkneys, the Faroes, the rough coasts of Scotland, and perhaps even to Iceland. They were in the forests of Germany, the rugged hills of Gaul, the foothills of the Alps, the valleys of the Rhine and the Danube, and the cities and remote valleys of Italy. Sometimes they went singly and became hermits. Often they formed groups, frequently of thirteen in imitation of Christ and the apostles. Some of them were missionaries to pagans. Others sought to elevate the morals of the nominally Christian populations near whom they settled. Often they were an irritation to the churchmen of the Continent, for they did not readily fit into the diocesan pattern and their "wandering bishops" and their individualistic hermits did not prove amenable to customary ecclesiastical discipline. Yet they were numerous and were a characteristic feature of Western Europe through most of the period from 500 to 950. Here was an extensive movement of a people, akin to the migrations which were flooding Europe, but transformed by a Christian purpose.

Much more widely influential than Cassiodorus and than even the Irish monks was Benedict of Nursia. A contemporary of Cassiodorus, he also was an Italian. He was born about the year 480 at Nursia, among the Apennines northeast of Rome, and was of good family. As a youth he went to Rome to study, but the scholastic life held no attractions for him. He was distressed and disgusted by the vices and frivolities of the city, and, when about fifteen or twenty years of age, he took up the life of the hermit. Fame began to come and the monks of a neighbouring monastery urged him to become their abbot. He proved too strict for them and returned to his hermit's routine. High and low sought him, eager to share with him what was deemed the complete Christian life, or brought their sons to have him train them in it. There, at Subiaco, up a valley east of Rome, twelve monasteries arose, each with twelve monks and a superior. About 528 or 529, when he was not far from fifty years of age, Benedict moved to Monte Cassino, not quite half way between Naples and Rome, and there, on its summit, destroying a pagan temple where worship to Apollo was still maintained, he established a monastery. The monastery grew and, although he remained a layman, bishops and priests as well as the laity came to consult him. He seemed to carry with him an atmosphere of quiet peace. He died some time after 542, preceded shortly by the twin sister who had also adopted the monastic life and lived in a convent not far from his own.

Benedict's great contribution was the rule which he gave to his monastery. In devising it he learned what he could from predecessors, especially Basil of Cæsarea but also John Cassian, founder of a famous monastery near Marseilles, and other monks. However, he was not a slavish borrower, for his rule bears indelibly the mark of his own experience as monk and abbot. He was aware of the various kinds of monks, some anchorites, some wanderers, some living by twos and threes but without wise guidance. He believed the best form of the life of a monk to be the cenobitic, that of the community, and it was for this that he devised his rule. In it he displayed that genius for order and administration which we associate with those who created and governed the Roman Empire.

That it was Benedict who had never had the experience of civil administration rather than the seasoned Roman statesman, Cassiodorus, who devised a rule which embodied the qualities which we regard as characteristic of Rome is surprising and seems to belie that comment. Yet Benedict, with his background of Roman culture and probably without at all being aware of the significance of what he was doing, worked out a monastic organization which stood the test of the centuries.

As Benedict envisaged it, the monastery was to be self-contained and self-supporting, with its fields and workshops. Over it was the abbot, chosen by the entire community. He was to have complete authority, but was to remember that his title meant father and that he was ultimately accountable to God. The monastery was to have other officers, especially if it were large—among them a prior (or provost), deans (each over ten monks), a cellarer, a novice-master, and a porter. Monks were to be admitted first for a novitiate of one year. After that time their decision was irrevocable. Upon entry the monk was to surrender all his property, either distributing it to the poor or giving it to the monastery. He was to think of nothing as being his own. The nobles and wealthy who brought their sons to be entered in the monasteries, even though they made large gifts to the foundation, were to expect no special favours. The ideal was a kind of Christian communism, like that of the early Christians in Jerusalem, whom Benedict cited for his precedent, where no one called anything his own, but all shared in the common stock.

The life was orderly but was not unduly severe and was probably more comfortable than was that of the great masses of the population. Clothing and meals were simple but adequate, and special provision was made for the ill, the aged, the very young, and those doing heavy manual labour. There was to be fasting at regular times, but this was not of the kind practised by the extreme ascetics whom we have met. Much weight was given to humility. Provision was made for various degrees of discipline, from private admonition to physical punishment, excommunication, and, as a last resort, expulsion. Idleness was declared "an enemy of the soul." The entire round of the twenty-four hours was provided for, with eight services, one every three hours, and with periods for sleep, including a rest early in the afternoon, for eating, and for labour. The labour might be in the fields or in the library, according to the aptitude of the monk. There was also time for directed and supervised reading and for meditation and private prayer. Silence was encouraged and was the rule at meals and after compline, the last of the services of the day. Joking and laughter were frowned upon. There was reading aloud at meals from religious books by those assigned to that function. Stress was placed on worship by the entire community and directions were given for the services. These were to include the Psalms, so that the whole of the Psalter was recited each week, reading from the Old and New Testaments with accepted commentaries on them, hymns, prayers, among them the Lord's Prayer, and the frequent use of the *Gloria,* the *kyrie eleison,* and the canticle *Benedictus.* Although hospitality was enjoined and practised, provision was made for keeping the monks from having more contact with the outside world than was absolutely necessary. There was a place for priests, for they were needed to say mass, but they were to obey the rule as fully as the lay monks.

The rule was wisely designed for a group of men of various ages living together in worship and in work for the cultivation of the full Christian life as that was conceived by the monk.

The rule of Benedict became standard in the West, probably because of its intrinsic worth. Pope Gregory the Great did much to give it popularity. It was taken to Britain by missionaries sent by Gregory from Rome and of whom we are to hear more in a moment. In the seventh century it began to gain in Gaul. Charlemagne admired it and furthered its adoption. By the latter part of the eighth century it was generally accepted. No central organization existed for its enforcement and to bring uniformity: each monastery was independent of every other. Modifications might and often were made in the rule by individual houses. Yet it became the model from which many other rules stemmed.

In an age of disorder the Benedictine monasteries were centres of quiet and orderly living, communities where prayer, work, and study were the custom, and that in a society where prayer was ignored or was regarded as magic to be practised for selfish ends, where work was despised as servile, where even princes were illiterate, and where war was chronic. Like other monastic establishments, Benedictine foundations tended to decline from the high ideals set by the rule. Many were heavily endowed and in numbers of them life became easy and at times scandalous. When awakenings occurred, they often took the form of a return to the rule or its modification in the direction of greater austerity. Even when the rule was strictly obeyed, the monasteries were self-centred and were not concerned with the salvation of the society about them, except to draw individuals from it into their fellowship. However, as we are to see, the missionaries of the Western Church were predominantly monks. It was chiefly through them, although often at the initiative and under the protection of lay princes, that the faith was carried beyond its existing frontiers. Later, moreover, monks of the Benedictine rule became prominent in the general life of the Church and of the community as a whole.

Even when the rule of Benedict was not adopted or where the full monastic way was not followed, the dream of Christian community life often made itself felt. It was seen, for example, in what were known as canons regular. A number of clergy attached to a particular church, perhaps a cathedral, would live together according to rule (*regula*). Not technically monks, these canons regular became a feature of the Catholic Church in the West. The parish churches to which they were attached were known, accordingly, as collegiate churches. The designation canon came from the term *vita canonica* which was given to this custom. The place in which the canons gathered for their official meetings was known as the *capitulam* or chapter, a name also used for the collective group of the canons. Augustine of Hippo had some such arrangement in his episcopal household. Further impetus was given to the development by Bishop Chrodegang of Metz not far from the year 760 and the custom spread under the encouragement of Charlemagne.

The Growing Power of the Church in an Age of Disorder

As the structure of the Roman Empire disintegrated, invasions multiplied, wars and disorder increased, and life and property became progressively unsafe, the Church stepped into the breach and took over some of the functions for which society had been accustomed to look to the state. It emerged as the protector of the weak, the poor, the widows, and the orphans. That was notably the case in Gaul. Here in the fifth and sixth centuries the bishops were largely recruited from the Gallo-Roman aristocracy. Drawn as they were from the wealthy, educated, Latinized provincials, they stood for the old order, but it was an order of comparative justice and stability in a day of an approach towards anarchy.

As time passed, in Western Europe, especially north of the Alps, bishops tended to become magnates not differing greatly from secular lords except in their titles and some of their functions. As the power of the central government declined and much of it passed into the hands of feudal lords, the Church, caught in the trends of the day, also in part conformed and its chief officials, notably its bishops, had their armies and bore arms. There were splendid exceptions, but we hear of bishops who were unchaste, gluttonous, and bibulous. Power of the secular kind entailed perils to true Christian living, and many there were who succumbed.

THE AUGMENTED POWER OF THE PAPACY AND GREGORY THE GREAT

In the general disorder, the Papacy, under some very able men, markedly increased its power and extended the geographical range of its authority. In principle, as we have seen, even before the year 500 its claims were sweeping. Whether those claims would be implemented depended upon the opportunity and upon the ability of the individuals in the Papal chair. The political disorders offered the challenge. Some Popes were weak and did not rise to the occasion. Indeed, as we are to see, towards the end of the period the Papacy fell victim for a time to the turbulence of the surrounding political scene and sank to an all-time low in its power. Yet it also had some very able and devoted men.

Of the Popes of this period the strongest was Gregory I, by common consent called the Great. Significantly, too, he was canonized by the Catholic Church and esteemed a saint, an exemplar of Christian faith and life. Occupying the throne of Peter from 590 to his death in 604, or for only fourteen years, he packed into that brief period a prodigious amount of work and achievement.

Gregory came from a prominent Roman house and had a Pope among his ancestors. The family was deeply religious. Three of his father's sisters dedicated themselves as virgins and two of them were eventually enrolled as saints. After his father's death his mother adopted the monastic life and later was canonized. Gregory was born about the year 540 and was given as good an education as the Rome of his day could provide. That city had been sacked again and again, it was greatly reduced in population, its aqueducts were no longer functioning, and many of the huge public buildings of imperial days were falling into ruins. Gregory knew no Greek and cared little for the classical pre-Christian Latin authors or for philosophy, astronomy, or mathematics. He early showed marked administrative ability and was appointed by the Emperor to head the civil administration of the city. Through the death of his father he inherited large wealth. Much of that wealth was in Sicily and with it he founded and endowed six monasteries on that island. He also turned his ancestral home in Rome into a monastery. The remainder of his fortune he gave to the poor. Whether he ever became technically a monk is in debate, but he was undoubtedly attracted to the monastery, frequented the one which he had founded in Rome, led an ascetic life, and was a warm admirer of Benedict. Indeed, most of our authentic information about the latter comes through him. The Pope appointed him one of the seven regionary deacons of the city, officers whose duty it was to look after the administration of alms. For six years he served in Constantinople as the Papal representative at the imperial court. When he arrived, Justinian had been dead for less than fifteen years, much of Italy, including Rome, was still in the Empire, and the Christological controversies had not yet been finally resolved. Always strictly and gravely orthodox, he was grieved by the large number of Monophysites who were separated from the Catholic Church. While in Constantinople he wrote voluminously in the clear but unadorned Latin which was characteristic of him. Returning to Rome about 585 or 586, he became secretary to the Pope.

In 590, through the popular acclaim of the clergy and people of Rome, Gregory was elected Pope. He was most reluctant to assume the duties of the office and is said to have written to Constantinople asking that the necessary imperial confirmation not be given. As Pope he faced a combination of problems which would have appalled and baffled a less able and resolute man, and he had to meet them under the handicap of physical frailty and recurrent attacks of indigestion, gout, and fever. His was the responsibility for seeing that the population of Rome was fed. Shortly before his accession the city had suffered from an inundation of the Tiber and the ensuing pestilence, and this aggravated his problem. The Lombards were expanding their power in Italy. In addition to the military threat of their arms and to the ruthless pillaging which is associated with invasions, they presented a religious challenge, for, to the extent that they were Christians, they were Arians. Gregory had the responsibility for the very large physical possessions of the Church of Rome, including its buildings in Rome and its endowments, chiefly in lands, in Italy, Sicily, Gaul, and North Africa. He held to the traditional claims of his see for priority in the Catholic Church, and as Patriarch in the West felt especial responsibility for Italy, Gaul, and Spain. At the outset he may almost have despaired of saving from shipwreck what he called "the rotten old vessel of which God had given" him "the charge."

Gregory rose to all the manifold obligations and reached out beyond them to new enterprises. He saw that Rome's poor were fed and that the church fabrics of the city were repaired and maintained. He managed the estates of the church so successfully that their revenues were increased, but with humane treatment of those who cultivated their lands. He raised armies, kept Rome inviolate from Lombard attacks, negotiated with both Lombards and imperial officials, and on his own authority made peace with the Lombards. During his pontificate he was the outstanding figure in Italy, in its political as well as its ecclesiastical life. He exercised authority in Gaul and Spain, attempted to reform abuses in the church in the Frankish domains, reached out into Illyricum, and inaugurated the Roman mission to Britain of which we are to hear more in a moment. He maintained contacts with the other patriarchs of the Catholic Church and insisted on the primacy of Rome, especially against the claims of the Patriarch of Constantinople.

Gregory preached frequently. He also gave thought and effort to the public services of the Church, including its liturgy and music. He introduced changes in the liturgy. The type of music called Gregorian and which attained wide and prolonged popularity has been attributed to him. Just how much, if anything, he had to do with it has been in dispute, but it is clear that he was interested in the music of the Church and it is probable that he at least made decisive modifications by editing what had come down from the past. He maintained strict discipline among the clergy, sought to enforce the rule of clerical celibacy which had long been the ideal in the West, and gave especial oversight to the bishops who were in the ecclesiastical province of which the Bishop of Rome was metropolitan. He was greatly interested in monasteries, gave them increased liberty from the supervision of the bishops to govern their internal secular affairs, and was zealous in reforming those foundations which had lapsed morally and spiritually. He deposed unworthy abbots, sought to prevent monks from wandering about from one monastery to another, and, to obviate causes for scandal, decreed that women's convents be kept far apart from men's monasteries.

While one of his favorite designations of himself, *servus servorum Dei* ("servant of the servants of God") had been employed before him, and not exclusively by Popes, it seems peculiarly appropriate for him. When, in the ninth century, it began to be used only by the Popes, it may have been in part because of his example. There was fully as great aptness in a phrase which was on an epitaph of Gregory, *consul dei* ("God's consul"), for to a preeminent degree Gregory brought to the Church the administrative gifts which characterized the great Romans. Like the more eminent consuls he was a builder of empire, an empire centred in Rome. It was an empire, too, which like that of the consuls and the Cæsars who bore the title of consul guarded the heritage of Græco-Roman civilization, *Romanitas*. Yet Gregory was not just another consul: he was a consul of God and the empire which he sought to strengthen was, as he saw it, the kingdom of God in which Christ was ruler and the Pope, as Peter's successor, Christ's vicegerent. In an age of mounting chaos that empire of Christ's Church stood for decency, order, justice, and the high values of the spirit. More than any other one man, Gregory laid the foundations for the power which the Church of Rome was to exercise in the Western Europe of the next nine centuries.

The contrast with the Eastern wing of the Catholic Church is significant. The latter developed no such able administrators as did the Papacy. In this respect it had no one to compare with Leo the Great or with Gregory the Great. The obvious reason for the difference is that in the West the Empire waned and the Popes stepped in to take its place in preserving order while in the East the Empire continued and the leading Patriarch of that region, he of Constantinople, was overshadowed by the Emperor and the state. Even when men came to that Patriarchate from the civil service, as did Photius, they had been subordinates and not rulers and tended to conform to the tradition of cæsaropapism. There may be deeper but more subtle reasons, such as the distinction between the Roman and the Greek genius, the one practical, the other, in its later Neoplatonic form, stressing spirit at the expense of flesh. It will be recalled that Monophysitism, belittling the human element in Christ, had much greater vogue in the East than in the West. Whatever the reasons, the contrast was real.

This trend towards regarding the Popes as the successors of the Cæsars and the Papacy as the exponent and protector of *Romanitas* brought with it both beneficent results and perils. On the one hand it gave to the Church of the West a structural unity, helped to hold Europe together, and made for civilization. On the other, it substituted, perhaps fatally, visible organizational unity for the unity of love and mixed the kind of power represented by the Roman Empire with that of the Cross and the resurrection. The latter was not completely lost, but it suffered by its conjunction with *Romanitas*.

Gregory was not only an administrator. For centuries he was even more famous as a theologian. Here he was not an originator, for his primary talents were not those of the scholar. His preaching was simple and practical. In common with his times, he employed the allegorical interpretation of the Scriptures, held the relics of the saints in great reverence, and believed in and emphasized miracles. He was intimately familiar with the text of the Bible and made much use of it. He was a warm admirer of Augustine and it was to a large degree the latter's thought that he endeavoured to transmit. Gregory did not exactly reproduce Augustine. While, with the latter, he held that the number of the elect is fixed, he seemed to make less of predestination by God than of God's foreknowledge. He believed in the divine initiative in the salvation of the individual, but held that once grace had begun to act, enabled by it, the individual could coöperate with it. To him sin was more weakness than the basic corruption of man's nature which Augustine stressed. He was substantially in accord with the modified Augustinianism of the Council of Orange.

Gregory put into written form much of the popular Christianity that had been growing up. He had more to say of purgatory than Augustine and was more certain of it than was the latter. Purgatory, so Gregory taught, is a state, a fire, in which Christians are purged of light sins before the final judgement.

Men must repent of sins committed after baptism. He held that God's forgiveness is conditioned solely on men's contrition for their sins, but that works of penance lighten the load which would otherwise have to be borne in purgatory as disciplinary and cleansing, and that masses for the souls in purgatory are a help. For Christians this side the gate of death masses and the aid of the martyrs and saints are also to be sought, not that they ensure forgiveness, but because they aid in the discipline which the Church prescribes for those who repent of post-baptismal sins. Gregory also wrote extensively on angels and demons, systematizing what was generally believed in the circles of his day. He gave to both an hierarchical arrangement. He thought that the end of the world was at hand.

The writings of Gregory became standard and were much read in succeeding centuries. He was regarded as the last of the great fathers of the Latin Church and did much to fix its beliefs.

Other Contemporary Theological Activity

Contemporary with Gregory was Isidore, Archbishop of Seville and head of the Church in Spain from about 600 to 636. His brief summary of Christian doctrine incorporated in his *Book of Sentences* was to be studied for centuries in the West as a text-book in theology. His *Origins* or *Etymologies,* a kind of compact collection of the secular and ecclesiastical knowledge of his age, was also widely used in the Middle Ages as a *vade mecum* to theology and the wisdom of Græco-Roman antiquity. Isidore, like Gregory, was not original. In the storms of the age theological activity was dying and, except for a brief revival in the heyday of the Carolingians, was not again to awaken until the eleventh century.

The Donation of Constantine and the Pseudo-Isidorian Decretals

Two other literary creations of this era need to be noted, for, while largely forgeries, they were made to strengthen the authority of the Papacy in an age when the Church in Western Europe was in danger of falling apart into a welter of tribal, royal, and feudal churches, dominated by secular princes, and when the unity provided by the See of Peter afforded cohesion. One of these was the Donation of Constantine. Probably written about the middle of the eighth century, it purported to be from early in the fourth century and by the Emperor Constantine. It described the latter's conversion, baptism, and miraculous healing from leprosy through Pope Sylvester I, and said that out of gratitude he was making over to the Pope and his successors his palace in Rome and "the city of Rome and all the provinces, districts, and cities of Italy or of the Western regions."

About the middle of the ninth century there arose, from the region around Rheims, the *Decretals of Isidore,* professing to have been compiled by one Isidore Mercator and to be a collection of decisions of councils and Popes from Clement of Rome late in the first or early in the second century to the eighth century. They included the Donation of Constantine. Some of the material was genuine, but much was spurious. The *Decretals* depicted the Popes as claiming supreme authority from the beginning, permitted all bishops to appeal directly to the Pope, thus limiting the authority of archbishops, and regarded bishops and Popes as free from secular control. In an uncritical age it was accepted as genuine and, although not the work of the Popes, was used to reinforce their claims.

THE SPREAD OF CHRISTIANITY IN THE WEST

One of the striking features of these centuries of disorder in Western Europe is the fashion in which, in spite of the near-anarchy, Christianity continued to spread. While many factors contributed to this expansion, it would not have been except for the inner vitality of the faith.

In Italy, Spain, and Gaul the native pagan cults which survived at the end of the fifth century disappeared and those imported by the invaders, except for Islam, were replaced by Christianity.

More serious than overt paganism were the sag in morals and the increase in superstition of those who bore the Christian name. In Gaul the later Merovingians were a sorry lot, weak and vicious. Under them the quality of living of laity and clergy deteriorated.

A gleam in the growing darkness issued from Ireland. The Irish *peregrini* who came to the Frankish domains were distressed by the low level of morals which they found among professing Christians and struggled manfully to raise it and to win to the faith such openly avowed heathen as remained. They encouraged the laity to come to them to confess their sins and as a means of discipline worked out penitentials, with penances prescribed for specific sins.

The most famous of the Irish missionaries in the Frankish domains was Columban. He was a contemporary of Gregory the Great, perhaps born in the same year. Handsome, full-blooded, attracted by and attracted to the opposite sex, as a youth, against his mother's tears, he entered the monastic life. From the famous monastic community of Bangor, in what is now County Down, he led a band of twelve across the sea and preached in the Merovingian realms more earnest faith and living. In the Vosges Mountains he founded monasteries which attracted many and to which he gave a more austere rule than that of Benedict. Eventually he aroused the ire of the Merovingian rulers, partly because of his frank speaking against the king's habit of taking concubines, and perhaps because of his unwillingness to submit to the bishops of the Frankish realm on the date for the celebration of Easter. To avoid deportation he left the Frankish domains and resumed his wanderings. These took him to a monastic community in the mountains between Milan and Genoa and there he died, probably in 615. Monasteries which followed his rule multiplied in the lands of the Franks.

The Irish *peregrini* were not an unalloyed asset to the religious life of the Continent. Unaccustomed to the diocesan form of church organization which they found there, they tended to disregard it. Their bishops wandered about as they pleased, ordaining whom they would. Their monasteries were reluctant or entirely unwilling to accord jurisdiction to the diocesan bishops. Some of the *peregrini* were accused of holding and teaching erratic and heretical doctrines. Yet in the main the Irish made important contributions through their missionary labours among Christians and non-Christians.

One of the most striking and important territorial gains of Christianity during this period, both in its immediate and its long-term results, was the conversion of the pagan peoples of the island of Great Britain. We have noted that Britain was part of the Roman Empire and that before the end of the fifth century the large majority of the population who had conformed to Latin culture had also accepted the Christian faith. It was in this Christian Britain that Patrick had been reared and from it that he went as a missionary to Ireland. However, not all the population of the island had adopted the Christian name. North of the Roman *limes,* in the later Scotland, were areas which had not been won to the faith and perhaps had not even been touched by it. Moreover, and more significantly, Germanic peoples, mainly Angles and Saxons, all of them pagans, had settled in the eastern portions of the island and had been formed into a number of petty kingdoms. The descendants of the Roman provincials, Christians, had moved to the western parts of the island or to Britanny or had been killed off.

In the sixth and seventh centuries within the span of approximately a hundred years the conversion of these Germanic settlers, the English as we had best call them, was accomplished. In it the British Christians in the west of the island had little or no part. Presumably their clergy were not concerned to give the Gospel to these invaders and chronic enemies. The missionaries were from two sources, Ireland and Rome. Both began their labours late in the sixth century. These gain added significance from the fact that in the seventh and eighth centuries English missionaries had a large share in the conversion of Germany and in the improvement of the Christianity of the Carolingian realms and that in recent centuries British Christianity, mainly that of England and Scotland, has been carried to much of the world.

The Irish missionaries to the English were largely associated with the names of Columba (also known as Columcille) and Iona. Columba was born in Ireland, of royal blood, probably in 521, and so was an older contemporary of Gregory and Columban. He seems early to have dedicated himself to the monastic life and in due time was ordained deacon and priest. He was never a bishop. In 562 or 563, when in the full vigour of middle life, moved, so his friend and biographer says, by "the love of Christ," he left Ireland with twelve companions and established his headquarters on Iona, a rocky island about three miles long and about a mile and a half wide off the west coast of Scotland. He was a man of striking personality, a born leader, forceful, with quick wrath for injustice to the weak, with tenderness for the poor and for the brute creation, and with a simple and deep faith in God. He is said always to have been occupied—with study, prayer, writing, fasting, and watching. Iona was his centre and there he was head of the monastic community which he founded. From Iona he made frequent journeys, some to Ireland, but more in what is now the mainland of Scotland. In Scotland there were immigrant Scots from Ireland, Celtic and probably largely Christian. There, too, were other Celtic folk, Picts, many of them pagans. The Christian faith had already been planted among these Celts, partly by Ninian, a younger contemporary and warm admirer of Martin of Tours, in the fore part of the fifth century. Kentigern, probably the same as Mungo, a shadowy figure about whom little certain information has survived and whose headquarters are said to have been at Glasgow, had been active as a missionary in the north of Great Britain in the sixth century. Columba also won some of the Celtic folk of Scotland. His disciples told of miracles performed through him which had much to do with gaining respect for his teaching.

Long after Columba, the community at Iona carried on his tradition. It was from Iona, a generation or so after the death of the founder, that a notable contribution was begun towards the conversion of some of the English. In a struggle for power in Northumbria, one of the Anglo-Saxon kingdoms in the north of England, two princes of the blood royal took refuge on Iona and there were baptized. When one of them, Oswald, came into control in Northumbria, he asked Iona for a missionary for his people. Christianity had already been introduced into the kingdom by the Roman mission of which we are soon to speak, but it was to Iona that Oswald turned for a bishop. The first to be sent proved poorly adapted to the assignment, but the second, Aidan, was remarkably successful. To him Oswald gave headquarters on the island of Lindisfarne, off the east coast, larger than Iona but, like the latter, a convenient centre. Aidan travelled through the little kingdom mainly on foot, winning pagans, confirming believers, caring for the poor, ransoming slaves, and educating and ordaining priests. Aidan's successor, Finan, also from Iona, baptized the king and royal entourage of Mercia, an Anglo-Saxon kingdom in the heart of England, and aided in the conversion of the East Saxons. Cuthbert, later Bishop of Lindisfarne, famous as a saint, had much to do with extending the work of conversion in the North. It was the English Bishop Wilfrid, educated on Lindisfarne, who was instrumental in bringing the South Saxons to the baptismal font and who directed the conversion of the Isle of Wight, said to have been the last of the "provinces" of Britain to be brought to the faith.

Quite apart from the stream which issued from Iona, there were other Irish who aided in the conversion of the English. To the monasteries of Ireland, too, went many English boys for education and training in the ascetic life.

The inauguration and initial direction of the Roman mission to the English were part of the enormous labours of Pope Gregory the Great. The members of this mission did not effect the conversion of as many of the English as did the Irish, but they brought the English Church into close fellowship with Rome and were the means of organizing it into the pattern of territorial dioceses and parishes which prevailed on the Continent.

How Gregory first became interested in the English we do not know. Oral tradition declares that before he became Pope he saw some lads in the slave market in Rome who attracted him by their fair bodies, fine hair, and winsome features. On inquiring, he was told that they came from Britain, that the population was pagan, and that the boys were Angles. "Right," he said, "for they have an angelic face and it becomes such to be co-heirs with the angels in heaven." When he learned that they were from the province of Deiri, he exclaimed, "Truly are they *De ira,* withdrawn from wrath and called to the mercy of Christ." When told that their king's name was Ælla he exclaimed, "hallelujah, the praise of God the Creator must be sung in those parts." The tradition went on to declare that Gregory offered himself to the Pope as a missionary to Britain, but that the Roman populace would not let him go.

Whether or not this story is true, Britain was traditionally within the patriarchate over which Gregory presided and, as we have seen, he sought to fulfil what he deemed his responsibility in various parts of that vast area. It is not strange that with his devotion and wide-ranging vision, as Pope he endeavoured to win its pagans to the faith and to give the church there an ecclesiastical organization. He seems to have redeemed some English slaves with the funds of the Church and he expressed himself as grieved that the British bishops were doing nothing for the conversion of their pagan neighbours.

To inaugurate the mission, Gregory chose men from the monastery which he had founded in his paternal mansion in Rome. It was a small company. Headed by Augustine, not to be confused with the famous Bishop of Hippo, it set out from Rome in 596, a century after the baptism of Clovis and thirty-nine years before A-lo-pên brought the faith to China, at the other extreme of Eurasia. Here was to be a new kind of conquest of Britain from Rome. The contrast with that earlier one was striking. Across a valley from the monastery rose the Palatine Hill, with the remains of the palaces of the Cæsars from which Britain had once been ruled. As a physical power Rome was now feeble. Yet this little band, unsupported by arms, was to inaugurate a conquest which was to continue centuries longer and have more enduring effects than had that which had been achieved and maintained by the legions. When the group reached Gaul they became terrified by the dangers in the way and Augustine returned to Rome to ask permission to discontinue the enterprise. Gregory sent him back with a kind but firm letter ordering them on.

Augustine and his band landed on the coast of the Kingdom of Kent, just across the English channel from the Continent. The King of Kent had a Christian wife, a Frankish princess, and with her was a Frankish bishop. After a little hesitation, the king gave the mission his consent to establish themselves in his capital, Canterbury, and turned over to them an existing church building, named for Martin of Tours. Before long he was baptized and thousands of his subjects followed him to the baptismal font. Augustine went to Arles, in the south of Gaul, for consecration as archbishop, and thus became the first Archbishop of Canterbury. At Canterbury Augustine began a monastery, using a pagan temple which had been given him by the King. Following the Benedictine rule, it became the prototype of many Benedictine houses in England.

Gregory kept in touch with the mission, sent it reinforcements, and counselled it through letters. He authorized Augustine to appoint twelve diocesan bishops and to place a bishop at York who, as the Christians increased in that region, should also become an archbishop and ordain twelve bishops. Thus was extended to England the diocesan system which had been developed on the Continent after the pattern of the Roman Empire. To this day Canterbury and York have remained the seats of the two metropolitans of the Church of England. Gregory advised the adaptation of ritual to local circumstances and counselled that pagan temples be transformed into churches rather than destroyed. With occasional reverses, the Roman mission was carried into portions of the east and north of England. While, as we have said, it did not win as many converts as did the Irish, it effectively forged a connexion between the Church in England with the Papacy which was not to be severed until the sixteenth century and then not completely.

Not at first did all the Christians in Great Britain submit to the hierarchy connected with Rome. Through tactlessness or ignorance Augustine antagonized the British bishops in the west of the island, sensitive as they already were because of the gulf between the Britons and the English and their long isolation from Rome. Differences in customs between those who received their faith through the Roman mission and those who obtained it through Ireland and Iona also caused divisions. Only gradually were these healed.

The English Church owed a great debt to Theodore of Tarsus. As his name indicates, he was from Asia Minor. He was in Rome when the death of an Englishman who had been sent there by the Kings of Kent and Northumbria for consecration as Archbishop of Canterbury left that post in urgent need of an occupant. Although then sixty-six years of age, he accepted the appointment (668), went to England and put the church in order. He was well educated in Greek and Latin and in secular and ecclesiastical literature. He found the church in a bad way, for a recent pestilence had carried off many of the clergy and populace and only three bishops were left. He travelled widely, "the first bishop whom all the English Church consented to obey," created new dioceses, consecrated bishops, established a parish system, held synods which brought increasing conformity with Rome, spread the church music of Rome, trained men in Greek, Latin, the Bible, astronomy, and mathematics, and brought in stricter moral discipline. He lived until 690, or to the great age of eighty-eight. In his later years the Celts made a determined effort to regain control, for a time with some success, but his work had been well done and he is remembered as the real organizer of the Church in England.

Within less than a century after the arrival of Augustine, missionaries from the recently converted English were going to the Continent. There for several generations they led in the conversion of much of what are now Holland and Germany. They organized the Church there and tied it up solidly with Rome. Thus they justified the efforts which Rome had put forth on behalf of England. Two names stand out in the story, Willibrord and Winfrith or, as he is better known, Boniface.

Willibrord laboured in what is now Holland with his headquarters at Utrecht. He was by no means the first missionary in the later Belgium and Holland. Part of what is now Belgium had been in the Roman Empire and had been reached by missionaries before the fifth century. Irish *peregrini* and missionaries from the Frankish domains had been there and with much success. The English Bishop Wilfrid had preached among the Frisians while on one of his trips to Rome and had baptized many. Willibrord came from a devout English family and had his early training in a monastery at Ripon of which Wilfrid was the founder. When about twenty years of age he went to Ireland. In 690, then in his thirty-third year, he embarked for Frisia, after the Irish fashion with eleven companions, and established himself at Utrecht, by which the Rhine then flowed. He sought the aid of Pepin of Heristal and the latter, eager to extend Frankish power in that region, gave it to him. He also asked Papal support and in 695 or 696 was given archiepiscopal consecration in Rome, almost exactly a hundred years after Augustine had set out from the Eternal City on his hesitant mission to England. Quite understandably the Frisians connected Willibrord with Frankish imperialism and associated baptism with submission to Frankish rule. Baptisms decreased or increased with the ebb and flow of Frankish power. Yet until he was eighty-one Willibrord continued at his difficult task. He was aided by other missionaries from England, and while success was slow, by the time of his death he saw Christianity well established in the southern part of what is now the Netherlands.

Winfrith first came to the Continent to aid Willibrord. The precise year and place of his birth are not known, but the date was possibly 672 or 675 and the place not far from Exeter. In early childhood he expressed a wish to enter the monastic life, but only tardily won his father's consent. He received his training in monasteries near Exeter and Winchester and there displayed qualities of scholarship, Christian character, teaching ability, sound judgement, and administrative skill which marked him out for distinction. In 716 he went as a missionary to the Frisians and for a time was at Utrecht. Because of unfavourable political conditions the door seemed closed and for a year and a half he was back in England. In 718 he once more left for the Continent and was never again to see his native land. He went first to Rome to obtain Papal approval for his mission. Winning it and now with the Latin name of Boniface, in 719 he went north, first to Germany and then, because of a change for the better for missions in Frisia, for three years he served under Willibrord, destroying pagan temples and building churches. Willibrord wished him for his successor, but Boniface declined, pleading as a reason his commission from the Pope and his conviction that only the Pope could appoint to the episcopate. He then went back to Germany. There he organized and purified the existing Christian communities and also won pagans to the faith. In Hesse he had the most spectacular success of his career. At Geismar, in the presence of a large number of hostile pagans, he began cutting down an ancient oak which was sacred to the god Thor. Before he had quite felled the tree a powerful blast of wind completed the demolition and the hoary giant, crashing, broke into four fragments. The pagan bystanders were convinced of the power of the new faith and from the timber Boniface erected an oratory to St. Peter.

Boniface commanded the confidence of successive Popes and by them was made bishop and then archbishop. By accepting appointment as bishop and archbishop from Rome and swearing allegiance to the Pope he strengthened the authority of the Papal see in the North. As archbishop Boniface was authorized by the Pope to found new episcopal sees. Through him these could also be tied to Rome.

The Carolingians committed to Boniface the task of reforming the Church in the Frankish domains. He kept in touch by letter with his friends in England and from that land and on the Continent recruited many helpers. He made much use of women. He was an indefatigable traveller, teaching, organizing, founding monasteries. Chief of his monastic foundations was Fulda, in the initiation of which he was aided by his disciple, Sturm. It followed the rule of Benedict and became the main centre of learning and theological education for much of Germany. Boniface was appointed Archbishop of Mainz. Under his leadership synods were held in the Frankish domains which sought to enforce the celibacy of the priests, to reduce the worldliness of the clergy, and to exalt the authority of diocesan bishops and reduce that of wandering bishops. Working under the authority of the Popes, Boniface did much to extend the Papal power in the Frankish domains. He reformed not only the Frankish Church but also the Church in Bavaria and in Thuringia. Boniface longed to go as a missionary to the Saxons who remained on the Continent.

Finally, in his old age, and by his own wish, Boniface returned to the Frisians, among whom he had spent his first missionary years, and there baptized thousands, destroyed temples, and erected churches. The end came, probably in June, 754, and as he would have wished. He had set a day for the confirmation of neophytes and had summoned them from far and wide to meet him on the banks of a river. There a band of pagans, apparently intent on plunder, fell upon him and his companions. Enjoining non-resistance on those about him, he was killed by the attackers. Humble, a man of prayer, self-sacrificing, courageous, steeped in the Scriptures, a born leader of men, affectionate, a superb organizer and administrator, he was at once a great Christian, a great missionary, and a great bishop. The Church in Germany owed him an incalculable debt. By the end of the eighth century the remainder of the pagan Frisians, for whom Boniface had given his life, had accepted Christian baptism.

Except the Scandinavians, the last of the Germanic peoples to be drawn into the Christian fold were the Saxons who had remained on the Continent after so many of their number had migrated to Great Britain. This was not strange. Their lands lay north of the Frisians and the Hessians and it was late when the Frankish boundaries were extended to include them. They long resisted conversion, for they associated it with Carolingian imperialism. Several English missionaries laboured among them, and Boniface, armed with Papal authority to proclaim the Gospel to them, pled for helpers from England. Due largely to English efforts, by the last quarter of the eighth century a small minority among the Saxons had been won.

The conversion of the bulk of the Saxons was through the vigorous use of armed force by Charlemagne. Charlemagne was determined to bring the Saxons into his realm and in 772 reduced much of the region to ostensible submission. As part of the process of integration under his rule he insisted upon baptism. He could not always be in the Saxon territories and during his absences repeated revolts broke out. As often as they occurred he returned with fire and sword. He did not depend entirely upon armed force. Many of the recalcitrant he moved into the Rhineland among a professedly Christian population, thus to facilitate their assimilation. He encouraged missionaries, many of them Anglo-Saxons, to come to these kinsfolk of theirs and baptize and instruct them. He divided the land into dioceses and had bishops set over them, thus giving the area a comprehensive ecclesiastical organization.

Here was the most naked use of armed force for the spread of the faith which Christianity had yet seen. It is pleasant to record that it did not go unprotested and that the boldest critic of whom we know was Alcuin, the English scholar who had been brought to court by Charlemagne to aid in the revival of learning of which we are to hear in a moment. He spoke out quite fearlessly and pled that adults be not baptized until they had been properly instructed and that tithes be not exacted of the newly converted.

Whether by force or by quiet instruction by missionaries, the Saxons became staunch adherents of their Christian profession. In the next period they were to become bulwarks of the faith.

Before the year 950 beginnings had been made in the conversion of the Scandinavians, that last wave of pagan invasion which was to scourge Western Europe. Willibrord made an effort to plant the faith in Denmark, but without success. The most notable pioneer among the Scandinavians was Anskar (or Ansgar) (801–865), who was a native of Flanders and is said to have been of Saxon stock. Anskar began his mission at the instance of the son and successor of Charlemagne, Louis, whose usual designation, the Pious, is evidence of his deep interest in Christianity. Like his father before him, but without his exuberant energy, Louis wished to extend the Frankish domains and to do so in close association with the spread of Christianity. To further his purpose, he had an archiepiscopal see created with Hamburg as its centre, later associated with Bremen, and had Anskar appointed to it and given Papal confirmation and the title of Papal legate for the North. Anskar was courageous, travelled widely, had some missionaries as helpers, and won a few converts. However, the majority of the Scandinavians were not as yet minded to become Christians. Independent, they especially spurned the suggestion of accepting the faith from agents of the Carolingians, for that would imply and might actually entail submission to rulers whose realms they were raiding. When, late in the tenth and in succeeding centuries, Scandinavia received baptism, it was under the leadership of its own princes and through missionaries from subject England from which nothing was to be feared politically.

Before 950 some of the Scandinavians who settled within "Christendom" accepted baptism. This was the case in England. It was also true in what came to be known as Normandy. Here the first Duke, known variously as Rollo, Hrolf, and Hrolfr, concluded a treaty with the Carolingian king in 911 by which his holdings were given legal status and in return he and some of his followers agreed to be baptized. It was not until after 950, however, that the conversion of most of the Scandinavians was accomplished.

From the preceding summary, all too brief, of the conversion of the peoples of Western Europe, it will be seen how largely it was by mass movements of entire tribes or peoples, led by the chieftains or kings. As the numerical triumph of Christianity in the Roman Empire had been completed by mass conversion encouraged and latterly enforced by the Emperors, so in these much smaller units which made up Western Europe in this period, that faith was adopted as the religion of the community, usually at the command or at least with the energetic assistance of the prince.

Here we must note the contrast between the theology officially held in the Church in the West and the practice, a contrast which was to continue down to our own day, not only in the Catholic Church of the West, but also in large wings of its major offshoot, Protestantism. The theology was Augustinian and in theory held that only through God's grace could any one be saved, that the recipients of grace were predestined and that presumably, as Augustine had held, their number was infallibly fixed. As a corollary of predestination all chosen by God would be saved through irresistible grace and the perseverance of the saints. Those not chosen would not be saved, regardless of what they or others, such as missionaries, might attempt to do. In apparent contradiction of that conviction, whole tribes and peoples were baptized and given Christian instruction and the other ministries of the Church.

There seems to be no evidence that any of the missionaries were troubled by the paradox. If they were, they might have taken refuge in the findings of the Synod of Orange in 529, findings which had Papal approval and which held that by the grace transmitted through baptism all who had received that rite can, if they labour faithfully, do those things which "belong to the salvation of the soul." Since through mass conversions baptism was practically universal and was given in infancy to successive generations, it followed that all might be saved if they worked together with God, performing those things which were held to be commanded by Him through the Church.

That the Catholic Church acted on the assumption that this could be accom plished was evidence of a basic optimism which we are to see persisting in the West, both in that Church and in Protestantism. It was also in the Eastern Churches and particularly in the Greek wing of the Catholic Church. But here it was not so marked. That it was no stronger in the East may have been due to the greater obstacles which the churches there faced, nearer as they were to the heartland of Eurasia and to the vast populations of Asia. Especially did the prospect seem hopeless for those Christians who were confronted by Islam.

How far in these conversions in the West was the Gospel understood and really accepted? Could the professedly Christian communities be knit together into an inclusive fellowship exemplifying the basic Christian tie of love? Much of the alleged Christianity was obviously very superficial and quite without comprehension of the real import of the Gospel. However, most of the missionaries through whom the instruction was given were monks. That meant that they were in principle fully committed to the Christian faith and to carrying out thoroughly its precepts in their own lives. It is significant, moreover, that often second and even first generation converts became noted exemplars of the faith and that the nominal winning of the Anglo-Saxons had scarcely been completed before missionaries from England were going to the Continent. We find such characters as Willibrord and Boniface and scores of others whom we have not the space so much as to name who bear unmistakably the distinctive marks of Christian character and who as such were revered by many of their contemporaries, even though but few sought to emulate them.

These many tribal, embryonic national Christian communities possessed a common tie in the Church of Rome. The Popes were increasingly acknowledged as the visible head of the Church and to a greater or less extent exercised supervision. Rome was a centre of pilgrimage. From all over Western Europe the devout flocked to its churches and shrines. It was sadly shrunken from the days of its imperial splendour, but now was a period when nowhere in Western Europe were there cities of any size. Rome was impressive even in its ruins and it still possessed imposing churches and shrines sacred to the memories of the two greatest of the apostles, Peter and Paul. Here also were to be had miracle-working relics of saints and martyrs, to be carried back to the monasteries and churches of the several lands of Western Europe.

THE CAROLINGIAN REVIVAL

Christian living and the inner life and unity of the Church were furthered by the great Carolingians. For about two centuries the Carolingians brought under their sway much of Western Europe including at the widest extent of their realms the larger portions of what are now France, Belgium, the Netherlands, Western and Southern Germany, Switzerland, and Austria, perhaps half of Italy, slight footholds south of the Pyrenees, and much of the east coast of the Adriatic. Their rule stretched from the Elbe to Barcelona and from the North Sea to south of Rome. Their power reached its apex under Charlemagne and was symbolized by his coronation as Roman Emperor by the Pope in Rome in 800. Compared with that of the Cæsars of the second and third centuries Charlemagne's empire was a small, impoverished, and semi-barbarous affair. In splendour it was far inferior to the contemporary Byzantine Empire, the Abbasid Caliphate, and the waning T'ang dynasty in China. Yet its glories dazzled Western Europeans. The Carolingians assisted the Christianity of Western Europe by giving a measure of peace and political unity to a fairly large area, by actively furthering improvements in the Church, and by an alliance with the Papacy which gave protection to the Roman Pontiffs against local enemies in Italy, especially the Lombards and unruly factions in the city.

The earliest of the Carolingians who rose to prominence, Pepin of Heristal and Charles Martel, had no very deep religious interest. Indeed, in his pressing financial needs, the latter appropriated some of the property of the Church, a move which is not surprising in view of the fact that in his day, through the gifts of generations of benefactors, about a third of the land of the realm is said to have been in the possession of ecclesiastical institutions. However, Pepin of Heristal and Charles Martel were quite willing to give moral support to Willibrord and Boniface in their missionary labours, for these would aid in the extension of Frankish political power.

The two sons of Charles Martel, Carloman and Pepin the Short, who succeeded their father on his death in 741, were more religiously minded. Indeed, after six years Carloman retired to the monastery of Monte Cassino, leaving Pepin in undivided control. They reinforced Boniface in his efforts to reform the Frankish Church and much of his success was due to their aid. Beginning with Clovis, the Frankish rulers had exercised a large degree of authority over the Church in their realms, and Pepin wielded this to improve the quality of the clergy and to strengthen the Church's discipline. In the age of disorder the custom of holding annual synods of the bishops, summoned by the king, had almost lapsed. Synods now became more numerous and acted vigorously to improve the morals of the Frankish domains. After Boniface retired to resume his mission among the Frisians, Chrodegang, Bishop and later Archbishop of Metz, continued his reformatory labours. Outstanding among the Frankish bishops of his day, he was zealous in cleansing the Church.

Pepin the Short also established relations with the Papacy which accrued to the benefit of himself and the See of Peter. For several years the Popes had been in a very difficult situation. They were threatened by the Lombards. At the same time they had broken off relations with the Emperors at Constantinople over the iconoclastic issue. Under Pope Gregory III, who held the chair of Peter from 731 to 741, or, in other words, during the later years of Charles Martel, a Roman synod had excommunicated the opponents of the icons and in retaliation the Byzantine Emperor, an ardent iconoclast, had exercised his authority to remove Sicily and such portions of Italy as he could command from Papal jurisdiction. In theory Rome had been under the Emperor, but the breach now severed that connexion and Gregory III was the last Pope to seek and be given the approval of the Byzantine Emperor for his election. Gregory turned to Charles Martel, as the most powerful Christian political figure in the West, for aid against the Lombards, but in vain.

Pepin the Short was more friendly to the Church and the Papacy. He asked of Pope Zacharias, who succeeded Gregory III, approval for relegating the last of the Merovingian *rois fainéants* to a monastery and the assumption by himself of the royal title. He thus seemed to say that the Pope had the right both to depose monarchs and to grant crowns, a principle which was to be of enormous importance in succeeding centuries. Pope Zacharias gave the requested assent. In 752 Zacharias was followed in the Papal chair by Stephen II. The Lombards were a growing menace. In 751 they had taken Ravenna, long the seat of the Exarch, the chief representative in Italy of the Emperor, and were threatening Rome. Stephen journeyed north to seek the aid of Pepin and was housed in a monastery at St. Denis, near Paris. There he crowned and anointed Pepin, confirming the earlier coronation, said, somewhat debatably, to have been by the hands of Boniface. He also anointed Pepin's queen and the king's two sons, Carloman and the future Charlemagne. In return, Pepin waged two campaigns in Italy against the Lombards and compelled the latter to turn over to the Pope their recent conquests from the Emperor, including Ravenna.

In granting these lands to the Pope Pepin the Short is usually regarded as having inaugurated the temporal power of the Papacy and the Estates of the Church. This status the Popes have claimed from that day to this, although it was to be sadly weakened in the nineteenth century.

The step was not as revolutionary as might at first sight appear. As we noted when we spoke of Gregory the Great, the Church of Rome had long held vast properties which it administered, widely scattered in Italy, Sicily, Sardinia, Corsica, and Gaul. To be sure, in theory these were within the structure of the Roman Empire and thus were subject to the Emperors. In practice, however, the Popes had managed them through an elaborate bureaucracy almost as though they were independent. Because of the decline of the imperial power in Italy, the Popes had been the chief defenders of the city of Rome. Gregory the

Great, for example, had raised armies for protection against the Lombards. Even with these qualifications, the action of Pepin was highly significant.

Pepin the Short died in 768 and was succeeded by his sons Charles and Carloman. The latter followed his father to the grave in 771 leaving Charles, whom we best know as Charlemagne, "Charles the Great," as sole ruler. In Charlemagne the Carolingian power reached its height. His was a long reign, for he died in 814 and thus was on the throne for nearly half a century, for more than forty years without a colleague. A bold and skilful warrior, he greatly extended the borders of his realm. He was also an able administrator whose organizing and directing genius actively concerned itself with all aspects of the life of his domains. Under his vigorous hand important political and ecclesiastical innovations were made and for a time it seemed that permanent recovery had been effected from the disorders which had followed the decay of the Roman Empire. By his coronation as Roman Emperor on Christmas Day, in the year 800, and in Rome itself, it might almost have seemed that the preceding centuries had been a bad dream and that the glories of the Cæsars were not only to be revived but also enriched and transfigured by the Christian faith of ruler and people. The act was not regarded as an innovation, for Rome still held the imagination of the peoples of Europe, civilization was thought of as inseparable from it, the Roman Empire continued, even if with diminished borders and from Constantinople, and there was ample precedent for two Emperors, one in the East and one in the West. Eventually Charlemagne was recognized by two successive Byzantine rulers as entitled, with themselves, to the designation of Emperor.

Charlemagne was deeply and genuinely religious and conceived of himself as ruling by Christian principles. He was masterful, autocratic, cruel in at least some of his wars, and notoriously lax in his marital relations, but he was moderate in his eating and drinking. He could not write (although in his mature life he made some pretense of trying) and while he could read he preferred to be read to. He was fond of the history of antiquity but he took especial delight in the writings of Augustine, particularly his *De Civitate Dei*. This work gave him his political and social philosophy and he set himself so far as possible to making his realm the City of God.

Possessed of this masterful energy and this religious motive, Charlemagne continued the reformation and improvement of the Church which was already under way. In the newly conquered lands won from paganism he created bishoprics, established monasteries, and appointed the men who were their heads. In the older parts of his domains, where the bishops were elected by the chapters with the consent of the people, his license was necessary. As the tradition of elections was weakened, he used his authority to place in episcopal chairs men whom he believed to be suitable and to endow them with the revenues of abbeys. He encouraged the regular holding of synods. He himself presided at important synods which dealt with theological doctrines and had the major voice in the decisions.

Charlemagne concerned himself with improving the structure of the Church. The parish system had long been spreading in the Frankish domains and the countryside had been divided into parishes, each with its clergy. Many of the parishes and chapels had been endowed with lands by local magnates for "the salvation of their souls," but the donors retained to themselves and their heirs the privilege of naming the pastors. These rights could be transferred by sale, gift, or bequest. Under these circumstances the bishop, beyond his function of ordination, might be permitted very little if any control. Charlemagne insisted that the bishops have the power of discipline over the clergy in their respective dioceses. The bishops also had political and civil functions.

Charlemagne's measures did not prevent many ecclesiastical endowments being allocated for the support of his favourites, even laymen. Thus his biographer, Einhard, an intimate at his court and that of his son, Louis the Pious, enjoyed the income of several important abbeys and, although married and living with his wife, seems to have been an abbot.

Further to raise the level of the Church, Charlemagne revived and strengthened the existing system of archbishops. He increased their number. Each was in theory to supervise the bishops in his province. The *missi dominici* sent out to enforce the king's decrees had authority in matters ecclesiastical as well as civil and military.

Charlemagne perfected a system of tithes for the support of the bishops and the parish clergy. For authority for the principle the clergy cited the Mosaic Law. The custom had spread gradually. In 585 a synod of Frankish prelates asked that it be regularized. Pepin the Short gave tithes legal status as a recognized tax and Charlemagne further endorsed them. In the Frankish domains and elsewhere in the Western Church, the support of the clergy and the care of the poor also came from offerings, many of them mass stipends in return for which masses were said for the donors or for those whom they designated.

Charlemagne encouraged the repair, embellishment, and construction of churches and the improvement of public worship. Pepin the Short had already furthered the spread of the "Gregorian chant." Charlemagne sought to make universal the form of the liturgy which had developed at Rome.

He endeavoured to raise the morals of the laity and to improve the acquaintance of the common man with the main principles of the faith. To this end he commanded the clergy to preach on the Creed, prayer, and the Ten Commandments. In theory all Christians were to know the Lord's Prayer and the Creed.

Through ecclesiastical legislation he strove to inculcate and enforce the sanctity of the marriage tie, and that in spite of his own errant example.

Charlemagne also stressed the education of the clergy. Even after the reforms of Boniface and Chrodegang, great room remained for improvement. In many monasteries learning had lapsed and idleness and ignorance abounded. His purpose was the advancement of religion and the Church, but as a foundation the study of the great authors of Roman antiquity was stimulated. Indeed, that we have the works of these pagan writers is in many instances due to the copies made in this period of literary revival. The form of Latin script was encouraged, a vast improvement over what had immediately gone before it, which became standard in succeeding centuries and is familiar in our printed books of today.

To aid in this educational programme Charlemagne drew scholars from wherever he could find them. They came from Ireland, Spain, Italy, Gaul, and, notably, England. In the seventh and eighth centuries some of the Anglo-Saxon monasteries had become centres of learning. Most famous of all their scholars was Bede. Reared in a monastery in Northumbria in the present County Durham, he was diligent in his religious duties and in his studies. He used Latin easily, knew some Greek, and was master of such of the learning of the day as was available to him. He wrote voluminously and on many subjects, but is best remembered for his *Ecclesiastical History of England,* our fullest source for the conversion of the Anglo-Saxons and the early years of the English Church. Alcuin, the most distinguished of the savants at the court of Charlemagne, a scion of a noble family, related to Willibrord, and a younger contemporary of Boniface, had been educated at York under the direction of one of the disciples of Bede. He had headed the school in that city. A trusted intimate of Charlemagne, with no great originality, he was immensely learned, taught in the palace school which his royal master had set up, wrote extensively, and died (804), ripe in years and honours, as head of the monastery of St. Martin of Tours.

Charlemagne was not especially interested in furthering asceticism. He founded a few monasteries, but to him they were not important for the practice of the full Christian life, but rather as centres of education and civilization.

Charlemagne concerned himself with the Papacy. He renewed his father's grants to the see of Peter and treated the Popes with respect. However, he made it clear that he expected them to support him with their prayers while leaving to him practical matters of political action and administration. He may not have been entirely happy when the Pope took the initiative of crowning him Roman Emperor as he was kneeling at the high altar on that memorable Christmas Day. That act, however, had fully as far-reaching significance as the

Papal sanction to the assumption of the royal power by Pepin. It established
the precedent that the imperial coronation of the Western successors to the
Cæsars must be by the Pope and thereby accorded that pontiff an enhanced
position.

THE DECLINE OF THE CAROLINGIANS

With the death of Charlemagne (814) the Carolingian power entered upon
a decline. It was not sudden, but none of his line who followed Charlemagne
had his ability and the Carolingian structure depended so largely upon the
quality of the monarch that as the latter deteriorated the fabric fell apart.

Charlemagne's immediate successor, Louis the Pious, who reigned from 814
to 840, was deeply religious in a monastic rather than his father's lay fashion
but he did not possess the force and administrative gifts of his sire. The impetus
given by his predecessors carried the realm forward and he was crowned as
Roman Emperor. As was to be expected, he was active in ecclesiastical affairs,
and synods continued the reform movement.

True to his convictions, Louis was especially concerned with improving the
quality of monastic life. To this end he called to his assistance Witiza, better
known as Benedict of Aniane. Born about the year 750, Benedict was now in
his mid-sixties. The son of a Gothic count, he had served in the court under
Pepin the Short and Charlemagne. Then, in his twenties, he had renounced
the world and entered a monastery. Disturbed by the laxity in the house which
he had chosen, he founded a monastery of his own at Aniane in which he
sought to restore the observance of the rule of Benedict in its full strictness,
and with especial emphasis upon worship and self denial. His example proved
contagious and by the time of Charlemagne's death many other houses were
adhering closely to the Benedictine ideal. Louis made Benedict of Aniane his
adviser on monastic affairs and the order went forth that all monasteries in
the realm must follow the Benedictine rule as interpreted by him.

The death of Louis the Pious (840) was followed, in 843, by the division of
the realm between his three sons, Lothair I, who was given the imperial title
and who received the region which included the Frankish portions of Italy and
the valley of the Rhone, Louis, because of his assignment known as "the German," to whom went the area east of the Rhone, and Charles the Bald, who
was apportioned most of the modern France and who was eventually (875),
exactly seventy-five years after that had happened to his grandfather, to be
crowned Roman Emperor by the Pope on Christmas Day in St. Peter's. This
division, the civil strife which followed, and continued quarrels among the
subsequent scions of the Carolingian line brought added internal weakness.

Not immediately, however, did collapse come. The intellectual and religious activity which had been encouraged by the great Carolingians went on well into the ninth century. Charles the Bald was abler than his father and his court was a centre of learning. It was not until the latter part of the ninth and the fore part of the tenth century that the darkness became intense.

RENEWED THEOLOGICAL ACTIVITY UNDER THE CAROLINGIANS

The intellectual and religious revival made possible by the Carolingians was accompanied by fresh theological activity and controversies over doctrine. Indeed, as at so many other periods in the history of the faith, innovations in Christian belief and the consequent debates were evidences of vitality.

One of the controversies centred in Spain. For a time after the Arab conquest the churches which survived south of the Pyrenees, and they were many and strong, were in part cut off from Rome. In the second half of the eighth century an archbishop, Wilchair, came in from the Frankish domains, apparently charged by the Papacy with carrying out reforms analogous to those which Boniface was working north of the Pyrenees. A bishop consecrated by him as a kind of Papal legate attempted to bring the date for celebrating Easter in accord with that of Rome, to introduce other Roman customs, and to prevent mixed marriages of Christians with Moslems. The vigorous methods of one of his subordinates aroused resentment among Spanish churchmen.

More serious was a dispute over the nature of the Trinity. Here the Pope stepped in and reproved not only the extreme views of one of the most outspoken partisans of the Roman Church, but also those of Elipand, Archbishop of Toledo and as such the ranking ecclesiastic in the Spanish Church. Elipand held to a conviction about the relation of the divine to the human in Jesus Christ which may have come down from early Latin Christian thinkers and have persisted, distorted, because of the isolation of Spain from the theological discussions which had issued in Chalcedon. In an attempt to insist upon the full humanity of Jesus Christ, it held that though in his divine nature he was the Son of God, the human Jesus was only a son by adoption. To this doctrine Felix, Bishop of Urgel, also adhered, and Urgel was in the portion of Spain which late in the eighth century was brought under Frankish rule. Summoned to a synod at Regensburg in 792, Felix renounced the Spanish view. Out of deference to the Pope, Charlemagne sent him to Rome, where again he repeated his rejection of adoptionist views. He then returned to his diocese.

However, the bishops in Spain maintained their position. Thereupon Charlemagne summoned a synod which met at Frankfort in 794 and in which were represented most of the Latin Church except that in the part of Spain controlled by the Moslems. The synod condemned the Spanish christology and to the documents embodying its findings Charlemagne added a letter of his own to the Spanish bishops, urging them to comply with the Frankfort decisions. Like some of the Roman and Byzantine Emperors, he was setting himself up as competent on theological issues. Moreover, although he was not yet a Roman Emperor and so had no ground for a legitimate claim of jurisdiction in most of Spain, he was assuming the right to speak to the churches of all Spain. He pled as a reason a request from the Christians of that land.

Incidentally, it was this Council of Frankfort which condemned the pronouncement of the Council of Nicæa of 787 for its permission to pay reverence to images and regarded it not as an ecumenical gathering, but as one simply of the Greeks.

The Council of Frankfort did not end the controversy over Spanish adoptionism. Even before the council had met, Felix, in spite of his solemn rejection of that position, had entered into an epistolatory controversy with Alcuin on the issue and the two continued the debate after Frankfort. In 798 a council at Rome called by the Pope condemned Felix's adoptionism. In the year 800 Alcuin and Felix met in a theological joust in the presence of Charlemagne at Aachen (Aix-la-Chapelle). Felix professed himself convinced and forswore adoptionist terminology, but the authorities did not trust him and he was kept in confinement in Lyons until his death (818). Through lengthy letters Alcuin attempted to bring Elipand to renounce adoptionism, but the latter was obdurate and he and the other bishops in the Spain which was under Moslem rule continued to hold to it.

In one respect the Frankish Church agreed with the Spanish Church. We have seen that in 809 a synod at Aachen approved the custom which had originated in Spain of adding *filioque* to the creed.

More far-reaching in its consequences than the adoptionist controversy was a development of views over the nature of the Eucharist and the emergence of the conception of that central rite of the Church which was later called transubstantiation. Not far from 831 Radbert, or Radbertus, a monk in the famous monastery of Corbie, near Amiens, to whose name Paschasius is usually prefixed, a scholar widely read in Latin and Greek theology, wrote an extensive treatise on the Eucharist, which later, in a revised form, he dedicated to Charles the Bald. He held that while to the senses the bread and the wine in the sacrament remain unaltered, by a miracle the *substantia* of the body and blood of Christ, the very body which was his on the earth, is present in them. However, this change takes place only for those who believe it and accept it in faith, and it is not effective for the unbeliever. To the believer, as had been said centuries earlier, it is the medicine of immortality.

This view did not win immediate acceptance. A distinguished teacher, author, and scholar, Raban Maur (Hrabanus Maurus), a pupil of Alcuin and abbot of the famous monastery of Fulda, denied that "the sacrament of the altar is truly the body of Christ which was born of the Virgin, suffered on the cross, and was raised from the tomb," but he held that the body of the risen Lord is present, even though not physically, and that to receive the body of Christ is to be united with Christ by faith in such a manner as to form with him a single body. Gottschalk, a former monk of Fulda, now imprisoned in a monastery for views which we are to note in a moment, indignantly rejected the suggestion of Radbert that the Christ on the altar suffers anew and dies anew, but he also differed from Raban Maur who seemed to say that the Eucharist was only a sign of grace, and maintained that the body and blood of Christ are mysteriously present as an objective reality, quite independent of the faith of the communicant. Ratramnus, like Radbert a monk of Corbie, in a brief treatise written at the request of Charles the Bald, held that the view of Radbert worked harm to the religious life, for since the effects of partaking of the Eucharist are spiritual, the bread of the Eucharist must be spiritually and not physically the body of Christ. To hold that Christ is physically present would negate the spiritual power and healing which are the true fruits of the sacrament. In spite of these criticisms, the position set forth by Radbert was nearer to that which was eventually endorsed by the Roman Catholic Church than was that of his opponents. Final official action, however, was to wait until the thirteenth century.

Gottschalk was the centre of another controversy, that over predestination. As a child, the son of a Saxon count, he had been dedicated to the monastic life in Fulda. When he reached adolescence, he sought and obtained release on the ground that this had not been with his assent. Yet he did not return to the secular life and, although he left Fulda, was ordained to the priesthood and became one of the numerous itinerant monks of the time. He was a diligent student of the writings of Augustine and, attempting to support his position by quotations from that saint, held that, for reasons which we cannot fathom, God predestines some to eternal life and that those so predestined cannot fail of that life, while, on the other hand—and here was the chief point of debate— those who are not predestined to eternal life are predestined to eternal death.

Obviously this was contrary to the official view which had been set forth in 529 at the Council of Orange. It will be recalled that the Orange gathering, while affirming original sin, declaring that turning to God is wholly through God's grace, and anathematizing those who declare that our will can anticipate God's action, also condemned the teaching that some are predestined to evil and said that if they labour faithfully all the baptized can perform those things which are necessary to salvation.

Powerful opposition was ranged against Gottschalk. In it were the abbot of his old monastery, Raban Maur, and the aggressive and skilful controversialist, Hincmar, Archbishop of Rheims. They were willing to say that God foreknows the sin of those who are not elected to salvation, but they denied that He fore-ordains it. In 848 Raban Maur, now Archbishop of Mainz, had Gottschalk expelled from the realms of Louis the German. That action threw the unfortunate monk into the province of Hincmar and in 849 the latter caused him to be deposed from the priesthood and imprisoned in a monastery.

This did not end the controversy. Gottschalk had powerful friends who rose to his defense. They came out vigorously against Hincmar and some councils took their side. However, in a council in 860 in which most of the Frankish domains were represented, it was Hincmar who triumphed, with slight verbal concessions to his opponents. An attempt was made to take the case to Rome, but a few years later the unfortunate Gottschalk died in his monastic prison, unreconciled to the Church.

More radical than Gottschalk, but in another way, was Claudius, Bishop of Turin, who flourished under Louis the Pious. Said to have been a pupil of Felix of Urgel, he was an earnest student of Augustine. He vigorously denounced the reverence of images and the cross. In this he was in agreement with the general convictions in the Frankish Church. However, he also came out against the current practice of asking for the intercession of the saints. Even more striking was his attitude towards the Papacy. He was critical of the Pope, declaring that he is not to be called apostolic who sits in the seat of the apostle, but he who does the work of an apostle.

The most eminent intellectual figure of the reign of Charles the Bald, John Scotus Eriugena (also called Johannes Scotus), was drawn into the controversies over the Eucharist and predestination. An Irish scholar, he was familiar with the great Greek theologians and translated the works of some of them into Latin, including especially Dionysius the Areopagite. In his intellectual position he was more of a Neoplatonist than a Christian, but in words and perhaps sincerely, he subscribed to the Christian faith. Some questioned his orthodoxy but he was protected by the friendship of Charles the Bald and by his superior scholarship, equipped as he was with a knowledge of the Greek as well as the Latin writings to which the Church looked as authoritative. His was a powerful and philosophically subtle mind and in the disputes of the day he undercut both parties. For instance, in the issue of predestination and foreknowledge, he declared that from God's standpoint there is neither past nor future, for, since He is eternal, He sees all of us and at once. He declared the disjunction between foreknowledge and foreordination to be false, because God can know only what He does. He also held that evil has no real being. Eriugena was too formidable to be tried for heresy by his Frankish contemporaries, but in 855 and 859 his views were condemned by synods.

DEVELOPMENTS IN CHURCH DISCIPLINE

The Carolingian age saw not only intellectual activity but also important developments in the means which the Church employed to further Christian living. It will be remembered that the rule for forgiveness of post-baptismal sins had been public confession, exclusion from the communion, and, after the ecclesiastical authorities were satisfied with the penitent's sincerity as shown by the performance of prescribed acts, public and formal restoration. This custom had been maintained in the West after it had been given up in the East.

In the disorders attendant upon the breakup of the Roman Empire and the invasions, this form of discipline had been weakened or allowed to lapse. In place of it there had come, as we have suggested, largely from Ireland and the Irish *peregrini,* the practice of private confession to a priest. The latter prescribed to the sinner the works of penance which must be performed before restoration to communion. The Irish penitentials, with their instructions to those hearing confessions, probably did much to regulate morals in a stormy age.

However, early in the ninth century the reformers in the Frankish realms began to condemn these penitentials as too much dependent upon the whims of the priest and as being unregulated by ecclesiastical authority. They sought, therefore, to renew public confession and restoration, and councils, bishops, and theologians pronounced in favour of them. Since great difficulty was encountered in persuading the guilty to undergo this prolonged and humiliating ordeal, efforts were made to improve the procedure of private confession. Private confession and penance were continued, but with more careful episcopal supervision. Books of directions for priests hearing confessions were prepared by bishops or under episcopal supervision which sought to embody as much as possible of the earlier standards and practices of the Church.

DECLINING CAROLINGIAN AND GROWING PAPAL POWER

We have noted the fashion in which from the time of Gregory the Great the powers of the Popes north of the Alps had markedly increased. This was due to several factors, among them the great ability of Gregory himself, the success of the Roman mission in England culminating in Theodore of Tarsus, the Anglo-Saxon missionaries on the Continent, loyal as they were to Rome, and the support accorded these missionaries by the early Carolingians.

Pepin the Short and Charlemagne had protected the Popes from the Lombards and local disorders in Italy and had thereby enhanced their position

However, they two, and especially Charlemagne, were such powerful figures that they overshadowed the Popes. While paying them deference, they used them for their purposes.

When, after Louis the Pious, the power of the Carolingians declined, for a time that of the Popes increased. This was partly because the Carolingians no longer dominated the Popes. It was also because the bishops in the Carolingian domains looked to Rome for protection against the archbishops. We have seen how the numbers and authority of the archbishops had been augmented as a phase of the Carolingian reforms. So long as the throne was in the hands of Charlemagne it was able to keep these functionaries in check. However, under the weaker rulers who followed, some of the archbishops seemed to the bishops to be overbearing and to be treating them as subordinate officials. Hincmar of Rheims, aggressive and masterful as he was, especially aroused opposition. The bishops called upon the Popes for protection against their metropolitans. Then, too, as the authority of the Carolingian monarchs declined, lay lords infringed upon what many of the clergy held to be the rights of the Church and the tendency was to look to Rome for support. It was at this time and from the domains of Charles the Bald, perhaps from Mainz or possibly from Rheims, that the Isidorian Decretals were assembled. Partly genuine and partly spurious, this collection of documents was designed to curb the power of the metropolitans and the lay nobility by stressing the position of the Papacy.

The Papal chair also had the advantage of being occupied by some very able men. The most eminent of these, Nicholas I, who was Pope from 858 to 867, we have already met in the conflict with the Byzantine wing of the Catholic Church, and have noted how vigorously he acted in that complex situation. In the West he was appealed to by several of the Carolingians in their conflicts with one another. Like Charlemagne, but in a different manner, he sought to realize in history what he conceived to have been set forth in Augustine's *De Civitate Dei*. He held that the Church was superior to all secular rulers, that the Pope is the ruler of the Church, and that the bishops are his subordinates through whom he carries out his divinely commissioned functions. Nor were these convictions empty theories. Appealed to by a bishop whom Hincmar, as Archbishop of Rheims, had deposed, he compelled the latter to restore him. In a notorious divorce case in which Lothair II, son of Lothair I and greatgrandson of Charlemagne, had obtained the consent of a synod in Metz to put away his wife, Thietberga, that he might marry a concubine, Nicholas forced Lothair to take back Thietberga and excommunicated two archbishops for siding with the king. He also made his will felt against an archbishop of Ravenna who claimed independence of the See of Peter.

THE DESCENT OF DARKNESS

The last decades of the ninth century and the first half of the tenth century were for Western Europe and the Western wing of the Catholic Church years of deep darkness. The Carolingian realms were hopelessly divided among quarreling, weak scions of that famous line. Charles the Fat, the son of Louis the German and greatgrandson of Charlemagne, bore the imperial title and for a time most of the Carolingian domains were reunited under him, but he was deposed in 887 and died the following year. What had been the Frankish kingdom broke up finally into a number of fragments.

Feudalism rapidly developed. Its roots went back before the time of Charlemagne but it now began to flourish. It was partly the result of the weakening of the monarchy and the desire for security in an age of disorder. It was also in part the outgrowth of an agricultural economy in which commerce had dwindled, towns were few and small, and money was scarce. The weaker landowners put themselves under the protection of the stronger and in return made contributions to their lord in the form of contingents for his armed forces and in other forms of service. The system was based upon land which was usually cultivated by serfs who were half free and half slave and who could not be sold from the soil which they tilled but who could not leave it. The major occupation of the feudal lords was fighting and war among them was chronic. This warfare made commerce and other peaceful pursuits difficult and produced a sag in morals.

The internal disorder in Western Europe was augmented by foreign invasion. This was from several directions. From the North came the Scandinavians, sea raiders in long boats. They landed on the coasts and swarmed up the rivers, burning, murdering, and pillaging. Pagans, they did not spare churches or monasteries. Indeed, they found them easy and attractive prey. Here and there they effected permanent settlements, especially in the British Isles, Normandy, Iceland, and the western parts of the later Russia. They brought ruin to the monasteries of Ireland, which, hitherto all but immune from invasion on that far western isle, had been a centre of peaceful Christian living and a source of light to Western Europe. They dealt severe blows to that Anglo-Saxon Christianity from which so many missionaries and scholars had issued to convert the pagans and raise the level of Christian living on the Continent. Up the Seine they came and besieged Paris, up the Loire to Orleans, along the Garonne to Toulouse, and by the Rhone as far as Valence. In Italy a number of cities, including Pisa, fell to their arms. In the 890's the Magyars, a pagan people from the East, poured over the Carpathians and established permanent colonies in the later Hungary. Moslem raiders harassed the shores of Italy and in 846 even plundered the famous churches, St. Peter's and St. Paul's, in Rome itself, for both shrines were outside the then city walls. On the East the Slavs were a menace.

In this approach to anarchy the Church and its institutions suffered and the quality of Christian living declined. Feudal lords appropriated monasteries and churches and either named their incumbents or seized their properties. Bishops and abbots became feudal lords and had little to distinguish them from their lay neighbours except their titles and some of their functions. Bishops and clergy perished or were killed outright in the invasions. Thus in 882 Hincmar, the famous Archbishop of Rheims, died while fleeing from Norman raiders. An Archbishop of Canterbury, taken by the Danes and held for ransom, had no way of raising the sum demanded by his captors except by despoiling his people and courageously chose death.

Unprotected and caught in the welter of the chaotic Italian political scene, the Papacy sank to its lowest ebb. Some Popes of the fifteenth and sixteenth centuries may have been greater sinners, but they were men of force who counted in Europe and the Western Church as a whole. In the latter part of the ninth and the fore part of the tenth century the Popes were either vicious or too weak to cope with the overwhelming odds against them. The tenure of office of many was brief: between 897 and 955 seventeen followed in rapid succession. One, John VIII, who died in 882, is said, on evidence that is not entirely uncontestable, to have been poisoned by his attendants and, when the drug took effect too slowly, to have had his skull crushed by a mallet. In 897 the corpse of the ambitious Pope Formosus, who had died the previous year, was taken from its sarcophagus, tried before a council over which his successor presided, condemned, despoiled of its vestments, and cast into an unconsecrated tomb for strangers and then taken by the populace and thrown into the Tiber. But Formosus had friends and the conflict between them and his enemies continued. Within a few months another Pope salvaged the body of Formosus which, having been rescued and buried by a hermit, he gave honourable sepulchre among the tombs of the ancient Popes and had a synod reverse the condemnatory acts of the anti-Formosus council. In 903 a partisan of Formosus was Pope for about two months and was then thrown into prison by a palace revolution which put another on the Papal throne. This new occupant, in turn, was replaced by a Pope supported by an armed escort, was degraded, and was sent to the prison where his victim was incarcerated.

For more than a generation after 904 the city of Rome and the Papacy were controlled by one local family, whose most prominent members were Theophylact, his daughter Marozia, her husband Alberic, and a younger Alberic, the son of Marozia and Alberic. We have varying estimates of the moral quality of the family. Marozia especially has been given a bad name. They controlled the choice of the Popes. One of these, John XI, who held the post from 931 to 935, was reputed to have been the son of Marozia and Pope Sergius III, who had reigned from 904 to 911. Another Pope, John X, who was on the throne from 914 to 928, fell out of favour with Marozia. It is said that because of his opposition to her proposed marriage with Guy, Marquis of Tuscany (the elder Alberic had died) she had his brother slain before his eyes and then had him imprisoned and killed. In 932 the younger Alberic seized the control from his mother, Marozia, and confined her and John XI in the Castle of St. Angelo. Alberic, called "the glorious prince and senator of all the Romans," was now in power. He seems to have wished to reform the Church and to have put fairly sincere and religious men on the Fisherman's throne. However, they were his creatures and apparently feared to take important action without his consent.

With such conditions in Rome, the Popes could not wield the influence in European affairs or in the Church of the West that had been exerted by some of their great predecessors. Certainly they could not give the moral and religious leadership that would lift the Church and the Christianity of the West from the slough into which they had fallen.

Faint Gleams of Light

Here and there in the darkness were gleams of light which, as the event proved, were harbingers of a better day. As we are to see again and again, often in what have appeared to be the darkest hours for the Christian faith movements have begun which, at the time affecting only small minorities, have later assumed major proportions and have brought revival and advance. In England, in a remote corner of the then Christendom, in the last three decades of the ninth century a king, Alfred the Great, established his rule over much of the country, compelled one of the Viking leaders to accept baptism, and brought about a religious and intellectual revival which on a smaller territorial scale was not unlike the earlier one on the Continent under the Carolingians. While his death was followed by something of a relapse, the darkness was never again as intense as it had been before him and, as we shall see, England became the chief source of the missionaries who won the peoples of Scandinavia to the Christian faith and instructed them in it. In the year 910, when Sergius, one of the creatures of the notorious Marozia, was on the Papal throne, the monastery of Cluny was founded which, as we are to hear later, became a radiating centre and symbol of a renewed life that was to bring the Christianity of Western Europe to a fresh high level.

EFFECT OF THE ENVIRONMENT

What effects did the environment in Italy and the west of Europe have upon Christianity in that region in the four and a half centuries from 500 to 950? How different did the Christianity of the West become from that of the Eastern wing of the Catholic Church? Because of the political division and the difficulty of physical communication the two were drifting apart. Cultural and other factors were working for separation, and in the West there were conditions which were placing their imprint on the Catholic Church of that area.

One striking contrast was that Byzantine Christianity was Greek, while the Christianity of the West was dominated by Rome. In spite of its weakness in the last half of the ninth and the first half of the tenth century, the Bishopric of Rome, the Papacy, exerted an influence over almost all Western Christendom. Over only the far periphery, especially Ireland, and Spain under the Arabs did it have little control. The Papacy stood for *Romanitas,* the tradition of imperial Rome, partly Christianized but still unmistakably Roman in its administrative genius, its insistence on law and order, and its comprehensive organization.

The claims and the power of the Papacy were furthered by the absence in the West of a strong competing civil state headed by an autocratic monarch such as the Greek Church faced in the Byzantine continuation of the Roman Empire. Even Justinian did not possess as much power in the West or in Italy as he exercised in the neighbourhood of Constantinople. Increasingly the authority of his successors waned. It was not recognized beyond Italy, Sicily, and the east coast of the Adriatic, and even there it was dwindling. The restoration of the imperial title in the West by Charlemagne did not bring the same degree of control over the Papacy by the state as the Byzantine Emperors wielded over the Patriarchate of Constantinople, for strong though he was, Charlemagne spent most of his time north of the Alps, a precedent followed by his successors, and Rome was never his or their capital. Occasionally, as in the decades immediately preceding 950, the absence of adequate civil protection injured the Papacy, but at other times, under strong Popes, notably Gregory the Great, it was an advantage.

In the West the Catholic Church became the Roman Catholic Church and, with some relapses, the administrative power of the Bishops of Rome over that Church mounted. The tendency to split up into national, tribal, and ethnic churches which in the East proved so divisive was also present in the West, but the growing power of the Papacy partly nullified it and gave a degree of unity to Western Christendom which was in striking contrast with the increasing and enduring schisms in the East.

The Roman temperament was seen in monasticism. It was the rule of Benedict, developed only a short distance from Rome and with the moderation, the sense of practical possibilities, and the organization which were typical of the Roman spirit, which prevailed in the West.

As Rome and other cities in the West declined in population, Christianity in that area adapted itself to the prevailing rural life and economy. That was in contrast with the Greek wing of the Catholic Church, increasingly dominated as it was by a commercial city, Constantinople.

Towards the end of the period Christianity was beginning to conform to feudalism in its organization and thought as it was never to do in the East.

The thought of Augustine, an influence which grew in the West, gave to that branch of the Catholic Church a distinct character, especially since Augustine had little or no currency in the East.

In a confidence in miracles, both West and East were in accord. How far that can be ascribed to the environment, especially to the environment peculiar to this period, may be debatable. It is clear, however, that while from the very beginning Christians had believed in the miraculous and the power of the Christian faith to work miracles was one of the factors in the conversion of the Roman Empire, in the years after 500 miracles loom more prominently in the writings of the educated leaders of the Church in the West than in the centuries before that dividing line. Gregory the Great had very much more to say of them than did the pre-sixth century fathers of the Church. The same is true of Bede. It is also significant that Einhard, the intimate and biographer of Charlemagne and possessing a classical Latin style which was the fruit of the Carolingian intellectual revival and of familiarity with the writings of pagan Latin antiquity, sent agents to Rome who after prayer robbed one of the chief churches of highly prized relics and brought them back for one of his foundations and that he recorded the miracles wrought through them after they had come into his possession.

The Effect of Christianity on the West

What effect did Christianity have upon Western Europe? Here were the descendants of the Roman provincials, religiously the products of the mass conversions of the fourth and fifth centuries. Here, too, were the scions of the barbarian invaders who also had come into the Church by community movements. Could Christianity raise the life of this population so that it would approximate to the standards set forth by Christ? The odds seemed overwhelmingly against success. Not only did Christianity face the obstacle of human nature, basically corrupted by sin, as Augustine had so clearly pointed out, but it also was confronted by the remnants of Græco-Roman civilization, that civilization which had crucified Jesus and which Augustine had seen as in stark contrast with the City of God. Within the borders of Western "Christendom" there were chronic fighting and rapine, and on its borders were the aggressive Moslem and frankly pagan peoples who were constantly seeking to press into a partially and superficially Christianized area.

Among the effects we must first of all remind ourselves of what we have summarized in the preceding pages, the continued adherence to the Christian name of most of the descendants of the Roman provincials and the professed acceptance of the Christian faith by the overwhelming majority of the invaders. Although in Spain and Sicily there were substantial Moslem elements, some of them invaders and others converts from the traditionally Christian population, in the North Christianity had not only won those pagans who had settled within what had once been the boundaries of the Roman Empire, but it had also been carried beyond those borders and had been firmly established in Ireland, Scotland, and the lands of the Frisians and the Saxons. In Spain and Sicily strong churches survived the Moslem conquests and in later centuries were again to embrace the entire population.

An effect which has often been noted was the preservation through the Church and the monasteries of much of the civilization of the Roman Empire and its transmission to later generations. From the standpoint of the Gospel this was not an unmixed blessing, for, as we must never allow ourselves to forget, that civilization was basically antagonistic to Christ and his message and in utilizing it the Christian community might be preparing the way for its triumph over the Gospel. Here, as we are to see, has again and again been a major peril, notably beginning with the Renaissance and continuing into our own day. Could Christianity, while perpetuating much of Græco-Roman culture, so select from it and transmute it that it could be made to serve the Gospel? That, whether or not they were aware of it, was what outstanding Christians were attempting. That was the dream of some of the great Popes and was seen in the Carolingian revival. Men like Charlemagne and Pope Nicholas I were seeking to make actual the City of God in the regions where their influence could reach. That they did not completely succeed is obvious.

That they and others less outstanding than they did not entirely fail must also be recognized. In the new stage of culture which was emerging in Western Europe there was more conscious effort to bring all of human life into submission to Christ than there had been under the pre-sixth century Christian Roman Emperors. The effort fell far short of the goal. The visible Church was penetrated and at times seemingly captured by irreconcilably hostile forces. The majority of the laity had at best only a faint insight into the meaning of the Christian message. Large portions of the clergy were corrupt.

Prominent administrative posts, including the episcopate, tended to be captured by men ambitious for place and power in a fashion which quite contradicted the Gospel. The designation "servant of the servants of God" employed by some of the Popes and taken from the memorable words of Jesus that they who wished to be greatest among his disciples must be servants of all became in the mouths of some of the occupants of the throne of Peter sheer hypocrisy. The property owned by the Church, theoretically to be used for the welfare of men, became a major menace to the true genius of the Church. Even the monasteries, dedicated as they were in principle to the full realization of the Christian life, almost always departed from the ideals of men like Benedict of Nursia and Benedict of Aniane. Presumably this was unavoidable. At least in one way or another and to a greater or less extent it has been seen in all institutions which bear the Christian name. Yet Western Europe after 500 and especially, as a result of what had been achieved between the year 500 and the year 950, in the centuries which immediately followed the latter date, was more nearly moulded by the Gospel than it had been before the disintegration of the Roman Empire and the great invasions. This was seen in almost every phase of its life. It was also apparent in individual after individual. Even when the majority fell so far short of Christian ideals that they seemed not to deserve the Christian name, they recognized and honoured those rare men and women who unmistakably displayed the fruits of the Spirit. These they called saints, cults arose in their honour, their physical relics were venerated, and they were regarded as worthy of emulation by all Christians.

SELECTED BIBLIOGRAPHY

GENERAL WORKS

A. Fliche and V. Martin, editors, *Histoire de L'Église depuis les Origines jusqu'à nos Jours.* Vol. IV, *De la mort de Théodose à l'élection de Grégoire le Grand,* by P. Labriolle, G. Bardy, L. Bréhier, G. de Plinval (Paris, Bloud & Gay, 1948, pp. 612); Vol. V, *Grégoire le Grand les États Barbares et la Conquête Arabe (590–757),* by L. Bréhier, R. Aigrain (Bloud & Gay, 1947, pp. 576); Vol. VI, *L'Epoque Carolingiene,* by E. Amann (Bloud & Gay, 1947, pp. 511); Vol. VII, *L'Église au Pouvoir des Laïques (888–1057),* by E. Amann and A. Dumas (Bloud & Gay, 1948, pp. 544). By Roman Catholic authors, scholarly, and with their major interest in the Roman Catholic Church.

A. Hauck, *Kirchengeschichte Deutschlands,* Vols. I and II (Leipzig, J. C. Hinrichs'sche Buchhandlung, 1887, 1890) cover the period dealt with in this chapter. A standard work, with copious footnote references.

H. von Schubert, *Geschichte der christlicher Kirche im Frühmittelalter* (Tübingen, J. C. B. Mohr, 1921, pp. xxiv, 808). Confessedly a handbook, it is very useful as such.

IRISH MONASTICISM

L. Gougaud, *Christianity in Celtic Lands* (London, Sheed & Ward, 1932, pp. vii, 530). A translation of an enlarged revision of the author's *Les Chrétientés Celtiques,* it contains excellent footnotes and is the best single volume survey of the subject.

W. A. Phillips, *A History of the Church of Ireland from the Earliest Times to the Present Day* (Oxford University Press, 3 vols., 1933–1934). By various members of the clergy.

BENEDICT OF NURSIA AND HIS RULE

The Rule of Saint Benedict. Translated with an Introduction by Cardinal Gasquet (London, Chatto & Windus, 1925, pp. xxviii, 150).

J. McCann, *Saint Benedict* (New York, Sheed & Ward, 1937, pp. 301). Semi-popular, scholarly, with official Benedictine approval.

GREGORY THE GREAT

F. H. Dudden, *Gregory the Great. His place in History and Thought* (London, Longmans, Green & Co., 2 vols., 1905). The standard life in English.

H. H. Howorth, *Saint Gregory the Great* (New York, E. P. Dutton & Co., 1912, pp. lvii, 340). Semi-popular, scholarly, depending in part on Dudden, but based upon independent research.

THE SPREAD OF CHRISTIANITY IN THE WEST

Adamnan, *Life of Saint Columba, Founder of Hy,* edited by W. Reeves, in *The Historians of Scotland,* Vol. VI (Edinburgh, Edmonston & Douglas, 1874, pp. clxxxiv, 385).

J. T. Addison, *The Medieval Missionary. A Study of the Conversion of Northern Europe* (New York, The International Missionary Council, 1936, pp. xiv, 176). A careful survey and interpretation.

Bede, *Historia Ecclesiastica.* A standard translation is by C. Plummer (Oxford, The Clarendon Press, 1896). Another is J. A. Giles, *Bede's Ecclesiastical History of England; also the Anglo-Saxon Chronicle* (London, George Bell & Sons, 1907, pp. xliv, 515).

A. Grieve, *Willibrord. Missionary to the Netherlands, 691–739, Including a Translation of the Vita Willibrord by Alcuin of York* (London, The Society for the Propagation of the Gospel in Foreign Parts, 1923, pp. 139). Chiefly important for its translation of this standard early source by Alcuin.

K. S. Latourette, *A History of the Expansion of Christianity. Volume II, The Thousand Years of Uncertainty* (New York, Harper & Brothers, 1938, pp. ix, 492).

G. W. Robinson, *The Life of St. Boniface by Willibald* (Harvard University Press, 1916, pp. 114). The standard biography which was written at the request of Boniface's successor.

THE CAROLINGIAN REVIVAL; THE ENGLISH BACKGROUND

T. Allison, *English Religious Life in the Eighth Century as Illustrated by Contemporary Letters* (London, Society for Promoting Christian Knowledge, 1929, pp. xvi, 154).

E. S. Duckett, *Anglo-Saxon Saints and Scholars* (New York, The Macmillan Co., 1948, pp. viii, 488). Well written, scholarly.

The Life of Bishop Wilfrid by Eddius Stephanus, Text, Translation, & Notes, by B. Colgrave (Cambridge University Press, 1927, pp. xvii, 192). By an intimate associate of Wilfrid.

THE CAROLINGIAN REVIVAL

H. Bett, *Johannes Scotus Erigena*. A Study in Mediæval Philosophy (Cambridge University Press, 1925, pp. 204).

E. S. Duckett, *Alcuin, Friend of Charlemagne* (New York, The Macmillan Co., 1951, pp. xii, 337). A standard, charmingly written account.

Einhard's Life of Charlemagne. The Latin Text Edited, with Introduction and Notes, by H. W. Garrod and R. B. Mowat (Oxford, The Clarendon Press, 1915, pp. lix, 82).

A. Gardner, *Studies in John the Scot (Erigena). A Philosopher of the Dark Ages* (London, Henry Frowde, 1900, pp. xi, 145).

Chapter 14

RETROSPECT AND PROSPECT

The four and a half centuries covered in the preceding four chapters may seem disheartening for any who would share the dream of Jesus for the coming of the kingdom of God. What had happened to that vision with its confident assertion that the reign of God was at hand? Any student who seeks to understand the nature and the course of human history and especially any Christian who is concerned with the fashion in which the God in Whom he believes deals with men and with what can be expected in history from the Christian Gospel must take this period into his total purview.

In trenchant phrases and vivid parables Jesus had pictured the characteristics of the kingdom of God and of those who are its members. All men of good-will must gladly, or perhaps sadly, admit that if mankind were to conform to the ideals which he set forth, men would no longer hate one another and be obsessed with the competitive struggle for food, clothing, and shelter, but would live in friendly coöperation and in that living would find an abundance for their physical needs in humble, glad service to one another. Yet Jesus had been crucified. His disciples were convinced that he had risen from the dead in conquering, radiant life, and that through the Spirit which issued from the Father and Jesus men could be born into that life. They were impelled by the faith that ultimately God's gracious will would be fully done and all creation would be freed from bondage, entering into the glorious liberty of the children of God, and that God would sum up all things in Christ, whether in heaven or on earth.

In that faith the early Christians had gone forth. They had shared it with others. The seemingly incredible had happened. Although beginning as one of the numerically smallest of hundreds of competing religious groups in the Græco-Roman world, within five centuries Christianity, the religion which arose out of their faith, had won the professed allegiance of the vast majority within that world, a world which then embraced the largest single aggregation of civilized mankind. Out of that faith had grown the Christian churches, the

374

largest of them the Catholic Church. By an amazing burst of vitality within a culture which had ceased to think or to say much that was new, that faith had given birth to creative thinking in theology, to new forms of worship, to an Empire-wide ecclesiastical organization, and, even more significantly, had transformed thousands of individuals and had started them on the road towards the goal "of the high calling of God in Christ Jesus."

Then decline, slow but prolonged, had set in. In winning the professed allegiance of the peoples of the basin of the Mediterranean the process had been completed by a mass conversion which watered down the quality of living. Swamped by these millions, the Catholic Church had relaxed its discipline and in some areas had apparently all but given up attempts to enforce it. Efforts of growing minorities to a full attainment of the Christian ideal had issued in monasticism, with its communities and its solitaries. But many of the latter had gone to revolting extremes, sometimes of bizarre exhibitionism quite contrary to the Gospel ideal, and after the first burst of enthusiasm and devotion in their founding, the former tended to run down and to become characterized by uninspired routine or even by indolent self-indulgence.

Then the Roman Empire and with it the Græco-Roman world had disintegrated. Christianity had not saved it or brought it into conformity with the ideals set forth in the Gospels or the epistles of the early apostles. The Church itself was divided by bitter dissensions and the prey of power-loving ecclesiastics and princes. The invasion of the Moslem Arabs flooded about half of the territory which might be called "Christendom" and within it the churches dwindled and ceased to put forth new expressions of vitality. North of the Mediterranean, in regions unconquered by the Arabs, floods of barbarians poured in, most of them at the outset non-Christians and most of their Christians Arians and so bringing weakening division to the Christian ranks. These invaders from the north and north-east came in successive waves, and recovery, conversion, and partial assimilation had not been completed for one until another arrived and the level of Christian living was again lowered.

Christianity persisted, but the creative activity which it had shown in the first five centuries in fresh movements and in thought declined and in large areas disappeared. To be sure, it gave stability to the Byzantine realms and strengthened their resistance against invasions. Partly under its ægis much of Græco-Roman culture went on, and Christians were the chief channels through which it was transmitted to the Arabs. However, that achievement, as we have suggested, did not ensure the preservation of the Gospel, but rather might obscure and weaken it, for in its basic assumptions and convictions that culture contradicted the Gospel. Christianity had not brought into the likeness of the Gospel the remnants of the urban life of the Mediterranean world. The largest

"Christian" city was Constantinople, and in spite of its many churches and the disappearance of the pagan cults, one may question whether it more nearly approximated the ideals of the Gospel than had pre-Christian Rome. "Christian" Rome of the year 950, although it was the religious capital of Western Europe and was kept alive by its churches and the pilgrims who flocked to them, was very much smaller than the burgeoning metropolis of the early Emperors and probably was as iniquitous, even if not in all the same ways. Nor, although it was theoretically dominant in them, did Christianity bring to its high standards rural Asia Minor and Greece or the predominantly agricultural Western Europe of these dark centuries. Indeed, in chronic wars with their accompaniment of cruelty, callousness, robbery, sexual laxity, and the glorification of brute force, the Western Europe of the middle of the tenth century may have been further from the standards of the Gospel than was the same area five hundred years earlier. In its numerical strength Christianity was not nearly as important in the year 950 as it had been in the year 500, and the states which professed allegiance to it did not loom as large in the total world scene in the middle of the tenth century as they had at the close of the fifth.

Where, then, was the "exceeding greatness of the power"? The vessels were still palpably earthen: had they proved too much so for "the power"? Was the weakness of God as seen on the cross actually stronger than men as Paul had declared, or had the sin of man proved too much for it? We must frankly recognize the plain historical facts which we have summarized in the preceding paragraphs and the equally certain fact that Christianity has never regained most of the territory which it lost to Islam.

We may not be able to discern the full answer to the questions which the story raises. However, we must note that Christianity had won to a professed allegiance the earlier invaders from the North who had settled within what had been the boundaries of the Roman Empire and was even moving beyond the former Roman *limes* into fresh territories. We must recall the fashion in which many Christians protested against the non-Christian conduct of their fellows in both East and West and the forms of instruction and discipline which the Church in the West adopted to bring into partial conformity to its standards the rude barbarians of that region. We must remember that in much of the West in some of the darkest days the Church had endeavoured, not always unsuccessfully, to protect the weak and had preserved and furthered education and orderly living. We must, moreover, remind ourselves that even in this brief survey we have met individuals of outstanding and wide influence, such as John of Damascus, John the Almsgiver, Columba, Gregory the Great, and Boniface, who clearly bore the impress of the Gospel and were admired, and rightly so, as its exemplars. For every one whose memory our scanty records have preserved, presumably there were many thousands, also exemplars of Christian faith and life, of whom no trace survives. In them the kingdom of God was present and they were both light and salt. Through them the faith was spread and nourished. Always there continued to be darkness and decay but had it not been for them the darkness would have been more intense and the decay more noisome.

We must also call attention to the fact that although to a large degree the kind of power seen in governments and in institutions, including even those of the Church, was in contrast with that seen in the incarnation, the cross, and the resurrection, some governments proved less of an obstacle to the Gospel than did others. The Sassanid and the Arab states, for example, the one dominated by Zoroastrianism and the other by Islam, made the course of Christianity very difficult. The Christian Roman Emperors were both an aid and a hindrance. The order which they gave and their protection to the Church were of assistance, but their efforts at the control of the Church often compromised the Gospel and their friendship encouraged in the Church a kind of power which was the opposite of that seen in the Gospel. Much depended on the character of the monarch. Those who, like Alfred the Great, were earnestly endeavouring to rule as Christians were of more help than those who were not. The great Carolingians by their patronage, in spite of their use of armed force, facilitated the spread of Christianity and the reform of the Church by deeply Christian churchmen.

Moreover, as we have hinted, already, even in the darkest hours at the end of the ninth and the beginning of the tenth century, a fresh resurgence of vitality was evident in Christianity. It was fairly obvious in Byzantine realms but was also present in Western Europe. In the next four centuries it was to carry Christianity over a larger proportion of the earth's surface than until then had been true of it or any other one religion, it was to issue in more fresh movements than had been seen since the first three centuries of the faith, and it was to stamp far more deeply the civilization of Europe than it had that of the Roman Empire. These results were especially marked in Western Europe, but to a less degree they were also seen in parts of Eastern Europe. To that stage of our story we must now turn.

FOUR CENTURIES OF
RESURGENCE AND ADVANCE
A.D. 950 — A.D. 1350

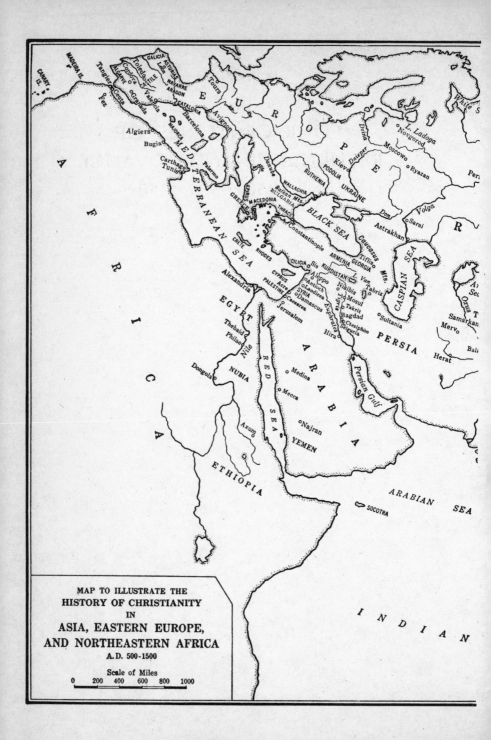

MAP TO ILLUSTRATE THE
HISTORY OF CHRISTIANITY
IN
ASIA, EASTERN EUROPE,
AND NORTHEASTERN AFRICA
A.D. 500-1500

Scale of Miles
0   200   400   600   800   1000

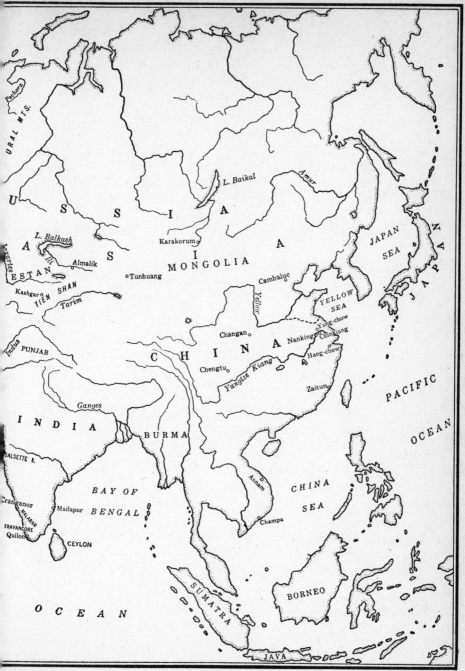

Chapter 15

THE MAIN FEATURES AND THE WORLD SETTING OF CHRISTIANITY

Not far from the year 950 a fresh surge of life was seen in Christianity which was to continue until about the year 1350. No precise dates can be set for either its beginning or its end. As we have seen, it commenced earlier in Byzantine or Greek Christianity than it did in Western or Latin Christianity. It was most marked in Western Europe but in some of its aspects, notably in the geographic extension of the faith, it had striking manifestations in the East, in Byzantine and Nestorian Christianity.

In these four centuries Christianity won the formal allegiance of most of such of the peoples of North-western and Central Europe as had not previously accepted it. It expanded into what is now Russia. It regained from Islam most of the Iberian Peninsula. On the north and west it was planted in Iceland and Greenland and possibly was carried to North America. It was professed by minorities in Central, East, and South Asia. By the year 1350 Christians were scattered from Greenland on the extreme north and west to the China Sea on the east, and to India on the south.

The main strength and the most abounding vigour of Christianity were in Western Europe. Here were most of the new movements which were expressions of the resurging life. From here the chief territorial spread of the faith was achieved. Here Christianity was more potent in shaping civilization than it had previously been anywhere, more even than in the Roman Empire after the formal conversion of that realm. In Western Europe it was so vital and so influential that in later centuries it was there and among peoples who migrated from Western Europe that it continued to display its greatest power.

Why this resurgence of Christianity and in these particular centuries? We do not know. We can recognize some of the contributing factors but we cannot be certain that they were the most important.

As we suggested in the last chapter, a revival of strength was seen in the Byzantine Empire in the second half of the ninth and the first half of the tenth century. It continued in the second half of the tenth and in the fore part of the eleventh century. At the end of the first quarter of the eleventh century the Byzantine Empire had reached an apogee which it was never again to attain.

In Western Europe, as we also saw, near the end of the tenth century the invasions which had racked that section from the fifth century ceased. There were still movements of peoples and chronic war, but not again were there major incursions of non-Christians into Western Christendom which left large deposits of settlers. The Northmen were the last of such waves to submerge much of Western Europe. Later invasions of non-Christians, notably of the Mongols and the Ottoman Turks, might threaten the region, but they did not penetrate effectively beyond its eastern and southern borders.

The cessation of the invasions was accompanied and followed in Western Europe by a growth of wealth, the beginnings of modern states, the inception of that expansion of its peoples which by the middle of the twentieth century was to revolutionize most of mankind, and the emergence of a fresh aspect of civilization.

Commerce revived and with it, both aided by it and aiding it, cities increased in numbers and population. This was first notable in Italy, where was the capital of Western Christianity, Rome.

In Western Europe kingdoms, nascent nations, began to emerge from the welter of feudalism. In 987 the feudal princes chose as King of France one of their number, Hugh Capet, Duke of France, with his capital at Paris. Although at the outset possessing one of the weaker of the feudal principalities, under successive heads the Capetian family gradually added to their domains and made of France a strong state. In 911, on the death of Louis the Child, the last of the Carolingians to rule in Germany, the great tribal princes of that area together with the chief clergy elected Conrad of Franconia king. The title of King of the Germans did not remain permanently in the Franconian house as did that of King of France in the Capetian family. In 919 it passed to a line of Saxon dukes. In 962 one of that dynasty, Otto I, who had been made King of the Germans in 936, was crowned Roman Emperor. The ablest of Western rulers since Charlemagne to gain that title, he had already driven off the Danes, had defeated the Hungarians, had established his effective power over the great dukes of Germany, had put men whom he trusted at the head of the main bishoprics and monasteries, and had made himself master of much of Italy. His coronation as Emperor by the Pope is often regarded as beginning what was known as the Holy Roman Empire of the German Nation, an institution which was to persist until 1806. At the time the step was not looked upon as an innovation, for by his coronation Otto was regarded as having come into the succession of Roman Emperors. The term "Holy" was meant to indicate that the Roman Empire was Christian and the words "of the German Nation" were intended to convey the principle that normally the imperial throne would be filled by a German. In this fashion the political leadership of Western Christendom passed to a Saxon, one of that people who less than two centuries earlier had been brought forcibly by Charlemagne to accept the Christian faith. In 1066 William the Conqueror began a strong state in England. The gradual expulsion of Moslem political rule from the Iberian Peninsula was accompanied by the rise of professedly Christian kingdoms, chief of which were Castile, Leon, Aragon, Navarre, and Portugal. There emerged other Christian kingdoms in Western Europe, among them Denmark, Norway, Sweden, Scotland, Poland, and Hungary.

The expansion of Western Europe may be said to have dated from the first of the Crusades, in 1096. Through the long line of subsequent Crusades and the commerce of the Italian cities, before 1350 it had touched not only Western Asia but also India and China.

These political and economic developments were paralleled by the coming in Western Europe of a distinctive stage of civilization. Many-sided, embodying fresh achievements of the peoples of that region and contributions from Græco-Roman culture, in every phase it bore the imprint of the revived Christianity of the era.

Expanding and vigorous though it unquestionably was, in these four centuries Western Europe and even all Christendom did not loom as prominently in the total world scene as had the Roman Empire from the first to the fifth century. Far richer, more populous, and more sophisticated was China of the Sung Dynasty (960–1279). Although, like Europe, divided politically, India was probably wealthier than the former and contained more people. The Arab realms were now in fragments, but the Moslem world stretched from Spain through Western Asia and Persia into Central Asia and India. In most of this area Islam was dominant. Moslem civilization reached a high level, and its thought, especially that of Averroes (1126–1198), exerted a marked influence on the intellectual life of Christian Europe. In the eleventh century the Seljuk Turks, Moslems, created a realm in Persia and Western Asia which was larger than that of any Christian state of that day. While it soon broke up, some of its fragments continued to be important.

In the latter part of the twelfth and in the thirteenth century there blazed forth in meteoric fashion an empire, that of the Mongols, which ruled over a larger area and over more people than any which up to that time had been created by man. It was not Christian. Although some of its princes had Christian mothers and were baptized as infants, it was frankly pagan. Its founder, best known by his later designation, Jenghiz Khan, "Universal Emperor," was the son of the head of a confederation of some of the tribes in Mongolia. After his father's death he fought his way to the headship which had been held by his sire. He extended his rule over several of his neighbours and before his death (1227) he had begun the conquest of China and Central Asia. Under the sons and grandsons of Jenghiz Khan the victorious sweep of the Mongol arms continued. By the close of the thirteenth century the Mongols were masters of China, Korea, most of Central Asia, Persia, Mesopotamia, Armenia, Georgia, and the south of Russia. Beyond the borders of that vast area their armies had been seen in Poland, Hungary, Moravia, North-west India, Burma, Annam, and Champa, and their fleets attacked Japan and Java. While within a century and a half of the death of Jenghiz Khan the Mongol realm had broken up and the Mongols had been expelled from China, large fragments of Eurasia were much longer under Mongol rule, notably in Central Asia and Russia, and in the sixteenth century conquerors of Mongol stock subdued much of India and founded a dynasty which lasted into the nineteenth century. Compared with the Mongol Empire as it was in the thirteenth and fourteenth centuries the Christian kingdoms and the remnants of the Byzantine Empire were petty principalities which escaped incorporation only because they were sufficiently on the periphery not to feel the full impact of the Mongol armies.

Although in 1350 Christians were more widely scattered geographically than in 500 or 950, they may not have been as numerous as in the former year. In the year 1350 Europe had been more profoundly shaped by Christianity than in the year 950 or than had the Roman Empire in the year 500. Yet the portions of the world which called themselves Christian were by no means as prominent in the total world scene as had been the professedly Christian Roman Empire in the year 400 or even, after an additional century of decline, in the year 500. In the year 1350, to the hypothetical visitor from Mars Christianity would probably not have appeared as much a factor in the life of mankind as Islam or Buddhism and possibly no more so than Hinduism or Confucianism. However, it had proved its ability to survive the demise of the realm and the culture in which it had achieved its first triumphs and with which it had seemed to be identified, and, winning the barbarian invaders from the North, it had been a major stimulus in stirring them to produce an advanced civilization.

As we pursue the narrative of Christianity in these centuries, we will first tell of the progress towards the conversion of the peoples of Europe. We will then trace the course of Christianity in Western Europe, for it was here, rather than in the waning Byzantine realms, that the faith was to have its chief centre into the twentieth century. Finally we will move eastward, to tell of what was transpiring there in the Christian communities.

Chapter 16

RENEWED AND CONTINUED PROGRESS IN
THE EXPANSION OF CHRISTIANITY

The century which was bounded by A.D. 950 and A.D. 1050 saw as wide a geographic advance of Christianity as any in the history of the faith until after A.D. 1500. It witnessed the conversion of those pagans who so recently had been a scourge of Christendom, the Scandinavians, in some of their home-lands—Denmark, Norway, and, incompletely, in Sweden—and in lands beyond the earlier borders of "Christendom" in which they had effected settlements—Iceland, Greenland, and, more notably, Kiev, the nucleus of the later Russia. It was the time when many of the Slavs of Central Europe came to the faith—some of those east of the Elbe through the efforts of Otto I, but especially the Czechs and Poles. During that period the Magyars were converted and Hungary joined the ranks of professedly Christian nations. In Spain the Christian reconquest of the peninsula made extensive strides. In Sicily the occupation by Christian Normans spelled the doom of Islam in that island. In Mesopotamia an Arab tribe accepted the faith. Thus those pagans who had threatened the very existence of Christianity were being won, and, as nowhere else by any other religion, the tide of Islam was being rolled back. In that same hundred years in Central Asia the Keraïts, who were later to be con-quered by the Mongols and to be the means of the infiltration of Christianity into the ruling line of that masterful people, adopted the Nestorian form of the faith.

The following two centuries were to witness a further geographic extension, but nothing as spectacular as this.

THE CONVERSION OF THE SCANDINAVIANS

We have noted the fashion in which the Scandinavians, the "Northmen," had ravaged much of Europe in the ninth and tenth centuries. We have also seen that their conversion had begun before the year 950. At the instance of Louis the Pious the Archbishopric of Hamburg had been created as a missionary outpost for that purpose and Anskar had been appointed to it, had travelled widely in the northlands, and had made some converts. After the death of Anskar (865) the prospect seemed so unfavourable for winning Scandinavia that late in the ninth century it was suggested that the see of Hamburg-Bremen be discontinued and it was only the reluctance of the Pope which prevented the step from being taken. However, some of the Northmen who settled in Great Britain and Ireland and the portion of the Frankish domains which later had its name, Normandy, from them, accepted baptism. Indeed, before the last quarter of the tenth century they had provided three archbishops for the Church in England. Under their contacts with the peoples whom they were attacking, the inherited religion of the Vikings was disintegrating and they were adopting both the faith and much of the culture of the conquered.

It was in the second half of the tenth century that Christianity began to make rapid headway in the three Scandinavian lands—Denmark, Norway, and Sweden. In each conversion was accomplished as a community affair by a kind of mass movement. In each the eventual triumph of Christianity came through royal initiative. In at least one of these lands, Norway, the kings took advantage of it to extend their authority over recalcitrant nobles. In each, as had been true in other states, the kings insisted upon controlling the church in their respective realms. Each obtained the creation of an archbishopric to head the church in his domains.

The actual instruction, baptism, and difficult nurturing of the infant churches was chiefly by missionaries from England. This appears to have been for two reasons. In the first place, through the repeated invasions and ultimately through the Danish conquest of England, close contacts had been established between the Scandinavians and that land. In the second place, since the English were a subject people, the Scandinavians had nothing to fear from them politically. Had missionaries been accepted from the Carolingian realms or from the archiepiscopal see of Hamburg-Bremen, they might have been the means of establishing Carolingian and then German political power in Scandinavia. As we have seen, missionaries were used by the Carolingians to extend their control over much of Germany. It would not have been surprising if a similar sequel had followed had the Church been founded in Scandinavia by missionaries from Carolingian and German territories. Since most of the missionaries were from England, the dream of Louis the Pious and Anskar that the Archbishopric of Bremen-Hamburg would be the radiating centre for Christianity in the North was largely although by no means entirely frustrated.

Denmark and Norway were brought to the Christian faith almost simultaneously, but the process of conversion began in Denmark slightly earlier than in Norway. That was probably to be expected because of the nearer proximity of Denmark to Christendom and the smaller size of the country. Not long before the year 950 a King of Denmark, Harald Bluetooth, was baptized. His son claimed for him that he had "made the Danes Christian," and we hear of bishops among that people. In the succeeding reign, that of Sweyn (Svend I), the conqueror of the larger part of England, a pagan reaction occurred. It was under Sweyn's son, Canute, that Denmark finally came into the family of professedly Christian states. From 1019 until his death in 1035, Canute was king in both England and Denmark and for a time he was also master of Norway. Canute was a Christian and beginning with 1020 he vigorously supported the Christian cause. He made a pilgrimage to Rome and is said to have commanded that all his subjects learn the Lord's Prayer and go to communion three times a year. Many missionaries came from England, but it was not until early in the twelfth century that Denmark was removed from the jurisdiction of the Archbishop of Hamburg and was given an archbishopric of its own.

In Norway the course of conversion was more spectacular than in Denmark. Harald Fairhair (died 933), a pagan, by much fighting had made himself master of most of Norway and had begun the establishment of a monarchy which would rule over that land. His son and successor, Haakon "the Good," had been reared in the English court as a Christian. He tried to win his people to his faith, but the opposition of the landowners proved too strong for him. Not many years after Haakon's death Harald Bluetooth of Denmark made himself lord of Norway and sought to spread Christianity in the land, but without much success. More effective were the brief efforts of a greatgrandson of Harald Fairhair, Olaf Tryggvason. A posthumous child, born about 963 or 964, from boyhood Olaf led an adventurous and colourful life. Early captured by the Vikings and sold as a slave, he was rescued by an uncle, adopted the life of a Viking, raided England, was baptized by a hermit on the Scilly Islands off the south-west coast of that land, and was confirmed by the Bishop of Winchester. Handsome, huge of stature, daring, fearless, he was the embodiment of the Viking ideal. In 995 he returned to Norway and there was elected king. He set about bringing all the Norwegians to acknowledge him and to receive baptism. The two processes seem to have gone hand in hand. He accomplished them by persuasion where possible and by force where necessary. Now and again he destroyed pagan temples and slew members of the opposition. Most of the land was nominally Christian when, in the year 1000, he perished in a great naval battle with the Danes, Swedes, and his Norwegian opponents.

The conversion of Norway was completed and the Church firmly planted by another Olaf—Olaf Haraldsson, or St. Olaf. Like the other Olaf, a posthumous child, he was also of the lineage of Harald Fairhair. Stocky, strong, skilful in sports, good to look upon, fair of hair, ruddy of face, keen of mind, with eyes before which, when they lighted up in anger, strong men quailed, he was a born leader of men. At the age of twelve he began his Viking career. He fought in England and France and raided the shores of Sweden. In his early twenties (in 1015) he went to Norway to claim the throne, defeated his enemies, and was rapidly acknowledged by *thing* after *thing*, the *thing* being the local assembly.

Once securely in power, Olaf sought to make his realm Christian not only in name but also in fact. Priests and bishops from England aided him in instructing his people, but not all these were strictly foreigners, for from their names it appears that three of the four bishops from England had Scandinavian blood in their veins. He travelled through the land to see that churches were built and priests set over them. He framed laws on what he believed to be Christian principles, proscribing paganism and customs which were contrary to Christian morals. Yet even he did not bring about the baptism of all his subjects. Many local magnates opposed him, partly because of his attempt to increase the royal power at the expense of their authority and partly because of his suppression of the pagan shrines which were their property and from which came much of their revenues and prestige. Aided by Canute of Denmark, they rose in rebellion and in a battle in 1030 Olaf was slain. A revulsion of popular feeling swept Olaf to canonization. Miracles were soon reported to have been wrought at his tomb, churches were erected in his honour, and he became the patron saint of the realm.

Although the formal conversion of Norway may be said to have been completed by the time of Olaf's death, the instruction of the populace in the tenets of the faith and the development of an organization for the Church required many decades. Monks and secular priests from England were of assistance. The *scald,* the bard who was an accepted feature of the old order, spread the message through his songs, and respected laymen who were committed to the new faith gave it prestige. By the latter part of the eleventh century the country had a diocesan organization. The division of the area into parishes and the provision of local clergy proceeded, although only gradually. Diocesan boundaries usually conformed to pre-Christian political divisions. The Archbishop of Hamburg attempted to exercise jurisdiction, but the king angrily objected and insisted on having his bishops consecrated in France or England. In 1152 Norway was given an archiepiscopal see of its own and its church thereby achieved the kind of national status which prevailed in several other kingdoms of Europe. Technically this was within the structure of the Catholic Church of the West over which the Pope was supreme, but Rome was far away and its power not so effective as in nearer lands.

The last of the three Scandinavian kingdoms fully to enter the Christian fold was Sweden. Christians were to be found there at least as early as the ninth century, and Anskar visited the land more than once. By 936 such Christian communities as had existed seem to have disappeared, but the faith was soon renewed. Many Swedes who had been in England as merchants or soldiers and had been baptized there returned home. In the second half of the tenth century there were bishops in Sweden. Early in the eleventh century a Swedish king, Olof Skötkonung, was baptized and inaugurated a bishopric, under the jurisdiction of the see of Hamburg-Bremen. Although most of the land was still pagan and the main shrine of the old worship was maintained as formerly at Uppsala, missionaries from England were preaching the new faith. As was to be expected and as was true in Norway, Christianity triumphed first in the South, nearer to Christendom, and paganism lingered longest in the North. It was not until the first decades of the twelfth century that Christianity was dominant. Monasticism entered through the Cistercians who, as we are to see, represented a revival in that movement. When, in 1164, Sweden was given its own archiepiscopal see, its first incumbent was a Cistercian, its seat was placed at Uppsala, and the cathedral was erected on the site of the head temple of the pre-Christian pagan cult. Thus was Christianity clearly victor and not in a lax form but headed by a member of that order, then young, which represented one of the latest and strictest attempts to conform fully to the Christian ideal.

THE SPREAD OF CHRISTIANITY IN SCANDINAVIAN OUTPOSTS IN THE ATLANTIC

The Viking explosion of the ninth and tenth centuries planted Scandinavian colonies, largely Norwegian, on westward-lying islands as far away as Greenland. In the latter part of the tenth and the fore part of the eleventh century Christianity was carried to them and their populations accepted it, but in some instances not without hesitation and with divided counsels.

The Orkney, the Faroe, and the Shetland Islands had something of a Christian population before the coming of the Vikings. The latter represented a pagan influx. Olaf Tryggvason is credited with the conversion of the populations of the Faroes and the Shetlands and with the forcible baptism of the head man of the Orkneys. Olaf Haraldsson helped to confirm and deepen the change.

The first settlers of Iceland seem to have been Irish monks, but, obviously, they did not give rise to a continuing population. The first large immigration appears to have been by Norwegians who disliked the centralizing measures of Harald Fairhair. Some effort at their conversion was made in the 980's. More vigorous and outwardly successful measures were taken at the instance of Olaf Tryggvason during his brief and stormy reign. Many were baptized and for a time civil war threatened between Christians and pagans. This was avoided by a compromise suggested by one of the leading men. It was agreed that all were to accept baptism, but that secret sacrifices to the old gods were to be met with only minor penalties. A few years later paganism was officially abolished. Olaf Haraldsson sent at least one bishop and a bell and timber for a church. The island long suffered from a shortage of clergy. This was partly met by training local boys and by a line of native bishops. The lads so prepared remained in subjection to the chiefs, and the bishops, while sent to the Continent for consecration, were elected by the island assembly, the *Althing*.

The first Norse settlement of Greenland was on the less insalubrious west coast and from Iceland, near the end of the tenth century. The leader was a pagan, Eric the Red. Christianity was introduced by his son, Leif, who had been won to the faith by Olaf Tryggvason and who, to his father's disgust, brought a priest to the island. The Norse population was never large, probably not much over two thousand. Churches and a cathedral were eventually erected and in the fore part of the twelfth century a bishop was consecrated. The bishop was henceforth the civil as well as the ecclesiastical head of the colony.

It was by the Norse that Christianity reached America. Leif Ericson himself is said to have been the first to touch the continent. How many Norse came in succeeding years we do not know. Nor do we know where they went, how many if any of them were Christians, or whether they made any converts among the Eskimoes and Indians.

The Winning of the Scandinavians in Russia and the Beginnings of Russian Christianity

It was not only in Western and North-western Europe and in islands in the North Atlantic that the Scandinavians became Christians. Almost simultaneously there was a movement towards the faith led by the Scandinavian rulers of a state which centred in Kiev, on the Dnieper, and which is usually regarded as the beginning of one of the numerically largest bodies of Christians, that of Russia. As was natural from the geographic location, this was not through the Latin but through the Byzantine or Greek wing of the Catholic Church.

In the ninth century in the great Viking movement, Scandinavians, most of them Swedes, made their way southward across the plains and along the rivers of what was later western Russia and became masters of the local, largely

Slavic, populations. They were known as Varangians or Rus and their chief settlements were Novgorod in the north and Kiev in the south, in the later Ukraine. Never more than a minority of the population, eventually they adopted the Slavonic tongue of the subject majority.

Christianity had long been present on the northern shores of the Euxine or Black Sea. Christians were there at least as early as the fourth and fifth centuries. To be sure, in the south of what is now Russia the rulers of the dominant people, the Khazars, had adopted Judaism, but in the second half of the ninth century the famous Patriarch of Constantinople, Photius, of whom we heard in an earlier chapter, organized a mission for the Russians which was so far successful that the latter asked for a bishop. Slightly later, also in that century, the Emperor Basil I, "the Macedonian," and the Patriarch Ignatius, whom we have also met, sent as a missionary to the Russians a bishop who is said to have made many converts.

Through these or other channels, by the middle of the tenth century Christianity had entered Kiev and at least one church building had been erected in that city. In the 950's, Olga, the dowager regent, was baptized and sent to Otto I of Germany for missionaries. These seem to have had no very marked success.

It was under Vladimir, the grandson of Olga, that the mass conversion of Kiev and the territory which was dependent on it began. Precisely when and how Vladimir became a Christian we do not know. An oft-repeated story declares that he was visited by representatives of Islam, Judaism, Latin Christianity, and Greek Christianity, each of whom sought to win him. It is further said that of all the delegations that of the Greeks made the greatest impression on him and that he took the decisive step after a deputation appointed by him had visited Constantinople and had reported the overwhelming splendour of a service in the cathedral of Saint Sophia at which they had been present. While this story is almost certainly a later fabrication, it at least reflects the choice which faced Vladimir as he saw the disintegration of the inherited religion of the Varangians and cast about for a faith to take its place. Islam, Judaism (popular among his neighbours, the Khazars), and the Latin and Greek forms of Christianity were the viable possibilities. The last may have won his support because it was the faith of the most powerful, the wealthiest, and the most civilized of the states which bordered on his domains. It will be recalled that the Byzantine Empire was not only near by but at that time was also approaching one of the heights of its might. Vladimir received delegates from the Pope and sent representatives to Rome, but it was to the Greek wing of the Catholic Church that he adhered.

In accepting Greek Christianity, Vladimir seems deliberately to have made it clear that for him baptism was not a token of submission to the then expanding Byzantine realm. He captured a Byzantine town in the Crimea and as a price of peace exacted the hand of a Byzantine princess to add to his collection of wives and concubines. It was after his return from the Crimea that he actively undertook the conversion of his people. The exact date is uncertain, but it was towards the close of the tenth century. It has been said, but this is questioned, that he required the populace of Kiev to betake themselves to the river for collective baptism and that he ordered the destruction of all the idols in the city. It is certain that he encouraged baptisms, built churches, founded monasteries, and sent clergy to other centres to spread what had been begun at Kiev. It was in 991 that the population of Novgorod was baptized by the bishop of the Crimean town which Vladimir had seized. By the end of his reign (1015) there were three bishoprics in his domains, but with characteristic independence he would not submit to ecclesiastical control from Constantinople.

After Vladimir and under the impulse given by him and with the encouragement of his successor, Christianity continued to spread in Russia. Still later it was carried to new areas. In the twelfth century, for example, monks from Novgorod planted it on the upper reaches of the Volga.

As in Western Europe, most of the active missionaries were monks and it was monastic Christianity which was held up as the ideal. Fully as much as in Western Europe, the Christianity of the masses was very superficial. Several generations passed before the majority would sufficiently conform even to so slight a degree as to attend the services of the Church and receive the sacraments. The dioceses were huge, the Metropolitan of Kiev, for centuries the head of the administrative structure, was appointed by the Patriarch of Constantinople and was usually a Greek and unfamiliar with local conditions, and a substantial minority of the bishops were from abroad and understood little of the customs or language of their flocks. The clergy were poorly trained and at best were too few for the size of the country. They were usually chosen by their parishioners and the bishops were selected by the local princes.

Superficial though much of this early Russian Christianity undoubtedly was, it began to take root. An extensive Christian literature was made available in Slavonic, the speech of the majority. This was partly through fresh translations from the Greek and partly by utilizing translations which had already been made for Bulgaria and which, as we have seen, were indebted to the initiative of Constantine (Cyril) and Methodius in the second half of the ninth century. A majority of the bishops and presumably almost all the parish priests were of the indigenous stock. Monasteries multiplied and from the outset were a normal part of the life of the Church. A famous one on the outskirts of Kiev had a profound influence.

THE CONVERSION OF BOHEMIA

Simultaneously with the rapid progress of conversion among the Scandinavians some of the largest groups of Slavs were being incorporated into Christendom. We have noted the labours of Constantine and Methodius in the second half of the ninth century, the winning of Bulgaria with its predominantly Slavic population, also in that fifty years, and have hinted at the activities of German missionaries among the Slavs of Central Europe. By the year 900 Christianity was strong in Moravia. The hundred years between 950 and 1050 witnessed the adherence to the faith of the two largest Slavic states in Central Europe, Bohemia and Poland.

The conversion of Bohemia was in part through the impulses which stemmed from Constantine and Methodius, but was chiefly from Germany. Famous near the beginnings of the Church in Bohemia was Václav, better known to most of us as Wenceslas, who came to the throne about 923–924 at the age of eighteen. A Christian, profoundly religious, he is said to have been a builder of churches, generous to the poor, ardent in his personal religious devotions, to have worn a rough shirt under his royal robes, and to have remained a virgin. He was a tributary of the German King and under him German missionaries entered. In 929 while on his way to mass he was murdered by his brother, Boleslav I, and an anti-German, anti-Christian reaction ensued. The combination of his piety and his tragic end made of Václav the national saint.

In the latter part of the century the climate again changed in favour of Christianity. Boleslav II, the son of the murderer of Václav, reigned from 967 to 999. In contrast with his father, he actively encouraged the spread of the faith. It was under him that the nominal conversion of Bohemia was substantially completed. He founded monasteries and built churches. Otto I was a power with whom to reckon and it seems to have been at his instance that the initial bishopric in Bohemia, that of Prague, was created. The first bishop was a Saxon and the second, Adalbert, although of Czech blood, was related to the family of Otto I, had been educated at Magdeburg, the seat of the bishopric which that German ruler had created as a centre for missions among the Slavs, and was strongly committed to the Cluny movement, with its strict standards of Christian living. He made himself unpopular by attempting to raise the semi-pagan life of his flock to the level advocated by the Cluny reformers, and was martyred (997) as a missionary to the pagan Prussians south of the Baltic. By that time Bohemia was regarded as a Christian kingdom.

THE CONVERSION OF POLAND

To the north of Bohemia lay Poland, that region whose absence of clearly defined geographic boundaries has rendered it the tragic victim of its strong neighbours. Here, as in Bohemia, Christianity entered partly under pressure from the Germans. Also, as in several of the lands which we have noted, its progress was associated with the growth of centralized political control by a king and was opposed by those local magnates who wished to preserve their independence and who associated it with the pre-Christian order.

We do not know exactly when the first conversions were made among the Slavs of the region which we know as Poland. In the second half of the tenth century a Slavic prince who ruled over part of the area accepted baptism, perhaps through the influence of his wife, the sister of Boleslav II of Bohemia. He was forced to recognize the overlordship of Otto I. In 968 a bishopric was created for the Poles at Poznań (Posen) and its first two incumbents were Germans.

The great growth of Christianity in Poland was under a son of this prince, Boleslaw Chrobry ("the Brave"), who reigned from 992 to 1025. Boleslaw brought together one of the largest states of the Europe of his day and sought to strengthen the royal authority at the expense of the local magnates. He encouraged missionaries. When Adalbert was martyred by the Prussians he had the body brought to Gniezno (Gnesen). That city was soon (1000) made the seat of an archbishopric, the brother of the martyr was put at its head, and three suffragan sees were created under it. Thus the Church in Poland was given a hierarchy, even though that might be inadequate for so large a realm. The creation of these bishoprics was at the initiative of the imaginative young Holy Roman Emperor, Otto III, grandson of Otto I, but the suggestion may have come from Boleslaw, for the act made the Polish Church almost independent of that of Germany.

After the death of Boleslaw what might have been anticipated took place. A revulsion set in against the royal authority and the faith which was so closely associated with it. For a time the Kingdom of Poland broke apart. Churches and monasteries were burned and bishops and priests were either driven out or killed. While the work of Boleslaw was never completely undone, for several generations the Christianity of the country was on a low level. Bishops were too few and their dioceses too large for adequate administration.

THE CONVERSION OF THE MAGYARS

It was late in the ninth century, while the Viking invasions of Europe were in full flood and the measure of order given by the Carolingians was declining, that the Magyars effected settlements in the modern Hungary. From there they repeatedly raided Italy and Western Europe as far as the North Sea. Pagans, they burned churches, plundered monasteries, killed some priests before the altars and carried others into captivity. They contributed to the low ebb of Christianity in the first half of the tenth century.

Rising German power checked the Magyar advance and in 955 Otto I inflicted a stunning defeat which freed Western Europe from the Magyar terror. Germans, Christians, moved eastward and colonized regions on the Danube on the Magyar borders. On the south-east the Bulgars had become Christians and the faith, as we have seen, was spreading in Bohemia and Poland on the Magyars' north. It is not strange that Christianity began making headway among the Magyars themselves.

The mass conversion of Magyars came late in the tenth and early in the eleventh century. It was chiefly accomplished through the royal family and especially by Vajk, better known as Stephen, who made of Hungary a monarchy of the type that was emerging in Western Europe.

It is said that two Magyar princes were baptized in Constantinople while on a political errand and that they brought back a bishop with them. However, it was to the West rather than to Constantinople that the leaders turned for their culture and their religion. In 973 Magyar envoys appeared at the court of Otto I and not far from that time German missionaries began to penetrate into Magyar lands. A Magyar prince, Geisa, was making himself master of the country and compelled many of his subjects to accept baptism. Baptism and submission to his authority appear to have gone hand in hand.

Geisa's labours were brought to a culmination by his son Vajk (Stephen). Stephen succeeded his father in 997 and continued the latter's measures for the unification of the realm and the adoption of Christianity. He himself preached to his subjects, urging them to accept the new faith. Although some question has been raised about the authenticity of the Papal letter which is our chief source of information, it is said that in the year 1000 Stephen asked of the Pope and received the royal title, a crown, and a hierarchy for his realm, with an archbishop and subordinate bishops. It is certain that many missionaries entered, a large proportion of them Slavs, and that by legislation Stephen enjoined respect for Sunday, decorum during church services, and the payment of tithes for the support of the Church. He also gave bishops judicial powers in matrimonial and ecclesiastical questions much as was customary in the West.

Stephen's innovations met stubborn resistance which from time to time flared up in open rebellion. When death removed his strong hand (1038) the almost inevitable reaction revived pagan rites and brought violence against the clergy. However, after a generation of internal dissensions and foreign wars and invasions, late in the eleventh century a succession of strong monarchs gave renewed support to Christianity and the Church.

CHRISTIAN COUNTER-GAINS AGAINST ISLAM IN SPAIN AND SICILY

As we have suggested, the four centuries which followed the year 950 witnessed a substantial reclamation of territories lost to Islam in Spain and Sicily.

In Spain the Moslem Arab conquest had no sooner reached its high-watermark than the small states which survived in the North under Christian leadership began to regain the lost territory. This, like the Arab domination, was achieved by armed force. The first stage of the Moslem retreat is usually dated from a battle in 718 in which the Christians were victors. Various Christian states arose—Aragon, León, Navarre, Castile, Portugal, and in the Asturias, Galicia, and Catalonia. These states often fought among themselves and thereby gave breathing spaces to the waning Moslem power. In the latter part of the tenth century Almanzor, the great minister and general of the Caliphate of Cordova, inflicted defeat after defeat on the Christian armies. However, in 1034 the Caliphate of Cordova came to an end and with it disappeared what had been the main centre and rallying point of Moslem power. The tide of battle ebbed and flowed, but by the middle of the thirteenth century the Moslem political power had been reduced to the small state of Granada, in the extreme south-east.

In the territories reconquered by Christian from Moslem princes little force was employed to bring about conversion from Islam. As in the Moorish states Christians had been tolerated and Christian bishops and clergy had continued to minister to their flocks, so now, under Christian rulers, such of the Moslems as chose to do so were permitted the free practice of their religion and were left in possession of their mosques, houses, and estates and for a time had magistrates of their own faith. Similarly as under Moslem rule Christians had been subjected to certain disabilities and special taxation, so Christian princes required Moslems to live in segregated districts and to pay tithes to the Church and a special tribute to the state.

Under these circumstances Islam declined in the Iberian Peninsula. Some of its adherents migrated to Africa to be under Moslem rulers. Others deemed it expedient to conform to the religion of their new masters. Active missionary effort was directed to the Moslems, especially beginning in the thirteenth century with the rise of the great missionary orders, the Franciscans and the Dominicans, of whom we are later to hear much. On at least one occasion an over-zealous bishop said mass in a mosque in violation of a pledge given by the Christian conqueror at the time of the surrender. It was long after 1350 that the last remnants of Islam disappeared from the Iberian Peninsula, but by that year the outcome was fairly well assured.

The extinction of Islam in Sicily was the result of the Norman conquest of that island in the second half of the eleventh century. The Normans, as their name indicates, were the descendants of Northmen who had settled in the area, Normandy, which took its name from them. In Normandy they had become Christians. The religious motive seems either to have been absent or distinctly secondary in their invasion of Sicily. A minority, they deemed it the part of wisdom to grant religious freedom to the diverse faiths of their subjects. Jews, Moslems, Greek Orthodox, and Roman Catholics enjoyed equal rights. Towards the end of the twelfth century, after a hundred years of Norman rule, Moslems were still numerous and influential and held high posts at court. However, the early Norman magnates strengthened the Church and founded additional bishoprics, thus in part undoing the damage which had accompanied Moslem dominance. Islam, never represented by more than a minority, declined. By the middle of the thirteenth century it had almost disappeared.

The Slow Completion of the Conversion of North-western Europe

The remarkable spread of Christianity in the hundred years after 950 brought into nominal adherence to the faith most of the major peoples of Western Europe who had thus far been outside its fold. The one important exception was the Moors in the Iberian Peninsula and these, as we have seen, were dwindling. Yet in 1050 by no means all those who dwelt in Western and Central Europe thought of themselves as Christians. In addition to the Moslems in the Iberian Peninsula and Sicily and the Jews, a small and widely scattered minority, there were still frankly pagan enclaves. They were principally along the southern and eastern shores of the Baltic. Chief among them were the Slavs north and east of the Elbe (Wends the Germans called them), the Pomeranians, the Lithuanians, the Prussians, the Estonians or Ests, the Letts, the Finns, and, in the extreme North, the Lapps.

After the middle of the eleventh century the geographic advance of Christianity in Western and Central Europe continued but at a much less marked pace. As we have repeatedly reminded ourselves, the effect of nominal conversion upon the majority of the peoples who had been won in the preceding hundred years was slight and the deepening of the faith through instruction, the recruiting and training of clergy, the development of dioceses and parishes, and the administration of the Church's sacraments was slow. In some lands, notably in Poland and Hungary, the first wave of conversion, associated as it was with vigorous and sometimes violent and ruthless expansion of the royal power, was followed by a pagan revival. Recovery always came, but it might be retarded. By the year 1350 conversion had been accomplished in all Western and Central Europe except for the Lithuanians, the Finns, the Jews, and the Moslem remnants in Spain. Beginnings had been made in all these and before long the Lithuanian pagan majority was to accept baptism.

Efforts for the conversion of the Wends commenced in a large way in the first half of the tenth century. Divided into many tribes, the Wends then occupied most of the later Germany east and north of the Elbe. The German rulers attempted to extend their control over them and their territories. This led to chronic warfare which was often waged with savage cruelty. Since the Germans professed to be Christians, both they and the Wends regarded baptism as a symbol of submission to German authority and the issue was compounded by racial bitterness. Otto I extended his domains, somewhat superficially, eastward to the Oder. He sought the conversion of his newly acquired Wend subjects. To this end he founded two bishoprics in Wendland and placed them under the Archbishopric of Magdeburg, inaugurated for this very purpose, on the left bank of the Elbe, looking across the river into Wend territory. After death had removed his strong hand, the Wends revolted and directed part of their spleen against the bishops, symbols as they were of German rule. German authority was later restored, but when it declined the Wends once more rose. Again and again the cycle was repeated. Some of the Wends were baptized, but the territory which had been theirs became solidly committed to Christianity only through the immigration of Germans, a process which required centuries.

The conversion of the Pomeranians, a Slavic people on the Baltic with their capital at Stettin, was accomplished during the twelfth and the fore part of the thirteenth century. In it Poles, Danes, and Germans had a part, but Germans were the chief agents. In the first quarter of the twelfth century a king of Poland invaded the region, captured some of the cities, and as a price of peace required the populace to pay him tribute and to accept baptism. His chief emissary for inducing the Pomeranians to fulfil their promise to be baptized was a German, Bishop Otto of Bamberg.

Otto was an organizer, a man of affairs, who had been Chancellor of the Holy Roman Empire. At this time probably in his sixties, he had the fearlessness and energy of youth. Twice he journeyed into Pomerania, both times in the 1120's, taking with him a band of assistants. He went unarmed, but with impressive pomp, with the endorsement of the Pope, and the second time with the authority of the German king. Under him numbers were baptized, but not until the close of the century do there seem to have been many Pomeranian priests. German and Danish monastic communities and the German farmers whom they encouraged to come to till their lands did much to complete the assimilation of the Pomeranians to the Christian faith.

It was in the latter part of the twelfth and the fore part of the thirteenth century that Christianity was firmly established among the Finns. This was largely through the Swedes, but it was an Englishman, Bishop Henry of the Swedish see of Uppsala, who, martyred, is esteemed the founder of the Finnish church. It was, however, a Swedish conquest which began in 1249 that led the majority to an outward conformity to the Christian faith. The Swedes also had missions among the Lapps, in the extreme north of the Scandinavian Peninsula, but by the middle of the fourteenth century only a minority had been won.

Late in the twelfth and early in the thirteenth century the Danes were especially strong in the Baltic. Through them conversions were made among the Ests, south of the Gulf of Finland. The Swedes and the Russians from Novgorod also had a part in bringing the Ests to accept the Christian faith. Indeed, there was unseemly rivalry among these nationalities in using baptism as a means of gaining support for their interests.

Except for the Lithuanians, the majority among the Baltic peoples south of the Gulf of Finland became Christians through the Germans. Early contacts with Germans were commercial. German merchants frequented the Baltic ports. Accounts brought by merchants led an elderly German monk, Meinhard, to go to the lower Dvina and preach to any who would listen. He was soon consecrated bishop for that area. The second of his successors, Albert, founded the city of Riga near the mouth of the Dvina and inaugurated (1202) a crusading order with the name, singularly inappropriate for Christian missionaries, Knights of the Sword, officially and slightly less offensively, *Fratres Militiae Christi*. By this time Crusades, of which we will have more to say in the next chapter, had become an honoured phase of the activities of Western Christendom and orders which combined monastic vows with the career of the soldier had come into being to further them. The Knights of the Sword conquered a fairly extensive area and required of pagans a pledge to accept baptism as a symbol of submission.

The Prussians, a non-Germanic people, were very resistant. Late in the tenth and early in the eleventh century they killed several missionaries. Undiscouraged, other missionaries came and baptisms followed. In the first half of the thirteenth century the Teutonic Knights undertook the task. They, too, had arisen from the Crusades, originally for the purpose of serving Christians in Syria and Palestine. In 1225-1226 they were called by a Pole for aid against a tribe of Prussians. Here they found their main field of endeavour. After a half century of fighting they conquered the land. They then ruled it for several centuries. Under them the Prussians outwardly conformed to the Christian faith.

The Teutonic Knights attempted to subjugate the Lithuanians, but the latter resisted both them and their religion. It was not until 1386 that as the price of an alliance with the Poles against the Knights the Lithuanians agreed to mass baptism and the destruction of their pagan temples. Obviously even then the conversion was superficial and pagan practices survived at least as late as the seventeenth century.

The Jews in Western Europe

Through most of Western Europe the Jews remained an unassimilated minority, largely city dwellers and keeping to their ancestral faith. There was much popular feeling against them and from time to time mobs attacked them. Some of the Crusaders on their way to the Holy Land slaughtered men, women, and children. Through the centuries there was a trickle of conversions which occasionally became a substantial stream. Many of these were forced and some were from motives of prudence, but others were from religious conviction. In general the Popes condemned the use of violence to bring conversions, but declared that if a Jew had been baptized he had thereby been made a member of the Church and was subject to its discipline if he reverted to the religion of his forefathers.

Jews were especially numerous in Spain. Throughout most of these centuries, with the exception of occasional spasms of persecution, they were treated with leniency by both Moslem and Christian rulers. Indeed, in the twelfth, thirteenth, and fourteenth centuries they often rose to high positions in the government and the administration of the finances of the Christian states was largely in their hands. Gradually, in the thirteenth and fourteenth centuries prejudice against them mounted and official measures were taken to compel them to attend sermons presenting the Christian faith. Presumably some baptisms followed. Not until 1391, however, does toleration seem to have ended.

The Further Spread of Christianity in Russia

In the first half of the thirteenth century Christianity in Russia entered upon grim days. The Mongols swept into the land and made themselves masters of the area north of the Caspian and Black Seas. They were pagans and the immediate effect of their conquest was adverse for the Church. Many Christians perished, numbers of church buildings were laid in ruins, and service books and vestments were destroyed. Eventually the dominant groups among the Golden Horde—the Russian Mongols—embraced Islam. It would not have been surprising if Russian Christianity, by the majority very superficially and unintelligently held, had disappeared.

However, the net effect of the Mongol conquest was to deepen the hold of Christianity on the Russians and to spread the faith into areas hitherto untouched. In general the Mongol rulers were friendly to the Church and did not attempt to force their Christian subjects to abandon their faith. The Church was given authority over its members in moral and religious questions, especially in marriage, sex offenses, inheritance, and the duties of children to parents. It was accorded immunity from some forms of taxation. The Church was regarded by Russians as the one institution which was peculiarly their own and became a symbol of what might be called Russian nationalism. It was the tie of Russian unity.

To escape the Mongol yoke many Russians migrated northward, beyond the border of Mongol rule. Numbers also sought release by abandoning the world and adopting the monastic life. Hermits made their way to the northern forests. In other places in the North monastic communities were established. Around many of the latter towns sprang up and the monasteries became schools in agriculture and the Christian faith. Through them pagans were converted, lands cleared, roads and canals built, marshes drained, and improved methods of cattle breeding and cultivating the soil were introduced. By them the Russian language was spread and various Finnish tribes were assimilated to the Russian church and Russian culture.

The Growth of Christian Minorities in Asia

Between 950 and 1350 more and more of the peoples of the western end of the continent of Eurasia made Christianity their official faith. Simultaneously, immersed in the dominant Islam, the churches on the north shore of Africa and in Western Asia east and south of Asia Minor slowly dwindled. Europe and Christendom were becoming synonymous.

For a time in these four centuries it seemed that Christianity, balked in the Moslem world, might not be so largely confined to an area which was on the periphery of civilization, but might win in Central and Eastern Asia. Converts were made in Central Asia and China and strong churches existed in India and on even one island, Socotra, in the Arabian Sea. At the outset of their conquests the hope was cherished by some that the Mongols themselves would be converted. If they, the rulers of the mightiest and most extensive empire that mankind had yet known, were to become Christians, all of the civilized and much of the uncivilized world might follow. Here was a major opportunity and challenge. The opportunity was not seized. Probably it could not have been. Yet during these centuries Christian communities, most of them small, multiplied in the regions in Central and East Asia which were subject to the Moslems. This was chiefly through the Nestorians but it was also in part through Catholics from Western Europe.

We have seen that Nestorians had won some of the Turkish peoples of Central Asia and were represented in the caravan cities of that region, radiating points of cultural influence. We have also noted that, carried to China in the seventh century by Nestorians, by the latter part of the tenth century Christianity had died out in that realm.

Early in the eleventh century Nestorian Christianity began to make fresh gains. Not far from the year 1000 the prince of the Keraïts, a Turkish folk in Central Asia, is said to have asked for baptism. In the thirteenth century that people were professing Christians. In that same century the Onguts, a Tartar folk dwelling to the north of the great northern bend of the Yellow River, also called themselves Christians, and among the Uighurs, a people long prominent in the area through which ran the trade routes from China to the West, were some of that faith. When or how they became Christians we do not know. In the thirteenth and fourteenth centuries European travellers found strong Christian communities in South India.

The Mongol advance seemed at first to favour Christianity. Among the early conquests of Jenghiz Khan was that of the Keraïts and in what seems to have been an attempt to strengthen his power he married one of his sons to a princess from the Keraït ruling family. She was a Christian and the mother of two of the most prominent of Jenghiz Khan's grandsons, Khubilai Khan and Hulagu. Hulagu's favourite wife was a Christian. Mangu, Grand Khan of the Mongols from 1251 to 1259, is said to have been baptized by an Armenian bishop. The inherited faith of the Mongols was a form of shamanism, a kind of "primitive" religion which yields easily to a "higher" religion. There was substantial ground for the hope that the Mongols might become Christians.

Under the Mongols Christianity once more appeared in China. At the Mongol capital, Cambaluc, the later Peking, the Nestorians had an archbishop. A native of North China, but probably not a Chinese, journeyed westward with an older companion and eventually became head of the entire Nestorian Church. Nestorian communities, presumably all foreign, were found in several Chinese cities. A Nestorian was governor of one of these cities and built several monasteries. Alans, Christians from the Caucasus, constituted a contingent of the Mongol garrison in Cambaluc.

The Mongol Empire opened the doors to wide-flung missions from the Catholics of Western Europe. In general the Mongols were fairly tolerant religiously and when once their rule had been established—although that was often by wholesale slaughter—they brought in a degree of peace and order. They accorded security to the east-west land trade routes across Asia. Many European merchants, mostly from the flourishing Italian cities, journeyed by them as far as China—which they knew as Cathay. They also went by sea to India and to the great marts of the China coast.

When the Mongol storm broke across Eurasia, two of the chief missionary orders of the Catholic Church, the Franciscans and Dominicans, were in the first flush of their enthusiastic youth. They took advantage of the new day to plant missions which were scattered from Russia to the China Sea. In the Mongol domains in Russia the rulers, as we have seen, were religiously tolerant.

The Pope assigned the region to the Franciscans and here, about 1300, the Brothers Minor had seventeen stations, including a monastery in the capital. Converts were made, among them members of the reigning family. The friars accompanied the nomads on their wanderings, preaching and administering the sacraments. Several bishoprics and two archbishoprics were created.

In Persia under the Mongols both Franciscans and Dominicans, principally the latter, were present. There were a Latin archbishopric and several bishoprics. These Western Catholics devoted their chief efforts to bringing to allegiance to Rome members of the other churches in the region—Nestorians, Jacobites, Armenians, Georgians, and Greek Orthodox.

In Central Asia Franciscans sought to establish missions and we hear of martyrdoms of Brothers Minor but also of baptisms and of at least one church building.

Both Franciscans and Dominicans were in India. Some suffered martyrdom, but some won converts and there was at least one Latin bishopric.

The most spectacular as well as the most remote of the missions of Western Christians which arose in the wake of the Mongol conquests was in China. China was the most populous and the richest of all the lands under Mongol rule. Its largest cities were said to surpass any in the rest of the world. To them came many merchants from Western Europe, the most famous, because of a narrative left by one of them, the Polos. In 1269 two Polos, brothers, arrived from Cathay at Acre, on the east shore of the Mediterranean, with letters from Khubilai Khan, then ruling all the Mongol domains from Cambaluc, asking for teachers of the science and religion of Europe. After a delay, two Dominicans started on the return trip with the Polos, who now had with them young Marco, the son of one of the latter, who was eventually to write the book at which we have hinted. Before they had gone far the friars took alarm at rumoured dangers and turned back, but the Polos kept on. In 1278 a report that Khubilai Khan had been baptized stimulated the Pope to start a group of five Franciscans towards China, but what happened to them we are not told.

So far as our records enable us to know, the first Catholic missionary to reach China was an Italian Franciscan, John of Montecorvino. He arrived in Cambaluc in 1294, bearing a letter from the Pope to Khubilai Khan. The latter had recently died, but his successor received John courteously. John encountered bitter opposition from the Nestorians, who were powerful at court, but he remained and by 1305 had built a church, had won about 6,000 converts, and had translated the New Testament and Psalter into what he described as "the language and character which is in most general use among the Tartars." By 1306 he had completed a second church at Cambaluc.

Letters from John telling of these successes reached the Papal court and caused something of a sensation. To reinforce him the Pope appointed seven Franciscans and created them bishops with authority to consecrate John as archbishop. Of the seven, one either did not leave Europe or soon turned back and three died on the way, so long was the journey and so formidable the hardships. From time to time other Brothers Minor came and missions were established in several cities. So far as we know, the last medieval missionaries to reach China were a party led by a Papal legate which arrived at Cambaluc in 1342 and reported to the Papal court on its return trip in 1353.

Missions to Moslems in North Africa and Western Asia

The Latin Catholics were not content with seeking to convert the Moslems in the Iberian Peninsula and Sicily or with turning the flank of the Moslem advance by taking advantage of the Mongol conquests to carry their faith into Russia, Central Asia, India, and the Far East. They also sought to win Moslems in those areas in North Africa and Western Asia which had been torn from Christendom by Islam and to bring into unity with Rome the Christian communities in these regions, chiefly in Western Asia, which had survived the Arab conquests. Much of this was in connexion with the Crusades. Most of the active missions were by Franciscans and Dominicans.

However, one of the most far-ranging in his dreams for missions, including the conversion of the Moslems, Raymond Lull, was disliked by the Dominicans and only late in life connected himself with the Franciscans. Born about 1232 on the island of Majorca, Raymond Lull was reared in aristocratic circles and until he had passed his first youth his was the life of a dissolute courtier. Then, converted by recurring visions of Christ on the cross, he made provision for his wife and family, gave the rest of his property to the poor, and devoted himself to religion. He wrote prodigiously. A mystic, some of his works were in that field. His chief concern was to see all men won to the Christian faith. He urged that the Mongols be reached before they accepted Islam or Judaism. He travelled extensively, pressing upon Popes and cardinals the founding of monasteries for the preparation of missionaries. He devised a system of presenting the Christian faith to non-Christians and lectured on it in some of the main centres of theological learning. It was on the Moslems that he concentrated most of his missionary zeal. He made three missionary journeys to North Africa. On the first two he was arrested and deported and on the third, in 1315 or 1316, when he was probably past eighty years of age, he was stoned so severely that he died.

Between them the Franciscans and Dominicans covered most of the Moslem world. In this they were supported by Papal letters to Moslem princes.

Both orders were in North Africa, seeking to serve the Christian sailors, merchants, and captives in that area and to revive the Christian cause which once had had a chief stronghold there but under the Moslem rule had all but disappeared. Bishoprics were created. In the twelfth and thirteenth centuries two other orders were formed to ransom or otherwise rescue the Christians who had been carried captive to that region.

Franciscans and Dominicans were widely scattered in Western Asia. Many were in cities which had been captured by the Crusaders. Others went beyond these centres. Their chief numerical successes were among the churches which were not in communion with Rome. One entire group, the Maronites, was drawn permanently into the Roman fold. From the others only minorities were gathered. Usually these became Uniates, that is, they were permitted to retain their ancient rites, customs, and languages, but brought their creeds into conformity with those of Rome and acknowledged the supremacy of the Pope.

Summary

As we have pursued our rapid way through this condensed account of the conversion of much of Europe, inevitably the question has again and again arisen to perplex us, as it has in earlier sections on the spread of the faith: to what extent, if at all, did these converts understand the Gospel, really commit themselves to it, and know its power? How far, from the standpoint of the true spirit of the faith, were mass conversions desirable? Was it true, as some one was later to put it, that Europe was inoculated with a mild form of Christianity in such fashion that it was immune to the real thing?

Probably full definitive answers are impossible. Yet certain facts are clear. At the outset the vast majority of the nominal Christians were quite unaware of the nature of the Gospel or of the kind of life entailed through the new birth wrought by it. Most of them were baptized either in response to a command from some ruler, their own or a foreign conqueror, or because those about them were receiving the rite. Traditionally religion had been a community affair. As peoples professed to exchange their former faiths for Christianity, it continued to be so. If they thought about it at all, the majority probably expected the new religion to do for them what they had asked of the old, but to do it better.

However, from the outset there were some who caught at least a faint glimmer of what was meant by the Gospel. We must remember that the active missionaries were usually monks and that monks were those who, in theory, had committed themselves fully to the commands of Christ as they understood them. As time passed, moreover, ethical standards that were believed to be Christian were accepted by almost all as ideal, even when they were far from being fully obeyed. Progressively in most lands of "Christendom" instruction was given which involved as a minimum familiarity with the creed, the Lord's Prayer, and something of the meaning of the sacraments.

Probably in the professedly Christian countries of Europe there was quite as much understanding of what was recorded in the New Testament and as much whole-hearted acceptance of it as in the minorities of Asia, whether these were recent converts who had come one by one or were ancient churches, encysted within the dominant Moslem or Hindu communities. Indeed, from Europe there issued, to a much greater degree than from these minorities, movements which we are to meet intermittently through the remainder of our narrative, some of them monastic and some of them from the Catholic standpoint heretical, which sprang from a deep desire to be fully Christian. It would seem that where either the overwhelming majority or a substantial minority profess to be Christian, fresh efforts for the perfect realization of the wonder of the Gospel have been more frequent than where Christians have been minorities which have been primarily on the defensive, seeking to hand down their faith from generation to generation to their children and grandchildren, set consciously in a hostile world, but despairing of winning that world to the faith.

Selected Bibliography

GENERAL WORKS

K. S. Latourette, *A History of the Expansion of Christianity. Volume II, The Thousand Years of Uncertainty* (New York, Harper & Brothers, 1938, pp. ix, 492). A survey of the years from 500 to 1500, with extensive footnote references.

J. T. Addison, *The Medieval Missionary, A Study of the Conversion of Northern Europe* A.D. *500–1300* (New York, International Missionary Council, 1936, pp. xiv, 176). A careful and accurate study of missionary methods.

The Cambridge Medieval History (Cambridge University Press, 1911 ff.) has several chapters which are pertinent to the subject of the conversion of Europe.

A. Hauck, *Kirchengeschichte Deutschlands* (Leipzig, J. C. Hinrichs'sche Buchhandlung, 5 vols., 1922–1929). Invaluable and has large sections which fall within the range of several of the areas and subjects treated in this chapter.

THE SCANDINAVIANS

Saxo Grammaticus, *Gesta Danorum* (edited by A. Holder, Strassburg, Karl J. Trübner, 1886, pp. lxxxviii, 724). Composed in the last quarter of the twelfth and the first quarter of the thirteenth century and least undependable when it deals with events of those years.

K. Lübeck, *Die Christianisierung Russlands* (Aachen, Xaveriusverlagsbuchhandlung, 1922, pp. 118). By a Roman Catholic, objective, scholarly, using Russian and Western European material.

POLAND

J. X. Seppelt, *Zur Einführung des Christentums in Polen* (in *Zeitschrift für Missionswissenschaft,* Vol. X, 1920, pp. 86–93). An excellent summary.

SPAIN AND PORTUGAL

C. R. Haines, *Christianity and Islam in Spain* A.D. *756–1030* (London, Kegan Paul, Trench, Trübner & Co., 1889, pp. viii, 182). Scholarly, based largely on original sources.

THE WENDS AND BALTIC PEOPLES

J. W. Thompson, *Feudal Germany* (University of Chicago Press, 1928, pp. xxiii, 710). Specializes on the northern and eastern expansion of the Germans and their culture, but has marked prejudices.

F. J. Tschan, *The Chronicle of the Slavs by Helmold, Priest of Bosau* (Columbia University Press, 1935, pp. xii, 321). A translation of a very useful twelfth century source.

ASIA AND NORTH AFRICA

W. F. Adeney, *The Greek and Eastern Churches* (New York, Charles Scribner's Sons, preface 1908, pp. xiv, 634).

B. Altaner, *Die Dominikanermission des 13 Jahrhundert* (Habelschwerdt, Frankes Buchhandlung, 1924, pp. xxiii, 247). Carefully done, with extensive footnotes.

L. E. Browne, *The Eclipse of Christianity in Asia* (Cambridge University Press, 1933, pp. 198). Useful.

E. A. Wallace Budge, *The Monks of Kûblâi Khân* (London, The Religious Tract Society, 1928, pp. xvi, 335). The best English translation of an important document.

L. Lemmens, *Die Hiedenmission des Spätmittelalters* (Münster, Aschendorffsche Verlagsbuchhandlung, 1919, pp. x, 112). Primarily concerned with Franciscan missions.

A. C. Moule, *Christians in China before the Year 1550* (London, Society for Promoting Christian Knowledge, 1930, pp. xix, 293). Translations, with excellent notes, of pertinent sources.

E. A. Peers, *Ramon Lull, a Biography* (London, Society for Promoting Christian Knowledge, 1929, pp. xviii, 454). By a specialist on the Spanish mystics.

E. A. Peers, *A Fool of Love. The Life of Ramon Lull* (London, Student Christian Movement Press, 1946, pp. 127).

H. Yule, *Cathay and the Way Thither: Being a Collection of Medieval Notices of China,* revised by H. Cordier (London, The Hakluyt Society, 4 vols., 1925, 1926). Long a standard.

Chapter 17

EXPANSION THROUGH THE CRUSADES

A phase of the life of Europe which loomed large through at least half of the four hundred years from 950 to 1350 was the Crusades. In spite of their name, they were not entirely religious movements. Indeed, they were a phase of the beginning of the expansion of Europe which, after a pause, was to be of major importance for the world and for Christianity in the ensuing generations and not least in the twentieth century. Ostensibly they had a Christian motive, they were with the authorization and in no small degree at the initiative of the Roman branch of the Catholic Church, they were permeated by religious, if not purely Christian, devotion, and they had marked effect upon the Christian communities, both in the West and in the East. However, important though they were, this is not the place for more than a brief summary of them. Our interest in them is primarily in their bearing upon our subject, the history of Christianity. From that standpoint they are significant partly because through them Western Christianity was projected into the Eastern Mediterranean, partly because of the effects, largely disastrous, on relations between the Western and Eastern wings of the Catholic Church, and partly because of the repercussions on Latin Christianity.

The Roots of the Crusades

Why were the Crusades? The causes were mixed and varied. They were in part that *wanderlust* which seems to have been one of the factors in the invasions of the Roman Empire and its successors in Europe of which we have had much to say in earlier chapters. They were in part economic. In the generation or more preceding the First Crusade Western Europe had repeatedly suffered from famine. To the thoughtful of that time Europe, sparsely settled by twentieth century standards, appeared to be overpopulated. It had more mouths than the economy of the time could feed and observers were not wanting who believed the land to be groaning under the weight of its inhabitants. Many sought release in these expeditions to the East. The Italian cities, now beginning to grow and looking eastward for trade, encouraged the Crusades as a means of furthering their commercial enterprises. There was the personal factor. Ambitious men saw in the Crusades opportunity for adventure, fame, and power.

At the outset the desire of the Byzantine Emperors for aid against the Moslem Seljuk Turks contributed to the Crusades. In the eleventh century the Byzantine Empire fell on evil days. These began in 1025 with the death of the Emperor Basil II and were accentuated when in 1056 the Macedonian dynasty which had brought to the realm large accessions of territory and of power came to an end. Internal dissensions combined with foreign invasions to threaten the very existence of the realm. In the West the Normans conquered Southern Italy, long a Byzantine possession. From the north barbarians forced their way to the very walls of Constantinople. Even more formidable were the Seljuk Turks. Originally from Central Asia, converts to Islam, in the eleventh century they built an empire which included Persia, Mesopotamia, Syria, Palestine, and Egypt. They fought their way into Asia Minor and in 1071, the year of a decisive victory of the Normans in Southern Italy, inflicted a stunning defeat on the Byzantine army in Armenia, near Lake Van, and overran much of Asia Minor. The accession (1081) to the imperial throne of Alexius Comnenus brought vigorous leadership to Constantinople. This was continued by his immediate descendants. Some territory was regained, but only by what proved to be a reprieve.

It is the religious factors which are here chiefly our concern. They were undoubtedly potent. First of all in the minds of many was the rescue from the Moslem of the places in Palestine, especially Jerusalem, which were sacred to the Christian. For centuries Christians from the West, like those from other regions, had been making them the goal of pious pilgrimages. To bring them into Christian hands and keep them was ostensibly the chief objective of the Crusades.

Another phase of the religious motive was the protection of the Byzantine Empire against the Moslem Turks. As we have said, the Turks were threatening this historic bulwark of Christendom. The Byzantine Emperors appealed to the Christians of the West for assistance and the Popes were disposed to give it.

Intimately related to this second religious motive was a third, the desire of the Popes to heal the breach between the Western and Eastern wings of the Catholic Church and to restore Christian unity. In the tenth and eleventh centuries relations between East and West had deteriorated. Greek Catholics were scandalized, perhaps not unwillingly, by the state of the Church in the West—by the weak Popes of that period of Papal decline, by the spectacle of bishops leading armies, something which their wing of the Church did not know, and by reports of the generally low state of the faith in the West before the reforms which were beginning to get under way in the latter part of the tenth century. With some of these reforms they were not in accord, notably the emphasis upon the celibacy of the priesthood. There remained, too, the chronic sources of irritation which we have repeatedly noted. In 1054 the friction had reached an acute point when, in negotiations between the Papacy and the Patriarchate of Constantinople, the Papal legates laid on the altar of Saint Sophia at the hour of solemn service a sentence of excommunication of the Patriarch. The latter replied with a strong denunciation of the Latin position. The rupture was not necessarily final, for there had been earlier ones which in principle had been healed, but it was serious, and the Popes wished to remove it.

THE FIRST CRUSADE

What is called the First Crusade began in 1096, the immediate outgrowth of an appeal by Pope Urban II in a stirring sermon at a synod at Clermont, in France, in November of the preceding year. The congregation, deeply moved, is said to have boomed out: *"Deus vult"* ("God wills it") and this was made the slogan of the enterprise. The Pope had been asked by the Eastern Emperor for aid against the Seljuk Turks. He was not the first Byzantine Emperor to seek such help. A predecessor had made a similar plea to Gregory VII, whom we are to meet again, as we also are Urban II, as a leader in reform in the Western Church and in seeking to enhance the power of the Church in the affairs of men. Urban called on the Christians of Western Europe to go to the succour of their Eastern brethren and also to free the holy places from the hands of the infidels. "Plenary indulgence," of which we are to hear more later, was promised to all who took part and eternal life to those who lost their physical lives in the enterprise. The cross was worn as a symbol by those who responded.

Preachers, conspicuous among them Peter the Hermit, spread the message through much of Western Europe. Popular enthusiasm mounted. Throngs, poorly organized, set forth, some of them attacking the Jews or pillaging fellow Christians as they went. Most of this wave perished, some before reaching Constantinople and others not long after they had crossed into Asia. Much better organized armies left in the summer of 1096, arrived in Constantinople that winter and the next spring, fought their way through Asia Minor, captured Antioch in June, 1098, with great slaughter, and the following year took Jerusalem, putting many of its inhabitants to the sword.

The most respected of the crusading leaders, Godfrey of Bouillon, was made Protector of the Holy Sepulchre. After his early death he was succeeded by a brother who had the title King of Jerusalem. Crusaders established themselves in various centres in Syria and Palestine, where the ruins of their strongholds can still be seen. Their political structure was feudal, as was natural for those coming from the Western Europe of that day. Rome appointed a Patriarch of Jerusalem and several bishoprics and archbishoprics were set up. Although reunion of all the Eastern Churches had not been accomplished under the ægis of Rome, the Western Church had largely extended its holdings, and in the East. The Crusaders were far from being ideal exemplars of the faith which they professed and few if any willing conversions from Islam were made by them.

THE LATER CRUSADES

The fall of Edessa in 1144 stimulated what was known as the Second Crusade, for Edessa was a key city in the defenses of the Crusaders' kingdom. That Crusade was preached by Bernard of Clairvaux, esteemed a model Christian by his own and later generations. It was, however, a failure, for many of its contingents perished before reaching Syria and it broke down in its attempt to take Damascus.

Moslem divisions had been one cause for the success of the First Crusade. Now the Kurdish Saladin built a strong Moslem state which enveloped the Latin kingdom on its land frontiers. In 1187 in a memorable and decisive battle at Hattin the European forces were cut to pieces. Jerusalem and most of the Crusaders' centres soon fell to the triumphant Islam.

It was to retrieve these losses that the Third Crusade was launched (1189). Three armies set out, led respectively by the Holy Roman Emperor Frederick Barbarossa, one of the most eminent of that long line, the scheming King Philip Augustus of France, and the adventurous King Richard, "the lion-hearted," of England. The Emperor came to his death in Asia Minor, the kings of England and France quarrelled, and the recapture of Acre was the chief tangible achievement of the costly expedition.

The dream of retaking the Holy Places would not be quieted, and in 1202 the Fourth Crusade set forth, stimulated by Pope Innocent III, whose tenure of that high office, as we are to see, marked the apex of the medieval Papacy. It was aimed at Egypt, where was Saladin's chief strength, for crushing him was believed to be a strategic prerequisite to the retaking and holding of Palestine. The Crusaders were dependent upon Venice for ships. Venetian influence turned the expedition to Constantinople. Venice had extensive commercial interests in the Eastern Mediterranean, wished an Eastern Emperor who would be compliant to its wishes, and supported a candidate for the post. The Crusaders stormed Constantinople (1204), plundered it, divided the

Eastern Empire's possessions, and placed one of their number, Count Baldwin of Flanders, on the imperial throne. Venice was given large possessions, chiefly islands which were important for her commerce. A Latin Patriarch of Constantinople was appointed. For the moment it seemed that the long cherished Papal ambition had been realized and that the Eastern and Western wings of the Catholic Church had been united under the undisputed rule of the Bishop of Rome.

The Crusading conquest of Constantinople was a major disaster for the Christian cause in the East. The Byzantine Empire, already enfeebled, was dealt a blow from which it never really recovered and which contributed to the weakness that ultimately (1453) put Constantinople into the hands of the Moslem Ottoman Turks. Except where overwhelming Latin military power compelled it to do so, the Greek Church did not submit to Rome but continued under its own Patriarch. The Greek masses loathed the Latins and the rift between the two wings of the Catholic Church was widened and deepened. The Byzantine Empire continued with headquarters at Nicæa, the city in Asia not far from Constantinople famous in the history of the councils of the Church. In 1261 it retook Constantinople and the Latin state came to an ignominious end.

Of the rest of the Crusades we need say very little. The distressful Children's Crusade of 1212 was the fruit of emotional appeals, chiefly notable as a vivid example of one phase of the religious temper of Western Europe of the day. Many of the youths who responded to it ended in slavery in Egypt. The sceptical Holy Roman Emperor Frederick II, whose stormy relations with the Papacy are one of the complicated sets of episodes of the Middle Ages, through negotiations and a treaty with Egypt obtained possession (1229) of Jerusalem, Bethlehem, Nazareth, and the roadstead of Jaffa and was crowned King of Jerusalem. In 1244 Jerusalem once more fell to the Moslems and was not again to be in "Christian" hands until the twentieth century.

Sacred alike to Jews, Christians, and Moslems, Jerusalem was desired by all three. Henceforth, for more than six centuries it was to be held by a succession of Moslem rulers. In the thirteenth century other efforts were made by Christians to regain it, but none as formidable as the earlier Crusades. Louis IX of France, the ideal Christian knight, led an expedition to Egypt in which he was taken prisoner. He died of disease in an attack on Tunis in 1270, where he had gone on his way to Palestine in the hope of baptizing the local ruler. Prince Edward, later King Edward I of England, took over the leadership, went to Palestine, stormed Nazareth, but did not capture Jerusalem. In 1291 Acre was lost and with it the last of the Crusaders' strongholds in Western Asia. Although the hope of renewing the attempt to seize Jerusalem was not surrendered for several generations, as expeditions with that objective the Crusades were over.

THE CRUSADING SPIRIT

The crusading idea, of a holy war commanded and blessed by the Church, had become deeply implanted in the Western European mind. Crusades were not confined to expeditions to retake or protect the Holy Places in Palestine. They were waged against Moslems in the Iberian Peninsula, against the pagan Wends and Prussians, against the heretical Cathari, and against still others, some of them Christians, whom the Popes adjudged enemies of the faith.

MILITARY MONASTIC ORDERS

Military orders arose from the Crusades. Their members took the standard monastic vows of poverty, chastity, and obedience, but were warriors who had dedicated their lives and their arms to the service of Christ. We have already noted the Knights of the Sword and the Teutonic Knights. More famous were the Templars and Hospitallers. The former were founded in 1119 with head-quarters near the temple site in Jerusalem. Their purpose was to protect pilgrims and fight in defense of the Holy Land. They were popular as symbols and guardians of the Holy Places and became wealthy through the gifts of the pious. Wealth brought them enemies and their independence of the bishops aroused the dislike of these ecclesiastics. In 1312 the Pope suppressed the order and much of its property went to the Hospitallers. The Hospitallers, or Knights of St. John, were based upon a hospital in Jerusalem near the church of St. John Baptist which had been originally founded by Charlemagne. As their name indicates, the first purpose of the Hospitallers was to care for the sick, but in the twelfth century they were made into a military order. They long maintained headquarters on the island of Rhodes and then (until 1798) on Malta. There were other crusading orders, among them one in Portugal, the Order of Christ, which succeeded to the property of the Templars in that kingdom. One of its Grand Masters, Prince Henry the Navigator, in the fifteenth century directed the exploring expeditions along the west coast of Africa which were to outflank the Moslem world and prepare the way for the extensive spread of Christianity in the South and East of Asia.

THE CRUSADING HERITAGE

The Crusades constitute one of the most striking and thought-provoking features of the history of Christianity. While in spirit many of the wars of the Eastern Empire were closely akin to them, they were primarily an outgrowth of the Latin or Western wing of the Catholic Church. They may be regarded as a phase of the activist temper of much of Western Christianity. Here was an effort to achieve the kingdom of God on earth by the methods of that world which the New Testament declares to be at enmity with the Gospel. To put it in Augustinian terms, it was the employment of the instruments of the earthly city to further the City of God. Arising from a mixture of motives, they enlisted much devotion. Here and there were Christians who questioned whether basically they were true to the Gospel and many more deplored the cruelty, immorality, and pride which went with them. However, the great majority of the Christians of Western Europe accepted them and endorsed them. In this the Papacy, the head of the Western Church, led.

The Crusades constituted a complete reversal of the attitude of the early Christians towards war. As we have seen, that was predominantly one of condemnation. By the majority, participation in it as a soldier was deemed inconsistent with the Christian ideal. Later the theory was developed that wars could be just. Now some wars were regarded as holy and in fulfilment of the purposes of God. *Deus vult* ("God wills it") was the cry.

The Crusades had important consequences. They stimulated the growth, already beginning, of the commerce of the Italian cities. They brought Western Europe into intimate contact with the high civilizations of the Near East. Yet they failed in their primary objectives. They did not put the Holy Places permanently into the possession of Christians. They weakened rather than strengthened the Greek Church and the Eastern Empire in their resistance to aggressive Islam. Minorities from the Eastern Churches were won to fellowship with Rome, but the Crusades deepened rather than bridged the widening rift between the Western and Eastern wings of the Catholic Church. Probably they intensified the hatred and the scorn of Moslems for the Christian name. The Crusades aided somewhat in the geographic spread of Christianity, principally along the south and east shores of the Baltic and to a lesser extent in the ephemeral Franciscan and Dominican missions in Central Asia and the Far East. However, they may actually have retarded the understanding of the Gospel. They were an aspect of the partial capture of the Church by the warrior tradition and habits of the barbarian peoples who had mastered Western Europe and had given their professed allegiance to the Christian faith.

Selected Bibliography

Ambroise, *The Crusade of Richard Lion-Heart,* translated by M. J. Hubert, with notes and documentation by J. L. La Monte (Columbia University Press, 1941, pp. xi, 478).

T. A. Archer and C. L. Kingsford, *The Crusades* (New York, G. P. Putnam's Sons, 1894, pp. xxx, 467).

M. W. Baldwin, *Raymond III of Tripolis and the Fall of Jerusalem (1140-1187)* (Princeton University Press, 1936, pp. viii, 177).

The Cambridge Medieval History, Vol. V (Cambridge University Press, 1929).

Villehardouin and DeJoinville, *Memoirs of the Crusades* (Everyman's Library No. 333, New York, E. P. Dutton & Co., 1908, pp. xli, 340).

Chapter 18

REVIVAL THROUGH MONASTICISM: THE RICH AND VARIED DEVELOPMENT OF THE MONASTIC IDEAL IN WESTERN EUROPE

Recovery from the decline which Christianity had suffered in Western Europe between the years 500 and 950 found expression and was furthered through fresh monastic movements. These became more numerous and took on greater variety than ever before. Indeed, in diversity they were much more marked than in the Eastern wing of the Catholic Church or than in any of the Eastern Churches.

Here, we may note, is one of the criteria of vitality in the Christian community. At the times when the tide of life is running low, few new movements appear. When the Christian faith is coursing with vigour through its visible manifestations, old movements are rejuvenated and new ones are born. In the Catholic Church some of the major manifestations of these revivals have been in monasticism. Seeking to attain to the Christian standard of perfection and so to obtain eternal life in heaven, men and women reared in the Catholic Church quite understandably turn to the monastic ideal and either enter existing orders or form fresh ones. In their zeal they may create novel forms of monasticism.

It is, therefore, one of the chief evidences of the awakening that came in the Western wing of the Catholic Church that in the second half of the century many existing monasteries were reformed and that new monastic communities sprang up. Closely associated with these movements were others which sought to embody the Gospel and to win nominal Christians to conform to it but which the Catholic Church deemed heretical. More intimately related than the latter were efforts to purge the whole Church of the corruption that was so obvious and so tragic, to bring all of Western Christendom to a closer approximation to Christian standards, and to spread the Western faith to peoples who

416

had not yet accepted it. Monastic movements continued to multiply throughout the four centuries from 950 to 1350 and reached a crest in the thirteenth century.

As we have seen, monastic life had fallen to a low level in the latter part of the ninth and the fore part of the tenth century. The invasions of Northmen, Moslems, and Magyars had laid many monasteries in ruins. Countless monks had been killed or driven into the cities. In numbers of monasteries secular princes had diverted the endowments to their own purposes. They turned over to the monasteries only part of the revenues and allowed the enrolment of monks to fall off. In many others lay patrons had appointed as abbots men who valued the post as a means of livelihood, who were married, and who brought to the monasteries their families, their warriors, their horses, and their hunting dogs. Numbers of monks married and dwelt in the monastic buildings with their wives and children. The canons, members of the groups of clergy who lived by a semi-monastic rule in collegiate churches and cathedrals, conformed even more easily to the world than did the monks. In some monasteries canons were substituted for monks, for they did not have to hold as closely to the Benedictine rule as did the latter.

First Hints of Awakenings

A generation or more before 950 there had been stirrings of reform. Now and again synods deplored the decay of monastic life but did little to effect a change. Some monasteries, but how many we do not know, maintained a fairly strict observance of the Benedictine rule. Here and there new ones were founded. The influence of Benedict of Aniane waned but did not die. Thus (c.933) John of Gorze refounded the abbey by which he is known. It was near Metz and its influence made itself felt from Cologne to Toul. Near Namur Gerhard inaugurated the monastery of Brogne and gave a stimulus to better monastic life in Flanders. Both Gorze and Brogne followed in part the lead of Benedict of Aniane with his emphasis upon liturgical prayer, his lengthening of the services, and his tendency to discourage both agricultural labour by the monks and the teaching of those not of the monastic community.

The Cluny Movement

The revival was given conspicuous leadership by the monastery of Cluny and its abbots. Cluny was north of Lyons, not far from Macon and the Rhone River. Its first abbot and real founder was Berno. A Burgundian, Berno had already made a record as abbot of another monastery where he had held to the strict observance of the Benedictine rule. So many youths were attracted by his zeal that he deemed it necessary to begin an additional house. This he did in 910 at Cluny on land given by William the Pious, Duke of Aquitaine. To prevent his successors from corrupting the foundation and diverting it from its original purpose, as lay princes had done with many other monasteries, Duke William placed it directly under the protection of the Pope. Like Gorze and Brogne, Cluny was profoundly affected by what had been done by Benedict of Aniane in his modifications of monastic life and ceremonies.

Many were hungry for the type of leadership given by Berno. As we have suggested, Christians of the day believed, as had many before and have many since, that the salvation of their souls was to be best attained by the monastic road. Men and women denied themselves here that they might win heaven hereafter. It was this impulse that constituted the wellspring of monasticism. Many entered upon the life from other motives, such as ease and physical security, or were committed to it by parents who wished to provide for their offspring, but had monasticism rested on these foundations it would not have endured. It was the urge for the attainment of wholeness of life, of meaning to life that would endure through eternity, which was the persistent source of recurring monastic revivals. To those who were impelled by it Cluny made a profound appeal.

Cluny grew in its enrollment and attracted gifts. Devout lay lords who had the nomination to abbacies asked Berno to accept the post and to undertake the reform of their houses. He acquiesced. On his retirement (926) because of age, he transferred most of his abbacies, including that of Cluny, to Odo.

Odo, who was abbot from 926 to 942, travelled extensively in France and Italy to promote the reform of monasteries. Of some he was made abbot. In others those in charge asked his advice. In the monasteries which he visited for that purpose he usually left one or more monks who had been trained at Cluny and whom he could trust to inculcate the spirit of that house.

For about two and a half centuries, with one exception, Cluny had a notable succession of able and devoted abbots. Scions of noble families, well educated according to the standards of the time, they gave themselves unstintedly to the work of their office, some of them refusing high ecclesiastical position to do so, and made their weight felt in Church and state. Under the fifth of the line, Odilo, who held the post for about fifty years (994–1048), the number of monasteries affiliated with Cluny rose from thirty-seven to sixty-nine. In addition, there were still more smaller groups, *cellae,* "cells," affiliated with the larger units. Although he was slight in build, short of stature, and nervous, Odilo inspired respect and was a forceful leader. Yet in discipline he inclined to mercy. By the beginning of the twelfth century the number of associated monasteries had risen to more than three hundred. Hugh the Great, who was abbot for approximately sixty years, from 1049 to 1109, ruling as he did eventually over more than three hundred widely scattered monasteries, was for years an efficient ally of the reforming Popes and was canonized a little over a century after his death. He had an unworthy successor who held the post for thirteen years, but the latter was followed by Peter the Venerable who was abbot from 1122 to 1157, or for thirty-five years, and who did much to restore the discipline of Cluny and its affiliated houses.

Cluny thus became the centre of a "congregation" of monasteries, the precursor of such orders as the Franciscans, Dominicans, and Jesuits. Heretofore each monastery had been independent of every other. Through Cluny a family of monasteries arose.

In theory Cluny held to the rule of Benedict of Nursia. In practice it modified it. It stressed silence, except in group worship. As had Benedict of Aniane, it lengthened and elaborated the services. No longer did the monks work with their hands in the fields. That labour was left to serfs while the monks devoted themselves to prayer. Their abbey churches tended to be huge. That of Cluny, begun late in the eleventh and completed in the first half of the twelfth century and dedicated by the Pope himself, was said to have been at the time the largest church in Western Europe. Scholarship was not encouraged and the study of the non-Christian authors of classical antiquity was either forbidden or deprecated.

The influence of Cluny spread widely beyond the monasteries which were closely associated with it. Many existing houses were made to accord with its practice. That was true even of the mother Benedictine house on Monte Cassino. Numbers of new foundations were on the model or under the inspiration of Cluny. Moreover, as we shall see in a later chapter, from it came bishops and Popes who led in the reform of the Western Church.

The Rising Tide of Monastic Life

In the tenth and eleventh centuries, partly but by no means entirely through the inspiration and example of Cluny, the tide of the monastic life continued to mount.

In England there was Dunstan (c.909–988). Of noble Saxon stock, monk and abbot of Glastonbury, later Archbishop of Canterbury, he and some of his friends who became bishops led in the improvement of the monasteries and of the Church as a whole in that land. There were similar movements in France, Italy, and Germany which in the last two countries were encouraged by some of the Holy Roman Emperors.

More and more it became the practice, somewhat after the manner of Cluny, for monasteries to be put in the ownership or under the control of some famous abbey. This was partly to escape the debilitating influence of a lay proprietor and partly to insure the strict observance of the monastic rule in the subordinate houses. Thus the abbey devoutly named Chaise Dieu (Casa Dei, the House of

God), founded in Auvergne in 1046, eventually had about three hundred dependent priories.

Fleeing from the Turkish invasions, Greek monks brought their traditions, chiefly to Italy but also to France.

In Italy new foundations were made, several of them through devoted scions of noble stock who had abandoned the world for the life of prayer and asceticism. Famous was Romuald (c.950–1027) of the ducal family of Ravenna who turned monk to expiate a crime of his father. He soon left the Cluniac Benedictine monastery which he had entered and became a hermit. An extreme ascetic, he was a wanderer and inspired many by his example. From him there arose a type of hermit community in which the members were strenuously ascetic and dwelt in separate houses, but had some of their liturgical services and meals together. From time to time they went forth as preachers. From this eventually came the Camaldulian Order, named for its centre at Camaldoli.

Peter Damian (c.1007–1072) was also of Ravenna, but from a lowly, poverty-stricken family. Through hard labour he acquired an education and taught at Parma. Then, from an inward urge to the perfect Christian life, he entered a monastery, became a hermit noted for extreme austerity, eventually was made abbot, and, inspired by the example of Romuald, whose biography he wrote, organized monasteries which were affiliated with his own. As were so many others of this new burst of monastic devotion, he was deeply concerned for the purification of the Church as a whole and urged the Popes to further it. One of the latter made him Cardinal Bishop of Ostia, the ancient seaport of Rome, and he became prominent in the inner circles of the Papal entourage, where we shall meet him again, labouring to carry out his dreams.

John Gualbert (c.990–1073) as a youth also came under the influence of Romuald. He was for a time at Camaldoli and then founded a monastery at Vallombrosa near Florence which soon became the head of a family of monastic houses. In them perpetual silence was the rule. The manual labour was performed by *conversi,* lay brothers, to leave the "choir monks" free for prayer. The choir monks were those who devoted themselves to the services in the chapel.

Noted, but in a somewhat different way, was Bernard of Menthon (923–1008). Born in a rich family of noble blood, he refused an honourable marriage to which his family urged him, entered the ranks of the clergy, and in his mid-forties was Archdeacon of Aosta, near the southern outlet of the famous pass across the Alps which now bears his name. Distressed by the savagery and poverty of the folk who dwelt in the mountains and who robbed travellers crossing the pass, he gave himself to them, won them, and then at the head of the pass founded a monastery and dedicated it to the care of those who journeyed by its doors. In 1213 Pope Innocent III put it under the rule of the Augustinian canons.

Still different was the Monastery of Bec, in Normandy. Like Cluny, it was to be a wellspring of vitality for large areas, especially Normandy and England. In contrast with Cluny, it was a centre of intellectual life and theological activity. It was begun in the fore part of the eleventh century by Herluin. Herluin was of noble birth, a warrior who in his late thirties turned to religion. He learned to read, was ordained priest, and gathered a small monastic community. To this in 1042 came Lanfranc. Lanfranc was from the North of Italy. He had been a teacher of law and letters and in his late thirties, after having taught in the cathedral school of Avranches, on the south-west coast of Normandy, he turned monk and entered Bec. Somewhat later, in the 1050's, Anselm joined the community. He was of Lombard stock and was born in a valley in the Italian Alps. Studious and deeply religious, he had long wished to adopt the monastic life, but in this met the bitter opposition of his father. It was not until he had crossed the Alps that he felt free to take the step. He proved to be the greatest theological intellect between Augustine and Thomas Aquinas and in this capacity we shall meet him again. Lanfranc and he were successively Archbishops of Canterbury and we shall also find him courageously standing for the purity and independence of the Church as against rulers who wished to use the Church for their own purposes. Lanfranc and Anselm gave Bec its distinctive character—the combination of deep religious devotion, in which they reinforced what came through Herluin, with scholarly pursuits. Bec became famous as a school, wealth poured in, and many subordinate priories were attached to it, notably in England.

The Monasteries Gain Special Privileges

Part of the tenth and eleventh century revival was a movement, largely successful, to free the monasteries from the control of lay lords and diocesan bishops. The power of lay lords had been one of the sources of the decay in the monastic life. To circumvent it, increasingly monasteries were removed from the power of the feudal nobility and were placed directly under the Pope. Theoretically the Pope could not divert their properties to other uses than those prescribed by the founder and was the guardian rather than the proprietor. Nor could he legally use the income from the endowments for himself or his favourites. The proportion to be given to him was usually fixed by the donor in the founding charter.

The diocesan bishops had proved a source of annoyance to the monasteries. In principle each bishop had extensive powers over all the ecclesiastical activities and institutions in his diocese. In monasteries he could hold services, consecrate altars, ordain such of the monks as were raised to the priesthood, and exercise discipline through excommunicating the obdurate or interdicting services.

Restrictions on these functions had been begun as early as the sixth or seventh century. In the tenth and eleventh centuries on behalf of house after house the episcopal authority was further reduced or annulled by Papal action. In many instances even the right of ordination was taken from the diocesan bishop. While episcopal ordination was still necessary, the monastery might ask any bishop whom it chose to administer the rite.

The kings also increasingly granted to monasteries immunity from the jurisdiction of royal officials and took the houses under their special protection.

This movement to free monasteries from all local secular or ecclesiastical interference and so to ensure them liberty to pursue the full Christian life was to continue into at least the thirteenth century. Thus there arose autonomous communities each with its own endowments in land, independent of the secular order and from the economic structure about it, for unhampered and full conformity to the Christian ideal in individual and group living as the monks and other Catholic Christians of the time understood it.

Here were centres of life from which issued impulses which helped to raise the level of the Christianity of almost all of Western Europe. The rude barbarians who had been converted in mass were taught something of the meaning of the faith which they had professed to accept. They were challenged by it. Many did not respond or responded only to react against it. Indeed, the grossness, superstition, stark depravity, cruelty, and callous self-seeking of millions in medieval Europe is one of the striking features of the age. On the other hand, thousands rose to the appeal. Never has the contrast between sinner and saint been greater. Not all life was transformed, but all aspects of Western Europe were profoundly affected.

The Cistercian Movement

In the twelfth century the leadership in creative, vigorous monastic life passed to the Cistercians. As we have suggested more than once, each great revival of the monastic life tended to be followed by decline. A leader of flaming devotion and high idealism would attract youth, and austerity would characterize the first years of the new house or houses. Then would come popularity and wealth, either through the labour of the monks themselves or by gifts from devout admirers, zeal would wane, and the quality of life would sink to mediocrity and uninspired routine or worse. In the twelfth century this began to happen to Cluny. The number of its affiliated monasteries continued to mount, although more slowly than earlier, but it was no longer in the van.

Other and younger movements took its place as pioneers. Chief of these were the Cistercians.

The Cistercians began with Robert, a Benedictine monk who by his zeal for reform and strict observance of the monastic ideal attracted a number of hermits. After being an abbot of a new community at Molesme in Burgundy in huts made of boughs (begun c.1075), eventually, as that foundation fell away from its first fervour, he removed (1098) to a new centre at Citeaux, not far from Dijon, in the eastern part of what is now France. Citeaux became the mother house of what were soon to be the Cistercians (from the Latin name, Cistercium, for Citeaux). The basic features of the Cistercian movement were given it by Robert, and especially by the second and third abbots of Citeaux, Alberic and Stephen Harding, the latter an Englishman.

In general the Cistercians held to the Benedictine rule. However, they had five distinct characteristics which set them off from other monks. First, and least important, was their garb. Instead of the black habit of the Benedictines, they wore greyish white, and are often referred to as the "white monks."

Second was an attempt, quite usual in new monastic movements, to observe the rule of strict poverty. This the Cistercians sought to accomplish by reducing to a minimum the physical accompaniments of their common worship. In contrast with the great churches and elaborate and costly liturgical vestments and ornaments of the Cluniacs, they had crucifixes of painted wood, chalices of silver rather than gold, and unadorned vestments of linen or fustian rather than of silk. They refused to derive the income for their houses from tithes, offerings, altar and burial dues, or from estates worked by serfs. Their clothing and food were to be of the simplest.

In the third place, in contrast with many of the foundations of the black monks which were near the cities, the Cistercians established their houses far from other habitations. Their lands were to be cleared and tilled by their own labour and not that of serfs. Some of this was done by the choir monks. Most of it was by the more numerous *conversi,* or lay brothers. The *conversi* were illiterate, they memorized only the creed and a few of the prayers, their prayers at the canonical hours were brief, and they were allowed more sleep and food than the choir monks. They followed the rule of silence except such exchange of words as was necessary for their work. The use of lay brothers made servants unnecessary.

A fourth feature was the reduction of the time spent in the liturgical services, for it will be remembered that these had been lengthened by Cluny and had become the chief occupation of the monks. Instead, room was made for more private prayer. There was to be no school for oblate children, namely, those of tender years who had been dedicated by their elders to the monastic life. No novices were to be accepted who were less than sixteen years of age. Thus all the monks were supposed to come by their own choice and from a sense of divine vocation.

The fifth distinct characteristic of the Cistercians was the provision for welding all the houses together into an integrated order, the first of its kind and the precursor of many others. The Cluniac houses were under the theoretical supervision of the abbot of the mother house, but they early became too numerous for effective oversight by one man. In the Cistercian system each monastery retained a large degree of autonomy, but identical service books were provided for all, each abbey was visited annually by the abbot of Citeaux or the abbot of one of the four other oldest foundations, and every year all the abbots of all the houses assembled at Citeaux in a general chapter to maintain fellowship and to take such legislative and disciplinary measures as might be necessary. Citeaux itself was visited and inspected regularly by representatives of its four eldest daughter houses.

The Cistercians quickly achieved wide popularity. Ardent youths were attracted by their devotion. In country after country their houses arose in desolate places. Forests were cleared, swamps were drained, and the necessary monastic buildings were erected.

Bernard of Clairvaux

The early popularity of the Cistercians was due in no small degree to Bernard of Clairvaux. Bernard was the most influential individual in the religious life of Western Europe of his generation. The first half of the twelfth century was marked by many men eminent in the Latin Church, but in the weight which he carried with his contemporaries Bernard stood head and shoulders above them all.

Bernard of Clairvaux was born in 1090 about two miles from Dijon and therefore not far from Citeaux. He was of Burgundian noble stock and of devout parents. At their birth his mother dedicated each of her children to God. Frail of physique, charming, from boyhood Bernard was deeply religious. It was probably in 1112, when he was about twenty-two years of age, that Bernard became a monk of Citeaux. With him he brought about thirty friends and relatives, including five of his brothers, who had been won by his ardent persuasiveness. The last remaining brother, the youngest, followed them later. In 1115, at the age of twenty-five, Bernard became abbot of a new foundation, the fourth of the Cistercian houses, at Clairvaux, in a rugged mountain valley near some of his own kinfolk and about a hundred miles from Citeaux. He was to remain head of that house until his death, in 1153.

Combining the qualities of both the mystic and the man of action, Bernard rose fairly steadily to his position of preëminence. As a mystic, his devotion was to the Virgin Mary and especially to Christ. He was moved by the love of Christ and was committed to him not only as God but also as man. He did much to promote a revival of adoration of Jesus in his humanity. This is seen in the hymn which is usually ascribed to him, *Jesu, dulcis memoria,* portions of which in their English translations are the hymns which begin with the lines "Jesus the very thought of thee with sweetness fills my breast" and "Jesus thou joy of loving hearts." If not written by Bernard, *Jesu, dulcis memoria* is akin to his spirit. Humble and yet bold and on occasion caustic, Bernard became the mentor of Western Europe. Eloquent and persuasive as a preacher and orator, he was a major force, as we have seen, in promoting the Second Crusade. He carried on a prodigious correspondence and travelled seemingly incessantly. He was the author of several books. He interested himself in the affairs of the Church at large and was the major influence in healing a schism which had been produced by the nearly simultaneous election of two Popes. In striving to maintain what he deemed orthodoxy, he sought to win heretics by preaching and was a vigorous and persistent critic of Abélard, whom we are to meet later as a leading intellectual figure in Western Europe in the twelfth century. One of his own monks from Clairvaux became Pope. Bernard's great popularity attracted hundreds and possibly thousands to the Cistercian way of life. Largely because of him, the Cistercians became active in reforming and elevating the quality of the Church.

OTHER TWELFTH CENTURY MONASTIC MOVEMENTS

The Cistercians were the leading but by no means the only new monastic movement which rose to prominence in the twelfth century.

Next to the Cistercians, the most prominent were the Carthusians. They were founded in 1084 by Bruno, who had been a canon and a distinguished teacher at Rheims and who four years earlier had abandoned the world for the monastic life. He and a small group established themselves in a wild spot, Chartreuse, later to be called the Grande Chartreuse, approximately twelve miles north of Grenoble in a mountain valley of about 3000 feet elevation. It was from Chartreuse that the order took its name, and from it were derived the English designation, Charterhouse, and the Italian title of its houses, Certosa.

Bruno soon moved on to found other colonies of hermits and the chief impulse to the order was given by the fifth prior of the Grande Chartreuse, Guigo I, a friend of Peter the Venerable and Bernard of Clairvaux. Guigo founded additional houses, attracted men to them, and put into detailed writing the customs of the mother monastery.

The Carthusians were profoundly influenced by the early monasticism of Egypt. Their way was one of great austerity. Those who followed it lived in separate little houses, wore hair shirts, fasted rigorously, and gave themselves to reading, prayer, and labour, especially the copying of manuscripts. Each community met together for worship in a common chapel, for some of their meals, and occasionally for conversation. Never nearly as numerous as the Cistercians, the Carthusians were to persist with rules which were not to be basically altered.

Less numerous and prominent than the Carthusians and much less so than the Cistercians were several other movements which in origin were roughly contemporary with these two. One was the order of Grandmont, begun about the year 1074 or 1100 by Stephen of Muret near Limoges, in what is now the west central part of France. Stephen was of French aristocratic stock and had been a hermit in the south of Italy before returning to his native land. Grandmont carried the rule of poverty even further than did the Cistercians or the Carthusians. Its monasteries were not permitted to own churches, tithes, lands, animals, or fixed revenues. It required its monks never to leave the monastic enclosure. To free the choir monks for their spiritual duties, Grandmont entrusted to its lay brothers all responsibility for the material side of the community's life.

An order which spread widely through France was that of Fontevrault. It was founded about 1101 by Robert of Arbrissel. Robert as a priest in Rennes had vigorously attacked abuses in the Church, had then become a hermit, and later had recruited many, both men and women, for the monastic life. The mother house, at Fontevrault, near Saumur, in the west of France, was ruled by an abbess and was primarily for women. It also contained men who had dedicated themselves to the service of the nuns. It especially attracted the daughters of the royal family and the high nobility.

Another family of monasteries sprang from a foundation at Tiron made by one Bernard in 1109. Like the Cistercians, it reduced the time given to liturgical services that the monks might devote more of their hours to labour.

Vitalis, who died in 1122, founded a monastery in the forest of Savigny, in France. It inspired the formation of a number of houses in the north of France and in England. Their programme closely resembled the Cistercians and in 1147 they were absorbed by the latter.

The eleventh and twelfth centuries also saw the development of canons regular who took their inspiration and some of their rule of life from Augustine of Hippo. It will be remembered that Augustine and the clergy who lived with him formed a community which followed a discipline devised by him. We have noted that in Carolingian times groups of clergy attached to churches had begun to govern their fellowship by semi-monastic rules. In the revivals of the eleventh and twelfth centuries the Augustinian Canons multiplied in France, England, and Germany. In the twelfth century some of these communities of canons came to be very much like monasteries, and differed from the latter chiefly in leaving their members free to exercise their ministry, especially that of preaching, outside the walls of their houses.

An order of the Augustinian Canons which spread widely was the Premonstratensians. Its founder was Norbert, who was a great friend of Bernard of Clairvaux, was later Archbishop of Magdeburg, and had wide influence in the Church. The mother house, begun in 1120, was at Premontre, in the northwest of France. Norbert at first thought of affiliating it with the Cistercians. To give its members greater freedom to move about in the world preaching than the rules of Citeaux permitted, he made it into a house of canons regular, but the austerity of the mother and daughter houses resembled closely that of the Cistercians.

Late in the twelfth century an order, the Trinitarians, much like the Augustinian Canons, came into being. The purpose was the ransom of Christians who had been taken captive by Moslems. Usually the ransom was effected by the payment of money, but in extreme instances individual Trinitarians offered themselves as substitutes for those whose release they sought.

We must also recall that in the twelfth century the monastic ideal was both sufficiently potent and flexible to give rise to the Templars, the Hospitallers, and the Teutonic Knights. In Spain and Portugal, partly out of the long wars for the Christian reconquest of the Iberian Peninsula, crusading orders arose, the chief of them in Spain being that of Santiago and that of Calatrava, and in Portugal, as we have seen, the Order of Christ.

THE COMING OF THE FRIARS

As Western Europe passed on into the thirteenth century, new forms of monasticism emerged. Many of the old ones continued. The Benedictine rule was still standard. However, the impulse which produced monasticism gave evidence of its amazing creativity in bringing into being a new type of movement which, while clearly in the monastic stream and deeply indebted to the past, had in it much that was novel. This displayed itself in what are called the friars or the mendicant orders. They are usually thought of as four in number, the Franciscans, the Dominicans, the Carmelites, and the Augustinians. These were known respectively as the Brothers Minor or Grey Friars, the Preachers or Black Friars, the White Friars, and the Austin Friars. To these four were added a few similar but much smaller bodies. They all combined the monastic life and its ideals of poverty, chastity, obedience, and community living with preaching to those outside their fellowship. They were missionaries both to the nominal Christians of Western Europe and to non-Christians in various parts of the globe. This was especially true of the two largest, the Franciscans and Dominicans. To this day these two orders have had a leading part in the world-wide extension of the Roman Catholic form of the faith. The Franciscans have vied with a much younger order, the Society of Jesus, in providing the Roman Catholic Church with a larger number of missionaries than has any other of the orders and societies.

The emergence of the mendicant orders was associated with the growth of cities in Western Europe. By the thirteenth century that part of the world was beginning to move out of the almost exclusively agricultural economy which had followed the decline of the Roman Empire and the disappearance of the urban civilization which had characterized that realm. Cities were once more appearing. It was to deepening the religious life of the populace of the cities and towns that the friars devoted much of their energy. Most of the earlier monasteries had chosen solitude and centres remote from the contaminating influences of the world. In contrast, the mendicant orders sought the places where men congregated and endeavoured to bring the Gospel to them there. The older monasteries were associated with a prevailing rural and feudal milieu. The medicant orders flourished in the rapidly growing urban populations.

Here was a striking enlargement of the monastic movement. It had been foreshadowed by the participation of outstanding monks, among them Lanfranc, Anselm, and Bernard of Clairvaux, in the affairs of the Church and of the secular world. Some Benedictine monasteries had conducted schools for youths who did not take their vows and through their guest rooms had given hospitality to many from the world. The Templars and Hospitallers were examples of orders which did not remain within their cloisters but instead gave themselves to the physical care of others. Bernard of Menthon had inaugurated a community which served travellers across the Alpine pass which bears his name. The Trinitarians were ransoming captives. The Augustinian Canons and especially the Premonstratensians had been moving in the direction of service to the world outside monastic walls. The friars were a further and substantial stage. The trend was to be continued. In subsequent centuries, as we are to see, monastic orders and congregations arose, either of men or of women, who gave themselves primarily to teaching and nursing. Yet several orders whose houses cut themselves off from the world persisted and from time to time new ones like them came into being. Much more than in the Eastern Churches, in the West monasticism developed many and varied forms. Here was evidence of the amazing vitality and of the ability of Christianity to adapt itself to fresh environments.

THE FRANCISCANS

As we have suggested, what was eventually the largest of the mendicant orders in its numerous branches was what officially is designated as the Order of Little Brothers or Friars Minor (*Ordo Fratrum Minorum,* abbreviated as O.F.M.), but popularly is known as the Franciscans. The name Franciscan is appropriate, for not only was the order begun by Francis of Assisi, but it has never ceased to be challenged by the ideals of its founder. From time to time efforts, often stormy, have been made to bring its practice to conform to the difficult standards of that compelling genius.

Francis is one of the most winsome figures of Christian history. He was born in 1181 or 1182 in Assisi, an ancient town on heights overlooking the gorge through which the Tiber emerges from the mountains. His father was Pietro Bernardone, a well-to-do cloth merchant. He had little formal education, but he knew a little Latin and could read and write. He also knew French. His baptismal name was Giovanni, but the nickname of Francesco—Francis—was given him and was the one by which he was best known and remembered. He was ardent, charming, and sensitive. At first he was a play-boy, a boon companion of the gay young scions of the local aristocracy, and a leader among them in their revelries. Yet he seems to have possessed an innate refinement and is said not to have succumbed to grossness in speech or act.

The conversion of Francis to the life of religion was not a sudden dedication, but came as the result of a spiritual pilgrimage of many months which began in late adolescence. It was partly induced by illnesses and disappointments and was marked by painful and intense struggles of the spirit and in its earlier stages by relapses into the former way of life. Francis began giving himself to the service of the poor and in spite of his loathing for their disease, visited lepers and cared for them. He spent much time in solitude in the fields and hills. He was inspired by the love of Christ which had been driven home to him in the contemplation of a crucifix in a nearby chapel. His fellow-townsmen at first thought him insane. His father, enraged, kept him in confinement at home until his mother released him. Finally his father took him before the bishop to disinherit him and Francis, stripping himself of the clothing which he had had from his sire and standing naked before the bishop, declared that henceforth he desired to serve only "our Father which art in heaven." He set himself to repairing with his own hands the chapel where was the crucifix which had come to mean so much to him, begging stones and also his food. That task completed, he addressed himself to the restoration of other chapels.

Among these his favourite was Santa Maria degli Angeli, the Portiuncula, a humble affair which after Francis became famous was enclosed by a large but gaudy church.

It was in 1209 at the Portiuncula during the reading of the Gospel at the mass that Francis, then in his upper twenties, heard the call which sent him forth on his life mission. He felt impelled to become a travelling preacher, proclaiming the kingdom of God and calling men to repentance, doing so in complete poverty, subsisting on whatever food might be given him, and radiating the love of Christ. He sought to imitate Jesus and to obey him to the letter.

Francis at once set about preaching in his native town. Others, attracted, joined themselves to him. As their rule he gave them the command of Jesus to sell all and give to the poor and to go forth without staff, food, money, or a second coat, preaching the kingdom of God and healing the sick. They called themselves the penitents of Assisi. They made the Portiuncula their headquarters and built near it huts of boughs. For a habit, they wore tunics of the brown coarse cloth from which peasants made clothing. They went about, barefooted, two by two, preaching and helping the peasants in the work of the fields.

These early days were marked by mingled opposition and cordial response. Many deemed the brothers mad, pelted them with mud, insulted them, and tore off their clothing. Others were impressed by their patent sincerity and by their joyousness under persecution and in their espousal of their Lady Poverty.

Francis and his companions were not entirely unique. The time was one of religious ferment. There were numerous wandering preachers, many of them ascetics and some of them frowned upon by the Church as disobedient heretics. Contemporary Italy also had many bands or guilds whose members went about together singing hymns of penitence and praise.

Francis was no heretic. A humble son of the Church and a layman, he submitted himself to the constituted ecclesiastical authorities. In 1210 he and eleven companions went to Rome to seek Papal permission to pursue their manner of life. Innocent III, one of the greatest of the Popes, was then on the throne of Peter. After some hesitation and a careful investigation by members of his *curia,* for he professed fear that their manner of life was too severe, Innocent gave them tentative approval and permitted them to continue preaching. However, he made the quite natural condition that in each diocese where they preached they must first obtain the consent of the bishop and that they elect a superior who could be held responsible for their conduct. Francis was the inevitable choice for the headship of the group. Thus the Penitents of Assisi, a few years later called by Francis in characteristic fashion the Minor, or Humbler Brethren, became an order.

Returning to Assisi, Francis, now reinforced by Papal approval, was received with acclaim and throngs flocked to his preaching. He sought, with success, to heal civil strife in his home city between the feudal nobility and the townsfolk. His followers multiplied and obtained from the proprietors, a Benedictine monastery, the Portiuncula as permanent headquarters.

In these early days of the order, the Brothers Minor worked with their hands for their livelihood, supplementing the labour with begging when food was not otherwise to be had. Francis insisted upon absolute poverty, would not permit any of the brethren to have money, and is said on one occasion to have forbidden a brother to own even a psalter, saying that if he possessed one he would wish for a breviary, and that if he owned a breviary he would soon be haughtily commanding one of his fellows to bring it to him.

The Brothers Minor not only preached but also sang. Some of their hymns were improvised by Francis, for his was always the soul of a poet. Especially famous was his *Praises of the Creatures,* better known as the *Canticle of the Sun.*

Closely related to the poetic strain in Francis was a love for all creation and a joy in it. One of the stories which his early disciples cherished was that of a sermon which he preached to the birds, exhorting them to praise and love their Creator. They also declared that once when Francis was preaching the swallows made so much noise that he could not be heard and that on his charging them to be quiet until he had finished they meekly subsided. At another time he made nests for turtle doves that they might lay eggs and rear their young under the protection of the brethren. This love of nature seems to have increased with the years and never to have been more keen than in his last months when his body was racked by pain.

The preaching of Francis and his associates was unstudied and direct. It stressed the adoration of God, repentance, generosity, and the forgiveness of wrongs done to one by others. It made much of love for one's neighbours and one's enemies, humility, and abstention from vices, including especially the vices of the flesh. It advocated fasting and encouraged the confession of one's sins to a priest.

By his sincerity, joyousness, earnestness, and radiant love Francis rapidly won an increasing number to the Brothers Minor. At first he admitted those who applied without the novitiate customary in the older orders. Among those who sought entrance was Clara, a girl of sixteen, twelve years younger than Francis, a scion of the Sciffi, one of the noble houses of Assisi. He welcomed her with great affection and in 1212, three years after the decisive call had come to him, received her into the order. In spite of the bitter opposition of her father, she persisted. To her father's even greater wrath, a younger sister followed her. Other women came and a house was found for them in Assisi. Thus a second order, a woman's branch of the Franciscans, the Poor Ladies or Poor Clares, came into being.

Early, although not formally until 1221, there also sprang up what is usually known as the Third Order, or, more accurately, the Order of Penitents. Its members were not fully to follow the way of Francis and were to remain in the world and hold property, but they were to be sparing in food and drink, give alms, abstain from vice, accept the sacraments, and remain loyal members of the Catholic Church. One of its earliest members north of the Alps was Elizabeth of Hungary (c.1207–1231). The daughter of a king of Hungary, devout from her childhood, she was early betrothed in one of the dynastic matrimonial alliances which were common and at fourteen was married to the Landgrave of Thuringia. Her husband perished in a crusade and in the later years of her brief life she gave much of her fortune to the poor, founded a hospital, and in Marburg with her own hands cared for the sick.

Francis was enthusiastically missionary in purpose and practice. He himself traversed much of Italy, preaching. He wished also to go to the Moslems. He sought to journey to the Holy Land, but was thwarted by shipwreck. He went to Spain to open a way to Morocco, there to reach Moslems who had recently been defeated by a coalition of Christian princes and had taken refuge in that land. Illness stopped him and compelled him to return to Italy. Eventually, in 1219, he went to Egypt, in company with what is usually called the Fifth Crusade. He was deeply grieved by the lack of discipline and the vicious lives of many of these champions of the Cross. Yet from among them he won some who helped to spread the Franciscan movement to Northern Europe. He also presented the faith to the Sultan and seems to have gained the latter's respect. He returned to Italy (1220) by way of Palestine and Syria. Not content with himself going on missions he sent out his friars to various parts of Europe and to Morocco.

Francis quickly ran his course. October 3, 1226, when only in his mid-forties, he breathed his last in the church of Portiuncula where, seventeen years earlier, he had heard the call which had sent him forth preaching. In his later years he had been increasingly frail and had more and more withdrawn from the management of the order. His ardent devotion to Christ and his meditation of Christ's passion were crowned by the appearance of the *stigmata,* the wounds of his Master, on his own body. Death came peacefully and in the end painlessly. Two years later, in 1228, he was formally proclaimed to be a saint by his friend and the patron of the order, the former Cardinal Ugolino of Ostia, now Pope Gregory IX.

Before death claimed him, Francis had the mingled joy and pain of seeing the Order of Brothers Minor quite outgrow him and the deep grief of knowing that it was already beginning to depart from the simplicity and poverty of its first days. In his last months he sought to stem the tide by dictating his will. In this he commanded all the brothers to work at some honourable occupation, not for gain but for a good example, and to flee idleness. Only when they were not paid for their work were they to beg. They were not to receive churches or habitations. The will expressly forbade the brothers to seek a bull which would relax this interdiction or to introduce glosses or modifications in the rule or the will.

Yet before and after the will was dictated the worldly wisdom of Innocent III in declaring the primitive Franciscan ideal too severe for human flesh and blood had been confirmed by the event. Organization proved necessary. Early the Brothers Minor assembled annually at Portiuncula. In 1216 at the request of Francis, Ugolino became the protector of the brotherhood. His guidance had much to do with shaping the next stages of organization. In 1220 a Papal bull prescribed a novitiate of one year as a prerequisite for full membership, fixed the garb, and declared the vows to be irrevocable. In 1221 the order was given a new rule, much longer than the original one. Francis was not an organizer or an administrator. He was too impulsive, too subject to changes of mood, too unpredictable, to carry the load of running a great organization. The actual management passed into the hands of others, within a few months to one of the first companions of Francis, Brother Elias, whom Francis, as minister general, appointed his vicar. In 1223 another rule was adopted which made begging rather than labour with the hands the normal method of support. To the intense indignation of Francis, Brothers Minor were beginning to establish themselves in the universities which were arising in Europe. Francis distrusted scholarship as a perversion of the original purpose. Preaching was not being given its former primary place, but Brothers Minor were becoming advisers in the Papal *curia*. No longer was the marriage to Lady Poverty being strictly observed, but collectively property was beginning to be acquired. Theoretically the property was not held by the order, but by friends or by the Pope in behalf of the order. Structurally the order had become fairly elaborate. Every group had its *custos,* or head. The groups were organized by territorial provinces, each of which had its minister and its chapter. Over all was a general chapter and a minister general.

After the death of Francis further relaxation of the primitive ideals entered and a sharp division disrupted the pristine brotherhood of love. On the one extreme were those who wished to hold to the manner of life which had been followed by Francis in the initial years of the fellowship, with its absolute poverty and its itinerant preaching. This group, a minority, who came to be known as the Zealots or Spirituals, were given prestige by the presence of several of the earliest companions of Francis. On the other extreme were those who desired a complete relaxation of the rule of poverty. In the middle were the majority, moderates, who would maintain something of the primitive poverty, but who wished the order to establish itself in the universities, develop scholars, and acquire influence in the Church. The conflict between these strains was acute. Indeed, no large order of the Catholic Church has had so explosive a history or has been rent by so many schisms.

It was the moderates who before many years obtained control. The first minister general after Francis, John Parenti, who served from 1227 to 1232, favoured strict conformity to the wishes of the founder. Yet it was under him that Pope Gregory IX declared (1230) that the will of Francis was not binding. In 1232 John retired under pressure, and Elias was elected in his stead. Although he had had the confidence of Francis, Elias departed from the strict observance of the latter's wishes. He was an extraordinarily able promoter and administrator. Before his election as minister general he had, with the support of the order's great patron, Pope Gregory IX, begun the erection of a huge church in Assisi as a memorial to Francis, a structure which was a visible denial of the ideals of the Poverello. For it Elias gathered funds from many quarters. Under him the order grew rapidly, its missions were extended, new provinces were organized, and its strength was augmented in the universities, institutions which then were in the first flush of their youthful popularity. He encouraged scholarship. Elias was autocratic and the pressure which he employed to raise the huge sums for the memorial church provoked criticism. Opposition arose, not only from the Zealots, against whom he had taken stern measures, but also from the moderates, especially in some of the universities. In a dramatic session of the general chapter in the presence of Gregory IX in 1239 Elias was deposed. Under his immediate successors further relaxation in the rule of poverty was effected. John of Parma, who became minister general in 1247, although of aristocratic stock and an accomplished scholar, was of the Zealots and insisted upon a strict observance of the will of Francis. However, after a decade he resigned and was followed by Bonaventura. Bonaventura was a philosopher and mystic, was known as the Seraphic Doctor, and was eventually canonized. He held the post for more than a quarter of a century, until in 1273, having been made a cardinal, he also resigned. A man of action, courteous, humble, cheerful, tactful, courageous, a stirring preacher, he has been called the second founder of the order. A moderate, he brought the Brothers Minor more and more into conformity with the monastic tradition. He took action against the Zealots and during his administration some of the more extreme of them were imprisoned.

The Spirituals or Zealots did not tamely submit to the trend towards moderation. In a variety of ways they protested. Some of them were profoundly influenced by the writings of Joachim of Flora (or Fiore).

Joachim was born in 1130 in Calabria in the extreme south of Italy and except for his wanderings spent his life there. He early began preaching, then entered a Cistercian monastery, eventually was ordained priest, and, reluctantly, was made abbot. Desiring a stricter way of life than he had found there, he left that post. Disciples came to him and he founded a monastery, that of St. John of Flora (Fiore). He was released from his obedience to the Cistercians and in 1196 the new order, that of Flora (Fiore), obtained Papal approval. It never became large. Joachim himself died in 1202. He was, then, an older contemporary of Francis of Assisi.

Through his writings Joachim exerted a wide influence. He was esteemed a prophet. He gave an interpretation of the human drama for which he claimed Biblical foundation. To his mind history had three ages, or dispensations, that of the Father, the Son, and the Holy Spirit. He complicated this pattern by others, three of them of five ages each, another of seven ages, and still another of eight ages. The three ages, of Father, Son, and Holy Spirit received his chief emphasis. They overlapped. That of God the Father began in Adam and ended in Christ. In it men followed a carnal life, marrying and giving in marriage. The second age, that of God the Son, began with Uzziah and was to be consummated in the year 1260. In it life was a mixture of flesh and spirit and it was the age of the clerics. The third age, that of God the Spirit, is that of the monks. In it men are to live a purely spiritual life. It was inaugurated with Benedict of Nursia and is to last until the end of the world. The third age is to be marked by a gift of the Holy Spirit, that of contemplation, and in it the whole Church is to become a contemplative society. The first period was one of law, fear, labour, and slavery. The second was one of grace, humility, truth, discipline, and filial service. The third is to be one of love, liberty, happiness, and contemplation. Here is to be the culmination of history.

It can readily be seen that this bold scheme of history would have an appeal for many, including those of the tradition of Francis of Assisi. The teachings of Joachim profoundly shaped the thought of the Spirituals and also of many outside Franciscan ranks. They reinforced those who attacked the corruption in the Church and the Papacy. Quite understandably the latter hit back. In 1225 one of Joachim's books and in 1259 his other works were officially condemned by the Church. Any who favoured his views, including the Spirituals, were under suspicion and some of them fell afoul of the Inquisition and were killed.

The Spirituals were eventually in several schools and in various parts of Europe. Fascinating though their story is, we must not take the space to recount it. Some were in Ancona, others in that hotbed of heresies, Provence, and still others in Tuscany. Some completely withdrew from the Order of Brothers Minor. The extremists among the seceders were known as the Fraticelli, or "Little Brothers." They exalted the ideal of poverty and the mission of Francis of Assisi. Some of their groups were protected by one or another member of the nobility.

Fairly typical of the Spirituals—if anyone can be called typical of so diverse ᴀ set of movements and of men—and also of the sharp contrasts and the religious ferment seen in Italy in the thirteenth century, was Jacopone da Todi (c.1230–1306). A scion of the nobility, wilful, high-spirited, extravagant, vain, arrogant, perhaps a Doctor of Laws from the University of Bologna, disdainful of religion, a brilliant intellectual, in his late thirties he was shocked into the religious life, perhaps by the death of his young wife. He revolted against his earlier habits, gave his goods to the poor, and, dressed meanly, seemingly half-mad, urged his fellow-townsmen to repentance and fought his besetting sin of pride. He joined the Franciscans and became a leader of the Spirituals. Mystic, poet, drinking of that fountain of mediæval mysticism, Dionysius the Areopagite, a wandering lay missionary, he became involved in Italian politics, for five years languished in prison at the command of the Pope, was released by a new Pope, and spent his later years in contemplation and in communion with the "Infinite Light."

Various attempts were made to restore unity in the Order of Brothers Minor. For a time a Papal bull following the Council of Vienne, in 1312, seemed to give promise of success. However, the vigorous measures against the Spirituals taken by John XXII, who came to the Papal throne in 1316 and who instituted a severe persecution of them, drove some of the extremists to declare that the Pope was Antichrist or the forerunner of Antichrist, that the Roman Church was the harlot of Babylon described in the Apocalypse, and that the sacraments of the Church were obsolete. The tension was heightened when, in flat contradiction of the findings of the general chapter of the Franciscans in 1322 which declared that Jesus and the apostles had stood for absolute poverty, John XXII, in a bull in 1323, denounced this view as false and heretical. In 1322 John ended the fiction by which the Pope held property for the use of the Franciscans and turned it over directly to the order.

In spite of these internal difficulties and secessions and its departure from strict adherence to the ideals of Francis, the Order of Brothers Minor continued and never ceased to play an important role in the Church.

THE DOMINICANS

The Dominicans, officially the Order of Preachers (*Ordo praedicatorum*) or the Preaching Brothers (*Fratres Praedicatores*), like the Franciscans, arose early in the thirteenth century. The two had many similarities. They also displayed marked differences. At times they were unfriendly rivals. In contrast with the Franciscans, whose founder was deeply distressed by the drift towards the universities, from the outset the Dominicans were dedicated to teaching and scholarship as well as to preaching. It was no accident that from them came Thomas Aquinas, whom Roman Catholics were eventually to regard as having made the authoritative systematic intellectual statement of their faith. Moreover, while committed to poverty, the Dominicans were not as haunted by the ideal of complete abnegation of all worldly goods as were Francis and some of his followers. With notable exceptions they tended to be recruited from the aristocracy. Also with outstanding exceptions the Franciscans were from the humble classes. Nor did the sons of Dominic have about them the explosive quality which so punctuated the early centuries of the Brothers Minor. From them issued no movement comparable with the Spirituals or the Fraticelli.

Of Dominic, the founder of the Order of Preachers, we have a far less vivid picture than we do of Francis of Assisi. He seems not to have been nearly so colourful a figure. Yet he appears to have been even more the creator of the order which is usually known by his name than was Francis of the Brothers Minor. He was born in Castile about the year 1170. He was, therefore, an older contemporary of Francis. In his youth and until his mid-twenties he was for several years a student in one of the cathedral schools of Spain. Then he became an Augustinian canon in the cathedral of his native bishopric and eventually under a reforming bishop rose to be prior of the chapter. In other words, his was the somewhat conventional course of an able, scholarly clergyman who was committed to the conscientious pursuit of his calling. He was humble, for he later refused two bishoprics and shortly before his death attempted to resign from the headship of the order of which he was the chief creator. He was stern with himself in his strict asceticism. He gave himself to prolonged prayer. He was gentle, and in spite of his austerities left the impression of always being joyful.

Dominic might have passed his life in comparative obscurity had he not been confronted by a major challenge. This was the defection from the Catholic Church of a large proportion of the population in what is now the south of France. That region had not yet been assimilated to the rising kingdom of France and was largely distinct in culture. In the latter part of the twelfth and in the thirteenth century the Catholic Church in that area was weak and was represented by a body of clergy who were predominantly ignorant and corrupt. As we are to see more at length in the next chapter, what the Church deemed heresy was rife. The major movement was that of the Cathari, and the leaders of that sect seem to have been better morally than the rank and file of the Catholic clergy. In Dominic's lifetime, as we are also to say later, the Inquisition and armed force in the form of a crusade were being brought to bear on them. Heresy was being wiped out by blood. Early in the thirteenth century, when he was in his thirties, Dominic travelled in the south of France with his bishop, Diego d'Azévédo, and was stirred to the depths by what was to him the appalling religious state of the populace.

It seems to have been Diego who took the lead in devising and carrying through the first stages a peaceful method of bringing into the Church those who had revolted from it. This was to be by bands of missionaries who in poverty, ascetic holiness, love, and intellectual calibre were to win respect for the Catholic faith and converts to it. A nunnery was founded at Prouille, near Toulouse, in 1206. It eventually grew to large proportions and in a sense was the mother house of the future order.

When Diego returned to his diocese, Dominic took over the leadership of the enterprise. The first few years were difficult and discouraging. Yet, with characteristic determination, he persisted. Kindly, winsome, possessed of deep convictions, he persevered, driven by a love of souls and sustained by a life of prayer. In 1214 or 1215 a citizen of Toulouse gave him a house and he gathered about him a small company of men who lived in community. In 1215 Dominic went to Rome to the Fourth Lateran Council, a gathering to the importance of which we are to recur in a later chapter. He sought from Pope Innocent III approval of the new order. The Pope was reluctant, partly because the Lateran Council, alarmed at the multiplication of novel monastic movements, had ordered that any one who wished to found a new religious house must accept its rule from one which had already been approved. The Pope gave his consent, but on condition that Dominic would adopt the rule of some established order. In conformity with this command, Dominic chose the rule of the Augustinian Canons. He may have been moved to do this by the fact that he had already been a member of a community which was of this pattern. In framing the constitution of his order, Dominic was especially influenced by the structure and experience of the Premonstratensians who, it will be remembered, were a widely spread development from the Augustinian Canons. Late in 1216 and early in 1217, at the request of Dominic, Pope Honorius III confirmed the order. The name, Friars Preachers, seems to have been suggested by Innocent III.

Dominic was profoundly moved by his contacts with Francis and the Franciscans. He met Francis in Rome in 1218 and attended the general chapter of the Brothers Minor at Portiuncula in that year. At their general chapter in 1220 the Dominicans decided to wed Lady Poverty. How far this was in imitation of the Franciscans is a matter of debate. That the Franciscans were an important influence in the step seems certain. Precisely how determinative they were we cannot tell. Like the Brothers Minor, the Dominicans became mendicants, begging their daily bread from door to door.

The Dominicans spread almost as rapidly and widely as the Franciscans. Dominic spent most of his later months in Rome. He died in 1221, shortly after presiding at the second general chapter of the Order. By that time the Dominicans are said to have had sixty houses. They were already represented at the new university centres of Paris and Bologna. The number of houses is reported to have grown to 404 in 1277, a little more than fifty years later.

The Franciscans and the Dominicans resembled each other not only in being "begging friars." In organization each had territorial provinces with chapters and a head, a general chapter of the entire order, and a single head of the whole. Each had a second order for women, and each a third order for the laity. Both were intensely missionary and by widely flung enterprises in Europe, Asia, and Africa sought to bring nominal Christians to a deeper faith and to win non-Christians. Both established themselves in the universities and the members of both did much preaching.

However, in contrast with the Franciscans, who sought the moral conversion of their hearers by the witness of untutored simplicity and a life of absolute poverty and self-giving love, the Dominicans strove to overcome ignorance and error through all the skills of trained minds. They stressed the education of their members. Each of their houses was a school and each must have at least one doctor of theology to direct the study of that subject. Scholarship was given an honoured place. But scholarship was for the purpose of preparing preachers who were to become missionaries to the masses.

THE CARMELITES

The Franciscans and the Dominicans were by far the largest of the mendicant orders. So popular did they become and so mightily did they stir the imagination of earnest Christians in Western Europe that they stimulated the development of similar bodies. Of these the most prominent were the Carmelites and the Augustinian Hermits or Friars.

The Carmelites ascribed their origin to Elijah who, it was said, founded a community of hermits on Mt. Carmel which continued to the time of Christ. Some of its members, so it was claimed, were then converted to the Christian faith and enrolled the Virgin Mary and the apostles as members. The order, it was maintained, then persisted unbroken as a Christian fellowship.

Actually, what became the Order of Our Lady of Mount Carmel can be traced only to the twelfth century. At that time a few pilgrims who took advantage of the Crusades to go to Palestine established themselves as a company of hermits on Mt. Carmel. About the year 1210, namely, while the Franciscans and Dominicans were taking shape, they were given a rule by the Latin Patriarch of Jerusalem. They were not unlike the Carthusians and and the Camaldulians. They were to live in silence and retirement far from other human habitation and were to meet only at specified times but not for meals. Eventually several other affiliated groups arose in Palestine.

The reconquest of Palestine by the Moslems constrained the Carmelites to scatter. They went to Cyprus and to several countries in the south and west of Europe. In 1229 they won Papal recognition as mendicants. Many were attracted to their ranks. The younger group found the old way of the hermit unfitted to conditions in Europe and wished, like the other friars, to preach and in preparation for that mission to frequent the universities. A crisis arose which threatened the existence of the order. Rescue from this outcome was chiefly by some of its English members, led by Simon Stock, who became general of the order in 1247. He obtained modifications which brought the order more nearly into the pattern of life of the Franciscans and Dominicans. In spite of protests Simon's ideas eventually prevailed and at a chapter general in London in 1281 closer approximation to the programme of studies of the Dominicans was achieved. The Carmelites established themselves in the universities. Yet the love of the older type of life, that of the hermit, persisted among some of the members.

The Augustinian Hermits

The Friars Hermits of St. Augustine or the Augustinian Order sprang from several communities in Italy which early in the thirteenth century sent colonies into Germany, Spain, and the south of France. They were among those movements towards the semi-hermit life which abounded in Italy late in the twelfth and in the fore part of the thirteenth century and were expressions of the religious awakening of those decades. In general they followed the rule ascribed to Augustine of Hippo, for, as we have hinted, this had become common among non-monastic groups devoted to religion.

It was largely through the initiative of the Papacy that a number of these bodies were brought together under a common organization. The Popes were disturbed by the multitude of new movements, some of which smacked of heresy or were in danger of becoming heretical. Quite understandably, they sought to draw them together into a structure which could meet Rome's approval and through which they could serve the Church. In 1243 Pope Innocent IV brought hermits in Tuscany under the Augustinian rule and appointed Cardinal Richard Annibaldi as their supervisor. More than any other one man, Annibaldi was responsible for the growth of the order. A Papal bull of 1256 which merged several bands of hermits into a closer union is usually regarded as the decisive landmark in making the Austin Friars an order. Before the close to the thirteenth century the Augustinians had conformed to the pattern of the Dominicans. They became a preaching order and based that preaching upon theological training and scholarship.

Other Mendicant Orders

The popularity of the great medicant orders contributed to the creation of still other bodies which resembled them. Most of them were ephemeral, partly because the Council of Lyons (1274) sought to discourage them. However, some persisted. Prominent were the Servants of Mary, usually known as the Servites. They were founded in 1233 by seven youths from aristocratic families of Florence who, giving up their wealth, established themselves on a mountain near that city. The community grew and in 1240 became an order which followed the Augustinian rule and also consciously borrowed from the constitutions of the Dominicans. In the 1240's the Servites received Papal approval but not until 1304 was that made final. Eventually they were ranked with the four great mendicant orders. We hear as well of the Friars of the Cross, also called the Crutched Friars. There were several bodies known as Fratres Cruciferi, one of which went back at least to the twelfth century and another to the thirteenth century.

The Friars Multiply and Clash with the Secular Clergy

As we have suggested, the movements represented by the friars quickly attracted large numbers of members and spread rapidly through Western Europe. Why this was so is not entirely clear. It may have been because they combined the sort of complete devotion to the Christian ideal that was seen in the traditional monasticism with service to others in the form of missions to nominal Christians and to non-Christians. Whatever the reason, they became one of the most familiar features of the Europe of the thirteenth century and continued to grow.

This growth brought the mendicant orders into repeated conflicts with the secular clergy. By the term "secular clergy" or "seculars" is meant those clergy who are not members of monastic bodies but who live *in sæculum,* namely, in the world. Before the end of the thirteenth century, the Popes had, by successive steps, made the friars independent of the bishops and responsible only to their own superiors and to the Holy See. While older orders had also enjoyed this immunity from control by diocesan bishops and were directly subject to the Pope, this status made the friars unusually irritating to the episcopacy, for, unlike most of the earlier monks, they did not live apart from the world, but went everywhere preaching, hearing confessions, and saying mass. Preaching had been a prerogative of the bishops and hearing confessions and giving the communion were among the functions of the parish clergy. Many bishops and parish priests, accordingly, felt aggrieved. In 1254 Pope Innocent IV, yielding to the complaints which had come to him, especially from the University of Paris, where the Dominicans were in open conflict with the university authorities, forbade religious orders to receive into their churches on Sundays or feast days the parishioners of others, to preach even in their own churches before mass, to preach in parish churches, or to hear confessions without the consent of the parish priest. Before the year was out, this edict had been revoked by Innocent's successor and the mendicants continued to flourish. Many of them also rose to high office in the Church. Here was a new and permanent element in the Catholic Church of the West.

OTHER THIRTEENTH AND FOURTEENTH CENTURY MONASTIC MOVEMENTS

The popularity of the friars did not fully eclipse the older monastic orders. In the thirteenth and fourteenth centuries, as we have hinted, while the former were coming into being and catching the imagination of Western Catholics, the older forms of monasticism persisted. The Benedictines, the Cluniacs, the Cistercians, the Carthusians, and others still constituted an important feature of the religious life in Western Europe. Indeed, a few new orders arose on the older patterns.

Thus in 1231 the Sylvestrines were founded by Sylvester Gozzolini. They followed the primitive form of the rule of Benedict and went beyond it in austerity and the practice of poverty. Italian in origin, they did not spread extensively beyond that peninsula. Although never numerous, they survived into the twentieth century.

In 1319 the Olivetans were officially constituted, taking their name from their original hermitage on Monte Oliveto and in memory of Christ's agony on the Mount of Olives. They sprang from a small group of aristocrats of Siena who in 1313 went to a mountain fastness to follow the ascetic life as hermits. The bishop whom the Pope appointed to direct them gave them the rule of Benedict. To this they adhered with great strictness. Their houses multiplied and were formed into an order with a general chapter and a superior general.

SUMMARY

This rapid survey of the development of the monasticism in Western Europe in the four centuries between 950 and 1350 will at least give evidence of the abounding vitality of the Christianity of that region in these years. As we look back across the story eight generalizations stand out.

1. For a large proportion of Christians the monastic way seemed to be the road through which to pursue the perfect Christian life and to attain the goal of the salvation of one's soul.

2. All the efforts to attain the Christian ideal through monasticism tended to spend their force and the institutions to which they gave rise to become prosaic and even corrupt.

3. From time to time, often in protest against this laxity, new monastic movements sprang up and flourished.

4. These fresh movements displayed increasing variety. Some of them, like the earlier ones, sought complete separation from the society about them, there to live uncontaminated by the evil which seemed an integral part of the world. On the other hand, a mounting trend was towards active participation in the world in an effort to save it and to win more and more men and women to the Christian faith.

5. The overwhelming majority of the new monastic movements had their origin in Italy and in what had once been Gaul, areas which had long been professedly Christian. Few arose in regions such as England, Scotland, the north of Germany, and Scandinavia, which had recently been won to the Christian faith, or in Spain, where Islam had not yet been fully vanquished. To this there were a few exceptions. One of them was Bec, where the founder was from Norman stock which only two or three generations earlier had been pagan, but even in Bec Lanfranc and Anselm, the leaders who did most to give the foundation distinction, were from Italy. It may be noted, by way of anticipation, that in subsequent centuries most of the new monastic movements had their birth in Latin Europe, while in contrast the movements which issued in Protestantism were especially strong outside Latin Europe.

6. The initiators of the new orders were chiefly from the aristocracy. Francis of Assisi was an outstanding exception, but even he was from the merchant class and not from the peasantry.

7. Here was a swelling tide seeking to deepen and make more intelligent and effective the loyalty to the Christian faith which had become nominal through the mass conversions of the earlier centuries.

8. Finally, we must note what we have already suggested and what will become more apparent in the next two chapters, that the monastic develop-

ments were but one phase of an even more inclusive mounting wave of religious life. This was concurrently making itself felt in other movements, some of them within the Church and some denounced by the latter as heretical, in efforts to purify the Church and with it to lift to a higher level the entire population which bore the Christian name.

SELECTED BIBLIOGRAPHY

GENERAL WORKS

G. G. Coulton, *Five Centuries of Religion* (Cambridge University Press, 4 vols., 1923, 1927, 1936, 1950). The first three volumes cover this period. Voluminous, enormously erudite, they are unsympathetic with monasticism.

D. Knowles, *The Monastic Order in England. A History of Its Development from the Times of St. Dunstan to the Fourth Lateran Council 943-1216* (Cambridge University Press, 1940, pp. xix, 764). Valuable not only for its description of conditions in England, but also for its account of monasticism on the Continent of Europe. By a Roman Catholic, singularly objective.

D. Knowles, *The Religious Orders in England* (Cambridge University Press, 1948, pp. xvi, 348). Carries the story of the preceding volume from 1216 to 1340. Like its predecessor, it contains valuable summaries of the course of Continental monasticism.

H. B. Workman, *The Evolution of the Monastic Ideal from the Earliest Times down to the Coming of the Friars* (London, The Epworth Press, 1927, pp. xxi, 368). Approximately the last third of this general, semi-popular survey covers the period of this chapter.

CLUNY

J. Evans, *Monastic Life at Cluny 910-1157* (Oxford University Press, 1931, pp. xii, 137). Carefully done.

L. M. Smith, *The Early History of the Monastery of Cluny* (Oxford University Press, 1920, pp. x, 225). Based upon extensive use of the sources.

L. M. Smith, *Cluny in the Eleventh and Twelfth Centuries* (London, Philip Allan & Co., 1930, pp. xxviii, 348). Like the earlier volume by the same author, carefully done and based upon the sources.

THE CISTERCIANS AND BERNARD OF CLAIRVAUX

M. H. d'Arbois de Jubainville, *Études sur l'État Interieur des Abbayes Cisterciennes et principalement de Clairvaux au XII ͤ et au XIII ͤ Siècle* (Paris, Aug. Durand, 1858, pp. xviii, 489).

Life and Works of Saint Bernard, Abbot of Clairvaux, edited by J. Mabillon, translated and edited with additional notes by S. J. Eales. (2d ed., London, Burns, Oates, & Washbourne, no date, 2 vols.). Made up chiefly of the letters of Bernard.

Cæsarius of Heisterbach, *The Dialogue of Miracles,* translated by H. von E. Scott and C. C. Swinton Bland, with an introduction by G. G. Coulton (London, George Routledge Sons, 2 vols., 1929). Stories told by a Cistercian in the first half of the thirteenth century which throw light on the religious life of the times and especially on that of one Cistercian abbey.

R. S. Storrs, *Bernard of Clairvaux, the Times, the Man, and His Work* (New York, Charles Scribner's Sons, 1907, pp. xvi, 598). Semi-popular, well-written lectures, based upon the sources.

W. W. Williams, *Studies in St. Bernard of Clairvaux* (London, Society for Promoting Christian Knowledge, 1927, pp. vi, 160). A well-written, sympathetic account of Bernard, with special emphasis upon his early years and the first part of his career, with extensive footnote quotations from the sources.

THE CARTHUSIANS

E. M. Thompson, *The Carthusian Order in England* (London, Society for Promoting Christian Knowledge, Part I, 1930, pp. x, 550). About a fourth of the whole is on the history of the order outside of England.

FRANCIS OF ASSISI AND THE FRANCISCANS

Out of the enormous amount that has been written on the subject, the following will be found useful.

T. S. R. Boase, *St. Francis of Assisi* (London, Gerald Duckworth & Co., 1936, pp. 137). A popular, well-written account.

P. Cowley, *Franciscan Rise and Fall* (London, J. M. Dent & Sons, 1933, pp. x, 212). A popular account, chiefly on Francis and the order until his death, with a brief summary of later developments—"the fall"—by a warm admirer of Francis.

P. Robinson, *The Writings of Saint Francis of Assisi Newly Translated into English with an Introduction and Notes* (London, J. M. Dent & Sons, 1906, pp. xxxii, 208). By a Franciscan.

"The Little Flowers" & the Life of St. Francis with the "Mirror of Perfection" (London, J. M. Dent & Sons, 1910, pp. xxii, 397. In *Everyman's Library*). The Little Flowers (*Fioretti*) and *the Mirror of Perfection* (*Speculum*) record the memories of Francis transmitted orally or in writing, as cherished by the saint's intimate friends. They have much of the miraculous and are told with the bias of the Spiritual Franciscans. The *Life* is the official one by Bonaventura, not as colourful as the other two books in this volume.

R. M. Huber, *A Documented History of the Franciscan Order (1182–1517)* (Milwaukee, The Nowiny Publishing Apostolate, 1944, pp. xxxiv, 1028). A useful summary by a Franciscan, of the history of the Franciscans, based upon the documents and with extensive references to them.

A. G. Little, *Guide to Franciscan Studies* (London, Society for Promoting Christian Knowledge, 1920, pp. v, 63). A useful introduction to the sources.

J. R. H. Moorman, *The Sources for the Life of S.Francis of Assisi* (Manchester

University Press, 1940, pp. xiv, 176). A critical description and evaluation of the various sources.

P. Sabatier, *Life of St. Francis of Assisi* (New York, Charles Scribner's Sons, 1909, pp. xxxv, 448). A standard life by a Protestant who was a warm admirer of Francis.

THE SPIRITUAL FRANCISCANS

D. M. Douie, *The Nature and the Effect of the Heresy of the Fraticelli* (Manchester University Press, 1932, pp. xix, 292). A scholarly study which, while specializing on the Fraticelli, embraces the entire movement of the Spirituals.

H. C. Lea, *A History of the Inquisition of the Middle Ages* (Vol. III, New York, Harper & Brothers, 1888, pp. ix, 736).

D. S. Muzzey, *The Spiritual Franciscans* (New York, American Historical Association, 1907, pp. 75). A prize essay, in the form of a brief, comprehensive summary with excellent references to the sources.

V. D. Scudder, *The Franciscan Adventure. A Study in the First Hundred Years of the Order of St. Francis of Assisi* (London, J. M. Dent & Sons, 1931, pp. 432). Well written, scholarly, with special emphasis upon the internal struggles in the order and the development of the Spirituals.

E. Underhill, *Jacopone da Todi, Poet and Mystic 1228-1306: a Spiritual Biography* (London, J. M. Dent & Sons, 1919, pp. xi, 521). A careful study by a distinguished specialist in mysticism.

JOACHIM OF FLORA

H. Bett, *Joachim of Flora* (London, Methuen & Co., 1931). Brief, but an excellent comprehensive summary conscientiously based on wide use of the sources and pertinent secondary works.

DOMINIC AND THE DOMINICANS

R. F. Bennett, *The Early Dominicans. Studies in Thirteenth-Century Dominican History* (Cambridge University Press, 1937, pp. xii, 189). An important survey, treating phase by phase various aspects of the Dominican life, practice, and achievement.

A. F. Drane, *The History of St. Dominic, Founder of the Order of Preachers* (London, Longmans, Green & Co., 1891, pp. xvii, 485).

G. R. Galbraith, *The Constitution of the Dominican Order 1216 to 1360* (Manchester University Press, 1925, pp. xvi, 286). A carefully documented study of the Dominican organization.

P. Mandonnet, *St. Dominic and His Work*, translated by M. B. Larkin (St. Louis, B. Herder Book Co., 1945, pp. xviii, 487). A comprehensive account, by a Dominican, with chief emphasis upon the order in its early years, and its varied activities and achievements.

Chapter 19

POPULAR RELIGIOUS MOVEMENTS:
MOVEMENTS OTHER THAN MONASTIC
FOR THE FULL PRACTICE OF THE
CHRISTIAN LIFE BOTH INSIDE
AND OUTSIDE THE CHURCH

The abounding vitality of Christianity in Western Europe in the four centuries between the years 950 and 1350 did not find its only expression through monasticism, vigorous and increasingly rich in its variety though that was. It also displayed itself in many minority movements which arose, like monasticism, from a desire for a more thoroughgoing commitment to the Christian faith. Some of them were ardently missionary, seeking to win others from the nominally Christian population. Many remained within the Catholic Church. Others were outside it, either by their own choice or because they were expelled for what that Church deemed their heresies. These movements are the subject of this chapter. In the following chapter we shall deal with the efforts to raise the entire Church in the West, which meant practically all of Western Europe, to a higher plane of life, and to do this through a comprehensive ecclesiastical structure.

As we enter upon these extra-monastic minority movements, we must remind ourselves again of the general situation in Western Europe during these centuries. Here was an area, still sparsely settled when compared with the Europe of the nineteenth and twentieth centuries, or even with the China and India of that day, but which was emerging from a prolonged series of foreign invasions. Cities, though small and unsanitary, were growing, commerce was increasing, distinctive art, architecture, and literature were appearing, and the first beginnings were being seen of that expansion of European peoples which was to be so outstanding a feature of the history of the world after the fifteenth century.

There had been a mass conversion of this Europe to Christianity. Much of it had been while the Roman Empire was still intact, well before the year 500. Some of it had been that of the barbarian invaders as they settled within the former borders of the Roman Empire. Several of the mass conversions, especially in the period after 950, either had carried or were carrying the boundaries of Christendom far beyond those of the Roman Empire at its widest extent. Could this mass conversion become more than nominal? Could either the entire body of these professed Christians, together with their collective life, be lifted to an approximation to the high standards set forth by Christ, or, if not, could substantial elements be brought towards those standards? We have seen how the effort was made through monasticism first to draw minorities from this mass of ostensible Christians into ideal Christian communities and then, increasingly, especially beginning with the thirteenth century through the friars, groups presumably completely dedicated to Christ, to lift all of Western Christendom to a higher level and to carry the Christian message to other parts of the world. In the next few pages we will go on to the non-monastic movements at which we have hinted.

POPULAR MOVEMENTS WHICH REMAINED WITHIN THE CHURCH

Movements of laymen outside monasteries which in one way or another sought a more earnest practice of the Christian faith multiplied during these centuries.

Prominent among them were the third orders of the various bodies of friars, to which we have already referred.

Confraternities, associations of lay folk, bound together by rules and vows under the authorization of a bishop, were a growing feature of the life of the Church. One is said to have been founded not far from the beginning of the thirteenth century.

Earlier we have noted the singing guilds which began in Italy in the twelfth century. In the second half of the thirteenth century they became organized, with chapels and other meeting places and with written constitutions. They went in procession through towns, or met in the evenings on piazzas or before some shrine to sing hymns of penitence and adoration. Their singing was in the vernacular.

A movement which is said to have begun in Perugia in 1259 was that of the Flagellants. By a kind of mass contagion men, women, and children bewailed their sins and many of them marched through the streets, naked except for loin cloths, crying to God for mercy, and scourging themselves until the blood ran. Old enmities were forgiven and enemies were reconciled. Criminals confessed their misdeeds and where possible made restitution. Murderers asked pardon of the relatives of those whom they had killed. In some places priests headed the processions and led them to churches where the penitents prostrated themselves before the altars. The Flagellants spread beyond Italy to Germany and Bohemia, but subsided almost as quickly as they arose.

The beguines comprised a variety of lay groups which seem not to have been confined to any specific set of forms and to have displayed wide variety. They were made up originally of women, but the designation later was also given to men. The origin of the name is in dispute. At the outset and to a certain extent for some centuries, the term appears to have been applied to an unmarried woman who followed the life of virginity while living in the world. The beguines wore a distinguishing garb. Some of them lived alone or with their families. Others had a collective life in beguine houses. These houses were not monasteries. No vows of poverty were taken. Some beguines were wealthy and others were from the poorer classes. Occasionally widows were in the houses. Many of the beguines were assimilated to the third orders of the friars. Indeed, the growth of the beguines seems to have been stimulated by the example of the Franciscans and Dominicans and some of the beguine houses were associated with houses of the Franciscans. In 1311 the Council of Vienne under Pope Clement V took action against the beguines on the ground that they were channels for the spread of heresy. However, in one form or another they survived into the sixteenth century.

Heretical Movements

In centuries which saw so much ferment in the religious life of Western Europe, it is not surprising that movements arose which could not be reconciled with the Catholic Church. We shall probably never learn even the names of all of them. Of those which we know, we must take the space to mention only the more prominent. We hear of heresies in the tenth and eleventh centuries, but in the twelfth century they reached more formidable dimensions.

As we enter upon their description it is well to note a feature which most of them had in common. The leadership and the bulk of the membership were not from the aristocracy but were primarily from the urban populations, merchants and artisans, and, to a less extent, from the peasants. In contrast, most of the monastic movements were initiated and led by members of the landed aristocracy. The striking exception was the Brothers Minor, who, as we have more than once reminded ourselves, were begun by a scion of the city merchant class. Yet it will be remembered that the extreme wing of the Franciscans, composed of those who deemed themselves most loyal to the ideals of their founder, tended to be critical of the Catholic Church and many of them broke with it. In this contrast is possibly to be seen the beginning of the rootage of the Christian faith among the masses and the consequent stimulation to independent thought and action. The governing groups, on the other hand, as is true of most aristocracies, were conservative and held to the established order.

One of the movements which was frowned upon by the Catholic Church had as its leader Tanchelm. He began to preach in the diocese of Utrecht and early in the twelfth century his views had fairly wide currency in the Low Countries and the Rhine Valley. He attacked the entire structure of the Catholic Church, denied the authority of the Church and of the Pope, and held that at least some of the sacraments were valueless. He was accused of teaching that irregular relations between the sexes affect only the body and not the soul and so are permissible, but this may have been a complete misrepresentation by his enemies. For a time he was imprisoned by the Archbishop of Cologne. In 1115, after his escape, he was killed, allegedly by a priest.

Not far from the same time, early in the twelfth century, Peter of Bruys, himself following a strictly ascetic way of life, rejected the baptism of infants, the Eucharist, church buildings, ecclesiastical ceremonies, prayers for the dead, and the veneration of the cross. He held that the cross, as the instrument of Christ's death, should be despised rather than honoured. He burned crosses and himself is said to have been burned by an infuriated mob. His followers are sometimes called Petrobrusians. They re-baptized those who joined them, profaned churches, burned crosses, and overthrew altars.

Sometimes classed with Peter of Bruys, but perhaps mistakenly, was Henry of Lausanne. Like the former he preached in what is now France and in the first half of the twelfth century. Before his death in 1145 he is said to have attracted a wide following, called Henricians. He taught that the sacraments were valid only when administered by priests who led a life of asceticism and poverty. He condemned the clergy of the day for their love of wealth and power. He was a contemporary of Bernard of Clairvaux. The latter, quick to attack all that he regarded as heresy and so endangering the salvation of souls, preached against Henry and his views in the areas in which they had gained currency.

Arnold of Brescia

Roughly contemporary with Peter of Bruys and Henry of Lausanne was Arnold of Brescia. Born in the city in the north of Italy by which he is known, he studied theology at Paris. Returning to Brescia, he was ordained priest and became the head of a community of canons regular. From his youth he had been noted for his purity of life and his espousal of poverty. He was earnestly eager to see the Church conform fully to the Christian ideal. Believing that this could not be so long as its leaders compromised with the world, he attacked the bishops for their cupidity, dishonest gains, and frequent irregularity of life and urged that the clergy renounce all property and political and physical power. Ardent by temperament and uncompromising, he aroused the antagonism of his bishop, and was ordered by Pope Innocent II to leave Italy and not to preach without Papal consent. A friend of Abélard, a distinguished scholar and teacher and a centre of controversy whom we are to meet later, he was lumped with the latter by Bernard of Clairvaux and was vigorously attacked. Bernard obtained his condemnation by the Council of Sens (1140). In 1145 or 1146, after protracted wanderings, Arnold was given absolution by Pope Eugene III. Soon, however, he again broke with the Pope. He denounced the temporal power of the Papacy and sided with a republic which had been set up in Rome under the local aristocracy and which had driven the Pope out of the city. The effort at a republic collapsed. Eugene III returned to Rome, and his successor, the able Hadrian IV (Nicholas Breakspear, the only Englishman to occupy the Papal throne), had Arnold expelled from the city. At the instance of Hadrian Arnold was seized by order of the Holy Roman Emperor Frederick I (Barbarossa), was delivered to the civil authorities of Rome, and in 1155 he was hanged, his body was burned, and his ashes were thrown into the Tiber. Some of his followers survived him and, a dissident sect, like him lived chastely and austerely and denounced the clergy and the Pope.

THE WALDENSEES

More numerous than the followers of Arnold of Brescia and more lasting as a fellowship were those who were known as the Waldensees or the Vaudois. The origin of the name is in debate. It is said to have been from the *vaux* or valleys or *vallis densa,* shaded valley, in which the Waldensees long persisted. It is also conjectured to have come from Peter Waldo, or Valdez.

Peter Waldo, a rich merchant of Lyons, became impressed with the brevity and insecurity of life and went to a theologian to ask the way to heaven. In reply, he was given the injunction of Jesus to the rich young ruler: "If thou wilt be perfect, go sell that thou hast, and give to the poor." Waldo proceeded resolutely (1176) to carry out the command. Paying his creditors and providing for his wife and children, he distributed the rest of his property among the poor and began begging his daily bread. He made a diligent study of the New Testament through a translation into his native tongue. Inspired by it, he undertook to imitate Christ. Garbed as Christ had commanded his apostles to be in their special missions during his lifetime, and, like them, taking no purse, he preached in city and countryside.

Peter Waldo soon attracted followers. They called themselves the "Poor in Spirit" or the "Poor Men of Lyons." Imitating him, they dressed as he did and went about preaching. So far they resembled the movement which Francis of Assisi was to inaugurate three decades or so later. When the Archbishop of Lyons forbade them to preach, Peter Waldo appealed to the Pope. The Pope at first looked favourably on their vow of poverty and gave them permission in dioceses where the bishops would allow them. Soon they found this restriction too hampering and disregarded it. They asked authorization of the Third Lateran Council (1179) but were denied it. Still they persisted and in 1184 the Pope excommunicated them. Believing that they ought to obey God rather than men, they continued to preach. Their numbers multiplied and they were joined by many of the Humiliati, who had arisen in and near Milan and in that same year (1184) had come under Papal prohibition.

In their tenets and practices the followers of Waldo continued to seek to conform to the New Testament. They memorized large portions of its vernacular translations. Following what they believed it commanded them, they went about two and two, preaching, simply clad, barefoot or wearing sandals, and subsisting on what was given them by those who listened to them. They refused to heed Pope or bishop and taught that the Church of Rome was not the head of the Catholic Church but was corrupt. They held that women and laymen could preach, that masses and prayers for the dead were without warrant, that purgatory is the troubles which come to us in this life, and that to be efficacious prayer need not be confined to churches. They criticized prayers in Latin on the ground that they were not understood by the people, and derided church music and the canonical hours. They declared that while priests and bishops who lived as had the apostles were to be obeyed, sacraments administered by unworthy priests were invalid and that a layman was as competent as a priest to hear confessions. They taught that every lie is a deadly sin, that oaths, even in law courts, are contrary to Christ's commands, and believed that all taking of human life is against God's law. They observed the Eucharist together and held that, if necessary, any layman might administer it. Their only forms of prayer were the "Our Father" and grace at meals. They had their own clergy, with bishops, priests, and deacons, and a head of their fellowship.

The Poor Men of Lyons spread rapidly and widely and were soon to be found in Spain, Italy, Germany, and Bohemia, as well as in their native France. Internal conflicts developed, partly because Peter Waldo, the first head, was deemed arbitrary in his rule, and in 1210 many in the north of Italy withdrew. Other variations developed in organization and doctrine. Many continued to think of themselves as members of the Catholic Church.

Pope Innocent III sought to take advantage of their differences to win the Poor Men back to the Church. He encouraged (1208) the formation and spread of *Pauperes Catholici* ("Poor Catholics") who under ecclesiastical direction would follow such of the practices of the Waldensees as the Church could approve. By this means many who had been attracted by the Poor Men were held or won back.

For the most part the Waldensees were humble folk. Even their enemies described them as dressing simply, industrious, labouring with their hands, chaste, temperate in eating and drinking, refusing to frequent taverns and dances, sober and truthful in speech, avoiding anger, and regarding the accumulation of wealth as evil.

Yet, branding them as heretics, the Catholic Church and the civil authorities sought to eliminate them, by persuasion if possible and if not by force. Such Waldensees as survived persecution sought refuge in the valleys of the Italian Alps, where we are to meet them again at the time of the Reformation.

THE CATHARI OR ALBIGENSES

A movement further removed from the faith of the Catholic Church than the Waldensees was that of the Cathari ("Pure") or, as they were known from one of their chief centres, Albi, in the south of France, Albigensees. In some places they also were called Patarini or Patarenes, although that appellation was not confined to them and was sometimes made to include all heretics. Like the Waldensees, they flourished in the twelfth century and were most numerous in Northern Spain, Southern France, and Northern Italy. Indeed, the two movements had much in common and seem to have interacted upon each other.

It is interesting and perhaps significant that the major new monastic order of the twelfth century, the Cistercians, originated in the same general region, although slightly farther north and east, and that the two chief monastic movements of the thirteenth century, the Franciscans and Dominicans, also had their rise and early growth in that geographic belt. The Cathari were but one expression of the religious ferment, chiefly Christian in its forms, which profoundly moved the Latin South of Europe in these centuries.

Yet the Cathari were not confined to Latin Europe. They were also found east of the Adriatic, among the Slavs. There they enjoyed an advantage over the Catholic Church in their use of the vernacular in their services. We also hear of them in Constantinople, where they had both a Greek and a Latin church.

What is now southern France, where the Waldensees and the Cathari had their chief strength, was fertile soil for such a movement. As we know from the statements of some of its own leaders, the Catholic Church in that region was unusually corrupt and had forfeited the respect of earnest souls. Some of the clergy compiled indecent books and permitted immodest songs to be sung in church. Many priests were luxury-loving, illiterate, indolent, profane, and tolerated simony and clerical concubinage. In such a situation a religion with high moral appeal and practice would gain a ready hearing.

The Cathari were dualists, believing that there are two eternal powers, the one good and the other evil, that the visible world is the creation of the evil power, and that the spiritual world is the work of the good power. They were, quite understandably, accused by their enemies of being Manichæans. Some later scholars have asserted and others have as vigorously denied the Manichæan origin. It is less debatable that they were influenced by the Paulicians and the Bogomils, dualists whom we have already met in the Eastern Church and who were strong in Bulgaria and the Balkans. Whether they owed their beginnings to contacts with these groups we do not know. As early as the first half of the eleventh century there were those in the south of what is now France who were arraigned by the ecclesiastical authorities for holding a dualistic heresy. In the twelfth century their numbers mounted.

The Cathari claimed to find in the Bible support for their convictions. Some of them rejected parts of the Old Testament, holding that they were the work of the Devil, but they all stressed the New Testament and gave especial weight to *The Gospel according to John*. Their views were by no means uniform, but on several they seem to have been agreed. They held, as we have suggested, that there are two powers, the one evil and responsible for the material world and the other good and the maker of the immaterial world. Some put forth a variant of this dualism, saying that the good God had two sons, one of whom, Satanal, rebelled, and the other, Christ, became the redeemer. All maintained that there were two churches, the one their own, that of Jesus Christ, good, and the other that of Rome, evil. Accordingly, they rejected the orders and laws of the Roman Catholic Church and taught that its sacraments were quite useless. As dualists, believing flesh to be evil, they endeavoured to shun all that had to do with the reproduction of animal life.

The Cathari were of two grades. Those who had fully embraced their way of life were called the "perfect" (*perfecti*). Admission to the "perfect" was by a kind of spiritual baptism, called "consolation." It was administered by one who had already received it and through it forgiveness of sins and entrance into the kingdom of the good power were obtained. The perfect must remain continent. If unmarried they must continue celibate, and if married, husband must separate from wife and the man must never again so much as touch a woman. They were never to eat meat, milk, or eggs, since these were the fruits of reproduction. They were not to engage in war or to own property. "Believers" (*credenti*) who had not yet become "perfect" might marry, hold property, and even outwardly remain members of the Roman Catholic Church and share in its sacraments. "Believers" looked forward to salvation through "consolation," although that step might be postponed until old age or fatal illness. At least some of the Cathari believed in the transmigration of souls and taught that Christ came to redeem those who had fallen and to enable them to return to their Creator.

In their communal worship the Cathari followed very simple forms. They had no church buildings. They held that since flesh is evil, Christ could not have had a real body or have died a real death. Accordingly they had no use for crosses or crucifixes. They read from the Scriptures, heard sermons, and shared a common meal from bread which, held in the hands, was blessed, broken, and distributed to the seated believers. We hear of other forms of the common meal in which bread, fish, and wine were used, and which was preceded by the washing of the feet of the participants by the "major" who presided. There seems to have been another form, on Easter, in which bread and wine were the elements.

In organization the "perfect" corresponded to the clergy of the Catholic Church. The Cathari were said to have majors (bishops), presbyters, and deacons, but they appear to have been without a comprehensive ecclesiastical structure.

As is so often true of persecuted groups with secret meetings, tales gained popular credence which accused the Cathari of the grossest immoralities. However, some of their most caustic critics bore witness to their high moral character. They were ardent missionaries. They seem to have been recruited largely from peasants and artisans, but they included some scholars and produced an extensive literature in the vernacular, including translations of the Bible. While, as we have said, strongest in Northern Italy, Southern France, and the north of Spain, the Cathari also won converts in Northern France and Flanders, chiefly in the cities.

The Suppression of the Heresies

One of the striking features of the movements of these centuries which the Catholic Church branded as heresies was that they either completely died out or, in the case of the Waldensees, dwindled to small groups. This disappearance appears to have been due in part to inherent weakness and the lack of an effective organization and in part to measures adopted by the Catholics.

It is of the actions taken by Catholics of which we hear most. In spite of the corruption within its ranks, the Catholic Church possessed striking advantages. In its system of parishes and dioceses directed from one common centre, Rome, reinforced by monastic orders and supported by secular rulers, it had a comprehensive structure which could operate on a wide front and from varied angles. Several Popes and councils of the Church formally condemned the heretics. Numbers of preachers, among them, as we have seen, Bernard of Clairvaux, Dominic, and the original group which the latter gathered about him, used eloquence and persuasion. The ecclesiastical combined with the civil arm to arrest heretics and punish them. In 1179 the Third Lateran Council proclaimed a crusade against them. This is said to have been the first occasion in which that device was employed against those who called themselves Christians. Recruited and led by a Papal legate, in 1181 a crusading army appeared to have some success, but it was soon disbanded and the Cathari once more raised their heads. In the ensuing quarter of a century, both the Cathari and the Waldensees multiplied, especially in Southern France.

It was Innocent III who initiated measures which dealt the decisive blows against the dissidents. At first his efforts seemed to meet with as little success as had those of his predecessors. The outstanding lord in Southern France, Count Raymond VI of Toulouse, evaded Papal efforts to induce him to take positive action and Philip Augustus, the King of France, hesitated further to complicate his own difficult problems, including his chronic troubles with England, by risking a prolonged internal war to enforce the Papal commands. Then, in 1208, the Papal Legate, Peter of Castelnau, was murdered in Raymond's domains and perhaps at his court. Innocent took advantage of the widespread horror evoked by the crime to call forth a crusading army. Religious zeal represented in an outstanding leader of the crusading armies, Simon de Montfort, combined with quite secular motives, sectional jealousies, and the desire of the nobles of Northern France to reduce the power of the South and to profit by its wealth.

Years of warfare followed, with wholesale destruction. It is said that when one of the first cities to be taken, Beziers, was entered, and the Papal Legate was asked whether the Catholics should be spared, the latter, fearing that the heretics would feign orthodoxy to save their lives, commanded: "Kill them all, for God knows His own." Louis VIII of France (reigned 1223–1226), the son of Philip Augustus, pressed the crusade against the Albigenses. He was followed by Louis IX, who reigned from 1226 to 1270. Deeply religious, esteemed by the Middle Ages the ideal Christian monarch, Louis IX regarded himself as the champion of the Catholic faith and was quite willing to press the campaigns against heretics.

By the Treaty of Paris, in 1229, Count Raymond VII of Toulouse promised loyalty to the Catholic Church and to give his daughter in marriage to one of the king's brothers. This ended the crusade. In that same year, to make certain that the peace was effective, an ecclesiastical council at Toulouse outlined a stern procedure for the eradication of heresy in the South. Among other measures, the council forbade to the laity the possession of copies of the Bible, except the Psalms and such passages as were in the breviary, and condemned vernacular translations. It thus sought to remove one of the prevalent sources of heresy.

To aid in the suppression of the heresies resort was had not only to crusades but also to the Inquisition. In principle the Inquisition was not new. The very words *inquisitio* and *inquisitor* came from Roman law and, like so much else in canon law, were taken over from the Roman Empire. Now and again in earlier centuries persons accused of heresy had been tried by ecclesiastical or secular authorities and on some the death penalty had been inflicted. In theory the bishops had jurisdiction in detecting and punishing heretics, but in practice many, perhaps most, had been lax or indifferent. Opinion within the Church was not uniform nor were all civil rulers content to commit to the Church full jurisdiction over their subjects on such issues. To complete the work begun by the crusades and to eradicate whatever heresy remained, the Council of Toulouse of 1229 systematized and elaborated the inquisitorial process. Further developments were due to the then reigning Pope, Gregory IX, and additions and modifications were made by later Pontiffs. In other words, the trend, then marked, of strengthening the administrative and judicial control of the Papacy over the entire Western Church was extended to the systematic eradication of heresy. Early inquisitors were chosen largely from the Dominicans. Soon members of other mendicant orders, especially the Franciscans, were used.

In contrast with what had been the custom under the Roman civil law, in the practice of the Inquisition the accused was regarded as guilty until proved innocent and was not confronted with the witnesses against him. Torture might be employed. Eventually the system spread to most countries in Western Europe and usually had the support of the kings as well as of the ecclesiastical authorities.

As a result of the internal weaknesses and lack of cohesion of the heretical movements and of the action of the Catholics through the state, crusades, the preaching and teaching of the mendicant orders, the activities of some of the bishops, and the measures taken by the Inquisition, by the middle of the fourteenth century the heresies which had flourished in the twelfth and thirteenth centuries had largely died out.

We shall see how in the fourteenth and fifteenth centuries and especially in the sixteenth century fresh bursts of life in Western Europe led to the emergence of other movements which could not be contained within the Catholic Church. At the appropriate place we must raise and seek to answer the question why, in contrast with the earlier dissenting movements, those of the sixteenth century persisted and for the most part increased until in the nineteenth and twentieth centuries a major spread of the Christian faith was through them. To enter into that problem at this point would be premature, but we must not pass on from the "heresies" of the twelfth and thirteenth centuries without pausing to note it and to call attention to its importance.

Selected Bibliography

E. Comba, *Waldo and the Waldensians before the Reformation,* translated by T. E. Comba (New York, Robert Carter & Brothers, 1880, pp. 69). Contains extensive footnote references to the sources.

G. G. Coulton, *Inquisition and Liberty* (London, William Heinemann, 1938, pp. xiii, 354). Enormously learned, with a strong anti-Catholic slant.

D. L. Douie, *The Nature and Effect of the Heresy of the Fraticelli* (Manchester University Press, 1932, pp. xviii, 292). A scholarly study.

R. W. Emery, *Heresy and Inquisition in Narbonne* (Columbia University Press, 1941, pp. 184). Based largely upon local manuscript archives.

E. Holmes, *The Albigensian or Catharist Heresy. A Story and a Study* (London, Williams & Norgate, 1925, pp. 138). A popular survey.

H. C. Lea, *A History of the Inquisition of the Middle Ages* (New York, Harper & Brothers, 3 vols., 1888). A standard work of prodigious scholarship.

A. L. Maycock, *The Inquisition from Its Establishment to the Great Schism* (London, Constable & Company, 1927, pp. xxiii, 276). A Roman Catholic account, somewhat apologetic and defensive.

A. Monastier, *Histoire de l'Eglise Vaudoise depuis son Origine et des Vaudois du Piédmont jusqu'a Nos Jours* (Paris, Delay, 2 vols., 1847). By a Waldensian pastor.

A. Muston, *The Israel of the Alps. A Complete History of the Waldensees and Their Colonies; Prepared in Great Part from Unpublished Documents.* Translated by J. Montgomery (London, Blackie & Son, 2 vols., 1875). By a French Protestant pastor.

H. Nickerson, *The Inquisition. A Political and Military Study of Its Establishment* (Boston, Houghton Mifflin Co., 1923, pp. xvii, 258). A semi-popular, serious account, chiefly of the Albigensees and the Crusade and Inquisition invoked against them.

D. Phillips, *Beguines in Medieval Strasburg. A Study of the Social Aspect of Beguine Life* (Stanford University Press, 1941, pp. ix, 252). A doctoral dissertation.

A. S. Turberville, *Mediaeval Heresy & the Inquisition* (London, George Allen & Unwin, 1920, pp. vi, 264). The earlier part of the volume deals with this period.

E. Vacandard, *The Inquisition. A Critical and Historical Study of the Coercive Power of the Church.* Translated by B. L. Conway (New York, Longmans, Green & Co., 1926, pp. xiv, 195). By a Roman Catholic.

H. J. Warner, *The Albigensian Heresy* (London, Society for Promoting Christian Knowledge, 2 vols., 1922, 1928). Especially valuable for its extensive translations from the sources.

Chapter 20

THE EFFORT TO PURIFY THE ENTIRE
CHURCH, ESPECIALLY THROUGH
THE PAPACY

Could all Western Christendom be really Christian? More than once we have called attention to the problem. Western Europe had adopted the Christian name by mass action, usually tribe by tribe. Baptism had become a social convention. A vast distance separated the living of the ordinary Christian from the high demands of Jesus for discipleship. Could that distance be narrowed?

In the preceding two chapters we have noted efforts which deepened the living of minorities. Some were monastic. Others were non-monastic. Some remained within the Catholic Church. Others denounced the Catholic Church or were expelled from it as heretical. As the centuries passed these several kinds of movements increased in numbers and endeavoured to reach a larger proportion of the population. The earlier ones were primarily monastic, despaired of the world at large, and sought salvation by withdrawal from it. Those caught up in them lived either as hermits or in communities apart from the other dwellings of men. They regarded themselves as good Catholics and asked the approval of the Pope but were largely independent of the normal ecclesiastical structure of parishes and dioceses. Increasingly monastic movements appeared, notably but by no means exclusively the Franciscans and Dominicans, which strove to combine distinctive Christian living in communities with reaching and serving the entire population. They were paralleled by non-monastic movements, some of them heretical, which also endeavoured to win others to what they deemed conformity to the standards of Christ.

Contemporaneous with these minority efforts were men who hoped to raise the level of all Western Christendom through the geographically inclusive structure of the Catholic Church. With its parishes and their priests, its dioceses and bishops, all heading up in the Roman Pontiff, the Catholic Church could touch all those in Western Europe who called themselves Christians. There were those who strove to utilize this inclusive organism to produce a society which would fully conform to the Christian ideal and which would eventually embrace all mankind. Some of these dreamers were humble folk. Others were bishops whose efforts were confined chiefly to their own dioceses. Numbers were monks. Others were laymen or members of the secular clergy. Many sought to operate through synods, either regional or universal, or endeavoured to make of the Papacy an instrument for attaining this goal. Among the latter were some who occupied the Papal throne. Often secular rulers took a hand in the effort. But, as we are to see, repeatedly the ecclesiastical authorities clashed with nobles, kings, and emperors.

The dreamers worked against mountainous handicaps. As we have more than once noted, in the five or six centuries before the year 950, invasion had succeeded invasion and each wave had interrupted the recovery from its predecessor and had brought fresh disorder. Fighting was chronic. Commerce had dwindled. Crude agriculture was the major means of livelihood. After the hopeful Carolingian revival, learning had again declined. The emerging feudalism was dividing Europe into a multitude of political entities which combined with the wars and the bad state of the roads, piracy, and banditry to render an inclusive Christian fellowship extraordinarily difficult. That unity faced an additional obstacle in the existence of what were in effect tribal churches, in each of which the chieftain, whether under the title of king, count, or duke, strove for control and to that end sought to appoint to its leading positions men whom he could dominate. In one fashion or another, offices in the Church were bought and sold. The practice was called *simony,* from Simon Magus, who, according to *The Acts of the Apostles,* had offered to purchase of Peter the power to confer the Holy Spirit. A large proportion of the clergy were notoriously lax in their sex relations and were married or kept concubines. This was known as *nicolaitanism,* from a practice denounced in *The Revelation of John.*

The efforts of the reformers were directed in large part to the purification of the clergy from these abuses, for it was hopeless to seek to improve the quality of the spiritual and moral life of the masses if the pastors were corrupt. Many looked to the Papacy for leadership and to advance the reform sought to place worthy men upon the chair of Peter. They conceived of the Catholic Church as embracing all true Christians and as finding its unity by conforming to the Church of Rome and by submitting to the head of that church. Periodically, indeed almost chronically, Popes and many of the bishops and archbishops strove to free the Church from the control of lay lords. The most ambitious of the Popes endeavoured to dominate not only the ecclesiastical but also all other aspects of life, including especially the political.

The battle for the cleansing of the Catholic Church and the achievement of an ideal society was always being fought but was never won. The vision of making the Church worthy of the designation *Corpus Christi,* the body of Christ, and of Christendom a society which could be described as the *Corpus Christianum,* was not to be fully realized. Probably it could not be. The ideals set forth by Christ are too high to be reached within history. Throughout this period, as both before it and after it, the struggle was a continuing thread in the history of Christianity. Sometimes it was pushed with vigour and gains seemed to be made. At other times it was allowed to lag. Yet always consciences made sensitive by the demands of Christ were grieved by the gap between the ideal and the actual. Nearly always there were those who were nerved by their faith to seek to close it.

The movements for reform through the reinvigoration of the existing monastic institutions or the creation of new ones were usually closely interrelated with those for the improvement of Church and society as a whole. In its effects the Cluny revival spread far beyond the Cluny houses. The same was true of the Cistercians. As we have seen, Bernard of Clairvaux was outstanding in the affairs of the Church and one of his protégés from Clairvaux became Pope. It was not long after the birth of the Franciscans and Dominicans before members of those orders were occupying high places in the Church.

Early Reform Efforts by Bishops

Here is not the place even to name all the bishops who were active in trying to lift the level of Christian living in their dioceses. To enumerate them would extend these pages far beyond any reasonable length. As fairly typical of many we must pause to speak briefly of a few who were active early in this period. We must especially name two who, although in different countries, were contemporaries.

In England in the tenth century that recovery continued from the destruction from the Viking invasions which had been begun under Alfred the Great. To be sure, the land was later to be ruled from Denmark and in 1066 it was conquered by descendants of the Vikings, the Normans, but these alien monarchs did not deal the severe blows to orderly life and to the Church that had been given by their pagan predecessors. Part of the recovery was seen in the improvement of the religious life of the realm. This was through the reinvigoration of old monastic houses, the founding of new ones, and efforts to purify the life of the entire nation. Of the many who were both the children of the revival and aided it, Dunstan was outstanding. We have already met him as a leader in monastic reform.

Dunstan was born about 909 in the south of England. He was related to the royal house and members of his family had occupied important episcopal sees. He is a controversial figure, but from his youth until extreme old age, for he died in 988, when he was nearly eighty, he was influential in the Church, and in his maturity he was also outstanding in affairs of state. He was one of the most learned men in the realm. Indeed, as was so often the case in Western Europe in that age, the repute of his scholarship and mechanical skill led to a popular report that he was an adept in the black arts. He had force of character and initiative which aroused opposition but which also had the capacity to inspire others and to win their veneration and love. There was about him, too, an aura of authentic sanctity which made a profound impression on many.

In his youth, as a result of a severe illness, Dunstan became a monk. In his mid-thirties he was made Abbot of Glastonbury and the monastery which he built there became the centre of a religious awakening. He attracted able followers, some of whom in time became leaders in the Church. An unfriendly king exiled him to the Continent and there he came in touch with some of the new tides of life. Brought back to England in 957 by a new and devout young monarch, Dunstan became a leader in a widespread monastic revival which seems to have been modelled in part upon what he had seen on the Continent but which was also distinctively English. Appointed to the see of Worcester, he was soon transferred, or, to use a later technical term, "translated," to the see of London and then, as Archbishop of Canterbury, to the primacy of the entire Church in England. He did much for the political unification of England, strove to improve the administration of justice, and sought to win the Scandinavian elements. In the more strictly religious aspects of life he endeavoured to eradicate what was left of paganism, to improve the quality of the secular clergy, and to bring the entire body of laity to a higher moral and spiritual level. He was supported and supplemented by two other extraordinarily able and devoted monks who were made bishops. One of them, Oswald, of Danish ancestry, who lived on until 992, as Bishop of Worcester and then as Archbishop of York strove not only to further the monastic movement but also to be a father of all in his dioceses.

While the awakening in England was taking place, a somewhat similar advance was being registered in Germany. As we have seen, in 911, when the Carolingian line died out in that land, Conrad of Franconia was elected king, and was followed in 919 by Henry the Fowler, Duke of Saxony. Conrad was in close alliance with the Church, for an archbishop had been chiefly responsible for putting him on the throne and a bishop was his chief adviser. Henry the Fowler had little use for the Church. Henry the Fowler in turn was succeeded by his son, Otto I, "the Great," who was descended from Charlemagne in the female line and who, as we have recorded, reigned from 936 to 973 and in 962 was crowned Roman Emperor. Otto made extensive use of the Church. He strengthened the great bishoprics. Since they were non-hereditary, he could control the elections to them and make their incumbents his allies to offset the power of the hereditary lay nobility. He also used frontier dioceses to push forward German rule over the Slavs east of the Elbe. Under him there was a literary revival which centred at his court and which was led by Irish and English monks and by Greek and Italian scholars. Next came Otto II, son of Otto I. He reigned from 973 to 983 and died before he was thirty. Otto III, son of Otto II and a Byzantine princess, was brought to the throne at the age of three by his father's death and died in 1002 in his early twenties. Reared by his mother and under ecclesiastical influence, he purposed restoring the glory of the Roman Empire and was also very devout and deeply concerned for the welfare and purity of the Church. Henry II, who reigned from 1002 to 1024, was also genuinely religious. He was eventually canonized, along with his queen. While firm with the clergy he was generous with them and was an ardent furtherer of reform. Conrad II (reigned 1024–1039), a strong ruler, was politically rather than religiously minded. He was followed by Henry III (reigned 1039–1056), an extremely able monarch. Earnestly Christian, he was reinforced by a queen of similar convictions. Thoroughly committed to the Cluniac reforms, he fought simony, went on pilgrimages, and in 1043 proclaimed the Day of Indulgence, using it to announce forgiveness to his foes and to urge that his subjects follow his example. With such a succession of monarchs, several of them vigorous and seeking to strengthen the Church, and a few of them ardent reformers, it is not surprising that movements for improving the quality of Christian living should be making headway. To this also contributed the cessation of the destructive incursions of barbarians.

Revival in the Church did not come entirely or even primarily by the initiative of the monarchs. Nor, at the outset, was it from the movement which was associated with Cluny. In the first half of the tenth century, as we have seen, Gerhard as founder and abbot of a monastery at Brogne, south of Namur, in what is now Belgium, was the outstanding pioneer of an awakening which spread through much of Lotharingia, a territory which was roughly the region of the Rhine Valley. Reinforcement came, as we have also noted, especially from the monastery of Gorze, in the diocese of Metz, a centre in which the new life sprang up quite independently of both Brogne and Cluny. But it was not long before Cluny was also making its influence felt.

In the second half of the tenth century and the first half of the eleventh century this German reform movement was augmented by the enhanced position given the bishops by Otto I and by the zeal of Henry II and Henry III. Great prelates cleansed monasteries, built churches, promoted education, fostered art, and in other ways strove to improve the spiritual and moral life in their dioceses.

Among the best of these bishops was Bernward of Hildesheim, who, born about the year 960 and dying in 1022, was a contemporary of Dunstan. He was of noble Saxon stock, from a family which had provided several prominent Church officials. As a younger son he was reared for a high post in the Church and seems from the beginning to have had a genuine religious interest. Educated in the cathedral school at Hildesheim, the seat of a bishopric which had been planned by Charlemagne nearly two centuries earlier as part of his programme for pacifying and giving religious training to the Saxons, Bernward became a tutor of Otto III and was later a trusted friend of the zealous Henry II. He was made Bishop of Hildesheim and in that post built churches, fought nicolaitanism among his clergy, gathered relics, and promoted art and education. He was canonized in the century after his death.

THE REFORMING SPIRIT CAPTURES THE PAPACY

It was largely through the initiative of the German monarchs of the tenth and eleventh centuries that the Papacy was rescued from the low state into which it had fallen in the latter part of the ninth and the fore part of the tenth century. Like the Carolingians before him, Otto the Great succumbed to the lure of restoring the glories of the Roman Empire. Three times he led an expedition across the mountains. He assumed the throne of Italy and, as we have more than once reminded ourselves, in 962 was crowned Roman Emperor by the Pope. For centuries this imperial will-o'-the-wisp, this *ignis fatuus,* was to lure German monarchs to dissipate their strength south of the Alps and was to keep them from constructing a unified Germany comparable to the kingdoms of more limited territorial ambitions which were built by royal houses in other parts of Europe.

These German Holy Roman Emperors were a recurring and, indeed, a fairly constant factor in Papal affairs. In theory Christendom was to have two heads, both divinely commissioned, the one civil, the Emperor, and the other spiritual, the Pope. In practice it was the Papacy which exerted the geographically more extensive influence, but for nearly a century it was Otto the Great and those who followed him in the imperial office who were responsible for putting on the Papal throne most of the worthy Pontiffs of that period and who eventually made the revival dominant at the Papal court. However, that control was not quickly achieved. Not until Pope Leo IX, who held office from 1049 to 1054, was reform firmly seated. In the preceding ten decades the record was very chequered.

The details of the story of the steps by which, with the vigorous support of the German Holy Roman Emperors, the new element obtained control of the Papacy are confusing. We need not here attempt to recount them all. However, some of the more important features and incidents, together with a few of the main figures, must claim our attention.

When, in 961, Otto the Great made his second expedition into Italy, it was said to have been in response to an appeal from Pope John XII. John wished the protection of Otto against Berengar II, who as titular King of Italy constituted a threat. John XII was the son of Alberic and the grandson of Marozia, whom we have met earlier as prominent members of a family which for some time had controlled Rome and the Papacy. John XII was only in his teens when he became the head of the Church of Rome and was more devoted to the chase and to pandering to his passions than he was to the duties of the supposed head of Western Christendom. It was John XII who in 962 crowned Otto Roman Emperor. The two concluded an agreement, the *Privilegium Ottonis,* whereby Otto conceded to the Pope temporal jurisdiction over about three-fourths of Italy and the Romans were not to consecrate any one as Pope who did not take an oath of fealty to the Emperor. John XII soon fell out with Otto and the latter had him deposed and another elected in his place.

There ensued a struggle for the Papacy between the Romans on the one hand and successive German Emperors on the other. The former insisted on their traditional right to elect their bishop. The latter, impatient with the quality of the men so chosen, especially since it was by a populace now shrunk to small dimensions and swayed by local leaders who had scant regard for the Emperors, strove to put their own nominees on the Papal throne. For a time the Roman family Crescentius dominated the city and sought to have their creatures made Popes.

The contest lasted for several reigns with Popes and anti-Popes each claiming to be legitimate. In 985 he who went by the title of Boniface VII died suddenly, perhaps poisoned, and his body was dragged through the streets of Rome and left naked and unburied. In 996 the youthful and ardently religious Otto III had one of his relatives placed on the Papal throne as Gregory V, the first German to hold the office. On the latter's death, in 999, Otto obtained the election of his tutor, Gerbert, a Frenchman, reputed to be the most learned man of his age. As Sylvester II Gerbert laboured to eradicate simony and clerical marriage and concubinage, but the demise of his imperial patron (1002) left him without powerful support and within a few months he too was dead.

After two Crescentian Popes, a faction headed by the nearby Counts of Tusculum was in control in Rome and had its nominees placed in the See of Peter. One of these, Benedict VIII (reigned 1012–1024), who was of the family of the Counts of Tusculum, was a friend of the Abbot of Cluny and favoured reform. Indeed, he and the Holy Roman Emperor Henry II collaborated to that end. However, another of the Tusculan Pontiffs, Benedict IX, nephew of his two predecessors and who became Pope in 1032, is said to have been one of the most profligate ever to occupy the post and degradation seemed again to triumph. Opposition to him arose, partly through the Crescentian faction, and for a time there were three rivals in Rome, each claiming to be the lawful Pope. It is not surprising that earnest leaders in the monastic revival, such as Peter Damian, were scandalized and longed for a cleansing of the Augean stables.

Decisive change came through the intervention of Henry III, soon to be crowned Holy Roman Emperor. As we have seen, Henry III was deeply religious. In 1046 synods held at his instance and under his direction deposed two of the competing Popes and constrained the third to resign. Neither of the first two men whom Henry caused to be placed successively on the Papal throne lived long. The next whose election he obtained was Leo IX, who held the post from 1049 to 1054. Under Leo IX the tide of reform swept into the Papacy and held it.

Leo IX, elected in his mid-forties, was of a noble family of Alsace. As Bishop of Toul in Lorraine, he had already made a record as administrator, organizer, and reformer. The integrity of his character is attested by his eventual canonization. Chosen at an assembly at Worms, in Germany, at the instance of Henry III and with the concurrence of delegates from Rome, he would not assume the title and functions of Pope until, after reaching Rome, garbed as a humble pilgrim, his election was confirmed, as long custom required, by the people and clergy of the Eternal City. In other words, he would not consent to the Pope being a mere creature of the Emperor. A friend of the Abbot of Cluny and of Peter Damian, he could be counted on for vigorous measures. He travelled extensively in Italy and beyond the Alps, holding synods which took action against the purchase and sale of Church offices, insisted that bishops should not be appointed by lay lords but be elected by clergy and people, and commanded clerical celibacy. He did much to restore the prestige of the Papal see.

Leo IX broadened the scope of the Roman cardinalate by appointing to its ranks men of reforming zeal from outside the environs of Rome. He thus made it more representative of the Western Church as a whole and surrounded himself with men whom he could trust. The "cardinals" had been, as the name indicates, the leading clergy in and near Rome. They included the priests in the chief or "title" churches in Rome, the deacons in charge of the districts into which Rome had been divided in the third century for the administration of poor relief, and the bishops in the immediate neighborhood of the city. From them, quite naturally, had come the Pope's advisers. Originally the designation cardinal had not been confined to Rome but had been given to outstanding clergy anywhere in the Catholic Church. The action of Leo IX enhanced the position of the Roman cardinals in the Church at large, for it established the precedent of drawing into the inner circle of the Papal entourage and the central administration men of ability from any part of the Church regardless of their country.

Leo IX had difficulties with the Patriarch of Constantinople of which we are to speak later and which, in 1054, led to another stage in the separation of the Eastern and Western wings of the Catholic Church. He died in 1054 and was soon followed, in 1056, by the Emperor Henry III. The latter's six-year-old son came to the throne as Henry IV under a regency.

The Rising Power of the Reformed Papacy

The new spirit could not tolerate with complacency the continued control of the Papacy by the Holy Roman Emperors. Even though the latter had been largely responsible for putting strong men on the Papal throne, their action represented a domination by lay lords which threatened the secularization of the Church. To the ardent among the reformers this was simony. Their dream was a Christian society in which Church and secular rulers would coöperate, but in which the Church would be independent of the latter and, in case of a conflict of authority, would be supreme. To them this seemed inevitable logic, for, as they saw it, the Church was the custodian of the Gospel, its officers were accountable for the eternal welfare of the souls of their flocks, and in a social structure ordered by Christian principles theirs must be the decisive voice.

A struggle was to ensue, one in which the leaders of the Church, operating in the name of the power displayed in the crucifixion and resurrection of Christ, were to utilize the kind of power represented by the state. In so doing, although they acted from what seemed to them the highest of motives, they were to make of the Roman Catholic Church an hierarchical structure which was so nearly captured by this other kind of power that it became an enemy to the power seen in the cross and the empty tomb. Because of the methods which the reformers employed to purify the Church the evils against which they laboured came back with redoubled force. However, we are anticipating our story.

Following Leo IX there came two Popes, both favouring reform but both with too brief a tenure of office to make their purpose effective. On the death of the second, in 1058, the Tusculan faction attempted to reassert their control of the Papacy and put up a Pope of their own.

The return of the old subserviency of the Papacy to one or another of the coteries of Roman families was prevented by the decisive courage of a man who was to be the chief actor in the Papal scene for nearly three decades. This was Hildebrand.

HILDEBRAND EXALTS THE PAPACY

Hildebrand was born about the year 1025, possibly not far from Rome, and was reared in Rome. His ancestry is not clearly established, but he seems to have had aristocratic blood from both sides of his house. His mother was related to a family of bankers and had him educated in a monastery in Rome of which her brother was abbot and where the rule of Cluny was partly in force. In late youth he continued his education in the Lateran Palace, closely associated with the Papacy. He therefore knew Rome and the Papal curia intimately and in some of its most corrupt years. Although educated in a monastery, he did not become a monk until he was in his early twenties. He may have taken the step at Cluny. Also while in his early twenties he was for a time in Germany. He returned to Rome in the train of Leo IX. Leo admitted him to minor orders. He was likewise a friend of the earnest Peter Damian. His rise was not sudden. Swarthy, small of stature, slightly deformed, only his piercing glance gave physical evidence of the genius which lay within. A practical man of affairs, he was also deeply devout. We know very little of his inner life, but he clearly belonged with those who wished to purify the Church. By the time he was thirty-five he was being noted as a young man of promise.

In 1059 it was Hildebrand who was largely instrumental in obtaining the election of Nicholas II, thus defeating the efforts of the Roman nobility to revive their earlier control of the Papacy.

The brief pontificate of Nicholas II, for it lasted only from 1059 to 1061, was marked by momentous steps. In the chief of these, the enactment of highly important legislation determining the procedure for elections to the Papacy, Hildebrand appears to have had little part. Indeed, it was Humbert, a cardinal-bishop, who seems to have been chiefly responsible for them. A monk from the diocese of Toul and an exponent of the Lotharingian revival, he had written a treatise, *Adversus simonaicos,* in which he outlined a programme for the purging of the Church.

This new legislation was in the form of a Papal decree of 1059. It has come down to us in two different versions. The two agree that in the election the cardinals were to take the initiative, that in case disorders in Rome made a meeting in that city inadvisable, they might hold the election elsewhere, that if a suitable man could not be found in the Roman Church the Pope might be chosen from any other church, and that if war or intrigue prevented the Pope from being enthroned according to custom he might nevertheless exercise all the functions of his office. The two forms differed chiefly in that one required the cardinal-bishops to take the lead and gave little recognition to the Emperor, while the other made no distinction among the cardinals and required imperial consent to the person chosen. With modifications, the principles expressed in the decree still govern elections to the Papacy, namely, that the choice is to be by the cardinals, that the cardinals are not required to meet in Rome, that the Pope need not be a Roman, and that, in case of necessity, he may exercise his functions from some other centre than Rome. Although still the Bishop of Rome and holding his place in the Catholic Church because of that fact, he was made more representative of the Western wing of the Catholic Church as a whole and was not as subject to the factional strife in the city of Rome as had been all too often the case in the preceding three or four generations. The reform wave had captured the Papacy.

The death of Nicholas II in 1061, preceded as it was by a few weeks by that of Cardinal Humbert, deprived the reformers of two outstanding leaders. Hildebrand now stepped into the breach. Utilizing the procedure for Papal elections which had been promulgated in 1059, he brought together in Rome the cardinals and other leading churchmen. At his instance and by his prompt action, they elected to the Papacy a friend of Peter Damian, who took the title of Alexander II and held the post from 1061 to his death in 1073. The Roman nobles, wishing to revive their control of the Papacy, collaborated with the bishops of Lorr' irdy, who disliked the reform movement, and sent a delegation to Germany to ask Henry IV, still a child of eleven years, to appoint one of their friends, an Italian bishop, Cadalus, to the post. The regency, glad of an opportunity to assert the traditional practice of the German kings in controlling the Papal succession, had the young Henry give his approval. Thus the Roman nobles and the German monarchy combined to frustrate the reformers' efforts for the independence of the Papacy of the secular arm. For almost the entire reign of Alexander II Cadulus was an annoying rival. Part of the battle was fought in Rome itself with the use of arms on both sides. Tortuous and complicated diplomacy was involved, with the lavish use of money by both sides to purchase the favour of the Roman populace. In the struggle Hildebrand was deeply involved. Thanks in part to him, Alexander II maintained his authority.

Alexander II proved to be an able Pope, and while he owed much to Hildebrand, his achievements were by no means due entirely to the latter. Nor was Peter Damian, who was also one of his advisers, to be credited with more than a fraction of the advances made under this pontificate. Indeed, Damian, fiery advocate of reform though he was, did not prove to be as wise in counsel as Hildebrand. Under Alexander II substantial progress was registered towards the realization of the dream of rendering the Papal power effective in all aspects of the life of Western Europe. In the political realm Alexander II compelled young Henry IV, potentially the mightiest monarch in that region, to surrender his purpose to divorce his wife. He gave his approval to William the Conqueror's conquest of England and to the invasion of Sicily by the Normans of Southern Italy. In each instance he sent a gonfalon, or standard, which he blessed, to be carried by the army. In the ecclesiastical realm he deposed the Bishop of Florence on the charge of simony, he aided William the Conqueror in putting Norman bishops in English sees, he induced the mighty Lanfranc, now Archbishop of Canterbury, to come to Rome to receive the *pallium* instead of sending it to him, as Lanfranc had requested, and he humbled the proud Archbishop of Cologne by compelling him to enter Rome walking, and barefooted. Legates appointed by the Holy See intervened again and again in ecclesiastical affairs in various countries. Appeals to Rome were encouraged from the wide reaches of the Church. Alexander II made his power felt in Denmark, only recently won to the Christian faith. In portions of Spain under Christian rulers he obtained action against simony and clerical marriage and encouraged the substitution of the Roman liturgy for the local Mozarabic liturgy which had long been in use in the peninsula. Alexander II was engaged in a head-on conflict with Henry IV over the control of the appointment to the important Archbishopric of Milan when death removed him from the scene and bequeathed that contest to his successor.

Hildebrand as Pope Gregory VII

That successor was Hildebrand. Hildebrand was the sole survivor of the band of able reformers who had gathered about Leo IX, for Peter Damian had died a few weeks before. At the funeral of Alexander II in the great church of St. John Lateran the crowd began to shout "Hildebrand for our Bishop." The mob carried him forcibly across the city to St. Peter's and there, with scant regard for the procedure which had been prescribed by Nicholas II and which he himself had supported, the cardinals hurried through the election with the consent of the bishops, abbots, monks, and laity, and, although only a deacon, Hildebrand was enthroned and took the title of Gregory VII. Not as great a man as Pope Gregory I, of whom he was a student and ardent admirer, he was to make the Papal power more widely felt and more potent in Church and state than had that distinguished predecessor. His reign, which, lasting as it did from 1073 to 1085, was only two years less than that of the latter, was like that other, one of the high-water marks of the Papacy.

Gregory VII's conception of the Papal office was sweeping. In its most inclusive form it is expressed in the *Dictatus Papae,* which was probably his own work, although it has sometimes been ascribed to others. Whether or not it had Gregory as its author, that document undoubtedly reflected his mind. It defined the Papal position in twenty-seven affirmations. Among them the following stand out: the Roman Church was founded by God; the Roman Pontiff alone deserves the title "universal"; he alone can depose or reinstate bishops; he alone may use the imperial insignia; he is the only man whose feet princes must kiss; he can depose emperors; he may transfer a bishop from one see to another; he may divide rich bishoprics and unite the poor ones; he has the power to ordain a cleric of any church and he who is ordained by him may not receive a higher grade from any other bishop; no synod can be called general without his authorization; a sentence passed by him cannot be reversed by any one except himself; he may be judged by no one; to him should be referred the important cases of every church; the Roman Church has never erred, nor will it err to all eternity; he who is not at peace with the Roman Church shall not be considered Catholic; the Roman Pontiff may absolve subjects from their allegiance to wicked men. Many of these claims were not new, but never had they been expressed in more positive fashion.

It is important and significant that these and the others of the twenty-seven points dealt with what in the broadest sense of that term was the administrative and disciplinary position of the Pope. In other words, in promoting the health of the Catholic Church the Papacy's function was to ensure correctness of doctrine and effective executive and judicial action. The tides of life upon which, in the last analysis, the vitality of the Church, as of any religious body, depended must be looked for elsewhere. We have seen them coming through monasticism, which the Pope and hierarchy accepted, and through movements which the Papacy and the hierarchy deemed subversive. Some of the Popes, including Hildebrand, were regarded as exemplary Christians and were eventually canonized. Presumably they would be channels for renewals of vigour in the Church. However, they constituted a minority of the Popes and a very small minority of the officially recognized saints. Administration, by an autocratic hierarchy heading up in the Pope, could not produce that vigour. At the most it could remove handicaps to it by the negative procedure of purging the Church of such moral abuses and doctrinal aberrations as were amenable to executive and judicial action.

Gregory put the Papal claims into effect. He compelled archbishops to come to Rome to receive the *pallium* as the mark of their office and to maintain contact with the Holy See. He strove to keep all bishops dependent on the Pope and stood against their appointment and investiture by lay princes. He not only sent out legates on special missions, as had his predecessors, but he also appointed some men to be his resident representatives in particular regions and countries, thus ensuring closer supervision from Rome and the enforcement of the Papal edicts. He held frequent councils in Rome and through legates encouraged and supervised provincial councils to enforce his measures. He sought to stamp out simony and clerical marriage and concubinage. He ruled the Papal states in Italy. He claimed suzerainty, in the feudal sense of that term, over some of the Norman princes in Italy, over Aragon in Spain, Hungary, the kingdom of Kiev, and the kingdom of Croatia-Dalmatia. In some instances this suzerainty was created at the request of princes who thereby sought legal recognition for their position. He endeavoured to bring under the control of Rome the churches in the newly converted countries of Denmark, Norway, Poland, Bohemia, and Hungary.

Gregory's greatest and most famous struggle was with Henry IV. It was prolonged and intricate. We must not take the space to go into it in detail, but it was so important that we must note its outstanding features. The issue was central in the programme of the reformers, the independence of the Church from the control of the laity. Its focus was the right of investiture. In Germany, thanks largely to the policy initiated by Otto the Great to offset the power of the hereditary lay princes, the bishops and archbishops had become great territorial magnates. To control them, the monarch insisted upon the right of appointing them and of compelling them to swear fealty to him. This the reformers would not tolerate, for it seemed to them to be diverting the bishops from their proper functions, the spiritual oversight of their flocks, and to make of them secular princes with predominantly secular interests.

The issue between Gregory VII and Henry IV was first joined over the Archbishopric of Milan, a dispute which had begun under Gregory's predecessor. In the spring of 1075 a synod at Rome had come out afresh against lay investiture, thus denying Henry any part in creating bishops. Later in that year Henry made an appointment to the Archbishopric of Milan. In December, 1075, Gregory took him to task not only for this act but also for some other episcopal appointments. In January, 1076, Henry IV, after a council of German nobles and bishops at Worms, denounced Gregory as "not Pope, but false monk," and demanded that he descend from the Papal throne. In this he was joined by a number of German and Italian prelates, who declared that Gregory had perjured himself by not abiding by an oath which he was said to have given to Henry III not to ascend the Papal throne or permit any one else to do so without the consent of that monarch or his son. Accordingly, they renounced their allegiance to him.

Gregory countered, in February, 1076, by deposing Henry, forbidding any one to serve him as king, and anathematizing him. Here was the most drastic step which any Pope had thus far taken in the political realm, the attempted dethroning of the mightiest monarch of Western Christendom. Henry's enemies in Germany seized the occasion to ask Gregory to preside at an assembly of the German notables at Augsburg in February, 1077, for either the condemnation or absolution of Henry. Pope Gregory accepted and prepared to go to Germany. To forestall Gregory and the proposed assembly, Henry hastened to Italy in the dead of winter, sought out the Pope, who, for fear of violence from Henry, had taken refuge in the friendly fortress of Canossa, and there for three days stood barefoot, in a penitent's garb, before the castle gate, asking mercy. Pressed by some of his supporters, including the Abbot of Cluny, Gregory relented and granted Henry absolution in return for the latter's solemn oath to do justice according to the Pope's judgement or to conclude peace according to his counsels. Henry had won a tactical victory, but the memory of his abject submission at Canossa remained as a vivid demonstration of Papal power.

In spite and in part because of the startling episode of Canossa, Henry IV emerged victor. To be sure, Henry's enemies in Germany rose in revolt and elected a rival king, and in 1080 Gregory, reluctantly taking sides, again declared Henry deposed. But Henry had a synod pronounce Hildebrand deposed and elect a Pope in his place, invaded Italy, entered Rome, and had him whom he had made Pope crown him Emperor (1084), while Gregory VII, still unyielding, helplessly kept within the walls of the castle of San Angelo in Rome. Normans from the south came to Gregory's relief, took Rome, and carried him off with them (1084). The following year (1085) Hildebrand died in exile at Salerno, apparently a beaten man.

HILDEBRAND'S SUCCESSORS CONTINUE THE BATTLE FOR REFORM

Hildebrand's seeming defeat did not halt the work of reform. His immediate successors continued in the path which he had followed. This was not without opposition. Henry IV insisted on controlling the bishops until his forced abdication, in 1105. Some of the bishops came out for the imperial position. From time to time rival Popes were set up.

The son of Henry IV continued his father's struggle until what proved to be a working compromise was reached, in 1122, a generation after the death of Hildebrand, in the Concordat of Worms, between Henry V and Pope Calixtus II. By that agreement elections of bishops and abbots in Germany were to take place in the presence of the Emperor, but according to church law and without simony or violence. In case of dispute the Emperor was to give his judgement after consultation with the metropolitan and other bishops of the ecclesiastical province. Nothing was said about the imperial presence being necessary at elections in Italy. Investiture with ring and staff, the symbols of spiritual authority, was relinquished by the Emperor to the Church. In return, the Pope agreed that investiture with the temporal possessions attached to the office was to be by the Emperor and should carry with it such obligations to the Emperor as legally went with it. The Concordat of Worms did not end the conflict between Popes and Emperors. We shall meet it again later in the twelfth century.

In spite of the chronic friction between the two centralizing powers of Western Europe, the Pope and the Emperor, Roman Pontiffs, inspired by the purpose of raising the moral and spiritual level of all Christendom, continued to labour to make the dream a reality. This was true of Pope Urban II, who came to the Papal throne in 1088, only three years after the death of Hildebrand, and held it until 1099. A scion of a noble family, he had been educated under the direction of Bruno, the founder of the Carthusians, had been a monk at Cluny, and had been made Cardinal Bishop of Ostia by Gregory VII. Deeply religious, thoroughly committed to reform, experienced in administration, he was fully as courageous as Gregory VII and as convinced of the right of the See of Peter to supremacy, but was less tactless. Nourished as he had been in the Cluny tradition, he vigorously and persistently fought the purchase and sale of church offices, condemned admitting to major orders any who were not celibates, and opposed the lay investiture of church offices. By extending the Papal control over monasteries he augmented the power of the Holy See as against the bishops and lay princes. He excommunicated King Philip I of France for putting aside his wife to marry the wife of one of his vassals. In his struggle with Henry IV inherited from Gregory VII, he excommunicated the Emperor. In initiating the First Crusade as an enterprise of all Western Christendom he added to the prestige of the Papacy. The Council of Clermont, held in 1095, over which Urban II presided, and which was the scene of the launching of the Crusade, also took other important actions. It renewed earlier Papal decrees against simony, nicolaitanism, and lay investiture. It ordered deposed all non-celibate priests, deacons, and sub-deacons. No fees were to be asked for confirmation, extreme unction, or burials. No one was to receive any ecclesiastical office from a layman. No bishop or other cleric was to take a feudal oath of loyalty to a king or any other lay lord.

We must pause to remark that one result of the First Crusade and its successors was the enhancement of the prestige and power of the Popes. The Crusades were begun by the Papacy. No Crusade was valid without Papal endorsement. The Crusades were an additional and important channel through which the Popes asserted, and often effectively, their leadership of Christendom.

One other action of the Council of Clermont requires special note, not because it was new but because it is illustrative of a persistent attempt by the Church to bring society to a closer approximation to Christian standards. That was to enforce the Peace of God. The Peace of God and the Truce of God were efforts by the ecclesiastical authorities to reduce the destructiveness of the wars between feudal lords which were chronic during these centuries.

The Peace of God had been first attempted towards the end of the tenth century as a local project in France. At the outset it sought to exempt from attack by the combatants all persons and places consecrated by the Church—clergy, monks, virgins, churches, and monasteries—and to estop fighting on Sundays. Exemption was later also claimed for all those protected by the Church, such as the poor, pilgrims, crusaders, and merchants on their journeys. The Peace of God spread and had the endorsement of many synods and bishops. To enforce it numbers of dioceses formed what were known as confederations of peace.

The Truce of God dated from early in the eleventh century. At first it forbade fighting from Saturday night to Monday morning. Later it was extended to the days of the week connected with central events in the life of Christ, to Thursday as ascension day, to Friday as the day of the crucifixion, to Saturday, when Christ's body lay in the tomb, and to Advent and Lent. The penalty for violation of the Truce of God was excommunication. Like the Peace of God, the Truce of God spread from France to Germany and Italy. Never fully enforced, it exercised some restraint upon the disorders of the times.

In an attempt to curb war, the Church also endeavoured to eliminate jousts and tournaments, since these gave popularity to private feuds and the shedding of blood. For instance, in 1139 the Second Lateran Council (called the tenth ecumenical council by the Western Church) forbade them.

THE REFORM MOVEMENT SPREADS IN VARIOUS COUNTRIES

As we have again and again said or hinted, it was not only through the Papacy that efforts were made to bring the rank and file of Western Christendom to a closer approximation to the standards set forth by the Christ and the apostles. We have seen how in the early years of the reform movement, before it had captured the Papacy, it was being carried forward by bishops, usually bishops who were monks or who had been profoundly influenced by monastic revivals. Similarly, as the reform gathered momentum, it found expression on the national level, partly through Papal legates, partly through outstanding bishops, and partly through monasteries and local or regional synods. We must here take a moment to hint at some of the reforms in particular regions and nations.

Early in the twelfth century, substantial advance was made in France in curbing simony, the violation of clerical celibacy, and the control of the Church by lay lords. At times the king, in his struggle to increase the royal power at the expense of the nobility, while himself insisting on a voice in the naming of bishops, endeavoured to restrain the domination of the Church by his great vassals. Many of the feudal gentry, moreover, surrendered, apparently voluntarily, the authority which they had possessed to name the priests for the parishes in their domains. Here and there better bishops appeared, more devoted than their immediate predecessors to the spiritual and moral care of their clergy and their laity.

In Germany and North Italy the prolonged struggle between Popes and Emperors militated against reforms. In Germany, however, we read of bishops who were diligent in preaching and who encouraged the parish priests to visit the sick among their flocks, faithfully administer the sacraments, and give religious instruction to their flocks. In Germany diocesan synods seem to have been frequent. We also hear of religious literature in German for the masses—hymns, long poems setting forth Biblical stories and the drama of salvation, and translations of Latin works of theology. In Germany, as elsewhere, painting and sculpture were employed to depict themes from the Bible and the lives of the saints, thus making them vivid to the illiterate who could not have access to them through the written page.

Hungary, only recently the scene of the conversion of the Magyars and the emergence of a Christian monarchy, saw several reforming councils in the early years of the eleventh century.

The measures associated with the name of Hildebrand also penetrated to England. Here the Norman kings had insisted upon controlling the Church. William the Conqueror had endeavoured to use his authority to improve the quality of the Church and had seen to it that the ranking archbishopric of England, that of Canterbury, was filled by Lanfranc, who had become outstanding as a teacher in the monastery of Bec and who was a champion of the Cluniac reforms. Lanfranc pushed those reforms in England. Wulfstan or Wulstan (c.1007 or c.1012–1095), who as Bishop of Worcester was the one pre-Conquest prelate who was permitted to retain his see under the Normans, was a spiritual child of the Dunstan movement and was canonized by Pope Innocent III. Anselm, also of Bec, who on the insistence of King William II succeeded Lanfranc as Archbishop of Canterbury and held the post from 1093 to 1109, had a prolonged struggle with William II and Henry I in an effort, mixed in its outcome, to achieve the independence of the Church from royal domination and to insist upon its close subordination to the Pope. Under the civil strife which marked the reign of the weak Stephen the Church wrested concessions from the king. Henry II attempted to restore the royal authority over the Church and in doing so came into conflict with Thomas Becket whom he himself had placed in the Archbishopric of Canterbury. The contest reached its climax in 1170, in the murder of Becket. That tragedy made of the latter

England's most popular saint of the period and enabled the Pope to obtain recognition of the claims of the Church for which Becket had died.

The Improvement in Various Aspects of the Morals of the Laity

Through education and legislation the ecclesiastical authorities endeavoured to lift the various aspects of life more nearly to the Christian ideal. We have already noted the attempt to reduce the destructiveness of war by the Peace of God and the Truce of God. The reform movement of the tenth and eleventh centuries also sought to induce the warrior to govern his conduct by Christian principles. Thus when the young noble reached his majority and formally assumed his arms, the Church blessed his sword with the prayer that he would use it to defend churches, the widows, the orphans, and all the servants of God. Thus arose chivalry, the code of the Christian warrior of gentle birth. Additions were made to it as the years passed. It demanded that the knight keep his plighted word and be loyal to his lord. He was to fight against the infidel and when death came was to make his confession and receive the communion. The *Chanson de Roland,* composed in the first half of the eleventh century, was a poetic form of a legend of a much earlier struggle against the Moslem in Spain which helped the wide circulation of some phases of the ideal. Even more striking were the accounts of Arthur and his Knights of the Round Table which in the dress that they were given late in the twelfth century idealized Christian chivalry. The story of Parzival (Perceval), an ancient folk tale, as it was put into poetry by Wolfram von Eschenbach late in the twelfth or early in the thirteenth century centered around the Holy Grail (the platter or the cup used by Christ at the last supper), suffering, atonement, and the knightly virtues, and was a notable expression of the standard set up for the Christian knight.

The Church sought to purify marriage and sex relations for the laity at large. In feudal society, not yet recovered from the demoralization of the centuries-long series of invasions and plagued by chronic fighting, sex relations were notoriously lax. Kings and nobles divorced their wives almost with impunity and spawned illegitimate children. With such examples at the top, the masses could not be expected to be much better. At the end of the eleventh and the fore part of the twelfth century, as a part of the general wave of reform, synods and canon lawyers sought, so far as legislation could do it, to enforce continence and render divorce difficult. Here and there efforts were made to give stability to the families of slaves.

The Church also strove to bring the economic phase of society to conform with what it deemed Christian standards. For instance, it forbade the taking of interest.

THE PAPACY ATTAINS ITS HEIGHT AS A COMPREHENSIVE LEGISLATIVE AND ADMINISTRATIVE STRUCTURE

In the last half of the twelfth and the fore part of the thirteenth century the Papacy reached the high point of its power in Western Europe. Never before had its influence been so strong in so many aspects of the life of that region. Never again did it make its weight felt so potently in so many phases of the culture of that area.

This apex of Papal might came as a climax to the religious revival which had captured the Holy See. It also paralleled the crest of the urge to attain the perfect Christian life which had expressed itself both through monasticism and in movements which the Church deemed heretical and which had culminated on the one hand in the emergence of the mendicant orders and on the other hand in the Albigensees and Waldensees. With it, too, were associated the growth of commerce and intellectual developments, including the rise of universities and the flowering of scholastic theology of which we are to speak in the next chapter. This coincidence of several movements seems to have been more than fortuitous. Precisely what was cause and what was effect we may not know, but that all were closely allied features of a particular stage in the history of Europe is certain.

It seems also significant that the Papacy and the Holy Roman Empire reached a climax not far from the same time. The struggle between Pope and Emperor continued and in some respects was intensified. Both contestants were reinforced by the revival of scholarship and with it the study of law.

The development of canon law attained a high point in the *Decretum* of Gratian, compiled about the middle of the twelfth century. Canon law, or the law of the Church, had its roots in the first century, but has been the product of a development which has been in progress from then until the present. Gratian's was by no means the first treatise on it. Many collections had been made, notably in the tenth and eleventh centuries. The *Decretum* of Gratian was in part a compilation, but it was more. It embodied the considered opinions of the author. Since Gratian had his spiritual fellowship with one of the strictest groups of the revival of the Benedictine rule with its passion for the reform of the Church, it was natural that he should exalt the position of the Pope. He was a master of his subject, did his work at Bologna, the main centre of the awakening interest in both canon and civil law, and his *magnum opus* was long regarded as standard.

On the other hand, the renewed study of Roman law, especially in the compilations made under Justinian which had been introduced to Bologna early in the twelfth century and which had spread to other centres, exalted the position of the Emperor. It was the Emperor as absolute monarch who was prominent in the Justinian code, and Justinian and the stronger among his Christian predecessors had often been dominant in ecclesiastical affairs. Civil lawyers, therefore, would tend to declare that any imperial edict, even in Church matters, should be obeyed.

Italy was deeply divided by the struggle. Two parties, Guelphs and Ghibellines, were prominent in Italian politics and civil strife between them was chronic. The Guelphs upheld the independence of the Church as against the Emperor and also stood for the autonomy of Italian cities, since these had less to fear from the Pope than from the Emperor. The Ghibellines supported the authority of the Emperor.

By the close of the thirteenth century both the Papacy and the Holy Roman Empire had passed the crest of their power. Neither was ever fully to recover the position which it had held in Western Europe. For the Empire the decline was to be permanent. Technically the Holy Roman Empire survived until early in the nineteenth century. The title of Emperor long added prestige to him who held it. Yet the time of its glory had passed. The efforts of the German monarchs who held it to make it effective south of the Alps was long to prevent the unification of Germany and Italy. After more than two centuries of decline, under new conditions the Papacy was to rise to a far wider geographic influence than at any earlier time. Yet that influence was exerted in a fashion different from that which had been seen in its great era which followed the triumph of the eleventh and twelfth century reformers and never again was it to achieve a full recovery in North-western Europe.

Even after the medieval Papacy and Empire had passed their peak, the contest between the two did not immediately cease. Indeed, as the authority of the Emperors waned, some of the most forceful and intellectually powerful treatises in its defense appeared. Thus early in the fourteenth century Dante Alighieri, the greatest poet of his age, wrote his *Monarchia,* in which he maintained that a universal monarchy is necessary for the peace and welfare of mankind, that this had been conferred upon the people of Rome, and that the Emperor held his authority directly from God and not through the Pope. While Dante declared that the Emperor must reverence the Pope, it is not surprising that the latter placed the *Monarchia* upon the index of forbidden books.

In the opening years of the fourteenth century John of Paris, a Dominican, wrote a treatise on the relationship between royal and Papal powers in which he placed restrictions on the latter but sought a balance between the two.

Much more radical and devastating was the *Defensor Pacis,* completed in 1324 by Marsilius of Padua and John of Jandun. Marsilius (Marsiglio Mainardino), an Italian physician and for a brief time Rector of the University of

Paris, was an ardent Ghibelline. John of Jandun, a Frenchman, was an out-standing teacher in the University of Paris. The *Defensor Pacis* attacked the claims of the Papacy to supremacy in state and Church. It had no use for the idea of a universal Christian empire. It held that there must be many states, each based upon the law inherent in nature, and that the Church should not have jurisdiction over them. The law for the several states was to be made by assemblies of all male adult citizens. The executive, which might be either one man or a council, was to be elected by the assembly and was to have authority over all other executive and judicial authorities. The *Defensor Pacis* maintained that since Christ did not claim temporal power but submitted himself and his property to the state and since, in accordance with his commands, the apostles did likewise, the clergy must hold to that example. It taught that the clergy must follow the way of absolute poverty, and that they and the Church must have no temporal authority. It came out sharply against the claims of the Papacy. It held that in the early Church there was no distinction between priests and bishops, and that all the bishops were equal and were all successors of the apostles. To obtain united action in the Church, the *Defensor Pacis* advocated the holding of general councils made up of priests and laymen elected by the voting assemblies of each of the states, assemblies which, as we have seen, were to be composed of all adult male citizens. Papal supremacy was attacked, with its emphasis upon the privileges of the clergy and its claim of suzerainty over the Holy Roman Empire. The canon law was denounced. It is not surprising that the Pope condemned the book even more emphatically than he did Dante's *Monarchia*. The *Defensor Pacis* was quite impracticable, but it was not without effect.

In the first half of the fourteenth century an earnest Franciscan, William of Ockham (Occam), whom we shall meet again as an outstanding theologian, advocated the independence of the state from the Church. He held as un-necessary Papal confirmation of the election of an Emperor or the investiture of an Emperor by a Pope. The Pope, he said, should be subject to the Emperor in secular matters. Ockham also insisted that the Papacy is not a necessary form of government for the Church. He declared that the Scriptures do not teach that Christ appointed Peter as the prince of the apostles. He held that not the Pope but only the Scriptures are infallible and that Popes may fall into error and be deposed. He taught that even the college of cardinals or a general council of the Church may err.

GREAT POPES OF THE TWELFTH CENTURY

Here is not the place for a complete list of the Pontiffs under whom the Papacy attained its greatest power. We must, however, pause to mention those who were outstanding. Some of them reigned in the twelfth century.

Innocent II (1130–1143), supported by Bernard of Clairvaux, was dominant as against the Holy Roman Emperors of his reign and triumphed over two rivals who claimed the Papacy. He told the bishops that they held their sees of him as vassals held their fiefs of their sovereigns and that they could not retain them without his consent.

Eugene III, a pupil of Bernard of Clairvaux, was in office from 1145 to 1153. It was he who appointed Bernard to preach the Second Crusade. He demonstrated the authority of the Papacy over the Church by deposing the powerful Archbishops of York, Mainz, and Rheims for disobedience. He strengthened the prestige of the Pope in distant Scandinavia. He reformed abuses in France. Yet for a time he was driven from Rome by the republic which had as one of its officials that Arnold of Brescia who had denounced the temporal power of the Papacy.

Adrian IV (1154–1159), who, as we have seen, was the only Englishman to sit on the Papal throne, was able to expel Arnold from Rome and was stout in his maintenance of Papal authority against the mighty Frederick Barbarossa. Frederick I (Barbarossa), who was German King from 1152 to his drowning on a Crusade in 1190, had been crowned Emperor in 1155, emulated Charlemagne, and was one of the strongest of the Holy Roman Emperors. He sought to make good the claims of the Emperors as against the Popes and during much of his reign carried on the traditional struggle.

Alexander III, Pope from 1159 to 1181, was an expert in canon law, and further augmented the power of the Holy See over secular princes and the Church. This he did in spite of the fact that during almost all his reign he had to contend with a succession of rivals who were set up by the opposition and that he came into head on collision with the ambitious and able Frederick Barbarossa. The latter was defeated and in a memorable scene at Venice in 1177 knelt and kissed Alexander's feet. Alexander took advantage of the murder of Thomas Becket to obtain recognition from Henry II of England of some of the Church's claims. Appeals to Rome increased, together with the nomination by the Papal Curia of bishops and holders of benefices in many parts of Europe. At the third Lateran Council (counted as the eleventh ecumenical council by the Western Church), held in Rome in 1179, further measures were taken for reform.

It was Alexander III who commanded that in the future canonization should be only with the authority of the Roman Church. Earlier, individual bishops had formally recognized the cults which had arisen around particular individuals who because of their character, their virtues, and the miracles believed to have been performed through them had become those by whose intercession God was approached. Abuses had crept in, and Alexander decreed that henceforward none should be officially enrolled among the saints without Papal consent. Not all the bishops obeyed and it was the seventeenth century before a Papal bull finally succeeded in reserving canonization to the Holy See.

INNOCENT III

The climax of the Papacy is usually regarded as having been reached under Lotario de' Conti di Segni who under the title Innocent III reigned 1198 to 1216. Of aristocratic Lombard lineage on his father's side and of the Roman nobility on his mother's side, he was born not far from Rome in 1160 or 1161. Educated in Paris, the main centre for the study of philosophy and theology, and at Bologna, noted for its emphasis on law, Innocent III was one of the most learned men of his day and was equipped in both theology and canon law. Made a cardinal-deacon at the age of twenty-nine by Pope Clement III, who is said to have been his uncle, he was early in the central administrative machinery of the Holy See. Because the next Pope, Celestine III, was of a rival Roman family, the young cardinal was out of favour for seven years. On the very day of the death and funeral of Celestine III, although not yet forty years of age and only in deacon's orders, he was hurriedly but unanimously elected to the vacant see by his fellow-cardinals and was enthusiastically acclaimed by the clergy and people of Rome. After a decent interval he was ordained priest and consecrated bishop.

A man of singleness of purpose, iron will, and great executive and diplomatic ability, Innocent III brought the Papacy to the apex of its influence in the political life of Europe and markedly extended its administrative control of the Church. A prodigious worker, he drove his own body mercilessly. To curb a fever he is said to have subsisted for some time chiefly on lemons. It may be significant, however, that in contrast with such predecessors as Leo I, Gregory I, and Gregory VII, who were, like himself, distinguished for enlarging the power of the Papacy, he has never been canonized. Nor, unlike the first two, has the designation "Great" ever been associated with his name. Perhaps that was because he was too prone to use the worldly tools in his effort to make actual the City of God. Yet he clearly recognized the distinctive Christian virtues and could speak most feelingly of them and of the life of the spirit.

Innocent III had an exalted conception of the position and mission of the Papacy. There seems to have been in it little if anything that was really new or that had not been asserted by some among his predecessors. Yet in letters, sermons, and other pronouncements he gave it forcible expression. He dreamed of Christendom as a community in which the Christian ideal was to be attained under Papal guidance. As the successor of Peter, the Pope, so Innocent held, had authority over all the churches. On at least one occasion, moreover, he declared that as Pope he was the vicar of him of whom it had been affirmed that he was king of kings and lord of lords. He wrote that Christ "left to Peter the governance not of the Church only but of the whole world." He also said that Peter was the vicar of Him whose is the earth and the fullness thereof, the world and they that dwell therein. How far he believed this to mean that the Pope should be a temporal ruler is in dispute. He certainly made his weight felt in affairs of state, especially but by no means exclusively in Italy. He conceded that kings were given certain functions by divine commission, but he held that God had ordained both the pontifical and the royal power, as he had the sun and the moon, and that as the latter draws its light from the former, so the royal power derives its dignity and splendour from the pontifical. Moreover, as a true successor of the great reforming Popes, Innocent insisted that the power of the secular ruler did not extend to the clergy, but that the clergy were to be independent of the law of the state and subject only to the Church.

Several features of the times combined to facilitate or to call forth by their challenge the exercise of the powers claimed by Innocent III for the Papacy. As we have earlier seen, his tenure of that office coincided with a swelling tide of religious life which displayed itself in the emergence of the Franciscans, the Dominicans, and other mendicant orders and in the prevalence of the Waldensees and the Cathari. The wealth of Europe was mounting. The Holy Roman Empire was declining. The Emperor Henry VI, the able son and successor of Frederick Barbarossa, had been a serious threat to the Papacy, for by his marriage with the heiress of the Norman kings who had ruled in Sicily and South Italy he controlled both the north and the south of that land and made it difficult for the Roman Pontiff to play off the one against the other as he had long been able to do. However, Henry VI died the year before Innocent III became Pope, leaving as his heir an infant son, Frederick II. The lad's mother died the year that Innocent ascended the throne of Peter and left the Pope as guardian of her son and regent of Sicily. A contested succession to the throne of Germany gave Innocent the opportunity to mix in the affairs of that distracted country. The kingdoms which were already in existence in Western Europe were assuming larger stature in comparison with the Empire but were not yet supported by a national sentiment which was strong enough successfully to defy Rome. Under these favouring and challenging circumstances Innocent III made good the claims of the Papacy to a greater degree than had any of his predecessors.

Innocent III further extended the Papal control over the Church. It was under his Pontificate that the Crusaders captured Constantinople. Although the diversion of the Crusade from its supposed purpose, the retaking of Jerusa-

lem, had been made against the wish of Innocent, the conquest of Constantinople had been followed by the setting up of a Latin hierarchy and a Patriarch
for that city and the other Byzantine territories which were subservient to
Rome. Latin rule in Constantinople enabled Innocent to extend the control of
Rome over the churches in Illyria, Bulgaria, and Wallachia which had formerly
been orientated towards the Byzantine wing of the Church. He also used the
occasion to bring the Church in Armenia within the Roman orbit. The
Maronites in the Lebanon, who had been monothelites, were won to conformity with Rome. No Pope had previously brought so much of the Church
in the East under the administrative control of the See of Peter. While most of
the gains proved to be only temporary, that they were achieved at all was
noteworthy. Innocent III authorized a crusade against the pagans on the south
and east shores of the Baltic, sent missionaries to the Prussians, and brought
the newly converted in that region under Papal direction. He reformed the
Church in Poland. He asserted the right of the Pope to give the decision in
all disputed elections to the episcopacy. He insisted that the Pope alone could
authorize the transfer of a bishop from one see to another. He declared that
only the Holy See could create new dioceses or change the boundaries between
existing dioceses. He was emphatic in seeking to further the high moral
character of the episcopate and the priesthood and continued the struggle to
enforce the celibacy of the clergy. To strengthen and purify the Church he
ordered that tithes for the support of the Church be given precedence over all
other taxes, he excluded all lay interference in ecclesiastical affairs, and he
prohibited any one man from drawing the income from more than one church
office. He affirmed the right of Rome to review important cases and thus added
to the trend to take appeals to the Holy See. He gave the Papal chancery the
best organization that it had thus far had.

In his effort to raise the level of Christian life in Europe, Innocent fought
what he deemed heresy. To this end he employed various means. Among them
was the Crusade against the Cathari.

It was Innocent III who called and dominated the most important of the
assemblies of the Church of the Middle Ages, the Fourth Lateran Council,
regarded by the Roman Catholic Church as the twelfth ecumenical council.
This convened late in 1215 and addressed itself to a wide range of problems.
It enacted a more comprehensive body of legislation than did any succeeding
council until that of Trent, nearly three hundred and fifty years later. It sought
not only the reform of the Church but also the improvement of the life of
the general Christian community. It laid down rules for the better education
of the clergy. It gave more precise definitions to several Christian doctrines.
Among them were a formula on the Trinity, transubstantiation, and the con-

demnation of what were deemed the errors of some of the heresies of the day. It sought to further the union with the Greek wing of the Catholic Church, then seemingly facilitated by the Latin conquest of Constantinople. It endorsed the new crusade which was a dream of Innocent III. It sought to raise the level of marriage and family life. It condemned the taking of interest and to prevent Jews from exacting it of Christians it forbade the latter to have any commerce with the former.

An act of the Fourth Lateran Council which was of major importance in the effort to raise the level of the rank and file of the laity was that which enjoined upon all Christians the duty of making their confession to a priest at least once each year. The early practice of penance, as we have seen, was public penalty and public restoration. Gradually in the Western wing of the Catholic Church the custom had spread of private confession to a priest, the private prescription by the priest of discipline, and the reconciliation of the penitent by the priest, also private. We have pointed out that as far back as the previous period penitentials, or books of directions to priests for examining penitents, had gained circulation. The custom of private oral confession had grown. Now a council representing the entire Western Church declared it to be obligatory upon every Christian.

It was especially in political affairs and in his dealings with kings and other princes that Innocent III exercised more power than any of his predecessors or successors. Here especially he seemed to be rendering effective the purpose of making the Papacy the instrument for bringing all the life of Christendom into conformity with Christian standards. He brought Papal dominance in much of Italy. In Rome itself he required the civil officials to acknowledge him rather than the Emperor as their sovereign and substituted his own appointees for the imperial judges. He won from the Tuscan cities acknowledgement of his suzerainty and obtained from the Emperor Otto IV the cession of lands claimed by the Papacy as grants from earlier rulers. In Germany he became the arbiter between two claimants to the throne and in return for his favour exacted from one of them, Otto IV, a promise to protect the possessions of the Church of Rome. Insisting that the Pope had the right to pass on the validity of elections to the imperial office, Innocent III crowned Otto IV Roman Emperor, but later, when Otto proved obdurate, excommunicated him and played a significant part in stirring up the opposition which cost him his throne. When he turned against Otto, Innocent gave his support to Frederick II, obtained his election as King of the Romans and King of the Germans, and wrung from him the freedom of the Church in Germany to elect its bishops and the concession of the right of appeal to Rome. So long as Innocent III lived, Frederick, able and ruthless though he was and quite sceptical religiously, was largely dominated by him. Innocent insisted upon the Papal overlordship of Sicily.

In France Innocent compelled Philip Augustus, as strong a monarch as Western Europe of that day knew, to take back the wife whom he had divorced and to restore to the Church lands which he had confiscated. Innocent was active in Spanish affairs. He crowned the King of Aragon at Rome as his vassal. He compelled the King of Leon to put away the wife whom he had married despite prohibitory canon law. He induced the Kings of Navarre and Castile to make peace and unite to fight the Moors. Portugal, Poland, Hungary, and Serbia became Papal vassals. In Norway he intervened to bring to time a priest who, having slain the king, had compelled the bishops to crown him.

Especially notable was the triumph in England. Here Innocent came into conflict with the notorious King John by insisting that the latter accept as Archbishop of Canterbury the able Stephen Langton in place of one whose election John had sponsored. John, furious, seized church property and drove many of the bishops into exile. Innocent excommunicated John, deposed him, and transferred the crown to Philip Augustus. To save his throne, John abjectly submitted, surrendered his kingdom to the Pope, and received it back as a Papal vassal. For many years thereafter, and under several Popes, Papal legates were prominent in the government of England.

The Slow Decline of the Papacy

Never again, as we have suggested, was the Papacy to be so potent in so many phases of the life of Europe. After Innocent III a decline set in which slightly less than two centuries later was to bring the See of Peter to a nadir that, while not as low as that of the tenth century, was in sad contrast with the purposes cherished for it by the great Popes of the eleventh and twelfth centuries.

The decline was not sudden. The thirteenth century saw several strong and high-minded Pontiffs, and some of them continued to make their office a force in Christendom. Thus the successor of Innocent, Honorius III, who held the post from 1216 to 1227, took measures to improve the education of the clergy and through his legates had great weight in the affairs of England during the minority of John's son, Henry III.

Yet even some of the strong Popes met serious reverses. Honorius III was followed by Gregory IX, a nephew of Innocent III. Although he came to the Papal throne in his early eighties and held it for fourteen years (1227–1241), until his mid-nineties, Gregory IX acted with vigour in a prolonged contest with the Emperor Frederick II, fostered learning, canonized Francis of Assisi and Dominic, strengthened the Inquisition, and sought to bring about the reunion of the Western and Eastern wings of the Church. But his excommunication of the Emperor failed to bring the latter to terms. Although Innocent IV (Pope from 1243 to 1254) had a general council of the Church excommunicate and depose Frederick II, he was unable to unseat that Emperor. Alexander IV (Pope from 1254 to 1261), nephew of Gregory IX, failed to dislodge the illegitimate son of Frederick II from his rule in Sicily and Southern Italy or to unite Europe against the threatened invasion of the Mongols.

The growing weakness of the Papacy was vividly demonstrated in 1294 when, after a Papal interregnum of two years caused by the rivalry of two powerful families and dissensions among the cardinals which prevented an election, the latter placed on the Papal throne a Benedictine monk, the organizer of a monastic congregation, who had the title of Celestine V. Although he was acclaimed by idealists and the Roman populace, Celestine, inexperienced in ecclesiastical politics and nearly eighty years of age, proved quite unable to meet the administrative demands of the post and after a few months resigned. In spite of the fact that less than twenty years after his death he was canonized, Dante pilloried him as he who had made the great refusal.

The decline of the Papacy became even more marked during the reign of Celestine's successor, Boniface VIII (Benedict Gaetani), who held the See of Peter from 1294 to 1303. Related to several Popes, among them probably Innocent III, with long experience in the Papal curia and as Papal legate, he brought scholarship and undoubted ability to the post. He was a lover of learning and promoted the founding of universities. He made as great claims for Papal authority as were ever promulgated. In his bull *Unam Sanctam,* issued in 1299, he declared "that it is altogether necessary to salvation for every human creature to be subject to the Roman Pontiff." He sought to make good this sweeping assertion. But, tactless, quick-tempered, lordly, and a lover of magnificence, he was far from being the equal of the greatest of his predecessors in ability or character and was defeated in his chief efforts to enforce his will. In spite of a Papal excommunication and interdict, a prince whom he opposed became ruler of Sicily. In the bull *Clericis Laicos,* promulgated in 1296, Boniface emphatically condemned the taxation of the clergy and Church property in France for royal purposes. A prolonged struggle followed between him and Philip IV of France, and at one point the Pope prepared to excommunicate and depose the king. A band of mercenaries instigated by the Pope's enemies seized the Pontiff at Anagni and held him prisoner. Although the burghers of Anagni rescued him and returned him in seeming triumph to Rome, within less than a month, an aged and broken man, he died of chagrin and melancholy.

Why the Decline of the Papacy?

The reasons for the decline of the Papacy were complex. Among them, however, was the growth of monarchies reinforced by a rising tide of a sentiment akin to nationalism. Kingdoms were not new but they were becoming stronger. As communications improved and cities and commerce grew, Western Europe began to emerge from its exclusively agricultural economy and endless division into large and small units associated with one another through feudal ties. Yet the dream of drawing together all Christendom into one unit dominated by the Holy Roman Empire and the Papacy was not fulfilled. Instead, Western Europe remained divided into numbers of states, large and small. Each monarch sought to control that portion of the Church which was within his domains and resented Papal interference. In this he was supported by the majority of his subjects, for they were averse to seeing foreigners placed in ecclesiastical posts by Papal appointment and were especially angered by the taxes imposed through the Church for the support of the Papal curia.

The debilitating conflict between Empire and Papacy was another source of the decline of the Papacy. The efforts of the reformers to free the Church from secularism by making it independent of the state and the vision which sustained the great Popes of a society in which the Christian purpose would be predominant through the guidance of the Bishops of Rome as Vicars of Christ had led to prolonged internecine strife in which Popes resorted to measures which were quite inconsistent with Christian standards of conduct. The Empire suffered more than the Papacy, but the latter was weakened, especially in moral stature.

Furthermore, the very machinery which the reforming Popes developed to make their power effective in purifying the Church and raising the moral and spiritual level of society proved a source of weakness. Their measures entailed the multiplication of officials, many of them at Rome and others scattered throughout Christendom, an elaborate and expensive bureaucracy. Positions in that bureaucracy were sought by ambitious men, for they brought prestige, physical comfort, even luxury, and a kind of power which was antithetical to that of the Gospel. Here, in the name of the Gospel, was a perversion of the Gospel which eventually became a noisome scandal. The taxes required for the support of the bureaucracy aroused resentment which challenged, often successfully, the authority of the Papacy to impose and collect them.

The Papacy Goes into Captivity at Avignon

The decline of the Papacy became vivid in what is often called the Babylonian Captivity. From 1309 to 1377 the Popes resided at Avignon, and although that city was not in France, it was overshadowed by that realm. All the Popes of the period were Frenchmen and were subject to French influence which at times became domination by the King of France. The Papacy was almost a French institution. This weakened its prestige in nations and regions at enmity with France and after 1350 issued in the Great Schism which, as we are to see, weakened not only the Papacy but also the Western Church.

It was under Clement V, Pope from 1305 to 1314 and the second after Boniface VIII, that the headquarters of the Papacy were removed to Avignon. Clement had been Archbishop of Bordeaux which, although under the King of England, was French soil. Under pressure from the King of France he annulled the acts which had been directed against that monarch by his two predecessors. He was noted for appointing his relatives to high office in the Church, including six whom he made cardinals. All but two of the twenty-four cardinals whom he created were French, a precedent which was to be followed by his Avignon successors.

The longest reign of the Avignon Pontiffs was that of John XXII, from 1316 to 1334. Coming to the office when he was sixty-seven, John XXII lived into his eighty-fifth year. In spite of his advanced age, his was a vigorous rule. Austere and simple in his private life, he left behind him a large personal fortune. He was involved in extensive wars over German and imperial affairs, for the struggle between Popes and Emperors continued to plague both lines of potentates. Possessing outstanding organizing and executive gifts, he increased the centralization of the affairs of the Church in the Papal curia and departmentalized the administration. He faced serious financial problems, for the removal to Avignon had cost the Papacy some of its Italian revenues and his extensive participation in war consumed almost two-thirds of his budget. Yet he proved to be something of a financial genius in augmenting the Papal funds and in introducing an efficient financial system. Among other measures he reserved for his treasury the income for three years of all minor benefices which fell vacant in the Western branch of the Church and also claimed the personal property of bishops on their death.

In general, the Avignon years were marked by luxury in the Papal entourage and the enlargement of varied forms of Papal taxation and exaction. Palatial residences for Pope and cardinals were erected. These and the style of living maintained within them were costly. The Papal bureaucracy and the Papal ventures in politics also demanded large expenditures. Among the sources of funds were what were technically known as Papal reservation and provision. By reservation was meant the right of nomination to a vacant benefice. Provision was appointment to a benefice before it fell vacant. From each new appointee the Pope expected the annate, approximately one year's revenue of the post. The income from vacant benefices the nomination to which was in Papal hands was also an increasing source of revenue, especially since the posts might be deliberately kept unfilled. In their effort to control the moral and religious life of Western Christendom the Popes, as we have seen, had encouraged or required appeal to their court. Under the Avignon Pontiffs the fees exacted for such appeals were another source of funds.

These enlargements of Papal powers and taxes aroused widespread resentment. In England, for example, in 1351 there was enacted the Statute of Provisors which forbade Papal interference in elections to ecclesiastical posts. This was followed, in 1353, by a law, *Praemunire,* which prohibited appeals to courts outside the kingdom. Although the Pope was not specifically named in the act, the intent was clear.

Some of the Avignon Pontiffs were upright men who strove to correct abuses and to improve the life of the Church, but the tide was against them. The Papacy was in a decline which in the next period was to be a scandal to the Christian name, first because of a prolonged and bitter division of Western Europe among rival claimants of the see and then because men of quite unworthy character manœuvred themselves into Peter's Chair.

Summary

It is a record of contrasts, frustrations and triumphs, this effort through the hierarchy to bring all Western Christendom to a near approximation to the Christian ideal. Here was a noble ambition. With the exception of small minorities, the peoples of Western Europe either had been won or were being won to an avowed acceptance of the Christian faith. Yet the majority had only a vague conception of the nature of the religion whose name they had taken. The habit of war was strong. Injustice and immorality were rife. At the outset of the period all too frequently even the monasteries, supposed conservers and exemplars of Christian living, had departed from their professed standards, and the clergy, by profession the guardians and shepherds of the masses, were notoriously corrupt.

In the course of the centuries between the years 950 and 1350 potent impulses had raised the level of Christian living in the monasteries and in some of the movements which were branded as heretical by the Catholic Church. In spite of the fact that they were zealously missionary, the mendicant orders and such bodies as the Waldensees succeeded in reaching only minorities. On the other hand, great dreamers, some of them monks and some of them of the secular clergy, strove to bring the entire body of mass converts and their descendants to what Paul had called "the high calling of God in Christ Jesus." To accomplish this purpose they strove to cleanse the vast body of clergy from the parish priests to the Pope and through this purified hierarchy to reach not minorities but all who bore the Christian name.

The struggle proved unending. Successes were registered, some of them striking. Many among the bishops and parish priests were exemplary Christians. More and more of the laity were being brought to an intelligent appreciation of the faith and to a disciplined observance of it. The reformers captured the Papacy. Yet abuses, even in the hierarchy, were never fully eliminated. At times they seemed to mount and the age-long efforts of the reformers to be vain. Indeed, in time the very machinery which had been developed by the dreamers to make their vision a reality proved an obstacle to the realization of the purposes of its creators. Increasingly Europe was ostensibly Christian. For the majority the Christian faith was at best nominal and in actual practice they denied it. That majority included many of the clergy and even bishops and Popes. Yet increasingly Europe numbered individuals and groups which were earnestly committed to the Christian faith. Nor can we say that the efforts of those who strove for a fully Christian society were entirely fruitless. As we are to see in a later chapter, more phases of the life of Western Europe were profoundly influenced by Christianity than was true in the Roman Empire after the seeming triumph of the faith in that realm. But for the dreamers that would not have occurred.

SELECTED BIBLIOGRAPHY

GENERAL WORKS

A. Fliche and V. Martin, editors, *Histoire de l'Église depuis les Origines jusqu'à Nos Jours*. Carefully done, by Roman Catholics and from the Roman Catholic standpoint, stressing the role of the Papacy, but with an honest attempt at objectivity and with helpful references to the sources and the literature. The volumes which cover this period are E. Amann, *L'Église au Pouvoir des Laïques (888–1057)* (Paris, Bloud & Gay, 1948, pp. 544); A. Fliche, *La Réforme Grégorienne et la Reconquete Chrétienne (1057–1125)* (Bloud & Gay, 1946, pp. 502); A. Fliche, R. Foreville, and J. Rousset, *Du Premier Concile du Lateran a l'Avènement d'Innocent III (1123–1198)* (Bloud & Gay, 1948, pp. 204); and A. Fliche, C. Thouzellier, and Y. Azais, *La Chrétienté Romaine (1198–1274)* (Bloud & Gay, pp. 512).

A. C. Flick, *The Rise of the Mediaeval Church and Its Influence on the Civilization of Western Europe from the First to the Thirteenth Century* (New York, G. P. Putnam's Sons, 1909, pp. xiii, 623). Approximately the second half of the volume deals with this period. Valuable as a summary and for its bibliographies.

A. Hauck, *Kirchengeschichte Deutschlands*. Of this standard work, dependable and with extensive references to the sources, Vols. 3, 4, and 5 (Leipzig, J. C. Hinrichs'sche Buchhandlung, 1920, 1913, 1920) cover this period.

A. Lagarde, *The Latin Church of the Middle Ages,* translated by A. Alexander (New York, Charles Scribner's Sons, 1915, pp. vi, 600). A standard summary.

H. K. Mann, *The Lives of the Popes in the Middle Ages* (London, Kegan Paul, Trench, Trübner & Co., 2d Ed., 18 vols., 1925–1932). Vols. IV–XVIII cover this period and go through the year 1304. Enormously learned, the work is by a Roman Catholic priest and tends to give a favourable picture of the Popes.

J. McCabe, *Crises in the History of the Papacy* (New York, G. P. Putnam's Sons, 1916, pp. xiv, 459). A history of the Papacy centering on outstanding figures, of whom three fall within this period.

THE EFFORT TO ENFORCE THE CELIBACY OF THE CLERGY

H. C. Lea, *History of Sacerdotal Celibacy in the Christian Church* (New York, The Macmillan Co., 3d ed., rev., 2 vols., 1907). Of this standard work more than half of Vol. I deals with this period.

DUNSTAN

J. A. Robinson, *The Times of Saint Dunstan* (Oxford University Press, 1923, pp. 188).

BERNWARD

F. J. Tschan, *Bernward of Hildesheim* (University of Notre Dame, Vol. I, 1942, pp. vii, 235).

HILDEBRAND

S. Gregorii VII Romani Pontificis Epistolæ et Diplomata Pontificia, being Vol. CXLVIII of J. P. Migne, *Patrologia Latina* (Paris, 1853, columns 1472).

A. J. Macdonald, *Hildebrand: A Life of Gregory VII* (London, Methuen & Co., 1932, pp. ix, 254). Well written, semi-popular, with frequent references to the sources.

A. H. Mathew, *The Life and Times of Hildebrand Pope Gregory VII* (London, Francis Griffiths, 1910, pp. xi, 308). Semi-popular, based upon the sources, but with almost no footnote references to them.

LANFRANC

A. J. Macdonald, *Lanfranc. A Study of His Life, Work and Writing* (Oxford University Press, 1926, pp. vii, 307). Based upon a careful and critical use of the sources.

WULFSTAN

J. W. Lamb, *Saint Wulfstan, Prelate and Patriot: a Study of His Life and Times* (London, Society for Promoting Christian Knowledge, 1933, pp. xiii, 218).

THOMAS BECKET

W. H. Hutton, *Thomas Becket, Archbishop of Canterbury* (Cambridge University Press, 1926, pp. vii, 315).

LAW, WAR, MARRIAGE, ECONOMIC LIFE

B. Jarrett, *Social Theories of the Middle Ages* (Westminster, Md., The Newman Bookshop, 1942, pp. ix, 280). A semi-popular survey, by a Dominican.

E. Troeltsch, *The Social Teachings of the Christian Churches,* translated by Olive Wyon (Vol. I, New York, The Macmillan Co., 1931, pp. 445). Slightly more than half of this volume is on medieval Catholicism.

JOHN OF PARIS

J. Leclercq, *Jean de Paris et l'Ecclésiologie du XIII ͤ Siècle* (Paris, Librairie Philosophique J. Vrin, 1942, pp. 268). By a Dominican. Contains the text of *De Potestate Regio et Papali.*

MARSILIUS OF PADUA

The Defensor Pacis of Marsilius of Padua, edited by C. W. Previté-Orton (Cambridge University Press, 1928, pp. xlvii, 517). The Latin text with an extensive introduction.

E. Emerton, *The Defensor Pacis of Marsiglio of Padua. A Critical Study* (Harvard University Press, 1920, pp. 81). By a distinguished specialist in Church history.

INNOCENT III

L. Elliott-Binns, *Innocent III* (London, Methuen & Co., 1931, pp. xi, 212). Popularly written.

A. Luchaire, *Innocent III* (Paris, Hachette et C ͥ ͤ, 6 vols., 1905–1908). Extensive, but weak in its lack of footnote references to the sources.

BONIFACE VIII

T. S. R. Boase, Boniface VIII (London, Constable & Co., 1933, pp. xv, 397). Very well done.

L. Tosti, *Pope Boniface VIII and His Times,* translated by E. J. Bonnelly (New York, S. R. Leland, 1933, pp. 546). By a Roman Catholic strongly biased in favour of Boniface VIII.

CONFESSION AND PENANCE

H. C. Lea, *A History of Auricular Confession and Indulgences in the Latin Church* (Philadelphia, Lea Brothers & Co., 3 vols., 1896). A standard survey.

O. D. Watkins, *A History of Penance. Being a Study of the Authorities* (London, Longmans, Green & Co., 2 vols., 1920). Valuable for its extensive citations from the sources and its excellent summaries. The latter part of Vol. II deals with this period.

THE BABYLONIAN CAPTIVITY

A. C. Flick, *The Decline of the Medieval Church* (New York, Alfred A. Knopf, 2 vols., 1930). Nearly two-thirds of Vol. I is devoted to the Babylonian Captivity. An objective account based upon the sources and secondary works.

Chapter 21

CREATIVE THOUGHT IN THE WESTERN CHURCH

One of the most striking features of the Christianity of Western Europe in the four centuries from 950 to 1350 was intense intellectual activity. The vitality which was seen in the geographic spread of the faith, the creation of many new forms of monasticism, the emergence of movements deemed heretical by the Catholic Church, and the efforts through the hierarchy led by the Papacy to render the faith dominant in all aspects of life also gave rise to theological ferment. A large proportion of the intelligentsia of Western Christendom directed their attention to the problems presented by the Gospel. Theology became a major subject of study, "the queen of the sciences." Some of the ablest minds that mankind has ever known were stimulated by it to profound thought. Thousands of lesser minds were engaged by it. What the Roman Catholic Church of the twentieth century adjudged the standard formulation of theology was by Thomas Aquinas, of the thirteenth century, but it was the culmination of three centuries of discussion and debate.

As order began to reappear in the West after the centuries of invasions and cultural decay, it was not strange that men applied their minds to the faith which was part of their heritage. They availed themselves of what had been written in the years before the darkness had descended. They addressed themselves to the New Testament, to the scholars of the early Church, and especially to Augustine and Gregory the Great. We have noted the rebirth of theological activity under the peace and security given by the great Carolingians, a revival which the decay of that line and the coming of the Vikings made abortive. Now the tide of thought once more rose.

As in other expressions of Christianity, in this period there was much more of vigour and creativity in the Western wing of the Catholic Church than in the churches of the East. The reasons for the contrast in the intellectual realm are probably those which accounted for it in the other aspects of the faith. We have already sought to discover them and we will recur to them in a later chapter.

THE RISE OF SCHOLASTICISM

Thought about Christianity in Western Europe in this period was closely associated with what is usually called scholasticism. Scholasticism was the achievement of the school men. It arose from the schools of the period and found its most marked development in connexion with them. Its inception was in the intellectual and religious revival under the Carolingians and its first great figure was John Scotus Eriugena. It was renewed in the eleventh century in some of the monasteries, notably Bec, in Normandy, and in schools maintained under the auspices of cathedrals. It continued in the universities which arose late in the twelfth and in the thirteenth century. Paris was the chief but by no means the only centre of scholastic theology. Near or associated with its cathedral were schools made famous by great teachers. Here sprang up the institution which was to be the type for numbers of universities in the north of Europe. An association or guild of teachers, it made theology its major subject. The other outstanding early university, Bologna, was, as we have seen, especially famous for law. Universities multiplied in the thirteenth and fourteenth centuries. They were chiefly ecclesiastical foundations, obtaining their charters from the Pope. While one might be best known for law and another for medicine, normally theology was an honoured subject in them all.

An outstanding objective of the school men was to ascertain the relation of faith and reason. It was a problem which had confronted Christian thinkers long before the school men and which continued to challenge them long after scholasticism was considered by many to be outmoded. Is what the Christian believes to have been given by God in the long process of revelation which culminated in Christ consistent with reason or are the two contradictory? If they are compatible, which should have priority, the faith by which the Christian accepts and commits himself fully to what has been given in the divine revelation and transmitted through the Church, or man's reason? Can reason demonstrate as true what the Christian believes about God? If it cannot, does what is received by faith complement what is reached by reason or do the two contradict each other? If reason seems to deny what the Christian accepts on faith as given by God, shall the Christian accord his reason priority and throw over as false what he has received through faith or can he find some way of holding to both? These were among the basic questions with which scholasticism wrestled.

In addressing itself to its task scholasticism employed the intellectual apparatus which it had inherited from the pre-Christian Græco-Roman world.

This was Greek philosophy, and especially what had been written by Plato and Aristotle. At the outset few of the school men could read Greek. Their lectures and discussions were carried on in Latin. Only portions of the works of Aristotle and of those in the Platonic tradition were available to them in that language. However, enough of Aristotle was accessible to enable them to employ Aristotelian logic. It was by means of this logic or dialectic with its syllogisms that they engaged in intellectual activity. They also were familiar with a work by the Neoplatonic Porphyry.

As the centuries wore on, more of the writings of Greek philosophers reached the school men. Especially notable was the influence of additional works of Aristotle. Some of these came in Arabic translations. The Moslem Arabs had first made contact with the Greek philosophers through the Nestorians, especially through Nisibis, that centre of Nestorian theological education. Nestorian scholars possessed Syriac translations of the Greek originals. By them translations were made into Arabic for their new rulers. Jewish philosophers were also seeking to work through their faith in terms of Greek thought. In the portions of Spain ruled by Moslems were schools controlled by the Arabs in which Christians and Jews as well as Moslems studied. Partly through them more of Greek thought became available to the Christian scholars of Western Europe.

Western Christendom also became acquainted with Jewish and Moslem Arab thinkers who had been influenced by Greek philosophy. Among the Jews Maimonides (1135–1204), a warm admirer of Aristotle, was especially read. Among the Moslems were Alfarabi, Algazel, and particularly Avicenna. Outstanding in his effect upon later scholasticism was Averroes or Averrhoes, a daring and prolific native of Cordova of the twelfth century. By the end of the twelfth century much of his work was available in Latin translations.

Under the impact of this Greek thought, either coming directly or through Moslem Arab intermediaries, the active and eager minds of the Christian scholars of Western Europe were stimulated and shaped as they addressed themselves to theology.

As we describe the theological activity of these centuries it will become apparent that it differed markedly from that of the first five centuries of Christianity. In general it took as settled the issues around which had centered that earlier period of creative Christian debate. Gnosticism had disappeared. The stark dualism represented by Marcion was present in the Cathari but for the majority of Christians in the West it was no longer an open question. The relationship of Christ to the Father and of the balance of the divine and human in Jesus were accepted as defined in the historic creeds of the Catholic Church.

At times, indeed, the school men seemed to be following slavishly what had come to them from the first centuries of their faith. They quoted as authoritative the Scriptures and the Christian thinkers whom they esteemed as the fathers.

Yet the greatest of the school men were far from being parrots. Men like Anselm and Thomas Aquinas had as acute and powerful intellects as had Origen or Augustine. In inquiring into the relation between faith and reason they were wrestling with issues quite as basic as those presented by the Gnostics, the Marcionites, the Arians, and the Monophysites. Although using the thought forms of Greek philosophy which were at their hands, the best of them were bringing to bear as keen, courageous, and honest minds as had either the pre-Christian or the Christian predecessors whom they revered. Building on the answers given by earlier generations, they were either asking whether these could be validated afresh or were putting in new ways old questions, such as the meaning of the death of Christ. Moreover, they were concerned more with the nature and attributes of God than had been their predecessors in the first five centuries.

REALISM AND NOMINALISM

An issue which appeared early in scholasticism and continued throughout its course was that between realism and nominalism. The division led to vigorous and often bitter debates. Philosophical in its origin, it had important religious implications.

Realism, which went back to its early formulator, Plato, declared that universals have an existence which is independent of the mind of the thinker. According to this view, general terms represent reality. Species and genera exist apart from the individual units embraced by them. For instance, "man" is not a figment of the imagination which the mind constructs to lump together the millions of beings called men, but in itself is an entity. Among other things, when applied to theology this means that man or mankind has a unity which has been corrupted by the sin of the first man, Adam. The saving work of Christ is for all mankind and not for isolated individual men, and the Church is more than the sum of individual Christians or local congregations. We can more readily believe in the Trinity if we regard as real a divine inclusive essence which is in Father, Son, and Holy Spirit. The realist held that the idea of the universals in the mind of God becomes the ground for the existence of individual things and beings.

Nominalism, on the other hand, maintained that only particular things are real, and that universals are merely words coined by the intellect. To put it in another way, such terms as man, city, nation, animal, and Church are concepts of the mind and only individual objects and events exist. Men, seeing what they believe to be resemblances between objects, invent abstract terms and group individual objects under them.

Between extreme realists and nominalists gradations were found. For example, some moderate realists held that the idea in God's mind is not precisely reproduced in the characteristics of a species and that the concept which is nourished in a man's mind of what constitutes a species is not entirely the same as the actual characteristics of the species. To give one illustration: the species "cow" does not exactly reflect what was in the mind of God; and what man perceives in the species "cow" is not altogether what is in that species.

Great Landmarks in Scholasticism: Anselm

It would be aside from our purpose to give a detailed account of the history of scholastic theology. We must content ourselves with saying something of its outstanding figures, individuals who loom up as landmarks. Of these the first to draw our attention is Anselm (c.1033 or c.1034–1109).

We have had occasion to mention Anselm more than once. Coming from Italy, he joined the monastic community of Bec in Normandy and became the outstanding intellectual light in an early expression of the monastic revival. Called by the execrable William Rufus in a moment of panic-stricken remorse to succeed Lanfranc as Archbishop of Canterbury, Anselm took the post only from a sense of duty. In it he had a prolonged conflict with the difficult William and with the latter's successor, the much stronger Henry I, over the issue of the lay control of the Church. His whole-souled committal to the reform movement is attested by the welcome given him at Cluny during his exile from his see. Through reluctant necessity Anselm was an administrator. He was also, but not unwillingly, a man of prayer who left behind him a guide for meditation and spiritual self-examination. He was, moreover, a pastor who as prior, abbot, and archbishop had much at heart the welfare of his flock. He cared for them one by one as individuals as well as in groups.

Anselm combined charm with firmness, gentleness with strength, sanctity with sagacity. Humble in spirit, without ambition for personal power or preferment, he was painfully conscious of his unworthiness in the sight of God. A contemporary of Hildebrand, he left as deep an impress upon Christian theology as the great Pope did on the See of Peter. Highly disciplined, penetrating, careful, and precise, much of Anselm's writing on theology was packed into small compass and yet is amazingly clear. Some of it was done in his days at Bec. Much of it was accomplished during his sojourns on the Continent, exiled because of his conflicts with the monarchs of England. Steeped in Augustine, Anselm did not slavishly reproduce that great master, but did his own thinking. He was a realist in philosophy and theology. Seeing no conflict between faith and reason, he took the familiar position of believing that he might understand and accepted through faith what was taught by the Church, but he held that the truth of what was thus received could be demonstrated by the processes of the intellect and could be supported by reason. Indeed, he maintained that the major tenets of Christianity, such as belief in God, the nature of God, the Trinity, immortality, and the incarnation, death, and resurrection of Christ, could be reached by reason and were the inescapable accompaniments of a rational view of the universe. His most famous theological works were his *Monologium* (*A Soliloquy*), *Proslogium* (*A Discourse*), and *Cur Deus Homo* (*Why God-man*).

The *Monologium* was composed at the insistent request of students. In it Anselm engaged in a meditation on the being of God. He was keenly aware of Augustine's writings and believed that he was not setting forth anything which was contrary to them. He held that there is a Being which is the best, the greatest, and the highest of all existing beings; that whatever is, exists through Something; that this Something, this Nature, derives existence from Itself, not from something else, and all beings derive existence through this Nature; and that this Nature created all things out of nothing, but that before their creation the idea of them existed in the mind of the Creator. Thence Anselm goes on to deduce by rational processes the main features of this Nature, this Supreme Being. Without appealing to the Bible he seeks to prove and describe the Trinity, the Father, the Son, and the Holy Spirit proceeding from the Father and the Son, and to arrive at the conclusions set forth in the great creeds of the Catholic Church.

The *Proslogium* seems to have come to Anselm as the culmination of long mental and spiritual struggle with the problem which it sets forth. The agony was so intense that it deprived him of appetite and sleep and robbed him of peace in his devotions. Then, suddenly, in the night, light broke and he quickly wrote down what it brought to him. Here, in a treatise of only a few pages, Anselm set forth what is often called the ontological argument for the existence of God. Anselm held that God is that Being than which nothing greater can be conceived to exist. This Being is obviously greater than one which can be conceived not to exist. God must exist in reality and not only in man's thought, for if he were merely a figment of the imagination, a Being which has actual being as well as being pictured in man's mind could be conceived of as existing. The latter must be true. To put it in still other words, reason demands the idea of a perfect Being, lacking in nothing; the idea of a perfect Being is of necessity the idea of Being which has existence, for a Being which lacks existence would not be perfect. God, so Anselm held, is not only that Being than which nothing greater can be conceived, but is greater than can be conceived. From this point Anselm went on to develop the characteristics, or attributes of God much as in the *Monologium*. In subsequent centuries, it must be noted, several of the most acute philosophical minds of the Occident, among them Descartes and Kant, examined Anselm's argument for the existence of God, some to refute it and some to affirm it.

In *Cur Deus Homo* Anselm dealt with the incarnation and the atonement. To put it in somewhat different language from that which he employed, Anselm held that since by his sin man had flaunted the will of God, God whose will governs the universe, God could not disregard that sin without upsetting the moral order of the entire creation. Even though in His mercy He might wish to overlook man's transgression He could not do so without being immoral, and this would be contrary to His nature. To maintain the moral order satisfaction must be given. That satisfaction must be fully equal to the offense. Since the sin is man's, satisfaction must be given by man. Yet man has nothing which he can offer to God over and above what he already owes to God, for even if he always perfectly conformed to God's will he would be but doing his duty. However, if man were not to be redeemed from his sin, God would be frustrated, for in creating man God intended him to choose and enjoy the supreme good, which is God Himself. While none but man can make the satisfaction to compensate for man's sin, only God can make that satisfaction, for the satisfaction must be greater than anything in the universe except God. That satisfaction, therefore, must be made by one who is both God and man. For that reason God became incarnate in Jesus. God did not undertake a fresh creation of man, for a fresh creation could not have made satisfaction for the descendants of sinful Adam. He was born, therefore, of Mary, of the seed of Adam. Of the three persons of the Trinity, only the Son, begotten of the Father before all worlds, could be incarnate, for if one of the other persons had been born of Mary there would have been two sons. By the incarnation, Jesus Christ, fully God and fully man, and only he, could make the needed satisfaction and enable God to forgive man without doing violence to the moral balance of the universe.

It has often been suggested that in his view of the atonement Anselm was influenced by the legal patterns of his day. These permitted the substitution of a money payment for the return of an eye for an eye or a life for a life. Anselm, so it is said, regarded the God-man, Jesus Christ, as making that substitution by his sufferings and death. It may be that Anselm thought in these terms. However, his insight was more penetrating and his view more comprehensive than the conventions of feudal society and their Teutonic background. There are hints of similar insights in Gregory the Great, with his rootage in Roman law, and, still further back, in the Old and New Testaments.

Anselm's theological contributions were not limited to the three treatises which we have summarized, important though these were. He opposed the doctrine of the Trinity as set forth by John Roscelin, who seems to have been a nominalist, denying the reality of universals, and thus to have thought of the Trinity as Three Gods. Anselm so forcefully argued against him that for several generations nominalism was discredited in the Catholic Church. He cogently presented the argument for the procession of the Holy Spirit from the Father and the Son, justifying the *filioque* clause as against the Eastern wing of the Catholic Church. In his very last hours he was wrestling with the age-long problem of how to reconcile the freedom of man's will with the omniscient foreknowledge and the predetermination of God. To these as to the other problems with which he dealt, Anselm brought the clarity of thought and the facility for verbal expression which were characteristic of him.

Great Landmarks in Scholasticism: Abélard

From Anselm we move on to one of his younger contemporaries, Peter Abélard (or Abailard). Probably born in 1079, Abélard was about thirty years of age and in the flush of his fame and his stormy career when the great archbishop breathed his last. Dying in 1142, he lived a third of a century after Anselm had been gathered to his fathers. Also a contemporary of Bernard of Clairvaux, with whom he was to have unhappy relations, his life was set at a time and in a country in which great tides of spiritual awakening were flowing. It was a period of intellectual ferment when students were thronging the schools which, flourishing, were the precursors of the university movement of a generation or two later. Daring architects were venturing from the inherited heavy Romanesque into the soaring Gothic. Here was an era to stir the pulses of sensitive, intellectually alert spirits.

Abélard both shared and contributed to the brilliance of the age. He was a striking and somewhat contradictory figure. Possessed of a rapier-like intellect, he thrived on debate. Charming, keen, a stimulating teacher to whom the atmosphere of the lecture room was as the breath of life, he attracted throngs of students. Intellectually eager and inquiring, but also arrogant, he rejoiced in challenging accepted beliefs and in worsting rivals in debate, including his own elders and teachers. Yet there was in him a deep strain of religious sensitivity and insight and from him came one of the most influential interpretations of the atonement. In spite of his questioning, he was a sincere Christian and held it to be the function of reason using Aristotelian logic to refute error and illumine the truth which comes through divine revelation and is apprehended by faith.

Abélard was born in Brittany not far from Nantes and of aristocratic stock.

His father had a bent towards learning and since both parents later adopted the monastic life, supposedly they were more than conventionally religious and surrounded their son's infancy with a devout atmosphere. Abélard early developed a hunger for learning. He went to various centres, in some places worsting his teachers, and eventually became the most popular of the lecturers in Paris. At first primarily a student and teacher of philosophy, later he gave himself more to theology.

At the height of his early fame Abélard was attracted by the beautiful and educated Héloïse, niece of a canon of the cathedral in Paris, sought her companionship by becoming her tutor and an inmate of her uncle's home, and won her love. Then came heartbreak. He had a child by her and against her protests, for she wished not to hamper his career by the more formal bond, was secretly married to her. Her uncle, infuriated by the entire affair, had ruffians break in on him and emasculate him. At Abélard's desire Héloïse became a nun. She declared that she had ever wished to please him more than God. He became a monk and had a tempestuous time in the monastic houses of which he became successively a member. Some of the letters of Abélard to Héloïse after their separation are among the most poignant in literature.

Students continued to flock to Abélard. He wrote extensively. One of his more famous books was *Sic et Non* (*Yes and No*). Intended for beginners, it listed several scores of questions on science, ethics, and theology, and for each gave quotations from the Scriptures and the Fathers which seemed to support contradictory answers. The book was meant to be provocative and to stimulate independent thinking. Yet Abélard never made reason supreme. To him faith and reason went hand in hand.

Abélard antagonized many. His enemies had him haled before a council at Soissons in 1121 for heresy. In 1140, largely at the instance of Bernard of Clairvaux, who regarded as subversive to the faith some of his teachings, including his views on the Trinity, the atonement, free will, and original sin, Abélard was condemned by a council at Sens. The two men were opposites in temperament. Abélard, while honestly Christian and conforming and submitting to the Catholic Church, was the intellectual, daring, acute, not content to accept conventional phraseology. Moreover, in reacting against nominalism which tended to think of the Trinity as three Gods, Abélard took a position which verged on monarchianism and laid himself open to the charge of Sabellianism. Bernard was a mystic, stressing the divine love, and was not a speculative theologian. Intensely committed to the historic formulas of the faith and the generally accepted views, he regarded Abélard as a dangerous rationalist. Since both were prominent, they could not but clash. Bernard, more forceful and more influential in ecclesiastical circles, carried the authorities with him. Abélard appealed to Rome, the Pope confirmed the condemnation, and he was excommunicated. Cluny gave him refuge, he and Bernard were reconciled, and his last months were spent in prayer and reading.

In philosophy, in his penetrating fashion Abélard pointed out weaknesses in both nominalism and realism. In addition to his *Sic et Non* and his remarkable stimulus to individual pupils, Abélard's distinctive contributions to theology were chiefly his teaching about ethics and the atonement.

In ethics Abélard held that sin is not alone in the overt act but primarily in the motive. He rejected the view of original sin which was found in Augustine. He held that mankind does not share in the guilt of Adam's sin, but that all, through the sin of Adam, share in the punishment meted out to Adam. However, so he maintained, every human being can coöperate with the grace of God and by good works escape that punishment. To be sure, men have weaknesses which incline them to sin, but in themselves these do not bring guilt to men. Men also have tendencies to good. By reason, which is the gift of God to man, individuals can discover what is good. They can then employ their wills to follow the good. Sin or the absence of sin lies in the motive, the intention, with which men act. The growing practice of auricular confession to a priest, Abélard held, could not be for the purpose of obtaining absolution, for the power to retain or remit sins which Christ gave his apostles was not transmitted to the bishops, and unless the verdict of the bishop accorded with divine justice it would possess no validity.

Abélard's view of the atonement is usually called, but not with precise accuracy, the moral influence theory. He rejected the position set forth by Anselm that the satisfaction made by Jesus Christ was necessary for the forgiveness of sins, for, he pointed out, God had forgiven sins before Christ came. If, he argued, forgiveness is an act of grace, it must be free and without demand for compensation for sin. In contrast, Abélard declared, God is love and has voluntarily assumed the burden of suffering brought on by man's sin. This act of God's grace, taken freely and without the necessity of making satisfaction for sin, awakens in men gratitude and love for God. In Jesus Christ, who is both man and God, men see what men should be, by contrast are brought to a realization of their sin, and by God's love seen in Christ are won to a response which releases new springs of love which issue in right conduct. In this fashion the sinner becomes a new creation, a different self.

Opinions differ as to the effect which Abélard had on later theological thought. Some hold it to have been transient. Others believe it to have been marked and continuing. Without attempting to determine which of these estimates is correct, we can at least be certain that here was an outstanding figure in the theological activity of the Europe of that period.

GREAT LANDMARKS IN SCHOLASTICISM: HUGO OF ST. VICTOR

A contemporary of Abélard and Bernard of Clairvaux, a critic of the former and a friend of the latter, was Hugo (or Hugh) of St. Victor (1096–1141). Son of a Saxon count and educated in Germany, he spent most of his adult life as a member of the community of Augustinian canons of St. Victor, in Paris. This community had a school which was famous at the time. Hugo taught in it and wrote extensively. His works included commentaries on several books of the Bible and the rule of Augustine, and disquisitions on the moral life, the way of the mystic, and various questions of theology. By far his largest treatise was *De Sacramentis Fidei Christianae*. Although this work had the sacraments as its title, it was actually a comprehensive survey of theology, beginning with the creation, God, and the Trinity, going on to the fall of man, original sin, and the incarnation, and then dealing more at length with the sacraments. Hugo divided knowledge into two branches, theology and philosophy. He saw no necessary conflict between them. Some truths in theology, so he held, are to be proved by reason; some, while not demonstrable through reason, are in accord with reason, while still others cannot be discerned through unaided reason but come through revelation apprehended by faith. Man has three gates or organs through which knowledge comes to him—his physical eye, the eye of the mind, and the eye of the spirit. Hugo was a mystic, and he valued highly what entered through the eye of the spirit by what he called contemplation.

We are to say more of the sacraments in the next chapter, but we must pause to notice that Hugo defined a sacrament as a "physical or material element presented clearly to the senses, by similitude representing, by institution signifying, and by consecration containing an invisible and spiritual grace." In other words, a sacrament is not only a sign or symbol of a sacred thing but it is the physical medium through which grace operates. Hugo came out clearly for transubstantiation in the Eucharist. This view was by no means novel, but it had recently been a subject of vigorous debate. Berengar, head of the cathedral school at Tours, had fairly recently denounced transubstantiation and in doing so had aroused Lanfranc to step forward in its defense. Within less than a century after the death of Hugo, the Fourth Lateran Council, as we have seen, made it the official position of the Western wing of the Catholic Church.

GREAT LANDMARKS IN SCHOLASTICISM: PETER LOMBARD

Peter Lombard was chiefly distinguished as the author of the *Sentences*, the most widely used text-book in theology in Western Europe during the Middle Ages. Because of that fact he was often known as the Master of the Sentences or just the Master. A contemporary of Abélard, Bernard of Clairvaux, and Hugo of St. Victor, he was a native of Novara, a few miles west of Milan, then regarded as being in Lombardy. Educated at Bologna, he went to Paris, taught there in the cathedral school, and for a brief time in his later years was Archbishop of Paris. Although critical of him, he was influenced by Abélard. Hugo of St. Victor also made an impression on him. He was deeply indebted to Augustine, John of Damascus, and Gratian the canonist.

The *Quatuor Libri Sententiarum* is briefly described by its title. It was made up of four books. The first treated of God, His nature, the Trinity, the attributes of God, and predestination. The second was devoted to God's creation, including angels, but principally man, sin, free-will, and the need of redemption. The third dealt mainly with the work of redemption through Christ, including the question of whether Christ had not only love for man but also faith and hope, in other words, whether Christ was fully human. The fruits of the Spirit were covered, and the seven cardinal virtues. The fourth book was chiefly concerned with the sacraments and eschatology. The method of treatment was to assemble pertinent quotations from the fathers revered by the Catholic Church.

In a certain sense the *Sentences* were pedestrian and not a work of creative thought. However, had they been merely pedestrian they would not have enjoyed the popularity and prolonged and extensive use that was theirs. They were extraordinarily comprehensive and skilfully compiled. They covered the field of Christian theology and the subjects which were of interest to the teachers and students of the time. They raised the pertinent questions, and, employing the prevalent dialectic method, explained and interpreted them and brought together passages from the outstanding authorities which would best throw light on them. In the day before printing had reduced the cost and when teachers and students could own few books, the Bible and Peter's Lombard's *Sentences* provided what were deemed the essentials for a theological education.

The High Tide of Scholasticism

In the latter part of the twelfth and in the thirteenth century scholasticism reached the peak of its popularity and creativity. Commerce was increasing, towns and cities were growing, new ideas were flooding in from abroad through Jewish and Arab scholars and contacts with the East by way of merchants and Crusaders. More works of the great Greek philosophers were becoming available in Latin, partly through translations from Arabic, and partly through the Latin occupation of Constantinople, bringing as it did Western Europe into intimate touch with that centre of Greek learning. Especially was more of Aristotle becoming known. He was often called the

Philosopher, so head and shoulders above the other masters of thought was he regarded. Universities were springing up and were covering a wider range of knowledge than had the earlier monastic and cathedral schools. At the same time the mendicant orders were coming into being, both stimulants and products of the religious awakening. As we have seen, the Dominicans and Franciscans early attached themselves to the rising universities, the one through the deliberate plan and the other in spite of the protest of the founder. Among the many caught up in these two orders were some minds of high quality. Inspired by their faith and having their energies channeled through it by their dedication to the religious life, they devoted themselves to theology. From these orders came the men who in the thirteenth and fourteenth centuries brought scholastic theology to its apex.

We can simply make brief mention of a few of the outstanding names. In general, the Franciscans tended to hold the traditional Platonic and Augustinian views and, while not unfamiliar with him, were less committed to Aristotle than were most of the Dominicans and at times were very critical of him.

Prominent among their great scholars was John of Fidanza (1221–1274), better known as Bonaventura and called the *doctor seraphicus*. We have already met him as a head of the Franciscans. He refused the Archbishopric of York but towards the end of his life, reluctantly and at the insistence of the Pope, became Bishop of Albano and cardinal. A mystic, influenced by Neoplatonism through Augustine and the writings ascribed to Dionysius the Areopagite, he held that the highest knowledge comes through union with God, a union which is to be reached through meditation and prayer. For him Aristotelianism was anathema, an error on which to pass judgement. He knew and used the scholastic dialectic and his theological writings won respect.

Bonaventura had as one of his teachers an Englishman, Alexander of Hales, who in his mid-fifties became a Franciscan and was known as the *doctor irrefragabilis*. Alexander of Hales was familiar with Aristotle and sought to reconcile Augustinianism with it. Robert Grosseteste, who died in 1253, while not a Franciscan, was friendly to the members of the order and was their first teacher of theology when they established a house at Oxford. A great scholar, he was expert in the mathematics and natural sciences of the day. He wrote commentaries on Aristotle and helped to give currency in Western Europe to that philosophy. But he also knew Neoplatonism, John of Damascus, and the writings of the pseudo-Dionysius, and tried to bring Augustinianism into accord with Aristotle. As Bishop of Lincoln from 1235 to his death in 1253, Grosseteste was known as a leader in reforming the clergy and stood out for the independence of the bishops from royal control. He also protested against the financial exactions of the Pope and the Papal curia.

At the outset of the growing interest in Aristotle, many of the bishops feared it as a threat to the inherited faith, coming as that had so largely through Augustine and those influenced by Augustine and hence with a Platonic slant. Moreover, the additional works of Aristotle had first become known through the Spanish schools and were interpreted with an Averroist slant, a trend which was subversive to historic Christian teachings. For instance, Averroes denied personal immortality. Averroism held that reason is supreme as a way to truth and there were Averroists who maintained that some things are true when reached by faith but false when tested by reason. Even more basically the Averroists believed that the material world is without beginning or end, that all the universe, including God and man, is governed by immutable necessity, and that far from having free will and reaching out to discover truth, we receive it passively from the cosmic mind. In this cosmic mind with its denial of persons who are free agents lay the ground for the rejection of individual immortality. In the light of such views, it is quite understandable that the authorities of the Catholic Church took alarm at the popularity of Aristotle as interpreted by Averroes. Here was a heresy which might lure the intellectuals from the Christian faith and be even more of a peril than the Cathari and Waldensees. Good churchmen were, accordingly, critical of those who attempted to reconcile Christian theology with Aristotle.

Yet the great Dominican theologians boldly thought through the Christian faith in terms of Aristotelian patterns. Their work was facilitated by fresh translations of Aristotle made directly into Latin which removed some of the fears of the conservatives. The two most prominent of the Dominican school men were Albert of Cologne, better known as Albertus Magnus and called *doctor universalis,* and Thomas Aquinas.

Albertus Magnus (c.1193 or c.1206–1280) was born in Germany, possibly of aristocratic and certainly of wealthy stock. He studied at various centres, among them some Italian cities. In his youth, while in Italy, he was caught up in the enthusiasm of the early days of the Order of Preachers and joined himself to it. He taught in several places in Germany and became famous as a lecturer in Paris. He later taught at Cologne, was head of the German province of his order, for a brief time was Bishop of Ratisbon, a post which he took reluctantly at Papal behest that he might work a reformation in the diocese, and then, that task accomplished, at his own request was permitted to lay down the burden. Later he travelled widely in Germany, preaching. He spent most of his last years in Cologne.

Although actively engaged in the affairs of his order and of the Church for much of his life, Albertus Magnus was a scholar of no mean dimensions. He did much to popularize Aristotle among the learned circles of Western Europe. Deeply interested in wide ranges of natural science, he studied those portions of Aristotle which were devoted to that subject and added the fruits of his own independent observations. Some of the latter anticipated the results of nineteenth and twentieth century science. He was also intimately familiar with the Bible and wrote commentaries on it. He was, too, a distinguished theologian. He was not unacquainted with Neoplatonic thought. However, he systematically employed Aristotle in his approach to theology and attempted to make this great pre-Christian Greek an aid to Christian thought.

The Prince of the School Men: Thomas Aquinas

One of the major contributions of Albertus Magnus was to the thought of Thomas Aquinas. In Thomas Aquinas we come to the high point in the achievement of scholasticism. Endowed with a penetrating and synthesizing mind, he applied the methods of the school men to theology and employed Aristotle in such fashion that he produced what the Roman Catholic Church was eventually to regard as its standard formulation of theology. A close student of Aristotle, he made full use of that philosopher in his attempt to think through and set forth in systematic fashion the whole range of Christian theology. Yet he did not follow him slavishly.

Thomas Aquinas, known also as *doctor angelicus* and *doctor communis,* was born at the end of the year 1224 or at the beginning of 1225, at Roccasecca, not far from Monte Cassino. His father was Count of Aquino and was related to the imperial house of Hohenstaufen. At a tender age Thomas was placed in the monastery of Monte Cassino, the mother house of the Benedictines, there to be educated under the supervision of his uncle, the abbot. He early showed an inquiring mind and an aptitude for study. At about the age of nineteen he was attracted, as were so many others of the high born young intellectuals of the day, to the Order of Preachers. His mother and brothers, angered by this step, seized him and kept him in confinement for over a year, hoping to dissuade him. However, he persevered, made his escape, went to Paris, and there studied with Albertus Magnus. He was in Paris midway in the reign of Louis IX, the Saint, when the university was in the heyday of its youth. After about three years he went to Cologne, there to continue his education under the direction of Albertus Magnus. For a time he was known as the "dumb ox," so quiet was he and so large of frame. Yet before long his unusual mental capacity became apparent. In his mid-twenties he declined appointment to be Abbot of Monte Cassino. Back once more in the University of Paris, he was a friend of Bonaventura. He began teaching at an early age and soon rose to distinction.

Years of teaching and writing followed, some of them in Paris, some in Spain, many of them in several centres in Italy, then again in Paris, and at the last in Naples. Several of his years in Italy were spent as a member of the Papal court. On one occasion he refused the Archbishopric of Naples urged on him by one of the Popes.

Thomas Aquinas regarded his vocation as that of the scholar, teacher, and writer. To this he gave himself with single-minded commitment. His labours were prodigious and his literary output enormous. Calm, kindly, quietly charming, chary of words except in the line of duty, he concentrated on thought. Yet he was primarily and deeply religious. He wrote hymns and commentaries on the Scriptures as well as philosophy and theology and assisted in the inauguration of the feast of Corpus Christi. Although unusually tall and bulky, his body was frail and could not indefinitely stand up under the strain to which his devotion to study subjected it. He died when about forty-nine years of age, deeply mourned, especially by his fellow Dominican and former teacher, Albertus Magnus.

Almost unfailingly calm and modest, Thomas Aquinas was from time to time drawn into controversy. In the struggle of the secular clergy to oust the friars from the University of Paris he came out boldly and eventually successfully on behalf of the Dominicans. He entered into debate with Averroists who were prominent in the University of Paris and argued that their distinctive views which were giving offense to the orthodox were based upon a false interpretation of Aristotle. An Aristotelian, intimately familiar with that scholar's work, he contended for the Philosopher against the conservatives who feared him as endangering the Augustinian theology which had been dominant in the Western Church. Among his opponents were a few in his own order but especially some of the Franciscans, for the members of that order, as we have seen, were inclined more towards Augustine and his Platonism.

Thomas Aquinas had the gift not only of clarity of mind, but also of facility of statement and a comprehensive intellect. Deeply indebted to Albertus Magnus, he put into orderly form what the latter had given him. He was by no means a slavish transmitter and on some points differed from his great teacher. He was not as much interested in natural science as was Albert, for he was exclusively a philosopher and theologian. Here he surpassed his mentor in range and inclusiveness of thought and systematic statement.

The great achievement of Thomas Aquinas was setting forth the relation of reason and faith in such fashion that those to whom the Aristotelian philosophy was definitive could feel that they might consistently remain Christians. As we have seen, the introduction to the full range of Aristotle's thought by the translation of his works into Latin had brought stimulus to the minds of

Western Europeans. In the thirteenth century he enjoyed a great vogue among a large proportion of the intellectuals of Western Europe. The task to which Aquinas set himself was the reconciliation of Aristotle with the Christian faith. He did this from profound conviction, especially since he believed that Plato, whom many were following, did not have the correct answers to man's quest.

Of the many works which came from the pen of Thomas Aquinas, the two which present his thought most comprehensively are his *Summa Contra Gentiles,* designed to equip missionaries to the Moslems with arguments in the presentation of their faith, and his *Summa* or *Summa Theologiae* (less correctly *Summa Theologica,* a form legitimatized by long usage), a massive work left uncompleted by his early death.

As we have said, Aquinas was critical of Plato. To Plato ideas or forms were real. Aquinas rejected this position. He was not a realist in the scholastic meaning of that term. He therefore also differed from Augustine and his Neo-platonic framework. To him, as to Aristotle, knowledge is based upon what the senses perceive. The data provided through the senses when interpreted by reason are a road to knowledge. Yet, while holding to the principles of Aristotle, Aquinas went beyond Aristotle, for the latter was not a Christian and Aquinas was preëminently held by that faith. To Aquinas faith is also a road to truth. Much of truth is not to be reached by reason. It comes by way of revelation from God and is to be appropriated by faith, that is, by feeling and will. As part of nature, man can know nature through his senses and reason, so Aquinas held. But Aquinas believed that man is also supernatural, and that man's ultimate happiness consists in contemplating God. That goal, so he declared, is not to be fully attained in this life, nor can it be reached by man's unaided intellect. The vision of God which is man's highest goal can come only through the outpouring of the divine goodness. Through that vision man is made a partaker of eternal life. However, so Aquinas taught, since God is the origin of both nature and revelation, both reason and faith are from Him and cannot be in conflict with each other, nor can the knowledge reached through the senses and reason contradict the truth which is given through revelation and apprehended through faith.

Aquinas held that the existence of God can be demonstrated on the basis of the knowledge which we obtain through our senses and our reason. He rejected both the view that the existence of God is self-evident, as Anselm had maintained, and that it cannot be proved but must be accepted on faith alone. He also taught that the attributes of God, such as that He is one, good, and infinite, can be confidently affirmed, partly through reason and partly through faith, and that God can be known by man. Aquinas went on to maintain that everything which exists has been created and is sustained by God. God creates what is out of what is not.

Having dealt extensively with God, Thomas Aquinas proceeded to speak of man. He described his soul and the various powers of the soul. Aquinas was to a certain degree a determinist, although in a somewhat masked form. To be sure, the will, so he held, is moved only by itself and not by its environment. But, he taught, God moves all His creatures, including man, in accordance with their natures. Yet Aquinas was not a determinist in the Moslem Averroist sense of that term. In stressing the competence of human reason he went far towards free will, even though he believed it to be limited.

As we have said, to Aquinas the end of man is the vision of God. All beings, including man, are subject to the law of God. This law has eternally existed in the mind of God. In the created world it is reflected in the law of nature, or the natural law. To assist man in knowing that law, God gave the divine law as it is seen in the Old Testament. That law was meant to guide man. Man, through his will, can conform to the law of nature, but partly through ignorance and partly through the misuse of his will he has failed to do so. Although marred by sin, man can still cultivate the four natural virtues—prudence, justice, courage, and self-control. However, it is only through God's grace that the distinctively Christian virtues, faith, hope, and love, can come to man. Only by God's grace, which man can never earn, can man be changed and attain to the vision of God. Grace, according to Aquinas, is both the divine act of God, undeserved by man, and its effect in "a certain supernatural thing in man coming into existence from God." He agreed with Augustine that "without grace men can do no good whatever" and that by its light they know what to do and by its help do what they know. Grace is a new birth wrought in the Christian by the creative act of God. Aquinas regarded grace as prevenient, that is, it is what stirs a man to the repentance on which the new birth is conditioned, and it enables man to repent. When the new birth has been wrought, grace continues to enable the Christian both to will and to work in such fashion as to please God.

Because man sinned, so Aquinas said, God became incarnate in Christ, the God-man. Christ was born of the Virgin Mary. Aquinas could not go as far as the Franciscans, who held to the immaculate conception, that is, that Mary was herself conceived without the taint of original sin, a view which in the nineteenth century the Roman Catholic Church explicitly and formally endorsed. He declared that it is proper to venerate Mary as the mother of Christ, but he did not believe it to be necessary to hold that she was miraculously conceived. It is primarily through Jesus Christ, so Aquinas said, that God's grace is mediated to man. Jesus Christ is teacher, Messiah, priest, and sacrifice.

Through the sufferings and death of Christ man is freed from the power of evil and from the penalty for sin and is reconciled to God. Aquinas combined the views of Anselm and Abélard on the atonement, holding that Christ both made satisfaction for man's sin and moved men to love.

Grace, so Aquinas maintained, comes to man through the sacraments. The sacraments derive their efficacy from the passion of Christ. The sacraments are means through which the grace operates which comes through Christ. God works through them. They are dependent for their power upon God and not upon the attitudes of those to whom they are administered. Their effect, so Aquinas declared, is *ex opere operato,* namely, from the act of performing them.

THE SIGNIFICANCE OF AQUINAS

How significant was Thomas Aquinas? Why is it that we have called him the prince of the school men? He was not an innovator in Christian doctrine. That must be apparent even in the brief summary which we have given of his teachings. What he wished to do was to present the historic Christian faith as held by the Catholic Church. We have seen that in his treatment of the immaculate conception of Mary he differed from what became the accepted teaching of the Church. However, he kept so closely to the central core of Catholic teaching that even now, as we have seen, his work is basic in the study of Roman Catholic theology.

Indeed, much of his significance lies in just that achievement. He lived in a day when Western Europe seemed to be in danger of departing from the Christian faith. Although they were being stamped out, the Cathari had only recently passed the apex of their spread. Professing to be Christians, probably sincerely so, and prizing the New Testament, they had rejected some of the most fundamental of the apostolic teachings. In the University of Paris, the chief centre for the study of Christian theology, Averroism, with its contradiction of some of the central Christian convictions, was gaining in popularity. The Aristotelian vogue and the use being made by the Averroists of him whom the scholars of the day called the Philosopher was a further threat. By employing Aristotle and by doing so in such fashion as to make him a bulwark of the Christian faith, and by presenting that faith comprehensively and clearly, Aquinas, more than any one else of the four centuries between 950 and 1350, provided Christianity with a firm intellectual foundation.

Moreover, by his use of reason and in delimiting the boundaries between reason and faith, Aquinas gave to reason an honourable place in Christian thought. To him there was no conflict between the two. Both are from God.

In this conviction he was not alone, nor was he a pioneer. However, he mightily reinforced it. In another chapter we will recur to the contribution which, in the use of reason and confidence in an orderly universe, Aquinas and other school men made to the general intellectual development of Western Europe.

We must also see Aquinas in relation to the other religious movements in Western Europe in the thirteenth century. The climax of scholasticism of which he was the outstanding representative was paralleled by a flood tide in other currents in the religious life in that part of the world. The amazing deepening of the Christian faith of the masses which was stimulated by the mendicant orders and which found part of its expression in them was still in the first flush of its pristine power. Indeed, Aquinas was in no small degree its product. It is one facet of his significance that he, as a Dominican, carried out the purpose of the founder of his order to devote scholarship to the cogent presentation of the Christian faith. We must also remember those popular movements, the most extensive being the Albigensees and the Waldensees, which, although condemned by the Catholic Church, were efforts to bring to a better understanding of the Gospel and a full commitment to it some of the millions who through the mass conversions of earlier generations had inherited a professed allegiance to it. The heyday of these movements had been not far from the boyhood of Aquinas. So, too, the effort to purify the hierarchy of the Catholic Church from parish priest to bishop, archbishop, and Pope, and through it to make of Christendom the *Corpus Christianum,* a truly Christian society, attained its climax under Innocent III, only a decade before the birth of Aquinas. To no small degree the significance of Aquinas was in the fact of this synchronization. He was a part of one of the great waves of Christian advance. In him the spirit which was pulsing through all these related movements had seized and stimulated a first-class mind to notable achievement.

THE BEGINNING OF THE DECLINE OF SCHOLASTICISM

Scholasticism never again attained the heights that it reached in Aquinas. After him there were able minds which devoted themselves to its dialectic. However, they did not use it as successfully to solve the intellectual problems presented by Christianity as had such men as Anselm and Aquinas. In them there appeared a gulf between reason and faith, a gulf which might prove disastrous to both. Why this was so is not entirely clear. Then, too, the intellectual life of Europe began to turn away from the methods and the interests of the school men. The latter continued, but new currents were passing them by, currents which were to be especially potent after 1350.

JOHN DUNS SCOTUS: A STEP TOWARDS THE DIVORCE OF FAITH AND REASON

Aquinas did not at once attain to the preëminence which was later accorded him. He had vigorous critics among his contemporaries and in the centuries immediately after him.

Among the more severe critics of Aquinas, but himself not merely a negative but also an independent and positive thinker, was John Duns Scotus, who is also called the *doctor subtilis*. About the biographical data of Duns Scotus there has been much uncertainty. He seems to have been born in the south of Scotland not far from the English border, perhaps in 1265 or 1266, and to have become a Franciscan when in his early or middle teens. He was, then, a younger contemporary of Albertus Magnus and Aquinas, being a child at the time of the latter's death and having become a Franciscan in the former's last years. He studied in Paris and perhaps in Oxford, briefly taught in Oxford, took his doctorate of theology in Paris, and died in Cologne in 1308, when still in his early forties. As a Franciscan, he was eventually accorded a position in theology in his order akin to that held by Aquinas among the Dominicans. The controversies between the two schools of thought were accentuated by jealousy between the two orders, for rivalry, sometimes bitter, has been chronic among the various monastic bodies of the Catholic Church. The inclusive structure of that church, whether in the West or in the East, has not ensured the bond of love which is central in Christian unity as conceived in the New Testament. Being a Franciscan from early adolescence, Duns Scotus was predisposed to dissent from Aquinas.

The differences between the theologies of Aquinas and Duns Scotus went deep. Like the former, the latter had a first-class mind and was inspired by his Christian faith to use it. He was in the Franciscan tradition which made much of Augustine, but he was more influenced by Aristotle than Bonaventura had been. In Duns Scotus there was a trend towards a disjunction between reason and faith which was to become acute in the next century in another Franciscan, William of Ockham, and which was to mark a breakdown in the scholastic attempt to bring the two into a consistent synthesis. Anselm and Aquinas had attempted to show that Christian beliefs were at least not inconsistent with reason and that some of them could be established through reason. Duns Scotus entered a path which, when followed further, issued in the denial that the major Christian convictions can be demonstrated by reason or are even consistent with it, and in the affirmation that they must be believed simply on the authority of the Church or of the Scriptures. We must note, however, that a degree of doubt is thrown on the thought of Dun Scotus by the uncertainty which exists as to whether some of the works attributed to him were written by him, at least in the form in which they have come down to us.

The path which Duns Scotus entered but which he did not follow to its end was the one into which he was led by his emphasis upon the freedom of God's will. Aquinas held that God's will acts in accordance with reason. To put it more extremely than Aquinas would state it, God is bound by reason, and the very nature of God is such that He does not act in a way that is not consistent with reason. This means, therefore, that since human reason is derived from God, nothing which God is or does is out of accord with man's reason. Through the use of his reason man can know much about God, and even though some of God's acts, notably the incarnation and the work of Christ, could not have been discovered through reason, they are not contrary to reason. In contrast, Duns Scotus viewed God as being completely free and not bound by reason. As he saw it, God is not under the necessity of conforming to reason. His acts, therefore, by implication, may even be contrary to reason. Yet Duns Scotus did not think of God as capricious or as making for chaos. But it was God's will and not His reason or His mind which brought the world into being.

Duns Scotus also regarded man as having more freedom of will than had either Augustine or Aquinas. He believed in original sin, but held that by it men have not lost the power of free decision. He had no thought of denying the incarnation or the atonement. Indeed, along with his fellow-Franciscans, he taught that Mary was without original sin. Yet he did not believe, as had Anselm and some others, that if God wished to forgive man He was bound to become incarnate and to be crucified that the moral order of the universe might be preserved. He did not hold that the incarnation and crucifixion were the wisest way to achieve man's salvation, as had Aquinas, for that would limit God's freedom. All he would say was that they were the way chosen by God.

Duns Scotus stressed the authority of the Church and the duty to believe what the Church teaches and to conform to what it commands. What the Church teaches may not be supported by reason and may even seem irrational, but is to be accepted because the Church says so.

Duns Scotus differed from Aquinas and others of his predecessors in the value which he gave to what is technically known as attrition. By attrition is meant sorrow for sin from fear of the punishment which follows sin. Aquinas maintained that this was not the true repentance which is prerequisite to the forgiveness of God, but that really to be repentant one must have contrition, that is, sorrow born of love of God for having slighted God's love. In contrast, Duns Scotus held that attrition is a sufficient starting-point towards God's forgiveness. This is not because through it a man deserves forgiveness, but because God wills it so.

The Breakdown of Scholasticism: William of Ockham: The Completion of the Divorce of Faith and Reason

A symbol and a decisive contributor to the decline of scholasticism was the Englishman William of Ockham (or Occam), known as *doctor invincibilis* and *venerabilis inceptor*. Born about 1300, at Ockham, in Surrey, he early became a student at Oxford and there joined the Franciscans. A radical, rebel, and controversialist by temperament and conviction, he eventually identified himself with the Spirituals of his order. He championed the cause of the Emperor as against the Pope. As we saw in the preceding chapter, he held highly unconventional views of the structure and authority of the Church.

Given· such a character, it is not strange that William of Ockham was daring, provocative, and argumentative in theology. In philosophy, in contrast with Duns Scotus, who held to a modified form of realism, he was a nominalist, although not in an extreme sense, and a vigorous critic of realism. He emphatically rejected the universals which were essential in realism. All that we can know, he held, are individual things. These we know by what he called intuition. Intuition is caused by objects, but even it can give incorrect information. We know not only external objects through our senses. We also know, and even more convincingly and immediately, our inner experiences such as joy and sorrow. An Aristotelian, he attempted to apply the principles of the Philosopher fearlessly and ruthlessly.

Turning from philosophy to theology, Ockham maintained that none of the Christian beliefs can be proved through reason by the logic employed by the school men. Even the existence of God, he held, cannot be demonstrated, and he found inconclusive all the arguments which Aquinas had adduced to support it. He declared that we must accept the tenets of Christianity, including such basic ones as the existence of God and the immortality of the soul, because the Church teaches them and because they are contained in the Bible. They cannot be proved but are to be accepted only on faith.

Here was the complete divorce between reason and faith. Scholasticism had come to the point where it had accepted defeat in the struggle towards what had been its great objective, to employ the tools given by the Greek pre-Christian philosophers to demonstrate by reason the validity of the great Christian affirmations.

William of Ockham and those who agreed with him had given up hope of reconciling the wisdom of man with the wisdom of God. To them, as to Paul, the cross and all that was involved in it were foolishness when judged by the wisdom of the Greeks, and man through his wisdom had not known God. They might not go as far as Paul and declare that God had made foolish the wisdom of the world, but they would insist that between truth as reached by the methods of logic derived from the Greeks and the truth made known through the Gospel a gulf existed which reason could not bridge.

Ockham's views did not win universal acceptance among the school men. The debate went on, often acrimoniously, but in scholastic circles Ockham's theology gained wide popularity.

It seems significant that the decline of scholastic theology which was evidenced by its progressive failure to support Christian faith by reason paralleled the ebbing of vitality in other phases of the Catholic Church of the West. As in these other aspects of the Church's life, it began to be seen in the later decades of the thirteenth century but did not become pronounced until the second half of the fourteenth century. As the climax of scholasticism attained in Thomas Aquinas was roughly coincident with the peak reached in monasticism with the emergence and early growth of the mendicant orders and in the Papacy in Innocent III but was slightly later, so the first indications of decay in scholasticism approximated in time the early hints that the ecclesiastical structure of Western Europe was to suffer from the changes in the on-going stream of history but lagged slightly behind them. No new monastic orders comparable in power and extent with the Franciscans and Dominicans appeared between the first quarter of the thirteenth century and the first half of the sixteenth century and no Pope after Innocent III (who died in 1216) was to wield as much power as he in so many facets of the life of Europe. Yet, as in these other expressions of the vigour of the Catholic Church, the decay in the intellectual approach did not become spectacular until the second half of the fourteenth century. Although William of Ockham not only registered the sharp disjunction between reason and faith which gave evidence of the breakdown of scholasticism but also was a leader in the attack on the political power of the Papacy, his was a vigorous mind and he was still within the scholastic tradition. It appears to be more than a coincidence that he died late in the 1340's and that he may have been a victim of the plague, that Black Death whose scourge, which first became striking in 1347 and 1348, was to speed up the passing of the old order in Europe and was to contribute to the next period of sharp recession in the course of Christianity.

SUMMARY

The problem of the school men was not new. From their very early days Christians had been struggling with the relation between philosophy, the search of man for truth by his rational processes on the one hand, and the Gospel on the other. Could the affirmations of the Christian faith be supported by reason? Indeed, might they be reached concomitantly but independently of revelation? In seeking the answer, the school men took advantage of the tools provided them by the pre-Christian Greek philosophers, especially Plato and Aristotle. The answers at which they arrived were varied. It is significant and sobering that the longer the scholastic method was employed the greater was the tendency to conclude that the truth of the basic Christian convictions could not be proved by the dialectical apparatus. Anselm had proceeded on the confident conviction that through reason implemented by logic man could demonstrate at least some and perhaps all of the major tenets of Christianity. Aquinas held that some of the truths affirmed by Christianity could be supported by reason and that while others could be arrived at only by the path of faith, none was inconsistent with reason. William of Ockham taught that none of the essential features of Christian belief could be proved to the satisfaction of man's reason but that they must be accepted on the authority of the Church and of the Scriptures. To be sure, not all Catholic scholars agreed with him. Many held to those who taught the contrary, especially to Anselm and Aquinas. As the centuries passed, Aquinas was more and more honoured. Yet in 1350, the trend was away from him. Here was poor preparation for meeting the intellectual challenges which the age into which Western Europe was moving posed to Christianity.

SELECTED BIBLIOGRAPHY

GENERAL WORKS

M. H. Carré, *Realists and Nominalists* (Oxford University Press, 1946, pp. vi, 128). Four essays which cover Augustine, Abélard, Thomas Aquinas, and William of Ockham.

F. Copleston, *A History of Philosophy. Volume II. Mediæval Philosophy Augustine to Scotus* (London, Burns, Oates & Washbourne, 1950, pp. x, 614). A competent, objective survey by a Jesuit.

R. Seeberg, *Text-Book of the History of Doctrines. Volume II, History of Doctrines in the Middle and Modern Ages,* revised, 1904, by the author, translated by C. E. Hay (Philadelphia, The United Lutheran Publishing House, 1905, pp. xii, 492). A standard treatment by a Lutheran, of which about the first third covers this period.

B. Smalley, *The Study of the Bible in the Middle Ages* (Oxford, Basil Blackwell, 2d ed., 1952, pp. xxii, 406). Carefully done.

LANFRANC

A. J. Macdonald, *Lanfranc. A Study of His Life Work & Writing* (Oxford University Press, 1926, pp. vii, 307). Carefully done.

ANSELM

Texts of Anselm's works are in J. P. Migne, *Patrologia Latina,* Vols. CLVIII and CLIX (Paris, 1853, 1903).

St. Anselm, *Proslogium; Monologium; an Appendix in Behalf of the Fool by Gaunilon; and Cur Deus Homo,* translated from the Latin by S. N. Deane (Chicago, The Open Court Publishing Co., 1903, pp. xxxv, 288).

St. Anselm's Book of Meditations and Prayers. Translated from the Latin by M. R. (London, Burns, Oates & Washbourne, 1872, pp. xvi, 294).

Eadmeri Historia Novorum in Anglia et Opuscula duo de Vita Sancti Anselmi et Quibusdam Miraculis Ejus, edited by M. Rule in *The Chronicles and Memorials of Great Britain and Ireland during the Middle Ages* (London, Longmans, Green & Co., 1884, pp. cxxvii, 460). By a friend and admirer of Anselm.

J. M. Rigg, *St. Anselm of Canterbury. A Chapter in the History of Religion* (London, Methuen & Co., 1896, pp. 294).

ABÉLARD

Petri Abælardi Abbatis Rugensis Opera Omnia juxta editionem Parisiensem anni 1626, suppletis quæ in ea desiderabantur opusculis accedunt Hilarii et Berengarii Abælardi Discipulorum Opuscula et Epistolæ, in J.-P. Migne, *Patrologia Latina,* Vol. CLXXVIII (Paris, 1885).

Abailard's Ethics. Translated with an introduction by J. R. McCallum (Oxford, Basil Blackwell, 1935, pp. x, 93).

Abélard, Peter, *Historia Calamitatum. The Story of My Misfortunes. An Autobiography,* translated by H. A. Bellows (St. Paul, Thomas A. Boyd, 1922, pp. xxi, 96).

The Letters of Abélard and Heloise, translated from the Latin by C. K. S. Moncrieff (New York, Alfred A. Knopf, 1942, pp. xiii, 264).

J. McCabe, *Peter Abélard* (New York, G. P. Putnam's Sons, 1901, pp. vii, 402). A semi-popular account.

J. K. Sikes, *Peter Abailard* (Cambridge University Press, 1932, pp. xvi, 282). A careful study based upon an extensive use of the sources.

HUGO OF ST. VICTOR

Hugonis de S. Victoris . . . Opera Omnia in J.-P. Migne, *Patrologia Latina,* Vols. CLXXV, CLXXVI, CLXXVII (Paris, 1879).

Hugh of St. Victor, *Explanation of the Rule of St. Augustine,* translated by A. Smith (London, Sands & Company, 1911, pp. xi, 121).

PETER LOMBARD

P. Lombardi . . . Opera Omnia . . . Accedunt Magistri Bandini . . . Senten-tiarum Libri Quatuor, in J.-P. Migne, *Patrologia Latina,* Vols. CXCI, CXCII (Paris, 1879, 1880).

BONAVENTURA

Breviloquium by St. Bonaventure, translated by E. E. Nemmers (St. Louis, B. Herder Book Co., 1946, pp. xxii, 248).

The Franciscan Union. Translation of St. Bonaventure's Itinerarium Mentis in Deum (London, Burns, Oates & Washbourne, 1937, pp. ix, 74).

Holiness of Life. Being St. Bonaventure's Treatise de Perfectione Vitae ad Sorores, translated by L. Costello (St. Louis, B. Herder Book Co., 2d ed., 1928, pp. xxxi, 103).

E. Gilson, *The Philosophy of St. Bonaventure,* translated by I. Trethowan (New York, Sheed & Ward, 1938, pp. xiii, 551). A modern expert treatise by a Roman Catholic.

ROBERT GROSSETESTE

F. S. Stevenson, *Robert Grosseteste Bishop of Lincoln* (London, Macmillan & Co., 1899, pp. xvi, 348). Well done.

ALBERTUS MAGNUS

H. Wilms, *Albert the Great: Saint and Doctor of the Church* (London, Burns, Oates & Washbourne, 1933, pp. xxi, 226). Based upon extensive research and sympathetic with Albertus Magnus.

THOMAS AQUINAS

Sancti Thomae Aquinatis Doctoris Angelici Ordinis Praedicatorum Opera Omnia secundum impressionem Petri Fiaccadori Parmae 1852–1873 photolithographice reimpressa (New York, Musurgia Publishers, 25 vols., 1948–1950).

The Summa Contra Gentiles of Saint Thomas Aquinas, Literally Translated by the English Dominican Fathers from the latest Leonine edition (London, Burns, Oates & Washbourne, and New York, Benziger Brothers, 4 vols., vol. 3 being in two parts, 1924–1929).

The Summa Theologica of St. Thomas Aquinas, Literally Translated by Fathers of the English Dominican Province (London, Burns, Oates & Washbourne, 2nd and rev. ed., 19 vols., 1920–1922).

Introduction to Saint Thomas Aquinas, edited with introduction by A. C. Pegis (New York, Random House, 1948, pp. xxx, 690). A useful volume, made up principally of translations from Aquinas.

R. Garrigou-Lagrange, *The One God. A Commentary on the First Part of St. Thomas' Theological Summa,* translated by B. Rose (St. Louis, B. Herder Book Co., 1943, pp. viii, 736). By a competent scholar.

E. Gilson, *The Philosophy of St. Thomas Aquinas,* translated by E. Bullough, edited by G. A. Elrington (Cambridge, W. Heffer & Sons, 1929, pp. xv, 372). A standard work.

M. Grabmann, *Thomas Aquinas. His Personality and Thought,* translated by V. Michel (New York, Longmans, Green & Co., 1928, pp. ix, 190). A brief, semi-popular account.

R. L. Patterson, *The Conception of God in the Philosophy of Aquinas* (London, George Allen & Unwin, 1933, pp. 508).

A. D. Sertillanges, *Saint Thomas Aquinas and His Work,* translated by G. Anstruther (London, Burns, Oates & Washbourne, 1932, pp. ix, 150). A popular, sympathetic account.

DUNS SCOTUS

M. Heidegger, *Die Kategorien- und Bedeutungslehre des Duns Scotus* (Tübingen, J. C. B. Mohr, 1916, pp. 241).

R. Seeberg, *Die Theologie des Johannes Duns Scotus* (Leipzig, Dieterich'sche Verlags-Buchhandlung, 1900, pp. vi, 705). Very carefully done.

P. Vignaux, *Justification et Predestination au XIVe Siècle. Duns Scot, Pierre d'Auriole, Guillaume d'Occam, Gregoire de Rimini* (Paris, Ernest Leroux, 1934, pp. viii, 189).

WILLIAM OF OCKHAM

The De Sacramento Altaris of William of Ockham, edited, Latin text, and English translation by T. B. Birch (Burlington, Iowa, The Lutheran Literary Board, 1930, pp. xlvii, 576).

Le Tractatus de Principiis Theologiæ attribué a G. d'Occam, édition critique, L. Baudry (Paris, Librairie Philosophique J. Vrin, 1936, pp. 159).

R. Guelluy, *Philosophie et Théologie chez Guillaume d'Ockham* (Louvain, E. Nauwelærts, 1947, pp. xxiv, 383). Based upon extensive research.

Chapter 22

PARISH LIFE, PUBLIC WORSHIP, DISCIPLINE, AND PRIVATE WORSHIP AND DEVOTION IN WESTERN EUROPE

How did the Christian faith operate among the masses of the people in Western Europe during the four centuries between 950 and 1350? We have had much to say of the monastic movements, but they centered their efforts upon the small minority of the population who were their members. To be sure, their effects were felt in much wider circles. As the centuries wore on, especially after the rise of the mendicant orders with their missionary zeal, the influence of those fully committed to the Christian life affected more and more of the common run of mankind about them. But we have thus far said little of the commonalty and of its religion and morals. We have spoken of the movements which the Catholic Church condemned as heretical, but except in certain sections these did not reach beyond minorities. We have told of the efforts of the reformers to make of the Catholic Church an instrument for raising all of Christendom to a nearer approximation to the Christian ideal, but in doing so we have focussed our attention on the directing centre, the Papacy and the councils of the entire Church, with here and there an excursus to outstanding bishops and archbishops. Only incidentally have we hinted at the fashion in which these struggles at the top had repercussions among the multitude. We have recounted in summary the intellectual approach to the Christian faith, but this also directly affected only the small minority who were scholars. We have not stopped to ask how far if at all echoes of the discussions were heard by the illiterate who constituted the bulk of Western Europeans.

We must now pause to inquire the way in which Christianity was mediated to the rank and file and the nature and features of the response. This will lead us to say something of the structure of diocesan and parish organization and life, of worship, both public and private, of the methods employed to acquaint the ordinary Christian with the tenets and practices of his faith, and of the discipline applied to guide or constrain the millions of individuals who were the supposed concern of the Church. The scene with which we have to deal is extraordinarily varied and generalizations are correspondingly perilous, but if we are to essay to paint the picture at all we can do so only with broad strokes, with here and there an illustrative detail.

THE DIOCESAN AND PARISH STRUCTURE

In reaching the masses with the Christian faith the chief channel of Christianity was the Catholic Church. That Church inherited the ecclesiastical structure which had evolved in the Roman Empire. It continued this, but with important modifications. That structure, it will be recalled, was territorially comprehensive and its main divisions reflected roughly the administrative units of the Empire. It had its dioceses, each with its bishop. Dioceses were grouped by provinces, and in each of these the bishops might meet in synods and the bishop in the leading city had a kind of preëminence and came to be known as the metropolitan. The bishops in the outstanding cities of the Empire, of which the chief were Rome, Antioch, Alexandria, Constantinople, and, because of its historic significance for the faith, Jerusalem, were termed patriarchs and exercised their authority over a still wider area. In the course of time parishes, much smaller divisions than the dioceses, developed for the care of the faithful in the local scene. This form of organization carried over into the period with which we have been dealing.

Important modifications were made. In the early days of the episcopate, vacancies were filled on nomination by neighbouring bishops and were approved by the clergy and laity of the diocese. As metropolitans emerged, each usually supervised the election and consecrated and installed the bishops in his province. Beginning with the sixth century in the West the assent of the king was generally required and the king often controlled the appointment. In theory the choice of the bishop was by the clergy and people of the diocese. By the middle of the twelfth century the election in most of Western Europe was by the canons, the clergy attached to the cathedral, the bishop's church. As we have seen, between 950 and 1350 a major struggle developed for the determination of the succession to the episcopate between the Pope on the one hand and the kings on the other. Under the great Popes the Roman See was an increasing power, but the conflict was not fully resolved.

Parishes multiplied. Especially did they do so as cities declined and Western Europe became prevailingly rural. In principle each had its resident priest or priests who administered the sacraments. This priest was called *presbyter* or *rector*. Because he had as his charge the *cura animarum,* the care of the souls in his parish, in time he might also be known as *curatus,* from whence comes the French *curé*. The priest might be known as the *parson,* or the *person* (from Latin *persona*), the most important man in the parish. At least in England, the resident clergyman might be called *vicar*. In this case the income from the parish had been assigned to a monastery or had been appropriated in some other way, perhaps by the bishop. The *vicar,* who was a *vicarius* or substitute for the parish priest, and who might not be in full priest's orders, was employed for a fraction of the revenues, to give spiritual care to the parish. In principle the parish priest was responsible to the bishop of the diocese and was supervised by him. In practice the chief layman in the parish, the local lord within whose domain the parish lay, was often more to be reckoned with than the bishop. It was he or his predecessors who had founded and endowed the parish. He therefore often made the appointment and controlled the appointee.

The clergy constituted a special class. They had their own courts and stoutly maintained that they could not be called to account by the civil courts or be taxed by the secular rulers. Here, as we have seen, was a source of chronic conflict between the state and the Church.

The Parish and Its Life

The parish was the unit around which revolved many of the community activities of the local population, especially in rural districts. The parish church and its services were a focus where baptisms were administered, marriages were consecrated, and the dead buried. Mass was supposed to be said daily and it might be preceded, especially on Sundays, by matins and succeeded by evensong. Sunday masses were well attended, but were often poorly conducted and scarcely listened to by the congregation. Parish churches and church yards were used for community dancing, games, banquets, sports, buffoonery, festivals, fairs, and markets.

Presumably the quality of Christian life in the parish depended primarily upon the parish priest or his substitute. He it was who gave religious instruction, administered the sacraments, and looked after the spiritual and moral welfare of his flock. In theory the priest was celibate and had been trained for his calling in the cathedral church of the diocese. From there he was supposed to go to the cathedral church of the metropolitan of the province for additional instruction and the Fourth Lateran Council ordered that in each of the latter there should be a chair of theology.

In practice the ideal was not fully attained. That there were some worthy priests is certain. How large a percentage of the whole they constituted cannot be determined and probably varied from region to region and from time to time. Many were palpably unworthy. There were periods and areas in which the majority are said to have been married or to have had concubines. Some had irregular relations with the women of the parish. Many frequented taverns. A large proportion were avaricious. Indeed, avarice was one of the main charges leveled against them. Numbers eked out their incomes by keeping taverns, buying and selling, and lending money.

Support of the parish clergy was partly through tithes levied on the fruits of the field, on merchandise, and on handicrafts. From the tithes not only were the clergy supported, but aid also came for the poor of the parish and for the maintenance and repair of parish buildings. Offerings were made at the mass, baptisms, marriages, and funerals. Technically voluntary, in practice they became obligatory fees paid for services rendered by the priest. Obviously they lent themselves to exactions and disputes.

Investigations made from time to time by reforming bishops and archbishops showed that substantial numbers of the parish priests did not understand the Latin of the services which they conducted, not even that of the mass. Very few were familiar with the Bible. The rise and multiplication of the universities in the thirteenth and fourteenth centuries might have been supposed to bring improvement, especially since in some of them the major subject was theology. However, canon law seems to have been more studied than theology, for it was a better road to preferment. Then, too, not many parish priests were university graduates. University men tended to go into the higher ranks of the clergy or into teaching, or to be absorbed in the central administrative structure of dioceses and the Papacy. Not all metropolitan cathedrals had occupants for the chairs of theology which were required in principle.

As we have suggested, the revenues from the parish might be diverted to absentees, individuals or monasteries, and the actual work be done by substitutes who were not always priests or even deacons. They were usually poorly trained men hired for a pittance, and that in spite of the protests of reforming bishops. Pluralism was widespread. By this was meant that one man might draw the revenues of several parishes and, an absentee incumbent, live in luxury and employ a *locum tenens*. This was regarded as so usual that many men, otherwise excellent, connived with it to their own profit. Thus we hear of one thirteenth century English bishop, later canonized, who, before he was elevated to the episcopate, held the rectorship of at least ten parishes in addition to other stipends.

The situation was complicated, both for worse and for better, by other factors. There were wandering priests, ordained, but not adequately controlled by bishops, who intruded in parishes, administering the sacraments in disregard of the resident priest. There were assistant clergy, deacons or sub-deacons. There were the parish clerks. There were chantry priests. These last said masses on behalf of the souls of the dead and were supported by endowments left by pious benefactors for that purpose. Frequently they had other duties and were really assistants to the *rector*. All too often their time outside that spent in saying mass was frittered away in idleness or worse. In some parishes there were also chaplains in charge of chapels which were erected to serve those who lived at inconvenient distances from the parish church. Again and again members of the mendicant orders disregarded parish boundaries and conflicts ensued with the secular clergy. However, by their preaching and example, especially during the first flush of devotion in the early days of the orders, the friars helped to raise the level of intelligence and living of the rank and file of the laity. This they did both as the result of their direct impact upon them and indirectly by stimulating the seculars to be more faithful in their ministry.

The instruction given the great body of the laity seems to have increased as the centuries passed. Much of this was through preaching. Originally chiefly the function of bishops, preaching was more and more by parish priests and, after the mendicant orders came into being, by the friars. In a day when books were few and expensive and illiteracy was the rule and literacy the exception, the oral word through the preacher was very important not only for exhortation but also for imparting the basic tenets of the faith. Some energetic bishops commanded the priests of their dioceses to preach and outlined the contents of the sermons. Thus in 1281, John Peckham, a highly educated Franciscan, Archbishop of Canterbury, had his provincial synod command the priests to preach each quarter, instructing their parishioners in the articles of the faith, the Ten Commandments, the seven deadly sins, the seven principal virtues, and the seven sacraments. In more than one country books of sermons were prepared and circulated to assist the priests in their preaching. Instruction also came through the religious plays that were given in churches and churchyards. It was furthered through paintings on the walls of churches, sculpture, and stained-glass windows.

Episcopal Supervision

Ideally the life of the parish was the concern not only of the priest but also of the bishop. Some bishops were too much caught up in the administration of the kingdom to give much care to their dioceses. That was especially the case since such posts as chancellor of the realm were often filled by them. Many bishops were too worldly to trouble themselves much with the details of their official responsibilities. Yet there were bishops who took their duties seriously. Their number multiplied through the mounting religious devotion and the reforming zeal of the age. They made regular journeys of visitation, carefully inspecting the parishes of their dioceses, recording what they found, and seeking to encourage the faithful among the clergy and to discipline the negligent or corrupt.

THE SACRAMENTS

Much of the religious life of the laity centered in the sacraments. In the last chapter we said something of the developing beliefs about them. It was not until 1439 that their number was finally officially fixed. Some authors revered by the Church had spoken of only two, baptism and the Eucharist. Peter Damian had enumerated twelve and Hugo of St. Victor thirty. Peter Lombard seems to have been the first to limit them to seven and to give the list which the Roman Catholic Church eventually made final. By the fourteenth century these had gained general acceptance. They were baptism, confirmation, penance, the Eucharist, extreme unction, marriage, and ordination.

BAPTISM

Baptism of infants had become universal for the offspring of Christian parents. It was believed to effect the new birth. It was, therefore, necessary for salvation. Infants dying unbaptized, so it was held, being still tainted with original sin, could never enjoy that beatific vision of God which is heaven. Popular belief had it that they went to hell. Children were, accordingly, to be baptized as soon after birth as possible. Water was to be used and the ceremony might be by immersion or by affusion, namely, pouring water over the child as the sponsor held it over the font. If the newly born child was in danger of dying, water must be cast on it "in the name of the Father, and of the Son, and of the Holy Ghost." Even though the words were uttered in the vernacular rather than Latin, and imperfectly, the intention was believed to make them effective. It was said, however, that many adults were uncertain whether they had been baptized and that baptism was often neglected.

CONFIRMATION

Confirmation was by the bishop. In at least one region it was to be administered in the child's fifth year. By it the child was supposed to become "God's champion." From various countries come reports that through indifference large numbers had not been given the rite.

PENANCE

Penance had, as we have repeatedly hinted, developed from the forms in use in the first five centuries of the Church. No longer was confession made in public to the congregation nor was the bishop the usual officer of the Church who declared the penitent forgiven and received him back into communion.

Public penance persisted for a time alongside private confession, but it gradually disappeared, especially after the eleventh century. The practice of private confession to a priest with the accompanying penance is usually said to have spread from the Irish monasteries, but the way for it seems to have been prepared quite independently of them.

Penance now entailed contrition for sin, oral private confession to a priest (inviolate secrecy was only slowly observed), the performance of whatever work of satisfaction was commanded by the priest, and the declaration of forgiveness or absolution by the priest. It was recognized that forgiveness rested ultimately with God and that it was conditioned upon the true repentance of the sinner. But it was held that God had granted to Peter and the apostles and through them to the priests the power to remit sins.

In one way or another instructions were developed for the priests to enable them to probe the consciences of those who came to confession. These involved questions of conduct, both of omission and commission—for example, whether things had been borrowed and not returned, whether the children had been taught good manners, the creed and the Lord's Prayer, and whether the churchyard gate had been left open so that animals wandered in. Then there were what were known as the mortal or deadly sins, declared to be seven in number—pride, covetousness, lust, anger, gluttony, envy, and sloth.

The priest prescribed good works to be done as discipline and in satisfaction for sins and graded according to the seriousness of the offense. These might be fasting, the giving of alms, pilgrimages, gifts to the Church, self-flagellation, or some other specific act. Absolution was conditioned upon the performance of these works. In principle, reinforced by the Fourth Lateran Council in 1215, every Christian was to go to confession at least once a year. Thus all the baptized were to come under the disciplinary ministrations of the Church.

INDULGENCES

In connexion with penance there developed the theory and practice of indulgences and of the treasury of the Church. At first indulgences seem to have been of a limited kind, and were the remission of some of the prescribed works of penance in return for some other act, such as gifts to a monastery or a church. It was also held that if the "temporal" penalties for sin were not met in this life, they would be required after death, in purgatory, before the soul was cleansed from its sin and was capable of the beatific vision of God. In the eleventh century the custom began, at first not widely, of granting plenary indulgences, that is, remission of all the temporal penalties for sins. True repentance was, of course, still a prerequisite to forgiveness, but the Church claimed the power to remit the temporal penalties. This was done by local bishops and the Popes. One of the early instances of plenary indulgence was the granting of it by Pope Urban II to those who enlisted in the First Crusade. Later plenary indulgence was extended to those who enabled others to go on a crusade or who performed some other specified good work.

In support of the practice of indulgences the school men, among them notably Alexander of Hales, Albertus Magnus, and Thomas Aquinas, elaborated the principle of the treasury of the Church. It was held that the apostles and saints had done far more than was necessary to assure themselves of heaven and had thereby added to a surplus of merit already enriched by what Christ had done. It was maintained that the Church had been granted the power to transfer some of it to reduce or cancel the good works required of penitent sinners in satisfaction for their offenses. In 1343 Pope Clement VI gave official endorsement to the principle.

Some of the school men, although clear that the Church could remit such penalties in this life, were not convinced that indulgences could accomplish more for the souls now in purgatory than encouragement to pray that the penalties in that state might be lightened. Others held that indulgences granted by Popes and bishops were effective not only in this life but also in purgatory. In the thirteenth century the belief spread that one person could obtain an indulgence for another, and that the living might even obtain indulgences for the souls in purgatory. Here, in the sixteenth century, was to be one of the moot points between Protestants and Catholics.

Indulgences, we must note, were not permissions to commit sin. Nor could they release souls from hell, where the punishment for sin was not temporal, that is, limited in time, but was eternal. Nor did they make repentance unnecessary. They presupposed genuine penitence. Yet here was a growing practice which later was to be grossly abused.

The Eucharist

As in the earlier centuries, so in this period, the Eucharist, which we may also call the Lord's Supper, holy communion, or the mass, was the high point and centre of Christian worship. In the Catholic Church the liturgy of the mass underwent no drastic change in this period. He who had known it in the year 500 in Rome, had he come back to the Eternal City in the year 1350 and gone to mass, would have noticed some modifications but would quickly have felt at home. The Roman rite spread through much of Western Europe, but was adapted to incorporate elements from local or regional usages. Variations existed in several areas. In England, for example, the missal according to the Use of Sarum (Salisbury) differed somewhat from that of Rome and became widespread in the British Isles.

The major developments in the Eucharist during these four centuries were not in the liturgy but in the affirmation of transubstantiation, the withdrawal of the cup from the laity in the communion, the extensive use of excommunication, the feast of Corpus Christi, and the adoration of the reserved sacrament.

We have already seen that in 1215 the Fourth Lateran Council expressly declared transubstantiation to be the teaching of the Church. While in theory the dogma was not new but went back to Christ himself in his institution of the Lord's Supper, the formulation made binding in 1215 had been developed in terms of scholastic philosophy. It had been a subject of debate among the school men and had on occasion provoked acrimonious controversy. Now that what the Western Church regarded as an ecumenical council had spoken, only heretics would dare openly to challenge the decision.

The denial of the cup to the laity came slowly and was a natural concomitant of the growing acceptance of transubstantiation. If through the words of consecration by the priest the bread and the wine in the Eucharist actually become the body and blood of Christ, great care must be taken to prevent any profanation of these elements. Particularly was there danger of spilling some of the wine as the cup was given to the laity. Gradually, therefore, the custom arose of giving only the bread or wafer to the laity and having only the priest take of the cup.

Excommunication was not new. We have met it from the early days of the Church. In the first five centuries it was invoked against those Christians who became flagrant sinners or in ecclesiastical disputes over doctrine or jurisdiction. It continued to be so employed. In addition it was now used as a weapon in contests between the clergy on the one hand and princes on the other. It was also increasingly resorted to by the clergy to coerce the laity in such matters as the observance of feasts and the payment of tithes. Theoretically intended to bring the sinner to repentance, it became a means of constraining the unwilling to compliance with the wishes of those who had the power to exclude from the Eucharist.

Related to excommunication and, indeed, called that until the time of Innocent III, who gave it the designation by which it was afterwards known, was the interdict. Employed at least as early as the ninth century, it became a potent instrument in the hands of the great Popes of the latter part of this era. In its broadest application it was the prohibition of the public administration of the sacraments and of the services of the Church in a given area. Private marriages and the baptism of infants were usually permitted, but most of the ministrations of the Church were suspended until the offending prince or city submitted. For example, Innocent III made effective use of it against John of England in placing under it all of the latter's kingdom.

The feast of Corpus Christi arose in the thirteenth century to commemorate the institution of the Eucharist. It is said to have been begun at the instance of Juliana, a nun, who urged it upon the Bishop of Liege and upon him who in 1261 became Pope Urban IV. In 1246 the Bishop of Liege ordered its observance in his diocese and in 1264 Urban IV instructed the entire Church to honour it. It was placed on the Thursday after Trinity Sunday, of which we are to say more in a moment. The office for it, composed by Thomas Aquinas, was of singular beauty. In spite of Papal endorsement, the feast made but slow headway. However, by the middle of the fourteenth century it was fairly general in Western Europe.

Another custom which arose from the emphasis on transubstantiation and which spread widely in the latter part of the period was the worship of the consecrated bread and wine. They were reserved or exposed all day on the altar in a transparent receptacle called a monstrance and the faithful would come individually or in groups and adore them.

Ideally the Eucharist was to be celebrated reverently and with great dignity. This was often observed, as in the Cluniac houses, with much pomp, and at other times, as in the Cistercian monasteries, with studied austerity. All too often, however, especially in parish churches, the mass was performed perfunctorily and carelessly, and neither the priest nor the congregation took it very seriously.

We must note that the fact that mass was said in Latin, a language understood by fewer and fewer of the laity in Latin Europe as the vernacular departed further from it, and never by more than a handful among the laity in Northern Europe, tended to remove it from the multitude. In the early centuries it was in the vernacular and the congregation understood it and shared in the responses. As its language became unintelligible to the laity and even to some of the priests, it was a spectacle which at best was staged with impressive beauty and at the worst was hurried through in slovenly fashion, with ragged vestments and dirty or tarnished altar furnishings.

EXTREME UNCTION

Pastors were strongly encouraged to give the communion to the sick who were in danger of death and to administer to them extreme unction. Scriptural authority for extreme unction was sought in Mark vi:13, where the apostles are described as anointing the sick with oil and healing them, and in James v. 14, 15, where the sick is instructed to call upon the presbyters of the Church, who are to pray over him, anoint him with oil in the name of the Lord, with the promise that the prayer of faith will save him that was sick, and that if he had committed sins they will be forgiven him.

Anointing with oil had a long history in Christian practice. It was partly for physical healing, and its use had often been abused. It was also connected with penance, for the forgiveness of sins. In this period it came to be separated from penance and was regarded as the distinct sacrament. Down to the twelfth century the practice in the West was to give it to all the ill who asked for it, except those who were doing public penance, but in the twelfth and thirteenth centuries it came to be regarded as only for those believed to be dying. The oil, properly consecrated, was held to make for mental and possibly bodily health, and to work pardon for sins. The priest was to be available day or night to administer it.

MARRIAGE

Marriage was now esteemed one of the sacraments. Here the Christian conscience and the Church faced a difficult and complex problem. Could the strong urge of sex be directed and controlled by the Christian ideal? Could customs of betrothal and marriage, some of them of pre-Christian origin and many of them, even of post-Christian development, with little of the Christian in them, be made to conform to Christian standards? What were Christian standards? Much of marriage was governed by property or power interests, such as the desire for an heir to inherit the estate or the union of two families to strengthen the position of each. A marriage might be arranged with scant regard to the personal wishes of the bride or the groom. Often betrothals were entered into apart from the Church and cohabitation begun, perhaps to see whether the union would be fertile and produce the wished for heir, before the blessing of the priest was asked. Under what circumstances could a marriage be annulled? These were some of the problems which perplexed the canon lawyers. In this period the Catholic Church in the West was struggling to find the answers and to enforce the regulations which it developed. On by no means all issues was a common mind attained. It was held, probably with increasing emphasis, that marriage was a sacrament, that the formal blessing by the Church through a priest was obligatory upon Christians when they entered into matrimony, and that questions of the validity of a particular union and possible termination were for ecclesiastical and not for civil decision. However, on many details and concrete applications there was as yet no agreement.

ORDINATION

We must not take the space to say much about ordination. It was regarded as a sacrament and was normally administered by a bishop, as one of the successors of the apostles. In very exceptional circumstances a priest might be delegated to serve for the bishop.

FUNERALS

Burial was not among the sacraments. However, it was attended by Christian ceremonies. Normally mass was celebrated. Eventually what was known as the office for the dead was said. Masses and prayers for the dead did not cease with burial but were continued, and petitions for the dead were part of the Sunday services.

THE FESTIVALS OF THE CHURCH

For the rank and file of Christians, as for the clergy, the Christian year, with its holy days and festivals, was of major importance. It entered into the warp and woof of every-day life and the observances connected with its special days did much to give instruction and to stimulate worship and devotion. Long before the tenth century the main structure of the Christian calendar had come into being. Sunday, Lent, Easter, Christmas, Pentecost, and some other days gave it rhythm and helped to remind even the careless of the main events in the life of Christ and of the Church.

In this period additions were made. They came largely out of the rising tide of Christian faith which marked these centuries. We have seen that in the thirteenth century the feast of Corpus Christi was inaugurated. Pentecost, or Whitsunday, commemorating the coming of the Holy Spirit, was the seventh Sunday after Easter. Its observance went back to early Christian times, but it was not until the eleventh century and later, possibly as a concomitant of the deepening religious life of the area, that it became generally prominent in Western Europe. It was known as Whitsunday because of the white garments worn by those coming to baptism in the days when Europe was being converted and because those not baptized on Easter were given the rite at Pentecost. The observance of Trinity Sunday, the first Sunday after Pentecost, in honour of the Trinity, seems to have originated early in the tenth century. It spread gradually, partly through the influence of Cluny, but was not made obligatory on the whole Church until the first half of the fourteenth century.

Feasts in honour of the Virgin Mary were largely of Eastern origin. This seems to have been especially true of the feast of the Conception of the Virgin (although it may have been of Irish provenance). Its extension in Western Europe appears to have begun in the eleventh century and to have been furthered by the Benedictine monks, but Bernard of Clairvaux was critical and it was long in being accepted at Rome.

When a saint was canonized, a day was set for his or her commemoration. As the centuries passed the numbers of the official saints multiplied and the days for the most notable of them also increased. A day for prayers for all of the dead, eventually known as All Souls' Day, was slow in developing. Late in the tenth century an abbot of a distinguished monastery spoke of it as being of long standing in his house. Early in the eleventh century Odilo, an abbot of Cluny, ordered a day for the annual commemoration of all the departed. Backed by the prestige of Cluny, the custom spread widely among other families of monasteries.

The Popularity of the Saints and the Virgin Mary

To Christians of that age the unseen world of spirits was very real. The Devil and his hosts were believed to be the source of many and perhaps most of the ills which beset the human race. Stories were abroad of those who had sold their souls to the Devil. Equally vivid were those forces and spirits which were opposed to evil. Indeed, a major contribution of Christianity was the confidence that men need not be subject to the demons but that they could be protected from them and, if their victims, could be delivered from them. Since in his crucifixion Christ had triumphed, the sign of the cross was believed to be effective against the machinations of the allies of darkness and many stories were told of its potency as a guard against them. The angels of God were also real to believers. The saints, in whom grace had triumphed, were revered. Not only by their good works had they added to the treasury from which the Church might draw to reduce the temporal punishments for the penitent. They also could be invoked and their aid obtained as intercessors.

Especially was the Virgin Mary honoured. It was a man's world, this era that we call the Middle Ages of Europe. Men controlled state and Church. In a time of warfare they did the fighting. The majority of the saints were men. Men were the theologians and the founders of the great monastic orders. Yet the Virgin Mary was exalted, perhaps partly in semi-conscious appreciation of the imbalance of the masculine and the hunger for the ideal which womanhood could supply. As we have seen, the Virgin Mary had early been accorded a high place and her designation, Mother of God, had been a battle cry in theological controversies in the Eastern wing of the Catholic Church. In this era of religious revival the devotion paid her in the West mounted. Special chapels for her were a normal feature of the churches. The faithful in all walks of life, confident in her mercy and concern, pled with her to intercede for them with her Son and also to give them her direct aid. In the early years of the twelfth century collections of legends gathering around the Virgin began to be made.

It was in the eleventh century, not far from 1050, that we first begin to hear of the prayer to the Virgin, the *Ave Maria,* or the Hail Mary. Made up in part of a portion of the angelic salutation at the time of the Annunciation, in part of the greeting of Elizabeth to Mary, with the addition of a plea that the Virgin pray for the petitioners, its origin is obscure and not all of even its brief length appeared at once. Like so much of the religious devotion of the age, it seems to have originated in the monasteries. However, before the end of the eleventh century at least one bishop and local synod enjoined the clergy to see that their parishioners knew it, and in the thirteenth century, encouraged by bishops and synods, it spread rapidly to many countries in Western Europe.

Connected with the *Ave Maria* was the Angelus. The Angelus was in honour of the incarnation. In later centuries the faithful were summoned to it three times a day, at morning, noon, and evening, by the ringing of a bell, and were to respond with a triple repetition of the *Ave Maria*. In this period the Angelus seems to have been only in the evening. Its origin is obscure, but we begin to hear of it as early as the thirteenth century. It spread rapidly as a parish custom and was a means of increasing the devotion of the rank and file of the laity, reminding them of the incarnation and drawing them to prayer to the Virgin. In the first half of the fourteenth century, John XXII, one of the ablest of the Avignon Popes, recommended it and gave an added impetus to its spread throughout the Church.

Many hymns were written in honour of the Virgin. One of them, *Ave Maris Stella,* is probably much older than this period, but it was popular during these centuries and in that era several other hymns were founded on it.

A Great Surge of Christian Poetry

The four centuries from 950 to 1350 were marked by a luxurious flowering of religious poetry, including hymns. In view of the rising tide of devotion and enthusiasm, this was to be expected. A large proportion of the composition was by members of the new monastic orders which sprang from the religious awakenings of the period. As we have seen, hymns were not new, and many of those most widely used, including the *Te Deum Laudamus,* dated from much earlier centuries. Now, however, in contrast with the Greek wing of the Catholic Church, where hymn writing had passed its zenith, in the Latin portion of the Church religious poetry flourished, its forms became richer and more varied, its rhythm more regular, and its rhyme purer. Much was in Latin. Many hymns were also in the vernacular and were popular among the laity. We have noted the guilds of singers who in the twelfth and thirteenth centuries were widespread in Italy.

Hymn writers were numerous and some of the greatest of the school men were among them. Thus Peter Abélard prepared a hymn-book for Héloïse and her nuns. Thomas Aquinas and Bonaventura were notable composers. In the Abbey of St. Victor in Paris, an outstanding centre of scholastic theology.

Adam, who died in 1142, is said by some to mark the zenith of medieval hymnody. It was to be expected that Cluny, with its earnest life of devotion and worship, would give rise to hymns. One of the most famous poems to come from it was the lengthy *De Contemptu Mundi,* said to have been written by Bernard (not to be confused with Bernard of Clairvaux), about the middle of the twelfth century. Sections from it translated into English in the nineteenth century by the Anglican, Neale, have gained popularity in English-speaking Protestantism under the titles, "For thee oh dear, dear country" and "Jerusalem the Golden."

The Breviary Is Collected, Standardized, and Attains Wide Circulation

A type of work which originally had its formulation and chief use among monks, but which eventually spread to the secular clergy and had wide influence upon the laity, was the breviary. It had its major development in this period.

As the name indicates, the breviary was an abridgement. It was also and primarily a compilation. Its purpose was to put in convenient form what the monks and the clergy needed in their collective services and their private devotions.

Earlier (Chapter 7) we have noted that long before this period the custom had arisen in the Church of praying six or seven times a day at specified intervals. The services connected with these "canonical hours" came to be known as offices. In time patterns for them were developed, with Psalms, readings from the Scriptures, hymns, antiphonaries, and prayers. They varied from place to place and from age to age. Special days, such as the great festivals and those in honour of the saints, had offices appropriate to them. As was natural, the offices were assembled in books for the use of the clergy.

Before the end of the sixth century what was known as the Roman usage had been elaborated. In the time of Charlemagne we hear of an abbreviation, or breviary, of the offices for the canonical hours prepared for lay folk. With their emphasis upon the offices for the canonical hours, various monasteries developed set forms. Some monks recited all the Psalms daily, but this was excessively time-consuming. Many monasteries, accordingly, arranged to spread the recitation of the entire Psalter over a week, and assigned to each of the seven daily services its appropriate Psalms. The oldest known breviary which contained all the canonical offices is said to date from 1099 and to have been in use at Monte Cassino. Under Pope Innocent III the breviary began to spread beyond Benedictine circles.

It was the Franciscans who developed the breviary which, with modifications, came into general circulation in much of the Western Church. Travelling as they did, they wished books with the offices for the canonical hours in such compact form that they would not be a handicap on their journeys, made as these usually were on foot. They wished, not large tomes for choirs who were resident in particular churches and monasteries, but a light volume from which the offices could be recited as they tramped the roads. The Franciscan breviary, regarded as the "modern office," became the chief basis for a breviary which had the endorsement of Rome. To the Franciscan breviary were added features which had been traditional at Rome. The Franciscan breviary thus modified gained wide currency among the secular as well as the regular clergy and through the clergy could not but have an effect upon the laity.

CHARITABLE LAY ENTERPRISES

An expression of the Christian faith of the laity which was seen in hundreds of parishes was care for the unfortunate. With the deepening of the religious life of Western Europe through the revivals, especially those of the twelfth and thirteenth centuries, and with the growth of cities and the increase in wealth, works of Christian charity multiplied. Many bishops, clergy, and monks had long made it part of their duty to care for the sick and the afflicted. Now the laity increasingly shared in this labour. Sometimes they formed associations and confraternities for this purpose. Hospitals and asylums for the ill, the crippled, and the aged were founded and maintained. Sufferers from leprosy, a disease which was especially feared by Europeans of the day, aroused compassion and houses for them were created, often under the protection of St. Lazarus or St. Magdalen. Hospices were also conducted for pilgrims and travellers.

PILGRIMAGES WERE POPULAR

One of the most widespread accompaniments of the religious life of the period was pilgrimages. Like so many other practices, these were by no means new. They were present from the early days of the Christian faith. Nor are pilgrimages an exclusively Christian phenomenon. They are found in many other religions. Back of them lies not only the religious impulse but also the desire to travel. The Christians of Medieval Europe were not behind the faithful of other ages in their zeal to visit sites esteemed sacred to their faith. Palestine, the Holy Land par excellence, associated with the scenes of the birth, life, death, and resurrection of Christ, attracted thousands. Rome with its churches and its memories of Peter and Paul lured other thousands. Tombs of saints, like that of Thomas Becket at Canterbury, were the goal of many.

Relics of saints were prized as highly as they had been in earlier centuries and shrines which housed them were the objectives of countless pilgrimages.

THE WIDENING AND DEEPENING OF THE APPEAL OF THE WAY OF THE MYSTIC

It was inevitable that the rising tide of religious life in Western Christendom should have as one of its outlets the way of the mystic and the life of private prayer. The first flush of enthusiasm in the early stages of each new monastic order invariably gave rise to a deepening mysticism, the cultivation of the sense of the presence of God. We have already said something of the impetus to mysticism given by Bernard of Clairvaux and Francis of Assisi, especially through their emphasis upon the human side of Christ and the events in his life. There was much of the mystic in Thomas Aquinas and, as we have noted, he held the crown of human existence to be the vision of God. His contemporary and friend, Bonaventura, was a notable mystic as well as an outstanding theologian, and his *Itinerarium Mentis in Deum (The Soul's Journey to God)* is evidence of the depth of his experience and insight. The Franciscan tertiate, Raymond Lull, whom we have already met as a missionary to the Moslems, was known equally well for writings which were expressions of Christian mysticism.

There were women among the mystics. Famous among them was Hildegarde (1098–1179). At the tender age of three she began to see visions and increasingly she felt the light of God enveloping her soul. At eight she was given as an oblate to a Benedictine monastery and when nearly fifty she founded a monastery of her own. Like many mystics, she concerned herself actively with the affairs of her time in Church and state. She carried on an extensive correspondence with Popes, Emperors, princes, princesses, bishops, and saints. Her visions were often in the form of allegories. She also prophesied, admonishing those in authority and speaking of Antichrist and the end of the world.

The Cistercian foundation for women at Helfta, near Eisleben, in Saxony, was a school of mysticism. Among its daughters was she who is known as Gertrude the Great (1256–c.1302). Reared from childhood in the monastery, she came under the spell of the writings of Bernard of Clairvaux and had such a special devotion to the heart of Jesus that on one Christmas night she felt her heart united to that of the Child Jesus. She had an abiding sense of the presence of God and had felt the imprint of the Trinity. On one occasion in the mass she believed that she saw Christ face to face. With Gertrude the Great are often grouped Mechtilde of Hackborn (died 1310) and Mechtilde (1217–1282), a beguine of Magdeburg who was a Dominican tertiate.

Also renowned was Bridget or Birgitta of Sweden (c.1303–1373). A daughter of the high aristocracy, the wife of a prominent noble, she was the mother of eight children. From her childhood she had been devout and had had visions in which she believed she talked with Christ and the Virgin. In her maturity these increased, especially after the death of her husband (1344). She had what she was convinced were revelations, she prophesied, and she felt impelled to rebuke the King of Sweden for onerous taxation and injustice to the humble among his subjects. Like some others among the mystics, especially in the West, she had marked organizing and administrative ability. She founded an order, at first associated by the ecclesiastical authorities with the Augustinian Canons, but eventually distinct, that of Our Most Holy Saviour, better known as the Bridgettines, which was carried on by her daughter Katherine and which expanded to other lands.

There were notable mystics among those at whom the Catholic Church looked askance or condemned outright as heretics. Among them were Joachim of Flora, of whom we have already spoken, and his contemporary, Amaury of Bena, in the diocese of Chartres, who, like Joachim, believed that the age of the Holy Spirit had come. In spite of the efforts of the Inquisition to root it out, Amaury's influence long persisted.

In the Abbey of St. Victor the writings ascribed to Dionysius the Areopagite had a profound influence. The house was a famous centre not only of scholasticism and hymnody but also of mystical piety. The philosophy and theology of St. Victor were shot through and through with it. The Victorines looked upon the universe as a book written by the hand of God and as a mirror in which the thought of God is reflected. They taught that that thought is expressed in the Scriptures and that these are to be read as allegories. To discover the mind of God, the method of dialectical logic is not enough and may even be misleading. It may be sought and reached through intuition and meditation. This approach is crowned by contemplation with its insight into truth and by ecstasy. The divine light which shines through contemplation enables us to know truth which cannot be attained by the path of reason and which may even be contradicted by reason. Thus said the men of St. Victor. Outstanding among the Victorines were Hugo or Hugh (1096–1141) of whom we have already spoken because of his prominence in scholastic theology, Richard, who died in 1173 and was the leading mystic of the house, and Adam, his contemporary (died 1177), the chief poet and hymn-writer.

Early in the fourteenth century there was a notable mystical movement in Germany which had Dominicans among its outstanding leaders and which was to persist into the latter part of the fourteenth century where we are to meet it again in the work, *Theologia Germanica,* which was to have a profound influence on many, including Martin Luther. Indeed, in this movement and others contemporary with it, we see a transition from the high tide of the period of 950 to 1350 through the ebb of 1350 to 1500 to the resurgence of the tide after 1500. In it Neoplatonism, partly mediated through Dionysius the Areopagite, was to be influential, a strange contrast with the Aristotelianism which was so potent in much of Dominican theology.

The strain which was channeled through the Dominicans was paralleled by that of the beguines and their male counterparts, the beghards, whom we have already come to know and who persisted into the fourteenth century. They were especially strong in Germany. So, too, were the Brethren of the Free Spirit, mystics, who formed themselves into secret associations, notably in Cologne, and, proscribed by the ecclesiastical authorities, were hunted out by the Inquisition. The Friends of God, as they were known, were less subject to suspicion by the hierarchy. Grouping themselves in circles whose member-ship was made up of both clergy and laymen, they sought to foster the mystical life in themselves and others, followed a course of strict asceticism, and tended to be critical of the majority of the clergy. Some of the Dominican mystics had close contacts with the Friends of God. Indeed, the greatest among the former, John Eckhart, is sometimes regarded as their father.

Why this movement should have come at this time and in this region we do not know. The period was one of distress, with civil strife and recurrent epidemics of the Black Death, but the mystics had begun to emerge before the environment reached its nadir and they were not necessarily a reaction from the sufferings of the age. Yet the insecurity and fears of the day may have contributed to them.

John ("Meister") Eckhart (c.1260–c.1327) was the chief founder of the four-teenth century German Dominican mysticism. Born in Thuringia, he early entered the Order of Preachers, then studied in the University of Paris, and, returning to Germany, was prior of at least two monasteries, was for a time head of the Saxon province of his order, was vicar-general of his order for Bohemia charged with reforming its houses, taught, was a notable preacher in the vernacular, with a clear, simple style, and, late in life, while professor of theology at Cologne, partly because of the anti-Dominican animus of the Franciscans, was accused of heresy. He appealed to the Pope, and died before verdict was given.

Eckhart protested, sincerely, that he was orthodox. Yet he verged on pan-theism. He knew scholastic theology but at times seemed to scorn it. He showed the influence of Dionysius the Areopagite, Eriugena, Hugo of St. Victor, Averroes, and Avicenna, as well as Aristotle. He held that in the human soul there is a spark, a light, which is of the same nature as God and that nowhere is God so really God as in the soul. It can be seen how he laid himself open to the charge of erasing individuality in men. In 1329 Pope John XXII branded as heretical seventeen propositions drawn from his works.

Eckhart had what he believed to be direct experience of God. His preaching grew out of his own profound religious life and he wished to help others to share it. He did not prize ecstatic emotion, but calmness and quiet. Yet he lived an active life and believed that to have peace in a life of pain was far better than to have a life of rest and peace in God. His writings were popular with some of the leading German intellectuals of the nineteenth and twentieth centuries and may have helped to shape their ideas, even if only by confirming them, especially those of Hegel.

John Tauler (died 1361), also a Dominican, was profoundly influenced by Eckhart. An earnest preacher, he was not a great scholar, but sought to strengthen ordinary folk to bear the distresses of the day. Another disciple of Eckhart was Henry Suso (c.1295 or 1300–1365), a native of Constance, who entered the Dominican Order at the age of thirteen. Deeply religious and highly imaginative from his youth, frail of body and often ill, sternly ascetic in self-flagellations and abstinence from food, he was subject to moods of deep depression and long periods of intense mental suffering. He also knew moments of high ecstasy. Not an original genius, he showed in his writings a capacity for a sentimental but surging love of God. In his later years many were drawn to him for spiritual counsel.

Ranking with Eckhart was one of the high peaks of the mysticism of the fourteenth century was John Ruysbroeck (1293–1381). A Fleming, born near Brussels, at the age of eleven he came under the instruction of his uncle, a canon in a church in Brussels, and was reared by that uncle and the latter's colleague. Educated by them, he became familiar with the works of Augustine, Dionysius the Areopagite, Gregory the Great, Bernard of Clairvaux, the Victorines, Bonaventura, and Aquinas. Ordained when he was twenty-four, he became chaplain to his uncle. In mature life the latter had a sudden soul-shaking experience which made him over from a somewhat conventional priest into a completely devoted spirit. Caught by the contagion of that dedication, the uncle's colleague and Ruysbroeck began a more austere way of life. Ruysbroeck, too, grew in his knowledge of God's love, a love which flooded his heart, and sought to present what was to him the true way of God's lovers against some of the local mysticism which seemed to him to be departing from the faith.

When he was fifty, Ruysbroeck and his two older companions withdrew to Groenendael, or Green Valley, in a forest near Brussels, and formed the nucleus of a community which eventually adopted the rule of the Augustinian Canons. There to an advanced age he gave himself to contemplation, prayer, the humble manual work of the community, joy in the birds and the animals of the wild-wood, and writing. The fruits of his pen were to have a wide influence. Tauler may have visited him and some of his books became the familiar property of many among the Friends of God. We are later to note his contribution to the early years of the Brethren of the Common Life. The best known of his works is *De Ornatu Spiritualium Nuptiarum* (*The Adornment of the Spiritual Marriage*), in which he developed the three stages of the life of the Christian mystic. His great stress was upon love.

Contemporaneous with this fourteenth century flowering of mysticism in Germany and Flanders was a somewhat similar movement in England. Whether it was the fruit of the Continental mystics we do not know. Like them it carried over beyond 1350 and we are to see it again. Its chief figure in the first half of the century was Richard Rolle, who was born in Yorkshire somewhere between 1290 and 1300 and died, perhaps of the Black Death, in 1349. He seems to have come from a well-to-do family but, restless with a longing which was unsatisfied by the pleasures which money made possible, he found peace only when he gave himself to following Christ in poverty. He was educated in Oxford and perhaps in Paris. Fleeing the world, he lived for a time as a hermit, but moved about, alternating between solitude and giving spiritual counsel and service. He was possessed by the love of God and devotion to Christ. He wrote extensively, put the Psalms into English, and poured out his soul in lyric poetry of praise.

SUMMARY

As the centuries passed, Christianity more and more became the conscious property of increasing elements in the population of Western Europe. The religious awakenings which in part expressed themselves in the succession of new monastic orders and in lay movements, some of them branded as heretical by the Catholic Church, were paralleled by tides which spread in ever widening circles among the rank and file. By no means all in Western Europe were profoundly affected. The majority were probably touched only superficially. The period was characterized by depths of depravity and heights of sanctity. The pessimist and the cynic have much to support their claim that by and large the clergy were ignorant, slovenly, and greedy, and followed their profession as a livelihood and not a vocation, and that the laity were irreverent and looked upon the ritual of the Church as at best a form of magic by which what they wished in this life and hereafter could be wrung from a hostile or indifferent universe. Yet the impression which one gets from the records is not only one of this side of the picture, indubitably dark and real though it was, but is also one of a growing and more intelligent commitment to the Christian faith by an enlarging proportion of Western Europeans. The attempt of the earnest idealists to effect this result through the inclusive hierarchical structure of the Church had given rise to a vast ecclesiastical machinery which was already in danger of defeating the purpose which the reformers had in bringing it into being. Yet, partly through that machinery and partly in spite of it, Christianity was making an ever deeper impress upon the rank and file of the population.

Selected Bibliography

PARISH LIFE, THE SACRAMENTS, AND THE CULT OF THE VIRGIN MARY
AND THE SAINTS

G. G. Coulton, *Ten Medieval Studies* (Cambridge University Press, 1930, pp. xi, 297). Readable, erudite, and critical of Catholicism.

G. G. Coulton, *Life in the Middle Ages: Selected, Translated & Annotated* (Cambridge University Press, 4 vols., 1928–1930). Selections from original sources.

E. L. Cutts, *Parish Priests and Their People in the Middle Ages in England* (London, Society for Promoting Christian Knowledge, 1898, pp. xvii, 579). Readable, with extensive translations from the sources.

H. Gasquet, *Parish Life in Mediaeval England* (London, Methuen & Co., 1906, pp. xix, 279). A semi-popular account.

A. Hauck, *Kirchengeschichte Deutschlands,* Vol. IV (Leipzig, J. C. Hinrichs'sche Buchhandlung, 1913, pp. viii, 1070). The initial chapter has material bearing on this topic.

H. C. Lea, *A History of Auricular Confession and Indulgences in the Latin Church* (Philadelphia, Lea Brothers & Co., 3 vols., 1896). Very useful.

J. A. MacCulloch, *Medieval Faith and Fable* (Boston, Marshall-Jones Co., 1932, pp. 345). A somewhat disparaging view.

A. J. Macdonald, *Berengar and the Reform of Sacramental Doctrine* (London, Longmans, Green & Co., 1930, pp. xii, 444). Carefully done.

J. T. McNeill and H. M. Gamer, *Medical Handbooks of Penance. A Translation of the Principal Libri Poenitentiales and Selections from Related Documents* (Columbia University Press, 1938, pp. xiv, 476). A useful compilation.

J. R. H. Moorman, *Church Life in England in the Thirteenth Century* (Cambridge University Press, 1945, pp. xxviii, 444). A thoroughly competent study, with extensive references to the sources and an important bibliography.

R. C. Mortimer, *The Origins of Private Penance in the Western Church* (Oxford University Press, 1939, pp. 195). A competent study.

B. Smalley, *The Study of the Bible in the Middle Ages* (Oxford, Basil Blackwell, 2d ed., 1952, pp. xxii, 406). Based upon extensive research. Declares that "the Bible was the most studied book of the Middle Ages" and that its language and content permeated medieval thought.

O. D. Watkins, *A History of Penance* (London, Longmans, Green & Co., 2 vols., 1920). Comprehensive.

THE BREVIARY

P. Batifol, *History of the Roman Breviary,* translated by A. M. Y. Baylay (London, Longmans, Green & Co., 1912, pp. xiv, 340). Erudite, with a strong bias in favour of the older Roman offices.

THE MYSTICS

C. Butler, *Western Mysticism. The Teaching of SS Augustine Gregory and Bernard on Contemplation and the Contemplative Life* (New York, E. P. Dutton & Company, 1923, pp. xiii, 344). Contains stimulating but debatable generalizations.

T. W. Coleman, *English Mystics of the Fourteenth Century* (London, Epworth Press, 1938, pp. 175). An excellent survey.

M. M. Comper, *The Life of Richard Rolle Together with an Edition of His English Lyrics (Now for the first time published)* (London, J. M. Dent & Sons, 1928, pp. xx, 340).

Meister Eckhart. A Modern Translation, by R. B. Blakney (New York, Harper & Brothers, 1941, pp. xxviii, 333). The translation preserves something of the easy colloquialism of the original.

R. M. Jones, *The Flowering of Mysticism. The Friends of God in the Fourteenth Century* (New York, The Macmillan Co., 1939, pp. 270). The best brief survey in English. By a distinguished American Quaker, it is sympathetic, well written, and based upon prolonged research into the sources and the pertinent secondary works, including especially Denifle.

P. Pourrat, *Christian Spirituality in the Middle Ages,* translated by S. P. Jacques (London, Burns, Oates & Washbourne, 1924, pp. xiii, 341). The second volume of a three-volume comprehensive survey by a Roman Catholic.

H. M. D. Redpath, *God's Ambassador: St. Bridget of Sweden* (Milwaukee, The Bruce Publishing Co., 1946, pp. xv, 216). A popularly written account by a Bridgettine nun.

Yorkshire Writers. Richard Rolle of Hampole, an English Father of the Church and His Followers, edited by C. Horstman (London, Swan Sonnenschein & Co., 1895, pp. xiv, 442). A useful collection of texts.

John of Ruysbroeck, *The Adornment of the Spiritual Marriage, The Sparkling Stone, The Book of Supreme Truth,* translated from the Flemish by C. A. Wynschenk Dom (London, J. M. Dent & Sons, 1916, pp. xxii, 259).

A. G. Seesholtz, *Friends of God. Practical Mystics of the Fourteenth Century* (Columbia University Press, 1934, pp. viii, 247). An excellent survey.

The Life of Blessed Henry Suso by Himself, translated from the original German by T. F. Knox, with an introduction by W. R. Inge (London, Methuen & Co., 1913, pp. xxxviii, 254). A poignant self-revelation.

E. Underhill, *Ruysbroeck* (London, G. Bell & Sons, 1914, pp. viii, 193). By an outstanding specialist on mysticism.

Chapter 23

THE SHAPING OF WESTERN EUROPE

When we shall have completed the chapter on which we are now embarking we will have devoted almost as many pages to the course of Christianity in Western Europe in the four centuries between 950 and 1350 as we did to the entire range of Christianity in the first five centuries of its history. Why have we done this? At first sight it may seem to be a strangely disproportionate allotment of our space, a space all too limited for the narration of so vast and important a story as the entire course of Christianity in the first nineteen and a half centuries.

It was natural that we should spend so much time on the first five hundred years. It was then that Christianity inspired the writings which comprise the New Testament, formulated its basic creeds, produced a vast body of literature, developed its organizational structure, gave rise to the monastic life, and inaugurated forms of worship which, with modifications and additions, have been standard for the large majority of Christians from that time to this. It was then, too, that Christianity achieved the seemingly impossible. From being what looked like an obscure sect of Judaism, competing with scores of other cults, it won the professed allegiance of the overwhelming majority of the population of the most powerful and the wealthiest state of that day, the Roman Empire.

In contrast, Western Europe from 950 to 1350 was by no means as populous as had been the Roman Empire at its height and was far less prominent in the total world scene than that realm had been in its heyday.

Yet the apparent distortion of perspective can be amply justified. That is partly because of the intrinsic interest of the developments in Western Europe, for here, as we have seen, Christianity displayed an amazing vitality which expressed itself in a wide variety of creative achievements. It was also because, in the face of untoward conditions, different from those which confronted it in the Roman Empire, but in their way fully as difficult, Christianity profoundly influenced more aspects of the life of Western Europe in these four centuries than of the Roman Empire in five centuries. More important still, within the next six centuries the peoples of Western Europe, so largely shaped by Christianity, were to dominate all of the human race to a degree that has never been true of any other segment of mankind. This they did partly by vast migrations, partly by political and economic mastery, but even more in ideas and cultural patterns. Those nations who in the twentieth century revolted against the political and economic imperialism of the West paid Western Europeans the largely unconscious homage of adopting the science and the machines which were first developed by them, and Communism, the ideology which through Russia sought to supplant the dominion of Western civilization, had its origin in Western Europe and was deeply indebted to Christianity. It was chiefly through Western European peoples that after A.D. 1500 Christianity had an astounding geographic spread, more extensive than that of any other religion in all history.

In the next few pages we must attempt to summarize the effect of Christianity upon Western Europe during the four centuries between 950 and 1350. We need not give much space to the topic, for, important though it is, not a little has already been hinted at or covered piecemeal in the preceding seven chapters. However, we must endeavour to draw together what has been scattered through those pages, here and there adding to it, and interpreting it. This is especially important, because in that effect lies part of the answer to the questions which are a major concern of this survey, the fashion in which the Christian Gospel has operated in history and the way in which, through it, God works—if, as the Christian faith declares, God exists and interests Himself in mankind.

At the outset we must note the contrast between the situation which confronted Christianity in the Roman Empire in the first five centuries of the faith and that which it faced in Western Europe from 950 to 1350. In the Roman Empire Christianity entered a high civilization which in material wealth and power was approaching its zenith but at a time when the creative genius of Græco-Roman civilization had about spent its force and when, except for Christianity itself and in the political realm, little that was basically new was being thought or done. Many were hungry for a dependable word on the questions which men ask about the nature of the universe and the meaning and possible destiny of human life. Christianity was only one of many systems which were offering answers. It came into the scene with a minimum of institutional and creedal equipment. Such of that as it possessed it inherited mainly from Judaism. Its compelling attraction was unique, "Jesus Christ and him crucified," "risen from the dead," and to him it owed its ultimate victory, but at the outset there were no fixed forms of organization or worship and only simple, if profound and breath-taking, affirmations. As we have seen, Christianity's most striking effect upon the Roman Empire was in the realm of religion. There it eliminated most of its rivals or, as in the case of the Greek philosophies, utilized them for its purposes. With a sense of the community and unity of all the followers of Christ, it brought into being the churches, especially the Catholic Church, an extensive literature, and formidable and largely original theologies. However, upon other aspects of civilization the influence of Christianity, while noticeable, could scarcely be called revolutionary. Græco-Roman culture was by no means completely reshaped.

The situation with which Christianity had to do in Western Europe between 950 and 1350 differed strikingly from that which it met before the year 500. In name the Roman Empire still existed and stirred the imagination of the peoples of both Western and Eastern Europe. Actually it had disappeared, although the Byzantine realm claimed the designation and was in the unbroken succession, and the German kings sought added prestige in the imperial title. In Western Europe internal decay and a series of barbarian invasions which continued for more than six centuries had brought civilization to a low ebb. Near-anarchy prevailed, learning and morals had sunk to a low level, and superstition was rife. The cessation of the invasions not far from the middle of the tenth century gave opportunity to create a new civilization. In its shaping Christianity had a very large share. From the beginning it was an integral part of the whole, challenging it and entering into the warp and woof of every aspect of the newly emerging culture.

The Christianity which so profoundly moulded Western European civilization was not that which in the first century had begun its victorious course in the Græco-Roman world. It still centered about Jesus Christ and drew its inspiration from him. However, it had become all but identified with a great institution which, far more than the realm which had its capital at Constantinople or what was called the Holy Roman Empire, was the heir of the Eternal City. Much more inclusive geographically than either, more nearly than they it perpetuated the Roman genius of universality, administrative skill, and justice based on law. Its capital was Rome and its greatest Popes were born in or near Rome and had something of the political sagacity of the ablest of the Cæsars—yet partly transformed and shot through and through with what had come from the Christian heritage. As we have seen, increasingly the Church of Rome controlled the Catholic Church in Western Europe. The word Roman prefixed to Catholic in the designation of that church is accurate, both because of the growing domination by the Church of Rome and the genius which that church imparted to the whole.

The Roman Catholic Church was the major means of the transmission to this new culture of Western Europe of what went into it from the Græco-Roman past. It was not the only channel. Much came through the Greek East, much by way of the Arab world (although it was through Christians of the East that the Arabs learned most of what they acquired from the earlier Mediterranean world), some through Irish monasticism which at most had only slight ties with Rome, and some survived in Italy apart from the Church. Yet for better or for worse it was mainly to the Catholic Church that Western Europe was indebted for whatever it inherited from Greece and Rome.

We have said for better or for worse, because from the standpoint of Christ and the Gospel the Græco-Roman heritage was by no means an unmixed blessing. In many ways the Gospel and Græco-Roman culture were reciprocally contradictory. From the time that an official representative of Rome had crucified Jesus a basic tension had existed between the Gospel and that culture. As Paul so clearly declared, to Greek philosophy the cross and what it stood for were stark foolishness. It is not surprising that the attempt to reconcile the two which was undertaken by the school men began to break down before the Middle Ages were spent. Here, however, was more than a conflict between the Gospel and a particular culture. It was a symptom and a symbol of a tension between the Gospel and all civilization, between the two cities of Augustine's famous survey of history.

Something of the effect of Christianity upon the newly forming civilization of Western Europe can be seen if we take up briefly one by one the major phases of that culture.

THE CHRISTIANIZING OF RELIGION

First of all we naturally place the religious aspects of Western Europe. Here Christianity faced an appalling array of problems. It had to try to bring more nearly to its standards the nominally Christian descendants of the population of the western sections of what had been the Roman Empire. For the large majority of these peoples conversion had been very superficial and the Church had great difficulty in making its discipline effective. The long series of invasions with their attendant disorder made for the deterioration of even the shoddy quality of what went by the name of Christianity. To the offspring of the Roman provincials were added the invaders and their progeny. Those from the North came with a crude polytheism, a disorderly array of many gods, and a belief in innumerable spirits, many of them malignant. While before many generations they accepted baptism, they did so largely *en masse,* by group action led by their tribal chieftains, and were loosely fitted into the fellowship of a church which was already embarrassed by the sub-Christian level of its existing constituency. In the Iberian Peninsula and Sicily, more over, Christianity was confronted by an aggressive Islam and when it slowly won back territories which it had lost and effected the outward conversion of the former Moslems, it found that these accessions, even when their pre-Islamic ancestors had been Christians, carried over some of their Islamic beliefs and practices. It is not surprising that under these circumstances the religious life of Western Europe fell far short of the high standards set forth in the New Testament and that it had in it so many contradictions.

Yet the Gospel was making headway. This was seen in part in the many movements which we have described in the preceding chapters—in the appeal which it made to the ardent spirits who founded the new monastic orders; in individuals and groups and societies among lay folk, some of them accepted and others rejected by the Catholic Church, who sought to live the full Christian life; and in the many efforts by princes, Popes, bishops, and humble priests to make of the Catholic Church an agency for shaping all of Western Europe into a *Corpus Christianum,* a true Christendom. When only these aspects are viewed, enthusiasts hail the age as preëminently Christian, look back on it with nostalgic admiration, and regard all that followed as departure from the faith and as the progressive de-Christianization of Europe.

There is another side of the picture at which we have more than once hinted. Undoubtedly there were many lives which reflected the power of the Gospel and are rightly viewed as exemplars of Christian faith and virtue. In appalling contrast there were depths of human depravity. Among high and low, in city, village, and country, among clergy, laity, and even monks, there were flagrant brutality, gross sensuality, and unrelieved arrogance and self-seeking. To be sure, nominal assent was almost universally given to the Christian faith. There was little overt denial of what was ostensibly the community religion. In practice, however, Christian ethical standards were widely denied, and the most sacred rites of the Church were repeatedly and even habitually performed carelessly. At times they were parodied. Church offices were bought and sold and their incomes diverted to purely selfish luxury, and to gratify their lust for power ambitious men strove for place and position in the Church. Even the ablest of the Popes who had at heart the reform of the Church sought to attain that end by measures which contradicted the Gospel and therefore eventually brought frustration. Here and there, notably in the brilliant circle which surrounded the extraordinarily learned, intellectually curious, charming, arrogant, and pitiless Emperor Frederick II, while there was a half-mocking prudential conformity with the faith, there were also cynicism and the use of the Church and the faith for purposes which were in complete denial of the Gospel. Notorious scoffers were found in high places. Among the devout as well as the merely conventionally religious there were superstition, con-

fidence in astrology, and customs and beliefs which employed Christian ceremonies, sacraments, and symbols as magical means to avert disaster or to attain
desired objectives.

Indeed, here was a vivid example of what has so often been seen in the history of Christianity. The Gospel accentuates contrasts. Beginning with the
opposition aroused by Jesus which led to his crucifixion by official representatives of as high a religion and as good a government as man had thus far
known, down into the nineteenth and twentieth centuries, in periods and
regions in which the Gospel has especially displayed its power and Christianity
has been the most vigorous, that very vitality has been paralleled by heightened
opposition. At times, as in the first centuries of Christianity, that has shown
itself in persecutions; in other times, as in the one with which we are here
dealing, it has been by outward assent but by denial in practice; in still other
eras, notably the nineteenth and twentieth centuries, it has been by frank rejection by large elements in traditionally Christian lands and by the adoption of
methods by presumably Christian nations which have contradicted Christian
principles.

Challenging Morals with Christian Standards

Intimately associated with religion were morals. Here, as we have repeatedly
seen, Christianity was the chief means of disciplining the population. This was
done in many ways, partly through sermons, partly through the teaching of
the Ten Commandments, partly through story and drama, and partly through
the sacrament of penance with its confession, prescription of penalties, and
absolution. A major deterrent from sin was the fear of hell and the Devil and
his hosts, for these were very vivid to the peoples of the period. Scoffers who
professed not to believe in them might on their death beds turn in terror to
the priest. Yet in principle the chief motive for repentance and righteous living
was the love of God. There is no denying the vast gulf between the ideal held
up in the Gospel and the behaviour of a large proportion of the population. It
was a robustious age in which life was cheap, warfare chronic, and for many,
perhaps the majority, the daily routine drab and sordid. Yet the Gospel did
not allow to go unchallenged the degradation accentuated by centuries of disorder. It created a tension. Thousands responded to it and other thousands
who fell lamentably short of the ideal paid homage to the characters of those
who to their minds approximated it.

Adequately to appraise the effect of Christianity on the religious and moral
character of Europe we must recall the honour paid men and women like
Bernard of Clairvaux, Francis of Assisi, Clara, Elizabeth of Hungary, Dominic,
Bonaventura, and Aquinas. Many were canonized by popular acclaim before

the Catholic Church gave its official imprimatur. Thousands who did not attain to their standards either sought to emulate them or felt themselves rebuked by them. Numbers of those labelled heretics but who sought to embody the Gospel were revered by the rank and file of their followers.

SHAPING THE INTELLECTUAL LIFE

One of the striking features of the period is the close association of religious and intellectual awakenings. We have seen that in the dark ages between the years 500 and 950 in large areas the only schools were the ones maintained in monasteries, those islands of orderly living in a time when civilization was at a low ebb. We have also noted that as the invasions subsided and the shadows began to lift, monasteries and cathedrals were the main centres of study and teaching. Some of the new monastic houses distrusted the pagan authors whose writings were regarded as a normal basis of education and not all cathedrals had significant schools. However, in contrast there were such houses as that of Bec, founded out of deep religious conviction, which within a generation became a major seat of intellectual creativity. St. Victor, the famous community of Augustinian Canons, was noted both for its earnest spiritual life which brought it fame for its mystics and for its philosophers and theologians. Some of the schools maintained in connexion with cathedrals for the preparation of clergy attracted great teachers and were thronged by eager students. The universities which began to appear at the end of the twelfth century and which multiplied in the thirteenth century were largely church foundations. As we have said, that of Paris, the model for most of the universities for Northern Europe, developed from a cathedral school. The rise of the universities coincided with the revival which found expression in the mendicant orders. The Dominicans, with the emphasis placed on scholarship by their founder, gravitated towards them almost automatically. It is significant that, in spite of the opposition of Francis, the Brothers Minor also early established themselves in the universities. There seems to have been something in the Christian faith which inspired many of those who committed themselves fully to it to intellectual inquiry and adventure. Thus Roger Bacon, a first-class mind, caught by the enthusiasm and devotion of the first flush of the Franciscans and sharing the somewhat stormy and unconventional character of that order, became a forerunner of modern science. We have already seen something of the wide range of the intellectual inquiries of the Dominican Albertus Magnus.

This stimulus by Christianity to fearless intellectual activity should not surprise us. We have already met it in such outstanding minds in the earlier centuries as Origen, Augustine, and Eriugena. We shall run across it increasingly as the centuries pass. To the northern peoples who had invaded Western

Europe and to whom the world about them had neither order nor meaning, the Christian faith brought the conception of a universe created by One Whose august purpose is shot through and through with love and Who governs the worlds by uniform law. In that universe the Christian must move reverently but he can also move confidently. History, so Christianity teaches, is not sound and fury, signifying nothing, as the barbarians had believed, nor is it a weary repetition of cycles as the Greeks had regarded it. It had a beginning in the creative act of God and moves towards a culmination determined by Him. It is not strange, therefore, that the beginnings of the science and the machines of Western Europe are found in this period and among those whose spirits and minds had been gripped by the Christian faith. It has been said that the first machines were the clocks developed in monasteries in connexion with the canonical hours. Whether or not this is true, it was to those who were moved by the Christian faith that the beginnings of the scientific outlook and method in Western Europe must be traced.

Moreover, we must remind ourselves that much of the literature of the period concerned itself with Christian themes. This was true of philosophy and theology. It was also true of the poets. Walther von der Vogelweide (c.1170–c.1230), the prince of the Minnesingers, from the beginning had a serious moral and religious strain which deepened with the years. That most famous of all the European poets of the period, Dante (1265–1321), wove his greatest work, the *Commedia,* around the Christian faith. The popular tales which centered about the Holy Grail and which later were given literary dignity are evidence of the fashion in which the Christian drama of redemption had taken possession of the imagination of large circles in Europe.

CHRISTIANITY AND ART

Any who travel widely in Western Europe cannot but be aware of the fashion in which the religious awakenings of these centuries were contemporary with striking outbursts of artistic creativity. The evidence is still there for all who will to see, in monasteries, churches, cathedrals, and museums. Only a fraction of what was produced has survived wars, revolutions, and the tooth of time. Yet even the remnants are impressive. Not all art and architecture was religious. Castles reflected the place of the king and the feudal noble, and town halls bore witness to the communal spirit of the growing cities. Yet most of the largest structures were churches. Some of them were monastic, and it is thought-provoking that they do not owe their size to the desire to accommodate large congregations. They were for use by the monks, and seldom were those in any one house numerous enough to fill more than what was called the choir. They were for the worship of God and to enshrine the

Eucharist with its mystery and wonder. To be sure, the abbots who directed the building were probably often moved as much by ambition to promote their own fame or the prestige of their monastery as by the desire to glorify God, but the latter was at least the ostensible purpose. So with parish churches and cathedrals: priests, benefactors, and bishops may have urged on the building from ambition to perpetuate their own memory or from the sheer joy of achievement. Yet the theme was Christian. The Biblical story was told in sculpture, mosaic, painting, and stained glass, and the altar with its bloodless sacrifice was the focus of the whole. The wish to equip the altar and its services in a fashion which would honour the Presence so confidently affirmed inspired the lavish expenditure of imaginative skill on vessels, furnishings, and vestments. Most of the painting of the period had Christian subjects. Monkish devotion found expression in the painstaking and often beautiful illumination of the manuscripts whose transcription was part of the labour prescribed by the monastic rule.

This is not the place to tell the story of the architecture of the age, with its accomplishments in various forms of the Romanesque, developed, as the name indicates, from Roman antecedents, and in its most notable examples not a debasement of its prototypes, but a fresh and stirring creation, or in the Gothic with its ingenious flying buttresses which made possible its great windows and soaring pinnacles and towers. Nor can we do more than mention the stiff and stylized painting and sculpture, seemingly fearful of distracting the attention from their religious purpose by obtruding fleshly beauty. Even the multitudes of figures and carvings which ornamented the Gothic structures and which often were faithful pictures of forms from everyday life or else grotesque or humorous expressions of the imagination could be interpreted as the consecration of all of His creatures to the service of God. Here was an overflowing, exuberant genius which gave itself to divine themes and which was at least in part evoked by them.

Ruthless Power and the Christian Faith

One of the notable groups of effects of Christianity in this period was in the political realm. It was in this area of life that at the outset power seemed most ruthless. Governments were set up and dominated by strong men who had won their position by intrigue and war. The class with the most prestige was not the scholars, as in theory in China, or the priests, as in Hindu India, but the warriors. The clergy were tempted to ape them. The Roman Empire had been welded together by conquest and diplomacy which relied on arms. Its head, Emperor (Imperator), by his very title was commander-in-chief and depended upon the legions for his position. Western Europe added to that tradition the many states which were carved out by war. Its dynasties were founded by successful warriors and its kings and nobles felt themselves compelled to resort to battle to hold their possessions and to extend them. This was true not only in the centuries of the invasions but also after the invasions had ceased.

As Christianity spread and members of the ruling class accepted it, it had an effect upon the theory and practice of government and upon the conduct of war and the manners of the warrior. As we have seen, most of the new monastic movements were begun by members of the nobility. There were even kings who divested themselves of their crowns to enter a monastery. Yet this was withdrawing from the burdens of civil office and had little direct effect on government. However, there were many who retained their titles and positions and who attempted to bring to them Christian insight. Coronations were normally by Christian rites. No one could be Holy Roman Emperor except through coronation by the Pope. Kings and Holy Roman Emperors were in theory bound to conduct themselves as Christians and to rule for the benefit of their subjects. For many, perhaps the majority, this was only a matter of form. Some, however, took the obligation seriously. For example, we have seen that the Emperor Henry III proclaimed a Day of Indulgence in which he professed to forgive his enemies and urged his subjects to emulate him.

We have noted something of the manner in which the Christian conscience attempted to deal with war by initiating the Truce of God and the Peace of God and by developing and inculcating chivalry, the code of conduct for warriors of gentle birth. We read, too, that in 1119 the Council of Rheims instructed chaplains to discontinue religious ministrations in castles to which booty from unjust wars was carried. A much more pretentious proposal was made in the twelfth century for Papal prohibition of all wars between princes, for Papal arbitration of all disputes, for the excommunication and deposition of any ruler who failed to observe a decision when it was once rendered, and for armed assistance by the clergy and lay rulers to one who was attacked after submitting to the Papal verdict. Obviously this was not adopted. However, the sense of being part of Christendom, of membership in a family of nations, laid the foundations for a body of law designed to govern the relations among princes.

Christian scholars elaborated political theory in the light of their faith. They held that both Church and state, Papacy and Empire, were founded by God and in the last analysis were responsible to Him. Aquinas taught that a ruler exercises his power as a divine trust and that a monarch who has betrayed that trust has lost his right to the obedience of his subjects. Some radicals, notably the Dominican John of Paris and Marsilius of Padua, maintained that the powers of both the civil and ecclesiastical officials are based upon the sovereignty of the people. There were dreamers who, like Dante in his *Monarchia,* envisioned a mankind-embracing Christian society in which the Pope and the Emperor were to be the leaders.

The conviction was widely held that the state is a divine concession to human weakness, but that its purpose is the maintenance of righteousness; that law, as the embodiment of justice, is above the king and must be obeyed by him; and that the relation between the king and his subjects is based upon a reciprocal obligation to maintain peace and justice. Some of the concepts of the Roman law which became influential in much of Europe were rethought in Christian terms. Thus the term *justitia* might be employed where the purpose was the salvation of the soul rather than the ownership of tangible property.

Christian conviction strove to eliminate some of the crude methods of determining justice which had been inherited from a pre-Christian Teutonic past. Prominent among them were trial by fire and water and by battle. Some bishops might defend and even advocate them. However, again and again Church councils and Popes condemned them.

To be sure, many official spokesmen for Christianity conformed to the tradition of resorting to intrigue and armed force. Popes fomented wars, summoned armies to their aid, sought to offset one monarch by calling another to their assistance, and preached Crusades. The Crusading orders attempted to combine the calling of the monk with the profession of the soldier. Yet there was a persistent conviction that members of the clergy should not bear arms. Here, as in so many aspects of life, the Christian ideal created a tension by challenging men to attain what was seemingly impossible, but what, prodded by Christian teaching, they knew to be right.

Christianity and Economics

In the keen competition for livelihood, how far was Christianity effective?

It is clear that through monasticism Christianity did something to give dignity to labour and added greatly to agriculture and so to the increase in the supply of food. Under the Benedictine rule work was obligatory. Although in many of the Benedictine houses food and clothing came from estates cultivated by serfs and while in several monastic orders manual work in the fields was assigned to lay brothers and the choir monks gave themselves to prayer and study, in others all the monks, even those of aristocratic birth, toiled in their gardens or on the lands of the monastery. Whether by all members of the community or only by the lay brothers, monasteries did much to clear land, bring it under cultivation, and develop improved crops and methods of tillage.

The first use of marl to enrich the soil is attributed to them and they were noted for their vineyards and their wines.

In industry and trade the impact of Christianity was uneven. In principle all taking of interest was strictly condemned and absolution could be had only by full restitution of the sums so acquired. In practice the Knights Templar became famous as bankers. In theory the ideal was believed to be communal ownership and individual use, for God was held to be the supreme owner and the world to be for the benefit of mankind. From the common store each should have whatever he needed. There were those who maintained that Christ and his apostles had followed the way of absolute poverty and insisted that those who fully gave themselves to him, especially the clergy and the monks, should follow their example. The official Church condemned this view and it was argued that because of the taint of sin in man community of property was impossible and private property permissible. Yet in practice, as we have seen, the monasteries held their property as a community possession. There were, moreover, many non-monastic communities of lay folk, among them beguines and beghards, who owned their property in common or adopted apostolic poverty.

Much of the trade and commerce of the age was carried on through guilds. Guilds had religious features and supposedly were guided by Christian standards. The ideal of a just price was generally acknowledged, that is, that a merchant or artisan should ask for his goods only what was fair. Theorists attempted to determine the principles for ascertaining it. The just price was applied to wages as well as to the sale of the products of labour.

THE CHRISTIAN IMPRESS ON WIDE RANGES OF THE IDEALS AND LIFE OF THE COMMUNITY

In addition to those aspects of life which were religious, moral, intellectual, æsthetic, political, and economic, Christianity affected profoundly the ideals and to a large extent other phases of the practice of the society and civilization of Western Europe. More and more as the period wore on it made itself felt in all ranges of the life of the community.

This was seen in the growing value placed on the individual as possessing an eternal soul for whose salvation the Son of God had given his life. Thus Meister Eckhart said that authorities usually taught that all persons are of equal rank by nature and went beyond this and held that the meaning of the incarnation is that by becoming man God meant to lift not just a few, as might have been the case had Jesus Christ been merely a man chosen from his fellows to be exalted, but entire human nature and with it all men into His likeness and His fellowship. We may recall that Bridget dared to rebuke the King of

Sweden for his callous exploitation of the poor. Centuries earlier, King Olaf Haraldsson of Norway, who was largely responsible for the conversion of his country, forbade the exposure of infants (except monstrosities) and decreed that at the opening of the national *thing* (the assembly of notables of the realm) a slave should not be sacrificed as heretofore, but freed. These instances could be multiplied many fold.

Socially Western Europe of the Middle Ages, as later, was a fairly tightly stratified society. At the lowest level were the slaves and the half-free serfs. Yet with the growing permeation of society by Christian ideals, consciences were becoming uneasy. No one could hear, day after day or Sunday after Sunday, the *Magnificat,* with its affirmation that God had put down the mighty from their seats and exalted them of low degree and that He had filled the hungry with good things and had sent the rich empty away, without sometime becoming aware of its contradiction of what he saw about him. The Christian teaching was that slaves had souls and equally with their masters could be heirs of eternal salvation.

Manumission of slaves was frequent and was often done by the master shortly before his death as a service which would work for the salvation of his soul. Significantly, the motives assigned in the formal documents which implemented the act were the brotherhood of man, the example of Christ, love for God, and the hope of salvation. In 1102 a Church council in London forbade the slave trade. In 1179 the Third Lateran Council, theoretically acting for all the Catholic Church, declared that no Christian should be subjected to slavery. When in the thirteenth century Bologna emancipated its serfs, it professed to have derived from Christianity the motive which prompted the act. While in political life it was practically impossible for one of lowly birth to rise to high position, the Church was much more flexible. Although scions of the nobility had a better opportunity for advancement in office than those of low degree, instances were not wanting of sons of humble parentage becoming bishops. To mention only one instance out of many, Robert Grosseteste, scholar and reforming Bishop of Lincoln, was of very obscure birth. Some of the canons of his cathedral were disgruntled by his elevation, but the fact that this was possible for sheer ability and character is evidence that in the Church these could win recognition.

The Christian faith also stimulated care for the sick, the poor, and the stranger. In a society where strife was chronic and survival seemed to depend on ruthless struggle which had no use for the weak, monasteries regularly entertained travellers, parishes cared for the indigent, and in the name of Christ hospitals were founded and maintained for the ill and the aged.

The position of women was affected. To be sure, as we have said, it was **a** man's world. In an age and a society in which warfare was chronic and the aristocracy were bred to arms, women were subordinate and men played fast and loose with them. However, it is evidence of the growing influence of Christianity that in the thirteenth and fourteenth centuries there were numbers of women who were eventually canonized, thus being recognized by the Church as worthy of emulation by all Christians. The cult of the Virgin Mary could not but make for reverence for womanhood and motherhood. Chivalry extolled loyalty to the lady who had won the devotion of the knight. There may be more than a coincidence in the fact that the accentuation of the cult of the Virgin and the development of chivalry were features of the same centuries. Closely associated with chivalry were the troubadours and the minnesingers, poets who extolled love. It may have been because of the impact of the Christian ideal that they sang of the objects of their affection not only for their physical charms but also for the beauty of their souls.

Here, as in so much of life, especially where it was challenged by the Christian faith, there were striking contrasts. Within the Church these were represented by Eve, subordinate to man and an agent of his fall, and the Virgin Mary and some of the women saints, and between the monastic conception, on the one hand, which viewed woman as a temptation and prized celibacy and, on the other hand, the teaching that marriage is a sacrament and therefore a channel of grace. In courtly lay circles there was the exaltation of the kind of love found in the poems of the pagan Ovid, and also the inculcation of loyalty to God and to one's lady in such fashion that these two were believed not to be contradictory.

As we have seen, marriage was regarded by the Church as a sacrament. In the midst of a society made chaotic by repeated invasions and chronic war and where for millions abject poverty was normal, the sex urge, always a problem with possibilities either for degradation or for noble achievement, often gave rise to grave irregularities among high and low. Here the Christian faith continued to point to the possibility of worthy direction and the Catholic Church by both negative prohibitions and the positive investing of the marriage tie with sanctity sought to make the Christian ideal a reality. While for multitudes, probably the majority, practice fell far short of what the Church taught, thousands, whether those who voluntarily chose the road of celibacy as a divine vocation or those who entered into the marriage tie, demonstrated that sex could be a blessing and not a curse. Marriages were normally arranged by the parents and were without romantic love. The latter was widely sought outside the marriage bond, although it did not necessarily go beyond what the Christian ideal could permit. Yet perhaps more often than not, between husband and wife there were, if not love, genuine affection and respect.

The effort was made to keep Sundays and other holy days free from the ordinary occupations of the week. Stories were told of the dire calamities which descended upon those who persisted in labouring or in holding or going to markets and fairs on these days. Some of the great festivals of the Christian year were the occasion for drunkenness and rowdyism, but the attempt was made to stress their religious significance.

Among the themes of sermons, including those of the friars, was the denunciation of extravagance and luxury in dress, of gambling, of dancing, and of masques, and at times the preachers had such effect that bonfires were built into which women cast what were pilloried as the instruments of sinful frivolities. Hunting and gaming were also condemned, but some writers and preachers held these to be contrary to the Christian profession only if carried to excess.

CONTRASTS AND AN UNRESOLVED QUESTION

On the area where once the Roman Empire had flourished there arose three civilizations, the Byzantine Greek, the Arab, and the Western European. Each was an heir of Greece and Rome and incorporated much from these great predecessors. To each distinctive features were added. Of the three that of Western Europe proved by far the most dynamic. By the twentieth century it was to spread over all the earth and by the mid-twentieth century varying elements from it were to be adopted by every people and tribe. Why was this? Why was it the civilization of Western Europe rather than that of the Byzantine Empire or the Arabs which was to prove so creative and potent? Presumably the world traveller of the middle of the tenth century would not have predicted that outcome. Probably he would have chosen Arab civilization first, Byzantine culture second, and Western Europe last as the one carrying with it the wave of the future. What made the difference? Was it race? That is too mixed a factor to be separated out and proved to be the cause. Was it natural resources? In these, if all natural endowments are included, the three seem to have been too nearly equal to account for the contrast. Was it climate? There, again, the three were too nearly alike to warrant regarding it as the decisive element.

Was the cause to be found in religion? As between the Byzantine and Western European civilization on the one hand and the Arab civilization on the other, here was a clear-cut and striking contrast. In the one Christianity was the professed faith and in the other Islam. Moreover, it may be significant that it was largely through Christians that the Arabs were introduced to Greek thought, that in the centuries of greatest Arab creativity the Christian communities in the Arab realms were still large, and that as they dwindled the cultural ferment in the Arab world declined. Yet Western Europe proved to be far more continuously creative than did Byzantine Greek culture, and both were adherents of Christianity and, indeed, of Catholic Christianity.

May it be that the answer is to be found primarily in a combination of the contrast in religions and in the conditions under which the religions operated? May the decisive factor in the dynamic in Western Europe have been Christianity and the conditions by which it was surrounded? Can it be that Western Europe forged to the fore because in it, largely through history and geography, Christianity had freer course than in the Byzantine realms? By history we mean the fact that the Roman Empire more nearly disintegrated in Western Europe than in the Byzantine continuation and that therefore Christianity was less shackled by the state. The geographic element is seen in the circumstance that, being on the Western tip of Eurasia, Western Europe was less subject to the pressure of non-Christian invaders, and especially of the Moslem invaders, than was the Byzantine Empire, and that therefore Christianity was less handicapped by being constantly on the defense and ultimately being subject to Moslem rulers.

We cannot be sure of the answer. Probably it is not to be found solely in one factor. However, that the presence of Christianity was the major cause is at least an arguable hypothesis. It is certain that it was in this period which we have been covering that Western Europe began to give indications of its future dynamic and prominence, for it was then that a distinctively Western European culture began to emerge. It was then, as we have seen, that Western Europeans first began the expansion which later, after a pause between the middle of the fourteenth century and the latter part of the fifteenth century, was to carry them all over the globe. Even between 950 and 1350 they had penetrated from North America to the Far East and from Greenland to South India and the Malay Peninsula, over more of the planet than had any other group of mankind. It was also precisely in these centuries that a striking revival in Christianity occurred and that the faith was increasingly moulding every aspect of the newly emerging culture.

Again and again we shall have occasion to remind ourselves that Western European civilization has by no means been an unqualified blessing to mankind. Indeed, in it and through it some of mankind's chronic evils have had their most colossally destructive effects. Outstanding are the wars, the materialism, and the exploitation of men by their fellows which have followed the development of science and machines. If Christianity is even partially responsible for the creativity and dynamic of Western civilization, it may have contributed to the phenomenal and tragic growth of these evils, evils which are direct contradictions of the Christian ideal for men. Has, then, Christianity miscarried? Has it been twisted to curse rather than to bless mankind? Can we gain here any inkling of the fashion in which God works in history? To this question we will recur again and again.

Before we seek to suggest more in detail, as we hope to do later, a possible answer to this searching and sobering query we will do well to remind ourselves that Christianity began in seeming weakness in a homeless birth in an inn, and that its most frequent symbol, a cross, records apparent frustration and defeat. Yet even by the year 1350 that faith had spread more widely than had any religion up to that time and in Western Europe it was entering deeply into a culture which was throbbing with vitality, a culture which presented stark contrasts and striking tensions which were accentuated and to no small degree due to the challenge of the Christian ideal.

Selected Bibliography

The Art of Courtly Love by Andreas Capellanus with introduction, translation, and notes by J. J. Parry (Columbia University Press, 1941, pp. xi, 218). A twelfth century author.

G. G. Coulton, *Five Centuries of Religion* (Cambridge University Press, 4 vols., 1923–1950). Of this monumental work, with its constant reference to the sources and its sturdy debunking of the idealization of the Christianity of the Middle Ages, *Volume III, Getting and Spending* bears more upon this chapter than does any of the others.

G. G. Coulton, *Life in the Middle Ages Selected Translated & Annotated* (Cambridge University Press, 4 vols., 1928–1930). Selections from the primary sources.

C. G. Crump and E. F. Jacobs, editors, *The Legacy of the Middle Ages* (Oxford University Press, 1926, pp. xii, 549). Essays by various experts covering a wide range of aspects of the life of Western Europe in the Middle Ages.

C. Dawson, *Religion and the Rise of Western Culture* (New York, Sheed & Ward, 1950, pp. xvi, 286). Gifford Lectures by a scholarly Roman Catholic layman.

S. C. Easton, *Roger Bacon and His Search for a Universal Science. A Reconsideration of the Life and Work of Roger Bacon in the Light of His Own Stated Purposes* (Oxford, Basil Blackwell, 1952, pp. vii, 255). Excellent. Based upon extensive research.

Bede Jarrett, *Social Theories of the Middle Ages 1200–1500* (Westminster, Md., The Newman Bookshop, 1942, pp. ix, 280). By a Dominican.

J. A. MacCulloch, *Medieval Faith and Fable* (Boston, Marshall-Jones Co., 1932, pp. 345). A somewhat disparaging view.

H. Rashdall, *The Universities of Europe in the Middle Ages,* rev. ed., edited by F. M. Powicke and A. B. Emden (Oxford University Press, 3 vols., 1936). The standard account.

H. O. Taylor, *The Mediæval Mind. A History of the Development of Thought and Emotion in the Middle Ages* (London, Macmillan & Co., 2 vols., 1911). A standard survey from the barbarian invasions to and including Duns Scotus, Ockham, and Dante.

E. Troeltsch, *The Social Teaching of the Christian Churches,* translated by Olive Wyon (New York, the Macmillan Co., 2 vols., 1931). The second half of the first volume of this standard work covers this period.

Chapter 24

THE EASTERN CHURCHES FROM A.D. 950 TO A.D. 1350

While the developments in Western Europe which we have been describing were in progress, what was happening in the churches in the East? Here Christianity had begun. Here it had its earliest numerical strength. Here had lived most of its creative minds of the first five centuries, and here monasticism had arisen. Yet these churches were more exposed to Islam than was the Christianity of Western Europe. They were nearer to the sources of the successive waves of invasion from the heart-land of Eurasia, in this period chiefly Turks and Mongols, and they were more divided by cultural, racial, and regional barriers, by ancient feuds, and by theological controversies than were the Christians of Western Europe.

We have seen the threat and the opportunity which came to them through the Mongol conquests and we have said something of their geographic expansion. We have noted how through the Byzantine wing of the Catholic Church the faith spread into Russia. We have watched the wide extension of Nestorian Christianity among minorities scattered across Asia from Mesopotamia into India and to the China Sea and have noted that through one of these minorities, the Keraïts, some of the Mongol princes were baptized as infants and there seemed some possibility that the rank and file of the Mongols might follow. Here was a geographic expansion of vast extent which for the time being appeared to hold promise of a further growth that might embrace Eastern Europe and most of Asia. When taken together with the contemporary vigour in the Christianity of Western Europe and the even greater areas traversed by missionaries of that branch of the faith, they constituted a forward surge in the Christian tide which was astonishing after the recession which accompanied the decline and disintegration of the Roman Empire. We have also recorded how through the Crusades the leaders of the Western wing of the Catholic Church were hopeful for the reunion of the severed branches of that comprehensive Catholic Church which had arisen in the Roman Empire but which had broken apart as that realm went to pieces. It was an era of achievement and of even greater possibilities.

We must now take up these Eastern Churches one by one and tell briefly the story of each.

THE BYZANTINE WING OF THE CATHOLIC CHURCH

First of all we must turn to the largest of these bodies, the Greek or Byzantine wing of the Catholic Church. Here there was high tragedy. We have seen that recovery from the blows given by the decline of Rome and the great invasions appeared to have begun earlier than in the West. Here the period 950–1350 opened hopefully with the conversion of the state which centered about Kiev, the nucleus of the future Russia, the empire where the largest member of the family of Orthodox churches was to arise. Yet the mother church, that of Constantinople, was to be dealt a nearly fatal blow by its fellow-Catholics of the West, a blow much more weakening than any thus far suffered from that traditional foe, Islam.

It was not until the period was far along that tragedy came. The advance which had been begun in the ninth century continued into the first half of the eleventh century. From the standpoint of geographic extent and economic power the Byzantine Empire expanded and reached a high point not far from the middle of the eleventh century. Under various rulers of what was called the Macedonian Dynasty Byzantine prestige was enhanced and partial control was renewed in South Italy and along the Adriatic, Bulgaria was subdued, the Crimea was an important outpost, the peoples of the Caucasus were tied to Constantinople by heavy subsidies to their rulers, much of Armenia was annexed, and Byzantine might was acknowledged in Northern Syria. Won by commercial concessions, the Venetians added their fleets to Byzantine naval power. In spite of the drain of the wars of conquest, the imperial treasury was replenished by taxes on industry and trade and by revenues from the newly annexed lands. Constantinople, the cultural and political centre of the realm, was the wealthiest city in Christendom. Although by no means as extensive or as rich as was China under the contemporary Sung Dynasty, or as the Roman Empire had been even as late as Justinian, this Byzantine Greek successor of the Roman name was staging a notable recovery.

Then, in dramatic fashion, came a series of political reverses. The death of Basil II in 1025 after a long reign marked the removal of the monarch under whom the realm had reached its apex. The Macedonian Dynasty faded out in a succession of mediocre Emperors. Domestic anarchy was paralleled by the successful advance of the Seljuk Turks, folk from Central Asia who, converted to Islam, had made themselves masters of the decaying Abbasid Caliphs at Baghdad. By 1081 the Turks were dominant in most of Armenia and Asia Minor. In South Italy by 1071 Byzantine rule was erased by the Norman conquest and there were revolts on the east shore of the Adriatic.

In 1081 Alexius Comnenus founded a dynasty, that of the Comneni, which lasted until 1185. Under Alexius Comnenus, who reigned from 1081 to 1118, and under his son, John II Comnenus, who followed him and died in 1143, a partial recovery was achieved. Partly through the aid of the First Crusade, Byzantine suzerainty was again established over much of Asia Minor and even over Antioch. Late in the dynasty Byzantine troops once more landed in Italy, but at the expense of alienating Venice, whose friendship was already waning. But within a few years Byzantine forces finally left Italy, never to return. Moreover, the interior of Asia Minor was again lost to the Seljuk Turks.

However, under the later Comneni there was something of a cultural renaissance. Art and letters flowered again and the great literature of pre-Christian Greece still had its students.

We have already spoken (Chapter 17) of the conquest of Constantinople in 1204 by the Fourth Crusade and the setting up of a Latin empire in that city. That event was a culmination of encroachments from the aggressive West which had long been in process. From the time of the First Crusade, warriors from Western Europe ostensibly on their way to the Holy Land, although at times a help, had been an embarrassment to the Byzantine rulers. In South Italy the Normans advanced on the traditionally Greek areas and in time expelled the Byzantine forces. In 1147 the Normans had invaded Greece, even more an integral part of the Byzantine realms. The rising tide of anti-Western nationalist feeling in Constantinople had come to a climax in the slaughter of the Latins in that city in 1182. Partly in retaliation, in 1185 the Normans had sacked Salonika.

By no means all the Byzantine territories were incorporated into the Latin empire. In them an aroused Greek nationalism supported princes who claimed to be the legitimate Roman Emperors. In 1261 one of these, Michael Paleologus, took Constantinople and ended the feeble Latin regime. From the Paleologi were to come Byzantine Emperors until the capture of Constantinople by the Turks in 1453 established the Moslems in that Christian capital. Yet never was their empire to approach in size that of the Macedonian Dynasty. Western Europeans, among them Venetians and Genoese, were long to retain parts of what had been Byzantine territory, including Athens, some of the islands in the Ægean, Crete, and a section of Asia Minor. It was fellow-Christians from the West quite as much as the Moslem Turks who were responsible for the final collapse of Christian Byzantium.

These political disasters could not but affect the Eastern wing of the Catholic Church and deepen the widening gulf between it and the Western wing of that church.

OUTSTANDING FEATURES OF THE BYZANTINE CHURCH

Several features must be noted of that branch of the Catholic Church which looked to the Patriarch of Constantinople as its ranking bishop. Most, if not all of them, had appeared earlier but were now intensified.

One of them was the lack of creative movements comparable to those which were surging in the Christianity of Western Europe. No new monastic orders appeared which could be regarded as counterparts of those in the West. Nor were there dissident movements—"heresies"—which were as vigorous as those in the West, unless it was the Bogomils, and these were Slavic rather than Byzantine. Much attention was paid to theology, but no fresh approaches were made which equalled those of the school men. While occasionally, as we shall see, showing a critical and independent attitude towards the state, the Byzantine Church had no such numerous and determined succession as had the West of men who sought through the hierarchy to purify the Church, to make it an instrument for raising the spiritual and moral level of all society, and to that end to free the Church from the control of the civil authorities.

Somewhat and perhaps closely related to this characteristic was the conviction of the Eastern wing of the Catholic Church that it was the champion and guardian of the true Christian faith as that had been taught by the early apostles. It regarded itself as orthodox, so much so, indeed, that Orthodox eventually became the designation by which it distinguished itself from other churches. The family of national churches whose major member in these centuries was that of the Byzantine Empire regarded as of its essence the conservation of the Christian faith, changeless, and looked askance not only on those churches in the East which earlier had separated from the Catholic Church, but also at what it deemed the innovations of the Western wing of the Catholic Church.

The reasons for this relative absence of fresh movements and for this sturdy adherence to what was deemed orthodox Christianity were probably complex. The chief of them, however, may have been the fact that the Byzantine Empire was chronically on the defensive. That realm was the waning continuation of the Roman Empire and of the Græco-Roman and especially the Greek heritage. It was a major bulwark of Christendom against Islam. Like the other churches of the East which geography compelled to face a triumphant Islam, it sought to preserve its existence by holding uncompromisingly to what had come down to it from the fathers and to distrust all variation as enervating disloyalty which would be productive of divisions and so of weakness. In contrast, the Christianity of Western Europe was not so immediately under pressure from Islam and, when in the tenth century the barbarian invasions subsided, it began a vigorous territorial expansion and was freer to reach out in new ways to meet the challenges in its central domains.

Another and a very striking characteristic of this Eastern wing of the Catholic Church was the fact that it possessed sufficient vitality to survive the state with which it had been intimately associated. This was seen more clearly in the next period when the Byzantine Empire finally succumbed to the conquering Turk. However, it was also true of the eleventh, twelfth, and thirteenth centuries when, as we have seen, that realm was shrinking. As the Byzantine state tottered towards its slow death the Church survived and in Greek areas became the refuge of Greek nationality. Moreover, as we are to say more at length a little later, even during these centuries of the fatal illness of the Byzantine Empire, the Christianity which looked to the capital as its main centre was spreading and showing renewed vitality on some of its geographic frontiers.

Limited Cæsaropapism

We must call attention to the fact that the Church was not always tamely subservient to the Byzantine or Eastern Roman Emperors. In earlier chapters we have noted how from the time of Constantine in the fore part of the fourth century the Emperors had taken an active part in the affairs of the Church. Continuing the pre-Christian tradition that religion and religious cults must be subservient to the state, they had sought, usually successfully, to dominate the Church. They called general councils, expressed themselves on theological issues, and controlled the election of the Patriarchs of Constantinople. Here was preëminently what was known as Cæsaropapism, the kind of control of the Church and its hierarchy by the prince to which the lay rulers of Western Europe aspired but which they were not uniformly able to achieve.

Yet even in Constantinople the Emperors did not always fully have their way. Earlier (Chapter 11) we have seen how in the case of the Patriarchs Photius and Ignatius the Emperors met determined opposition in their attempts to control the Church. The able Nicephorus II, who reigned from 963 to 969, ordered that the bishops reach no decision and make no nominations or promotions without imperial consent. Yet the Patriarch refused to crown the next monarch, John Tzimisces (reigned 969–976), ostensibly because he had murdered his predecessor, until he had abrogated this command. Nicephorus II also attempted to curb the power of the Church and of the monasteries by forbidding the creation of new religious foundations or the enlargement and enrichment of those already in existence. But in 988 pressure from the Church and the monks was sufficiently strong to bring about the rescinding of this edict. Michael Cerularius, Patriarch 1043–1058, sought to make the Church independent of the state somewhat in the fashion that the contemporary reformers in Western Europe were endeavouring to do, but by no means necessarily in imitation of them. For a time he appeared to be succeeding, but the Emperor whom he had helped put on the throne turned against him, he was deposed near the end of 1058 and, exiled, died a few days later. However, almost immediately he was canonized by popular acclaim, the Emperor was compelled by public opinion to give him an elaborate funeral, and the next Patriarch instituted an annual feast in his honour. The Patriarch Arsen Autorianus had the courage to refuse pardon to the powerful Emperor Michael Paleologus, who had restored the Byzantine rule at Constantinople, because that monarch had blinded his rival for the throne. Arsen's act cost him his post, but a loyal minority, presumably as much for political as religious motives, refused to concede the validity of the ordinations of the Patriarch who was put in his place and for a time constituted a dissident sect.

BYZANTINE MONASTICISM

Still another feature of the Eastern wing of the Catholic Church was the distinctive character of Byzantine monasticism. Monasticism continued to be prominent. The monastery of Studius, in Constantinople, long exerted a large influence in both Church and state. The communities on Mt. Athos grew and became famous. There were other mountains noted for their monastic establishments. Some of the latter had been founded before 950 and others were inaugurated after that year. Houses existed for women as well as for men. No orders existed comparable to those which arose in the West during these centuries, such as the Cistercians, Franciscans, and Dominicans, in which numbers of houses were brought within the structure of a single organization and under a common rule. The reforms carried through in the preceding period by Theodore of Studius had a wide influence, but Studius did not become the mother house of an order. Nor did monks give themselves to widespread preaching and to the care of parishes as was increasingly true of the friars of the West. Monasteries were primarily for the perfection of their members by prayer and ascetic practices. Some monks, usually a minority in any one house, were hermits and lived a life of solitude. However, the monasteries often were associated with philanthropic enterprises and had hospices for the aged and the poor and hospitals for the care of the sick. Usually they were self-governing and in at least some instances efforts were made by the founders to prevent any outsider, even the Patriarch or the Emperor, from taking possession of them.

As in Western Europe, so in the Byzantine realms, monasteries tended to depart from the high ideals of their founders and the enthusiasm and devotion of their initial years. Numbers entered them for the purpose of obtaining an easy livelihood. Many monks were ignorant, indifferent to their religious duties, and morally reprehensible. Some retained their personal property instead of holding all in common. Several of the monasteries sought to add to their collective wealth. Many came into the possession of laymen. Originally this was done on the condition that the lay proprietor repair or rebuild the physical plant. Eventually, however, this became only a pretext or might not be honoured even nominally. The one to whom the monastery had been granted appropriated the revenues for his own ends and gave only a pittance for the support of the monks. From time to time efforts were made to correct these abuses, but no such sweeping waves of reform were seen as were common in these centuries in the West.

HESYCHASTIC MYSTICISM

In the Eastern as in the Western wing of the Catholic Church there was mysticism. In the Eastern branch this took distinct forms. There were, as we have noted, monks who gave themselves to solitary contemplation. A special form of contemplation arose which is known as Hesychasm. It seems to have had as its father Simeon Neotheologus (or "New Theologian"), a Studite monk of the eleventh century. In the fourteenth century it flourished especially on Mt. Athos. It sought through special practices to attain the beatific vision of God. It held that the divine light can be attained and that it is of grace, bringing justification, joy, and peace. The Hesychasts claimed that by holding their breath, fixing their eyes upon their navels, and making the spirit reënter the soul, they could be enveloped by the light which shone around Christ at the time of his transfiguration on Mt. Tabor.

Hesychasm led to violent controversy. In its defense it was urged that the light was not the divine essence, for God Himself could never be seen by man, but that it was an operation or agency of God, divine grace. The critics contended that such a light could only be of the essence of God and that to separate the essence from the operation was to be guilty of falling into the error of believing in two Gods. The champion of the Hesychasts was Palamas, a monk on Mt. Athos, later (1349–c.1360) Archbishop of Thessalonica. The chief opponent was Barlaam, a native of Calabria, in Italy, a monk who had sought the union of the two wings of the Catholic Church. The issue was complicated by the widening gulf between the Latin and Byzantine Churches. The Roman Catholics held with Barlaam. The Byzantine Church, at first divided, eventually came out emphatically for the Hesychasts. In 1341 a synod in Constantinople supported them and this decision was confirmed by a second. A third synod sided with the adherents of Barlaam's views, but a fourth, in 1351, approved the Hesychasts and excommunicated Barlaam and his chief supporter, the Archbishop of Ephesus. Its decision was final and Hesychasm had the official endorsement of the Byzantine Church. We shall see that it persisted and that in the nineteenth century it enjoyed something of a revival, especially in the largest member of the family of Orthodox churches, that of Russia.

The fact that Hesychasm, with its quietism, loomed so prominently in the Orthodox Church is evidence of still another feature of that wing of Christianity. Here was a meditative, passive, non-activistic faith which specialized on the interior life. It had parallels in the West and in some respects resembled the mysticism which was prominent in various sections of Latin Christianity in the fourteenth century. However, Orthodox monasticism was not as varied in its expressions as was that of Western Europe.

THE WIDENING RIFT BETWEEN EAST AND WEST

Probably it was to be expected that the Eastern and Western wings of the Catholic Church would drift farther apart. Here was one of the outstanding features of the history of Christianity in the four centuries between 950 and 1350.

The causes were many. The ostensible reasons were such differences as the *filioque* clause in the Nicene Creed, the contrast between the Western custom of clean-shaven clergy and the Eastern bearded clergy, the Latin tradition of fasting Saturdays in Lent, the singing of the Alleluia only on Easter, the eating of animals strangled and of blood, the celibacy of the parish clergy in the West as against the married clergy in the East (a cause of friction which became more marked as the reformers in the West sought to enforce the rule of celibacy within their jurisdiction), the use in the West of unleavened bread (azyme) in the Eucharist instead of the leavened bread which was employed in the East, and the custom in the Greek Church of rebaptizing Latins who wished to come into its fellowship.

Vigorously and often bitterly though these issues were debated, in reality they were superficial. Underneath were far more weighty and basic factors. The enveloping structure of the Roman Empire within which the Catholic Church had arisen and which facilitated its unity had further disintegrated. While both claimed to be heirs of the Roman Empire, the Holy Roman Empire and the Byzantine Empire had become clearly separate and the fiction that they were the Western and Eastern wings of the same realm was progressively more difficult to maintain. Rivalry between the Roman Pontiffs and the Patriarchs of Constantinople continued. The East resented the claims of the Popes to universal dominion over the Church. The encroachments of Western European peans upon the Byzantine realms which culminated in the capture of Constantinople and the setting up of a Latin Patriarchate in that city aroused hot resentment among the masses of the Greeks which their leaders, eager for political reasons to effect a reconciliation, could not successfully over-ride. Then, too, the Greeks looked upon the Latins as barbarians.

In addition to these sources of friction there were differences which went far back into the history and outlook of the Latin and Greek wings of the Catholic Church and which had been sharpened with the years. To be sure, both repeated the Nicene Creed as standard and in theory held to the Chalcedonian theology. However, the Greek wing tended to emphasize the divine side of Christ and to give a truncated view of his humanity. In its long struggle with Monophysitism it had come to verge on that position. Its typical picture of Christ, which may have been adapted from the pre-Christian representations of Zeus, portrayed him as Pantocrator, the Lord Omnipotent. In contrast, the West stressed not only the full deity of Christ but also his full humanity and at times may have seemed almost Nestorian in its tendency. In the twelfth century there developed in the West, partly through the stimulus given by Bernard of Clairvaux, a devotion which while not denying the incarnation, dwelt on the man Jesus. It has been said that Byzantine Christianity tended to minimize the Christ of the Gospels and to act as though its faith was in a mythical heavenly saviour. In contrast the West did not forget the Jesus of the Gospels. Perhaps for this reason and possibly because of the Roman tradition, Western Christianity was activist and ethical. It tended to believe that the moral standards of the faith could be met and through auricular confession and penance sought to bring the masses to them. Christianity did not mould Byzantine culture as deeply as it did the civilization of Western Europe. Eastern Catholicism was not so intent upon reshaping all of life as was its Western counterpart. The Byzantine liturgy was much more elaborate and the Eucharist more removed from the congregation than was usually true in the West. The iconostasis, a partition, separated the congregation from the altar and what the priest did at the altar to a much greater degree than did altar screens in the West.

The rupture between East and West did not come at once and not until after 1350 was it clearly final. Important incidents marked its course. Of these some were in the Patriarchate of the able and vigorous Michael Cerularius. Cerularius was alarmed by the conquest of Southern Italy by the Normans and the prospect of the transfer of the ecclesiastical supervision of that area and of Sicily from Constantinople to Rome. Moreover, at the time when Cerularius came to the Patriarchate (1043) the utterly unworthy Benedict IX was on the Papal throne. It may have been for this reason that at the outset he did not notify the

Pope of his election or have the Pope's name on his diptych, namely, that he did not make mention of him in the prayers at the Eucharist. However, in 1049 a very different man became Pope, the able and reforming Leo IX, who held the post until 1054. Leo IX endeavoured to extend the sway of Rome to Sicily and Southern Italy and campaigned against the clergy who, in accordance with the Greek custom, were married. This aroused Cerularius and in retaliation he and Leo of Ochrida, the Metropolitan of Bulgaria, closed the churches and monasteries of the Latin rite in their territories. At the same time Leo of Ochrida wrote to a bishop in Southern Italy warning him against what he held to be the errors of Rome and the churches in the West.

Cardinal Humbert, a monk who was a leader in the reform in the West, a sturdy opponent of lay investiture, translated the letter from Greek into Latin and was empowered by the Pope to reply. In that letter the commission given to the Roman See through Peter was emphatically asserted, together with the promise that the faith of Peter and so of the Church of Rome should not fail, the spurious Donation of Constantine, then accepted as genuine, was quoted to uphold the Papal claims in Italy, and the fact was stressed that in contrast with Rome's record of orthodoxy some of the Patriarchs of Constantinople had been heretics. The letter also pointed out that in his clemency the Pope had permitted churches and monasteries of the Greek rite to continue in Rome. For political reasons the Byzantine Emperor wished to have harmonious relations with the Pope. Presumably at his instance Cerularius returned a moderate reply. The Emperor also wrote in the same vein. Both expressed the desire to maintain the unity of the Church. Leo IX was not conciliatory. He protested to the Emperor the arrogance of Cerularius and in a letter to the Patriarch set forth strong strictures on the latter's conduct. Thus the Pope asserted the claim of the See of Peter to supremacy over the entire Catholic Church and held that this was incompatible with the autonomy of national churches.

Leo IX appointed a delegation to carry these letters to Constantinople. On it were three high ecclesiastics, one of them the uncompromising Cardinal Humbert and another the future Pope Stephen IX who, like Humbert, was an ardent reformer and an advocate of the authority of the Roman See. The Emperor was still conciliatory, for he wished an alliance with the Pope to restore and maintain Byzantine influence in Italy. However, Cerularius, noted for his independence of imperial domination, was obdurate and on July 16, 1054, the Papal legates dramatically laid on the altar of St. Sophia, as it stood ready for the Eucharist, a sentence of excommunication of the Patriarch and his supporters and left the cathedral, shaking the dust off their feet. In his turn, within a few days, at a solemn synod Cerularius excommunicated the legates.

These acts of the Papal legates and of Michael Cerularius and his synod by no means effected a final breach between the Roman and the Orthodox churches. The Catholic Church was still regarded as one. The Patriarch of Antioch, as a leading figure in the Catholic Church, sought to mediate between the disputants. In the ensuing centuries when Crusaders and pilgrims from Western Europe were numerous in the East, coöperation between members of the hierarchy in the East and the Latins was not uncommon and from time to time the latter were given the communion by Eastern clergy. Although at one time the Byzantine Emperor Alexius Comnenus was excommunicated by the Pope and in return forbade the Latin churches in Constantinople to use unleavened bread in the Eucharist, in 1089 Pope Urban II, who was deeply concerned to heal the breach, removed the excommunication and the Emperor advised the synod of his church provisionally to place the Pope's name on the diptychs. Urban had as a chief motive in promoting the First Crusade the reunion of the churches, and in 1098, while the Crusade was in progress, he convened a Council at Bari, in the south of Italy, of both Latin and Greek bishops. The Greek bishops, however, were only from Italy and possibly Sicily and not from the Byzantine Empire, for the purpose was primarily local, to make Papal power effective in the domains recently conquered by the Normans. The main point of discussion seems to have been the *filioque* phrase. Anselm was the chief advocate of the Papal position and the Greeks are said to have been won over by him.

In spite of the hopes of Urban II, the First Crusade and its successors widened rather than bridged the gulf between the Western Church on the one hand and the Eastern churches on the other. The Crusaders tended to regard the Greeks as well as the other Eastern Christians as heretics. Latin clergy supplanted the Eastern clergy or were placed alongside them. Some Eastern Christians were won to union with Rome, but the majority held aloof and their antipathy was accentuated by the behaviour of the Crusaders. The conquest of Cyprus by Western Europeans late in the twelfth century and the creation of a Latin hierarchy with special privileges as against other Christians accentuated the tension, for the island had long been under the Greek wing of the Church. The Latin conquest of Constantinople in 1204 and the setting up of a Latin Patriarch in that city heightened popular resentment. Greek nationalism rallied around the Byzantine Church and made it a symbol of resistance. The conquest was effected during the high tide of Papal power under Innocent III. At the time it looked as though reunion was about to be accomplished under that great Pontiff, but the majority of the Greeks kept aloof. They could not bring themselves to concede the supremacy of the Pope.

Yet efforts for reunion continued to be made. During the Latin occupation of Constantinople John III (Ducas Vatatzes), one of the Byzantine Emperors who maintained a capital at Nicæa, in an effort to regain territories which had been lost to the Latins, hoped for peace between the two churches. At his request made through the Byzantine Patriarch Pope Gregory IX sent envoys to see whether an accord could be reached. No agreement followed; each side stated (1234) its grievances against the other and would not yield on crucial issues. Negotiations were resumed not far from 1250, this time between John III and Pope Innocent IV. They dragged out for three years or more and when they seemed about to succeed they were terminated by the death (1254) of both the Emperor and the Pope.

Discussions over reunion were resumed under the Emperor Michael VIII Paleologus, the first of his dynasty, who in 1261 restored the Byzantine rule in Constantinople. Michael's object appears to have been the security of his throne, for he was faced by internal as well as foreign enemies and felt himself in need of Papal support. He was especially afraid of Charles of Anjou who from his base in Sicily and Italy was attempting to build an empire in the Mediterranean. Eventually, in May, 1274, at the Second Council of Lyons, regarded by the Roman Catholic Church as the Fourteenth Ecumenical Council, the goal seemed to have been attained. The Greek delegation conceded all that was asked by the Pope and unity was declared to have been restored. However, the overwhelming majority of the constituency of the Byzantine Church would not assent. Nationalism ran high and with it resentment against any hint of submission to the hated Latins. Yet the Emperor Michael attained his purpose of security for his throne. In 1282, a revolt against Charles of Anjou, known as the Sicilian Vespers, removed the menace from that prince. After Michael's death his son and successor felt himself strong enough to renounce the arrangement made at Lyons and the breach between the churches was deepened.

The advances of the Ottoman Turks led some of the Byzantine Emperors to seek accord with Rome in the hope of obtaining military help from the West. Suggestions were put forward that a general council of the severed branches of the Catholic Church be held, to include the Papal representatives and the Patriarchs of Constantinople, Antioch, Jerusalem, and Alexander. The conversations came to nought. In 1369 the Byzantine Emperor John V while on a visit to Rome made his submission to the Pope, but he could not carry his tottering empire with him. As we shall see, another effort, at the time seemingly successful, was essayed in 1439, but it, too, proved futile. The once outwardly united Catholic Church was fractured, presumably beyond repair.

NON-BYZANTINE MEMBERS OF THE FAMILY OF ORTHODOX CHURCHES: THE BULGARIANS

The story so briefly summarized on the preceding pages of this chapter may give the impression that for Byzantine in contrast with Latin Christianity the period from 950 to 1350 was one not of advance but of almost unrelieved recession, especially after the middle of the eleventh century. That, however, would be far from the truth. To be sure, politically the Byzantine succession of the Roman Empire was in a fatal decline which was only partly interrupted by the brilliant rulers of the Macedonian Dynasty. Moreover, the churches within its borders were suffering, both from the conquests of the Moslem Turks and the incursions of the Crusading Christians from the West. Yet the northward geographic spread of Christianity from the Byzantine nucleus which had begun before 950 continued. By it the faith was carried far beyond the boundaries which it had reached before the barbarian invasions. Through it new national bodies were added to the family of Orthodox churches which looked towards Constantinople and its Patriarch as their centre.

First of all we must note briefly the somewhat sadly chequered course of the faith in Bulgaria. We have already seen (Chapter 11) how in the second half of the ninth century and the fore part of the tenth century, under the royal leadership of Boris and his son Simeon, the Bulgars and their Slavic subjects had been brought to accept Christianity and how under the latter Bulgaria had enjoyed a golden age, with Simeon adopting the designation Tsar and having the bishops of his realm declare their church independent with one of their number at its head as patriarch.

However, after death had removed the strong hand of Simeon (927) a decline set in which lasted until 1186. The great Emperors of the Macedonian Dynasty extended their sway, first over the eastern and then over the western part of the country, and the church lost its independence and was dominated by Greek bishops and clergy. The heads of the church were appointed from Constantinople and Greek was enforced as the ecclesiastical language.

The Bulgarian Church was also troubled by a religious movement which we know as Bogomilism. This seems to have arisen in the tenth century. Its origin is obscure. It is said to have been begun by a Bulgarian Orthodox Christian priest named Bogomil or at least to have found an early leader in him. It is also declared to have been indebted to the Paulicians and even to have been a continuation of them—that set of sturdy religious groups whom we met earlier (Chapter 11) and who were condemned by the Orthodox as heretics. There had been active Paulician settlements in the Balkan Peninsula from at least the eighth century and contagion from them is quite within the range of possibility.

Bogomilism had in it Christian elements which were set in a basic context of dualism such as we have repeatedly seen in our story. It rejected the Old Testament, for the latter told of the creation of this present evil world by God. It accepted the New Testament, but rejected the miracles of healing by Christ since these had to do with the flesh, and held them to be parables of healing from sin. The Bogomils maintained that all branches of the Christian Church were in error and would have nothing to do with their doctrines, rites, sacraments, orders, holy days, crosses, icons, and saints. They repeated the Lord's Prayer four times each day and four times each night. While disapproving of marriage, they enjoined abstention from it only on "the perfect" and permitted it for the rank and file, "the hearers." "The perfect" were active missionaries and spread their faith against severe persecution. We have already noted the similarity between the Cathari and the Bogomils, a resemblance which may indicate that the former were derived from contact with the latter.

Bogomilism was associated with a Slavic particularism and reinforced the revolt against the domination of the Byzantine Empire and the Greeks, including the Orthodox Church, associated as that was with Byzantine and Greek imperialism. It also seems to have championed the cause of the oppressed slaves and serfs against their masters, who were largely Greeks.

In the weakness which fell upon the Byzantine Empire after the disappearance of the Macedonian Dynasty and especially after the divisions brought by the Latin conquest of Constantinople, the Bulgarians rose and threw off the Greek yoke. The first effective revolt was in 1186. Bulgarian bishops were gradually substituted for Greek prelates. To obtain recognition of the legitimacy of the new order, the Bulgarian ruler entered into long negotiations with the powerful Pope Innocent III, whose prestige in the East had been heightened by the setting up of the Latin empire on the Bosporus. As a result, the Bulgarian prince, Kaloyan, acknowledged himself to be subject to the Roman See and was crowned by a Papal legate. The Bulgarian hierarchy, including its primate, accepted the supremacy of the Pope. This, however, seems to have made little difference in the life and internal organization of the Bulgarian Church.

As under a later ruler the renewed Bulgarian empire continued to expand, the Byzantine Emperor, in the hope of assistance against his Latin rival, recognized the Bulgarian monarch as Tsar or Emperor, and therefore on a legal equality with himself, and in 1235 the Greek Patriarch, with the consent of the other three Patriarchs of the Greek Orthodox Church (namely, those of Antioch, Alexandria, and Jerusalem) conceded patriarchal rank to the head of the Bulgarian Church. Yet the latter, who three years earlier had deserted the Roman allegiance and had recognized the authority of the Greek Patriarch of Constantinople, continued to be subordinate to him. The Popes attempted to assert their suzerainty over Bulgaria, but in vain. The reunion of the Roman and Greek churches officially effected at the Second Council of Lyons included the Bulgarian Church. However, as we have seen, that act, which ignored the rank and file of the constituency, was rejected by popular clamour in the Greek domains. For most practical purposes it was also ignored in Bulgaria.

In the fore part of the fourteenth century Hesychasm was carried into Bulgarian monasticism and gained an influential following.

In the latter half of the thirteenth century Bulgaria entered upon another period of political decline. In the fore part of the following century this was accentuated by invasions of the Serbs and the Turks. In the half century after 1350, as we are to see in the next period of our story, the Turks eliminated the Bulgarian state and brought fresh problems to the Christianity of that unhappy land.

Non-Byzantine Members of the Family of Orthodox Churches: the Serbs

We have already noted (Chapter 11) the introduction of Christianity among the western neighbours of the Bulgarians, the Serbs, in the seventh and ninth centuries. This was under Byzantine auspices and in the ninth century was by compulsion. In the latter part of the ninth century a marked impulse was given to the acceptance of Christianity by the indirect influence of Constantine (Cyril) and Methodius through the Christian literature prepared in Slavonic by them and their pupils. During the latter part of the ninth and into the eleventh century Byzantine, Bulgarian, and then Byzantine power dominated most of the Serbs. This tied the Serbian churches to the Orthodox wing of the faith.

However, since the Serbian territory was a border land between Rome and Constantinople, some of the Serbs and especially their neighbouring Slavs, the Croats, adhered ecclesiastically to Rome. In 1076 the mighty Hildebrand as Pope Gregory VII conferred the royal dignity upon a Croatian chieftain and the following year granted it to Michael, a Serbian chieftain, in return for the latter's recognition of Papal suzerainty. This, of course, meant that ecclesiastically Michael's growing realm passed into the Roman orbit. A few years later the Pope raised the bishopric of Antivari to archiepiscopal rank, giving the church among the Serbs a degree of administrative unity.

The realm which Michael had erected proved ephemeral. After the death of his son and successor (1101) the domains which had been assembled fell apart. For a time Byzantine influence mounted. However, the decline of the Byzantine Empire in the latter part of the twelfth century and the added weakness brought by the Latin conquest of Constantinople enabled a Serbian prince, Stephen Nemanya, who ruled from 1168 to 1195, to bring most of the Serbs under his sway—with the notable exception of Bosnia and Hum. Religiously the domains of Stephen Nemanya were divided. Part adhered to Rome, part to Constantinople, and Bogomils were numerous. Stephen had been baptized in the Latin rite, but he was enthusiastically Orthodox. While he tolerated the churches of the Latin rite, he gave his support to the Orthodox wing of the Church. Moreover, he conducted a crusade against the Bogomils and drove most of them out of the country. They found refuge in Bosnia and Hum. Stephen Nemanya founded a dynasty which consolidated Serbia into a kingdom and survived until 1371. It was Stephen Nemanya's son, also Stephen, who assumed the title of king.

The creation of a Serbian national church was the work of a younger son of the first Stephen, Rastko (1174–1236). Rastko was reared at the court of his father. When in his impressionable mid-adolescence, not far from the age of eighteen, he was won to the monastic life by a Russian monk from Mt. Athos. Fearing parental opposition, he fled secretly to Mt. Athos and there took monastic vows and the name of a famous Serbian saint, Sava, by which he is best remembered. Not many years thereafter (1195) his father left his throne to become a monk and his queen became a nun. Stephen, now known as Simeon, founded the monastery Studenitsa and joined his son Sava on Mt. Athos. There the two built and richly equipped a monastery which soon became the major Serbian literary centre and the school in which the leaders of the Serbian Church were trained.

Simeon's death in 1200 seemed to throw the Serbs into the Roman camp. Civil strife over the succession broke out between two of his sons, brothers of Sava. The then Pope, Innocent III, used the opportunity to extend Roman influence over the land. To obtain the help of Hungary one of the rivals, through the astute diplomacy of Innocent, was compelled to acknowledge Roman supremacy. In his turn, to win Papal support, the other rival, the second Stephen, divorced his wife, the daughter of the Byzantine Emperor, married a Venetian, received from Innocent's successor a royal crown, and vowed obedience to the Pope. The Papal legate proceeded to set up a Latin hierarchy.

However, Sava, loyal to his Orthodox convictions, was not to be frustrated. He had returned to Serbia in 1208 and the clergy, many of whom had been trained by him, stood by him. Moreover, popular opinion was with him.

He had travelled the length and breadth of the land, reforming the Church and raising the level of its life. The people knew him and supported him. Sava went to Nicæa, then the capital of the Byzantine Empire, obtained from the Emperor, Patriarch, and synod recognition of the independence of the Serbian Church, and was consecrated archbishop to head the new autocephalous hierarchy. Returning home, he easily gained from his brother recognition as head of the national church, for the king presumably welcomed an arrangement by which that body would be autonomous and under the control of a member of his family. The Papal legate withdrew, together with his Latin clergy, and Sava set about the ecclesiastical organization of the country. He established schools, one of them in connexion with Studenitsa. He resumed his journeys over the realm, supervising, inspiring, and when necessary disciplining the clergy. He adjusted inherited pre-Christian customs to Christian purposes. After the death of his brother, the king, he crowned the latter's son, his nephew. Eventually he passed on his own office to a man whom he had trained. More than any other one man Sava shaped the Christianity of Serbia. That Christianity perpetuated the Byzantine tradition of the close association of Church and state, a national church, and the type of monasticism which had its chief exemplars on Mt. Athos. Under Sava Greek Christianity, adapted to Serbian traditions, became firmly rooted.

We must here pause to note the important place which that variant of Christianity, Bogomilism, came to have in Bosnia and the adjoining Hum, later known as Herzegovina. Both areas bordered on Serbia, to which they were closely related in race. The Bogomils, or Patarenes as they were known in this region, had found a refuge there after their expulsion from Serbia. They multiplied and spread into the nearby Croatia, Slavonia, Hungary, and Dalmatia. One reason for the strength of Bogomilism in Bosnia and Hum seems to have been that, being neither Greek Orthodox nor Roman Catholic, it reinforced local particularism against the Orthodox Serbs on the east and the Roman Catholic Hungarians on the north, peoples who sought to extend their control over these two districts. Apparently from a politic desire to divert Hungarian aggression, in 1204, in the Pontificate of Innocent III, the ruler in Bosnia and some of the leading Patarenes formally abjured their heresy in the presence of Papal representatives. However, when the danger lapsed, Bogomilism revived and in the third quarter of the thirteenth century the majority of the Bosnians and their nobles are said to have been Patarenes. Even the Catholic bishop was reported to have been one of them. In spite of persecutions, a crusade, the Inquisition, and the labours of Dominican and Franciscan missionaries, until long after 1350 Patarenism continued to flourish in both Bosnia and Hum.

Non-Byzantine Members of the Family of Orthodox Churches: the Russians

It was in Russia that Greek Orthodox Christianity made its most extensive gains during this period. Earlier (Chapter 16) we told of the introduction of Christianity to the state which centered around Kiev, the historic nucleus of the later Russia. We also saw that the invasion and conquest by the non-Christian Mongols, at first destructive, actually deepened the hold of Christianity on the Russians, partly because the Church, as the one institution which was clearly theirs, was the symbol and bulwark of Russian nationalism. Moreover, during the centuries of the Mongol occupation, Christianity was carried north of the Mongol domains. Between 950 and 1350 this Greek Christianity which had Constantinople as its focus, through the conversions to it effected in Russia, approximately doubled the area in which it was the religion of the majority. There was no proportionate increase in the number of its adherents, for Russia was still sparsely settled. However, it probably added far more to its fold than in the same centuries it lost to Islam through the Turkish encroachments on its traditional territories.

Since we have already summarized the geographic spread of Christianity in Russia we must here content ourselves with saying something of the internal developments which contributed to the distinctive characteristics which the faith in that land eventually presented.

Contributions to Russian Christianity came through a number of channels. The major foreign source was the Eastern wing of the Catholic Church. Much of the Christian literature was translations from the Greek into Slavonic which entered by way of Bulgaria, for the vernaculars of the two regions were sufficiently akin to make this possible.

The fact that these translations into the vernacular were available had a negative effect. For centuries few of the Russian clergy and monks troubled themselves to learn Greek, for what they wished was at hand in their native tongue. This meant that the vast treasures of pre-Christian Greek literature and philosophy were closed to them. Russian literature of these centuries centered on practical, moral, and ascetic ends. This was in contrast with Western Europe in this period. Here the language of the liturgy and the Church was Latin. Priests and monks learned it and in doing so they acquired a key which unlocked to them the wide range of pre-Christian Latin literature and thought.

The Pechersk or Caves Monastery at Kiev was the most famous pioneer foundation and so had a large share in shaping the future monasticism of Russia. Hilarion, the first Metropolitan of Russian origin, a noted scholar and preacher, in his earlier days had dug a cave for himself near Kiev and there had practised meditation. A precursor of the later community of the Caves was Anthony, who had been a monk at Mt. Athos. The Caves Monastery eventually followed the rule of the monastery of Studius in Constantinople in the development of which Theodore the Studite had had so important a part. That rule became the norm for subsequent Russian houses. Through travellers and pilgrims contacts were made and maintained with other centres in Constantinople and with Mt. Athos. A Russian monastery was developed on that holy mountain and from it a fairly constant stream flowed into Russia.

For the first half century or so after the baptism of Vladimir (c.988) the church in his domains, thanks to his insistence, was autocephalous and so practically independent of the Patriarch of Constantinople. However, beginning with 1037, most of the Metropolitans of Kiev were selected by the Patriarch. Although in the twelfth century the Russian princes nominated the bishops, through the Metropolitans the tie with Constantinople was very close. The rich Byzantine liturgy was adopted by the Russian Church and made a profound impression on the Russian spirit.

Another channel through which influences from abroad came to Russian Christianity was Palestinian monasticism. Theodosius, who with his teacher Anthony was the founder of the Caves Monastery and so of Russian monasticism, was a warm admirer of the monks of Palestine. True to what he had heard of his Palestinian models, he avoided extreme asceticism, placed limits on silence, and sought a balance between the active and the contemplative life.

Still another medium through which Christianity came to Russia was the Catholicism of the Latin West. When the first conversions of Russians were being made the rift between the Eastern and Western wings of the Catholic Church was not nearly as great as it was to become in the eleventh century. The sense of unity, although weakened, was still strong. Therefore it was not deemed improper for lessons to come from both directions. We saw that it was to Germany that Vladimir's grandmother Olga had sent for missionaries. Missionaries from the West helped in the conversion of the Russians under Vladimir. Intermittent contacts with Rome existed in the eleventh century. It is possible that the system of levying tithes for the support of the Church which Vladimir adopted was suggested by Western practice. The Mongol conquest damaged the Kievan culture which, near to the West, had some elements from the Latin wing of the Church and separated Great Russia, that which later clustered around Moscow, from the West while enabling contacts to be maintained with Constantinople. However, some intercourse was continued through Dominican and Franciscan missionaries. Both, but especially the latter, were in Kiev in the thirteenth century. At the beginning of the fourteenth century the Brothers Minor had seventeen stations in the portions of Russia ruled by the Mongols, with several bishoprics and two archbishoprics. Some of the converts were Mongols. Presumably repercussions were felt in the Russian Church.

To these contributions from abroad the Russians added distinctive ones of their own. One was kenoticism, the emptying of self in humility. It is significant that the first to be canonized by the Russian Church and for centuries esteemed the patron saints of the land were Boris and Gleb, sons of Vladimir, who, without offering armed resistance, were killed by henchmen of their brother in the latter's desire to rid himself of them as possible rivals to the succession. The older of the two, Boris, is said to have spent the night before his death in prayer, waiting for his murderers. In the legends which recounted the tragedy, he is reported to have been moved by humility and love and a realization of the vanity of the kind of power represented by the state. Whether or not the reports are true, the fact that they were formulated and treasured gives insight into what was valued by many Russian Christians. The multitude esteemed the two brothers as saints because they were innocent sufferers. They were honoured in liturgical offices for having "forsaken the perishable glory of this world" and for "hating the kingdom of the world and loving purity."

Theodosius, or Feodosi (died 1074, and so an older contemporary of Hildebrand and Abbot Hugh of Cluny), the first Russian monk to be canonized (Boris and Gleb were not monks), the real organizer of the Caves Monastery, the chief pioneer and inspirer of Russian monasticism, was also noted for kenoticism. It is said that from childhood he was marked by humility, in spite of the pleas of his wealthy parents wore uncouth and patched clothing, and later worked with the slaves in the fields. He ran away from his mother to enter the monastery. Eventually, relenting, she yielded to his entreaties and herself became a nun. As head of the monastery he is reported always to have been merciful and mild, to have been loth to resort to punishment to discipline his monks, and to have welcomed back the wayward who had fled the cloister.

Theodosius made another contribution to Russian monasticism. He sought to have the monastery serve the world. From its income he supported a hospice for the beggars and the sick and sent food to the prisoners in the city jail. He was the spiritual counsellor of many and seems to have been responsible for the inauguration of a Russian tradition that monks should be the confessors and guides to lay folk. He went out into the world to make contacts with individuals and to rebuke and exhort the erring.

Kenoticism and practical service to the world were not the only trends in Russian monasticism. Even in the Caves Monastery there was a grim strain of extreme asceticism and fear of demons which was in partial contrast with Theodosius.

Another Russian monk, not canonized until the mid-sixteenth century, was

Abraham of Smolensk, of the second half of the twelfth and the fore part of the thirteenth century. It was after the death of his parents that he distributed his inherited goods among the poor and entered a monastery on the outskirts of Smolensk. He became an ardent student of the writings of the Fathers of the Church, was sternly ascetic, warned all who would listen of the impending wrath of God, and in his prayers implored God to have mercy on the people. The laity thronged to him, but the clergy and monks were hostile and for a time had him confined in a monastery and forbidden to say mass, why is not entirely clear. Eventually released, he became the head of a monastery, and there until his death at a ripe age taught and counselled those who came to him.

Much more influential was Sergius, the patron saint of Russia and the most widely beloved of her holy men. He was born sometime between 1314 and 1323 and died in 1392. He lived, then, after the Mongol conquest. He was the outstanding example of a new type of monasticism which arose after that event. Pre-Mongol Russian monasteries had been either in towns or near them. After the Mongol inroads, many monks settled in the northern forests, away from human habitation and Mongol rule. In many ways Sergius resembled Theodosius. He was marked by kenotic humility. He worked with his hands and even in the days of his greatest fame tended the monastic garden. He protected and comforted the oppressed. Unlike Theodosius, he was first a hermit. Then others began to gather around him, each dwelling in a separate cell. Eventually, against his will, for he feared the temptation to pride, he was ordained priest and was made abbot of the community. A monastery founded by him, the Troitsa (Trinity), about forty miles from Moscow, became famous and was the mother of many other houses. Also unlike Theodosius, Sergius was a mystic, a pioneer in Russia of that type of religious experience and devotion. He seems to have been affected by the Hesychast movement, newly arrived from Mt. Athos. But his was not only a life of prayer. He encouraged the prince of Moscow to resist the Mongols by force of arms. He gave his blessing to the force sent out to meet the Mongols and the notable victory which followed was attributed by the prince to his prayers.

It was only gradually that the Christian faith really penetrated to the masses of the population of Russia. Accepted first in the upper circles, it was slow in making its way to the rank and file. Paganism long survived. It seems significant that the *Tale of Igor's Campaign,* written at the end of the twelfth century by a professed Christian, and unique in early Russian literature for its intentionally artistic form, has in it almost nothing distinctively Christian but is prevailingly pagan and secular. As late as the eleventh century pagan magicians, *volkhvi,* had sufficient influence to stir up a popular anti-Christian uprising in Novgorod, the leading centre of Christianity in the North-west.

The Bible, read in Slavonic in the services of the Church, eventually became familiar to monks and the lay folk who attended the liturgy. Of the Old Testament the Psalms were the most prized. The New Testament was especially valued.

The Gospels made a great impression upon the early Russian saints. Here they got behind Christ the Pantocrator who had come to them in the Byzantine tradition and rediscovered the human aspects of Jesus. Through the Gospels and the saints the voluntary suffering and humility of Jesus contributed markedly to the kenotic quality in the Russian religious ideal.

By way of a Slavonic translation the Pseudo-Dionysius (Dionysius the Areopagite) became the possession of the Russians and, as in East and West, made its Neoplatonic contribution to mysticism.

Slow though the process was, Russian life was being moulded by Christianity. In contrast with Slavic paganism which did not inculcate responsibility, Christianity with its ethical teaching, reinforced by a belief in the future life and the last judgement, nurtured in individuals a sense of accountability for their deeds. It brought an awareness of sin and an urge to repentance and so introduced the element of struggle for moral perfection. As in Western Europe, it quickened men's social conscience. Some of the leaders of the Church objected to slavery, and monasteries had hospitals and asylums for the aged. Christianity stimulated legislation to end class feuds and bloody revenge. Rulers as well as subjects were held to be under the judgement of God. Good princes were praised and bad ones condemned.

Eventually Christianity became the conscious possession of the masses. Many flocked to outstanding monks for counsel. There was no formally regularized confession to priests as in the West, but there was preaching with practical instruction in Christian virtues. The emphasis was upon the love of God and one's neighbours and upon repentance, even with tears, and fasting. There were also the fear of God and humility.

By the middle of the fourteenth century Christianity in Russia, as in Western Europe, was in a new milieu.

When Christianity was being adopted Russia was composed of a congeries of loosely related political units. In the eleventh century the state which had centered in Kiev and in which the Russian hierarchy had its head tended to disintegrate. Then, in the middle of the thirteenth century, came the Mongol conquest. The Kievan culture largely disappeared. It was chiefly the Church which survived. Remnants of independence persisted in the South-west, in the North-west around the cities of Novgorod and Pskov, and in the forests in the North-east. In the North-west there were threats from the Swedes and the Teutonic Knights. Had either or both of these succeeded, the Church in that region might have been assimilated to the Latin Christianity of the West. However, Alexander Nevski, the Prince of Novgorod, defeated the Swedes (1240) and the Teutonic Knights (1242) and the Mongols made him Grand Prince of Kiev. In the following century he was canonized. In the South-west in the mid-thirteenth century a local prince, in an effort to obtain assistance from the West against the Mongols, accepted a crown from the Pope and permitted Roman Catholic missionaries to enter. The latter seem to have made little headway. In the first half of the thirteenth century, Lithuanians, still pagan, pressed southward and took Kiev. They were friendly to the Orthodox Church, some of them were baptized, and in their capital, Vilna, numbers of Orthodox churches and monasteries were erected.

It was neither in the North-west nor the South-west that the centre of the Russia of the future was to emerge, but in Moscow. Here Daniel, a son of Alexander Nevski, ruled. Daniel's son, Ivan, extended his domains, but as subordinate to the Mongols and accepted his title from them. He called himself Grand Prince of Moscow and of all Russia. He supported the Orthodox Church and under him Moscow became the seat of the Metropolitan of Russia. Through the influence of the Mongol pattern, the Grand Prince of Moscow became autocratic, insisted upon full control of all aspects of life, and demanded unquestioning obedience of his subjects. Here was arising the later Russia, with its centralized autocracy. In the next period it was profoundly to affect the course of Russian Christianity.

THE MONOPHYSITES OF EGYPT, NUBIA, AND ETHIOPIA

In contrast with Western Europe, the Balkans, and Russia, the period from 950 to 1350 cannot be said to have been one of renewed vigour in the Monophysite Christianity of Egypt, Nubia, and Ethiopia. In the third quarter of the tenth century a new line of rulers, the Fatimids, Shiah Moslems, took possession of Egypt and separated it from the Abbasid Caliphs of Baghdad. At first Christians hoped that the change would give them relief. To the south, in the upper part of the Nile Valley, in the tenth century most of Nubia held to the Christian faith and resisted the infiltration of Islam and the threatened conquest of the Moslem Arabs of Egypt. Yet the four centuries were, in general, marked by progressive gains of Islam at the expense of the churches and by deterioration in the quality of life in the surviving Christian communities.

During the first generation of the Fatimite rule restrictions against Christians were eased and there were conversions from Islam. Christians were in high places at court and at least one of the Caliphs had a Christian wife.

However, for a decade in the first quarter of the eleventh century there was severe persecution from the Caliph Hakim, who is said to have been insane. He was clearly a religious fanatic. He ordered the destruction of churches and put Christians under extreme disabilities. In succeeding generations times of relative toleration alternated at irregular intervals with more or less severe persecutions. In the first half of the fourteenth century the latter became unusually acute.

The Coptic Church, which had the majority of the Christians of Egypt, suffered chronically from corruption. Many bishops and Patriarchs charged fees for ordinations and consecrations and the practice bred abuses. Now and again reformers arose, some of them in high office in the Church, who sought to end the custom, but they were only temporarily successful. The ecclesiastical authorities found it wise to keep on good terms with the Moslem rulers. Repeatedly this led to the interference of these non-Christians in the affairs of the Church and at times to unseemly attempts by aspirants for ecclesiastical position to obtain the endorsement of the state.

There seem to have been no new creative currents in life or thought in the Coptic Church. Nor were there fresh monastic movements. Presumably this was because the Church was of necessity on the defensive, since conversions to it from Islam entailed the strong possibility of death to the convert and an accentuation of persecution for the Church. Innovations were feared as possible sources of division and weakness.

In the second half of the twelfth century controversy arose over a practice which was modifying the method of confession. The custom of the Coptic Church had been that confession of sin was to be either publicly and collectively in the congregation or privately to a priest. If made while in a congregation, the penitents were invited to confess their sins silently to God while a censer was being carried around the church. Eventually the Patriarch gave permission to the individual to make his confession on his knees in the privacy of his chamber, not to a priest, but in the presence of a lighted censer. To this a certain priest, Mark, objected. An eloquent preacher, he urged on thronging congregations that confession to a priest and absolution through him were necessary to salvation. Excommunicated, Mark continued to preach and also declaimed against the custom of circumcision which had long been a custom in the Church in Egypt. Facing deposition, he went over to the Melchites, taking some of his followers with him. This, however, cost him his popularity. Returning to his mother church, he died in obscurity.

As we have hinted, there were other Christians in Egypt. Melchites, that is, those who adhered to the Greek Orthodox Church, had a Patriarch, but were relatively few. Armenians came to escape intolerable conditions in their native land and kept their own ecclesiastical organization. They, too, were not numerous.

In Nubia Christianity remained the prevailing religion much longer than in Egypt. We hear that in the eleventh century a king in that region erected monasteries and churches. However, Islam, dominant as it was in the Egyptian part of the Nile Valley, almost inevitably gained ground in Nubia. In the thirteenth century mosques were being built and Christianity was waning. Yet it was to continue for centuries longer. Ecclesiastically it seems to have been subordinate to the Coptic Church in Egypt.

The Church in Ethiopia was also dependent upon that in Egypt. We know little of the course of Christianity in the country between the sixth and the twelfth century. Christian literature seems largely to have disappeared. Late in the tenth or early in the eleventh century a princess of the Jewish faith sought to stamp out Christianity. She was followed by Christian rulers and in the twelfth century a monarch attempted to increase the number of bishops and so make the Church independent of Egypt. In this, however, he failed. In the second half of that century a prince is said to have carried forward the frontiers of the faith in the South against paganism. In the thirteenth century Coptic monks translated the New Testament into one of the languages of the land and additional Christian literature came from Egypt. Islam was pushed back by successful military campaigns by the rulers (of the Solomonic dynasty which claimed descent from Solomon and the Queen of Sheba), monks increased in number, and some of them won converts from paganism on the frontiers of the country and within Ethiopia itself. Attempts by reformers among the monks to raise the level of morality at the court and among the nobility aroused opposition in high quarters. As an incident of the conflict, but important as an indication of vitality in the Church, the abbot of a leading monastery excommunicated the king and the latter took vigorous measures against the abbot.

THE JACOBITE SYRIANS

The Monophysites, or Jacobites, of Syria possessed an ecclesiastical structure which was headed by a Patriarch of Antioch. While in most places constituting only a minority of the population, they had a fairly wide geographic extension eastward into Persia and northward and westward into Asia Minor and Cyprus. In the twelfth century they are said to have had about twenty metropolitans and a hundred bishops. That same century and the fore part of the thirteenth century saw marked literary activity among them, including an outstanding work on the liturgy. Their most notable figure is reported to have been Barhebræus (1226-1286), famous as a scholar in several fields and reputed to have been one of the most learned men of his age. He was broad in his ecclesiastical contacts and on his death was honoured by Orthodox, Nestorians, and Armenians as well as Jacobites. A much smaller body than their fellow-Monophysites, the Copts, they were normally in communion with the latter and looked up to them with respect. At times the two churches were separated. Moreover, from time to time the Jacobites were troubled by internal dissensions. In the fourteenth century these and persecutions by Moslems reduced their morale and their numbers.

ARMENIAN (GREGORIAN) CHRISTIANITY

We have seen (Chapter 12) that the Armenians, a distinct people in the mountainous regions north of Mesopotamia, had a national church, Monophysite in its creed, and a bond and symbol of Armenian nationality. Pressed by strong peoples and states on its borders, the Orthodox Romans to the west and south-west, and the Zoroastrian Persians, then the Moslem Arabs, later the Turks, still later the Mongols, and eventually the Turks again from the east and south, the Armenians struggled to maintain their political and ecclesiastical independence. Not always were they successful, but their church proved more effectively resistant than their state.

The struggle continued during the four centuries between 950 and 1350 and with varying fortunes. From the second half of the ninth to the third quarter of the eleventh century a dynasty, the Bagratid, governed the country, but only semi-independent and under the suzerainty of the Caliph at Baghdad. Soon after the middle of the eleventh century the Bagratid rule disintegrated. That was due partly to Byzantine victories but chiefly to Turkish invasions. Because of the latter, the country split into several principalities under rulers who were either Turks or Kurds. About 1235 the Mongol invasion brought fresh disorders.

In the last quarter of the eleventh century an Armenian kingdom was set up in Cilicia, in Asia Minor, to the west of Armenia proper. That realm became the main centre of the Armenian Church and endured into the second half of the fourteenth century. The westward move of the Armenian Church brought it into more intimate contact with the Greek Orthodox. The coming of Crusaders from the West and the establishment by the Crusaders of strongholds in the adjacent Syria made for contacts with the Catholics of Western Europe and the Popes. Negotiations with the Byzantine Church failed to bring union. Latin influence was stronger. The Cicilian Armenian rulers sought support from the Crusaders and the West. Negotiations with the Papacy led to close relations between the Armenian and Roman Churches. Many of the Cicilian Armenian Christians submitted to Rome. Although they tended to maintain their traditional ecclesiastical customs, Latin contacts brought modifications. There were Italian colonies in Cicilia as well as Latin missionaries, and there were Armenian groups in Italy.

The decay and disappearance of the Crusaders and their principalities in Syria and Palestine were followed by the weakening of the Latin influence among the Cicilian Armenians and the collapse of the Cicilian Armenian state.

The Turkish invasions and rule in the main historic centre of their nation led many Armenians to emigrate. They went in various directions—eastward, westward, and southward. They constituted colonies, mainly in the cities, and maintained themselves by handicrafts and trade. Usually they preserved their language and customs and held to their church as a bulwark of their distinctiveness. In these respects they were not unlike the Jews, although differing markedly from the latter in many ways, including religion.

In Armenia the national church was troubled by separatists, most of whom seem to have been Paulicians. The Paulicians were not all of one kind, but they appear to have had strong resemblances to one another. Many of them were active in spreading their faith. From time to time there were also disputes with Nestorians and Jacobites who were on the fringes of the main strongholds of the Armenians.

In spite of conquests by non-Christians, pressures from Greek and Latin Christians, and secessions to the Paulicians, the majority of the Armenians held to their historic church. Moreover, these centuries were fairly fertile in the production of Christian literature in Armenian. This included the *Book of Lamentations,* or *Nareg,* written by one Gregory, a monk, early in the eleventh century, a widely read book of meditations and prayers of penitence and aspiration, and a lengthy prayer and many hymns by Nerses, Catholicos in the third quarter of the twelfth century. They are evidence of vitality in the Armenian Christianity of these centuries.

THE NESTORIANS

In our account of the geographic spread of Christianity in the period between 950 and 1350 (Chapter 16) we have seen the amazing extent of territory covered by that easternmost of the Christian communions, the one to which the name of Nestorian is usually but probably mistakenly given. It will be recalled that this was the church which arose in the Persian Empire, which had its main centres of numerical strength in the Tigris-Euphrates Valley, which persisted under Arab rule, and which during these centuries had its headquarters at Baghdad. It will also be remembered that in the thirteenth and the first half of the fourteenth century there were Nestorian communities, most of them small, in Central Asia and China, and that through intermarriage with the ruling family of the Keraïts, who were Nestorian Christians, some of the Mongol princes, descendants of Jenghiz Khan, had been baptized in infancy. That there were Christian communities on the west and east coasts of South India during these years we know from the reports of Western Europeans who found them there on their journeys to and from China. We have almost no information on their internal history in these centuries, but it seems clear that, although claiming to have been founded by Thomas of the original apostles, their ecclesiastical connexions were with the Nestorians in Persia and Mesopotamia. For several centuries, as we have said, the population of Socotra, an island near the eastern entrance to the Gulf of Aden, called themselves Christians, but whether they were originally Monophysites or Nestorians we do not know. In the fifteenth century they were reported to be predominantly Nestorians. Not far from 1350 there were said to have been Nestorian metropolitans in China, India, Samarqand, Turkestan, Kashgar, and two other centres, each with from six to twelve suffragan bishops.

Early in the fourteenth century the Nestorian Patriarch is reported to have had a hierarchy of twenty-five metropolitans and from two hundred to two hundred and fifty bishops. Under the Caliphs at Baghdad Nestorians had been prominent as officials and physicians, so much so that Moslems accused them of being arrogant. From time to time new church buildings were erected. When about the middle of the thirteenth century the Mongols supplanted the Caliphs, the Christians basked in the favour of the new rulers. Hulagu, the first of the Mongol conquerors in Western Asia, was believed by at least some of the Nestorians to have been baptized. He may have favoured the Christians to offset the Moslems. His successor was also friendly. As the Mongol power began to wane, Moslems took their revenge on the Christians. Yet in the middle of the fourteenth century Nestorianism seems to have been spread over more territory and to have been more prosperous than ever before.

SUMMARY

In general, the four centuries between 950 and 1350 saw a very considerable extension of the eastern frontiers of Christianity, with especially wide expansion in the thirteenth and fourteenth centuries. The faith had become firmly rooted among the Slavs of the Balkan Peninsula. It had spread to the plains of Russia and by 1350 was being carried northward into the forests on the edge and beyond the fringes of the Mongol occupation. Christian communities were to be found clear across Eurasia from the Atlantic and the western and eastern shores of the Mediterranean to the China coast and from Scandinavia and north of Moscow to South India. Some of the eastward extension was through Franciscan and Dominican missionaries, fruits of the great awakenings in the

Christianity of Western Europe. Most of it was through the Eastern Churches, especially the Greek Orthodox wing of the Catholic Church and the Nestorians.

Yet the Christianity of the East was in an extraordinarily precarious situation. The Byzantine Empire, its main political bulwark, was clearly waning. Almost everywhere in Asia Christianity was represented by minorities, many of which were slowly yielding ground to an aggressive and politically and socially dominant Islam. In few of these Christian communities were tides of fresh life showing themselves in fresh creative movements. Here was nothing comparable to the surging vitality in the Christianity of Western Europe. It is not surprising that it was in the East that the losses suffered after 1350 were the most sweeping.

SELECTED BIBLIOGRAPHY

GENERAL WORKS

A. Fortescue, *The Lesser Eastern Churches* (London, Catholic Truth Society, 1913, pp. xv, 468). By a Roman Catholic, but not polemical.

B. J. Kidd, *The Churches of Eastern Christendom from A.D. 451 to the Present Time* (London, The Faith Press, preface 1927, pp. 541). Chiefly valuable for extensive information and footnote references to the sources and secondary literature.

THE BYZANTINE CHURCH

W. F. Adeney, *The Greek and Eastern Churches* (New York, Charles Scribner's Sons, 1908, pp. xiv, 634). A comprehensive survey of the history of these churches.

N. Baynes and H. St. L. B. Moss, editors, *Byzantium. An Introduction to East Roman Civilization* (Oxford University Press, 1948, pp. xxxi, 436). Contains excellent summary chapters by experts and an extensive bibliography.

G. Every, *The Byzantine Patriarchate 451–1204* (London, Society for Promoting Christian Knowledge, 1947, pp. 212). Stresses the history of the relations between Rome and Constantinople and argues that the rupture of 1054 was not as important or as final as is often said.

A. Fortescue, *The Orthodox Eastern Church* (London, Catholic Truth Society, 3d ed., preface 1911, pp. xxxiii, 451). Historical and descriptive, by a Roman Catholic.

A. Fortescue, edited by G. D. Smith, *The Uniate Eastern Churches. The Byzantine Rite in Italy, Sicily, Syria and Egypt* (London, Burns, Oates & Washbourne, 1923, pp. xxiii, 244). Deals chiefly with the Italo-Greeks, their history and recent status. From a Roman Catholic point of view.

A. Michel, *Humbert and Kerullarios Studien* (Paderborn, Ferdinand Schöningh, 2 vols., 1924, 1930 (*Quellen und Forschungen . . . herausgegeben von der Görres-Gesellschaft*). Contains a good many texts of the original documents.

CHRISTIANITY IN BULGARIA AND SERBIA

M. Spinka, *A History of Christianity in the Balkans. A Study in the Spread of Byzantine Culture among the Slavs* (Chicago, The American Society of Church History, 1933, pp. 202). A competent survey based upon the sources.

CHRISTIANITY AMONG THE RUSSIANS

G. P. Fedotov, *The Russian Religious Mind* (Harvard University Press, 1946, pp. xvi, 438). By an outstanding expert, covering the Kievan period, from the tenth to the thirteenth century.

F. P. Fedotov, compiler and editor, *A Treasury of Russian Spirituality* (New York, Sheed & Ward, 1948, pp. xvi, 501). Translations of standard biographies or autobiographies of eight Russian saints, together with some of their works, from the eleventh to the thirteenth century.

G. Vernadsky, *Kievan Russia* (Yale University Press, 1948, pp. xii, 412). Contains important sections, by a thorough scholar, on the conversion of Russia and the religious life of the country.

G. Vernadsky, *Relations byzantino-russes au XIIe siècle* (*Byzantion,* Vol. IV, 1927–1928, pp. 269–276). By an expert.

G. Vernadsky, *The Status of the Russian Church during the First Half-Century following Vladimir's Conversion* (*The Slavonic and East European Review,* Vol. XX (1941), pp. 294–314).

N. Zernov, *The Russians and Their Church* (London, Society for Promoting Christian Knowledge, 1945, pp. v, 193). A semi-popular historical survey.

CHRISTIANITY IN EGYPT, NUBIA, AND ETHIOPIA

E. A. W. Budge, *The Egyptian Sûdân, Its History and Monuments* (London, Kegan Paul, Trench, Trübner & Co., 2 vols., 1907). By a distinguished specialist.

E. A. W. Budge, *A History of Ethiopia, Nubia, and Abyssinia* (London, Methuen & Co., 2 vols., 1928).

E. L. Butcher, *The Story of the Church of Egypt. Being an Outline of the History of the Egyptians under Their Successive Masters from the Roman Conquest until Now* (London, Smith, Elder & Co., 2 vols., 1897). An extensive but somewhat uncritical assemblage of material.

THE JACOBITES OF SYRIA

Chronique de Michel le Syrien Patriarche Jacobite d'Antioche (*1166–1199*), edited and translated into French by J.-B. Chabot (Paris, Ernest Leroux, 4 vols.). The portions of this history which deal with the period which here engages us are in Vols. I and II (1901, 1905). The work is valuable both for the Jacobites and the Nestorians.

ARMENIA

L. Arpee, *A History of Armenian Christianity* (New York, The Armenian Missionary Association of America, 1946, pp. xii, 386). Written by an Armenian Evangelical, it is warmly pro-Armenian and vigorously anti-Roman Catholic.

M. Ormanian, *The Church of Armenia. Her History, Doctrine, Rule, Discipline, Liturgy, Literature, and Existing Conditions,* translated from the French by G. M. Gregory (London, A. R. Mowbray & Co., preface 1910, pp. xxxiii, 271). By a former Armenian Patriarch of Constantinople.

THE NESTORIANS

The History of Yaballaha III Nestorian Patriarch and of His Vicar Bar Sauma Mongol Ambassador to the Frankish Courts at the End of the Thirteenth Century, translated from the Syriac and annotated by J. A. Montgomery (Columbia University Press, 1927, pp. 82). A fascinating contemporary picture of the Nestorian Church.

Chapter 25

RETROSPECT AND PROSPECT

In these four centuries between 950 and 1350, what had happened to the dream of the kingdom of God which had been proclaimed and cherished by Jesus? We have called the period one of resurgence and advance. In it Christianity had been carried over a wider reach of territory than even in those great first five centuries of accomplishment which had inaugurated its course. To be sure, Christianity had rewon only a small proportion of the territory which it had been forced to yield to Islam, but except in Asia Minor it had suffered no major fresh losses to that faith and it was in process of regaining the Iberian Peninsula and Sicily. In the lands in Western Europe which for centuries had been swept by successive waves of invasion, mostly of pagans, it had brought the conquerors to professed obedience. As with a rising tide, it had stimulated the emergence of movement after movement which made for a deepening of this nominal allegiance. It had entered significantly into every major phase of the new culture which was emerging in this formerly devastated area. It continued to be the professed religion of the waning remnant of the empire which still claimed the Roman name but was Byzantine and Greek. From that core it was spreading in the Balkans and Eastern Europe north of the Black Sea and there was beginning to affect cultures, although as yet not as profoundly as it was in Western Europe. In all this how far was the kingdom of God being realized? To what degree, if at all, were men and women rising to what Paul called "the measure of the stature of the fulness of Christ"? How far and in what ways was God's will being "done on earth as it is in heaven"?

Obviously God's will was not yet fully done. "The exceeding greatness of his power" was still in "earthen vessels." Even the institutions called churches and which were presumably both the expressions and the vehicles of that power were far from complete conformity with it. Indeed, the most imposing of those institutions, the section of the Catholic Church which had the Pope as its head, from the efforts of great dreamers to make God's will dominant had in part succumbed to another kind of power, the kind which had crucified Christ.

Monastic movements which had sprung from the ambition to embody fully the commands of Christ were never perfect expressions of those commands and as they grew older tended to depart further from them.

But the Gospel was not without effect. God's word was not returning to Him void. As in earlier centuries, lives were emerging which palpably bore the impress of Christ. Whether they were more numerous than earlier it is impossible to determine. They would have been the first to acknowledge, as had Paul so many generations before, that they had not fully attained nor were already made perfect. "The power" did not render even the greatest of the Christians infallible. Bernard of Clairvaux preached Crusades. Hildebrand helped to create a Papal organization which was corrupted by a kind of power which was opposed to Christ. They and others of those regarded as model Christians were evidence that "the power" did not overrule the freedom of man's will and thereby make men incapable of sin or error.

Yet out of the crude stuff of roistering and ruthless barbarian ancestry and descendants from the Roman provincial stock, most of it only superficially converted, men and women were appearing who were regarded by those about them as exemplars of the Christian ideal, products of the transforming power which had gripped Paul and the other apostles. The very fact that they were so esteemed was evidence that the masses of professing Christians, even when they themselves did not seriously attempt to emulate them, were sufficiently responsive to the Gospel to recognize its fruits and pay reverence to those who bore them.

Moreover, more than in the first five centuries and to a much larger degree than in the discouraging four and a half centuries of the great recession, the "power" was entering into those customs, institutions, and standards of conduct generally accepted in much of Europe, especially Western Europe, which were shaping the majority of the population. By no means all Europe was even nominally Christian. Such portions as bore the Christian name were palpably far short of deserving that designation. Those called Christians were as yet only a small minority of mankind. Yet the "power" was at work, irradiating some of the crude stuff of the "earthen vessels." It was sensitizing consciences, making them uneasy and ill content with anything short of the seemingly impossible "high calling of God in Christ Jesus" to be perfect as God is perfect and to be "filled with all the fullness of God." The "exceeding greatness of his power" was enabling men and women to approach that goal. It was also inspiring them to seek to raise the level of entire communities and of all human society towards the performance of God's will on earth. The contrasts between ideals and performance were striking, sometimes in individuals, more frequently in society. This, however, was evidence of the challenge given by Christ and an indication of the fashion in which the "power" worked.

Now followed another period when it seemed that the "power" was fading from the human scene. For something more than the century and a half between 1350 and 1500 Christianity was losing ground. As in the earlier periods, precise dates for the beginning and the end of the era cannot be fixed. In some areas of geography and of life the recession began before 1350. Here and there it was being overcome before 1500. In other places recovery either never came or was retarded until after 1500. Yet these dates can serve roughly as boundaries. In these fifteen decades the geographic frontiers of Christianity shrank alarmingly. The faith vanished from most of Asia and was hard-bested in Asia Minor and the Balkan Peninsula. Loss of morale and decay were apparent in Western Europe, the area in which Christianity had been the most potent in the preceding four and a half centuries. Yet the recession was not as severe or as prolonged as had been that between 500 and 950. Incipient recovery, too, was more marked and the ensuing advance more striking and far-reaching. To that recession, the second of major proportions in the history of Christianity, we must now turn.

GEOGRAPHIC LOSS
AND INTERNAL LASSITUDE,
CONFUSION, AND CORRUPTION,
PARTLY OFFSET BY VIGOROUS LIFE
A.D. 1350 — A.D. 1500

Chapter 26

THE SETTING OF THE SECOND RECESSION

Not far from the middle of the thirteenth century a number of important developments occurred in Europe and Asia which worked adversely for Christianity. They were not as nearly disastrous for the faith as had been those which brought the great recession that marked the four and a half centuries between A.D. 500 and A.D. 950. Yet they were serious and to the hypothetical traveller from Mars might have seemed to presage the disappearance of Christianity from the world scene. As in the great recession from the close of the fifth to the middle of the tenth century the menace came from two directions, namely, through pressures external to lands where Christianity had become rooted and through the disintegration of the political and cultural structure with which Christianity had become associated, so now in Eurasia at large events were transpiring which brought losses, and developments in Christendom itself spelled peril.

One of the most momentous and widespread of the changes was the disintegration of the Mongol Empire and the accompaniments and aftermath of that series of events. This took place in the second half of the fourteenth century. Presumably that wide-flung realm could not be long held together after the impulse given by the initial wave of conquest had been spent. It broke up into a number of fragments, large and small, and some of these soon disappeared. In 1368 the Mongol Dynasty in China came to an end and was succeeded by the Ming Dynasty, founded by a Chinese and brought to power in part by anti-foreign sentiment. This meant the expulsion, the assimilation, or the dying out of the minor foreign communities in China, among them those which professed the Christian faith. Indeed, so completely did Christianity disappear in China that we do not know either the date or the manner of its demise. The bulk of the Mongols became Buddhists, and this placed fresh obstacles to any possible conversion to Christianity. Islam became firmly established in the north-west of China and in what later was known as Sinkiang. It may well have been that some of the nominal Christians in that area went over to that faith. In Persia and Central Asia the Mongols turned Moslem, thus effectively precluding the spread of Christianity among them. The end of the Mongol Empire entailed difficulties for the trans-continental trade which had mounted under the relative security given the heart-land of Asia by the comprehensive Mongol rule. This rendered perilous if not impossible the journeys of missionaries from Western Europe to that region and thus helped to terminate the enterprises of the Franciscans and Dominicans in Persia and Central Asia. Timur (Tamerlane), the fanatical Moslem of Mongol stock whose life (1336–1405) spanned the second half of the fourteenth century, carried on extensive wars of conquest which radiated from his capital at Samarqand into Central Asia, Persia, Mesopotamia, and North-west India. They seem to have borne hard on the Christian minorities, mostly Nestorians, which were in Central Asia. Certainly these perished, leaving behind them only grave stones.

One phase of the aftermath of the Mongol Empire favoured the spread of Christianity. The decline of Mongol rule in Russia and the growing extent and power of the state which had its capital in Moscow made for the extension of Christianity in that region and for the emergence of a Russian Church which had distinct characteristics that we are to note in the following chapter.

Ominous for the future of Christianity was the continued advance of the Ottoman Turks. We have seen that this had begun before the middle of the thirteenth century and by 1350 had wrested much of Asia Minor from Christian rulers. In 1329 Nicæa was taken. Between 1350 and 1400 the Turks established themselves in Europe, mastered Adrianople, and conquered Bulgaria. In 1453 Constantinople fell to their arms. It became their capital. This meant the subjection of the Christian population to Moslem rule. The triumph of the Crescent over the Cross was dramatized by the conversion into a mosque of Saint Sophia, that great church which had been erected by Justinian and which for over nine centuries had been the chief cathedral of Greek Christianity. The Ottoman Turks swept on into Europe, reduced Greece and the Balkan Peninsula, conquered much of Hungary, besieged Vienna, and threatened Western Europe. In 1500 the Turkish tide had not quite reached its height. A politically divided Western Europe was unable to unite against it, and that in spite of the repeated and frantic appeals of the Popes. The age of the Crusades had passed. Once more the Crescent was in the ascendant. In the next chapter we are to see more at length the problems which this brought to Christianity.

In what had become the chief stronghold of Christianity, Western Europe, a new age was coming to birth which carried with it grave threats to the faith. Beginning a few years before 1350, successive epidemics of bubonic plague, the

"Black Death," swept over the region and are said to have reduced the population of Northern Europe by as much as a third and that of England by a half. By decimating the ranks of the Franciscans and Dominicans, the "Black Death" dealt severe blows to the missions and the quality of these orders. In recruiting their ranks to make good their losses the friars accepted men who fell below the earlier high standards. By reducing the labour supply the Black Death hastened social changes, including the decline of serfdom.

Even more serious were developments which were ushering in a new Europe. Nation states were emerging under the leadership of absolute monarchs. Gun powder was making more deadly the wars between them. The Holy Roman Empire, that combination of institution and dream which had given a measure of unity to Western Europe, was in hopeless decline. Its great rival for the mastery of Western Europe, the Papacy, survived, but with weakened political and moral influence. The vast machinery which great Popes had built up to implement their purpose of fulfilling what they believed to be Christ's commission to the See of Peter either proved beyond the capacity of well-meaning but mediocre Pontiffs or fell prey to ambitious men who employed it for selfish purposes. Popes still sought to be effective in the life of Western Europe, but their political activities were chiefly restricted to Italy. More and more the absolute monarchs who were strengthening their power over nation states were extending their control over the Church in their realms, a control which was to be augmented after 1500.

Feudalism, an expression of a predominantly rural economy, was passing. Commerce, banking, and cities were continuing the growth which had been prominent since the eleventh and twelfth centuries. In the *bourgeoisie* monarchs were finding allies, often restless and independent, in their efforts to increase their power at the expense of the feudal aristocracy. In its ambition to reach all men and transform society in Western Europe the Church had become closely associated with the feudal structure. Many of the endowments of churches and monasteries were in land and were integrated with the feudal economy. Now that feudalism was passing, the Church was handicapped by its earlier achievements. As the victory of Christianity in the Roman Empire had wrought an intimate tie between the faith and that realm which had proved embarrassing when the latter decayed, so the efforts of Christians, to a large degree successful, to make their faith effective in the feudal stage of Europe proved a liability when, in its turn, feudalism became moribund. Could "the exceeding greatness of the power" which Paul declared to be inherent in the Christian Gospel prove itself potent in this new Europe of commerce, cities, and aggressive, fighting nation states ruled by ruthless absolute monarchs?

Intellectually and spiritually Western Europe was moving into a new day. Here was an even more serious, if less immediately obvious threat to Christianity. Scholasticism, with which the theology of the Church had been closely associated, was decaying. It still dominated the universities and the monastic orders, including the Franciscans and Dominicans, but the main new currents of intellectual life were flowing in other channels. This seemed to augur ill of Christianity and the Church.

The Renaissance was in progress with its companion, humanism. No one date can be assigned for the beginning of the Renaissance. Preparation for the Renaissance went back before 1350, but not until the fifteenth century did it come to its flood tide. Literally Renaissance means new birth, as though during the Middle Ages Europe had been dead and had now again become alive. The term Revival of Learning is also employed for one phase of the Renaissance, as though the Middle Ages had been intellectually sterile. The designations are evidence of the pride of the age, somewhat narrowly self-conscious, and of its contempt for its immediate predecessor. Actually, as we have seen, the Middle Ages had been pulsing with life and intellectually had been highly creative. Indeed, to no small degree the Renaissance was the child of the Middle Ages and would not have been but for what had been accomplished through Christianity.

The Renaissance was multiform and complex. In its broadest sense it embraced most of the currents which were shaping Western Europe in the fourteenth, fifteenth, and sixteenth centuries. It ran parallel with discoveries in geography and astronomy, with growth in commerce, and with fresh movements in literature and art. It was intimately related to an enthusiasm for the pre-Christian literature of Greece and Rome and to an increased study of Greek.

Humanism was an accompaniment and manifestation of the Renaissance. An outstanding early humanist was Petrarch (1304–1374) who left behind him a large number of admirers and disciples. In contrast with the asceticism and contempt for the world in which the Middle Ages had professed to see the road to the goal of man's course, eternal life, Petrarch and humanists in general had an exuberant appreciation of life in this present world. They were attracted by what they saw in Virgil, Cicero, and Horace. Increasingly they became expert in the great poets, historians, essayists, and philosophers of Greece and Rome. They rejoiced in verbal expression and prized literature for the skill and grace which it displayed and the present enjoyment which it afforded. The men of the Renaissance took pleasure in nature and sought to explore and understand it. They were fascinated by the beauty of the human body and endeavoured to study its anatomy and to reproduce it in art. They waxed enthusiastic over the surviving examples of the sculpture of pre-Christian Greece and Rome with their faithful portrayal of the body in bronze or stone. They were self-confident, believing in themselves and man. They took joy in their critical faculties, and especially in challenging what had been accepted in the Middle Ages. They poured scorn on scholasticism and the school men. Admiring and reviving the architecture of Rome and Greece, they despised the architecture of the Middle Ages, contemptuously calling it Gothic, by which they meant barbarous. They sought satisfaction in human achievement and believed in man's power to understand the world and to master it. They thought of man as the competent architect of his own future. While paying lip service to the Christian faith, they tended to rule out God, the need of redemption, and the incarnation, and to ignore life beyond the grave. Often they flaunted Christian morality.

In a very real sense the Renaissance and humanism were an outgrowth of the Middle Ages and of the Christian faith which had so large a share in shaping the culture of that era. The confidence in the orderliness of the natural world, the belief that man and his environment constitute a universe and are not unintelligible chaos had been drilled into the mind of Western Europe by the school men, nurtured as they were in the Church and committed to the Christian faith. To be sure, the intellectual tools which they employed had been devised in pre-Christian Greece and increasingly they came to the conclusion that these would not enable man to demonstrate the truth of the main Christian affirmations. Yet they were confident that God had created and continued to govern the universe, and that, although He made high and inexorable demands, His purpose for man was beneficent. The Psalms, which were a large part of the services of the Church and the monasteries, took pleasure in the world of nature and overflowed with gratitude for it. The sayings of Jesus throbbed with the beauty, mystery, and tragedy of growing things, birds, sunshine and rain, and human joys and sorrows. Some of the greatest of the school men, among them Albertus Magnus, the teacher of Thomas Aquinas, had inquiring minds which ranged widely over nature.

As in so many others of the contributions which have come to mankind through the Christian faith, humanism, in part the product of Christianity, could be either an aid or an enemy of that faith and, in fact, was both. The typical humanist of the Renaissance was a member of the Catholic Church. Many, like Petrarch, held office in the Church and were supported by it. Humanists might and often did attack certain features of the Church of the day. Petrarch, for example, was very critical of the monks. Yet ostensibly in creed they remained orthodox. Numbers of humanists were not only nominal but also devout and sincere in their Christian faith. They combined their humanist enthusiasms with Christian devotion. While by no means entirely lacking in Italy, humanists of this stamp were especially prominent north of the Alps. On the other hand, humanism could and in many instances did lead to what in effect even though not overtly was a denial of the Christian Gospel. Perhaps it was more dangerous because it was not openly in opposition. It often passed over into an arrogance which had no deep sense of sin or of creatureliness and which felt no need for the forgiving grace of God. To a large proportion of the humanists heaven and hell were either non-existent or unimportant. This present life was what counted. Some might be personally humble but were convinced of man's self-sufficiency to solve his problems. More were vain, self-seeking individualists, nominally Christian, but patent contradictions of the Christian ideal. There was much scoffing at Christianity. This phase of the humanistic strain was to contribute to the secularism which then and in later centuries was to be one of the most serious threats to Christianity.

The intellectual life of Western Europe was given added impetus by the invention of printing by movable type. This occurred not far from the middle of the fourteenth century. The device spread rapidly and, replacing the slow and costly multiplication of books by manual transcription, vastly facilitated the circulation of ideas. It was furthered by the use of paper in place of the more expensive parchment. The manufacture of paper, probably derived indirectly from China, became common in Europe in the thirteenth and fourteenth centuries.

Towards the close of the fifteenth century came the renewal of that expansion of Europe which had been begun in the Crusades and the eastern commerce of the Italian cities and which had been halted by the Black Death, the break-up of the Mongol Empire, and the growth of the Ottoman Empire. It was furthered by the increase in the use of the mariner's compass. It was to continue into the twentieth century. Could the Christianity of Western Europe, handicapped by so many internal weaknesses, respond to the opportunity and the challenge given by that expansion, move into the lands opened to Western Europeans, and make the impact of the Occident a blessing and not a curse?

As we move on into the century and a half between 1350 and 1500 we will find the Eastern and Western wings of what had been the Catholic Church drifting farther and farther apart. We will see the effort at reunion break down, apparently with finality. Each wing was henceforth largely to go its own way. Much of the Orthodox Church was under Turkish domination. What became the largest member of the family of Orthodox Churches, that of Russia, was more and more separated by geography and genius from the Roman Catholic Church. While occasionally influenced from Western Europe, Russian Christianity was distinct from it. The other Eastern Churches dwindled and without repair. It was in the Christianity of Western Europe that the currents of life were chiefly pulsing. We shall deal first, but briefly, with Christianity in the East and then turn, and more nearly in detail, to that of Western Europe.

EUROPE 1500-1750

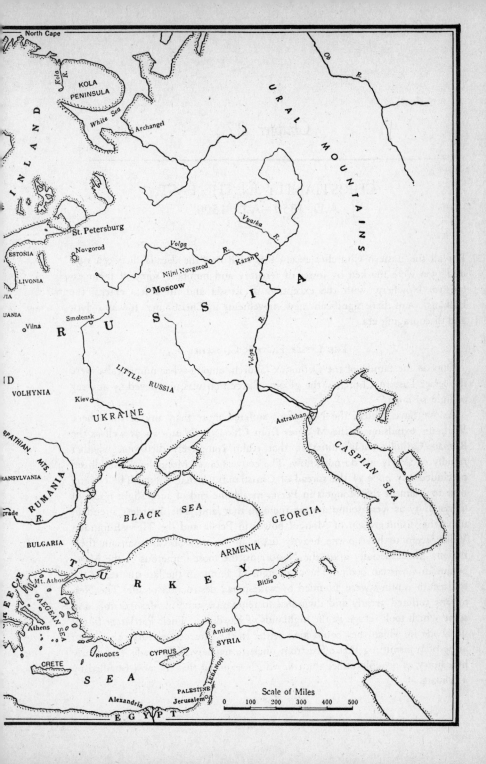

Chapter 27

CHRISTIANITY IN THE EAST
A.D. 1350 - A.D. 1500

For all the Eastern Churches except that of Russia the decades between 1350 and 1500 were marked by losses of territory and numbers, some of them extensive. Nowhere, with the exception of Russia and, to a less extent, the Balkans, were there significant new movements in Christianity. It was a dark and discouraging era.

THE LESSER EASTERN CHURCHES

Outside the family of the Orthodox Church, among what numerically were the lesser Eastern Churches, the gloom of recession was unrelieved by any ray of light or hope.

As we have hinted, the Nestorians suffered more than any of the others. With the expulsion of the Mongols from China the Nestorian as well as the Roman Catholic communities in that realm completely died out, whether rapidly or slowly we do not know. The conversion of Mongolia to Buddhism precluded any hope of the spread of Christianity in that region. The coming over to Islam of the Mongols in Persia meant the end of such slight traces of Christianity as were found among them in that land. The disorders attendant upon the disintegration of Mongol power in Persia and the Tigris-Euphrates Valley seem to have borne heavily upon all varieties of Christians in these regions, and especially upon the Nestorians, the most numerous of the Mesopotamian Christian bodies. The campaigns of Timur in the last quarter of the fourteenth century were attended by widespread destruction of life. The Nestorians suffered greatly and dwindled to remnants, some in Mesopotamia and some which took refuge in the highlands of Kurdistan. Their Patriarchs found no abode in which they could long settle. In the fifteenth century the custom arose of transmitting that office from uncle to nephew. This made it as nearly hereditary as possible under the rule which required that the post be filled by a celibate.

Christian communities with Nestorian connexions survived in South India. We hear that in 1490 some of them sent to the Nestorian Patriarch for bishops, with the information that they had long been without episcopal ministrations. The lapse may have been due to persecution.

The island of Socotra ceased to be Christian, but how and by what stages we do not know.

From the reverses encountered in this period the Nestorians were never to recover. They persisted, but as small enclaves. Those in or on the edge of Kurdistan were subject to recurrent raids by the Kurds, a vigorous, rough independent mountain folk with a religion which was compounded of Islam, the professed faith, with non-Moslem elements. Few though they were, in the centuries after 1500 the Nestorians were divided, partly by internal schisms and partly by efforts of other Christians, Roman Catholic and Protestant, to win their allegiance.

The Monophysite Jacobites, with a Patriarch of Antioch as their ranking bishop, also suffered. Small communities, presumably largely merchants and handicraftsmen, had been scattered widely in Persia, Mesopotamia, and Central Asia. Like the Nestorians, they were at a grave disadvantage when the Mongols turned Moslem, in the disorders which accompanied the break-up of Mongol rule, and during the wars of Timur. They, too, died out completely in Central Asia and most of Persia and dwindled in Mesopotamia. In Syria, the major centre of their strength, they also fell on evil days. From 1292 to 1495 they were divided among themselves by rival Patriarchs. Much as in the latter part of the fourteenth and in the fifteenth century the Roman Catholic Church was weakened by the Great Schism between rival Popes, so in this much smaller body internal dissensions among claimants for the headship of the church brought sad enervation. Persecutions by Moslems added to the distress. By the time the schism was healed (1495) and one Patriarch, at least theoretically, had the allegiance of the entire body, the constituency is said to have shrunk to approximately fifty thousand poor families.

Between 1350 and 1500 Armenian Christianity did not meet as many or as grievous disasters as did the Nestorians and Jacobites. However, it, too, experienced reverses and, like the Jacobites, divisions. The Armenian kingdom which had arisen in Cilicia in Asia Minor in the eleventh century continued to 1375. It had been closely associated with the Crusaders and its last dynasty, that of Lusignan, was a Latin family. Through that association many Armenians had come into union with Rome. The Cilician kingdom declined and the *coup de grâce* was given by Egyptian forces in 1375. In the meantime, following the break-up of Mongol rule, much of the historic Armenia was divided into many principalities under Armenians, Turkomans, and Kurds. In the last two decades of the fourteenth century and in the opening years of the fifteenth century Timur and his armies repeatedly invaded Armenia, bringing their customary destruction. To escape them many Armenians migrated to other regions. After the death of Timur much of Armenia was ruled by a family of Turkomans until, early in the sixteenth century, it was supplanted by the Persians.

Largely in consequence of these vicissitudes, Armenian Christianity was divided. Some Armenians were kept in union with Rome as Uniates, that is, they preserved many of their customs but acknowledged the supremacy of the Pope and brought their creeds into conformity with those of Rome. Franciscan and Dominican missionaries laboured valiantly to bring this about. Armenian bishops were present at the Council at Florence when, in 1439, as we are shortly to see, the Pope seemed to have achieved the reunion of the Orthodox Church with Rome, and the union of the Armenians with the See of Peter was solemnly proclaimed. However, the majority of the Armenian Christians held aloof. Their church, in turn, presented a sorry spectacle of dissension and violence. It is said that each of the last six of its Patriarchs (1377–1432) who ostensibly had their headquarters at Sis, the capital of the Cilician Armenian kingdom, had obtained the post through bribery and the assassination of his predecessor. There were efforts, only partially successful, to reëstablish the Armenian Patriarchate at Etchmiadzin, near the foot of Mt. Ararat. Various claimants for the post came forward. A symbol of legitimacy was what was believed to be the right arm of Gregory the Illuminator, under whom the conversion of the land had been successfully begun late in the third century and who was regarded as the great saint of the church. Encased in a silver reliquary this grisly object was used in consecrations, thus in physical form conveying apostolic succession. During these decades it passed now to one Patriarch and now to another. Indeed, there were at least two which were asserted to be genuine.

After Constantinople became the capital of the Ottoman Turks, the conqueror, wishing an administrative head for the Armenians in his realm, gave to their bishop civil jurisdiction over all of their nation in the Turkish Empire and made him their sole representative to the government. This was in accordance with the pattern adopted for other Christian bodies in that realm. This bishop had the title of Patriarch, but was subordinate to the one in Etchmiadzin.

In spite of these many hardships, so debilitating to the inner life of the Church, Armenian Christianity continued. Clergy were trained and ordained and bishops were consecrated. Many Armenians of the dispersion remained loyal to their mother church. Indeed, the church produced a notable theologian.

Gregory of Datev (c.1346–1410) taught and wrote during troubled years and in the latter part of his life was forced to flee to escape the disorders which followed the death of Timur. A monk and a teacher of theology, he was a loyal Monophysite who wrote vigorously against those who sought to bring the Armenian Church into union with Rome. His *Book of Questions,* completed in 1397 during the invasions by the armies of Timur, was an outline of theology in which he sought to set forth the Christian faith in comprehensive fashion. He was familiar with the outstanding early writers of the Catholic Church, both East and West, including Augustine. He also knew the more recent theologians of the West, among them Albertus Magnus and Thomas Aquinas. Not a creative thinker, he presented the historic Christian tradition, but from a Monophysite angle. His work was to be cherished by his church as a standard.

The dates 1350 and 1500 had no especial significance in the history of the Coptic Church. To be sure, the 1350's were marked by a severe anti-Christian outbreak and in 1517 Egypt was taken by the Ottoman Turks. Yet persecutions were no new experience and the coming of the Turks, Moslems like their predecessors, a succession of Mameluke rulers, was by no means revolutionary for the Church. As often heretofore Moslem feeling against the Christians was aggravated by resentment at the prominence of Christians in official circles. The Moslem rulers found it to their advantage to employ them as clerks and administrators. Some Christians used their favoured position to ignore the discriminatory regulations against those of their faith. Many were wealthy and also seemed to the Moslems to be arrogant instead of humble as beseemed members of a minority religion. From time to time persecution broke out, accompanied by mob violence. Some Christians renounced their faith. We hear that in 1389 large numbers of these apostates marched through the streets of Cairo, lamenting that they had abandoned the religion of their fathers from fear of persecution and denouncing Islam. They were beheaded, both men and women, and a fresh persecution of Christians followed.

In Nubia Christianity was waning. Early in the period it was sufficiently strong to embolden a Nubian prince to protest against the persecution of his fellow-believers in Egypt. He seized Moslem merchants in his realm and would not release them until the Coptic Patriarch, incarcerated for his faith, had been given his liberty. However, by 1500 the Moslem rulers of Egypt were extending their influence in Nubia and Moslem merchants were bringing in their faith. Nubian Christianity was on the way out.

Little information has come to us of the history of Christianity in Ethiopia (Abyssinia) during this period. Presumably the connexion was maintained with the Coptic Church. It is probable, too, that the head of the Ethiopian

Church was still appointed from Egypt. That Christianity survived is clear, for we are to hear more of its history when we come to the next period.

The fact that, in the face of extraordinarily unfavourable conditions, the churches in the East survived is evidence of marked vitality. From within them came a succession of priests and bishops and men to staff the monasteries. To what extent if at all they produced men and women who were exemplars of Christian living we cannot know. That the majority fell far short of the ideal is clear. That some approached it is probable.

The Turkish Conquest of the Balkan Peninsula

The years between 1350 and 1500 witnessed the conquest by the Ottoman Turks of most of the Balkan Peninsula. It was not until after the larger part of the Balkan Peninsula had succumbed that Constantinople fell.

The Turkish conquest brought fresh problems and some changes to the Christianity of the region. In 1349 the Byzantine Emperor called on his son-in-law, the emir of the Ottoman Turks—for he had given his daughter in marriage to this magnate—to aid him against the Bulgars who were besieging Salonica. The Turks responded and thus began their widening incursions into Europe. In 1356 several thousands of them settled permanently in the Balkan Peninsula. The Balkan peoples were weakened by internal divisions and could not offer effective resistance. Early in the 1360's the Turks shifted the centre of their power to Europe and transferred their capital to Adrianople. Late in the 1360's they began the systematic reduction of Bulgaria. In 1389 at a decisive battle at Kosovo Polye the Turks defeated a Serbian-Bulgarian-Croatian coalition and reduced the several princes to a position of vassalage.

In spite of the Turkish advance the religious life of the Balkans did not at once decline. Indeed, in the second half of the fourteenth century the Bulgarian Church experienced a notable revival. The outstanding figures of the awakening were Theodosius of Trnovo (died 1367 or 1368) who, a monk and an ardent Hesychast, took a leading part in fighting the widespread Bogomilism, and Euthymius, a disciple of Theodosius and in the last quarter of the century Patriarch of the Bulgarian Church. A marked increase in the preparation of Christian literature was seen. Extensive revisions were made of works already existing in Slavonic, fresh translations were prepared from the Greek originals, and new books were written. Under Euthymius the Hesychast movement seems to have captured the Bulgarian Church.

However, the revival was short-lived. Towards the close of the fourteenth century, the loss of Bulgarian political independence was followed by the end of its ecclesiastical independence. The Bulgarian Church was brought under the Patriarch of Constantinople.

The mid-fourteenth century mark saw the Orthodox Church in Serbia on an upward surge. The great ruler of the country, Dushan, assumed the title of Emperor and a council made its archbishopric a patriarchate. The Patriarch of Constantinople was unreconciled to a step which seemed to threaten his preëminence in the Orthodox communion and retaliated by anathematizing the Serbian Church and its Patriarch. Yet under Dushan's vigorous regime the Church ignored the displeasure of Constantinople, improved its internal life, and took action against Bogomilism. In the second half of the fourteenth century a new monastery, the Great Meteoron, was inaugurated on a high crag in Thessaly in a region of hermits known as the Thebaïd of Staghi. Its founder was Athanasius, who had been trained on Mt. Athos. With the mounting of the Turkish menace a reconciliation was effected (1375) between the churches of Serbia and Constantinople by which the title of Patriarch was confirmed for the head of the former. When, in the second half of the fifteenth century, almost all Serbia was brought under Turkish administration, the Church became the symbol and the tie of Serbian nationalism.

In spite of the Turkish conquest of the Balkan Peninsula, in only one area, Albania, was there extensive conversion of the Christian population to Islam. In Albania, in contrast with Bulgaria and Serbia, the Slavs were in a minority. The dominant groups were descendants of peoples who had inhabited the region since the dawn of history. Protected by a mountainous terrain, they had maintained themselves against all invaders. They were chronically opposed to the Slavs. For centuries before the Turkish conquest they had been Christians, divided between the Latin and Greek wings of the Catholic Church. It was not until the fifteenth century that the Turkish conquest began. It was only slowly accomplished and Turkish rule was never firmly established over the sturdy highlanders. Yet eventually, probably not until the sixteenth and seventeenth centuries, the majority of the Albanians became Moslems. It has been suggested that the motives were the desire to be accepted as equals of the Turks and animosity against the Slavs, since most of the latter were of the Orthodox Christian faith.

THE TURKS ERASE THE BYZANTINE EMPIRE AND USE THE ORTHODOX CHURCH FOR THEIR PURPOSES

In 1453 Constantinople, long a bulwark of Christendom against the Moslem advance, fell to the Ottoman Turks. The night before the final assault the defenders—Emperor, Patriarch, and nobles, together with their Latin allies—knowing that this was the end, partook of the communion in Saint Sophia. The next day the Emperor died fighting in the breach. On May 30 the Turkish ruler, by fitting coincidence with the title Mohammed II, entered the city and held a Moslem service of thanksgiving in Saint Sophia. Mohammed seemed at last to have supplanted Christ in the capital of that state and Church which had prided themselves on being the perpetuators and champions of the faith, unadulterated, that had been proclaimed by the apostles. Constantinople became the Turkish capital, Saint Sophia was transformed into a mosque, early in the sixteenth century the Turkish Sultans obtained from the last of the Abbasids the title of Caliph, the successor of the Prophet and the religious head of Moslems the world over, and the quondam citadel of Eastern Christianity became the seat of the titular head of the Moslem faithful.

In the closing years of the fifteenth century and in the sixteenth century the Turkish Empire continued to expand. At its height, under Suleiman the Magnificent (1520–1566), it included all the Balkan Peninsula, except rugged Montenegro and a strip of the Dalmatian coast, it reached into Hungary, made the Black Sea a Turkish lake, and embraced Asia Minor, Armenia, Georgia, the Euphrates Valley, Syria, Palestine, Egypt, and the north coast of Africa as far as Morocco. Italy was threatened and a foothold, temporary as it proved, was obtained in that peninsula. Western Europe shivered in fear, but, divided, gave scant heed to the frantic appeals of the Popes for a crusade to stem the Turkish tide.

The Turkish conquest brought many accessions to Islam. As we have said, they were numerous in Albania. They were even more prevalent in Asia Minor. That region, the earliest large area in which Christianity had been the faith of the majority, now became predominantly Moslem. Christian communities survived, but chiefly in the historic Greek cities on the coast and among the Armenians. The motives for conversion varied. Wishing to be identified with the new rulers, some of the upper classes made the shift. Many Christian slaves of Moslem masters conformed to the faith of their owners. In the Balkan Peninsula, some of the Bogomils became Moslems to escape persecution by Orthodox and Catholic Christians. Systematic and compulsory conversion to Islam was common. Thousands of sons of Christians were torn from their parents, reared as Moslems, and enrolled in the armies. Out of the choicest of these converts recruits were chosen for the Janizaries, the picked fighting core of the Turkish forces. Many churches were transformed into mosques.

Yet Christianity did not perish. The Orthodox Church survived the Empire. Mohammed II had a synod elect a Patriarch and invested him with the insignia of his authority. As part of the administrative system by which the Turks governed their realms, the major divisions of Christians were regarded as distinct nations, or millets, each with its own laws and with an ecclesiastic at its head. The Orthodox were called the Rum Millet, or Roman Nation, and had their Patriarch as their responsible official. He exercised far more authority over his flock than had his predecessors under the Christian Emperors. He maintained his courts in which some categories of cases of the Orthodox were tried. Other Orthodox bishops and patriarchs in the Turkish realms were made subject to him.

This new status of the Orthodox had serious handicaps. The Patriarchs were chosen and held office at the pleasure of the Sultan. Frequently they were deposed after a brief term. They had to make heavy payments to the Sultan for the post and received from him the symbols of their office. In return they exacted fees, often onerous, from their bishops and clergy. What in the West was called simony became the rule. Under such circumstances numbers of the Patriarchs and bishops were unworthy men. Many of the wealthy and influential members of the Greek Orthodox community had their homes near the seat of the Patriarch, in the Phanar district of Constantinople. They tended to control the Church and to exercise a monopoly of its chief offices. The rule of the Phanariots had in it much of special privilege and corruption. Moreover, Christians were put under the disabilities which from early in the Arab conquests had been common in lands with Moslem rulers. In principle at least they were specially taxed, were required to wear a distinctive garb, and were to make no public display of their religion. Now and again fanatical sultans instituted persecutions and threatened to compel all Christians to accept Islam and either to destroy the churches or transform them into mosques.

In spite of these handicaps the Orthodox Church still had its clergy, its services, and its monks. It produced few if any great theologians and no major new movements issued from it. But it lived on, an expression not only of the Christian faith but also of Greek nationalism.

Russian Christianity Finds a Centre in Moscow, Expands, and Is Modified

In one region, Russia, the Orthodox Church continued to spread. Not only was there territorial expansion but there were also movements in Christianity which gave evidence of marked vitality. The Mongol occupation seems to have deepened the attachment of its Russian subjects to the Church. The Church became a tie of Russian unity, so far as that existed, and of Russian distinctiveness as against the conqueror. There was, too, the progressive permeation of the masses by Christianity due to the continued presence of the Church, its priesthood, and its services.

Much of this was in the Russia which centered about Moscow. The Grand Princes of Moscow, as they were styled, influenced by what they had seen in the Mongol regime, became autocrats with absolute rule over their domains. Supported by the Church, they brought under their control the free cities and the many local lords who had been part of a decentralization of power somewhat akin to the feudalism of Western Europe. Some Mongol princes also accepted their rule. In 1480 the Grand Duke of Moscow, Ivan III, threw off the last vestiges of the Mongol yoke and became fully independent.

Ivan III claimed to be the legitimate successor of the Byzantine Emperors. While he was still in his early teens Constantinople fell to the Turks. After the death of his first wife he married a daughter of the nearest relative of the last Byzantine Emperor. He adopted the double-headed eagle, symbol of imperial power, and the elaborate ceremonial of the Byzantine court, and demanded that his nobles be completely subject to him.

The older Russia, that which in later centuries was known as the Ukraine and which centered about Kiev, was not quickly drawn into the Muscovite orbit. In the middle of the fifteenth century, for instance, the Metropolitan of Kiev was independent of Moscow and was directly under the Patriarch of Constantinople.

Monks continued to be pioneers of the north-eastward expansion of Russia and its religion and culture. Many, moved in part by the desire to escape foreign rule, went beyond the Mongol frontiers into the forests and either singly or with a handful of disciples built cells. If a monk was of outstanding sanctity others joined him, the cell became a monastery, and around it a village might arise, at the outset made up of lay folk who came for spiritual counsel but later attracting merchants and artisans. The monasteries became schools, hospitals, and inns for travellers. Some had libraries and to them princes and nobles turned for information. Monasteries had a large part in shaping the culture of the state which centered about Moscow. More than before the Mongol invasion they were directing the intellectual and artistic phases of Russian life. They were noted for the skill which some in their communities displayed in painting icons. Most distinguished of these painters was the monk Andrew Rublev, who died about 1427.

In this fourteenth and fifteenth century Russian monasticism of the northeastern frontiers were many who, regarded as model Christians, were canonized. Sergius, whom we have already met, was one of the earliest as well as the most famous of them.

Two forms of monastic life developed which were to come into sharp conflict shortly after 1500. One of these had as its pioneer and outstanding exemplar Joseph of Volokolamsk, or Joseph Volotsky. Born in 1440 of a noble family, Joseph early became a monk and persuaded his parents and brothers to follow him. He eventually founded a monastery near Volokolamsk. This he made a model in protest against a relaxation of the monastic life which had become prevalent. The custom had been developing for the wealthy to enter a monastery in their old age, keeping their property, living on its proceeds, and leaving it to the community on their death. Monasteries were reluctant to accept any one as a novice unless he brought with him a substantial sum. They became comfortable places in which to spend one's years supported by the labour of serfs. Against this trend Joseph inveighed. In his monastery near Volokolamsk he enforced a strict rule which demanded severe fasts, hard work, and diligence in study. Learned, an eloquent preacher, he entered actively into the life of Russia. Although firmly insisting that the individual monk have no property of his own, he saw no sin in the collective possession of wealth by the monastery. Indeed, he encouraged the erection of great monastic buildings and espoused long services and gorgeous vestments, vessels, and altars. He made his monastery a school for the education of prelates, attracted to it the scions of the aristocracy, and encouraged the bishops and abbots who came from it to take part in public affairs. They could thus render Christianity a force in various aspects of the life of the nation. Before many years men trained in his tradition became outstanding in the Russian Church. Strict in their discipline, firmly orthodox in doctrine, strenuously opposed to all heresy, insisting upon the punctilious observance of traditional rites, they had little of the mystic about them and minimized meditation and the inner life of prayer. They were known as Josephites.

In striking contrast was a widespread trend in monasticism which had as its chief representative a contemporary of Joseph, Nilus (Nil) Sorsky (c.1433–1508). Monks of this kind were numerous in the North, beyond the Volga, and were known as the Transvolgians, the Transvolga "elders" (*startzi*), or the Non-possessors. They preferred to live alone and to have no property, either singly or collectively. They devoted themselves to solitary meditation and prayer, supported themselves by the labour of their hands, wrote few if any books, and beyond giving spiritual counsel to laymen did not mix in the affairs of the world. They may have been influenced by Hesychasm. They also perpetuated the kenotic tradition.

Probably of peasant stock and with the surname Maikov, as a young monk Nilus had journeyed to Palestine and Greece, had there known the Hesychast movement, and probably had acquired some competence in the Greek language. He was deeply learned in the literature of his church. Returning to Russia, for a time he was a member of a monastery founded by Cyril, a disciple of Sergius, in Northern Russia. In a spot in the forest a few miles from there he undertook the life of a hermit. A small group of his friends and disciples settled about him.

Nilus advocated a combination of the way of the hermit with that of the cenobite. He believed the religious life to be best nurtured in a small group, a *skete,* not exceeding twelve members, under the spiritual direction of a *starets* ("elder"), their superior. The members were to live far from the habitations of other men. They were to practice complete poverty and the greatest simplicity, owning no land and working with their hands for the bare necessities of existence. They were not to be averse to accepting alms, but always in moderation, and were never to obtain anything by force.

True to the kenotic tradition, while orthodox himself and permitting excommunication for heretics and apostates, Nilus opposed capital punishment for them and advocated a degree of tolerance. To him the goal of the religious life was the union with God of the soul which had fully given itself to the love of God. The road of that union could not be taught: it must be shared. He wished not to be called teacher but simply to be a friend. Even devout conversations might divert the soul from its true road. Any appeal to the senses through elaborate church services and beautiful and rich accoutrements of worship was a snare to be shunned. He advocated the repetition of short prayers to Jesus followed by interior prayer of the spirit, with no audible expression.

Probably it was inevitable that the Josephites and the Non-possessors should clash. The conflict seems first to have come to a head in 1503, in the later years of Nilus. At a council held at Moscow Nilus lifted his voice against the severe measures which were being proposed against the Judaizers, heretics of whom we are to speak in a moment. As might have been expected, the Non-possessors, with their kenotic principles of non-resistance, were defeated by the activist, zealous Josephites. Yet among them were many who were eventually canonized as ideal Christians and the tradition which they represented was again and again to make itself felt in Russian Christianity. The victory of the Josephites, advocating as they did the participation by monks in public life, furthered the close association of Church and state which, in part inherited from Constantinople, was to be a marked feature of Russian Christianity.

Two movements, branded as heresies, appeared in Russian Christianity in the fourteenth and fifteenth centuries. One of these was that of the Strigolniks or "barbers," seemingly so called because their outstanding leader, a deacon of Pskov named Karp, was barber to the clergy. Some of the Russian clergy felt the practice to be wrong of charging fees for the sacraments. They found a spokesman in a bishop who protested to the Patriarch of Constantinople against the Metropolitan of Moscow for upholding the custom. The Patriarch supported the Metropolitan. But Karp was not satisfied. He listened sympathetically to candidates for ordination as they complained of the charges made by the Archbishop of Novgorod. He came to believe that ordinations made in this fashion, being tainted with simony, were invalid. From that it was an easy step to the conviction that all sacraments administered by clergy who were guilty of simony were worthless and that to receive them would be condoning the sin and so would be sharing in it. Since simoniacal fees were universal, all the sacraments of the Church must be shunned by sincere Christians. Accordingly the Strigolniks left the Church and formed separate congregations which were served by laymen. The attempt was made to conform to the manner of life of the Christians of the first century and to have nothing to do with what they believed to be the apostate official church, with its wealth and formalism. The lay readers refused any financial remuneration, interpreted the Bible to their flocks, and set an example of humble, earnest living. The only sacrament which was observed by them was that of penance. Prayers for the dead were denounced as contrary to the Scriptures. Strict moral standards are said to have been observed. The conjecture has been offered that the Strigolniks were influenced by Bogomilism, but this appears to be unproved.

It was to be expected that the bishops and clergy would be opposed to a movement which was so critical of them. Two deacons who were the leaders, one of them Karp, were executed in Novgorod in 1375. Vigorous action against the Strigolniks continued until they seemed to have been stamped out. It may have been, however, that they were simply driven into a secret existence.

The other outstanding Russian heretical movement of this period was that of the Judaizers. This is said to have begun in the 1470's with the conversion to Judaism of two priests in Novgorod by a Lithuanian Jew. They kept their new faith secret and continued in the Church. They proved to be ardent missionaries. Through them Judaism spread and numbered among its adherents clergy who were high in Church and state or who, remaining crypto-Jews, attained high office, one of them as primate of the Russian Church and another as chancellor of the Grand Prince of Moscow. They did not go over completely to Judaism but showed the influence of that faith in various ways, some in opposition to the use of icons, and others in an interest in Jewish philosophy and science, especially in astrology and Kabbalah. If, as seems usual, they adopted some of the dogmas of Judaism they were not circumcised nor did they conform to the Jewish ritual.

In 1487 the Archbishop of Novgorod learned of the movement. At his request a church council was called, but the friends of the Judaizers and men who, like Nilus, objected to capital punishment, prevented stern measures from being enacted. The Grand Duke Ivan III seemed to favour the movement in his desire to curb the monasteries and seize their lands. His daughter-in-law went over to it. However, in 1503 another council met at Moscow and after prolonged debate, in which, as we have seen, Nilus again opposed harsh treatment, those who advocated drastic treatment triumphed. Several of the heretics were burned and others were sent to prison for life. That seems to have ended the movement, although it may simply have gone into hiding.

From these various movements, those within the Church and those branded as heretical, it was clear that Christianity had taken firm root in Russia. It was giving rise to indigenous expressions of the faith and was strong enough to cope successfully with serious defections. It was still emphatically loyal to what had come to it from Constantinople. Indeed, Moscow was beginning to be viewed by good Russians as the successor to that city as the headquarters of Orthodoxy. Sometime late in the fifteenth or in the fore part of the sixteenth century a Russian monk wrote a fulsome letter to the Moscow ruler in which he declared that since Rome had become heretical and Constantinople had fallen to the infidel Moscow had succeeded them as the third seat of the guardian of the apostolic faith and was never to be followed by a fourth. Indeed, the Russian Church probably better represented the Greek Orthodox Church as it was before the Turkish conquest than did the Greek Church of later centuries. The latter was to be influenced by the Roman Catholic Church in its scholastic forms and was less flexible. Yet modifications in the Russian Church were being made in practice though not in formal doctrine and at least one independent effort at basic reform, that of the Strigolniks, had appeared.

PAPAL EFFORTS TO WIN THE EASTERN CHRISTIANS

In spite of the weaknesses which, as we are to see, were afflicting it during the century and a half between 1350 and 1500, the Papacy did not give up the hope of bringing about the visible union under its control of all who bore the Christian name. In this it was aided by many ardent supporters.

We have noted the recurring attempts before 1350 to bring this about and have recounted how some of them had been made in connexion with the Crusaders and their footholds in the East. They had given rise to Uniate bodies, that is, as we have suggested, those drawn from Eastern dissident churches who submitted to the Pope but who kept their traditional liturgies and many of their inherited customs.

One of these, brought into union during the Crusades, was that of the Maronites, who seem to have had their origin in the Monothelite controversy in the seventh century and to have held to that position until their accession to Rome. Others were Greeks of the Byzantine rite. They had a complex history complicated by the relations between Rome and Constantinople and the breaks and the attempts at the reunion of those who held to these two sees. In Italy there had long been Greek-speaking churches and monasteries who observed the Basilian rule. The Greek rite was preserved, notably in the monastery of the Mother of God at Grottaferrata, a house founded early in the eleventh century on the Alban Hills not far from Rome and continued across the years into the twentieth century. There were also Greek Uniates in various cities in the East, including Constantinople itself. Some of the Armenians became Uniates before 1350 and a Uniate Armenian church persisted. Latin influence contended with Greek in the Balkan Peninsula, especially on the east coast of the Adriatic and in the North-west near to Austria and Hungary. It also penetrated into Russia. Between 1350 and 1500 it entered Russia chiefly by way of Poland and Lithuania. It was late in the fourteenth century (beginning in 1386) that the conversion of the upper classes of Lithuania was accomplished. This came about through an alliance which Lithuania sought with Poland against the Teutonic Knights. Since the Poles adhered to Rome, it was Latin Christianity which the Lithuanian aristocracy adopted. The Lithuanians extended their rule over part of Western Russia and some of the Russian nobility conformed to the Roman Catholicism of their new masters. However, the bulk of the Russian population, even under the Lithuanians, held to the Orthodox form of the faith.

The last great and seemingly successful effort of the Papacy to bring the Eastern Christians into union with it was through a council, regarded as ecumenical by the Church of Rome, at Ferrara and then at Florence in 1438 and 1439. The Byzantine Emperors, in desperate straits because of the advance of the Turk, had been seeking help from the West and to obtain it sent embassies to its courts and offered to enter into negotiations with the Pope. Pope Eugenius IV (reigned 1431–1447) was eager to assert his authority in the Church in his struggle with the councils of which we are to speak in the next chapter and to win the prestige which would accrue from the consummation of reunion under his auspices. To Ferrara came the Byzantine Emperor, the Patriarch of Constantinople, representatives of the Patriarchs of Antioch, Alexandria, and Jerusalem, and a score or more of Eastern bishops. Among the latter was Isidore, Metropolitan of Kiev, and thus, in a sense, a representative of the Russian Church. Another was Bessarion, Metropolitan of Nicæa. Prolonged discussions followed on the traditional and familiar points at issue and on questions of procedure and precedence. Agreement was reached, partly through compromises. The most thorny question of all, the authority of the Pope, was assented to in the ambiguous statement: "We recognize the Pope as Sovereign Pontiff, Vice-gerent and Vicar of Christ, Shepherd of all Christians, Ruler of the Church of God; saving the privileges and rights of the Patriarchs of the East." These "privileges and rights" were left undefined and vague, presumably intentionally so, for only thus could both Latins and Greeks be satisfied. The decree proclaiming the union was published in July, 1439. Most of the Greeks signed it with reluctance and one refused his assent.

As was true of the accord reached at the Council of Lyons in 1274, the union ostensibly effected at Florence was rejected by the overwhelming majority of the constituency of the Greek Orthodox Church. In spite of the Turkish peril, they were quite unreconciled to the arrangement even though it was intended to bring them military help. Moreover, the Patriarchs of Antioch, Alexandria, and Jerusalem jointly repudiated the acts of the Ferrara-Florence Council. On returning to his see, Isidore was promptly clapped into jail by his irate flock. Escaping, he made his way to Rome, was created cardinal, and was appointed Papal Legate to Constantinople. The Pope was able to send only a handful of troops to that beleaguered city. Some of these perished in the last desperate and fruitless stand against the Turks.

Officially the union stood until after the fall of Constantinople. Quite understandably, for he wished as little connexion as possible of the church in his realms with his enemies in the West, the victorious Turk sided with the foes of union. In 1472 a synod in Constantinople speaking for the Orthodox Church formally repudiated the action at Florence and anathematized those who adhered to it.

Yet gains there were for Rome. Some of the Greeks remained in communion with the Pope. Bessarion held true to the Ferrara-Florence agreements, made his home in Rome, became a cardinal, was a leader in the Renaissance, helped to encourage the study of Greek and Plato, was a benefactor of the Greek scholars who took refuge in Rome after the fall of Constantinople, and led in the reform of the Greek monasteries in South Italy. More important still, some of the other Eastern Churches had spokesmen at the Council of Florence. The head of the Armenian Uniates appointed legates to renew the accord of himself and his group and late in 1439 the appropriate decree was issued. The Coptic Patriarch of Alexander sent as a representative an abbot who also had authority to speak for the ruler of Ethiopia. Later, when the Pope transferred the council to Rome, delegates arrived from one of the factions of the Syrian Jacobites. A Nestorian bishop and delegates from those of the Maronites who had not yet submitted to Rome also came. Through the council, then, which the Church of Rome counted as clearly ecumenical, with representatives from almost all the severed branches of the Catholic Church, larger or smaller sections from these bodies which it regarded as dissident submitted to the Pope and brought their creeds into accord with his.

Although the Papacy registered gains in the East, the large majority of the Christians in that region remained aloof. The Roman programme for achieving the unity of all Christians had not proved successful. After 1500 it was to be dealt another major blow by its inability to hold the majority in Great Britain and North-western Europe who had heretofore accepted it. The section of the

Church headed by the Bishop of Rome continued to insist that conformity with it was the way which Christ had appointed for that unity of all who believed in him for which he had prayed. However, it was to be increasingly clear that the Papal pattern was an ecclesiastical continuation of the imperial dream of pre-Christian Rome and that great and growing numbers of those who bore the Christian name would not assent to it.

SELECTED BIBLIOGRAPHY

L. Arpee, *A History of Armenian Christianity* (New York, The Armenian Missionary Association, 1946, pp. xii, 386). By an Armenian Evangelical, warmly pro-Armenian and anti-Roman Catholic.

S. Bolshakoff, *Russian Nonconformity* (Philadelphia, The Westminster Press, 1950, pp. 192). A useful, comprehensive historical sketch, with an excellent bibliography.

L. E. Browne, *The Eclipse of Christianity in Asia from the time of Muhammed till the Fourteenth Century* (Cambridge University Press, 1933, pp. 198). Only the last few pages of this excellent survey fall within the period covered by this chapter.

E. L. Butcher, *The Story of the Church of Egypt* (London, Smith, Elder & Co., 2 vols., 1897). An extensive assemblage of material.

G. P. Fedotov, compiler and editor, *A Treasury of Russian Spirituality* (New York, Sheed & Ward, 1948, pp. xvi, 501). Useful translations of sources with excellent introductions.

A. Fortescue, *The Orthodox Eastern Church* (London, Catholic Truth Society, 1929, pp. xxxiii, 451). A good survey, in spite of a strong Roman Catholic bias.

A. Fortescue, *The Uniate Eastern Churches. The Byzantine Rite in Italy, Sicily, Syria, and Egypt* (London, Burns, Oates & Washbourne, 1923, pp. xxiii, 244). This careful, well-written Roman Catholic study deals almost exclusively with the Greeks who were in union with Rome. Most of it has to do with Italy.

A. H. Hore, *Eighteen Centuries of the Orthodox Greek Church* (London, James Parker & Co., 1899, pp. vi, 706). By a sympathetic Anglican.

B. J. Kidd, *The Churches of Eastern Christendom from A.D. 451 to the Present Time* (London, Faith Press, preface 1927, pp. 541). Not very readable but packed with data.

M. Spinka, *A History of Christianity in the Balkans. A Study in the Spread of Byzantine Culture among the Slavs* (Chicago, The American Society of Church History, 1933, pp. 202). An excellent survey based upon the sources.

G. Vernadsky, *The Heresy of the Judaizers and Ivan III* (*Speculum,* Vol. VIII, pp. 436–454).

Chapter 28

WESTERN EUROPE: DECLINE AND VITALITY

Increasingly after 1350 Western Europe became the main centre of Christianity. Here was the chief hope of that faith. Due to the several factors which we have noted in the preceding chapter, the Eastern Churches were waning in numbers and vigour. In spite of the mounting vitality shown by the Orthodox Church in Russia, the gains registered in that land, and the claim that Moscow had become the Third Rome, the citadel and guardian of the true faith, Eastern Europe was still on the periphery of Christendom. Moreover, in Western Europe Christianity had plowed more deeply into the entire life of the population than it had elsewhere. Entering the partial vacuum left by the collapse of Græco-Roman culture in that region, a collapse more profound and a vacuum more striking than in the area controlled by the Byzantine Empire, it held to its allegiance the descendants of the Latinized peoples and won the invaders from the North. Being the most nearly stable element in the culturally fluid society which followed, and containing a powerful spiritual and moral dynamic, it helped to mould every phase of the civilization which emerged.

Now that civilization was passing, to no small degree because of currents which issued from Christianity. In the new age into which Western culture was being hurried, there were forces which were threatening Christianity in both old and new ways. As a result, in Western Europe that faith appeared to be declining. For centuries there had been a struggle in the various institutions which bore the Christian name between lethargy and corruption on the one hand and reform and renewal on the other. Between 950 and 1350 the latter appeared to be winning. Now, in the period bounded roughly by the years 1350 and 1500 the former seemed uppermost. In aspect after aspect of the life of Western Europe, including especially the Church, deterioration, as judged by Christian standards, was under way. Yet it did not become as marked as in the dark centuries between 500 and 950. There was also evidence of sound life, some of it old and much of it new. Here and there were indications that the ebb would not always continue, that the tide was turning, and that eventually it would come to the flood. We must first sketch the grim side of the picture. We will then turn to the brighter side and point out the sound life that remained and the fresh expressions of "the greatness of the power."

The Decline of the Papacy as a Political, Moral, and Spiritual Force

The most striking of the symptoms of the malady which was afflicting the Christianity of Western Europe was the decline of the Papacy. In the preceding centuries great reformers had envisioned the See of Peter as the directing agency through which all Christians could be held to the true faith, all the universal Church be unified and kept firm in its mission, all of Christendom brought towards the high ideal of God proclaimed in Christ, and ultimately all mankind governed. The occupants of the Fisherman's throne had varied in ability and achievement, but the most outstanding of them had made their office a force in the major aspects of the life of Western Europe and one to be reckoned with in the Byzantine Empire and Western Asia. In their efforts to implement their dream the Popes had developed an ecclesiastical structure which reached throughout most of Western Europe and which made necessary an elaborate bureaucracy at its centre. In addition to the Pope the chief figures in the bureaucracy were the cardinals.

One of the striking indications that decline had begun was, as we have noted, the removal in 1309 of the seat of the Papacy to Avignon. Claiming their place as head of the Catholic Church by virtue of the fact that they held the post of Bishop of the Church of Rome, because of the disorder in Italy for which the centuries-long conflict between their predecessors and the Holy Roman Emperors was largely responsible, the Popes found residence in that city dangerous if not intolerable. The first Avignon Pope, Clement V, was subservient to Philip IV, "the Fair," King of France. That powerful monarch had been responsible for the death of Boniface VIII in a contest between the two over the taxation of the clergy and Church property in the former's domains in which the Pope had lost.

The Papacy remained at Avignon until 1377. Although technically that city was not then in France, during most of its years there the Papacy was under French influence. As we have seen (Chapter 20) life was luxurious for the cardinals and their dependents and the financial devices used to support them bore heavily on Western Europe and provoked much criticism. Seven Popes made Avignon their residence. None was as evil as some who were to follow.

All were university-trained and three were monks. At least half of them were upright. pious, and wished to give worthy leadership to Christendom. Most of them were able and several struggled to reform the Church, including Avignon with its throngs of idle benefice-seekers. Usually they were skilful administrators. In theory they held to the claims of Papal authority put forward by their great predecessors and some made their weight felt in European politics. Indeed, the Avignon Popes were the most powerful potentates in Western Europe in their day. So long as the Papacy was there, Avignon was more cosmopolitan and international than any other city in fourteenth century Europe.

Yet the system was too much for the Popes. Several of them succumbed, at least to the extent of putting their relatives in lucrative and important posts. The very complexity and weight of the machinery which had been constructed with the ostensible welfare of Christendom and of the millions of individuals who constituted its population as its purpose entailed abuses which even the strongest and most high-minded of the Avignon Pontiffs could not eliminate and could scarcely check. The Papacy was paying the price for having utilized the kind of power which seemed essential to the realization of its objectives but which entailed contradictions of Christian ethical and spiritual principles. Conditions continued to deteriorate and permeated the entire church of which the Papacy was the head. Pluralism (the holding of two or more benefices and drawing the incomes from them), absenteeism (not living in the post the income from which came to the titular holder), self-seeking greed, and loose-living among the clergy mounted.

Worse was to follow. Many, especially but not exclusively in Italy, were distressed by the prolonged absence from Rome. Some of the noblest spirits of the day, notably Catherine of Siena, of whom we are to hear more in a moment, pled with successive Popes to return to their proper place in the city from which they took their title and which was their immediate responsibility. The next to the last of the Avignon Popes, Urban V, went to Rome in 1367 and was there about three years. He found the city sadly dwindled in population and its churches and palaces almost in ruins. He set about repairing the churches, but conditions proved discouraging and he retreated to comfortable Avignon. His successor, Gregory XI, made it one of his purposes to move his seat to Rome and accomplished it early in 1377. The "Babylonian Captivity" had ended. Yet out of that return, so fervently desired by some of the most earnestly Christian spirits of that day, came what was remembered as the Great Schism of the West. For a generation, from 1378 to 1417, Western Europe was divided between rival Popes, always at least two, and latterly three, each supported by a section of the Church.

The Great Schism Begins

The Great Schism began soon after the death of Gregory XI, in 1378. The Roman populace were insistent that a Roman, or at least an Italian, be his successor. Although two-thirds of the cardinals who composed the electing conclave were French and would have preferred one from their own nation who would have led them back to Avignon, they were divided over which Frenchman to choose. Moreover, they were in Rome and were subjected to the clamour of the mob. Under pressure they selected a Neapolitan who took the title of Urban VI. A university graduate, an archbishop, and in charge of the Papal chancery, Urban was sixty years of age when he was put in the chair of Peter. He proved an unhappy choice. Although a scholar, an experienced administrator, austere in his private morals, and zealous for reform, he was tactless, obstinate, quick-tempered, and, so his enemies said, arrogant. He soon antagonized the cardinals, especially since he flatly refused even to consider going back to luxurious Avignon, publicly rebuked them for their worldliness, was peremptory in forbidding them their profitable pluralism and simony, and commanded them to live in the sees whose episcopal titles they bore.

The cardinals, some of whom were of noble blood, took umbrage at such treatment from a Pope whom they considered low-born. Moreover, at Avignon they had had the growing tradition of dominating the Pope and would not brook this new independence. Within a few months they left Rome. Declaring that Urban VI's election had been obtained under duress from the Roman mob and hence was illegal, they demanded that he resign. The overwhelming majority denounced him as an apostate and Antichrist. They insisted that they had the power to depose as well as to appoint and declared the post vacant. The French majority in the college of cardinals thereupon elected another Pope, one of their own number and a prince related to the King of France. A soldier, a shrewd politician, and not above reproach in his private life, he took the inconsistent title of Clement VII. Soon, with his cardinals, he had settled in Avignon. Urban VI, indignant, refused to recognize the legitimacy of the action and appointed a new group of cardinals but without deposing the old.

The countries of Europe now lined up on one or the other side. Spain, France and her satellite, Scotland, and part of Germany supported the Avignon Pope. Northern and Central Italy, most of Germany, England, Scandinavia, Bohemia, Poland, Flanders, and Portugal remained with Urban VI. Thus the growing nationalism was showing itself. Often before there had been two men who simultaneously claimed the Papal title. Never before had Western Europe been so nearly evenly divided between them by sharp territorial lines.

THE RESORT TO A GENERAL COUNCIL

Pained by this rupture of visible unity, many strove both to heal the breach and to purge the Catholic Church of corroding evils. Devout souls, scholars, the University of Paris, whose voice carried great weight in Europe, and some monarchs struggled with the problem. Eventually they had recourse to that instrument, a general council, which since the initial one at Nicæa early in the fourth century had been regarded as the means by which the mind of the Church could be expressed and appropriate action taken. Indeed, now that the Papacy was divided and had proved incapable of stamping out the grievous abuses which crippled the Church, many hoped that by gaining recognition of the authority of a general or ecumenical council as superior to that of the Pope, not only would unity be restored but the Church would be cleansed. This, in brief, was the conciliar theory. There followed what is sometimes known as the conciliar movement. Obviously it was entirely counter to the theory which had prevailed in the West for the past several centuries and which insisted that the Pope alone could call a general council, that either he or his representative must preside, and that none of its actions was valid without his approval. The movement succeeded in ending the schism, but not in making the council supreme as against the Pope or in purging the Church of the corruption which was threatening its life.

Several years elapsed before the proposal that a general council meet became a reality. To be sure, in 1324, half a century before the Great Schism, the *Defensor Pacis* had advocated a general council which would be above the Popes. In 1379 and 1380, soon after the two rival Popes had been elected, a specialist on canon law, then in Paris, proposed that the King of France invite other princes to join with him in calling a council. A similar suggestion was made in 1381 by a scholar at the University of Paris. When Urban VI died a successor was chosen who continued the Roman line. Clement VII carried on an inglorious course at Avignon for sixteen years and was followed by a much abler and more upright man, Benedict XIII, who held the post for more than a quarter of a century. Efforts were made to induce the Pontiffs of both lines to resign and permit the choice of a new one on whom the whole Church could unite. That was suggested, among others, by the University of Paris. At one time both Popes had agreed to abdicate. However, each found ways of evading his promise. Eventually cardinals from both Rome and Avignon jointly tried their hands at ending the schism and called a general council. This met at Pisa in 1409. It was attended by several hundred cardinals, patriarchs, archbishops, bishops, abbots, heads of religious orders, scholars, and representatives of universities and of kings and princes. It deposed both Popes and, without waiting to hear whether either would heed the decree, authorized the cardinals to elect a new one. This the cardinals did. Since neither the Avignon nor the Roman Pontiff would comply, there were now three who claimed the chair of Peter. Each had the support of one or another of the states of Europe.

More and more leaders among the European intellectuals were advocating the holding of a general council and, scandalized by the schism and because of it losing faith in Papal supremacy, were maintaining that such a body was superior to the Pope in the government of the Church. Among them were Peter d'Ailly (1350–1420), theologian, philosopher, chancellor of the University of Paris, confessor to the King of France, and eventually Archbishop of Cambrai, cardinal, and papal legate; and John Gerson (1363–1429), a pupil of d'Ailly, chancellor of the University of Paris, pamphleteer, and writer of books of devotion. These, with many others, laboured mightily for union and were earnest advocates of a general council. The idea spread, endorsed by clergy, synods, universities, and even cities, and promoted by a flood of pamphlets.

The Council of Pisa was an inauspicious beginning. Not only did it fail to heal the schism: it enhanced it. Moreover, it did not bring the reforms in the Church at large which had been hoped from it. The second Pope chosen by the cardinals to continue the Pisan line after the death of the first incumbent was Baldassare Cossa, John XXIII. Undoubtedly able and a commanding personality, he was an aristocrat who had led a wild youth, was more of a statesman and general than a spiritual leader, and was accused, probably with some ground, of being deceitful, cruel, tyrannous, and debauched in his private life. He had dominated the Council of Pisa and the first Pope chosen by that body. That the conciliar movement had put him in the chair of Peter could scarcely commend it to the conscientious and thoughtful spirits in Europe.

THE COUNCIL OF CONSTANCE

The Council of Pisa is not officially regarded as having been representative of the entire Church. A much larger council was held at Constance from 1414 to 1418. Unlike that of Pisa, it is counted as ecumenical by the Roman Catholic Church and is reckoned as the sixteenth in the series. While by no means accomplishing all that had been hoped from it, it ended the Great Schism. In doing so it prepared the way for the death of the conciliar movement, for by placing the Catholic Church under one Pontiff rather than two or three, it facilitated the triumph of the Pope over the council.

The Council of Constance was called by the newly elected German King and King of the Romans, Sigismund, who eventually (1433) was to be crowned Holy Roman Emperor. Thus Sigismund renewed the earlier tradition in which ecumenical councils had been convened by the Roman Emperor rather than by any bishop or group of bishops. He induced John XXIII to coöperate with him in summoning the council. Yet his call was sent out first and that of John XXIII went out soon afterward, and independently. Even more than Pisa, the gathering brought together a notable assembly of cardinals, archbishops, bishops, abbots, scholars, clergy, and lay folk. Indeed, it was the most widely representative of the Church that had ever met in Western Europe. Its first task was to end the Great Schism. In this Peter d'Ailly was prominent. Largely at his suggestion, the voting in the council was by nations, thus preventing it from being dominated by the large party which John XXIII had succeeded in drawing together to support his claims. This was a procedure without precedent in the history of the councils and was evidence of the place which nations were coming to have in Western Europe. By it the universities and laity were given a voice, for they were in the national delegations.

The council found it no easy matter to end the Great Schism. Under pressure, John XXIII, the only one of the three Popes present, solemnly promised to abdicate if the other two would do likewise. Soon thereafter, as sentiment in the gathering swung against him, he fled from Constance in disguise, pleading ill health. Some question arose as to whether the council could proceed without him. Sigismund saved the day by insisting that it continue and Gerson preached a sermon in which he declared that a general council was representative of the entire Church, that it might be called without the authorization of a Pope, and that it might require a Pope to abdicate. After futile negotiations, John XXIII was charged with a long list of misdeeds and immoralities and was formally deposed. The Roman Pope, Gregory XII, resigned, was made a cardinal and, honoured, died two years later at the age of ninety. The remaining Pope, he of Avignon, Benedict XIII, refused to abdicate, although a committee headed by Sigismund himself journeyed to him in Narbonne, in the south of France, to urge him to comply. The council thereupon declared him a perjurer, a heretic, an obstacle to the union of the Church, and deposed him. Until his death, c.1423, Benedict continued to insist that he was the rightful Pope. He was followed by two successors in the Avignon line but they attracted only a negligible following. Deputies from the five nations into which the council had been divided for voting purposes joined with the cardinals and elected as Pope Cardinal Oddone Colonna, a member of an old Roman family and a man of unblemished reputation. He took the title of Martin V and presided over the subsequent sessions of the council. The Great Schism of the West had been ended.

The council addressed itself to the reform of the abuses in the Church which were so clamant. However, it was too badly divided to accomplish much, especially since many of its members would have lost valued privileges had some of the measures advocated been adopted. Indeed, it was probably hoping too much to expect that a council made up predominantly of men who were profiting by the abuses which it was proposed to eliminate would consent to drastic measures. Some decrees were passed which were designed to check simony, to reduce the financial exactions of the Papacy, to end one form of conferring the income of several benefices on a single individual, and to prevent benefices being awarded to men who because they were unordained or unconsecrated were given dispensations excusing them from fulfilling the duties attached to them. In other ways the power of the Pope was abridged and the attempt was made to curtail some of the evils which had grown up in connexion with indulgences. The German delegation obtained from the new Pope a concordat, but one which was to run only for five years, placing restraints on some of the revenues drawn from their country by the Pope, cardinals, and Papal curia. The French delegation negotiated a somewhat similar agreement. The English also got a concordat, more limited in its scope but unrestricted in time. The cardinals were at most to be twenty-four in number and were to be more equitably distributed among the nations, and not, as had been the case, predominantly from one nation.

More important were decrees which were designed to ensure the implementation of the conciliar theory. Another general council was to meet in five years, a second after another seven years, and thereafter councils were to convene at least every ten years. Before the close of each council the place of the next meeting was to be set by the Pope with the consent of the council. Thus the general council of the Church was always to be either in session or to be expected at the end of a definite interval. It might be called more frequently in case of an emergency, but the time between councils could not be lengthened beyond the five, seven, and ten year spans set forth in the decree. It was declared that the council drew its power immediately from Christ, and that all, even the Pope himself, were "bound to obey it in all those things which pertain to the faith, to the healing of the schism, and to the general reformation of the Church."

There was one action of the Council of Constance, the condemnation and burning of John Hus, to which we are to recur later in this chapter. We must mention it here, however, as part of the effort to extirpate heresy. The Council was concerned not only with the administrative unity and moral reform of the Catholic Church. It was also intent upon preserving doctrinal unity and was resolved to root out all that smacked of heresy. In its eyes Hus stood out as the most dangerous contemporary heretic and it took vigorous action against him.

The Pope elected by the Council of Constance, Martin V, set himself to restore the damaged power and prestige of his office. Himself from a distinguished Roman family, he returned to Rome and repaired the city, its neglected churches and fortifications. He sought to bring order into the turbulent states of the Church, which were presumably directly under the government of the Pope. Comparatively modest in his own manner of living, he celebrated with great pomp the public occasions in which he officially appeared. He made his weight felt in ecclesiastical affairs in several countries in Europe. However, he was accused, justly, of favouring members of his family. Moreover, he was not disposed to concede the authority to the general council which had been enacted at Constance but wished to renew the prerogatives which had been claimed by his great predecessors. Nor did he do much to carry through even the limited reforms which had been outlined at Constance.

The Failure of the Conciliar Movement

Yet, in obedience to the command laid on him by the Council of Constance and prodded by that centre of the conciliar theory, the University of Paris, Martin V called a general council to meet at Pavia in 1423. The gathering had barely convened when an outbreak of the plague caused it to move to Siena. Attendance was slim and the Pope, never enthusiastic about the meeting, did not attend but contented himself with sending representatives to preside in his name. Measures for reform, which was one of the professed purposes of the gathering, were blocked by the Pope's supporters. After efforts lasting a little over a year the council was dissolved.

Martin V did little to effect the reforms which were so urgently demanded by widespread elements in the Church. To be sure, he appointed a commission of cardinals to suggest reforms in the Papal curia. They reported and, following their recommendations, in 1425 he ordered some changes. Among them were injunctions to bishops and archbishops to reside in their dioceses, to hold provincial synods three times a year to correct abuses, to set an example of Christian living, and to shun heavy financial exactions. However, little seems to have been done to enforce the decree. The old abuses continued and complaints were still loud.

When, in 1431, Martin V died, the cardinals, before electing a successor, drew up a document called a capitulation to which the new Pope was to be required to subscribe. It demanded, among other things, that the Pope respect the rights, the persons, and the property of the cardinals and turn over to them half the revenues of the Church of Rome, reform the Papal curia "root and branch," and call a general council.

The man chosen took the title of Eugene IV and held the post from 1431 to 1447. Of aristocratic Venetian stock, he was austere in his private life, deeply religious, simple in his tastes, vigorously opposed to nepotism, generous to a fault with money, dignified, and with an imposing presence. He is chiefly remembered for the fashion in which he made the Papacy master of the general council.

In accordance with the instructions of Martin V given on the eve of his death, the general council met in Basel in 1431. The Roman Catholic Church officially regards it as the seventeenth ecumenical council. The Pope appointed as the presiding officer in his stead Cardinal Cesarini (1389–1444), a man of humble birth who had risen to high office by sheer ability and character. Scholar, humanist, ascetic, devout, punctilious in his religious duties, affable, Cesarini made an ideal Papal legate. Members of the council were tardy in arriving and the sessions were slow in getting under way. Late in 1431 Eugene IV, made fearful by what he had heard of the gathering, ordered it dissolved and another council held at Bologna a year and a half thence. Cesarini wrote a strong letter protesting the unwisdom of this action. Sigismund advised the council to stand firm. Nicholas of Cusa (1401–1464), scholar, philosopher, theologian, mystic, and reformer, although later a firm supporter of Papal supremacy and a cardinal, at this point came out strongly for the authority of the council, maintaining that the Pope was simply one member of the Church, that the Church alone was infallible but could transfer that prerogative to a general council, and that the council was superior to the Pope and could depose him.

In February, 1432, the council pronounced itself legally assembled and declared that its authority rested upon acts of the Council of Constance and that any proceedings against its members were null. It organized itself by committees and gave seats and votes to members of the lower as well as the higher ranks of the clergy. It was thus widely representative. It told Eugene IV to withdraw his bull of dissolution and to appear with his cardinals before it within three months, either in person or through representatives. When they did not come the council held them guilty of contempt.

With so much opinion against him in the Church and in Europe at large, Eugene IV seemed to yield. He recognized the council as legal and sent four legates to represent him. When the legates, arriving, attempted to take charge of the council in the Pope's name, they were told that the Pope was subordinate to the council and must obey it. Early in 1434 the Pope made what appeared to be a complete capitulation, annulled all his bulls against the council, and gave it his support. That year a rebellion in Rome forced him to flee from the city. Papal prestige was at a low ebb. The council seemed to have won and the conciliar idea to be clearly in the ascendant.

The Papal cause was further handicapped by the disclosure during the Papacy of Eugene IV that the Donation of Constantine which had so long been important in the foundation on which claims for Papal civil sovereignty had been erected was a forgery. The spuriousness of the document was demonstrated independently by the critical acumen of two scholars of the new age, Nicholas of Cusa in 1433 and Laurentius Valla in 1440.

In another realm the Council of Basel appeared to have justified the principle on which it was acting. By negotiation and compromise it made peace with the moderate wing of the followers of Hus and thus seemed to have brought back into the bosom of the Catholic Church a numerous element who had been condemned as heretics.

When it came to the reform of the Church the Council of Basel failed, and failed conspicuously and lamentably. This was chiefly because thoroughgoing reform would mean sacrifices, some of them serious, by the majority or all the members of the council. Some measures were passed, among them ones to forbid simony, to enforce the celibacy of the clergy, and to forbid theatricals and other secular amusements in churches and churchyards.

Since the council was anti-Papal it was relatively easy to decree the abolishment of some of the sources of the revenue of the Popes and the cardinals which had long been a source of complaint, among them the annates, for this entailed no privation on any but a very few members of the council. So, too, legislation was put through to restore the election of the higher clergy by the chapters as against Papal appointment and to regulate the age and composition of the cardinalate and the election of Popes. In its antagonism to the Pope the council over-reached itself. Among other prerogatives, it claimed the right to grant indulgences. Some who had hitherto supported it, including the powerful and high-minded Cesarini and most of the Italians and later Nicholas of Cusa, disillusioned by what they believed to be its excesses, went over to the supporters of the Papacy.

The seeming success of the Council of Basel in limiting the power of the Papacy encouraged the French and the Germans to take similar steps and thus to reduce the administrative control and the financial exactions of Rome within their borders. In 1438 in the Pragmatic Sanction of Bourges the King of France recognized the supremacy of the general council, with the provision that it should convene once a decade, abolished annates and first-fruits, ordered that vacancies to the larger benefices be filled by election rather than by Papal appointment, and limited the number of cardinals to twenty-four. Less sweeping measures were taken in Germany and agreed to by the Pope.

The major crisis in the Council of Basel and one which issued in its final undoing came in connexion with the effort for the reunion of the Latin and Greek wings of the Catholic Church. In the last chapter we saw that the threat of the Ottoman Turk constrained the Byzantine Emperor and Patriarch to seek reconciliation with Rome in the forlorn hope of obtaining military assistance from the West. The majority of the council wished the Eastern delegation to come to Avignon. The Pope suggested an Italian city, and this the Greeks preferred as being more convenient. The Pope ordered the council transferred to Ferrara and a minority of its members, including Cesarini, complied. They convened at Ferrara and then at Florence. There, as we have noted, they met the Greeks and what appeared to be striking success crowned their efforts. Enormous prestige accrued to the Pope.

The departure of the moderate and pro-Papal minority left the Council of Basel in the hands of the radicals who wished further to curb the power of the Pope. In the spring and summer of 1439 a decree was enacted which declared a general council to be supreme in matters of faith. Another decree deposed Eugene IV, released all Christians from allegiance to him, and pronounced his acts null and void. In the autumn of 1439 it chose as Pope Duke Amadeus of Savoy. The latter took the title of Felix V. He was able to attract very little support and ten years later resigned. The small remnant of the Council of Basel, now in Lausanne, put the best face possible on the adverse situation. Eugene IV was now dead and had been succeeded at Rome by Nicholas V. The council voted to recognize him as the true Pope.

With that act of virtual abdication the conciliar movement may be said to have come to an end. It had failed to curb the power of the Papacy. Indeed, by ending the Great Schism of the West, itself no mean accomplishment and its major achievement, it had dug its own grave. When once the Church in Western Europe was reunited under one Pope, the Pontiffs, asserting the traditional claims of their predecessors, made their power effective against the councils, divided as these were and without adequate leadership. Moreover, like the Papacy, members of the councils were too deeply involved in the abuses against which much of Europe was complaining to work the sweeping reforms which the situation demanded.

The conciliar idea did not quickly die. Again and again in the fifteenth century, even after the Council of Basel had ended in a fiasco, there were those who wished to have recourse to a general council of the Church. Sometimes these were Popes who hoped to use it to rally Europe against the Turk. Now and again a monarch invoked the spectre of a general council to wrest some concession from the Pope. Many of those longing for the reform of the Church hoped against the hard facts that a council could accomplish it. We shall meet the idea again in the sixteenth century. Yet, whether or not men realized it, the councils had proved themselves unable to purify the Church or to construct machinery for its administration.

THE FURTHER MORAL DECLINE OF THE PAPACY

Still worse was to come. Administrative unity had been restored to the Catholic Church in Western Europe under the direction of the Papacy but the basic moral reforms for which sensitive souls had struggled had not been achieved. The ecclesiastical structure through which they should have been accomplished had in it so many in positions of authority whose comfort would have been compromised by basic changes that in spite of the labours of some earnest souls in high places the purging in "root and branch" which had been promised was not accomplished. Now that there was only one Pope and the effort to control him through a council representative of the entire Church had failed, the Papacy became even more a centre of corruption. It was captured by the Renaissance and secularistic humanism. Men ambitious for ostentatious luxury and for power and prestige of a kind which was entirely contrary to the genius of the Christian Gospel worked their way into the Papal curia and even into the college of cardinals and the Papacy itself. This did not come all at once. It was not until the close of the fifteenth century that the Papacy reached its lowest depths of moral degradation. Then it did so on a tragically grand scale in an individual of outstanding ability and force of character, but who was as nearly the opposite of the Christian ideal as it is possible for man to be.

The first of the Popes to represent the Renaissance was Nicholas V, who held the post from 1447 to 1455. He had struggled up from humble origins and in his student days in Florence, that centre of Renaissance art and letters, had caught much of the spirit of the new day. He combined humanism with earnest Christian purpose. Temperate in his personal habits, he was a collector of manuscripts, is credited with having founded the Vatican Library, and, a patron of artists, scholars, and men of letters, made Rome a centre of the new humanism and art. It was he who adopted the plans for the new St. Peter's. Although a lover of peace and genuinely religious, he was not the one to lead in the urgently needed reformation of the Church. He even attracted to Rome and gave support to humanists who were essentially pagan.

Callistus III, a Spaniard, who was Pope from 1455 to 1458, was chiefly memorable for the fashion in which he advanced the members of his family, the Borgias, including especially his nephew, Rodrigo, whom we are to meet again in a moment as the infamous Alexander VI.

Æneas Sylvius Piccolomini who with the Papal title of Pius II held the post from 1458 to 1464, had had a humanistic training, was late in seeking ordination, in youth and middle age had led a life which was far from blameless, had an illegitimate son, and was noted for promoting his interests by astute diplomacy. He had written much, some of it in the clever but low moral tone characteristic of the Renaissance. However, he confessed his faults and professed, perhaps somewhat theatrically, to have had a conversion comparable to that of Paul and Augustine. An indefatigable traveller, he was a true son of the Renaissance in his love of natural scenery and his glowing descriptions of it. His energy was largely spent in attempting to rally a divided Europe against the advancing Turk.

Paul II, who reigned from 1464 to 1471, represented an anti-humanist reaction. A nephew of Eugene IV, he was from Venice. Vain, a lover of pomp, charming, imposing, dignified, open-handed to the poor, he sought to expel from Rome those of the humanists who were thinly veiled pagans, and attempted to curb simony and to bring order in the Papal states. Yet he, too, could scarcely be expected to cleanse the Church.

Although he was the General of the Franciscans, the successor of Paul II, Sixtus IV (1471–1484), was more interested in making the Papacy the centre of a strong Italian state than in rendering it an effective moral and spiritual force in Europe. Of blameless personal life, a scholar, a distinguished teacher in various universities, as Pope he found himself surrounded by a turbulent Italy confronted by the threatening Turk. Italy was divided into many states. The largest were Venice, Milan, Florence, Naples (called the Kingdom of the Two Sicilies), and the States of the Church, the latter directly under the Pope. There were many lesser states, and complicated intrigue and war engrossed the attention of rulers and peoples and blocked all efforts to present a united front against the aggressive foreign foe.

True to the traditions of his predecessors of an earlier age, Sixtus IV strove to unite Western Europe in a crusade against the Turk. To that end he assembled a fleet which saw inconclusive action. Embroiled in the maze of Italian politics, he was more than once engaged in wars with cities and states. Vying with Italian princes who were patrons of Renaissance art and literature, he accorded support to humanists, enlarged the Vatican Library, built the chapel (Sistine) which fittingly bears his name, and spent large sums on new streets and building projects in Rome. In other words, he sought to make Rome the literary and artistic capital of Renaissance Europe. He lavished offices on members of his family.

All this, it need scarcely be pointed out, was in striking and utter contrast with the ideals and purposes of the founder of the order of which Sixtus IV had been the head. That contrast was symbolic of the fashion in which the Roman Catholic Church and the Papacy were succumbing to trends, seemingly dominant, which were threatening to de-Christianize Christendom. One observer, obviously unfriendly, dated the period of Papal decadence from Sixtus IV. While clearly an exaggeration, it is significant of the deflection of the Papacy from its professed status of Vicar of Christ that this could be said of that office when it was held by the successor of Francis of Assisi.

The Papacy Reaches a Nadir

He who had the title of Innocent VIII (1484–1492) owed his elevation to the Papacy in part to unseemly factional strife among the cardinals at the time of his election and to the powerful support of a nephew of his predecessor, Sixtus IV. Before ordination he had been married and had had a son by his wife and two illegitimate children. While in his private morals this widower seems to have reformed after being made a priest, he proved to be an amiable but weak administrator. He was largely under the influence of the corrupt nephew of Sixtus IV to whom he owed his promotion, and under him the morals of the Papal curia from the cardinals down were lamentable. In urgent need of income, partly because of his embroilment in Italian politics, Innocent VIII sold church offices and created new ones, also to be sold. Some of his appointees to the cardinalate were worthy men, but one was the illegitimate son of his brother and another was Giovanni de' Medici, the thirteen-year-old son of the powerful Florentine, Lorenzo de' Medici. Before he was eight years old that favoured child, designated for ecclesiastical preferment, had been given, with the consent of Sixtus IV, an abbacy, and before he was twelve he had two more, including that of Monte Cassino, the mother house of the Benedictines—that appointment in itself being evidence of the deterioration of both the Papacy and monasticism. To be sure, when under importunate pressure from the lad's father he designated him cardinal, Innocent VIII insisted that he be not formally installed for three years and that in the interval he give himself to the study of theology and canon law, but even then he was only sixteen when he undertook his full duties.

Several of the cardinals lived in luxury in the style of secular princes, hunted, gambled, entertained lavishly, and had mistresses. Outstanding among them was Rodrigo Borgia, nephew of Calixtus III. Handsome, able, genial, an orator, forceful, compellingly attractive to women, possessing a huge income from the benefices lavished upon him, he had been elevated to the cardinalate when he was still under thirty years of age and served prominently under five Popes. By his acknowledged mistress, married successively to three other men, he had four children, and by other mothers had two more children. For all of his off-spring he sought position and wealth. One of them, Cæsar Borgia, was designed by his father for a career in the Church. At the age of seven he was given benefices. Later he was made bishop and when his father became Pope he was made archbishop and then cardinal.

In 1492 Rodrigo Borgia was elected Pope and, taking the title of Alexander

VI, he held the post until his death in 1503. It was charged that he obtained the election by wholesale bribery of the cardinals. Yet in many quarters the choice was welcomed. He proved to be an able and strong administrator. He was hardworking and was expert in the business and etiquette of the Vatican. At one time he appeared to give himself to much needed reforms in the Church. He encouraged some of the religious orders. Like Sixtus IV, he was clearly on the side of those who, in the current disputes on the subject, held to the immaculate conception of the Virgin Mary. He gave his support to the Angelus which, as we have seen, was in honour of the Virgin and of the incarnation. He defended the prerogatives of the Church in the Low Countries against those who were encroaching on them.

Yet Alexander VI is chiefly remembered for his preoccupation with European and especially with Italian politics and for the shameless way in which he sought to further the advancement of members of his own family. Particularly notorious were the adventures of Cæsar Borgia and the Pope's support of them. Cæsar Borgia was obviously unfitted for an ecclesiastical career. Formally released by his father from his clerical obligations, he married and set about carving out for himself a state in Italy. In an age of unbridled ambition and intrigue in Italian politics, he was outstanding in courage, daring, calculating self-interest, utter perfidy, and cold-blooded cruelty to all who stood in his way. Deprived of Papal support by his father's death, his projects came to nought.

The exploits of Cæsar Borgia and the evil deeds of Alexander VI lost nothing in the telling. Both men had enemies who cared as little for the truth as did they. There have been those who have sought to defend their memory, especially that of the father. But while there have been exaggerations and although both were charged by contemporaries with crimes of which they have not been conclusively proved guilty, the evil characters of both are well established. While Alexander VI was certainly not as weak and may not have been as depraved as the worst of his predecessors, notably some of the tenth and the fore part of the eleventh century, under him the Renaissance Papacy sank to a nadir in morality. When the sixteenth century dawned the outlook for moral and spiritual leadership by the Popes in bringing Christendom to a high level such as had been envisioned by Hildebrand and other reformers of the Middle Ages was extremely grim. The Papacy was a liability rather than an asset.

Monarchs Curtail Papal Control

Not only did the Papacy sacrifice much of its moral leadership. It also had its administrative powers restricted. It was losing the struggle to free the Church from domination by lay princes and to make the Papacy supreme in all aspects of the life of Christendom, a struggle in which the great Popes of the Middle Ages had seemed to be succeeding. In some states the monarchs, supported by the rising tide of nationalism, curtailed the Papal revenues and judicial functions and limited the power of the Pontiffs to control the choice of the higher officers of the Church in their realms. Thus in 1438, as we have seen, the Pragmatic Sanction had reduced the Papal revenues from France. Not far from the same time, as we have also noted, similar actions were taken for England and Germany. Late in the fifteenth century Sixtus IV was constrained to concede to Ferdinand and Isabella the right to nominate to Spanish sees. In the fifteenth century the custom grew in France of taking appeals from the church courts to those of the king.

DECAY IN MONASTIC LIFE

The Christianity of Western Europe was suffering a decline in that feature of its life through which so much of the attainment of Christian perfection had been sought, the monasteries and religious orders. In the years around 1350 the Black Death took a heavy toll from them. While in some lands they recovered in numbers, the deterioration in discipline and morals which was one of their chronic threats seems to have been especially marked in the latter part of the fourteenth and in the fifteenth century. Conditions appear not to have been generally as bad as they had been before the reform movements of the eleventh, twelfth, and thirteenth centuries. Of this we cannot be sure, since data for accurate comparisons are lacking. However, it appears to be significant that in contrast with these centuries, in each of which major new orders arose, the only fresh monastic or semi-monastic movement that sprang up between 1350 and 1500 which attracted substantial numbers was that of the Brethren of the Common Life, of which we are to say more in a moment.

Along with this comparative dearth of fresh orders, we hear much of the sad condition of many of the existing houses. These reports may be an indication of a conscience which was becoming increasingly sensitive to contrasts between ideals and achievement. They may also seem to be more numerous because of the better state of our records for these decades. Yet they tell of widespread lethargy, luxury, laxity, and even stark immorality. In many monasteries poor financial management had brought evil days. Some others, heavily endowed, after years of earnest living, became vacant or all but vacant and their revenues went to the support of absentee and often worldly ecclesiastics. Nunneries were favorite places in which to domicile younger daughters of the aristocracy who were not provided with husbands. In them these scions of the nobility, having no inner call to the cloistered life, disregarded the rules, often went abroad, and had private incomes which made possible physical comforts. We read, too, of monasteries which were refuges for the sons of the nobility, of monks who were lazy, who spent much of their time in the chase, in frequenting taverns, and in frivolous and obscene talk, and who were avaricious. In Friesland monks and nuns mingled and are said often to have disposed of the results of their license by abortion or infanticide. We are told that in Spain some of the kings made their cast-off concubines abbesses.

THE STATE OF THE CLERGY

When conditions at the headquarters of the Church in Avignon and Rome are such as we have described, it is not surprising that in the rank and file of the bishops and priests there was widespread corruption. Clerical concubinage was prevalent, more so in some sections than in others. We hear repeatedly of bishops who behaved more like secular lords than fathers of their flocks, who were active in affairs of state to the neglect of their dioceses, and who went to war. In Spain it was said not to be uncommon for kings and other grandees to obtain support for their illegitimate sons by having them appointed bishops. We read of bishops with numerous illegitimate progeny for whom they provided. Reports were common of masses hurriedly and carelessly said, of colleges of chantry priests which were endowed for the purpose of prayers for the testators and the deceased of their families and where the stipulated services were neglected or grouped together. Absentee pluralists who drew the revenues from several, sometimes many benefices, and had the duties performed by poorly paid substitutes and lived elsewhere continued to be so numerous that attempts to end the scandal were futile.

THE SEEMINGLY IMPENDING DE-CHRISTIANIZATION OF WESTERN EUROPE

By 1500 it seemed that Western Europe, partially Christianized by the advances of the previous centuries, was being de-Christianized. The hardly won gains appeared to be in process of dissipation. Within the inner circle of the Church ill-concealed paganism was raising its head and in practice if not in word the Christian faith was denied by many of its official representatives. In much of the life of Western Europe there was a real though unavowed repudiation of Christian ideals. Much of what was being said would have shocked the high-minded even among pre-Christian pagans. This was true in literature. In his *Decameron* Boccaccio (1313–1375) mirrored the life of his day, and it was a life much of which clearly ignored Christian standards. Slightly more than a century later Machiavelli (1469–1527), a warm admirer of Cæsar Borgia and an active participant in Italian politics, in his treatises on political science, of which his *Prince* is the most famous, made expediency his rule in complete disregard of what the Christian must esteem as moral principles. His influence upon political theory, and he was a pioneer in later political thought, tended towards ruling out from the state and relations between states any attempt at regulation by Christian standards.

We scarcely need to say that in practice Western Europe had never been Christian. Yet it paid lip service to that faith, canonized some of its monarchs for what it deemed their approximation to the Christian ideal, and read with approval Augustine's *City of God*. Now it seemed to be throwing off even the pretense of honouring what great Christians had endeavoured to embody. It appeared to be in process of resolving the tension between the Christian demand on man and man's performance, so marked in the Middle Ages, by abandoning any attempt to live up to that demand.

Evidences of "The Exceeding Greatness of His Power"

Where, then, was "the exceeding greatness of his power"? The vessels were certainly earthen. The institutions which had been devised to conserve and further "his power"—the Papacy, general councils, monasteries, monastic orders, the bishops and clergy—were proving to be so much so that their earthiness seemed to have prevailed.

Yet "his power" was at work. It was welling up in many quarters, some of them quite unexpected. It was showing itself in thousands of lives, most of them humble, but some of them prominent. Here and there it was cleansing old vessels, such as existing monasteries and monastic orders. It was also giving rise to new movements. There were many more of these than in the dark centuries which followed the collapse of the Roman Empire. We must not take the space even to enumerate them all, much less to describe them fully. We will, however, say a little about some of the more outstanding individuals and movements in whom "the exceeding greatness of his power" was being manifested. While we shall mention them one by one and by certain classifications, we must remember that several of them were appearing simultaneously and that they were contemporary with the decay in the Papacy, the monasteries, and the clergy, and with the failure of the councils to effect thoroughgoing reform. Disease and health were both present in the Christianity of Western Europe. So "exceeding great" did "his power" prove to be that in the sixteenth and seventeenth centuries it rose to the challenge of mounting threats to the faith and broke out in a fresh forward surge in the Christian tide.

It is important to note that this forward surge was preceded by what might be described as a ground swell and to some degree issued from it. That ground swell was seen in several lands in Western Europe and had many different manifestations. While not apparent in the Papacy, only slightly making itself felt in the cardinalate, manifested in the general councils merely to be frustrated, absent from most of the monasteries, and seemingly negated by the majority of the bishops and parish clergy, it was potent. Moreover, to no small degree it arose from what had been accomplished through these institutions and agencies by devoted spirits of earlier years who had dreamed and laboured to make them instruments for cleansing the Church. Even if the moral and spiritual level of all Europe had not been lifted, a substantial proportion of the descendants of those who had come into the Christian faith through the mass conversions of the earlier centuries were growing in their intelligent commitment to it.

Two Outstanding Practical Women Mystics: Catharine of Siena and Joan of Arc

Always one of the evidences of the working of "the exceeding greatness of his power" has been the type of life to which it has given rise in individuals. Some of these have been officially pronounced to be exemplars of the Christian faith and have been canonized. Many, presumably not a few of them equally worthy, have missed such recognition. While they were not proportionately as numerous as in the centuries between 950 and 1350, the century and a half between 1350 and 1500 saw many of them. Several combined, to an unusual degree, a life of activity in the world with that of the mystic. Two of the most prominent of these "practical mystics" were Catherine of Siena and Joan of Arc.

Catherine of Siena (1347–1380) was one of twins, the youngest and twenty-third child of a prosperous dyer, Giaccomo Benincasa, and his wife, Lapa di Piagenti di Puccio. Due chiefly to her father's influence, the home was deeply religious. From early childhood Catherine dedicated herself to Christ and the celibate life. At six she believed that she had had a vision of Jesus and at seven she is said to have vowed herself to him in virginity. At twelve her parents wished to arrange a marriage for her, but, at first to their annoyance, she refused, saying that she had promised to be the bride of Christ. They yielded and, since she did not wish to enter a monastery, they allowed her to have a room to herself in which for three years she lived in solitary meditation and physical austerity, with much inward struggle. She then took the vows of a member of the third order of Dominic. There followed three more years of solitary prayer and meditation in a room set apart for her under the parental roof. These were for her a time of peace and joy, for she was by nature of a sunny spirit.

Then came the conviction that she must reënter the world and begin a more active life. She gave herself to the service of the poor and the sick, including a year when an epidemic of the Black Death swept across Siena. Both she and her contemporaries believed that she had the gift of healing, and many were the cures attributed to her. She also served prisoners and had a notable conversion of one who was condemned to death.

Combining the visions of the mystic with deep interest in people and in the affairs of every day, Catherine of Siena wrote hundreds of letters, some of spiritual counsel to humble folk and some to those prominent in Church and state, including the Pope himself. In spite of many critics and one period in particular when calumnies were spread in an effort to besmirch her good name, even within her brief life time her fame spread through much of Western Europe. She reconciled enemies and warring factions. She concerned herself with politics and sought, in vain to her intense disappointment, to stimulate a crusade to bring Palestine again into Christian hands. She endeavoured to heal chronic feuds among prominent families in Siena. She urged upon Pope Gregory XI, then at Avignon and engaged in war with the Tuscan cities, to make peace, even if that cost him loss in worldly goods, to give himself to the cure of souls, and to come back to Rome. To resolve a struggle between Gregory XI and Florence in which the Pope had laid that city under an interdict, she first went to Florence, where the authorities hailed her coming, and then journeyed to Avignon and saw the Pope, who held her in reverential esteem. Although she failed in her effort to bring Gregory XI to the desired accord with Florence, she strengthened his wavering will to make his residence in Rome and had the joy of seeing that accomplished and peace made between his successor, Urban VI, and Florence.

Deeply grieved that the return of the Papacy to Rome was followed by what became the Great Schism, Catherine vigorously took the side of the Roman Pontiff, Urban VI, and wrote blistering letters to the French cardinals who, fleeing the Eternal City, had elected Clement VII. Summoned by Urban VI, she went to Rome and there exerted herself on his behalf. In the midst of that turbulent city she attempted, on at least two occasions with some success, to bring internal peace. It was in Rome that she died.

It is significant that in the second half of the fourteenth century one frail woman of humble birth, who died before she had reached her mid-thirties, should have had so profound an influence. Hers was a life of meditation, prayer, ecstatic vision, and of so great a devotion to Jesus, whose bride she believed herself to be, that she felt that she had received the stigmata of his wounds spiritually even though not physically. By nature joyous, she had a profound sense of her own sinfulness, attributed to it some of her failures to accomplish what she believed to be her divinely commissioned ends, and had periods of inward struggle and depression. Yet her life was also one of intense activity in personal ministrations and in the stormy and intricate complexities of Italian and Papal politics. The fickle crowd sometimes adored her and sometimes spurned her. However, in that century of growing corruption in high ecclesiastical quarters and in the Western Europe torn by wars, visited by the recurring scourge of the Black Death, with its fear of death and judgement, its stark depravity and callous cruelty set in contrast with the spiritual sensitivity and high aspirations of many of its sons and daughters, this humble young woman, although sometimes, as in her advocacy of a crusade, giving herself to a cause which from the perspective of a later day appeared fantastic, was a major figure. The fact that she could attain that position, without aspiring to it but only because she was driven by a sense of duty to undertake causes which she deemed laid upon her, was both a tribute to her character and evidence of the regard in which the Christian ideal when incorporated in an individual was held by thousands in the Europe of that day.

To be classed with Catherine of Siena as combining the visions of a mystic with practical activity was Joan of Arc or Jeanne d'Arc (1412–1431), often known as the Maid or the Maid of Orleans. The daughter of a prosperous peasant household, in her early teens she began to hear what she believed to be the voices of God and of some of the saints and angels. As a result she vowed to remain a virgin and gave herself increasingly to prayer. This was during the Hundred Years' War between France and England, and at a time when, after invasions by their King Henry V, the English were occupying much of France and were opposed by rising national sentiment in that unhappy land. However, the French were handicapped by the weak leadership of the Dauphin, the heir to their throne. Joan believed herself commissioned by God to raise the siege of Orleans, then beleaguered by the English, and to bring the Dauphin to Rheims and see him crowned as the lawful king, as against the child Henry VI of England, for whom the crown of France was claimed by his supporters. She made her way to the Dauphin, was accepted by him after some hesitation and an examination by theologians, donned armour, and went with the French force which set out for the relief of Orleans. The English were defeated, Orleans was saved for the French, and the Dauphin, the Maid beside him with her banner, was crowned at Rheims as Charles VII.

In the ensuing complexities of diplomacy and war Joan fell into the hands of the Burgundians, who were allies of the English, was sold to the English, was tried by an ecclesiastical court which was heavily weighted against her, and was condemned on twelve counts, the chief of which was that she held herself to be responsible directly to God and not to the Church. She was then turned over to the secular arm at Rouen and burned, and her ashes were thrown into the Seine. A quarter of a century later Charles VII's government obtained Papal permission for the review of the case by a church court which was as strongly biased in her favour as the earlier one had been against her.

As a result she was declared orthodox and the judgement against her was annulled. She had undoubtedly been sincere and single-minded, an instance of religious devotion which identified obedience to God with loyalty to the emerging French nationalism that centered itself around the king. That she, a peasant girl who was executed before she was twenty, had so great an influence was, as with Catherine of Siena, evidence of the fashion in which many in the Europe of the fourteenth century were moved by one whom they believed to be inspired by God and wholly committed to Him.

PRACTICAL MYSTICS AMONG THE MEN

Those who combined the way of the mystic and its prayer and contemplation with that of intense activity in the affairs of Church and state were not confined to one sex. They were also to be found among men. We have already met three of them, Peter d'Ailly, John Gerson, and Nicholas of Cusa, as leaders in the effort to unite and cleanse the Church through the conciliar movement.

In the midst of a life crowded with study, university administration, and prominent participation in the affairs of the Church, both in France and in Europe as a whole, Peter d'Ailly (1350–1420) took time for prayer, and to such good purpose that he wrote guides to contemplation, meditation, and prayer which were so obviously the fruit of profound experience, not only in his own life, but also as a spiritual guide to others, that they found a wide and continuing circulation.

Peter d'Ailly's pupil and close friend, John Gerson (1363–1429), as chancellor of the University of Paris was an active partisan in French politics and had a large share in the Council of Constance. When in his early fifties implacable political enemies forced him into retirement and semi-exile. Much of that time he gave himself to the care of neglected children. He wrote extensively on the life of the spirit, partly to describe and condemn what seemed to him false mysticism and partly to give positive advice to those who would follow the road of true mysticism. He held that reason as well as feeling should have a part in the mystic's experience. In some monastic circles there had been a reaction against scholasticism which went to the extreme of so great a distrust of reason as to hold that men could never really know God, whether as truth or goodness, but could only say what He was not. With this Gerson took sharp issue. He also denounced some of the writings of Ruysbroeck for what he regarded as pantheistic tendencies.

Nicholas of Cusa (1401–1464) led an extraordinarily active life as monastic reformer, a participant in the conciliar movement, bishop, and cardinal. He was a friend of some of the humanists and had himself studied Greek. Yet he, too, went far in the way of the mystic. He was profoundly influenced by

Augustine and Dionysius the Areopagite. He had his early education at the hands of the Brethren of the Common Life and was an ardent friend of them and of the Windesheim community, of whom we are to hear more in a moment. While not as extreme an anti-intellectualist as some of his contemporaries, he moved in that direction. He believed that what came to the mystic through his experience of God could never be expressed in words and rejoiced in the term *docta ignorantia*.

The Way of the Mystic Has a Continuing and Growing Attraction

We have seen (Chapter 22) that the first half of the fourteenth century witnessed a luxurious flowering of mysticism in wide and not always inter-related circles in Western Europe. For this movement the year 1350 had no significance. It continued without interruption into the second half of the fourteenth century and had no diminution in the fifteenth century. It was not confined to those who, like Catherine of Siena, Joan of Arc, Peter d'Ailly, John Gerson, and Nicholas of Cusa, combined the way of the mystic with intense activity in the wider affairs of their nation, Europe, or the Church. It was also widespread among many whose lives were lived either in much narrower circles or entirely apart from the world. It seems not to have been affected by the corruption in the Papacy and the Papal curia or by the partial failure of the conciliar idea. It was an important phase of the ground swell which issued in the great awakenings of the sixteenth century.

In Germany the stimulus given by Eckhart, Tauler, Suso, and the Friends of God continued. The anonymous layman who was known as the Great Friend of God had his mature years in the second half of the fourteenth century. From the movement there came a number of works of devotion. Of these the most influential was the *Theologia Germanica,* probably written about the middle of the fourteenth century. It came to prominence in the sixteenth century through Luther. That great leader in the Protestant Reformation claimed that he had learned more from it of God, Christ, and man than in any other set of writings except the Bible and Augustine. He saw to it that it was circulated in printed form and through his endorsement it went through many editions.

The Brothers and Sisters of the Common Life, Windesheim, and the Imitatio Christi

In the Low Countries the long-lived John Ruysbroeck (1293–1381) did not die until well after 1350 and he and his writings made their effect felt throughout this period. For instance, the Franciscan Henry of Herp or Henry Harphius, Provincial of the Observants of Cologne and later attached to a monastery at Malines, was deeply impressed by them, especially in his work on *Mystical Theology.*

The influence of Ruysbroeck contributed to the rise and growth of what was known as the New Devotion. This found expression through the Brethren of the Common Life, the Sisters of the Common Life, and the Congregation of Windesheim, and had its crowning literary monument in *The Imitation of Christ.*

The chief moving spirits in the inauguration of the Brethren of the Common Life were Gerard Groote, or Gerard the Great (1340–1384) and Florentius Radewijns (Florence Radewin). Gerard was the son of a burgomaster of Deventer. Precocious as a student, he took a master's degree at the University of Paris, dabbled in magic, through family influence obtained the income of several benefices, and was living comfortably when the rebuke of a Carthusian whom he had known in the university led him radically to alter his life and to give himself to fasting, a hair shirt, and prayer. He began preaching, denounced current vices, including the concubinage of the clergy, stirred Utrecht and its environs, and then was silenced by the ecclesiastical authorities. He visited Ruysbroeck and, deeply impressed by him and his community, resolved to found others like it. In Deventer he began aiding school-boys, entertaining them at his table, and setting them to earning their living by transcribing books. His household grew, and presently, at the suggestion of his friend Florentius Radewijns, he formed it into a simple community in which all the earnings of the members were pooled. Characteristically Gerard Groote died of the plague caught from a sick friend whom he was endeavouring to help.

Out of this simple beginning, in spite of the opposition of the mendicant orders, houses of this kind multiplied, those for men under the name of the Brethren of the Common Life and those for women under that of the Sisters of the Common Life. They combined some of the principles of monasticism with the non-monastic life. They laboured with their hands and held in common the fruits of their toil. They had the practice of confessing their sins daily to one another. They prized books and aided in a revival of education which was already in progress. Their spread was chiefly in Germany and the Low Countries and it may well have been that the presence in these regions of houses of beguines and beghards served as a precedent and so furthered their popularity.

Florentius Radewijns, born near Utrecht, a graduate of the University of Prague, a convert of Gerard Groote, and to whose suggestion the action of the latter in founding the Brethren of the Common Life was in part due, took a further step, perhaps at the instance of Groote, and began a house at Windes-heim near Zwolle which followed the rule of the Augustinian Canons. He was head both of Windesheim and of the Deventer Brethren of the Common Life, but in 1400, after his death, the two became distinct, and although for at least a time the movements kept in close touch with each other, Windesheim became the centre of what in 1419 was a congregation of twenty monasteries, some of them older than itself. It gave a marked stimulus to monastic reform in Germany and the Low Countries.

It is not strange that out of the awakening of which the Brethren of the Common Life and Windesheim were expressions there issued one of the most widely used aids to devotion, prayer, and meditation, *The Imitation of Christ.* Gerard Groote had prized the Bible and the great writers of the Church. He and his disciples made much of prayer, but, while they read Ruysbroeck and collected passages from books which would help them in it and their daily lives, they were not interested in speculative mysticism. It was among the Canons Regular of Windesheim that the literature of the New Devotion arose. Some of it was in German and some in Latin.

Of the writers of the New Devotion, Thomas à Kempis is the most famous, and of his works (if indeed he is the author of it) *The Imitation of Christ* is the best known. Born at Kempen, near Düsseldorf, in 1379 or 1380, Thomas à Kempis went to Deventer for his education and when he was in his late teens was admitted by Florentius Radewijns into his community of copyists. When he was nineteen or twenty he entered the monastery of Mount St. Agnes, a recently founded community of Augustinian Canons near Zwolle of which his brother was prior. There he spent the rest of his days, dying in 1471 as sub-prior. His life was one of quiet, a monastic routine of books, services, and writing. He was a calligrapher of note and was the author of tracts, sermons, biographies of Gerard Groote, Florentius Radewijns, others of their group, and a contemporary Dutch virgin, a mystic who was later canonized. His tracts and sermons dealt with prayer, contemplation, meditations on Christ and the Virgin Mary, the mystical union with Christ, and the ethical problems of members of a monastic community. Whether he was the author of *The Imitation of Christ* has been hotly debated. The book has been ascribed to several others, among them John Gerson. The majority opinion has settled on Thomas à Kempis. It may well be that the author was anonymous, but there seems to be no doubt that whoever he was he belonged to the Windesheim circle, either to the mother house or to some other monastery in that fellowship, and that the book distils much of the collective experience of the type of piety represented by the Brethren of the Common Life and Windesheim.

It must be added that as it went on, the New Devotion tended to regulate prayer by a precise methodology and so to become formal and sterile.

In the thirteenth and fourteenth centuries the mysticism of Germany and the Low Countries also found expression among the Carthusians. Ludolph of Saxony, also known as Ludolph the Carthusian (c.1300–1370), prior of a monastery of his order in Strassburg, wrote a *Life of Christ* which was translated into several languages and which had a wide vogue for two centuries or more. Its aim was to promote the love and imitation of Christ and it was meant to be read slowly, to promote meditation. Dionysius (1402–1471), a native of Ryckel in Limburg and a member of a Carthusian house near Liége, had frequent ecstasies and divided his days between study and prayer. He wrote voluminously, giving instruction in asceticism and contemplation.

This German and Low Country mysticism had a dark side. There were those, although not in any of the movements which we have mentioned, who professed to have a union with God which rendered yielding to the impulses of the flesh a matter of moral indifference. It led to the antinomianism which in various places and times has broken out under the Christian name.

ENGLISH MYSTICS

The flowering of mysticism in Germany and the Low Countries was paralleled by one in England. In the first half of the fourteenth century its chief figure was Richard Rolle, of whom we have already spoken (Chapter XXII). Rolle exerted a marked influence upon Walter Hilton, whose work lay in the second half of the century and who died in 1396. An Augustinian canon, Walter Hilton was an experienced spiritual director and his counsel was sought by monks, nuns, and men of importance in the secular world. Three books of his have come down to us. One, *The Scale of Perfection,* directing the soul in its progress to God, is said to have been more widely read in fifteenth and sixteenth century England than any other devotional guide. It had a continuing fruitage. *The Scale of Perfection* is characterized by what we now think of as typically English, a distrust of extravagance and extremes and a middle way between them. It is concerned as much with ethics as with contemplation. In it, as in Bernard of Clairvaux, contemplation is the communion of love. Like Bernard, it makes much of the human side of Jesus. In it are passages which remind one of the later English Protestant Evangelicalism.

Also belonging to the second half of the fourteenth century was Juliana or Lady Julian of Norwich. She was an anchoress who seems to have had her solitary dwelling in a house in the yard of the Church of St. Julian, near Norwich. The book which made her famous, her *Revelations of Divine Love,* is largely autobiographical. It is compiled of insights which came to her and which she believed had been showed her by God or by Christ. Some have to do with Christ, some with sin, forgiveness, and grace, some with God, and some with prayer.

Less well known was Margery Kempe, a younger contemporary of Walter Hilton and Juliana of Norwich. Born in 1373, she was the daughter of a mayor and alderman of Lynn and was married to a burgess of that city to whom she bore fourteen children. After her first youth there came a sudden revulsion against the vanities of life and the conviction that she should live as a virgin. To this resolution she won her husband's reluctant consent. She undertook pilgrimages, one of them to Palestine. Visions and revelations came to her, and had to do chiefly with how she should act on particular occasions. She met much criticism, but was also consulted by her neighbours as an oracle and was often called to pray over the dying. Her autobiography is interesting in its frankness and perhaps as one that might have been duplicated in its beliefs and its sense of direct guidance by God in numbers of others of her day and age.

ITALIAN MYSTICS

Catherine of Siena was an outstanding but by no means the only mystic of Italy in the century and a half between 1350 and 1500. In spite of the widespread corruption in morals of the laity, the priesthood, the monasteries, and the Papal court, there were those who were completely devoted to God and believed that they had direct experience of Him. One of these was Catherine of Bologna (1413-1463), abbess of the Poor Clares in her native city. Through prolonged struggles with temptation she became expert in the battles of the spirit and had visions, ecstasies, and revelations.

Catherine of Genoa (1447-1510) came from a family which had provided the Church with two Popes and several cardinals. One of her sisters, an Augustinian canoness, had joined in founding a convent. Well educated, at sixteen she was wedded by her family to one of the patrician youths of the city. The marriage proved unhappy, for the two were unsuited to each other and he was unfaithful and extravagant. After a decade, perhaps because of her attempt to find solace, she had a profound religious experience which she regarded as her conversion. In that change of heart her husband soon followed her. They then began to live simply in one of the humbler sections of the city and gave themselves to the care of the poor and the sick. She established the habit of taking the communion daily and inflicted on herself severe penances. She undertook prolonged fasts. Eventually she and her husband moved into a hospital the better to devote themselves to the orphans, the sick, and the dying. As matron of the hospital she showed remarkable administrative gifts and served heroically through a prolonged epidemic of the plague. In 1497 her husband died and not far from that time her health became so impaired that she resigned as matron and discontinued her practice of fasting. From her conversion Catherine had given herself to the love of God and, deeply conscious of her own sinfulness and her remoteness from the supreme Purity, felt that love cleansing her from all pride and filling her with a deep yearning to be transformed into that Purity. To her the love which she felt for God and the love of God for her were like the cleansing fires of purgatory.

THE INCREASING ROLE OF WOMEN

The thoughtful reader must have noted that one of the features of the century and a half between 1350 and 1500 was the increasing prominence of women in the Christian story. Throughout the preceding centuries women had had an important role. Paul had declared that in Christ there is neither male nor female. A woman, the mother of Jesus, had been revered across the generations and never more so than immediately preceding 1350. There had been many women saints. Now women appeared more strikingly as leaders and exemplars of the faith. It was still a man's world. The clergy were exclusively male. The great theologians and the founders of most of the monastic orders were men. However, more than previously, women were coming to the fore as mystics and saints. This was to continue, notably in the Roman Catholic Church.

THE EFFECTS OF PREACHING

Much preaching was heard in Western Europe in the fourteenth and fifteenth centuries. It may even have increased in this period. Some of it was by friars and some by the ordinary parish clergy and the bishops. Much of it was routine and quite uninspired, but some of it was profoundly stirring and moved multitudes. It contributed substantially to the ground swell which preceded and in part issued in the forward surge of the tide in the sixteenth century.

Among the most memorable of the preachers was the Spanish Dominican Vincent Ferrer (1350–1419). He travelled widely in Spain, Northern Italy, Switzerland, and France, preaching as he went. He was from an aristocratic family which presumably was deeply religious, for he had a brother who was general of the Carthusians. He had had a prolonged education in philosophy and theology, had taught, and had served the Avignon Papacy before beginning the career which brought him fame. Severely ascetic, he declined high ecclesiastical office, including that of cardinal. It was not until he was nearly fifty that the Pope started him on his preaching mission. His main themes were sin, impending judgement, and repentance, and were put in such fashion that thousands were smitten in conscience and by fear. Speaking only in his native tongue, he drew enormous crowds. Some of his followers were organized as flagellants who marched in processions, scourging themselves as they went. One of the young men whom he inspired, Bernardine of Siena, continued his work in Italy. From 1408 to 1416, he was almost continuously south of the Pyrenees. There he is said to have won thousands of Jews and Moslems. He also concerned himself with Spanish politics, part of the time as a trusted counsellor of kings. Yet he also gave himself to the lowly and tended sick children. In an epidemic of the plague in Genoa he fearlessly ministered to the stricken. Many miracles of healing were attributed to him. It is not strange that he was formally canonized in 1455, less than a generation after his death.

Vincent Ferrer is one of the more outstanding in a great throng. The friars travelled widely, not only preaching dogma but also attacking the amusements and frivolities of both the noble and the commoner and pillorying the oppression by the lords, the extortions of the merchants, the corruption of the law, and the exactions of the retainers of the mighty. Drunkenness, gluttony, and profanity were denounced, and the saints were praised. Some of the hermits preached, and several wandered about from place to place attracting casual audiences. To aid the preacher there were numerous manuals and treatises on his art.

VARIOUS AIDS TO DEVOTION

In the course of the fourteenth and fifteenth centuries various aids to devotion for both laity and clergy appeared or were further cultivated. It seems to have been in this period that the Way of the Cross, also known as the Stations of the Cross, began to be set up in churches. In Jerusalem the scenes of Christ's sufferings had long been a goal of pilgrims and among them had been the traditional route, later called the *via dolorosa,* which he traversed to his crucifixion. Obviously only a small minority of Christians of Western Europe could make the journey to that distant region. The device began slowly to be adopted of setting up in churches what would be a partial reproduction of this way with reminders at intervals, usually in the form of pictures, of incidents in that memorable and sad progress. By following it and pausing for prayer and meditation at each station the faithful would have their imaginations quickened and their devotion deepened.

Hymns were composed, many of them in the vernacular, both expressions of religious devotion and aids in its cultivation.

Religious dramas were continued and elaborated as a means of instruction. However, they tended to be secularized, to be taken from the churches to the churchyards, and to have so much buffoonery attached to them that purists in morals began to denounce them.

Art also contributed to nourishing the religious life. Painters arose whose works were expressions of prayer and profound meditation on Christian themes. Notable was he who is known as Fra Angelico (1387–1455), the Dominican who is best remembered for his deeply moving paintings in Florence, especially in the monastery of San Marco. Along with the earlier Giotto (c.1267–1337), he was a forerunner of the flowering of Christian art which mounted in the fifteenth century in such men as Donatello (c.1386–1466), Filippo Lippi (1406–1469), the latter's natural son Filippino Lippi (1457–1504), and Botticelli (1444–1510), and which, a generation later, in the fore part of the sixteenth century, was to have its highest expressions in Raphael (1483–1520) and Michelangelo (1475–1564). The main themes of these artists, whether in painting, sculpture, or architecture, were Christian. Some of the masters, like Botticelli, a warm admirer of Savonarola, and Michelangelo, a Christian Platonist and Dante devotee, were profoundly moved by deep personal Christian faith. In them was seen much of the ground swell and, in the greatest and latest of them, the full flood of new tide of the Christian awakening.

MONASTIC REFORM

Here and there were attempts to recall Europe to the ideals which had sought expression in monasticism. No new orders appeared which captured the imagination of such large numbers as had the Cistercians, the Franciscans, or the Dominicans. Yet there were movements which showed that the monastic way to the perfect Christian life had by no means lost its appeal. There were the Brethren of the Common Life and the family of monasteries which centered around Windesheim. The Jesuates (*Jesuati*) received Papal authorization in 1367. They gave themselves to the care of the sick, especially those stricken by the plague, to the burial of the dead, and to strict self-mortification, including scourging. They arose from the life and work of a patrician of Siena, John Colombini (c.1300–1367) who, after a sudden conversion, devoted himself to the indigent sick, to reconciling estranged friends, and to inducing those who had wrongfully taken property to restore it to its rightful owners. Late in the fourteenth century the Hieronymites, taking their name and inspiration from Jerome and the community which he gathered about him in Bethlehem in the fourth century, came into being. They were given the rule of Augustine. Their chief cradle was in Spain and in 1415 they are said to have had twenty-five houses in that land. The Hieronymite nuns were founded in Spain in 1426. In the sixteenth century the order was one of the channels through which the Catholic Reformation found expression. In Rome in the time of its depravity, Frances (1384–1440), a mystic from an aristocratic family, remembered by the name of that city and later canonized, founded the Oblates of St. Benedict, a community of women who followed the Benedictine rule and gave themselves to prayer and good works.

The mendicant orders, recovering from the tragic reduction of their staffs by the Black Death, continued to attract many and thousands enrolled in the ranks of their tertiates. Within the Franciscans the struggle, almost as old as the order itself, continued between those who held to a complete adherence to the ideals of the founder and those who would relax it. The strict party, the Observants, at times seemed to gain as against the others, the Conventuals. The Observants appeared in various countries in the fourteenth and fifteenth centuries. Prominent in furthering them in Italy were Bernardine of Siena and John Capistran. In 1517 a Papal decree gave the Observants a separate structure and declared them to be the true order of St. Francis. Late in the fifteenth century Francis of Paula founded in South Italy and Sicily what are usually known as the Minims, who sought to follow fully the exacting rule of Francis of Assisi. They spread rapidly to France, Germany, and Spain. There was conflict within the Order of Preachers, between those desiring a stern order of life and those who would ease it. While the Observants seem to have been in the minority as against the Conventuals, they were active. So, too, the Augustinian friars experienced a reform in several countries in the fourteenth and fifteenth centuries. In Germany the Observants dominated the order and their organization, officially recognized in 1493, comprised almost all the existing houses. They acquired special significance from the fact that when Martin Luther suddenly decided to become a monk it was an Observant house that he entered. A leader in the reform, Staupitz, had much to do with one stage of Luther's spiritual pilgrimage. A purification of the Carmelites was begun in Italy early in the fifteenth century. In several different places in Europe efforts were made to recall one or another of the Benedictine houses to their earlier ideals. Some of them achieved at least partial success.

MONASTIC REFORM MOVES INTO THE CHURCH IN SPAIN

By the end of the fifteenth century the ground swell was making itself felt in Spain which in the sixteenth century was to mount to a great forward surge. It was first markedly apparent in some sections of the monastic life and from there moved into the Church at large and did much to raise the general level of the quality of clergy and laity.

The closing years of the fifteenth century and the first quarter of the sixteenth century witnessed the political unification of Spain. By the last quarter of the fifteenth century the Christian kingdoms which emerged in the course of the reconquest of the Iberian Peninsula from the Moslems had loosely coalesced into four—Portugal, Castile, Aragon, and Navarre. Castile and Aragon were brought into a personal union by the marriage (1469) of Isabella (1451–1504), Queen of Castile and Leon, and Ferdinand (1452–1516), King of Aragon. In 1512 Ferdinand acquired the part of Navarre which lay south of the Pyrenees. In 1492 the last remaining Moslem stronghold, the Kingdom of Granada, was conquered by Ferdinand and Isabella. While deep internal differences remained in language, traditions, and administrative organization, Spain was more and more a unity under centralized rule.

Isabella was earnestly religious, worked a moral reform in the corrupt court of Castile, endeavoured to purify the convents in the realm, and promoted learning. Ferdinand was of a different stamp and while known as the Catholic was crafty and boasted of his success in deceit in diplomacy. Yet Isabella was too able and vigorous to be ignored.

Improvement was very much needed in the Spanish Church. Concubinage among the clergy was widespread and the level of general morality was low. The reform in the Franciscans through the Observants had spread to Spain. It found a friend in Isabella and a dauntless and extraordinarily able leader in Ximénes de Cisneros (1436–1517) whose long life gave him time to carry through many of his projects.

Ximénes de Cisneros was late in rising to prominence. He was well educated in civil and canon law, spent several years in Rome, and returned to Spain with a Papal appointment to a benefice in the Archbishopric of Toledo when one should fall vacant. The Archbishop was unwilling to recognize the Papal document. Ximénes would not yield his claim, and as a result was imprisoned by the Archbishop for six years. Released when in his early forties, he was given office by another bishop and at once displayed remarkable administrative gifts. Then he joined the Observant Franciscans and began a rigorously ascetic regimen. For three years he was a hermit and found deeply satisfying the life of austerity, solitude, prayer, and meditation. In 1492, over his protests, Isabella chose him as her confessor. Two years later he was elected provincial of his order in Castile. With the support of the Pope and Isabella, he carried through, against severe opposition, a reform designed to bring all Franciscans in that province under the Observant discipline. In 1495 Isabella had him appointed Archbishop of Toledo, the most influential ecclesiastical post in her kingdom. He at first refused and finally accepted only on the express command of the Pope. Once installed, he continued to live as a strict Franciscan and devoted the huge revenues of the see to such purposes as the relief of the poor and the ransom of captives. Indeed, Pope Alexander VI, his opposite in moral character, admonished him to live more in accord with the dignity of his high office. His vision, inflexible will, and administrative ability were directed towards the purification of the Church. He continued his measures to bring the Conventual Franciscans to Observant standards. He took action to purge the secular clergy, obtaining for this purpose a free hand from the Pope. In all this he had the support of Isabella.

Although active in affairs of state, twice regent of Castile, and a cardinal of the Roman Church, Ximénes never lost sight of his purpose of improving the quality of the Church. Late in life he founded the University of Alcalá, gave to it much time, thought, and money, and made it a centre of the teaching of religion. To further the study of the Scriptures he had compiled and prepared for printing the Complutensian (from Complutum, the Latin name of Alcalá) Polyglot Bible, in which Greek, Latin, Hebrew, and Aramaic were used. He employed that new medium, the printing press, to multiply for circulation other Christian literature. He revived the use of the ancient Spanish Mozarabic liturgy as against that of Rome.

THE INQUISITION IN SPAIN

A side of the religious life of Spain in this period which was intended to cleanse it was the extension and intensification of the Inquisition.

In the middle of the fourteenth century, with the possible exception of Lithuania, Spain had more self-confessed non-Christians than any other country in Western Europe. Jews were numerous and prominent, there were many Moslems, and Granada remained a frankly Moslem state. Late in the fourteenth century Lithuania became officially Christian, but in the fifteenth century the conversion of Jews and Moslems in Spain was still incomplete. Early in the fifteenth century, partly from fear of the widespread massacres which were being visited on their co-religionists and partly through the eloquence of Vincent Ferrer, thousands of Jews accepted baptism. Many of the converted and their descendants rose to prominence in the Church. Others married into highly placed Spanish families. In 1492 Ferdinand and Isabella ordered all Jews who held to their ancestral faith either to be baptized or leave the country. More baptisms followed. The monarchs acted with similar vigour to bring about the conversion of the Moslems. By the terms of the surrender of Granada (1492) the latter were guaranteed protection for themselves and their property. The first Archbishop of Granada after the capitulation respected the pledge and sought the conversion of the populace by persuasion and tact. As a result, thousands were baptized. However, Ximénes believed those methods to be too lenient and adopted more strenuous ones. These goaded the Moors to a rebellion which was put down by ruthless force. Partly in retaliation, Ferdinand and Isabella gave them the choice of emigration or baptism. In 1502 an edict forced a similarly unpleasant alternative on the Moslems who remained in Castile. Many thousands elected the easier course and were baptized.

Under these circumstances, for many baptized Jews (called *Marranos* or *Conversos*) and converted Moslems (called *Moriscos*) the change in religion was purely nominal. There was much popular feeling against them, especially against the Marranos. They were widely accused, probably justly in many instances, of maintaining their non-Christian rites in secret. Presumably envy for their economic prosperity contributed to the clamour. To ferret out the crypto-Jews and hidden Moslems, in 1478 Ferdinand and Isabella, partly through the urging of Thomas de Torquemada, prior of a Dominican house in Segovia, and of a Dominican prior in Seville, but apparently without any widespread demand from the Church in that kingdom and with reluctance on the part of Isabella, asked Rome for the extension of the Inquisition to Castile. The Pope, Sixtus IV, agreed, and in 1480, with his authority, the step was taken. In accord with the rising power of the monarch as against the Papacy, the Inquisition was to be directed by men appointed by the crown rather than by Rome. It was to have jurisdiction only over the baptized and not over non-Christians. Directed primarily against the *Conversos,* it soon brought numbers of these to the stake. However, the majority of the condemned were not burned but were heavily fined and were subjected to humiliating penance. Torquemada was named Inquisitor-general, with power in Castile, Aragon, Valencia, and Catalonia. Learned, sternly ascetic in his private life, observing strictly the vow of poverty, deeply pious, uncompromising, Torquemada extended the operation of the Inquisition. After his death (1498) it was continued.

The Inquisition was developed by men who had the zeal of reformers and made for a certain kind of unity in Spain, but it can scarcely be said to have contributed to the religious awakening of the sixteenth century. The conviction with which it was administered was perilously akin to fanaticism. It may have prevented Protestantism from gaining a firm foothold in the country, but the kind of devotion which it nourished was a caricature of that which is the fruit of the "exceeding greatness of his power" of which the New Testament speaks.

It may be significant that none of those who were most outstanding in the fifteenth century reform in Spain—Isabella, Ximénes, and Torquemada—was ever canonized. In spite of their devotion and labours, in the judgement of the Roman Catholic Church they were not assuredly exemplars of the Christian ideal.

These developments in Spain were of peculiar importance because of the prominence which that country was to have in the ensuing century. She was to become the mightiest military power in Western Europe and was to build an enormous overseas empire. Through her colonial possessions Christianity was to have an opportunity for wide geographical extension and the quality of the faith that was propagated reflected the temper of the Church within her borders.

"The Power" Infiltrates Humanism

Towards the end of the fifteenth century the ground swell which was preliminary to the flood tide of the sixteenth century began to make itself felt among the humanists. As we have reminded ourselves, in its earlier days humanism made little positive contribution to the religious life of Western Europe. Few if any humanists openly repudiated Christianity. They were Catholics and some of them drew their support from the Church. The value which they placed on man was in part of Christian origin. Yet the earlier leading humanists were largely negative in their attitude towards the Church and its faith. They were scornful of scholastic philosophy and theology and were contemptuous of monasticism. Laurentius Valla (1405–1457) was fairly typical of the prevailing attitude of humanists. He used his critical skill to reveal the spurious character of the Donation of Constantine. He took delight in showing that the Apostles' Creed was not framed by the Twelve Apostles, as legend declared it to have been, and by advocating the study of the original Greek and Hebrew texts began to shake confidence in the Vulgate as the authoritative version of the Scriptures. In the second half of the fifteenth century a change began to be seen. There were outstanding humanists who were also earnestly Christian. They might still be critical of some aspects of the Church but they were concerned more for positive than for negative measures.

One strain of Christian humanism issued from the Platonic Academy at Florence. Founded about 1442 by Cosimo de' Medici, the most powerful personage of the day in that city, it was designed to emulate the famous pagan Academy of Athens. One of its leading members, Marsilio Ficino (1433–1499), a protegee of Cosimo de' Medici, a translator and ardent student of Plato and Plotinus, was deeply enamoured of Dionysius the Areopagite, that inspirer of so much of Christian mysticism, held Augustine in reverence, in his personal morals remained uncontaminated by the fashionable vices of the Renaissance, was ordained to the priesthood, believed that religion in its purest form was revealed in Christ, and held that Platonism and Christianity could be harmonized. To that circle belonged Pico della Mirandola (1463–1494), the brilliant youngest son of the Prince of Mirandola. Learned in Greek, Latin, Hebrew, Arabic, and Chaldee, he sought to prove the truth of Christianity from Kabbalah, that Jewish school of thought which lent itself to mysticism and to theological and philosophical speculation and which had a strange similarity to the more ancient Gnosticism. A restless traveller, in the latter part of his brief years he was profoundly impressed by Savonarola, of whom we are to hear more a few pages below, and had dreams of going barefooted about the world preaching.

In France a distinguished Christian humanist, the teacher of several others, was Jacques Lefèvre d'Étaples (c.1455–1536). A priest, he studied in the University of Paris and in Florence, Rome, and Venice, made himself familiar with Greek, and was deeply impressed with Plato. Returning to Paris, he taught in the University and there profoundly influenced some of those who were to be pioneers in Protestantism. He devoted much of his time to Biblical studies, translated the Bible into French (although his was by no means the first French version), and pled for a return to primitive Christianity and for the Scriptures as the primary authority for Christians. He was the devout humanist who wished to go back to the primary sources and so to know the Christian faith as it came fresh from Christ and the apostles.

Eminent among the early German humanists was Roelof Huysmann (1443–1485), better known as Rudolf Agricola. A native of the Low Countries, as a youth he studied with the Brethren of the Common Life, then in Italy, and taught in the University of Heidelberg. Earnestly religious, he helped to give German humanism a Christian orientation. He was much admired by Erasmus, of whom we are to say more in a moment. More prominent and eventually an unwilling but quietly courageous centre of controversy between humanists and those within the Church who opposed them was Johann Reuchlin (1455–1522). A master of classical Latin and Greek, he was especially noted for his familiarity with Hebrew. In this he drew his inspiration in part from Pico della Mirandola. From the latter he also acquired an interest in Kabbalistic studies. With the humanist's concern for digging into first-hand sources, he went back of the Vulgate to the original texts and pointed out errors in that revered translation of the Bible. A stormy controversy which stirred Church and scholarly circles arose over Reuchlin's refusal to recommend the proposed destruction of all Jewish books except the Old Testament. This was being stoutly advocated by a converted Jew, Pfefferkorn, as a first step towards bringing over his former co-religionists to the Christian faith. Against Reuchlin were the universities, the Inquisition, and the friars, especially the Dominicans. For him were the humanists. Some of the latter came out anonymously with a series of satires, *Letters of Obscure Men,* which, directed against Reuchlin's antagonists, set the humanists of Europe to laughing. In an appeal to the Pope, Reuchlin won out, but somewhat inconclusively. He remained within the Catholic Church, but we shall meet his grand-nephew, Philip Melanchthon, whom he looked upon almost as a son, as one of Luther's staunchest supporters.

Prominent among the English Christian humanists were John Colet (c.1467–1519) and his younger friend and admirer, Thomas More (1478–1535). The sole surviving son of a Lord Mayor of London, Colet was born to wealth. After taking a degree at Oxford, he travelled in Italy and, returning to England, began lecturing on the Bible in a fresh way which commanded attention. A student of Plato, Plotinus, and Dionysius the Areopagite, there was in him something of the mystic. Eventually he became Dean of St. Paul's Cathedral in London. He was chiefly remembered for his Biblical studies, his preaching, his advocacy of reform, and his founding of St. Paul's School as a centre of humanistic studies. We are to see Thomas More at a later stage in our story, but here we meet him as a charming, witty humanist, a translator of the writings of Pico della Mirandola.

Erasmus, Prince of Christian Humanists

As the crowning glory of the Christian humanists we move naturally to Desiderius Erasmus (c.1466–1536). This is partly because of his fame among his contemporaries and partly because it was through him that the aspect of the ground swell represented by the combination of humanism with Christianity made a major contribution to the flood tide of the sixteenth century.

Desiderius Erasmus was born out of wedlock in Rotterdam. He was cared for by his mother, but he early lost her and his father in the plague. As a child he was put to school in Deventer and had part of his education through the Brethren of the Common Life. A student and an intense individualist by temperament, he reacted vigorously against well intentioned efforts by his guardian and other friends to induce him to take up the monastic life. Eventually he was ordained to the priesthood, but he had no taste for that profession. He studied at the University of Paris, and at various times was in Italy, England, the Low Countries, and Germany. He craved books and friends, but would never be too closely bound by the latter. Not a profound scholar, his great talent was the skill with which he handled Latin. He was a man of letters whose books commanded a wide audience, an audience which was multiplied by the increasing use of the printing press.

Erasmus was sincerely Christian and wished for the reformation of the Church. He had no use for monks or scholasticism and cared little for theology or the sacraments. He wished to see the Church purged of superstition through the use of intelligence and a return to the ethical teachings of Christ. He desired no break with the existing Catholic Church. He initiated no innovations in doctrine or worship. Rather he pled for ethical living, and in a politically divided Europe, racked by chronic wars, he argued for peace. His approach was rational. He appeared to cherish the conviction that through the appeal to man's reason both Church and society could be vastly improved.

Among the more widely read writings of Erasmus were his *Enchiridion*

Militis Christiani, or *Handbook of the Christian Soldier,* meant to be a guide to Christian living, deprecating formalism and ceremonies and emphasizing morals; *The Praise of Folly,* a satirical description of current life from the Pope and cardinals down through kings, nobles, monks, preachers, philosophers, and merchants, to the lower strata of society; *Querala Pacis* or *The Complaint of Peace,* in which he praised peace and pilloried war; and his *Familiar Colloquies,* in which he held up to ridicule what he deemed the corruptions in the Church and the monasteries. He got out an edition of the Greek Testament with a fresh translation into Latin. He stimulated editions of some of the early Christian writers. His moral earnestness and his attempt to stress the New Testament, combined with the wide vogue enjoyed by his writings did much to incite to reform and to turn humanism from its secularistic and pagan tendencies.

WYCLIF AND THE LOLLARDS

What, in the meantime, was happening to scholasticism? Could it survive the scorn which the humanists were pouring on it? Although the tide was running against it, it continued. From those nurtured in it there appeared men and movements which in their effort to give expression to "the exceeding greatness of the power" of the Christian Gospel advocated such drastic measures that they were condemned as heretical by the Catholic Church. They, too, were part of the ground swell which was to issue in the flood tide of the sixteenth and seventeenth centuries.

Outstanding and making a major contribution to later movements was John Wyclif. There is much uncertainty about the date of his birth, but it is clear that he was a native of Yorkshire. His student years were in Oxford and he became a master of scholastic philosophy and theology. In time he was the outstanding scholar among its teachers and his lectures were largely attended. In an age when nominalism seemed to be sweeping all before it, Wyclif was an unabashed realist. He was profoundly influenced by Augustine and through him by Plato. In this he reflected the revival of Augustinian studies in the England of his day which had as a leader Bradwardine, an Oxford theologian and later Archbishop of Canterbury. Wyclif stood with Thomas Aquinas rather than with Duns Scotus, but the latter, who had been at Oxford only a generation or so before him, seems to have had a profound influence upon him. Like Duns Scotus, he was critical of some existing beliefs and also held to the omnipotence of the arbitrary will of God. He was probably even more deeply indebted to Robert Grosseteste, who had been a powerful figure at Oxford only a few years earlier and who was outstanding as the reforming Bishop of Lincoln.

We must think of Wyclif as spending the major part of his career as student and teacher, chiefly within the confines of Oxford, stimulated by the debates among the school men, holding various ecclesiastical appointments outside the university which gave him a livelihood and the means to pursue his university course, and occasionally performing the duties attached to these offices. He was often an absentee recipient of income from parish sources. In 1374, through royal appointment, he became rector of the parish of Lutterworth. On one occasion he went on a political errand to the Continent for the crown and thus established a connexion with John of Gaunt, a younger and influential son of King Edward III, which later stood him in good stead.

It was not until the last eight or nine years of his life that Wyclif engaged in the writing and the activities for which he became famous. In treatises on divine and civil dominion, he put forth the theory that all ownership is God's, and that God grants the use of property on the condition that the holder render faithful service. If the trust is not fulfilled the use is forfeited. While the principle applied to property held by civil as well as ecclesiastical dignitaries, what gave it force in England was Wyclif's declaration that if an ecclesiastic habitually misused his holdings, he could be removed from them by the secular power. He also maintained that Popes might err and that they were not necessary for the administration of the Church. A worldly Pope was a heretic and should be removed from office. In an England which was smarting from exactions by the revenue-hungry Avignon Papacy, these assertions were welcomed by many. They were in accord with actions of the "Good Parliament" of 1376 in seeking to curtail the collection of Papal revenues in England and the enjoyment of English revenues by absentee Papal appointees. The powerful John of Gaunt, completely self-seeking, was prepared to champion Wyclif since the latter's advocacy of the intervention of the civil arm to remove unworthy clergy from their benefices gave him support in his ambition to replace ecclesiastics whom he could not control by men who were his creatures. The protection of John of Gaunt and other nobles shielded Wyclif from the action against him attempted by the Bishop of London and the Archbishop of Canterbury.

Wyclif progressively became more radical in his views, and in doing so lost the support of John of Gaunt and some others among the powerful of the realm. About the time that Europe was being scandalized by the outbreak of the Great Papal Schism, in a treatise on the Church, taking a strict Augustinian view of predestination, Wyclif argued that the true Church is made up only of those elected by God and is invisible, and that since it is God's choice which determines membership, no visible church or its officers can control entrance or can exclude from membership. Nor can Pope or bishop know who are true members. To his mind, salvation does not depend upon a connexion with the visible Church or upon the mediation of the priesthood, but solely upon election by God. He was critical of monks and friars. Later he held that every one of the elect is a priest and that the New Testament recognizes no distinction between priests and bishops. Priests and bishops, he maintained, should be honoured because of their character and should set an example to their flocks. Clergy who tried to enforce the collection of tithes by that very fact were revealed as unworthy of their office. He condemned the cult of the saints, relics, and pilgrimages. Soon, while holding to the real presence of Christ in the bread and wine of the mass, he attacked transubstantiation and taught that under some circumstances a layman might officiate in the Eucharist. While not rejecting the seven sacraments, he did not believe confirmation to be necessary. He repudiated indulgences and masses for the dead but retained a belief in purgatory. He declared that intelligent sincerity in worship was of more value than the form. Indeed, formalism and elaborate services might hinder true worship.

For a time at Oxford Wyclif was supported by the secular clergy, partly because in coming out against the monks and friars he had taken sides in the chronic conflict between the seculars and regulars in the university. Moreover, Oxford, as the leading university in England and for a time second only to the University of Paris in prestige in Northern Europe, was jealous of its independence of king and bishop. Before long, however, the episcopacy succeeded in expelling or winning the friends of Wyclif and the university passed into the hands of his enemies. In the meantime Wyclif had retired to Lutterworth and was making that the directing centre of his activities.

In furtherance of his convictions Wyclif had the Bible translated from the Vulgate. He insisted that the Scriptures are the supreme authority, that priests and bishops should be familiar with them, and that even unlettered and simple men can understand them and should study them. To make the Bible accessible to the rank and file he had it put into the English vernacular of his day. Before Wyclif undertook the translation, the Psalms had been given an English form either by Richard Rolle or some one inspired by him. There had been other translations of parts of the Bible. But it was due to Wyclif and those kindled by him that the entire Bible was made available in the English of the fourteenth century. The first attempt was in somewhat crabbed style, but later revisions were more idiomatic.

To give wide currency to the Gospel as he understood it Wyclif sent out travelling preachers. They had no uniform designation. He called them "poor priests," "poor priests that preach," "unlearned and simple" men, "faithful and poor priests," "true priests," or, simply, "itinerant preachers." They were to preach wherever they could gain a hearing—on the roads, in village greens and churchyards, or in churches. They were to be garbed in russet robes of undressed cloth reaching to their feet, and were to go, long staff in hand, without sandals or purse, taking such food and shelter as were offered them, and teaching in the vernacular the Lord's Prayer, the Ten Commandments, and the seven deadly sins. They might have with them a few portions of the translation of the Bible, especially the Gospels and some of the Epistles. For their guidance Wyclif wrote tracts and sermon outlines and prepared paraphrases of the Bible. In his own sermons, in contrast with much of the preaching of the day which dwelt upon miracles, fables, and the lives of the saints, he stressed the exposition of passages from the Bible. That was what he desired of his preachers. He wished them to continue the itinerant life and never to settle down. At the outset some of them were university graduates and from families of some social standing. As time passed they were drawn almost exclusively from the poor.

Wyclif's writings and the work of his itinerant preachers won a large number of adherents. They were known as Lollards. Some were attracted by the attacks on the abuses of the time, for Wyclif and his preachers were outspoken in their denunciation of the corruptions in the Church and of the clergy. Others were presumably drawn by the appeal of the Bible in the speech of every day. Among the Lollards or at least among those friendly to them, were members of the gentry who protected the preachers and enabled them to deliver their messages. Much of the popular poetry of the time reflected views which were in accord with those of Wyclif's preachers.

Persecution was inevitable, vigorous, and prolonged. The bishops could not ignore a widespread movement which cut at the roots of their power and denounced some of the accepted beliefs and practices of the Catholic Church. John of Gaunt, far from model in his morals, prided himself on his orthodoxy and was alienated by Wyclif's attack on transubstantiation. The itinerant preachers were accused of stirring up the Peasants Revolt of 1381. The charge was probably ill-founded. The insurrection was a protest against taxation and maladministration. It was a climax to unrest which had long been seething and which was symptomatic of the economic and social changes that were under way. To be sure, the unrest had religious aspects and in part religious sources. *Piers Plowman,* the contemporary allegory which pictured the evils of the day, voiced the current dissatisfaction and may have added to it. The "mad priest" John Ball had a more direct association with the revolt and preached that all goods should be held in common and the distinction erased between lord and serf. Wyclif's preachers seem not to have been among the social revolutionaries. However, many of the possessing classes, frightened by the revolt, held them responsible. Wyclif himself died in peace in 1384. The Lollard preachers had powerful friends. Yet in 1401 a strong act against heretics passed Parliament, in 1406 an anti-Lollard measure was enacted, and in 1407 the Archbishop of Canterbury gave vent to a series of blasts which were confirmed by a synod in London in 1409 and which condemned the doctrines of Wyclif and the unauthorized translation of the Bible and prohibited unlicensed preachers. There were some burnings of Lollards.

In the reign of Henry V (1413-1422) sweeping measures were taken. That king was vigorously anti-Lollard and a Lollard outbreak in which a knight, Sir John Oldcastle, was involved was ruthlessly suppressed. In 1415 the Council of Constance condemned Wyclif on 260 different counts, ordered his writings to be burned, and directed that his bones be exhumed and cast out of consecrated ground. In 1428, at Papal command, the remains of Wyclif were dug up and burned and the ashes were thrown into a nearby stream. Action against the Lollards continued, but Lollardy persisted and seems to have enjoyed something of a revival in the reign of Henry VII (1485-1509). Certainly there was continued persecution. Lollardy became one of the contributory sources of English Protestantism.

THE HUSSITE MOVEMENT

While measures against the Lollards were proceeding, in another land, Bohemia, the writings of Wyclif were reinforcing and helping to shape a revolt against the Catholic Church which was to be accompanied by far more bloodshed than was the attempted extirpation of their influence in England.

The second half of the fourteenth century witnessed a rising tide of reform in Bohemia. There many of the clergy were worldly and corrupt. There, too, preachers were denouncing the evils in the Church and society, were appealing to the Bible as the rule of life, and were demanding more frequent communion.

Of this reform movement John Hus (c.1373-1415) became the outstanding leader. He was of humble birth and death early deprived him of his father. He was reared by his mother and was encouraged by her in his struggles to obtain an education. He studied philosophy and theology at the University of Prague, then newly founded and one of the most famous in Europe. Not distinguished for brilliance and with only an average record as a student, he nevertheless took degrees, lectured on the Sentences of Peter Lombard, and by 1403, when he was at most in his early thirties and perhaps still younger, he was ordained to the priesthood. Eventually he was dean of the faculty of philosophy and rector of the University of Prague. He must have had charm and gifts of leadership so early to have risen to prominence. Moreover, not even his bitterest enemies seem to have been able to find anything amiss in his private life and one of his eminent critics spoke of his reputation for unblemished purity, a striking tribute in an age when that could not be said of many in high ecclesiastical position.

In 1402 Hus became rector and preacher in the chapel of the Holy Innocents of Bethlehem in Prague. In that post, by his eloquence and earnestness he attracted all classes, from the highest to the lowest, and speedily became one of the most influential men in the country. During Hus's boyhood the King of Bohemia, Charles IV, who also became Holy Roman Emperor, had made Prague a centre notable in architecture and letters. It was a time of national awakening and prosperity. Hus preached in both Latin and Czech and by his use of the latter stimulated a patriotism which was already growing. Yet he was not concerned so much with national feeling as he was to reach the populace in the speech of daily life. He denounced the evils in the Church, from parish priests to Pope, held that Christ and not Peter was the foundation on which God had founded the Church, and that, far from being inerrant, many Popes had been heretics. He was marked by high ethical purpose rather than radical theological speculation and wished moral reform rather than ecclesiastical revolution.

The reform movement of which Hus was the outstanding spokesman was given added stimulus by the writings of Wyclif. By the marriage of Richard II of England in 1382 to Anne of Luxemburg, sister of the King of Bohemia, a close connexion had been established between the two countries. Anne seems to have been a woman of high character and to have been interested in a purer religious life, for she is said to have brought with her to England copies of the Bible in Latin, German, and Czech, and so long as she lived to have exerted a moderating and wholesome influence upon her royal spouse who, only a few years after her restraining hand was removed by death, came to an inglorious end through his own folly. In Anne's day a number of Bohemians were students in Oxford. Since in 1383 the Archbishop of Canterbury, the high-born William Courtenay, great-grandson of Edward I, had succeeded in having vigorous action taken against the Lollards in that university, the controversy must have been prominent in student discussions. Whether through Oxford or other channels, the writings of Wyclif were being read in Prague at least as early as the fore part of the 1380's. Presumably Hus knew of them in his student days. Before he had attained fame as a preacher he had copied with his own hand some of Wyclif's writings. However, Hus was no blind reproducer of Wyclif. He differed from him on many points, generally in the direction of moderation and conservatism.

As was to be expected, opposition developed. Hus was popular with the masses and many of the aristocracy. The Queen made him her confessor and she and her ladies came to his preaching. Reform sentiments were embodied in popular songs. However, the clergy whose manner of life was being attacked were critical and the honest conservatives were disturbed. The situation was complicated by domestic political dissensions, divided loyalties in the Great Papal Schism, and the traditional Czech resentment against the Germans, prominent since the latter were in Bohemia and especially in Prague. In the German-Czech tension, in 1409 the Czechs were given control of the university and the German contingent, disgruntled, left the country. Hus was looked upon as a champion of the Czechs. His influence and that of Wyclif became dominant in the university. The Archbishop of Prague was antagonistic and obtained a decree from the first Pisan Pope ordering the surrender to the Archbishop of all Wyclif's writings for burning and what amounted to the silencing of Hus. Hus refused to comply, and that in spite of the burning (1410) of several scores of Wyclif's books, and on excommunication by the Archbishop he appealed to the new Pisan Pope, John XXIII. Yet he soon placed himself against that Pope by openly denouncing the crusade which the latter was invoking against the King of Naples and the indulgences which were being sold in Prague to raise funds for that venture. In taking this step Hus alienated the theological faculty of the university. John XXIII retaliated by putting Hus under stringent excommunication and issued an interdict against Prague. To relieve the situation, Hus left the city (1412). Yet he continued to preach from place to place and generally in the open air. Czech sentiment was with him.

Hus and the writings of Wyclif had by now attracted an attention which was not confined to Bohemia and England. They had become of European moment. Sigismund, who had a large part in making possible the Council of Constance, was much concerned, especially since he was a brother of the King of Bohemia. He urged Hus to present his case to that body. Hus complied and journeyed to Constance under letters of safe-conduct from Sigismund. There he was arrested and imprisoned, for he was under the ban of John XXIII. The Council of Constance formally condemned Wyclif and his writings, an action which made clear its attitude towards Hus. Hus was tried by the council on several counts, among them his alleged support of the teachings of Wyclif, and especially statements in his own works. One of these statements was the assertion that if a Pope, bishop, or prelate was in mortal sin he was not Pope, bishop, or prelate. To this Hus orally added kings. Hus declared that he was being accused of maintaining positions which he did not hold, that he was willing to be informed by the council of his errors, and that he was prepared to submit to its judgement, but only if by doing so he did not offend

God and his conscience. Here, it may be added, he took a position which was closely akin to that maintained by Luther a little over a century later and which was of the essence of Protestantism.

The issue was clearly joined. The council, insisting as a matter of principle on its supreme authority in the Church, could not dismiss Hus without compromising the basic convictions of its competence held by the leaders of the movement which had brought it into being. Hus was condemned. It may be added that both John Gerson and Peter d'Ailly were against him and that d'Ailly had a leading part in the proceedings. In a formal meeting of the council the charges against Hus were repeated, and the prisoner, wasted by prolonged imprisonment, illness, and sleeplessness, still protesting his innocence and refusing to abjure his alleged errors, was silenced, degraded from the priesthood, and turned over to the secular arm. He was thereupon (July 6, 1415) burned at the stake. His last audible words were said to have been: "Lord, into thy hands I commend my spirit."

The burning of Hus did not end the movement of which he had been the leader. Indeed, it furthered it. Hus became a national hero. While he was in prison in Constance some of his followers began giving the cup in the communion to the laity. Hus approved. In Bohemia those who held to Wyclif and Hus soon fell into two camps. One, aristocratic, known as the Utraquists because in the communion they gave both the bread and the wine to the laity, wished the free preaching of the Gospel and a moral clergy and stood against only those practices of the Catholic Church which they regarded as forbidden by the Bible. The other, the Taborites, who took their name from their chief fortress and who were led by a blind general, Ziska, were from the humbler ranks of society and went on the principle of rejecting everything for which they could not find express warrant in the "law of God" as set forth in the Bible. The Utraquists and the Taborites could not agree but for a time united against the crusading armies which were sent against them. The Utraquists administered an overwhelming defeat to the Taborites in the decisive battle of Lipan (1434). They won from the Council of Basel certain concessions (1436), among them the use of the cup for the laity, and in theory were restored to the communion of the Catholic Church. Although Pope Pius II declared that agreement to be illegal, the Bohemian Parliament gave them full equality with the Catholics.

Another group, the *Unitas Fratrum,* or the Bohemian Brethren, appeared about the middle of the fifteenth century and seem to have been made up of elements from the Utraquists, Taborites, and Waldensees. We are to meet them again, especially as spiritual ancestors of the Moravians.

SOME OTHER EFFORTS AT REFORM

The movements which centered about Wyclif and Hus were not the only ones in Northern Europe which, in seeking for a purer expression of the Christian faith, were either cast out by the Catholic Church or were on the verge of heresy.

John Pupper of Goch (1400–1475), a native of the Low Countries, held that "only the Bible has irrefragable authority," and that the Church and even the fathers of the Church are subject to error and are of value only in so far as they are in conformity with the Scriptures. He had had a close connexion with the Brethren of the Common Life, was a priest, and for forty years was rector and confessor of a house of canonesses in Mechlin who followed the rule of Augustine. Deeply religious, he emphasized the love of God. Influenced by Augustine, he stressed grace in salvation. He opposed legalism and Pelagianism and emphasized the inner disposition of the soul and what seemed to him to be true Christian liberty. He appears never to have run afoul of the ecclesiastical authorities, perhaps because his quiet, contemplative manner of life kept him out of the public eye.

Far otherwise was the course of his friend, John of Wesel (c.1410–1481). A graduate of the University of Erfurt, a teacher in that institution, and later a distinguished preacher at Mainz and Worms, John of Wesel held as fundamental the conviction that he should not say or write anything contrary to what is contained in the Bible. He challenged the basis on which Papal indulgences were issued, declaring that while the Pope could absolve from the punishments imposed by man or positive law, he could not release any one from penalties inflicted by God for sin. He also challenged the accepted belief in the treasury of the Church and said that if the saints had acquired merit, it could be distributed only by God. He boldly asserted that no one has the authority to grant an indulgence. He held that the grace of God raises a sinner from his fall and that no reason exists for the mediation of the Church. Late in life he was haled before the Inquisition. He recanted, but was condemned to imprisonment in a monastery and to have his books burned.

A slightly younger contemporary of these two, John Wessel or Wessel Gansvoort (c.1420–1489), a native of Groningen, had part of his early training with the Brethren of the Common Life, was much impressed with *The Imitation of Christ,* and came to know Thomas à Kempis. Eager for learning, he travelled much in Western Europe, knew Paris and Rome, but seldom remained long in one place and did not tie himself by any continuing bonds. He was profoundly influenced by Plato and wrote extensively on theology. An earnest seeker for truth, in his mature years he was afflicted by doubts, but eventually had them resolved and declared that he knew nothing but Jesus Christ and him crucified. He held that, being inspired by the Holy Spirit, the Bible is the final authority in matters of faith. To him the Church was the communion of saints. He denied that the sacraments are of themselves effectual means of grace, and declared that the infusion of love in the heart is true baptism and that the priest is only a minister of God and can contribute nothing to the power of the sacrament. He completely rejected indulgences. He held that all that Christ did and suffered was for the purpose of exciting and nourishing love and that in the Eucharist, although the physical eating is important, the spiritual eating is alone profitable.

A quite different manifestation of the ground swell which prepared the way for the great tide of the sixteenth century was the Flagellants. We have met them earlier in the Middle Ages. Shortly before 1350 they appeared again, probably first in Italy and as a result of the Black Death and of earthquakes. The uncertainty of life and the imminence of death, always marked in the Middle Ages and accentuated by disasters before which man seemed helpless, drove men and women to penitence. The Flagellants were characterized not only by scourgings but also by folk-songs on Christian themes and by brotherhoods which combined penance with works of mercy and care of the sick. They often demanded that their members be reconciled to their enemies. By 1349 Flagellants had spread, among other places, to the Low Countries, Bohemia, Poland, Denmark, and England. North of the Alps they developed into a kind of organization, sometimes called the Brotherhood of the Cross, with a distinctive white habit and a severe discipline which involved a public scourging twice a day. At least some of these northern Flagellants cast doubt on the necessity of the sacraments. They also are said to have taught that their penances would work the salvation of the world. In 1349 they were condemned by the Pope. Yet they broke out again from time to time in the fourteenth and fifteenth centuries. We hear of them in Provence in 1399 and in Germany as late as 1481.

Extremes Meet: Savonarola and Alexander VI

Near the close of the fifteenth century Florence was the scene of a contest in which the extremes met. The ground swell of surging life dashed itself against corrupt power entrenched in the Papacy and apparently was completely dissipated. The monastic ideal of the Middle Ages for a time captured one of the major cities of Europe, a chief centre of the Renaissance and humanism, but was soon frustrated by its impotence to transform society and succumbed to the utter worldliness of Rome. The outstanding figures in the unequal contest were Savonarola and Alexander VI.

Girolamo Savonarola (1452–1498) was born in Ferrara of a Paduan family. His father was quite undistinguished, but his mother was a woman of marked nobility of character and his paternal grandfather was a deeply religious and learned physician who was devoted to the poor. Girolamo was a bookish, serious lad who did not mix with his contemporaries and was early enamoured of religion and the writings of Thomas Aquinas. Although Ferrara was then, under the ducal family d'Este, a brilliant centre of the Renaissance, the young Savonarola was little affected by the new tide except to revolt against it. Disappointed in love, in his early twenties he fled to Bologna and joined the Dominicans. Sensitive and intense, he was deeply grieved by the corruption which he saw in the Church and in the monastery gave himself to fasting, prayer, and teaching the novices. Sent to Ferrara by his superiors to preach, he seems to have made little impression on his native city. A war drove him from Ferrara to Florence (1481) and he there entered the monastery of San Marco, a house of reformed Dominicans which had been rebuilt and equipped with a valuable library by Cosimo de' Medici the Elder, had been inspired by a remarkably saintly man, its founder, and had been decorated by Fra Angelico.

It was nearly ten years after he became a member of the San Marco community before Savonarola acquired fame as a preacher. He was heard in several cities where his superiors sent him and about 1491 he began to stir the multitudes in Florence. He had a burning conviction that God's judgement was soon to be visited on the earth and called his hearers to repentance before it should be too late. Crowds thronged to him and to accommodate them he began preaching in the cathedral. About 1493 he was chosen prior of San Marco and was appointed head of his province of the Dominicans. In these posts he furthered a stricter life which proved contagious in several houses of the order. Late in 1494, when grave losses in a war with France had thrown the Florentines into deep perplexity and had brought distrust of the leadership of the Medici, long dominant in the city, the voice of Savonarola pled for repentance in the face of what he declared to be divine punishment for the sins and frivolities of the citizens and may have prevented rioting and near-anarchy. After the Medici had been expelled from the city and after the French king had given up his occupation of the city and had departed with his cohorts, Savonarola was generally held to have been a true prophet, to have exerted some control of the king when he entered Florence, and to have induced him to depart. The king had a profound respect for him and heeded him at critical junctures. The friar, accordingly, was very popular. He had a large part in framing the form of government, a republic, which was adopted after the French left. He became the most influential personage in the city.

Although often voicing the conviction that he himself would come to a violent death, Savonarola declared that the Church would be renovated after a period of scourging and that all unbelievers would be converted and the Gospel would triumph in the earth. He pled with the Florentines to accept Christ as their king. He urged Italy, Florence, the princes, and the prelates to repent and turn to Christ. He exhorted his hearers to give to the poor all beyond their barest needs. In a series of sermons during Lent in 1495 he called upon his fellow-citizens to live a godly life of union and concord and undertake a complete reformation of morals.

There followed a startling transformation of the life of the city. Women threw aside their finery and dressed plainly, bankers and tradesmen restored ill-gotten gains, there was much reading of the Bible and the works of Savonarola, churches were crowded, alms to the poor increased, and some scions of leading families and several mature men of outstanding ability entered San Marco as monks.

Savonarola inevitably made enemies. Some of them went to Rome and urged the Pope, Alexander VI, to act. In 1495 the latter courteously summoned the friar to the Holy See. Savonarola asked to be excused, pleading ill health and the urgent necessity of remaining in Florence if the reforms which had been begun were to be carried through. In October, 1495, the Pope commanded him to abstain from all preaching, whether in public or private. For a time the friar obeyed and gave himself to study. By personal persuasion he succeeded in 1496 in transforming the usually riotous carnival into a time of giving to the poor and of processions in which children marched through the streets singing hymns. In Lent, 1496, with Papal permission and at the invitation of the civic authorities, he returned to his pulpit. Later in the year Alexander VI attempted to curb him by putting the monastery of San Marco in a grouping of Dominican houses which would render it more directly subject to Rome. Savonarola defied the order.

Early in 1497 the influence of Savonarola in Florence was such that at the annual carnival season, indecent books and pictures and carnival masks and costumes were collected by bands of children and burned in a huge pyre in the main square to the sound of devotional hymns and denunciations of the carnival.

In Lent, 1497, the friar came out boldly against the evils in the Church and with thinly veiled allusions to the Pope. That Pontiff was all the more enraged because the republic in Florence which Savonarola was supporting was in alliance with France and against the league of Italian states of which the Pope was a member: the latter's enmity was as much on political as personal and religious grounds.

In May, 1497, Alexander VI launched a bull of excommunication against

Savonarola, on the ostensible ground of his disobedience of the Papal command to come to Rome and his blocking of the incorporation of San Marco in the new combination of Dominican houses ordered by the Pope. Savonarola again defied the Pope.

Savonarola was strong enough to make of the carnival season of 1498 another time of religious fervour with a public burning of "vanities."

However, the tide began to run against him. The Pope threatened Florence with an interdict and ordered the civic authorities either to silence the friar or send him to Rome for trial. Savonarola appealed to the sovereigns of Spain, France, England, Hungary, and Germany to call a general council of the Church and declared that Alexander VI was neither a true Pope nor a Christian. Yet, heeding the pleas of the civic authorities, he ceased preaching. Popular opinion began to swing away from him. A Franciscan publicly attacked Savonarola as a heretic, false prophet, and schismatic, and challenged him to prove his integrity by the ancient custom of ordeal by fire. In the discussions which followed, Savonarola finally agreed to the test. It was to be made by a representative Dominican and a Franciscan. But when a vast throng had assembled to witness it, the spectacle was delayed by a storm of rain and by disputes on procedure. The Franciscan ultimately slipped away and the disappointed crowd rioted against Savonarola and the Dominicans.

The city government, now in hostile hands, arrested Savonarola and tried him and two of his closest disciples, employing the familiar medieval device of torture. The trial was continued before two Papal commissioners who had their master's command to see that the friar died. Savonarola and the other two were condemned, hung, and their bodies burned (May 23, 1498) in the great piazza. Alexander VI had seemingly triumphed.

No large body of followers perpetuated the programme of Savonarola, as had the Lollards that of Wyclif and the Utraquists, Taborites, and the Bohemian Brethren that of Hus. The majority of Florentines returned to their old ways. Indeed, for a time there was a reaction and a distinct moral let down. Yet a faithful minority remembered and each year on the anniversary of the sorrowful event strewed flowers on the scene of the execution. Many individuals, moreover, were permanently changed. Among them were the painter Botticelli and the humanist Pico della Mirandola. Michaelangelo was a loyal admirer. While Florence did not heed the friar's exhortation permanently to accept Christ as king, and although his political activities quickly came to nought and a few years later the Medici were back in power, the memory of Savonarola's purposes, eloquence, and heroism did not die and he was honoured as one of Florence's great.

The Florence in which Savonarola rose to prominence illustrated, as in a kind of microcosm, the contrasts, contrasts which are so great as to constitute a paradox, between "the exceeding greatness of the power" of the Christian faith on the one hand and the palpably earthen vessels on the other. Here was one of the leading cities of the Europe of the fourteenth and fifteenth centuries. It was professedly Christian. In it were great wealth and extreme poverty. Its republican government had come under the control of the family of the Medici, and their expulsion and the attempts to restore republican methods were intimately associated with the career of Savonarola. Here had lived the great Christian poet of the Middle Ages, Dante. Here was the Platonic Academy, with its mixture of earnestly Christian and thinly veiled non-Christian humanism. Here were artists inspired by their Christian faith—Fra Angelico, Botticelli, and Michelangelo among them. In especially striking contrast were Savonarola and his younger Florentine contemporaries, Niccolò Machiavelli (1469–1527) and Francesco Guicciardini (1483–1540). Machiavelli, the hardheaded, experienced expert in government, a combination of crude immorality and obscenity, prodigious energy, and astute, almost cynical practicality, is often considered the father of modern political science and his name is synonymous with pure expediency. To be sure, he longed for the unification of weak and distracted Italy, did not ignore religion, and held private virtue to be essential to a healthy national life. Yet he would make religion ancillary to the purposes of the state and admired to the point of idolization Cæsar Borgia with his audacity, his skilful diplomacy quite unburdened with regard for the truth, and his resolute and ruthless use of cruelty and fraud. Guicciardini, who wrote what has been acclaimed the master history of Italy from 1494 to 1532, as a statesman sought to promote what he deemed his own interests with utter disregard for the principles and convictions to which he subscribed in theory.

This kind of contrast had been seen in earlier centuries and in later eras was to be marked and perhaps even accentuated. Indeed, one of the effects of Christianity appears to have been to heighten the contradictions in human society. By calling men to an ideal impossible of attainment within history and sensitizing men's consciences, it widens the gulf between those who give themselves to the ideal and those who either reject it outright or deny it in practice.

SUMMARY

In the century and a half between 1350 and 1500 all Western Europe was the scene of this contrast between the nominal acceptance but cynical and practical disregard of the Christian ideal on the one hand and on the other hand earnest efforts to bring men to it.

The nominal acceptance but actual denial of Christianity was striking in those institutions which the great dreamers of earlier ages had created and developed in the hope of bringing men to the Christian goal. With numerous exceptions, the hierarchy, from the parish clergy through the bishops and archbishops, and including the Papal curia and the Popes themselves, was corrupt. In much of Western Europe the structure which had been developed with the express purpose of serving the Christian community and lifting it towards the Christian standard had become a handicap rather than an aid. The Papacy especially, which many of the earlier reformers had strengthened in the hope that through it the entire Church would be purified and all society brought to conformity with the purpose of God in Christ, had become a scandal. For nearly two generations it retreated from its historic seat, and, in contrast with its claim to universality, fell under the control of one nation, the French. Then, in escaping from that thraldom, it was divided. When the schism was at last ended, the Papacy succumbed to the quite worldly side of the Renaissance and was mired down in the morass of Italian politics. The very machinery which the great dreamers had created to enable the Papacy to make their hopes for the Church a reality, by its weight and its temptation to an anti-Christian kind of power became a liability to the Christian cause. The general councils in which many believed they saw the remedy ended the Papal schism but failed to accomplish the cleansing of the Church.

Moreover, what to the far-seeing must have seemed fully as grave a menace, Western Europe was experiencing the rise of nation states under absolute monarchs, each of whom sought to control the Church and to make Christianity subservient to his purposes. The battle between the Papacy and the Holy Roman Empire to prevent the secularization of the Church was now being waged on many fronts, some of them new. Not only was it going against the Church. It was also threatening the degree of Christian unity, limited though that was, which had been achieved through the Church of Rome.

The monastic movement which had come into being from the longing to lead the perfect Christian life had in most of its members become either listless, humdrum, and comfortable routine or, among a minority, a handicap to morality and spiritual vision. Even the mendicant orders, which only four or five generations earlier had arisen from a great missionary passion to bring the masses of nominal Christians to a vital dedication to Christ and to win the non-Christian world, had almost ceased to reach out beyond the borders of Western Christendom and within that area had experienced a decline in morale.

It seemed that Western Europe, the scene of the most numerous and vigorous movements springing from the Christian faith in the great centuries between 950 and 1350, was being de-Christianized. The new forces of nationalism, a recrudescence of paganism through the Renaissance and humanism, and the obsession with wealth and secular power appeared to be stifling the manifestations of life which had been so encouraging to those who hoped that the Gospel was at last bringing order into the chaos which had followed the collapse of the Roman Empire and dreamed of it as moulding the emerging civilization of the region.

There was another side of the picture. Many movements were appearing, some of them revivals of earlier ones and others of them new, which were evidence of healthy vitality. Individuals were emerging, often in quite unexpected quarters, who were regarded as ideal exemplars of the Christian faith. In several regions the discipline of prayer and of devotion was taking new forms and was spreading. There were efforts to bring the monasteries and the mendicant orders back to their pristine purposes. Fresh forms of Christian communal living were emerging. Christianity was beginning to capture the new humanism. Here and there, notably in England and Bohemia, the new movements were unsubmissive to the existing ecclesiastical structure and were being expelled from it.

Two features of these expressions of vitality, of "the exceeding greatness of his power," are especially significant. One was that for the most part they were issuing from the grass-roots. Here and there, as in Spain, they were capturing the existing organization of the Church, but for the most part they did not begin with the upper levels of the hierarchy. As we have more than once remarked, they were a ground swell. They were an indication that Christianity had become, to no small degree, the conscious possession of the rank and file and not something imposed from above, as had been the fashion by which the nominal conversion of Western Europe had been accomplished.

A second feature, almost and perhaps quite as significant as the first, was one of geography. Within the areas which had been fully assimilated to Latin culture before the collapse of the Roman Empire and where conversion had taken place before the sixth century, the new movements tended to follow generally accepted patterns. That was true, for example, of Catherine of Siena, the reforms in which Ximénes led, the labours of Vincent Ferrer, and the Hieronymites. On the other hand, in regions which had not been so assimilated or where Latin culture had been erased, as in Britain, by the barbarian invasions, and among peoples where conversion had not come until after the sixth century, the movements tended to take on new forms. Some of these, among them the Friends of God, the Brethren of the Common Life, and such Christian humanists as Colet, Thomas More, and Erasmus, remained within the Roman Catholic Church. Others, notably the Lollards and those who had Hus as their outstanding figure, were so critical of that church and so refused submission to it that they were cast out by it.

Both of these facets were to take on special significance in the centuries which followed. The ground swell issuing from the rank and file of Christians was to come to flood tide. Within what had once been the Roman Empire that flood tide was for the most part to be contained within the Roman Catholic Church and was to purify it of some of its worst moral abuses. In great areas outside what had been the Roman Empire it was to break with the Roman Catholic Church and was to issue in one or another aspect of what is collectively known as Protestantism.

SELECTED BIBLIOGRAPHY

GENERAL WORKS

The Cambridge Modern History. Volume I, The Renaissance (Cambridge University Press, 1934, pp. xii, 724).

A. C. Flick, *The Decline of the Medieval Church* (New York, Alfred A. Knopf, 2 vols., 1930). It covers the fourteenth and fifteenth centuries. A large proportion of the space is devoted to the Avignon Papacy, the Great Schism, and the Conciliar Movement. It is good, but must be used with care.

P. Hughes, *A History of the Church. Volume Three, The Revolt against the Church: Aquinas to Luther* (New York, Sheed & Ward, 1947, pp. xvi, 556). By a Roman Catholic.

J. Huizinga, *The Waning of the Middle Ages. A Study of the Forms of Life, Thought and Art in France and the Netherlands in the XIVth and XVth Centuries* (London, Edward Arnold & Co., 1927, pp. viii, 328).

E. M. Hulme, *The Renaissance, the Protestant Revolution, and the Catholic Reformation in Continental Europe* (New York, Appleton-Century-Crofts, 1914, pp. 589). A useful summary.

J. Mackinnon, *The Origins of the Reformation* (New York, Longmans, Green and Co., 1939, pp. xi, 448). By an outstanding specialist.

THE GREAT SCHISM

G. J. Jordan, *The Inner History of the Great Western Schism. A Problem in Church Unity* (London, William & Norgate, 1930, pp. 216). Valuable for quotations from the sources.

C. Locke, *The Age of the Great Western Schism* (New York, Charles Scribner's Sons, 1900, pp. x, 314). A semi-popular treatment.

THE CONCILIAR MOVEMENT

E. F. Jacob, *Essays in the Conciliar Epoch* (Manchester University Press, 1943, pp. viii, 192). Carefully documented.

E. J. Kitts, *In the Days of the Councils. A Sketch of the Iife and Times of Baldas-*

sare Cossa (Afterward Pope John the Twenty-third) (London, Constable & Co., 1908, pp. xxiv, 421). Carries the story through the Council of Pisa.

E. J. Kitts, *Pope John the Twenty-third and Master John Hus of Bohemia* (London, Constable & Co., 1910, pp. xxx, 446). Continues the story through the Council of Constance and the death of John XXIII.

THE DECLINE OF THE PAPACY

A. H. Mathew, *The Life and Times of Rodrigo Borgia Pope Alexander VI* (New York, Brentano's, 1912, pp. 413). Portrays the seamy side of the life of Alexander VI, but places that life in its setting.

L. Pastor, *The History of the Popes from the Close of the Middle Ages*, translated from the German by various scholars (St. Louis, B. Herder, and London, Kegan Paul, and Routledge and Kegan Paul, 36 vols., 1902–1950). The standard work by a Roman Catholic scholar, using the archives of the Vatican. Vols. I–VI deal with the period treated in this chapter.

P. de Roo, *Material for a History of Pope Alexander VI, His Relatives and His Time* (New York, The Universal Knowledge Foundation, 5 vols., 1924). Written with a strong bias in favour of Alexander VI.

MONASTIC LIFE

H. Bett, *Nicholas of Cusa* (London, Methuen & Co., 1932, pp. x, 210). A biography of one who was noted as monastic reformer, mystic, scholar, and cardinal.

G. G. Coulton, *Five Centuries of Religion. Volume IV. The Last Days of Medieval Monasticism* (Cambridge University Press, 1950, pp. xv, 833). By a distinguished specialist, based upon an extensive use of the sources.

THE STATE OF THE CLERGY

W. W. Capes, *The English Church in the Fourteenth and Fifteenth Centuries* (London, Macmillan & Co., 1900, pp. xi, 391). A useful handbook.

A. H. Thompson, *The English Clergy and Their Organization in the Later Middle Ages* (Oxford, The Clarendon Press, 1947, pp. xv, 327). With reference to the sources and extensive selections from them.

FOURTEENTH AND FIFTEENTH CENTURY MYSTICS IN GENERAL

P. Pourrat, *Christian Spirituality in the Middle Ages*, translated by S. P. Jacques (London, Burns, Oates & Washbourne, 1924, pp. xiii, 341). A standard survey, by a Roman Catholic.

CATHERINE OF SIENA

The Dialogue of the Seraphic Virgin Catherine of Siena Dictated by Her while in a State of Ecstasy, to Her Secretaries, and Completed in the Year of Our Lord 1370, translated . . . with an Introduction on the Study of Mysticism, by A. Thorold (London, Kegan Paul, Trench, Trübner & Co., 1896, pp. vi, 360).

Saint Catherine of Siena as Seen in Her Letters, translated and edited with an introduction by V. D. Scudder (London, J. M. Dent & Sons, 1927, pp. x, 352).

J. Jorgensen, *Saint Catherine of Siena,* translated from the Danish by I. Lund (New York, Longmans, Green & Co., 1938, pp. ix, 446). Well documented, with a Catholic imprimatur.

M. Roberts, *Saint Catherine of Siena and Her Times* (New York, G. P. Putnam's Sons, 1906, pp. viii, 300). A semi-popular account.

THE MYSTICISM OF THE LOW COUNTRIES AND GERMANY

E. F. Jacob, *Gerard Groote and the Beginnings of the "New Devotion" in the Low Countries* (*The Journal of Ecclesiastical History,* Vol. III, pp. 40–57).

R. M. Jones, *The Flowering of Mysticism. The Friends of God in the Fourteenth Century* (New York, The Macmillan Co., 1939, pp. 270). Carefully and sympathetically done.

S. Kettlewell, *Thomas à Kempis and the Brothers of the Common Life* (London, Kegan Paul, Trench, Trübner & Co., 2 vols., 1882). Carefully done. A standard work.

J. E. G. de Montmorency, *Thomas à Kempis, His Age and Book* (London, Methuen & Co., 1906, pp. xxiii, 312). Well done.

Nicholas of Cusa, *The Vision of God,* translated by E. G. Salter with an introduction by E. Underhill (London, J. M. Dent & Sons, 1928, pp. xxx, 130).

A. G. Seesholtz, *Friends of God. Practical Mystics of the Fourteenth Century* (Columbia University Press, pp. viii, 247). A careful, sympathetic study.

Theologia Germanica, translated from the German by S. Winkworth (London, Macmillan & Co., 1924, pp. lxxvii, 227).

Thomas à Kempis, *The New Devotion. Being the Lives of Gerard Groote, Florentius Radewin and Their Followers,* translated by J. P. Arthur (London, Kegan Paul, Trench, Trübner & Co., 1905, pp. xlvii, 266).

Thomas à Kempis, *The Imitation of Christ* (New York, E. P. Dutton & Co., 1910, pp. xx, 284). The *Everyman's Library* edition.

ENGLISH MYSTICS

T. W. Coleman, *English Mystics of the Fourteenth Century* (London, The Epworth Press, 1938, pp. 176). Semi-popular, with selections from the sources.

Walter Hilton, *The Scale of Perfection,* newly edited from manuscript sources, with an introduction by E. Underhill (London, John M. Watkins, 1923, pp. lxvi, 464).

Julian of Norwich, *Revelations of Divine Love,* edited by G. Warrack (London, Methuen & Co., 5th edition, 1914, pp. lxxviii, 208).

The Book of Margery Kempe, edited by S. B. Meech, prefatory note by H. E. Allen, notes and appendices by S. B. Meech and H. E. Allen (Oxford University Press, 1940, pp. lxviii, 441).

CATHERINE OF GENOA

F. von Hügel, *The Mystical Element of Religion as Studied in Saint Catherine of Genoa and Her Friends* (London, J. M. Dent & Sons, 2 vols., 1923). A thoughtful, scholarly study.

PREACHING

G. R. Owst, *Literature and Pulpit in Medieval England* (Cambridge University Press, 1933, pp. xxiv, 616). Based upon an extensive examination of the sources.

G. R. Owst, *Preaching in Medieval England. An Introduction to Sermon Manuscripts of the Period c.1350–1450* (Cambridge University Press, 1926, pp. xviii, 381). Extensive use of the sources and numerous quotations from them.

THE BEGINNINGS OF SPANISH REFORM AND THE SPANISH INQUISITION

von Hefele, *The Life of Cardinal Ximenez*, translated from the German by Dalton (London, Catholic Publishing & Bookselling Company, 1860, pp. lvi, 581). A standard older work by a Roman Catholic scholar.

T. Hope, *Torquemada, Scourge of the Jews, A Biography* (London, George Allen & Unwin, 1939, pp. 245). Popularly written.

H. C. Lea, *A History of the Inquisition of Spain* (New York, The Macmillan Co., 4 vols., 1906, 1907). A standard work of which the first volume is on this period.

R. Merton, *Cardinal Ximénes and the Making of Spain* (London, Kegan Paul, Trench, Trübner & Co., 1934, pp. xiv, 279). Carefully written with an attempt at objectivity.

R. Sabatini, *Torquemada and the Spanish Inquisition. A History* (London, Stanley Paul & Co., 6th edition, 1927, pp. 404). Vividly written.

CHRISTIAN HUMANISM

F. Seebohm, *The Oxford Reformers of 1498: Being a History of the Fellow-Work of John Colet, Erasmus, and Thomas More* (London, Longmans, Green & Co., 1867, pp. xii, 440). A standard older work.

ERASMUS

P. S. Allen, *The Age of Erasmus* (Oxford, The Clarendon Press, 1914, pp. 303). A series of lectures.

P. S. Allen, *Erasmus: Lectures and Wayfaring Sketches* (Oxford, The Clarendon Press, 1934, pp. xii, 216). For a general audience.

E. Emerton, *Desiderius Erasmus of Rotterdam* (New York, G. P. Putnam's Sons, 1900, pp. xxvi, 469). A standard account.

D. Erasmus, *The Education of a Christian Prince*, translated with an introduction by L. K. Born (Columbia University Press, 1936, pp. viii, 277).

D. Erasmus, *Enchiridion Militis Christiani . . . The Manual of the Christian Knight* (London, Methuen & Co., 1905, pp. 287).

D. Erasmus, *The Complaint of Peace, Translated from the Querela Pacis* (A.D. *1521*) (Chicago, Open Court Publishing Co., 1917, pp. 80).

D. Erasmus, *The Praise of Folly,* translated by L. F. Dean (Chicago, Packard and Co., preface, 1946, pp. 152).

F. M. Nichols, *The Epistles of Erasmus from His Earliest Letters to His Fifty-third Year.* English translation (London, Longmans, Green & Co., 3 vols., 1901–1918).

P. Smith, *Erasmus. A Study of His Life, Ideals, and Place in History* (New York, Harper & Brothers, 1923, pp. xiii, 479). A semi-popular study by a specialist on the period.

WYCLIF AND THE LOLLARDS

H. M. Smith, *Pre-Reformation England* (London, Macmillan & Co., 1938, pp. xiii, 556). An excellent survey of the situation at the beginning of the sixteenth century. It includes a sketch of the Lollards.

G. M. Trevelyan, *England in the Age of Wycliffe* (New York, Longmans, Green & Co., 1929—preface 1899—pp. xvi, 380). A well-written standard work.

H. B. Workman, *John Wyclif, a Study of the English Medieval Church* (Oxford, The Clarendon Press, 2 vols., 1926). A standard account, very well done.

HUS

The Letters of John Hus, with introduction and explanatory notes by H. B. Workman and R. M. Pope (London, Hodder & Stoughton, 1904, pp. xxxi, 286).

The Count Lützow, *The Life and Times of Master John Hus* (London, J. M. Dent & Co., 1919, pp. viii, 398). An excellent account based on the sources.

D. S. Schaff, *John Huss—His Life, Teachings and Death—after Five Hundred Years* (New York, Charles Scribner's Sons, 1915, pp. xv, 349). Carefully done, distinctly favourable to Hus.

M. Spinka, *John Hus and the Czech Reform* (The University of Chicago Press, 1941, pp. 81). An excellent study, stressing the ways in which Hus differed from Wyclif and his continuing, largely independently of Wyclif, an indigenous movement which wished the moral reform of the Church.

OTHER REFORMERS

C. Ullman, *Reformers before the Reformation, Principally in Germany and the Netherlands,* translated by R. Menzies (Edinburgh, T. & T. Clark, 2 vols., 1885). An excellent account.

SAVONAROLA AND MACHIAVELLI

P. Misciatelli, *Savonarola,* translated by M. Peter-Roberts (New York, Appleton-Century-Crofts, 1930, pp. xi, 274). A popular account by a warm admirer of Savonarola.

R. Roeder, *Savonarola. A Study in Conscience* (New York, Brentano's, 1930, pp. 307). A well-written account for the general reader.

P. Villari, *Life and Times of Girolamo Savonarola,* translated by L. Villari (New York, Charles Scribner's Sons, first edition 1888, many times reprinted, pp. xlvii, 792).

P. Villari, *The Life and Times of Niccolò Machiavelli,* translated by L. Villari (London, Ernest Benn, first published 1891, many times reprinted, pp. xxiv, 510, 547). A standard account.

SUPPLEMENTARY
SELECTED BIBLIOGRAPHY

(Books printed since 1950)
For the Period Prior to A.D. 1500

Anderson, Charles S. *Augsburg Historical Atlas of Christianity in the Middle Ages and Reformation.* Minneapolis: Augsburg, 1967.

Bainton, Roland H. *Christendom: The Medieval Church.* Princeton: D. Van Nostrand Co., Inc., Anvil Books, 1962.

Baus, Karl. *From the Apostolic Community to Constantine.* New York: Herder & Herder, 1965.

Beck, H. G. and others. *From the High Middle Ages to the Eve of the Reformation.* (Translated by Anselm Biggs) New York: Herder & Herder, 1970.

Boyle, Leonard E. *A Survey of the Vatican Archives and of its Medieval Holdings.* Toronto: Pontifical Institute of Medieval Studies, 1972.

Bretano, Robert. Two Churches: England and Italy in the Thirteenth Century. Princeton: Princeton University Press, 1968.

Cannon, William R. *History of Christianity in the Middle Ages.* Nashville: Abingdon Press, 1960.

Carrington, Philip. *The Early Christian Church* (2 vols.). New York: Cambridge University Press, 1957.

Chadwick, Henry. *Early Christian Thought and the Classical Tradition.* New York: Oxford University Press, 1966.

———. *The Early Church.* Baltimore: Penguin Books, 1967.

Chadwick, Nora. *The Age of the Saints in the Early Celtic Church.* New York: Oxford University Press, 1961.

Chadwick, Nora, and others. *Celt and Saxon: Studies in the Early British Border.* New York: Cambridge University Press, 1963.

Chadwick, Nora, Kathleen Hughes, G. Brooke and K. Jackson. *Studies in the Early British Church.* New York: Cambridge University Press, 1958.

Conference on Christianity in Roman and Sub-Roman Britain. Christianity in Britain, 300–700. Leicester, Eng.: Leicester University Press, 1968.

Cowdrey, H. E. J. *The Cluniacs and the Gregorian Reform.* Oxford: Clarendon Press, 1970.

Daly, S. J. and J. Lowrie. *Benedictine Monasticism: Its Foundation and Development through the 12th Century.* New York: Sheed & Ward, 1965.

Dickens, A. G. *The Age of Humanism and Reformation: Europe in the 14th, 15th and 16th Centuries.* Englewood Cliffs, N.J.: Prentice-Hall, Inc., 1972.

Duckett, Eleanor Shipley. *Carolingian Portraits.* Ann Arbor: University of Michigan Press, 1962.

———. *St. Dunstan of Canterbury: A Study of Monastic Reform in the 10th Century.* New York: W. W. Norton & Co., 1955.

Dvornik, Francis. *Byzantine Missions among the Slavs.* New Brunswick, N.J.: Rutgers University Press, 1970.

———. *The Idea of Apostolicity in Byzantium and the Legend of the Apostle Andrew.* Cambridge, Mass.: Harvard University Press, 1958.

Foster, John. *After the Apostles: Missionary Preaching of the First Three Centuries.* New York: Macmillan, 1952.

———. *They Converted Our Ancestors: A Study of the Early Church in Britain.* London: SCM Press, 1965.

Frend, W. H. C. *Martyrdom and Persecution in the Early Church: A Study of a Conflict from the Maccabees to Donatus.* Garden City, N.Y.: Doubleday & Co., 1967.

Frohnes, Heinzgünter and Uwe W. Knorr, editors. *Kirchengeschichte aus Missiongeschichte, Band I, The Alte Kirche.* Munich: Christian Kaiser Verlag, 1974.

Gabrieli, Francesco, editor. *Arab Historians of the Crusades* (trans. from the Italian by E. J. Costello). Los Angeles: University of California Press, 1969.

Godfrey, C. J. *The Church in Anglo Saxon England.* Cambridge, Eng.: Cambridge University Press, 1962.

Gonzales, Justo. *A History of Christian Thought* (2 vols. to date). Nashville: Abingdon Press, 1970–1971.

Grant, Robert M. *Augustus to Constantine: The Thrust of the Christian Movement into the Roman World.* New York: Harper & Row, 1970.

Green, Michael. *Evangelism in the Early Church.* Grand Rapids, Mich.: Eerdmans, 1970.

Hanson, R. P. C. *St. Patrick: His Origins and Career.* New York: Oxford University Press, 1968.

Hardinge, Leslie. *The Celtic Church in Britain.* London: SPCK, 1972.

Hinnebusch, William A. *The History of the Dominican Order.* Vol. 2: *Intellectual and Cultural Life to 1500.* Staten Island, N.Y.: Alba House, 1973.

Hoare, Robert J. *Christianity Comes to Britain.* London: Chapman, 1968.

Hughes, Kathleen. *The Church in Early Irish Society.* Ithaca, N.Y.: Cornell University Press, 1966.

Jedin, Hubert and John Dolan, editors. *Handbook of Church History* (Vols. 1, 3, 4 of 4 translated from the German). New York: Herder & Herder, 1965–1970. *Note:* For titles of separate volumes, see Baus—Vol. 1, Kempf—Vol. 3, and Beck—Vol. 4.

Jedin, Hubert, Kenneth Scott Latourette and Jochen Martin, editors. *Atlas zur Kirchengeschicte.* Freiburg: Herder, 1970.

Kaegi, Walter Emil, Jr. *Byzantium and the Decline of Rome.* Princeton: Princeton University Press, 1968.

Knowles, Dom David. *From Pachomius to Ignatius.* Oxford: Clarendon Press, 1966.

———. *The Religious Orders in England.* Vol. 2: *The End of the Middle Ages.* New York: Cambridge University Press, 1955.

Lach, Donald. *Asia in the Making of Europe.* (2 vols.) Chicago: University of Chicago Press, 1965.

Lebreton, Jules and Jacques Zeiller. *The Triumph of Christianity.* New York: Collier, 1962.

Leclerq, Jean, O.S. *The Love of Learning and the Desire for God: A Study in Monastic Culture* (trans. by Catherine Misrahi). New York: New American Library of World Literature, 1962.

McNeill, John T. *The Celtic Churches: A History* A.D. *200–1200.* Chicago: University of Chicago Press, 1974.

Nigg, Walter. *Warriors of God: The Great Religious Orders and Their Founders.* New York: Alfred A. Knopf, 1959.

Obolersky, D. *The Byzantine Commonwealth: Eastern Europe, 500–1438* New York: Praeger, 1971.

Palanque, J. R. and others. *Church in the Christian Roman Empire* (4 vols.) (trans. by Ernest C. Messinger). New York: Macmillan, 1953.

Payne, Robert. *The Holy Fire. The Story of the Fathers of the Eastern Church.* New York: Harper & Row, 1957.

Pelikan, Jaroslav. *The Emergence of the Catholic Tradition* (Vol. 1 of the 5-vol. set entitled *The Christian Tradition: A History of the Development of Doctrine*). Chicago: University of Chicago Press, 1971.

———. *The Spirit of Eastern Christendom (600–1700).* (Vol. 2 of the 5-vol. set entitled *The Christian Tradition: A History of the Development of Doctrine*). Chicago: University of Chicago Press, 1974.

Petry, Ray C. *Late Medieval Mysticism.* (Library of Christian Classics, XIII) Philadelphia: Westminster Press, 1957.

Ramsey, William M. *The Church in the Roman Empire before* A.D. *170.* Grand Rapids: Baker Book House, 1954.

Runciman, Stephen. *A History of the Crusades* (3 vols.). Cambridge, Eng.: University Press, 1951–1954.

Setton, Kenneth M., general editor. *A History of the Crusades* (2 vols.). Madison, Wis.: University of Wisconsin Press, 1969.

Symons, Thomas, editor. *Regularis Concordia.* New York: Oxford University Press, 1953.

Talbot, C. H. *The Anglo-Saxon Missionaries in Germany.* New York: Sheed & Ward, 1954.

Von Campenhausen, Hans. *Men Who Shaped the Western Church* (trans. by Manfred Hoffman). New York: Harper & Row, 1965.

Walroud, F. F. *Christian Missions before the Reformation.* London: SPCK, n.d.

INDEX

Aachen, synod at (in 809), 304, 360
Abbas, 289
Abbasid Caliphs, 289, 319, 353, 566, 614
Abbots, 332, 334
Abel, 176
Abélard, Peter, 425, 450, 502-4, 536
Aberdeen: Episcopalians in, 774; University of, 772
Åbo (Turku), 739, 1149
Abraham, 11, 333
Abraham of Smolensk, 584
Absenteeism, 626, 641, 663
Absolution, 529
Abstinence from alcohol. See Temperance movement
Abyssinia. See Ethiopia
Acolytes, 133
Acre, 411, 412
Actium, 93
Activism, 314, 414, 572, 963, 973, 980, 1027, 1417
Acts of the Apostles, The, 66, 68, 123, 210, 460
Adalbert, 393, 394
Adam, 11, 142, 177, 195; sin of (in Augustine), 178, (to the Pelagians), 181, (unity of mankind corrupted by), 498, (to Calvin), 754
Adam of St. Victor, 537, 540
Address to the German Nobility, The (Luther), 710, 711-12
Adeodatus, 96, 97, 174
Adiaphoristic Controversy, 731
Admonitions to Parliament, 815
Adonai, 141
Adonis, 25
Adoptionism, 143-44, 146; Spanish, 360
Adornment of the Spiritual Marriage, The (Ruysbroeck), 543
Adrian IV, Pope, 481
Adrian VI, Pope, 861-62
Adrianople, 272, 602, 612; Treaty of, 1211
Adventist churches, 1259
Adversus simonaicos (Humbert), 468
Æons, 124
Æterni patris (Leo XIII), 1102
Africa. Christianity in, 926-28, 1205-7, 1302-11; White Fathers in, 1085, 1206, 1309, 1310; south of the Sahara, 1303-11, 1435-39; unrest in, 1353, 1392, 1435; growth of leadership in, 1436-37. See also North Africa,

South Africa, and various countries
African Methodist Episcopal Church, 1251, 1307
African Methodist Episcopal Zion Church, 1251
African slave trade, 967. See also Slave trade and Slavery
Afrikaans, 1306
Afrikanders, 1305, 1306
Against Celsus (Origen), 150
Against the Murderous and Thieving Hordes of Peasants (Luther), 725
Agape, 197, 203, 213, 263, 1385
Agatho, Pope, 285
Age of Reason, The (Paine), 1007, 1074, 1230
Aglipay, 1322, 1445
Agriculture: in Middle Ages, 330, 365; and monasteries, 556-57
Ahimsa, 1442
Aidan, 344
Aids to Reflection (Coleridge), 1172
Ailly, Peter d', 629, 630, 646, 669, 705
Akbar, 931
Alacoque, Margaret Mary, 878, 1089
Alais, Peace of, 768
Alans, 311, 402
Alaric, 95
Alaska, 1002, 1016, 1223, 1227, 1232, 1242
Alban, 90
Albania, 613, 614
Albanian Orthodox Church, in the United States, 1414
Alberic, 366, 367
Alberic of Citeaux, 423
Alberic the younger, 366, 367
Alberoni, 975
Albert (founder of Riga), 399
Albert, Duke of East Prussia, 726
Albert of Brandenburg, 708, 709
Albert of Cologne. See Albertus Magnus
Albert V, Duke of Bavaria, 873
Albertus Magnus, 508-10, 530, 552, 605
Albi, 453
Albigenses (Cathari), 438, 453-55, 484, 513, 577; crusade against, 456
Albright, Jacob, 1040
Alcalá, University of, 657, 845
Alcuin, 350, 357, 360
Aldersgate, 1025

Aleutians, 1016, 1223
Alexander, Bishop of Alexandria, 153, 154
Alexander the Great, 10, 23, 80, 103, 146, 237
Alexander of Hales, 507, 530
Alexander Nevski, 586
Alexander Severus, 87
Alexander II, Pope, 469-70
Alexander III, Pope, 481
Alexander IV, Pope, 487
Alexander VI, Pope, 636, 638-39, 656, 859, 862; and Savonarola, 673-74
Alexander I, Tsar, 1016, 1213, 1214, 1215, 1221
Alexander II, Tsar, 1214, 1216
Alexander III, Tsar, 1214, 1219
Alexandria, 15, 21, 25, 104; Church in, 66, 77, 80, 201, 243; school of Christian thought in, 146-51; synods in, 161, 167; divine element of Jesus emphasized in, 165, 166, 170; bishops of, 185; baptism in, 196; Patriarch of, 283, 319, 900, 1206, 1207; captured by Persians, 287; taken by Arabs, 288
Alexis, Tsar, 911, 913, 914
Alexius Comnenus, 409, 566, 574
Alfarabi, 497
Alford, Henry, 1167
Alfred the Great, 367, 377, 461
Algaze, 497
Algeria, 1206
All Souls' Day, 535
Allegory, use of, 14-15; in Scriptures, 150
Allen, William, 813
Allgemeine Geschichte der christlichen Religion und Kirche (Neander), 1133
Allgemeine lutherische Konferenz, 1135
Almanzor, 396
A-lo-pên, 324, 346
Alphonso XII of Spain, 1111
Alphonso XIII of Spain, 1111
Alsace, 888
Althing, 390
Alva, Duke of, 764
Amadeus of Savoy (Felix V), 635
Amalfi, 873
Amaury of Bena, 540
Ambo, 202
Ambrose of Milan, 98-99, 177, 238; Augustine and, 96, 97; and Theodosius, 184; hymn writing of, 208; and monasti-